CACHE Level 3

Child Care and Education

Marian Beaver
Jo Brewster
Sandy Green
Sally Neaum
Heidi Sheppard
Jill Tallack
Miranda Walker

Nelson Thornes

Published in 2008 by:
Nelson Thornes Ltd
Delta Place
27 Bath Road
CHELTENHAM
GL53 7TH
United Kingdom

09 10 11 12 / 10 9 8 7 6 5 4 3 2

A catalogue record for this book is available from the British Library

ISBN 978 0 7487 9996 1

Cover photograph by Jim Wileman
Illustrations by Pantek Arts Ltd. Archive illustrations by
Jane Bottomley and Angela Knowles
Page make-up by Pantek Arts Ltd, Maidstone, Kent

Printed and bound in Spain by GraphyCems

Acknowledgements

The authors and publishers wish to thank the following for permission to use copyright material:

p1: Photofusion Picture Library/Alamy; p3: Jack Sullivan/Alamy; p4: NCH, Home-start; p7:
Bubbles/Alamy; p8: Sure Start/Department for Children, Schools and Families; p20: Corel 588
(NT); p21: Vario Images GmbH & Co.KG/Alamy; p24, 26, 32: Image Source Black/Alamy;
p83: moodboard/Alamy; p87: Peter Glass/Alamy, Maggie Murray/Photofusion; p101: http://
publications.teachernet.gov.uk/eOrderingDownload/6840-DFES-ifchildabuse.pdf, p16; p105:
Brownstock Inc./Alamy; p119: Arclight/Alamy; p136: Janine Wiedel Photolibrary/Alamy; p142:
JUPITERIMAGES/Comstock images/Alamy; p147: Stockbyte/Alamy; p188: Cornwall Pics/
Alamy; p221: FogStock/Alamy; p225: Silverport pictures; p226: Martin Jenkinson/Alamy; p227:
British Association of Dermatologists/British Skin Foundation; p245: Digital vision/Alamy; p266:
www.standards.dfes.gov.uk/eyfs/resources/downloads/principles.pdf; p267: www.standards.
dfes.gov.uk/eyfs/resources/downloads/card4_4.pdf; p296: cbp-photo/Alamy; p298: Ryan
McVay/Photodisc 70 (NT); p242: Mark Passmore/Apex; p293: Yvette Cardozo/Alamy; p302:
Red Images, LLC/Alamy; p307: Charles Bowman/Alamy; p319: Digital Vision/Alamy; p325:
Blend Images/Alamy; p336: Design Pics Inc./Alamy; p343: Bloom Works Inc/Alamy; p357:
Jim West/Alamy; p360: Jim West/Alamy; p366: (clockwise from top left) Autism Independence
UK SFTAH, Scope, Dyspraxia Foundation, Diabetes UK, NDCS/The National Deaf Children's
Society, Dyslexia Action, Epilspsy Action/British Epilepsy Association; p367: Design Pics Inc./
Alamy; p372: http://www.teachernet.gov.uk/_doc/3724/SENCodeOfPractice.pdf; p375, 377:
Silverport pictures; p379: Jack Sullivan/Alamy; p382: JobCentrePlus/Silverport pictures; p384:
Digital Vision/Alamy; p391: Photodisc 24 (NT); p410, 460: Blend Images/Alamy; p431: Sally
and Richard Greenhill/Alamy; p467, 472: Corbis Premium RF/Alamy; p476: Ian Shaw/Alamy;
p481: Purestock/Alamy; p483: Design Pics Inc./Alamy; p487: fstop/Alamy; p505: ELC/Alamy;
p511: Photodisc/Alamy; p513: Digital Vision/Alamy.
For any other photographs, thanks are due to the parents, children and staff at ABC Nursery,
Playtime Out of School Club, Cullompton, Devon, The Clockhouse Pre-school Centre,
Nottingham and Staple Hill School.

Every effort has been made to contact the copyright holders and we apologise if any have been
overlooked. Should copyright have been unwittingly infringed in this book, the owners should
contact the publishers, who will make corrections at reprint.

Contents

Introduction

This book is a user-friendly, accessible guide to the Early Years care and education of children from birth to 16 years. It has been written for learners of the Council for Awards in Children's Care and Education (CACHE) Level 3 Award/Certificate/Diploma in Child Care and Education. It also covers the requirements for underpinning knowledge for National Vocational Qualifications (NVQs) in Children's Care, Learning and Development at Level 3. Learners on any of the many other courses that require a knowledge and understanding of Early Years care and education will also find this book useful. Child care settings may find it a valuable addition to their reference shelves and helpful in supporting in-service training.

Contents of the book

The book is divided into fourteen units which match the units of the CACHE Level 3 qualification. The mandatory units and five of the optional units are covered. CACHE learners complete differing units depending on whether they're undertaking the Award, Certificate or Diploma. The units in this book are colour coded to reflect this, so learners will easily be able to see which units apply to them.

Throughout the book, information is given in a style ideal for Level 3 learners. The role and responsibilities of practitioners are emphasised, and good practice is highlighted. Practical examples help readers to relate theory to real-life situations, and questions and tasks help readers to recall knowledge and develop understanding. You can read more about the text features on pages viii-ix.

Acknowledgements

The authors and publishers would like to thank the following people and organisations for permission to reproduce material in this book:

Jo Brewster: Thanks to Fay Beaver and Holly and Laurie Brewster for their photographs. Thanks to Lovers' Lane Primary School for the photographs of displays and equipment.

Sandy Green: As always I thank my husband John for his on-going support and love. Thanks also to family and friends for their interest and enthusiasm for all that I do, and a special thank you to Hannah and Alan for permission to use photos of my wonderful grandchildren, Jasmine, Harry, Alfie and Daisy. My love comes to you all.

Heidi Sheppard: I would like to thank Robert for his tolerance and support during the writing of this book, my wonderful boys Nicholas and Alexander for their energy, understanding and ability to make me smile! Viva Las Vegas guys! Thanks to the support and encouragement of my close family and friends, I now know that I can rise to the challenges that come my way. I would like to dedicate my work to the memory of my late father Eddie (I know you would be very proud).

Miranda Walker: Love and thanks to Nick Walker for his endless support and assistence with photography.

Every effort has been made to contact copyright holders and we apologise if anyone has been overlooked.

Marian Beaver has worked in social work, teaching and Early Years care and education. She taught for many years in FE at New College Nottingham and was an external verifier for CACHE. She inspected nursery provision for Ofsted, as well as writing. Prior to her recent retirement, she worked in Early Years and Childcare for Nottinghamshire County Council.

Jo Brewster has practised as a nurse, midwife and health visitor. She has taught for many years on Childcare courses in FE at New College Nottingham. She has inspected nursery provision for Ofsted and has worked as an internal and external verifier for CACHE.

Sandy Green has worked in a range of early years settings. She has inspected nurseries for Ofsted and worked as both an internal and external verifier. Having taught a range of early years courses in FE for many years, Sandy left full-time teaching in 2001 to work as a freelance consultant. She has contributted to many magazines and is an established author

Sally Neaum has taught in nursery classes and across the infant age range. She has also taught on a range of FE courses and has been an Ofsted inspector for nursery provision.

Jill Tallack has worked in schools across the whole primary age range, in a college of further education, training childcare students and as a registered nursery inspector. She is currently working as a local authority advisory teacher and area SENCo, supporting under-fives provision in the private, voluntary and independent sector.

Miranda Walker has worked with children from birth to 16 years in a range of settings, including her own day nursery and out of school clubs. She has inspected nursery provision for Ofsted, and worked at East Devon College as an Early Years and Playwork lecturer and NVQ assessor and internal verifier. She is a regular contributor to industry magazines and an established author.

Heidi Sheppard has worked with children from birth to 16 years in a range of settings including day and residential schools for children with learning difficulties and special educational needs. She has worked as a lecturer, NVQ assessor and internal verifier. Heidi is a qualified subject learning coach. She has recently joined an educational trust as training school programme manager.

Welcome to CACHE Level 3 Childcare and Education. This section explains the features of this book and how to use them as a tool for learning. **It's important that you read this section.**

CACHE Level 3 learners complete different units depending on whether they're undertaking the CACHE Award, Certificate or Diploma. This book is divided into colour coded units, so you will easily be able to see which Units apply to you.

Learners registered for the CACHE Level 3 Award will follow Units 1 and 2. Learners registered for the CACHE Level 3 Certificate will follow Units 1 to 5. Learners registered for the CACHE Level 3 Diploma will follow Units 1 to 9 and will also undertake four optional units. Five of the optional units available are covered in this book, but Diploma learners will only need to choose four optional units to study.

Learning Outcomes

All units are divided into 'learning outcomes'. The first page of each unit lists the relevant learning outcomes.

Focus on...

This feature appears at the beginning of each learning outcome to explain the focus of the outcome and makes a link to the CACHE Assessment Criteria.

Links

Links frequently appear in the text to direct you to other units in the book that relate to the subject currently being covered.

Key Terms

During your course you'll come across new words and terms that you may not have heard before. When these words and terms are first used in the book they will be highlighted in bold. A clear, simple definition of the word or term can be found at the bottom of the relevant page.

Learning Outcomes

In this Unit you'll learn about:

1. the range of provision for children

2. understanding roles and responsibilities in promoting children's rights

3. what is meant by professional practice

4. the principles and values that underpin working with children

5. how to develop relevant study and time management skills.

FOCUS ON...
The range of provision for children

This links with Assessment Criteria 1.1, 1.2

Further information about play and learning theory can be found in **Unit 7**.

Statutory sector = provided by the state

Practical Examples

Practical examples (case studies) are included to help you understand how theory links with practical work in real settings. After each case study a question or two is provided to help you think about how you can use your learning in real situations.

Have a go

'Have a go' sections ask you to do small tasks based on the text you have read. The tasks will help you to understand and remember the information. Some tasks are linked to your placement. These will help you to apply your learning to your practical work.

Good practice

It's important that you always work to high standards and do your best for the children in your care. This feature highlights good practice.

Fast facts

The 'fast fact' feature gives you bite-sized nuggets of information.

Progress Check

At the end of each learning outcome you will find a list of questions. Answering these will confirm that you have understood what you have read.

Weblinks

Each unit ends with the addresses of websites you may like to visit to further your learning.

New legislation

Some new legislation affecting childcare and education will be introduced in England from September 2008. Please turn to the appendix on page 542 for details. It's important that you are aware of this development.

CACHE statement of values

CACHE has developed a set of values that underpin their courses. These values are promoted within this book. The CACHE statement of values are:

You must ensure that you:

1. Put children first by
    *   Ensuring the child's welfare and safety
    *   Showing compassion and sensitivity
    *   Respecting the child as an individual
    *   Upholding the child's rights and dignity
    *   Enabling the child to achieve their full learning potential

2. Never use physical punishment

3. Respect the parent as the primary carer and educator of their child

4. Respect the contribution and expertise of staff in the care and education field, and other professionals who may be involved

5. Respect the customs, values and spiritual beliefs of the child and their family

6. Uphold the Council's Equal Opportunity Policy

7. Honour the confidentiality of information relating to the child and their family, unless its disclosure is required by law or is in the best interests of the child.

You can read more about this online at www.cache.org.uk

Unit 1

An introduction to working with children

The vast majority of children are brought up within their family. Childcare practitioners have differing contact with the parents of the children in their care, varying according to the setting in which they work. A thorough knowledge of both childcare legislation and the different types of childcare provision and support services available to children and families is essential to those who work with children and their families.

Learning Outcomes

In this unit you will learn about:

1 the range of provision for children

2 understanding roles and responsibilities in promoting the rights of children

3 what is meant by professional practice

4 the principles and values that underpin working with children

5 how to develop relevant study and time management skills.

Learning Outcome (1)

FOCUS ON...
the range of provision for children

This links to assessment criteria **1.1**

The role of statutory, voluntary, private and independent services in relation to children and families

There is a wide range of **statutory**, **voluntary**, **private** and **independent** services that support children and their families in the UK today. The UK has a welfare state that provides statutory services both through the local authority and central government. The government introduced this during the 1940s. The aim of the welfare state is to ensure that all citizens have adequate standards of income, housing, education and health services from 'cradle to grave'. The welfare state and the services provided by it have changed a great deal since they were introduced. Recent governments have supported the growth of private and voluntary provision to supplement state services provided by local authorities and central government.

The range of services for children and families

Care and education services for children and their families are provided by:

- the state, through either local authorities or central government departments organised in regions – these are referred to as statutory services
- volunteers or voluntary groups – referred to as voluntary services
- private individuals or companies – referred to as independent or private services.

What are statutory services?

These are provided by either local authorities or central government departments.

A statutory service is one provided by the government after a law (or statute) has been passed by parliament. Such laws say that either:

- a service must be provided (i.e. there is a duty to provide it), for example education for 5 to 16 year olds; or
- a service can be provided (i.e. there is a power to provide it if an authority chooses), for example local authority day nurseries.

Statutory sector = provided by the state
Voluntary sector = provided by voluntary organisations
Private sector = provided by individuals, groups or companies to meet demand and make a financial profit
Independent = not dependent or reliant on others

What do statutory services provide?

Statutory services provide for, among other things, education, health care, financial support, personal social services, housing, leisure services and public health. Government provision is sometimes referred to as 'the state sector'. Local authorities are mostly involved in the provision of education, social services, housing, public, health and leisure services. Central government provides social security benefits and the National Health Service.

How are statutory services financed?

Statutory services are financed by the state, which collects money through local and national taxation and National Insurance. There may be some fund-raising activities and charging for services (for example, prescription charges and charges for outings in schools). There has been increasing pressure on state services to be more accountable financially and to be run more like private organisations and give 'value for money'. This philosophy has affected the way that both state hospitals and state schools are funded and organised.

How are statutory services staffed?

Most of the people who work in statutory organisations are trained and paid for their work, but volunteers may carry out some tasks (for example, parent-helpers in schools, WRVS workers in hospitals).

What are voluntary services?

Organisations are referred to as 'voluntary' when they are founded by individuals who want to help certain groups of people who they believe are in need of support (i.e. they are formed voluntarily, like Barnado's and the NSPCC). The basic difference between voluntary and statutory organisations is that, unlike a statutory organisation, no legislation has to be passed in order for a voluntary organisation to be set up. The government is very positive about some services being provided by 'the voluntary sector', but it does pass laws to regulate them, requiring certain of them to register,

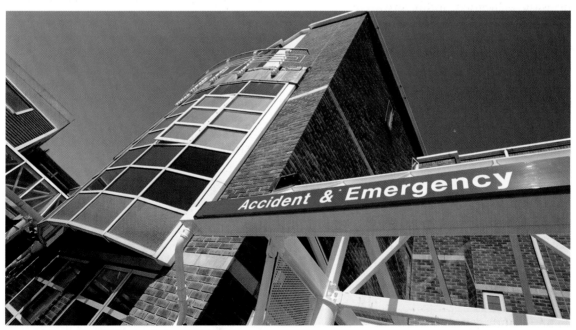

▲ A statutory service is financed by the state

so that the services they provide can be inspected by government officers in order to protect the people who use them (for example, playgroups and childminders, under the Children Act 1989, supported by the Children Act 2004).

What do voluntary services provide?

There is a long and varied tradition of voluntary work in the UK and as a result there is a wide variety of voluntary organisations. Voluntary organisations have a number of different functions. Some organisations combine more than one of these functions.

They:

- act as information and campaigning bodies (for example, Shelter and the Pre-School Learning Alliance or PLA)
- provide money to help people in particular circumstances – these are sometimes called benevolent funds or charities (for example, the Family Welfare Association)
- help and support some people who have health conditions or impairments (for example, Scope, Royal National Institute for the Blind or RNIB)
- support and care for families and children, and other individuals (for example, Barnado's and NCH day centres and family centres, Mencap, Relate).

FAST FACT

Did you know that Barnardo's was first set up in 1867? This was when Thomas Barnardo established orphanages for destitute children. These days, Barnardo's no longer runs orphanages but it does support 110,000 children and their families through a range of projects, including counselling children who have been abused and fostering and adoption services.

How are voluntary services financed?

Money for voluntary organisations comes from a variety of sources that include donations, fund-raising, grants from central or local government, lottery grants and fees for the services they provide.

How are voluntary services staffed?

Some people do work without pay and have no qualifications (for example, in self-help groups), and this is the reason that most people think they are called 'voluntary'. However, many people who work for voluntary organisations are professionally trained and qualified and receive a salary (for example, inspectors in the NSPCC or workers in NCH family centres). Some voluntary organisations may pay one person who then organises many unpaid volunteers (for example, Homestart), or pay several people a small amount (for example, playgroup workers). They may be run by a voluntary management committee, as is the case for many playgroups and community groups.

the children's charity

Support and friendship for families

▲ Do you recognise the logos of these voluntary organisations?

What are private or independent services?

Independent services are usually private services provided by individuals, groups of people or companies to meet a demand, provide a service, and make a financial profit. As with voluntary organisations, the government is also positive about certain services being provided by the private or independent sector.

What do private or independent services provide?

Independent services usually aim both to provide a service and to make a financial profit for their owners. They therefore need to be what is called 'financially viable', i.e. not run at a loss. They provide, among other things, nursery care, education, health care, counselling services, housing and leisure services. Nannies and childminders are part of the private sector.

How are private or independent services financed?

The financing of private services comes both from private investment by people wishing to make a return on their investment and from the fees that they charge for their use. In some cases the state may pay the fees for someone to use a private service. This happens when it has a duty to provide a service for a particular client but there is a lack of provision within the state sector in a particular area (for example, paying for day care with a childminder for a child who is considered to be 'in need' under the Children Act 1989).

How are independent services staffed?

Independent services are staffed according to the need of the organisation. In regulating some services the state may, for example, demand they employ a certain proportion of professionally qualified staff. Some users may also demand qualifications, for example those using qualified nannies.

The political structure for service provision in the UK

Statutory, voluntary and private or independent services for children and their families are provided within the political structure of a country. Political structures vary between countries and there are therefore differences between the UK and other European countries in their provision. In the UK, although some service provision is administered centrally, other provision depends on the choices made by politicians in different local authorities. Services may therefore vary from one area to another. Political parties change and services may be modified as a result.

Statutory services: central government provision

Some statutory services are provided by central government, through different departments. The political process that leads to this provision involves the following:

- In a general election, citizens elect politicians, called Members of Parliament (MPs). MPs make policy decisions about the services they want to provide, based on their political beliefs. They then pass laws (statutes) to say which services should be provided.

- MPs employ officers to put their policies into practice. These officers are called civil servants and they are paid from our taxes. These officers work in central and regional offices throughout the country.

For example, the Department of Health, HM Revenue and Customs and the Department for Work and Pensions are all organised as central government departments with regional offices.

Statutory services: local government provision

Local government, through a local authority, also provides some statutory services. The organisation of local authorities in the UK is varied and complicated. The main differences are as follows:

- Some areas of the country have two tiers (or layers) of local government, both of which have elected councils, which are:
  - a district council, which may represent a borough, city or district
  - a county council, which will contain several districts.

  In such areas the provision of services is divided between the two authorities.

- Other areas have just one tier (or layer) of local government and only one elected council. These are called unitary authorities, because one body provides all local services.

The political process that leads to the provision of services involves the following:

- Citizens vote for and elect councillors in district and county council elections. These councillors then form the local council. The party with the greatest number of councillors takes charge (this is called the democratic process). The powers of local councils are given to them by Acts of Parliament and through passing local by-laws.
- Councillors appoint officers to put their policies into practice and to

organise and provide services in that area. These are called local government officers and they are paid from local and central taxation. These officers work in town halls, civic centres and other offices in the area. Some schools and other education services, social services, leisure services and housing are provided in this way by local government departments.

The state in relation to private, independent and voluntary services

The extent to which the state encourages independent or voluntary provision depends on its political outlook. Conservative governments have traditionally been associated with support for the independent, private sector. However, it is a fact that recent governments of both political persuasions have increasingly encouraged the provision of private and voluntary services. In order to protect the people who use them, the state passes laws requiring these services to reach certain standards, to register and to be inspected by government officials (for example, childminders and private day nurseries, under the Children Act 1989 and Children Act 2004).

Apart from this, independent services can charge the amount that they believe people are prepared to pay for a service. They meet the demands of 'the market place'. Voluntary providers are usually controlled by some form of committee that decides who should be helped by their service. This may mean that services users may have to subscribe to a certain belief, or be 'deserving'. This is in contrast to state provision, which is available as a right to citizens if they are eligible.

Childcare and education services

Statutory provision of childcare and education services

The state is required by law to ensure that all children, including those with disabilities, receive education if they are of statutory school age.

Early years education

The structure of primary school provision varies between areas. Primary education may be provided for children in:

- one primary school until the age of 11
- an infant school until the age of 7, then a junior school until the age of 11
- a first school until the age of 8, followed by a middle school from 9 to 13 years.

Local management of schools

Local education authorities now give a large proportion of their education budget directly to schools. The headteacher and the governors of a school decide how to spend this money and how to staff the school. They are responsible for the financial and overall management of their school. This system is called the **local management of schools (LMS)**. Most people in education view this as a successful policy that has given power and discretion to schools to manage their own budgets.

National Curriculum and the Early Years Foundation Stage

All state schools are now required by law to follow the National Curriculum. This is to ensure that all children follow a broad-based and balanced curriculum. The content of the National Curriculum and arrangements for testing it have been amended several times. The Early Years Foundation Stage (EYFS) is the new single framework for children from birth to 5 years.

Nursery schools and classes

Local authorities have had the power to provide pre-school education for many

▲ Primary education must cater for all children

Local management of schools (LMS) = enables a headteacher and the governors of a school to decide how to spend the money and staff the school

years, but they have not used this power uniformly across the country or within their own area. As a result, state provision of nursery schools and classes varies nationally. Some councils provide separate nursery schools, others provide nursery units attached to a primary school, while others provide very little. Education in these settings is usually part time. The government now funds pre-school education for all 4-year-olds, but parents can choose whether this is in the state, voluntary or private sector. It has extended this funding to some 3-year-olds and aims to fund all 3-year-olds. To obtain funding, settings have to be inspected and judged to be offering provision that will satisfactorily promote the Early Years Foundation Stage. There is still a strong emphasis on play and exploration in all nursery education. State nursery schools are more often found in areas of highest social need.

Most European countries provide more nursery education than the UK but their statutory school age is usually older. For example, in France and Germany there is a legal entitlement to a place in a kindergarten for every child from 3- to 6-years-old. In Italy, children attend pre-primary education as part of the state system from 3 to 6 years. In Sweden, all parents who work or study are entitled to a place for their children in a publicly funded centre from the age of 1 year.

Day nurseries and family centres

The social services department (SSD) of a local authority has the power to provide day care for children in day nurseries and family centres, and a duty under the Childcare Act 2006 to provide for **children in need** in its area. Many of these powers in England have now been transferred to

the Department for Children, Schools and Families (DfCSF), which has done much of the work in developing policies for Early Years Development and Childcare Plans and Partnerships and for setting up the first Early Years Excellence Centres.

Government initiatives
Sure Start

Sure Start is an area-based government initiative. Launched in 1999 it aims to improve the health and wellbeing of families and children before and from birth, so children are ready to flourish when they get to school. Sure Start programmes started in neighbourhoods where a high proportion of the children are living in poverty and where it is hoped Sure Start could help them to succeed by pioneering new ways of working to improve all services for children and their families.

Sure Start is the responsibility of seven government departments working together. Programmes are run locally by partnerships, including voluntary and community organisations, health, local government, education and, most significantly, local parents.

SureStart

△ Sure Start's logo

Sure Start programmes provide the following as a minimum, but exactly how they do so depends on local circumstances and needs:

● outreach and home visiting
● support for families and parents

Children in need = a child is 'in need' if they are unlikely to achieve or maintain a reasonable standard of health or development without the provision of services, or if they have a disability

- support for good-quality play, learning and childcare
- primary and community health and social care
- support for children and parents with special needs.

Sure Start programmes work according to the following key principles:

- Coordinate and add value to existing services.
- Involve parents, grandparents and other carers in ways that build on their existing strengths.
- Avoid stigma by ensuring all local families are able to use Sure Start services.
- Ensure lasting support by linking to services for older children.
- Be culturally appropriate and sensitive to particular needs.
- Promote the participation of all local families in the design and working of the programme.

The National Childcare Strategy

The development by the Labour government of a **National Childcare Strategy** is also taking place. In May 1998 the government unveiled its plans to spend more than £300m on funding childcare places over the following five years. Its aim was to ensure good quality, accessible and affordable childcare for children aged up to 14 years in every neighbourhood in England. The strategy includes measures to make childcare more affordable, by including tax credits for working families, and more accessible, by increasing the number of places and encouraging diversity in provision to satisfy the preferences of parents. A similar strategy is in place for Wales.

The Children's Plan

In December 2007 the government published the Children's Plan. This wide-ranging initiative aims to:

- strengthen support for all families during the formative early years of their children's lives
- take the next steps in achieving world-class schools and an excellent education for every child
- involve parents fully in their children's learning
- help to make sure that young people have interesting and exciting things to do outside school
- provide more places for children to play safely.

It also means a new leadership role for Children's Trusts in every area, a new role for schools as the centre of their communities, and more effective links between schools, the NHS and other children's services so that together they can engage parents and tackle all the barriers to the learning, health and happiness of every child.

Children's Centres

The national development of children's centres is another initiative underway. The government has a commitment to delivering a Sure Start Children's Centre for every community by 2010. Multidisciplinary teams of professionals will be linked to the centres with the aim of providing integrated services for children under 5 years.

Children's centres will provide:

- good quality early learning with teacher input and day care for children
- child and family health-care services

National Childcare Strategy = a strategy introduced by the government in the UK in May 1998 to ensure good quality, accessible and affordable childcare for children up to the age of 14

- parental outreach
- family support services
- a central location for networking e.g. for childminder networks
- support for children and parents with special needs
- effective links with Jobcentre Plus to support carers and parents.

Further details and information can be found by contacting the Early Years Department of any local authority.

Extended Schools

The government launched the Extended Schools initiative in 2005 with the expectation that by 2010 wraparound childcare will be provided by schools or local providers from 8am to 6pm all year round. A broad range of provision will be available, for example breakfast clubs, sports clubs and homework clubs. In addition there will be support for parents, for example, family learning and parenting programmes. Specialist support will also be available, for example behaviour support and advice.

Voluntary sector provision of childcare and education services

Pre-school playgroups

The playgroup movement in the UK began in the 1960s with the formation of one group by a parent. The movement spread rapidly through the country. Over the years it has filled a much-needed gap in pre-school provision, but recent changes in funding and rise in provision by other sectors has led to a fall in the number of playgroups nationally.

To form a pre-school playgroup, local people usually join together, rent premises and form a committee that organises and appoints workers. Parents sometimes help on a rota at sessions. There are usually a number of part-time sessions available a week; a charge is made for each child, but 3- and 4-year-olds may be funded. Pre-school playgroups have traditionally provided play facilities and social contact. However, the inspection process has been very demanding for some pre-school playgroups; staff are relatively low paid and may lack professional qualifications. Playgroups also had to register with and be inspected by the social services department. However, both arms of this inspection process were brought together under Ofsted in September 2001.

Parent and toddler groups sometimes use the same facilities as playgroups. Parents and carers bring children from babies upwards, but supervise them while they play.

PLA

The Pre-school Learning Alliance (PLA) is a national educational charity with many years' experience in the field of pre-school education and care. It offers a national training programme for parents and pre-school staff, and publishes educational materials and advice for pre-school playgroups.

Nursery and family centres in the voluntary sector

Voluntary organisations that were initially more traditionally involved in providing residential care now fund many nursery and family centres in areas of high social need. Organisations such as Barnardo's and NCH Action for Children have diverted their resources into providing community day care and family support for those who are experiencing difficulties.

Private sector provision of childcare and education services

Childminders

Childminders look after other people's children in their own homes. They have a legal duty to register to care for children under 8 years of age, previously with the SSD, but now with the Department for Children, Schools and Families (DfCSF) Childminders must conform to standards in the guidance to the Children Act 1989 and the Care Standards. They must be of good health and character and have non-discriminatory attitudes. The Standards cover safety, floor space and ratios for children to childminders according to the different ages. Childminders are free to fix their own charges. They are sometimes paid by a social service department to care for children in need. The Early Years Foundation Stage will apply to the home learning environment (HLE) and will therefore encompass childminding. Inspections will be carried out in line with the EYFS.

The National Childminding Association (NCMA) is an influential body concerned with providing information and training, and acting as a pressure group for childminders.

Nannies

Nannies are privately employed by parents to look after children in the family home. Nannies may live in or out of the home. They negotiate their contract, which includes hours, pay and duties, with their employer. There has been a call for nannies to be registered under a national system. This raises numerous problems, and some experts believe that registration would be unworkable and not serve to protect children. The Federation of Recruitment and Employment Services (FRES) has published a set of guidelines for anyone wanting to employ a nanny. It provides a 10-point list for prospective employers to help them to choose the right nanny.

Private day nurseries

Private day nursery provision more than trebled in the period from 1987 to 1997, when there were an estimated 6,100 day nurseries in England, providing 194,000 places. Private day nurseries occupy many types of premises, including purpose-built nurseries and those in converted buildings; they vary in size. They all have to register with Ofsted for a specific number of children and conform to standards in the same way as childminders and to national regulations about qualified staffing levels. They provide full- or part-time care and education for children under school age and many provide for babies. Some also provide before- and after-school care and care during the school holidays. Charges vary and to some extent they reflect what people in an area can afford to pay. The National Day Nurseries Association (NDNA) aims to promote quality in the private sector.

Out-of-school clubs

Out-of-school clubs are provided in school, nursery or other premises and have had considerable financial backing from government in recent years. They provide invaluable support for the children of working parents in the periods between working hours and school hours. As already stated, the provision of wraparound care is in line with government requirements for Extended Schools.

Private nursery schools

Private nursery schools exist to meet a demand from parents who want their children to be educated in the private sector. They are often part of a private school for children up to the age of 11 years. These schools provide full- and part-time education for children from 3 years old during school hours; they may also provide before- and after-school care. Their fees vary. Small class sizes are a key feature of this form of provision. Schools have to register with the DfCSF and meet certain standards. If they are providing nursery education for funded children they have to register and be inspected by Ofsted.

Personal social services

Statutory provision of social services

Previously, local authorities provided personal social services through their social services department (SSD). The Children Act 1989 gave them a duty to provide services for 'children in need' in their area to help them to stay with their families and be brought up by them. Changes informed by the Children Act 2004 meant that from April 2006 the education and social services for children were brought under the directorate of children's services within each local authority.

Social services provide support and care for children and their families. These include:

- looked-after children – children looked after by the local authority through foster care or residential care
- families where children have been assessed as being in need; this includes children with disabilities

- children who may be suffering significant harm
- children placed for adoption.

The SSD tries to keep families together by offering them support in the community. It may provide social work support and counselling, practical support in the home, family centres, short periods of relief care, help with providing essential household needs and welfare rights advice. In certain cases it may look after children in need by providing them with foster care or residential accommodation and respite care (now known as a 'short-term break') for children with disabilities.

Children at risk

The SSD has a duty to investigate the circumstances of any child believed to be at risk of harm and take action on their behalf to protect them by using child protection procedures. It also provides care in residential or foster homes for children who are made the subject of care orders by a court.

Looked-after children

The SSD provides accommodation for children who, with the agreement of their parents, need a period of care away from their family. Foster carers, approved and paid for by the department, will often look after such children. It also provides community homes for some children. All SSDs provide an adoption service for children who need new, permanent parents.

Special needs

There is also a range of services that are provided for children with disabilities alongside those provided by the health and education authorities. Social workers are expected to provide a range of services for children and their families. These include supporting access to a range of services, such as short-term breaks, and providing assistance to enable children to participate in clubs and community activities alongside non-disabled peers.

Care Matters

In October 2006, the document *Care Matters: Transforming the Lives of Children and Young People in Care* was published by the government. This Green Paper set out ideas of how the care system can be made better for children in care in the future in seven areas:

- more help for families who are having problems
- a consistent adult throughout their lives
- a good, settled placement that is right for each child
- a place at a good school and support for each child to do their best
- more out-of-school support for children in care
- giving young people a say on when to move on from care, and the support they need to succeed when they do
- giving young people a say and holding people responsible for making care work.

(From www.everychildmatters.gov.uk)

Finding information about services

Information about local social services departments can be obtained from their offices, which are listed in the telephone directory and at local libraries. Your local authority website will be a good source of information. The SSD will have leaflets to inform the public about its services.

Voluntary provision of social services

National voluntary organisations

There is a wide range of voluntary organisations that help to support families and children; some of these are shown in the table on pages 14 and 15.

These organisations supplement the work of the social services department. Addresses and further information can be obtained from websites, telephone books, from the *Charities Digest* (published by the Family Welfare Association and available in public libraries) and at the volunteer bureau.

In most areas there are local voluntary organisations that have grown up to meet the needs of the local population. They are often listed and coordinated by a local Council for Voluntary Service (CVS). They are also listed under 'Voluntary organisations' in Yellow Pages directories and online. There is a wide range of these organisations. In some cases there is a national organisation which has local subgroups or affiliated groups, for example the National Autistic Society. Some are self-help groups; others meet the needs of people from a variety of ethnic and national backgrounds. They may provide specific information services, advice and support.

Independent provision of personal support services

Some support services can be purchased privately, for example personal and family therapy, different forms of counselling, domestic and care assistance. These services tend to be expensive and financially impossible for many people, but they can provide a very useful service for many people in need of personal support with family matters.

13

▽ Voluntary organisations

ORGANISATION	SERVICE
AFRICAN-CARIBBEAN, INDIAN, PAKISTANI COMMUNITY CENTRES	Exist in areas where there are numbers of people of Caribbean and Asian origin. They offer a range of advice and support services for local people. There is also a wide range of local organisations that aim to meet the needs of other minority communities. Some of these provide nurseries
BARNADO'S	Works with children and their families to help to relieve the effects of disadvantage and disability. It runs many community projects, including day centres where young children who are at risk can be cared for and their families supported. It also provides residential accommodation for children with special needs. It carries out research into areas of need and publishes the results of research
CHILDLINE	Provides a national telephone counselling helpline for children in trouble or danger. It listens, comforts and protects. Its free phone number is 0800 1111
THE CHILDREN'S SOCIETY	Offers childcare services to children and families in need. It aims to help children to grow up in their own families and communities
NATIONAL ASSOCIATION OF CITIZENS' ADVICE BUREAUX	Provides free, impartial (not biased), confidential advice and help to anyone. It has over 1,000 local offices that provide information, advice and legal guidance on many subjects. These include social security, housing, money, family and personal matters
CONTACT-A-FAMILY	Promotes mutual support between families caring for disabled children. It has community-based projects that assist parents' self-help groups, and runs a national helpline
FAMILY SERVICE UNITS	Provide a range of social and community work services and support to disadvantaged families and communities with the aim of preventing family breakdown
FAMILY WELFARE ASSOCIATION	Offers services for families, children and people with disabilities. It provides financial help for families in exceptional need, social work support and drop-in centres
GINGERBREAD	Provides emotional support, practical help and social activities for lone parents and their children
JEWISH CARE	Provides help and support for people of the Jewish faith and their families. Among other facilities, it runs day centres and provides social work teams and domiciliary (home) assistance

ORGANISATION	SERVICE
MENCAP	Aims to increase public awareness of the problems faced by people with mental disabilities and their families. It supports day centres and other facilities
MIND	Is concerned with improving services for people with mental disorders and promoting mental health and better services
NCH ACTION FOR CHILDREN	Provides support for children who are disadvantaged and their families. It runs many schemes, including family centres, foster care and aid and support to families. It also carries out and publishes the results of research
NATIONAL DEAF CHILDREN'S SOCIETY	A national charity working specially for deaf children and their families. It gives information, advice and support directly to families with deaf children. It helps them to identify local help and support
NATIONAL SOCIETY FOR THE PREVENTION OF CRUELTY TO CHILDREN (NSPCC)	Has a network of child protection teams throughout England and Wales. The RSSPCC works similarly in Scotland. Central to the NSPCC's services is the free 24-hour Child Protection Helpline – 0808 800 5000 – which provides counselling, information and advice to anyone concerned about a child at risk. It investigates referrals and also offers support in family care centres. It is very involved in research and publication, and provides information and training for other professionals. It also campaigns to change attitudes towards children and their care
PARENTLINE	Offers a telephone support helpline for parents who are having any kind of problem with their children – 0808 800 2222
PLAYMATTERS: THE NATIONAL TOY LIBRARIES ASSOCIATION	Exists to promote awareness of the importance of play for the developing child. Libraries are organised locally, loaning good quality toys to all families with young children
RELATE	Trains and provides counsellors to work with people who are experiencing difficulty in their relationships. People usually make a contribution to this service according to their means
THE SAMARITANS	Provides confidential and emotional support to people in crisis and at risk of suicide. The Samaritans is available 24 hours a day. Local branches can be found in the phone book under S, or phone 0845 909090

Health services

Statutory provision – the National Health Service

The NHS was created in 1948 to give free health care to the entire population of the UK. Since it was founded:

- the general health of both children and adults has improved
- the demand for services has continued to increase, despite improvements in general health
- more expensive technology and treatments has meant that the cost of the service has increased enormously and is continuing to do so.

This increase in cost has resulted in a series of reforms over the years aimed at achieving greater efficiency, and contributing to what some regard as a decline in standards, for example the increase in hospital waiting lists and the introduction and gradual increase in prescription charges.

Health authorities

The Department of Health (central government) is in overall charge of policy and planning for the health service and social care. It gives powers and money to health authorities in Britain.

The role of each health authority is to:

- determine the full range of health needs of the local population, from vaccinations, to mending fractures, to treating cancer
- plan the shape of the services required, including the services of dentists, pharmacists and opticians

- purchase the services required to meet local health needs
- review their effectiveness and make any necessary changes.

NHS trusts

More recently the concept of a 'market' for health care, introduced in 1990, has been modified, with health authorities co-ordinating groups of primary health care teams (GPs and community nurses) to commission the services that their patients need from NHS trusts. These are:

- primary care trusts (PCTs)
- community trusts, providing community services such as health visitors, midwives and clinics at health centres
- hospital trusts, providing a range of outpatient and inpatient services.

The work of the NHS trusts includes emergency and acute services, as well as meeting longer-term needs in mental health and disability.

National Health framework for children, young people and maternity services

This forms part of the government's strategy to tackle child poverty. It was set up in 2004 by the Department of Health (DH) and services are divided into three types:

- universal services – for all children, young people, their families and expectant parents
- targeted services – to encourage use of services by those who do not usually use the services
- specialist services – for those identified as having difficulties or medical conditions which need specialist care, support or treatment.

The framework is divided into three parts which are further divided into standards as illustrated in the table below.

Voluntary provision of health care

There is a long history of health care and provision through the voluntary sector in the UK. Many hospitals with voluntary status, however, including famous ones such as St Bartholomew's in London, became a part of the NHS when it was formed in 1948. Prior to this, people had to pay to see a GP, and if they could not afford this they sometimes went to a charitable hospital instead.

There are many voluntary organisations and self-help groups covering a very wide range of medical conditions and impairments that aim to help and support people, and to fund research.

The Sick Children's Trust is a national charity providing accommodation for the families of sick children at centres of specialist paediatric care. The Trust owns houses in different cities in which it aims to provide homely accommodation to families at times of great stress.

Private provision of health care

There has been a large growth in private sector provision since 1979. Increasingly, people who are able to, and wish to, pay into private insurance schemes and

▼ The National Health framework for children, young people and maternity services

PART 1	
Standard 1	Promoting health and wellbeing – identifying needs and early intervention including the Child Health Promotion Programme
Standard 2	Supporting parenting
Standard 3	Child-, young person- and family-centred services
Standard 4	Growing up into adulthood
Standard 5	Safeguarding and promoting the welfare of children and young people
PART 2	
Standard 6	Children and young people who are ill
Standard 7	Children who are in hospital
Standard 8	Disabled children and young people and those with complex health needs
Standard 9	The mental health and psychological wellbeing of the children and young people
Standard 10	Medicines for children and young people
PART 3	
Standard 11	Maternity services

then receive their treatment privately, or purchase care directly. This usually means that they do not have to wait for treatment, and the physical standards in private hospitals are usually better although not necessarily the standards of care.

However, not all services are provided in the private sector, including accident and emergency services. Some people believe that the presence of the private sector contributes to the growth of a two-tier health service, where those who can will pay for a good service, and those who cannot make do with a poorer service by the NHS (similar to the effect of having private and state schools). It is possible that private health provision will begin to play a greater part within the NHS.

✓ Progress check

1. What childcare and education services are provided by the state sector?
2. What childcare and education services are provided in the voluntary sector?
3. What childcare and education services are provided by the private sector?
4. Which Act of Parliament gave the local authority a duty to provide services for children in need in their area?
5. Who is a 'child in need'? Try to put the definition in your own words.
6. Which Act gave local authorities the responsibility for assessing the individual needs of clients?
7. What do the NSPCC, NCH and Barnado's provide?
8. Which voluntary societies provide telephone helplines for the public?
9. Which private support services can people purchase themselves?

Learning Outcome 2

FOCUS ON...
understanding the roles and responsibilities in promoting the rights of children

⊂◯◯⊃ This links to assessment criteria **2.1**

Main legislation concerning the rights of children

Children Act 1989

The Children Act 1989 came into force in October 1990. It aims to protect children in every situation – in their homes, in day care, or in full-time care. It provides extensive guidance on the regulation of services for children and families. It is based on a number of important principles that are embodied in the Act. These principles include the following:

- Children are entitled to protection from neglect, abuse and exploitation.
- The welfare of the child is the first consideration.
- Wherever possible, children should be brought up and cared for by their families.
- The child's wishes should be taken into account when making decisions.
- Unnecessary delay in procedures or court action should be avoided.
- A court order should only be made if it positively contributes to a child's welfare.
- Professionals should work in partnership with parents at every stage.

- Parents whose children are in need should be helped to bring up their children themselves.
- Although the basic needs of children are universal, there can be a variety of ways of meeting them. Patterns of family life differ according to culture, class and community. These differences should be respected and accepted.

Children Act 2004

The Children Act 2004 sets out the process of integrated services for children in order to promote the achievement of the five outcomes of the Every Child Matters legislation for every child.

Childcare Act 2006

The Childcare Act 2006 states the following:

- Local authorities must improve outcomes for all children under 5, close the gaps between those with the poorest outcomes and the rest by integrating services and ensuring these services are accessible and proactive.
- Local authorities should take the lead role in facilitating the childcare market to ensure the needs of working parents, in particular those with disabled children and those on low incomes.

- People must be enabled to have access to the full range of information they may need as parents.

- The Early Years Foundation Stage: [this was] introduced to support the delivery of quality integrated education and care for children from birth to 5.

- A reformed, simplified, childcare and early years regulation framework should reduce bureaucracy and focus on raising quality.

United Nations Convention on the Rights of the Child

Children's rights are most fully described in the United Nations Convention on the Rights of the Child. Created over a period of 10 years, with the input of representatives from different societies, religions and cultures, the Convention was adopted as an international human rights treaty on 20 November 1989. It entered into force in record time on 2 September 1990. It contains a comprehensive array of rights, bringing civil and political, economic, social and cultural rights, as well as humanitarian rights, together for the first time in one international instrument.

Overall, the Convention serves as a landmark in the promotion of the rights of the child, placing children alongside other population groups whose rights necessitate protection by way of an international treaty. It is based on the belief that all children are born with fundamental freedoms and the inherent rights of all human beings. This is the basic premise of the Convention on the Rights of the Child, an international human rights treaty that is transforming the lives of children and their families around the globe. People in every country and of every culture and every religion are working to ensure that each of the 2 billion children in the world will enjoy the rights to survival, health and education, to a caring family environment, play and culture, to protection from exploitation and abuse of all kinds, and to have their voice heard and opinions taken into account on significant issues.

▲ UN Flag

Human Rights Act 1998

The European Convention on Human Rights was a treaty ratified by the UK in 1951. It guaranteed the various rights and freedoms in the United Nations Declaration on Human Rights, adopted in 1948. The Human Rights Act 1998, which came fully into force on 2 October 2000, gives people in the UK opportunities to enforce these rights directly in the British courts, rather than having to incur the costs and delay of taking a case to the European Court.

Promoting the rights of children and young people

In order to promote children's rights, it is important to understand what these rights are and your role in promoting these rights. Under the UN Convention, children have the right to:

- be with their family or those who will care best for them
- enough food and clean water for their needs
- an adequate standard of living
- health care
- play
- be kept safe and not hurt or neglected
- free education.

In addition:

- children with disabilities have the right to special care and training
- children must not be used as soldiers or cheap workers.

Once you have considered the rights of children, it is hoped that you will be able to view and assume links to other aspects of the regulations and frameworks which apply to your work with children and young people, such as Every Child Matters, the Early Years Foundation Stage and the Special Educational Needs Code of Practice.

There is an expectation that every practitioner will, of course, view the welfare of the child as paramount and central to their practice. It is also fair to assume that promoting children's rights is not the sole responsibility of an individual adult; as in many aspects of work with children and young people, this promotion will be most effective if it is collaborative and understood by everyone.

In practice, within any setting, adults working with children are enabled through guidance, policies and procedures to support and promote the rights of children. Choices, respect and valuing the individual are all ways in which children's rights can be promoted.

How society promotes equal opportunities

Promoting equal opportunities means giving everyone an equal chance to participate in life to the best of their abilities, regardless of race, religion, disability, gender or social background.

▲ All adults have a role to play in promoting the rights of children

This will not be achieved by treating everyone the same, but by recognising and responding to the fact that people are different, and that different people will have different needs and requirements. If these needs and differences are not recognised, then people will not receive equality of opportunity.

Equality of opportunity is promoted in a number of ways:

- At government level, there are laws to combat oppression and discrimination.
- At institutional level, many organisations have policies, procedures and codes of conduct to promote equality.
- On a personal level, equality of opportunities are addressed as the awareness of individuals is raised, and they examine their own attitudes and views.

Government level

The role of legislation

Laws themselves do not stop discrimination, just as speed limits do not stop people speeding. However, the existence of laws sends out a very clear message that discrimination is not acceptable and that penalties exist for those who flout the laws.

Legislation to combat racism

The Race Relations Act 1965 outlawed discrimination on the basis of race in the provision of goods and services, in employment and in housing. Incitement to racial hatred also became an offence under this Act. This Act was amended in 2000 and placed a responsibility on public organisations to encourage racial and social harmony.

In 1976 the Commission for Racial Equality (CRE) was given power to start court proceedings in instances of racial discrimination. The Children Act 1989 required that needs arising from children's race, culture and language should be considered by those caring for them.

Disability legislation

This includes the following:

- The Education Act 1944 placed a duty on local authorities to provide education for all children, including those with special needs.
- The Disabled Persons (Employment) Act 1944 required larger employers to recruit a certain proportion of people registered disabled into their workforce.
- The Education Act 1981 laid down specific procedures for the assessment and statementing of children with special educational needs. This was superseded by the Code of Practice for Special Educational Needs, which was introduced as part of the Education Act 1993.
- The Chronically Sick and Disabled Persons Act 1970 and the Disabled Persons Act 1986 imposed various duties on local authorities towards disabled people.
- The Children Act 1989 defined the services that should be provided by the local authority for 'children in need'. Children who are disabled are included in this category.
- The Disability Discrimination Act 1995 was passed to ensure that any services offered to the public in general must be offered on the same basis to people with disabilities.
- The Special Educational Needs and Disability Act 2001 required LEAs to

provide parents of children with special needs with advice and information. It strengthened the rights of children with special needs to be educated in mainstream schools.

- The Special Educational Needs Code of Practice 2001 is the most recent code which applies to settings that receive government funding. It is divided into chapters that are intended to support and advise practitioners.

Promoting effective equal opportunities, anti-discriminatory and anti-bias practice

As individuals, people contribute to promoting effective equal opportunities, **anti-discriminatory practice** and anti-bias practice by:

- examining their own attitudes and values – this can sometimes be a difficult and disturbing experience
- challenging behaviour and language that is abusive or offensive
- undertaking training to increase their ability to provide for the needs of all.

Valuing diversity

The first step in implementing anti-discriminatory and anti-bias practice is to recognise the diversity of our society and to value this diversity as a positive rather than a negative factor. In order to be able to do this, childcare workers will need to adopt an approach that is non-judgemental when working with families. This means that differences in family style, beliefs, traditions and, in particular, ways of caring for children should not be judged as being better or worse but should be respected.

Different families will provide for their children in a number of different ways and childcare practice that is anti-discriminatory will seek to meet the needs of all families within a framework that respects their individuality.

Practical example

Dinh at playgroup

Dinh started at playgroup when he was 3. His family had recently moved to the small town where the playgroup was located. His mother and father spoke some English, but Dinh understood and only spoke Vietnamese. The playgroup staff had little experience of working with children who did not speak English, but they contacted the local education authority which was able to provide them with some support from a peripatetic 'English as an additional language' teacher and access to some specialised resources. Together with the teacher, the staff were able to support Dinh and he gradually gained confidence in English; he was soon able to join in and enjoy all of the playgroup activities.

1. What were Dinh's needs?

2. What would have happened to Dinh if playgroup staff had not responded to him in this way?

3. Think of some other situations where failing to respond would result in needs not being met.

Anti-discriminatory practice = practice that encourages a positive view of difference and opposes negative attitudes and practices that lead to unfavourable treatment of people

▲ It is important to value diversity – a language difference is an opportunity not a problem

Inclusion and differentiation

Inclusive environments and activities can be achieved when the needs of all children are considered. To meet the needs of all children it is essential to observe and learn about the children in our care.

In order to provide inclusive activities, settings should provide:

● equipment that all children can use

● a range of options for different activities, e.g. books, story tapes, story boards with characters and symbols

● a range of environments and furniture activities at different levels

● flexible and adjustable resources and equipment

● a range and variety of tools and implements

● effective adults to support and facilitate.

When providing for the needs of individuals, it is important to consider how we can extend and adapt the tasks and activities that interest and engage children. Encouraging and challenging children can support them to solve their own problems, extend their thinking and stimulate learning.

✓ Progress check

1. Which legislation applies to the promotion of children's rights?

2. How could you explain the terms 'inclusion' and 'differentiation' to a new practitioner?

3. List five ways in which all settings can promote diversity.

Learning Outcome ③

FOCUS ON...
what is meant by professional practice

○○ This links to assessment criteria **3.1** and **3.2**

○○ You will find further information about professional practice and effective professional relationships in Units 5 and 9 of this book.

Your role and the boundaries and limits to it

It is essential that childcare workers are clear about their role, how they fit into the organisation and how the roles of other workers and professionals complement each other in order to meet the needs of children and their families.

Professional practice means ensuring that you behave in a professional manner at all times; as such, the expectations for such behaviour are informed by laws and legislation as already mentioned in this unit. At a local level, within the organisation, policies, procedures and codes of conduct should be in place to support you to behave in the expected manner.

You should expect to be inducted into the setting and a supervisor should take time to ensure that you are aware of your role, the limits to this and what to do if you feel that your role is compromised at any time. Current and up-to-date policies and procedures which reflect current legislation should be accessible to you for further reference. It is important that you

check with a supervisor if at any time you are unsure about your role.

Characteristics that define an effective practitioner

There are certain characteristics that are possessed by an effective practitioner and these are shown in the diagram below.

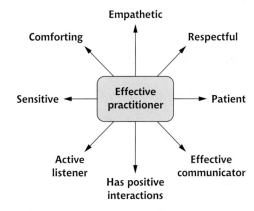

▲ Characteristics of an effective practitioner

Developing appropriate relationships with children, parents and colleagues

The quality and character of children's early close relationships are believed to be of central importance to their social and emotional development. Pioneering research into the nature and effect of early relationships, particularly concerning the development of attachments between infants and their main carers, was carried out in the 1940s and 1950s. During this period, John Bowlby, an influential British child psychiatrist, studied the long-term developmental effects on children who had been separated from their parents when they were orphaned or evacuated during the Second World War. He observed that many of these children suffered a range of behavioural, emotional and mental health problems.

The experience of secure attachments is very important to children's all-round development. Childcare workers are usually looking after children who are separated from their primary carers and therefore they need to understand:

- the possible long-term consequences for children who have insecure attachments
- the possible effects of an 'interruption' to an attachment caused by separation of the child from their main carers, either temporarily or permanently, or loss.

▲ **Attachments are close, affectionate two-way relationships**

Attachments are the affectionate two-way relationships that develop between infants and their close carers. When a secure attachment is established the infant will try to stay close to that adult and will appear to want to be cared for by them. By the end of the first year the infant will show a marked preference for that person and may show anxiety towards strangers. Infants then become distressed if they are separated from those adults to whom they are attached and will try to regain contact with them. Bowlby called this 'attachment behaviour'.

Bowlby concluded that babies have a biological need or instinct to form an attachment to the person who feeds and cares for them. He maintained that this was a survival instinct without which the helpless infant would be exposed to danger and might die.

In line with the professional values, childcare workers should ensure that the child or young person is central to their practice as the needs of the child are paramount. The adult must want to become emotionally involved and to spend time with the child. An attachment is not formed immediately. Carers who are sensitive to the signals given by an infant and respond to them encourage the bond to develop over a period of time.

When children's needs are met fully this encourages attachments to develop. The success and intensity of the attachments do not, however, depend on the amount of time carers spend with the child but on the quality of that involvement.

Relationships, as already stated, develop over time. Children will benefit in many ways if they have secure relationships. Benefits include confidence, resilience and independence.

Appropriate relationships
With children

It is important that childcare workers develop appropriate professional relationships with children; indeed the

Early Years Foundation Stage expects children to have the opportunity to develop secure relationships with adults. Within every setting, adults should be clear that the experiences of every child will be enhanced by the relationships that they have with the adults around them. It is also important for the adults to be clear about the relationships that they have with children and the limits to these; caring adults should be aware that they are in a privileged position and are working in partnership with parents. Practitioners should remember that they should never undermine the relationships that children have with their parents or carers. Professional relationships with children are supported by codes of conduct and policies within the setting.

With parents

All those who work with children will recognise that the relationship between the establishment and the parents (or primary carers) of the child is extremely important. Good relationships will benefit the child, the parent and those who work with the child. Parents have the most knowledge and understanding of their child. If they are encouraged through good relationships to share this knowledge, they will feel valued and involved and the child will clearly benefit. Initiatives such as the Parent's Charter emphasise the rights of parents to make choices and be consulted in decisions concerning their children's education.

Therefore, the practitioners who have daily contact with parents have a responsibility to ensure that they present a professional impression of themselves and the organisation. They need to keep parents informed about their child's activities and parents should be encouraged to contribute. Practitioners need to ensure

that the information they share is in line with the procedures of the setting; any information or questions beyond their role and responsibilities must be referred to the appropriate senior member of staff.

It is fair to suggest that, sometimes, childcare practitioners know some of the children and their families at the setting better than they know others. This could be for a number of reasons, including links through family and friends. It is therefore essential that practitioners maintain the highest level of professionalism both within and beyond the setting. Practitioners may be asked to baby-sit for or socialise with parents away from the setting. Practitioners should take time to consider the implications of overfamiliar and informal relationships with parents and the effect that overfamiliarity may have on the children and the setting.

GOOD PRACTICE

Some good practice points to remember:
- Be friendly and approachable. Remember that parents might feel uneasy in an unfamiliar setting and it is up to staff to make the right kind of approach.
- Be courteous and maintain a professional relationship.
- Encourage a meaningful exchange of information between the home and the centre.

With colleagues

Relationships with other adults are important within any professional organisation. The world of work puts many demands on the individual. It is important that whenever practitioners are within the setting they behave in a professional manner and ensure that the needs and welfare of the children are at the heart of everything they do. It is true that work with children and young people is challenging and demanding, both physically and emotionally. It is also fair to suggest that adults in such a position must always ensure they present a positive role model to children and young people. Children can learn from the relationships that adults share and the attitudes and interactions they exhibit.

If adults experience difficulty working with each other and conflict arises, a professional approach must be taken. Such situations should be explored with the support of senior colleagues or managers. Individuals need to feel that they are supported and that any situation which causes conflict is resolved. Procedures and codes of practice should be in place to enable practitioners to work effectively with one another.

 Further information about working with teams can be found in Unit 5 of this book.

Practical example

Kylie's night out

Kylie enjoys her job at the nursery where she is a key worker for some of the children. Owen is 2 years old; he has been to visit the setting and he will start full time on Monday – Kylie is going to be his key worker.

Tonight Kylie is going out with some friends. When she arrives at the local pub she notices Owen's mother is also there with a group of people. Kylie stops to chat to her and Owen's mother buys drinks for Kylie and her friends. As the night progresses, Kylie and her friends start to play drinking games. Eventually, they are asked to leave the pub because they are being too boisterous and other people have complained about them. The girls have to leave.

On Monday morning, Kylie nervously prepares for Owen to arrive at the nursery.

1 Why is Kylie feeling nervous?

2 What do you think Kylie should have done when she noticed Owen's mother was in the pub?

3 How do you think this first impression will affect the relationship that Kylie has with Owen and his mother?

✔ Progress check

1 Consider the qualities of an effective practitioner and write your own definition.

2 How will children benefit from the opportunity to develop secure relationships?

Learning Outcome (4)

FOCUS ON...
principles and values that underpin working with children

This links to assessment criteria **4.1**

If you refer to the Key Elements of Effective Practice described in Unit 5, you will be reminded of the expectations of the sector. Within Unit 5 you will also find information about effective communication (see pages 206–7).

Every Child Matters

Every Child Matters is the government's vision for children's services; the document was published in September 2003. It proposed reshaping children's services to help achieve the outcomes children and young people said were key to wellbeing in childhood and later life.

The following table gives details of the five outcomes. They are part of the Every Child Matters: Change for Children Outcomes Framework, which is used by children's services inspectorates to shape the criteria for Joint Area Views of local areas.

▽ **Every Child Matters: Change for Children Outcomes Framework**

OUTCOMES	AIMS
BE HEALTHY	Physically healthy
	Mentally and emotionally healthy
	Sexually healthy
	Healthy lifestyles
	Choose not to take illegal drugs
	Parents, carers and families promote healthy choices
STAY SAFE	Safe from maltreatment, neglect, violence and sexual exploitation
	Safe from accidental injury and death
	Safe from bullying and discrimination
	Safe from crime and anti-social behaviour in and out of school
	Have security, stability and are cared for
	Parents, carers and families provide safe homes and stability

▶▶

ENJOY AND ACHIEVE	Ready for school
	Attend and enjoy school
	Achieve stretching national educational standards at primary school
	Achieve personal and social development and enjoy recreation
	Achieve stretching national educational standards at secondary school
	Parents, carers and families support learning
MAKE A POSITIVE CONTRIBUTION	Engage in decision-making and support the community and environment
	Engage in law-abiding and positive behaviour in and out of school
	Develop positive relationships and choose not to bully and discriminate
	Develop self-confidence and successfully deal with significant life changes and challenges
	Develop enterprising behaviour
	Parents, carers and families promote positive behaviour
ACHIEVE ECONOMIC WELLBEING	Engage in further education, employment or training on leaving school
	Ready for employment
	Live in decent homes and sustainable communities
	Access to transport and material goods
	Live in households free from low income
	Parents, carers and families are supported to be economically active

(From *Every Child Matters: Change for Children in Schools*, DfES/1089/2004)

✔ Progress check

(1) Consider the table on pages 29–30. How does your practice and the practice at your setting ensure that Every Child Matters? You could consider each outcome in turn.

Learning Outcome (5)

FOCUS ON...
how to develop relevant study and time management skills

This links to assessment criteria **5.1**

Your learning style

It is useful to stop and consider yourself as a learner, to think about your preferred learning style and your needs as a learner. Being aware of the way that you learn can help you to understand why you find some tasks easier than others. Knowing your preferred learning style may also help you to make choices about the types of study and learning activities that you take part in or methods of study that you choose.

People learn in different ways. For example:

- visual learners may learn best through the use of visual aids or prompts, textbooks, diagrams, video
- auditory learners may learn best through listening to lectures, recordings and discussions
- kinaesthetic learners may learn best by doing things, using a hands-on approach to learning.

Most people learn through a combination of styles; there are different resources available both in books and electronically which could be used to help you to consider your preferred learning style.

See also Unit 7.

Study skills

It is important that you consider how you are going to study and organise yourself accordingly. When you participate in a programme of study, there should be no shortage of information about what is expected of you and the deadlines that have been set. Taking responsibility for recording and reviewing this information will ensure that you are able to plan and develop your work over time rather than in a hurry at the end. This appears to be sensible advice that we are not all good at taking on board; the result of a lack of planning is, of course, a rushed and stressful end-loaded experience.

Managing time

Planning does take time but a calendar, diary or planner will provide you with a visual prompt. You need to manage your time in order to achieve the tasks that you have planned to do. Prioritising, putting things in order of importance, should help you to organise the task and decide the order in which to do things.

It can be helpful to:

- make lists – if you do this, you will be more able to cope if things get stressful
- ask others – other colleagues and students may be able to share useful tips and ideas with you
- try setting targets that are SMART – these are described in Unit 5, page 211
- be honest with yourself and others – if you are worried or experiencing difficulties talk to someone who can support and advise you.

Setting the scene

Making time for study and ensuring suitable study space can some times be a challenge. We can all find other things to do; we can all suggest we are not in the mood. However, the task that we need to complete will still be there, hanging over us, until it is done.

▲ **Choose an appropriate study space**

So, set the scene:

- Choose an appropriate study space – for some this will be at home; others work best in a library away from distractions.

- Be comfortable and ready for study – feeling hungry or tired will not help you to work efficiently.

- Ensure that you have the resources that you need – books, computer, notepad to note down your thoughts or additional questions.

FAST FACT

Do acronyms help you to recall important information? Why not try reorganising the list of outcomes from the Every Child Matters Framework into the following order:

B – Be healthy
E – Enjoy and achieve
A – Achieve economic wellbeing
M – Make a positive contribution
S – Stay safe

- Avoid distractions – switch off your mobile phone; tell others that you are studying.

- Set targets 'By the end of the session I will have . . .'

- Reward yourself!

Using a range of resources

Reading and research are an important part of studying, so it is important that you make use of all of the resources that are available to you. Using the library is essential; here you will be able to access a range of resources including books, periodicals, reference books, videos, DVDs and the internet. Other information used to support study can also be located at the library: for example, literature from local organisations and the local authority.

Books are a very expensive resource and it is essential that they are respected and looked after; unless the book is your own property, you will not be able to write in it. When reading, if there is information that you would like to go back to, use sticky

▲ **A range of resources will help you when you are studying**

notes/tabs as you can add them to a page and remove them later without damaging the book.

When watching video, DVD or television, take notes that you can use later.

The internet is an invaluable resource and can be an effective way to find information. Using this resource can be quite time consuming so it is a good idea to make a list of the information or key points to research.

It is very important that you adhere to the centre and awarding body assignment advice and guidance; particular attention should be paid to **plagiarism**. Your centre should provide you with a plagiarism statement and the implications with regard to achievement. Centres will have no option but to disqualify candidates who are found to have copied work from books, published assignments and the internet.

Plotting mind maps

Mind maps are often used to enable students to plot their thoughts and ideas in a visual map. This strategy helps to focus thoughts and ideas and is a useful planning tool. Maps do not need to be complex, although often individuals map using different colours for different strands or sections of the map. The approach that you use is entirely up to you as this resource is your own.

Writing assignments

Planning is essential when you have an assignment to write. In order to ensure that the content, layout and information has been fully considered, an assignment plan will need to be in place. Therefore, a plan should include what you are going to do, how the assignment will be presented, the content of each section, a checking and reviewing strategy for you to use,

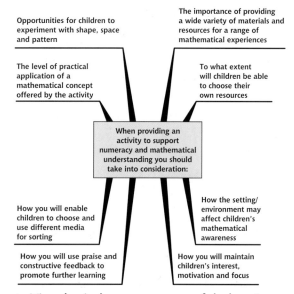

▲ Visual mind maps are a useful planning tool

references and quotes, etc. The plan should be specific to your needs.

Referencing and writing a bibliography

Referencing within an assignment should follow the expected model, often this is the Harvard system of referencing. Within your work, the reference should include the name of the author and the date of publication. All other details about the publication should be included in the bibliography.

A bibliography will need to be included with every assignment; all reading and referenced material will need to be included in alphabetical order.

You will need to include:

- the title of the book or article or website address
- author
- publisher
- date of publication
- place of publication.

Plagiarism = stealing from the work of others and claiming it as one's own

Progress check

1. What should you do before you start work on an assignment or project?

2. How can you set the scene for study?

3. What are the implications of plagiarising the work of others?

 Weblinks

- www.cwdc.org.uk
  The website of the Children's Workforce Development Council

- www.ndna.org.uk
  The website of the National Day Nurseries Association for information on current issues and professional practice

- www.everychildmatters.gov.uk
  For information about the Every Child Matters framework and extensive links to a range of relevant issues

- www.ncvo-vol.org.uk
  The website of the National Council for Voluntary Organisations

- www.scvo.org.uk
  The website of the Scottish Centre for Voluntary Organisations

- www.howtostudy.com
  A website where you can find information to help you to study effectively

- www.ofsted.gov.uk
  For information about the childcare and education sector

- www.dcsf.gov.uk
  For information about legislation, policy and practice

- www.move-on.org.uk
  For information on improving and developing literacy skills

- www.cache.org.uk
  Awarding website including a range of guidance and documents

- www.nch.org.uk
  The website of the National Children's Home charity, which is a leading children's charity and provider of services for children in need

- www.barnados.org.uk
  Barnardo's vision is that the lives of all children and young people should be free from poverty, abuse and discrimination. A leading children's charity, it provides direct support to children and young people through projects at home, school and in the local community

- www.mencap.org.uk
  Mencap works with people with a learning disability and their families and carers

- www.home-start.org.uk
  Home-start is a charity which helps to support struggling families with young children through a network of trained parent volunteers. The support offered is free, confidential and non-judgemental

Unit 2

Development from conception to age 16 years

This is a key unit in your qualification. In order to work successfully with children, you need to understand how they develop in all areas. Observing the children that you work with and making careful assessments of their development will enable you to understand a child's achievements and needs, and to plan for them.

Learning Outcomes

In this unit you will learn about:

1. how to apply the general principles and theoretical perspectives to all areas of development

2. how to use a range of observation techniques appropriate to different stages of development and circumstances

3. how to assess the development of children, and reflect upon the implications for practice.

Learning Outcome (1)

FOCUS ON...
how to apply the general principles and theoretical perspectives to all areas of development

⬭⬭ This links to assessment criteria **1.1** and **1.2**

Understanding child development

In this section you'll find tables that show you when children aged up to 16 years are expected to reach certain milestones in their development, such as learning to walk. The ages given in the tables are only approximate guides because:

● different children develop at different rates. This is completely normal. A group of children of the same age won't reach the same milestones at exactly the same time

● the same child may well reach milestones in some areas of their development earlier than expected, and reach milestones in other areas later. For example, a child may crawl and walk earlier than expected, but begin to talk a little later.

It is important for you to understand the **expected pattern of development** so that:

● you can offer appropriate activities and experiences to children of all ages and abilities

● you can monitor children's progress by comparing their current stage of development with the expected development pattern. Later in the unit,

you'll learn more about how to do this by observing the children in your care.

⬭ FAST FACT

Children generally develop in approximately the same sequence. Babies will learn to roll over before they sit up, and children will say single words before they string two or three words together in a basic sentence.

Areas of development

The tables on pages 40–53 show how children develop in the following areas of development:

● physical development

● social, emotional and behavioural development

● communication and intellectual development.

Although we refer to different areas of children's learning for convenience, in practice children do not learn in a compartmentalised way. Babies and children are people who are growing and developing physically at the same time as they are learning skills and experiencing new feelings.

Practitioners must have a good understanding of the expected child development patterns so that:

Expected pattern of development = when children are generally expected to achieve key development milestones. These milestones are sometimes called the 'development norms'

- they can carry out observation and assessment effectively. Practitioners evaluate individual children's development by making comparisons between a child's actual developmental stage and the expected development rates
- they can offer appropriate activities and experiences for individual children. This will be informed by observation and assessment of individual children
- they can anticipate the next stage of a child's development. This allows the practitioner to provide activities and experiences that will challenge and interest children, stimulating their development
- they notice when children are not progressing as expected. Although children develop at different rates, significant delays or many delays in several areas can be an indication that children need intervention and extra support.

Influences on development

There are two key factors that influence how development occurs:

- *nature*: development occurs in response to the way children are genetically programmed from birth to be able to do certain things at certain times. This is referred to as 'nature'
- *nurture*: development occurs in response to the experiences that individual children have from the time they are born throughout their lives. This is referred to as 'nurture'.

It is generally accepted that individual children develop as they do because of a combination of the two factors – nature and nurture. Language is a good example of this. Studies have shown that babies all over the world make coos, gurgles and other sounds that are very similar. The potential to speak and a common ability to make similar pre-language sounds would seem to be down to nature. But children learn to speak the language they are exposed to – this is down to nurture.

This means that individual children's development and levels of maturity will depend in part on the experiences they have had (or, in other words, the way they have been nurtured). To have realistic expectations about children's development and maturity, practitioners must take into account that:

- children develop within unique families. Different families influence children in widely different ways
- families exist within a social and cultural system. Social and cultural systems interact with and influence the family, and therefore the child's development.

Children have different experiences at different times and so they develop at different rates. Children cannot be expected to achieve aspects of development that are largely attributed to nurture if they have not yet been exposed to experiences that encourage this development. Practitioners must keep this in mind. The diagram on page 38 shows how nature and nurture influence aspects of children's development.

There are many books available dedicated solely to the topic of child development. It is advisable for practitioners to read widely about the subject. The tables on pages 40–53 give an overview of the expected rates of development from birth up to 16 years.

		Physical	Language	Cognitive	Emotional and social
NATURE	Heredity Genetic	Biological maturity	Language emerges	Children take in information through all five senses	Children need to be cared for
NURTURE	Environmental Learning	Food Activity Physical comfort	Children must hear language (or see it signed) and be responded to	Stimulation and encouragement through sensitive responses	Care that is consistent and appropriate

The importance of 'nurture' to different areas of development can be seen from the size of the shaded areas

Key

☐ Nature

▨ Nurture

▲ The influence of nature and nurture on children's development

Physical development

The neonate (newly born baby) has reflexes. These are physical movements or reactions that they make without consciously intending to do so. For example, the neonate will move their head in search of the mother's nipple or the teat of a bottle when their lips or cheek are touched (known as rooting), and they will also suck and swallow milk. These reflexes help the baby to feed, and therefore survive. You may have experienced the grasp reflex – a baby will clasp their fingers around yours if you touch their palm. You

will have probably seen the startle reflex too – a startled baby will make a fist and their arms will move away from their body. This can often be seen if there is a loud noise, or if the baby wakes suddenly.

Gross motor skills

Gross motor skills are an aspect of physical development. The term 'gross motor skills' is used to refer to whole-body movements such as sitting up, crawling and walking. These skills develop rapidly during a child's first five years.

Fine motor skills

Fine motor skills are also an aspect of physical development. The term 'fine motor skills' is used to refer to the delicate, manipulative movements that are made with the fingers. Fine motor skills and the development of vision are linked. This is often referred to as 'hand–eye coordination'. Fine motor skills and hand–eye coordination are used when a child is

▲ The neonate

threading cotton reels, for example; the child will look carefully at the position of the hole in the reel, and manipulate the string accordingly.

Crawling

Sitting from lying down

Bear-walking

Walking with two hands held

Walking with one hand held

Walking alone

▲ Gross motor skills

Holding and exploring objects

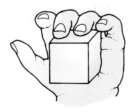

Palmar grasp using whole hand

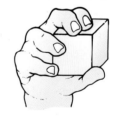

More delicate palmar grasp involving the thumb

Inferior pincer grasp

Exploring with the index finger

Delicate/mature pincer grasp

▲ Fine motor skills

Stages of development

▽ Rates of development for 1 month

PHYSICAL DEVELOPMENT – GROSS MOTOR SKILLS

In **supine**: head is on one side

In **prone**: head is on one side, can be lifted

When sitting: head falls forwards (known as head lag), and the back curves

Head will turn towards light and noise

Hands are closed tighlty

Reflexes help a baby to survive

PHYSICAL DEVELOPMENT – FINE MOTOR SKILLS

Gazes attentively at faces, particularly when fed and talked to

---

SOCIAL AND EMOTIONAL DEVELOPMENT

Totally dependent on others

Smiles from about 5 weeks

Senses are used for exploration

Begins to respond to sounds heard in the environment by making own sounds

COMMUNICATION AND INTELLECTUAL DEVELOPMENT

Communicates needs through sounds

Communicates needs through crying

Communication occurs through the physical closeness

Begins to coo and gurgle in response to interaction from carers

Prone = position of a baby lying on their front
Supine = position of a baby lying on their back

▼ Rates of development for 3 months

PHYSICAL DEVELOPMENT – GROSS MOTOR SKILLS

Turns from side to back

In supine: head in central position

In prone: head and chest can be lifted from the floor, supported by the forearms

When sitting: little head lag remains, back is straighter

Arms can be waved and brought together

Legs can be kicked separately and together

PHYSICAL DEVELOPMENT – FINE MOTOR SKILLS

Alert, the baby moves their head to watch others

Engages in hand and finger play

Holds rattle briefly before dropping

SOCIAL AND EMOTIONAL DEVELOPMENT

Through use of senses, a baby begins to understand they are a separate person

Baby begins to discover what they can do, and this creates a sense of self

May cry if a primary carer leaves the room, not yet understanding that they still exist and will return

Shows feelings such as excitement and fear

Reacts positively when a carer is caring, kind and soothing. If a carer does not respond to a baby, the baby may stop trying to interact

COMMUNICATION AND INTELLECTUAL DEVELOPMENT

Recognises and links familiar sounds such as the face and voice of a carer

Will hold 'conversations' with carer when talked to, making sounds and waiting for a response

Can imitate high and low sounds

▼ Rates of development for 6 months

PHYSICAL DEVELOPMENT – GROSS MOTOR SKILLS

Turns from front to back, and may do the reverse

In supine: head can be lifted and controlled when pulled to sitting position

In prone: head and chest can be fully extended, supported by arms, with the hands flat on the floor

Sits unsupported for some time, with back straight, and plays in this position

Uses hands to play with feet, and may take them to the mouth

Weight-bears when held in standing position

PHYSICAL DEVELOPMENT – FINE MOTOR SKILLS

Interested in bright, shiny objects

Watches events keenly

Uses palmar grasp to pick up objects. Takes them to the mouth for exploration

Passes objects from hand to hand

SOCIAL AND EMOTIONAL DEVELOPMENT

Shows a wider range of feelings more clearly and vocally. May laugh and screech with delight, but cry with fear at the sight of a stranger

Clearly tells people apart, showing a preference for primary carers/siblings

Reaches out to be held, and may stop crying when talked to

Enjoys looking at self in the mirror

Enjoys attention and being with others

COMMUNICATION AND INTELLECTUAL DEVELOPMENT

Sounds are used intentionally to call for a carer's attention

Babbling is frequent. The baby plays tunefully with the sounds they can make

Rhythm and volume are explored vocally

Enjoys rhymes and accompanying actions

▽ Rates of development for 9 months

PHYSICAL DEVELOPMENT – GROSS MOTOR SKILLS

Sits unsupported on the floor

Will go on hands and knees, and may crawl

Pulls self to standing position using furniture for support

Cruises around the room (side-stepping, holding furniture for support)

Takes steps if both hands are held by carer

PHYSICAL DEVELOPMENT – FINE MOTOR SKILLS

Uses an inferior pincer grasp to pick up objects

Explores objects with the eyes

Points to and pokes at objects of interest with index finger

SOCIAL AND EMOTIONAL DEVELOPMENT

Enjoys playing with carers, e.g. peek-a-boo games and pat-a-cake

Offers objects, but does not yet let go

Increasing mobility allows baby to approach people

Begins to feed self with support

COMMUNICATION AND INTELLECTUAL DEVELOPMENT

Initiates a wider range of sounds, and recognises a few familiar words. Understands 'no', and knows own name

Greatly enjoys playing with carers and holding conversations

Makes longer strings of babbling sounds

Intentionally uses volume vocally

▼ Rates of development for 12 months

PHYSICAL DEVELOPMENT – GROSS MOTOR SKILLS

Sits down from standing position

Stands alone briefly and may walk a few steps alone

Throws toys intentionally

PHYSICAL DEVELOPMENT – FINE MOTOR SKILLS

Clasps hands together

Uses sophisticated pincer grasp, and releases hold intentionally

Looks for objects that fall out of sight, understanding they still exist although they can't be seen

Feeds self with spoon and finger foods

SOCIAL AND EMOTIONAL DEVELOPMENT

The sense of self-identity increases, as self-esteem and self-confidence develop

Waves goodbye, when prompted at first, and then spontaneously

Content to play alone or alongside other children for increasing periods of time

COMMUNICATION AND INTELLECTUAL DEVELOPMENT

Increasingly understands the basic messages communicated by carers and older siblings

Can respond to basic instructions

Babbling sounds increasingly like speech, and leads to the first single words being spoken

Shows understanding that particular words are associated with people and objects, by using a few single words in context

▼ Rates of development for 15 months

PHYSICAL DEVELOPMENT – GROSS MOTOR SKILLS

Walks independently

Crawls upstairs. Crawls downstairs feet first

Sits in a child-sized chair independently

PHYSICAL DEVELOPMENT – FINE MOTOR SKILLS

Tries to turn the pages of a book

Makes a tower of two blocks

Makes marks on paper with crayons

Holds own cup when drinking

SOCIAL AND EMOTIONAL DEVELOPMENT

Curious. Wants to explore the world, as long as carers are close by

May show signs of separation anxiety (i.e. upset when left at nursery)

May 'show off' to entertain carers

Shows a keener interest in the activities of peers

Can be jealous of the attention/toys given to another child

Changeable emotionally. Quickly alternates between wanting to do things alone and being dependent on carers

COMMUNICATION AND INTELLECTUAL DEVELOPMENT

Will put away/look for very familiar objects in the right place

Uses toys for their purpose, e.g. puts a doll in a pram

Understands the concepts of labels such as 'you', 'me', 'mine', 'yours'

The use of single words increases, and more words are learnt

BEHAVIOURAL DEVELOPMENT

May respond with anger when told off or thwarted. May throw toys or have a tantrum

Can be distracted from inappropriate behaviour

Possessive of toys and carers. Reluctant to share

Child is 'busy' or 'into everything'

▼ Rates of development for 18 months

PHYSICAL DEVELOPMENT – GROSS MOTOR SKILLS

Walks confidently. Attempts to run

Walks up and down stairs if hand is held by carer

Bends from the waist without falling forwards

Balances in the squatting position

Pushes and pulls wheeled toys

Rolls and throws balls, attempts to kick them

PHYSICAL DEVELOPMENT – FINE MOTOR SKILLS

Uses delicate pincer grasp to thread cotton reels

Makes a tower of three blocks

Makes large scribbles with crayons

Can use door handles

SOCIAL AND EMOTIONAL DEVELOPMENT

Has a better understanding of being an individual

Very curious, and more confident to explore

Becomes frustrated easily if incapable of doing something

Follows carers, keen to join in with their activities

Plays alongside peers more often (parallel play), and may imitate them

Still very changeable emotionally

May show sympathy for others (e.g. putting their arm around a crying child)

COMMUNICATION AND INTELLECTUAL DEVELOPMENT

Understands a great deal of what carers say

More words spoken. Uses people's names

Uses trial and error in exploration (tries to post several shapes in the hole of a shape sorter)

BEHAVIOURAL DEVELOPMENT

Can be restless and very determined, quickly growing irritated or angry

May assert will strongly, showing angry defiance and resistance to adults

Can still be distracted from inappropriate behaviour

▼ Rates of development for 2 years

PHYSICAL DEVELOPMENT – GROSS MOTOR SKILLS

Runs confidently

Walks up and down stairs alone holding hand rail

Rides large wheeled toys (without pedals)

Kicks stationary balls

PHYSICAL DEVELOPMENT – FINE MOTOR SKILLS

Makes a tower of six blocks

Joins and separates interlocking toys

Draws circles, lines and dots with a pencil

Puts on shoes

SOCIAL AND EMOTIONAL DEVELOPMENT

Beginning to understand own feelings. Identifies sad and happy faces

Experiences a range of changeable feelings which are expressed in behaviour

More responsive to the feelings of others

Often responds to carers lovingly, and may initiate loving gestures (a cuddle)

COMMUNICATION AND INTELLECTUAL DEVELOPMENT

Completes simple jigsaw puzzles (or 'play-trays')

Understands that actions have consequences

Will often name objects on sight (e.g. may point and say 'chair' or 'dog')

Vocabulary increases. Joins two words together, e.g. 'shoes on'

Short sentences are used by 30 months. Some words are used incorrectly, e.g. 'I goed in'

BEHAVIOURAL DEVELOPMENT

May use growing language ability to protest verbally

May get angry with peers, and lash out on occasion (e.g. pushing or even biting them)

▼ Rates of development for 3 years

PHYSICAL DEVELOPMENT – GROSS MOTOR SKILLS

Walks and runs on tip-toes

Walks up and downstairs confidently

Rides large wheeled toys using pedals and steering

Kicks moving balls forwards

Enjoys climbing and sliding on small apparatus

PHYSICAL DEVELOPMENT – FINE MOTOR SKILLS

Makes a tower of nine blocks

Turns the pages of a book reliably

Draws a face with a pencil, using the preferred hand. Attempts to write letters

Puts on and removes coat. Fastens large, easy zippers

SOCIAL AND EMOTIONAL DEVELOPMENT

Child can tell carers how she is feeling. Empathises with the feelings of others

Uses the toilet and washes own hands. Can put on clothes

Imaginary and creative play is enjoyed

Enjoys company of peers and makes friends. Wants adult approval. Is affected by mood of carers/peers

COMMUNICATION AND INTELLECTUAL DEVELOPMENT

Child is enquiring. Frequently asks 'what' and 'why' questions

Use of language for thinking and reporting. Enjoys stories and rhymes

Vocabulary increases quickly. Use of plurals, pronouns, adjectives, possessives and tenses

Longer sentences are used. By 42 months, most language is used correctly

Can name colours. Can match and sort items into simple sets (e.g. colour sets)

Can count to 10 by rote. Can only count out three or four objects

Begins to recognise own name

BEHAVIOURAL DEVELOPMENT

Increasingly able to understand consequence of behaviour and the concept of 'getting in trouble'

Understands the concept of saying sorry and 'making up'

Less rebellious. Less likely to physically express anger as words can be used

▼ Rates of development for 4 years

PHYSICAL DEVELOPMENT – GROSS MOTOR SKILLS

Changes direction while running

Walks in a straight line successfully

Confidently climbs and slides on apparatus

Hops safely

Can bounce and catch balls, and take aim

PHYSICAL DEVELOPMENT – FINE MOTOR SKILLS

Makes a tower of 10 blocks

Learning to fasten most buttons and zips

Learning to use scissors. Cuts out basic shapes

Draws people with heads, bodies and limbs. Writes names and letters in play as the awareness that print carries meaning develops

SOCIAL AND EMOTIONAL DEVELOPMENT

May be confident socially. Self-esteem is apparent. Awareness of gender roles

Friendship with peers is increasingly valued. Enjoys playing with groups of children

Control over emotions increases. Can wait to have needs met by carers

As imagination increases child may become fearful (e.g. of the dark or monsters)

COMMUNICATION AND INTELLECTUAL DEVELOPMENT

Completes puzzles of 12 pieces

Memory develops. Child recalls many songs and stories. Fantasy and reality may be confused

Problem solves (I wonder what will happen if), and makes hypothesis (I think this will happen if)

Sorts objects into more complex sets. Number correspondence improves

As an understanding of language increases so does enjoyment of rhymes, stories and nonsense

BEHAVIOURAL DEVELOPMENT

If exposed to swearing child is likely to use these words in their own language

Learning to negotiate and get along with others through experimenting with behaviour

Experiences being in/out of control, feeling power, having quarrels with peers, being blamed, blaming

Has a good understanding of familiar, basic rules

Distraction works less often, but child increasingly understands reasoning

▼ Rates of development for 5 years

PHYSICAL DEVELOPMENT – GROSS MOTOR SKILLS

Controls ball well. Plays ball games with rules

Rides bike with stabilisers

Balance is good, uses low stilts confidently

Sense of rhythm has developed. Enjoys dance and movement activities

PHYSICAL DEVELOPMENT – FINE MOTOR SKILLS

Controls mark-making materials well (e.g. pencils). Writing more legible

Writes letters and short, familiar words

Learns to sew

SOCIAL AND EMOTIONAL DEVELOPMENT

Child will have started school. This transition may be unsettling

Enjoys group play and cooperative activities

Increasingly understands rules of social conduct and rules of games, but may have difficulty accepting losing

Increasing sense of own personality and gender

Keen to 'fit in' with others. Approval from adults and peers desired

Friends are important. Many are made at school

Many children will have new experiences out of school (e.g. play clubs, friends coming for tea)

Increasingly independent, undertaking most physical care needs for themselves

COMMUNICATION AND INTELLECTUAL DEVELOPMENT

Options/knowledge of subjects are shared using language for thinking

Enjoys books. Learning to read. Recognises some words

Thinking skills and memory increase as vocabulary grows

Spends longer periods at activities when engaged. Shows persistence

Children learn from new experiences at school. Learning-style preferences may become apparent

BEHAVIOURAL DEVELOPMENT

Feels shame/guilt when adults disapprove of behaviour

May seek attention, 'showing off' in front of peers

Keen to win and be 'right'. Adults need to mediate in squabbles

Often responds to 'time out' method of managing behaviour

▼ Rates of development for 6–7 years

PHYSICAL DEVELOPMENT – GROSS MOTOR SKILLS

Can hop on either leg, skip and play hopscotch

Rides bicycle without stabilisers

Confidently climbs and slides on larger apparatus in school and in parks

PHYSICAL DEVELOPMENT – FINE MOTOR SKILLS

Can catch a ball with one hand only

Writing is legible

Sews confidently and may tie shoe laces

SOCIAL AND EMOTIONAL DEVELOPMENT

Enjoys team games and activities

Towards age 7, a child may doubt their learning ability ('I can't do it')

May be reluctant to try or persevere, becoming frustrated easily

Personality is established. Attitudes to life are developed

Solid friendships are formed. The relationship with 'best friends' is important

More susceptible to peer pressure. Cultural identity also established

Has learnt how to behave in various settings and social situations (e.g. at school, play club, a friend's house)

COMMUNICATION AND INTELLECTUAL DEVELOPMENT

Imagination skills are developed. Fantasy games are complex and dramatic

Language refined and more adult-like. Enjoys jokes and word play

Many children read and write basic text by age 7, but this varies widely

Ability to predict and to plan ahead has developed. Understands cause and effect well

Can conserve number. Does simple calculations. Understands measurement and weighing

BEHAVIOURAL DEVELOPMENT

May sulk or be miserable at times (when under pressure or when conflict arises)

May be over-excitable at times, leading to 'silly' behaviour

May still rebel, but more capable of intentionally choosing behavioural response to conflict

Increasingly able to settle minor disputes and conflict independently

May argue over carrying out tasks (e.g. tidying up or doing homework)

Has a strong sense of right and wrong. May tell adults when another child has broken a rule

▼ Rates of development for 8–12 years

PHYSICAL DEVELOPMENT – GROSS MOTOR SKILLS

Physical growth slows at first, so there are fewer physical milestones reached

Puberty generally begins between 11–13 years
(see 13–16 years table)

Coordination and speed of movement develops

Muscles and bones develop. Has more physical strength

Begins to run around less in play

Interest in TV, computers, console games, DVDs may mean child is less active. A balanced, active lifestyle should be encouraged

PHYSICAL DEVELOPMENT – FINE MOTOR SKILLS

Does joined-up writing, which becomes increasingly adult-like

Has computer skills. May type well and control the mouse as an adult would

Can sew well, and may be adept at delicate craft activities such as braiding threads

SOCIAL AND EMOTIONAL DEVELOPMENT

May feel unsettled when making the transition from primary school to secondary school, and as puberty approaches

Stable friendships are relied upon. These are generally same-sex, although children play in mixed groups/teams

May be reluctant to go to a play club or event unless a friend will be there too

More independent. Makes more decisions. May play unsupervised at times. May travel to school alone by end of age band

COMMUNICATION AND INTELLECTUAL DEVELOPMENT

May read for enjoyment in leisure time

Can make up and tell stories that have been plotted out

Verbal and written communication is fluent, often with correct grammar usage. Enjoys chatting to friends/adults

Range of new subjects may be learnt at secondary school

Child may follow their interests, learning outside of school

Sense of logic develops. Thinking in abstract by 10 (can consider beliefs, morals and world events)

BEHAVIOURAL DEVELOPMENT

Mood swings may be experienced during puberty (see 13–16 years table)

Conflict with parents due to desire for increasing independence ('Why can't I stay home alone?')

May feel rules are unfair ('But all my friends are allowed to do it!')

May refuse to go along with some decisions made by parents (e.g. refusing to wear certain clothes purchased for them)

▽ Rates of development for 13–16 years

PHYSICAL DEVELOPMENT – GROSS MOTOR SKILLS

The bodies of both boys and girls change throughout puberty.
There is variation in the age at which this occurs
Girls generally enter puberty by 13 years, becoming women
physically by 16 years
Boys generally enter puberty by 14 years, becoming men
physically by 16 or 17 years
Sporting talents may become apparent

PHYSICAL DEVELOPMENT – FINE MOTOR SKILLS

May learn/refine new manipulative skills (such as drawing, stitching, carpentry, woodwork,
playing an instrument)
Talent in arts or crafts may become apparent

SOCIAL AND EMOTIONAL DEVELOPMENT

Desire to express individuality, but also a strong desire to
fit in with peers
Becomes romantically/sexually interested in others, and in
own sexuality
May express self creatively through art/music/dance or
creative writing
May worry about aspects of physical appearance
May express self/experiment with identity through appearance (e.g. dress, hairstyles,
piercings)
Pressure at school mounts as exam curriculum is followed
Young people may feel overwhelmed or anxious
A balance of school work/leisure time is important, especially if young people take on
part-time jobs
Developing own morals, beliefs and values outside of parents' influence
Likely to communicate innermost thoughts and feelings more frequently to friends than
to adults
May prefer to spend more time with friends than with family. May stay in bedroom more
at home

COMMUNICATION AND INTELLECTUAL DEVELOPMENT

Academic knowledge increases as exam curriculum is followed
Towards age 16, decisions are made about the future (college course/career)
Young people may be reluctant to directly ask adults for the advice or information they
need. They may prefer to access it anonymously

BEHAVIOURAL DEVELOPMENT

May swing between acting maturely, and saying/doing 'childish' things
(e.g. may watch a young children's TV programme, or sit on a swing in
the park)
May experiment with smoking, alcohol, drugs or early promiscuity. This
behaviour is linked with low self-esteem
May experience mood swings. Tense atmospheres are lightened when
adults remain in good humour
May disregard the opinions/values of parents if they conflict with those of the peer group
Acting on own values may cause conflict at home (e.g becoming a vegetarian)

Before birth

There are many books devoted to the subject of conception, pregnancy and birth. It's a good idea to read about this subject. This will help you to understand the development of babies who are born prematurely. Also see the Weblinks section at the end of this unit.

⊂⊃⊃ This links to assessment criteria **1.3**.

Theories about how children learn and develop

Psychologists and other theorists have studied play, learning and development for hundreds of years, and developed different theories about how children learn and develop.

Some key theories are outlined here, but there are many books dedicated to the subject of learning, development and play theories. You may find it interesting to learn about additional theories and the research and experiments that underpin them.

FAST FACT

Psychologists do not always agree with one another! There are many opposing theories about learning and development as you will read below.

Because theories conflict, it is best to learn about them with an open mind. Some theorists disagree with each other entirely while the theories of others are similar. Any theories that help practitioners to predict how children will develop and learn are helpful. But there is not one 'right' or 'true' version. How well theories are regarded will often depend on who the theorist is and the research that they have conducted.

In practice, most childcare workers will use a blended approach, drawing on aspects of various theories in their own approach to children's learning and development.

Piaget

Jean Piaget was born in 1896. He developed 'constructivist' theories that have been influential, although they have been challenged over the years. Piaget was the first to say that when children play they can make discoveries for themselves without being taught. He observed that children generally shared the same sequential pattern of learning, and he noted that children of the same age often made the same mistakes. This led him to believe that children's cognitive development (their ability to think, reason and understand) developed through a series of sequential stages of development. Piaget believed that children should not be hurried through these stages as that would have a negative effect. He said children should be allowed to pass through the stages naturally.

Piaget focused on children's cognitive development in isolation – he did not consider other areas, such as children's social and emotional development. He referred to children as 'lone scientists' and believed that adults should seek to provide environments where children could make their own discoveries. The idea that adults should intervene only sensitively in children's play stemmed from Piaget.

Piaget referred to children at play as 'active participants in their own learning'. He believed that children use their first-hand and previous experiences to learn. He thought children made assumptions based on experiences – he called these *schemas*. Piaget called the process of applying one schema to another circumstance *assimilation*. For example, imagine a child had only ever poured water through a funnel. They then discover that dry sand will also pass through the funnel. They have assimilated a new concept into their existing schema – sand and water can both pass through funnels.

Piaget believed that when children cannot fit a new experience into an existing schema, they create a new schema that will fit. He called this process *accommodation*. For example, Sally may assume she likes all biscuits even though she's only ever eaten custard creams (which she enjoyed). When she tries another type she finds out this is not the case – she hates ginger biscuits! She accommodates a new schema – different biscuits have different tastes, and she doesn't like them all. To take our first

example, accommodation may take place if a child discovers that wet sand will not pass easily through a funnel in the same way as dry sand or water.

Piaget believed that children pass through four stages of cognitive development. He did not believe that everyone would attain every stage, particularly stage four.

Vygotsky

Lev Vygotsky, born in 1896, was one of the first academics to disagree with Piaget. He died when he was only in his thirties, so his career was short, but he has had a major impact on current thinking. He believed that children learn through social interaction and relationships, through the social tool of language. Vygotsky's theory is called the 'social constructivist theory'.

▼ Piaget's stages of cognitive development

STAGE ONE: SENSORIMOTOR. CHILD'S AGE: 0–2 YEARS
Key aspects: babies use their sense to learn. They can only see things from their own point of view – they are 'egocentric'. They do not know that something they cannot see still exists, e.g. if a ball rolls out of view, they will not look for it. At about 18 months this changes. They have then achieved 'object permanence'
STAGE TWO: PREOPERATIONAL. CHILD'S AGE: 2–7 YEARS
Key aspects: children are still 'egocentric'. They believe animals and inanimate objects have the same feelings as people – they are 'animalistic'. They use language to express their thoughts, and use symbols in their play, e.g. they pretend a length of string is a snake
STAGE THREE: CONCRETE OPERATIONAL. CHILD'S AGE: 7–11 YEARS
Key aspects: now children 'decentre' – they can see other points of view and understand that inanimate objects do not have feelings. They are establishing complex reasoning skills, and they can use writing and other symbols, e.g. mathematical symbols. They can conserve number reliably and solve conversation tasks
STAGE FOUR: FORMAL OPERATIONAL. CHILD'S AGE: 11–ADULTHOOD
Key aspects: children can use logic and work methodically. They can think 'in abstract' – doing mental arithmetic and thinking things through internally. They can problem solve thoughtfully

Interested in children's play, Vygotsky was of the opinion that all play contains an imaginative element, and that this is liberating for children. He agreed with Piaget that children at play are 'active participants in their own learning'. However, he felt that the emotional aspect of play was as important as the learning aspect. He believed that play was a good way to learn, but he did not think it was the only way.

Vygotsky developed a concept known as 'the zone of proximal development' which centres around the idea that adults can help children learn, and that children can also help one another. This idea has become known as the 'Vygotsky tutorial'. The Russian word 'proximal' translates to the word 'nearby'. He used the term 'the zone of actual development' to describe the things that children can do without any help at all, and the term 'zone of proximal development' to describe the things that children could potentially do with assistance – the learning that was next or 'nearby'.

Vygotsky believed that children should always be challenged by some activities that are just beyond them, as this would motivate them and move their learning forward. The process of offering activities that will slightly stretch children in this way is referred to as 'scaffolding learning'.

In summary, through scaffolding learning with some challenging activities just beyond what a child can do, children can move from the actual zone of development to the proximal zone of development. This contrasts with Piaget's view that children should be allowed to pass through the stages of development naturally with little intervention.

Jerome Bruner

American Jerome Bruner (born 1915) extended Vygotsky's theories and called his new theory the 'spiral curriculum'. This makes reference to his belief that children learn through discovery with the direct assistance of adults who should provide opportunities for them to return to the same activities (in terms of materials and ideas) again and again. He believed that by doing this children would extend and deepen their learning of the concepts and ideas that adults introduce to them.

Bruner observed how children like to return to activities over a period of some years; he felt they are motivated to learn through the spiral curriculum. You may have noticed children who enjoy building the same model time and again, or drawing the same pictures. Resources like interlocking bricks can be a favourite of children for some years.

B. F. Skinner

American Burrus Skinner (1904–1990) established a theory known as 'operant conditioning'. He demonstrated how this worked in experiments conducted with rats. He gave rats food as a reward when they displayed behaviour he wanted, in this case pressing a lever. He did not feed them otherwise. The rats learnt to repeat the rewarded behaviour. They would systematically press the lever and then wait at the position in the cage where the food was dispensed. He called this 'positive reinforcement'. He also taught them not to display behaviour he did not want – he gave them electric shocks when they entered a specific area of a maze he created. They learnt to avoid the area.

This research was important, and Skinner's findings still influence the way we manage behaviour today. We reward behaviour we want (with praise for instance) and we discourage the behaviour we don't want with consequences (such as time out).

Language development theories

There is a debate about how children learn language. One group of theorists believes that just hearing and using language triggers an innate (meaning 'inbuilt') knowledge of how language and grammar work. In other words, the 'thinking' part of language is already there – it just needs to be triggered. Another group of theorists does not believe that this knowledge is innate at all. They believe that it comes from the way the way children hear and are taught language. This is the ongoing nature versus nurture debate.

Skinner (see page 56) believed that the acquisition of language is down to nurture. He thought that adults teach children to talk through imitation. According to this theory, when a baby starts to babble, carers give the baby special attention. This is pleasurable, and it encourages the baby to babble again, and eventually to babble more frequently. As carers babble back and talk to the baby, the baby imitates. Once again this is rewarded with special attention. Skinner believed that words and then sentences are learnt in the same way, by positive reinforcement. Critics of this theory say that adults often do not correct children when they make grammatical errors, and yet children still learn to use grammar correctly. They say this implies that children learn grammar in other or additional ways.

Vygotsky (see page 55) studied both thought and language to find out what impact language has on the way people think. He agreed with Skinner in that he believed that children initially learn language by imitating their carers. He said children first learn how to use language to make themselves understood – to convey messages and to express their feelings. This enables them to function in society, and they are using language for the social purposes of communication. But he believed a child would then go on to master language a second time, this time internally, within their own mind. Instead of being for communication with others, this language is just for the child themselves. He believed that this use of language was crucial to the development of children's thinking. He called it 'verbal intelligence'.

Have you heard young children talking to one another in a way that does not seem to make much sense? Or talking loudly to themselves? Vygotsky believed these things occur because young children cannot yet distinguish between language for communicating and language that is for themselves, and so they sometimes express their verbal intelligence.

Chomsky

American Noam Chomsky (born 1928) is another important theorist. In the 1950s, Chomsky helped to establish a new relationship between linguistics (the study of language) and psychology (the study of the mind). Chomsky believed that the process of language acquisition is more complicated than a child simply learning to talk through imitation which is rewarded. His theory is known as *nativist* as it promotes the idea that language acquisition is down to nature rather than nurture.

Chomsky developed a theory that humans are born with a biological brain mechanism, called a language acquisition device (LAD). According to the theory, the experience of using language is only needed to kick-start the LAD. He claimed that this accounts for the fact that children acquire language skills more rapidly than other abilities. (Children have generally mastered the basic rules of language by the age of 4.) He said all children were 'wired' by a 'deep structure' to instinctively know that language can be used to negotiate, question, command and affirm. This is common to all languages. He said children also had a 'surface structure', the use of which enables children to use the specifics of the languages they are exposed to.

Chomsky's research has shown that children are able to develop sentences they have never heard spoken. Some nativist theorists have gone on to say that if language is learned other intelligent species such as apes and dolphins would learn to acquire language. They believe the fact that this does not happen proves the ability is innate.

This links with the information given in Unit 16.

Psychoanalytical theory of social and emotional development

Freud

Sigmund Freud (1856–1939) grew up in Vienna before moving to England. He developed the psychoanalytical theory which has been the most influential theory of the 20th century.

Freud thought that the experiences we have in childhood are stored in our unconscious minds. He believed these experiences were so significant that they influence the way we feel as adults. He said that these feelings unconsciously direct our behaviour. In other words, according to Freud, we may not know why we behave in certain ways, but it will be due to unconscious feelings which stem from our childhood experiences. Freud's theory gave us the idea that childhood experiences are key factors in the development of personality, particularly if traumatic events occur in childhood.

Freud developed what he called *psychoanalysis*. This is a form of therapy, through which he believed he could help people to identify their unconscious feelings and to understand them. He came to believe his therapy could help people to change the way they feel and behave.

Freud believed that humans have three separate and conflicting aspects to their minds. These are known as:

- the *id*: the id is someone's animal instinct, responsible for their need to satisfy basic desires; it is the part that demands 'I want ... '
- the *superego*: this represents an individual's ideal of what sort of person they would like to be. This is based on demands from parents (currently or from childhood), and demands from society
- the *ego*: the ego is the force that regulates the id and the superego. It tries to resolve conflicts so that the id is satisfied within the limits of what the superego will allow. The ego is sometimes called the 'reality force'.

Freud said a person needed to have a mental balance between the id, ego and superego in order to behave normally. Freud also believed that people go through 'psychosexual stages of development' called *oral* (aged birth to 18 months), *anal* (aged 18 months to 3 years), *phallic* (aged 3 to 6 years), *latency* (aged 6 years to puberty) and *genital* (from puberty to adulthood). Freud believed that problems in passing through these stages could lead to problems in adulthood. For instance, if a child did not receive sufficient nourishment in the oral stage they might grow up to be overly dependent on others, as a nursing infant would be. You can find out more about Freud's psychosexual stages by following the Weblink at the end of the unit.

Erikson

Erik H. Erikson (1902–1994) studied under Anna Freud, Sigmund's daughter. He developed further theories about the superego. He believed that the life of a human can be divided into stages. The stages are explained in the diagram below. Each stage is summarised by a basic theme which highlights what may be learnt during that stage, depending on personal experiences. Erikson believed that what an individual learnt at each stage would influence them in the future.

Birth – 18 months	• Theme: Drive and hope • We either learn to trust life and have confidence and hope, or learn to mistrust life and develop feelings of worthlessness
18 months – 3 years	• Theme: Self-control, courage and will • We learn to master skills, gain bodily control and learn right from wrong. We are also vulnerable, and may feel great shame and guilt
3 – 5 years	• Theme: Purpose • We want to copy adults and purposefully play with small-world objects such as phones and dolls. Initiative develops, but following initiative may lead to feelings of guilt
5 – 12 years	• Theme: Method and competence • We're capable of learning much, and this gives a sense of 'industry' (being industrious). There can be also be feelings of inferiority and incompetence resulting on low self-esteem
12 – 18 years	• Theme: Devotion and fidelity • Development now depends on what we do ourselves rather than just on what is done to us. We must find our own identity. There will be role confusion and conflicts, but devotion to friends and causes
18 – 35 years	• Theme: Affiliation and love • We seek companions and love through friends and relationships. We can experience deep intimacy and may have children. If we do not find intimacy we may feel isolated
35 – 65 years	• Theme: Production and care • We now turn our attention to productive and meaningful work. We are 'in charge' and get strength from caring for others. If not, we may become 'stagnant' or 'self absorbed'
65 years – death	• Theme: Wisdom • If we can look back on a life of meaning we feel 'integrity'. If not, we feel despair at the life we had and fear death as we struggle to find a meaning to it all

▲ Erikson's Stages of Man

Current theorists

Margaret Donaldson

Margaret Donaldson (born 1926) is a developmental psychologist from Glasgow. In the 1960s, she was particularly interested in the thinking and language of children aged 2–7 years, although her theories can be applied to a wider age range. Her research showed that, compared with when they are placed in laboratory conditions (or test/exam conditions), children can think better and at a higher level when they experience everyday, familiar situations and contexts. This caused people to think differently about the research conducted by the theorists of the past.

Donaldson used the term *disembedded thought* to mean what we now generally call 'abstract thinking'. She said that problems which are unconnected from real, natural situations are harder for children to solve and should be made 'real'. For instance, children are often taught about fractions by being shown how to divide a cake into halves, quarters, eighths and so on, because this scenario makes sense to them.

Kathy Sylva

Kathy Sylva is an American educational psychologist who has been working in England since 1975. She was part of a team who studied every part of children's play and learning for five years and documented their findings in a series of books. After this work, Sylva was asked by the government of the day to look into an early education programme used in America. She also spent three years looking into British early years education. Sylva concluded that the more money that was spent on early years education, the better the quality of that education, and therefore the better the results.

Later, Sylva and four colleagues (Edward Melhuish, Pam Sammons, Iram Siraj-Blatchford and Brenda Taggart) embarked on a research project comparing the outcomes of different kinds of early childhood settings in England. This is known as the Effective Provision of Pre-School Education (Eppe) project. It involved looking at 3,000 children from birth to 7, in a range of settings including the home, pre-school, day care and nursery school, to see what impact everything that happened there had on children's learning. One key Eppe finding has been the subject of much debate. It was found that the most effective settings for learning are children's centres (with integrated day care and education) and nursery classes, which are staffed by graduate-level employees who are well paid.

It was also found that high-quality care and high-quality education can co-exist in the same setting. It had been previously thought that settings were either 'good at care' or 'good at education'.

Cathy Nutbrown

Cathy Nutbrown has conducted key research into **inclusion** in the early years. Nutbrown has demonstrated that inclusion is important not only for children with individual needs, but for all children. During her research, Nutbrown found out about practitioners' attitudes towards inclusion as well as their practices. She went on to write about the elements which can make inclusion successful, including curricula, professional development for staff and work in partnership with parents.

Inclusion = when children with disabilities or special needs are included within settings alongside non-disabled children

Neuroscientific discoveries

New theories about the way in which human beings think, remember and learn are being developed in the light of new technology that has emerged in recent years. Using advanced imaging techniques, neuroscientists (brain scientists) can now look right inside living, functioning brains. They can actually watch what happens when people are thinking, remembering and learning. Interesting new research is being carried out around the world. Practitioners are advised to themselves up to date with developme Professional journals are a good source o new information as it is released.

Theory of attachment, separation and loss

Details of this theory can be found on page 25.

Further information about play and learning theory can be found in Unit 7.

✓ Progress check

1. Why do practitioners need a good knowledge and understanding of child development?

2. Why should you learn about theories on learning and development with an open mind?

3. Why do you need to know about learning and development theories?

4. In relation to development, what is meant by the term 'nature'?

5. In relation to development, what is meant by the term 'nurture'?

This links to assessment criteria **2.1**

Why we observe children

We observe children all the time in our work. We watch them to make sure they are safe and to ensure that all their needs are met. But when we talk about making observations, we mean setting aside some time to specifically watch and record what a child does.

We observe children in this way for the following reasons:

- To understand the pattern of child development: the expected pattern of development you learnt about in section 1 was devised by experts who studied children's development through observation. In the same way, observing children regularly over a period of time will help you to understand the pattern of development. It is a special experience to witness children reaching for and achieving milestones.

- To assess a child's current stage of development: when a child first attends a setting, it is usual to observe them to see which milestones they have already met. This is called 'baseline' or 'formative' assessment. From then on, progress can be monitored.

- To ensure appropriate activities are provided to promote development:

when you are aware of a child's stage of development, you can provide appropriate activities. For instance, you might do a 12-piece jigsaw with a child who is close to 4 years, because they are expected to be able to complete one at around 4 years old. If a child is not given a 12-piece puzzle, they cannot achieve the milestone.

- To monitor ongoing development and plan for the next stage: it is important to check that development is progressing steadily. With a good understanding of development patterns, you can plan for the next stage. For instance, you might arrange to get a push-along baby-walker for a baby who has just learnt to stand up and will soon be ready to learn to walk alone.

- To identify any particular difficulties or individual needs a child may have: because observation helps us to focus closely on all aspects of development, we can detect if a child is having difficulties in any area. We can then plan how to help them. (You'll find out more about this later in the unit.)

- To know and understand an individual child better: we can learn about an individual child's likes and dislikes, how they interact with others and how they behave in different situations. We can share the observations with the child's parents and carers, using them as a starting point for discussion about development.

- To record any behaviour that causes concern: it is helpful to observe worrying behaviour so that it can be analysed later. Observations also provide written details of when and how the behaviour occurs. (You will learn more about this in Learning Outcome 3.)

- To monitor progress towards national targets which apply to the setting: you can find out more about this in Unit 7.

- To evaluate the standard of the provision: how well children are progressing can indicate how well the setting is meeting children's needs. This includes how good the quality of the learning experiences is, and how well the staff support and care for the children.

The reasons for observing children are summarised in the diagram below.

The observation cycle

Observation is carried out in a cycle. First, baseline information is collected to tell us about a child's current stage of

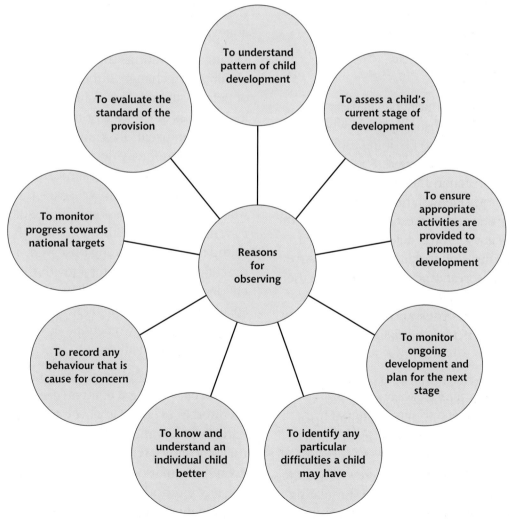

▲ Why we carry out observations

development. From then on, observations are carried out regularly. These help us to monitor the progress made since the **baseline assessment** information was collected. Over time, as regular observations continue, an ongoing record of children's development is built up. The observations are also used to help us plan how to support the next stage of children's development.

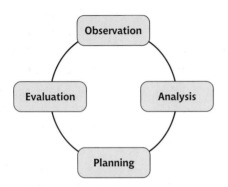

▲ The observation cycle

Sometimes practitioners will carry out general, broad observations of whatever children happen to be doing. But other observations are focused. For instance, practitioners may decide to observe a child playing outside with his peers because they are particularly interested in observing the child's gross motor skills and his social skills. This is referred to as the 'objective' of the observation. Settings will have their own policies and procedures about the way in which observations are carried out. Practitioners must work in line with these at all times.

In addition to monitoring general developmental progress, observation is particularly helpful for building up a picture of the social relationships and bonds children are making with their peers and with adults. It can also reveal whether children are provided with a stimulating environment, interesting activities and appropriate routines.

Regular observations can also help to highlight changes in children's behaviour patterns. This can be very helpful if a child has become quiet and withdrawn, or perhaps unsettled or angry, as there is a record of the change to refer to. Records are also helpful for reporting to parents, carers and other professionals if appropriate.

Methods of observation

There are several methods of recording observations. It is good practice for you to become familiar with all of the different methods over time. However, you should select the most appropriate method to suit your objective and purpose, and work in line with the requirements of your setting.

During observations the behaviour of children can change. If they are aware of being watched, some children may feel anxious or excited, or they may try harder than usual. To counteract this, the practitioner may decide to be a 'non-participant observer'. This means that the practitioner will be unobtrusive – they will settle themselves somewhere suitable to watch the child without alerting them to the fact they are being observed. The practitioner will not interact with the children during this time. They will not speak and so there will be no need to make a record of their own actions or words during the observation.

It is easier to be objective and to record what is happening when you are not involved in events. However, it can be hard to find somewhere unobtrusive that still allows you to see and hear everything that occurs. Although you can use any method of observation as a non-participant observer, if you are looking to observe certain aspects of development

Baseline (or formative) assessment = the first assessment of a child's current stage of development

or behaviour, you may not see them if you do not encourage children to carry out particular activities or tasks. However, this technique is well suited to the 'free-description' and 'target child' methods of observation, which are explained below and on page 67.

Alternatively, the practitioner can be a 'participant observer'. The participant observer can directly ask or encourage children to do things. This technique works well with the 'checklist method' of observation described on page 66, which is often used with babies and young children. Participant observers can ask questions to find out the reason for a child's behaviour – 'Why are you doing that?'

Childcare workers must plan their observation time with colleagues to ensure that it fits in with the overall plans of the setting. Sometimes it is necessary to abandon an observation: for example, if you see something unsafe about to happen or if a child in search of assistance cannot be redirected to another adult.

Whatever method of observation is used, the following key pieces of information are always needed:

- the name of child (or another method of identifying them – initials perhaps)
- date and timing of the observation
- where the observation was carried out
- name of the observer
- activity observed/objective of observation
- other children present
- other adults present.

The presentation of observations differs from setting to setting. However, this key information is often recorded on a separate piece of paper which accompanies the observation itself.

The key methods of observation are outlined below.

Free description

This is also known as written or narrative description. The observer focuses on the activity of the child, writing down everything seen during the allotted time. Free description observations are generally short, lasting for perhaps five minutes or less. They are helpful for focusing on areas of difficulty for children, for instance working out exactly what is happening when a child struggles to feed herself. These observations are often recorded in a notebook and written up afterwards.

You will need:

- a notepad
- a pen.

What to do

Write a detailed description of how the child carries out the activity being observed. Note their actions and behaviour, including their facial expressions. Record what the child says and any non-verbal communication such as gestures. This is intensive work, which is why this type of observation is usually used for just a few minutes. Observations are usually recorded in the present tense.

Example

Ben is sitting at the painting table next to Jessica. He picks up his paintbrush and looks at her. She looks back. He smiles and holds his brush out to her. Jessica takes it and smiles back. Ben says, 'Thank you.'

Checklists (also known as tick lists)

A form prompts the observer to look for particular skills or reflexes that a child has. The observer ticks them off as they are seen. This method is frequently used for assessing a child's stage of development. It is well suited to the observation of babies, whose physical development will typically progress rapidly. The observations may be done over time or babies and children may be asked to carry out specific tasks.

You will need:

- a prepared checklist (these can be purchased or developed by practitioners)
- a pen.

What to do

The checklist tells you what to observe and record. As a participant observer, encourage children to carry out the necessary tasks, ticking the relevant boxes to record the child's response – generally whether they could carry out the task competently. As a non-participant observer, tick the boxes as you see evidence of children's competence naturally occurring.

Example
▼ A checklist

ACTIVITY	YES	NO	DATE	OBSERVER'S COMMENTS
Rolls from back to front				
Rolls from front to back				

Time samples

The observer decides on a period of time for the observation, perhaps two hours or the length of a session. The child's activity is recorded on a form at set intervals – perhaps every 10 or 15 minutes. This tracks the child's activity over the period of time. However, significant behaviours may occur between the intervals and these will not be recorded.

You will need:

- a prepared form giving the times for the observations
- a pen
- a watch.

What to do

Keep an eye on the time to ensure you observe at regular intervals. At each allotted time, observe the child and record their activity in the same way as in the 'free description' method.

Example

10.00am

Ben is sitting at the painting table next to Jessica. He picks up his paintbrush and looks at her. She looks back. He smiles and holds his brush out to her. Jessica takes it and smiles back. Ben says, 'Thank you.'

10.15am

Ben gets down from the table. He goes to the nursery nurse. He looks at her and says, 'Wash hands.'

Event samples

This method is used when practitioners have reason to record how often an aspect of a child's behaviour or development occurs. A form is prepared identifying the aspect being tracked. Each time the behaviour or development occurs, a note of the time and circumstance is recorded. Samples may take place over a session, a week or in some circumstances longer.

Practitioners may want to observe how frequently a child is physically aggressive for instance, and in what circumstances.

You will need:

- a prepared form adapted for the objective of the observation
- a pen.

What to do

Watch a child, and each time the aspect of behaviour or development being observed occurs, record the circumstances along with the time.

Example

▼ An event sample form

EVENT NO.	TIME	EVENT	CIRCUMSTANCES
1	2.30 pm	Joshua pushed Daisy over	Joshua had left his teddy on the floor. He saw Daisy pick it up. He went over to Daisy and tried to take the teddy. She did not let go. Joshua pushed her over. Daisy gave Joshua the toy and started to cry. Joshua walked away quickly with the teddy

Target child

The observer will record a child's activity over a long period of time, but, unlike the time sample method, the aim is not to have any gaps in the duration of the observation. In order to achieve this, the observer uses a range of codes to record, in shorthand on a ready-prepared form, what is happening.

You will need:

- a prepared form with a key to the abbreviations that will be used
- a pen
- a watch.

What to do

With this type of observation the observer has to make decisions about which things are significant and should be recorded, because it is impossible to record every detail over a long period. (It is interesting for two people to observe the same target child over the same period and then compare their forms. They are likely to have recorded different things.) Language and activity are recorded in separate columns for ease. It takes practice to get used to using the codes.

Example

▼ A record of target child observation

TIME	ACTIVITY	LANGUAGE	SOCIAL GROUPING	INVOLVEMENT LEVEL
11.30	TC goes to the box of blocks. Uses both hands to tip the box up and get the blocks out	_TC_ 'Out'	SOL	1
11.31	TC sits down. Using right hand he places one block on top of another. He repeats this, building a tower of four blocks		SOL	1

Key:
TC = target child
_TC_ = target child talking to self
SOL = solitary grouping
1 = target child absorbed in their activity

Practical example

Nathaniel

Three-year-old Nathaniel bit two children at pre-school last week. He has attempted to bite on two more occasions this week. Pre-school leader Sarah discussed this with Nathaniel's dad, who said he had also been bitten by Nathaniel at home. Sarah decides to observe Nathaniel's behaviour, using the event sample method.

1. Why has Sarah chosen to use the event sample method?

2. What could Sarah ask her colleagues to do to help her with event sampling?

Reliability and validity

When practitioners carry out an observation, they aim to be objective. In other words, they aim to record exactly what is happening without interpreting events from their own point of view. Because we all use our past experience and knowledge to process what we see happening in the world, there is a danger that we will interpret events from our point of view. But when you are observing, you should only record what you see. Otherwise the observation is not valid.

Practitioners may sometimes be tempted to record that a child can do something, perhaps because the child can nearly do it, and the practitioner wants them to have a favourable outcome. Or, perhaps the practitioner thinks they have seen the child do something before, and so they want to give them the benefit of the doubt. However, again, the practitioner must only record what they see.

Sometimes there are factors outside the practitioner's control that may affect the reliability or outcome of an observation. If the weather is very windy or it's a very hot and sticky day, for example, children may be feeling fractious and irritable and they may behave differently from usual. This means that an observation may not give a reliable picture of the children's general behaviour. Alternatively children may be excited, or they may be feeling a little unsettled as they get to know a new child or adult who has joined the setting. If you identify a factor that is likely to affect the reliability of the observation, you should record it on the observation record. Failing to do so could make the observation misleading, as adults reading it may believe the behaviour recorded is representative of the way in which a child generally behaves. The outcome would then be compromised.

Objectivity (being objective) prevents:

- bias
- stereotyping
- labelling children
- jumping to conclusions
- relying on personal views.

Confidentiality

As the primary carers and guardians of their children, parents have the right to decide what personal information is collected and recorded about their child. It is essential that practitioners obtain written permission from parents authorising them to carry out observations and to keep relevant documentation on record. Many settings ask for parental permission on the registration form that parents complete prior to their child attending the setting. This must be signed and dated.

Any personal information about children or families should be treated as confidential unless withholding information would affect the wellbeing of the child. You must not disclose confidential details to anyone who does not need to know about them. This includes information about children's individual development, learning and individual needs. Further information about confidentiality is given in Unit 3 on page 88.

⟩⟩ FAST FACT

As a learner you must get permission from your workplace supervisor to carry out observations in the setting, before you approach parents. The supervisor will probably ask to see your completed observation and the child's family may also want to have a copy.

Baseline information

Before practitioners can evaluate the progress that children are making they must get a picture of their current level of development. It's important to document this baseline information carefully as all future observations build upon it.

Baseline information also informs the way in which practitioners approach their work with individual children. This is because the activities that practitioners offer, and the way in which they will relate with children, depend on individual children's abilities and understanding.

Baseline information can be collected from several sources including:

- discussions with parents and carers
- records that parents may have if their child has been to another setting previously
- information from assessments made by other professionals, such as health visitors, GPs or speech therapists
- baseline assessment carried out by the practitioner.

Although information will be gathered from the sources above, practitioners often conduct their own baseline observations to fill in the gaps. For instance, parents may not know if their child can stack bricks or sort shapes because they may not have the relevant resources at home. So the practitioner will observe the child playing with these resources at the setting in order to inform the baseline assessment.

Assessing and evaluating observations

Once an observation (or series of observations) has been completed, a practitioner will consider the observation carefully and then draw conclusions. The consideration aspect is known as 'assessment', and the conclusions drawn are known as the 'evaluation' or the 'outcome'. Some people refer to the whole process of assessing and evaluating as the 'interpretation'.

Settings will have developed their own techniques for interpretation and for the way in which the interpretation is presented in written format. You should follow your setting's guidelines. However, generally practitioners will follow an assessment procedure similar to the one outlined on page 70.

Go through the observation, noting sections that seem significant in terms of behaviour or development. Significant events could reflect achievement, progress, difficulty or the child's feelings. Unusual behaviour will also be of interest

Reflect on the significant events, considering what conclusions can be drawn. For example, if a 2-year-old has been observed getting out a box of blocks for himself, you may conclude that a level of independence has been achieved in selecting and accessing materials

Consider if the behaviour observed is consistent with what you know about the expected patterns of children's development. Is the child doing the things you'd expect them to at their age? Are they behaving as you'd expect? (Although it is not required by most settings, your tutor may ask you to make references to the child development theories on which you are basing your conclusions. This demonstrates that you have a sound knowledge base from which to make assessments.)

Consider what you already know about the individual child from baseline assessment and prior observations. Are they making progress? If so, how is this evident? If not, is this currently a cause for concern?

Once these assessments are finalised, practitioners will write up their evaluations, generally in a free-flowing style. It is essential to ensure that the final evaluation:
• is firmly based on what was recorded at the time of observation
• makes links between the development norms and the child's actual stage of development.

The last stage is to use the information gathered to inform the setting's planning
There is more about this in Unit 7 on page 262.

▲ Procedure for assessing and evaluating observations

FAST FACT

Remember that observations are only a 'snapshot in time' and cannot provide a complete picture.

Observations give us an indication of how children are developing, and what individual needs they may have. This means that observations give us a picture of what a child is doing and how they are behaving at the time the observation is done. But they cannot give us the full story – we cannot know for sure what a child is thinking or feeling for instance. The child may also do things differently or behave differently at another time for a number of reasons, including their mood. Observations date very quickly as children develop rapidly, especially in their early years when they may have new experiences on a daily basis. Different practitioners may interpret observations in different ways, depending on the developmental theories they choose to refer to.

When concerns arise

If you become concerned about a child following observation, it is important that you do not delay in reporting your concerns in line with your setting's policies and procedures. This means that children can get the help and support they may need as soon as possible. Early intervention can often make a difference to how a child with an **impairment** continues to progress in their development.

Identifying difficulties and individual needs

As mentioned in section one, observations can help practitioners to identify children's **individual needs** and difficulties. This relies on practitioners having good knowledge and understanding of expected development rates and patterns. This is because practitioners become aware of difficulties and individual needs by comparing children's actual development with what is generally expected. Childcare workers working in early years are often the first to identify individual needs. The older the children you work with, the more likely it is that children's individual needs will already have been identified. However, observation still has an important part to play in identifying how needs change over time as the child develops, and how strategies to support the child should also change. Below you will find out about the Special Educational Needs Code of Practice, which was introduced to ensure that early years settings work to identify children with **special educational needs**, and to meet their needs.

The Special Educational Needs Code of Practice

The Special Educational Needs Code of Practice (SEN Code) was introduced in 1994 and revised in 2002. It applies to schools and early education settings offering the Early Years Foundation Stage.

Children with special educational needs are identified as:

- children who learn differently from most children of the same age
- children who may need extra or different help to learn.

The SEN Code sets out procedures to be followed in order to meet the needs of children with special educational needs. Under the SEN Code, early years settings must:

- adopt the recommendations of the SEN Code
- train staff to identify and manage children with special educational needs
- devise and implement a Special Educational Needs policy in line with the SEN Code. This must explain how the setting promotes inclusion, which means how it includes children with disabilities and/or special educational needs within the setting
- appoint a **Special Educational Needs Co-ordinator (SENCO)**, who will have responsibility for overseeing how the setting meets the needs of children and follows the SEN Code.

Impairment = term used to identify an individual's child's disability, i.e. a visual impairment, hearing impairment, speech impairment or physical impairment. A child may have more than one impairment, e.g. a learning difficulty and a visual impairment. The word 'disability' may be used to mean the same thing

Individual needs/specific needs = terms used describe how an impairment impacts on the needs of an individual child. This will be specific to them; for example, Emily, a wheelchair user, needs assistance with toileting and dressing but Nina, also a wheelchair user, does not

Special educational needs (SEN) = children with SEN learn differently from most children of the same age and may need extra or different help to learn. Not all disabled children need extra or different help to learn. It depends on their individual needs. The term SEN is used by national and local education departments

Special Educational Needs Coordinator (SENCO) = an appointed person within the setting who has been trained to take overall responsibility for issues relating to special educational needs

Settings must do these things even if there are currently no children with SEN in attendance.

Assessment and intervention frameworks

Under the SEN Code, settings are required to intervene and take action to support children with SEN. There are two stages:

● Early Years Action: this is the first stage in which a child's special educational needs are identified. To meet the child's needs the setting should then devise interventions (strategies) that are additional to or different from those provided under the setting's usual curriculum.

● Early Years Action Plus: this is the second stage in which practitioners feel it is appropriate to involve outside specialists/professionals. These people can offer more specialist assessment of the child and advise the setting on strategies to support them.

Parents, carers and families are at the heart of provision as they know most about their child. Some parents are 'experts' with wide-ranging and in-depth knowledge of their child and their disability and/or special educational need.

Early Years Action

Staff working in early years settings are often the first to notice that a child may be experiencing difficulties with their learning

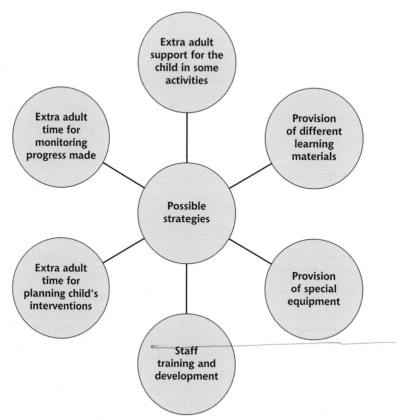

▲ Intervention strategies

and/or development, although sometimes it may be a parent or carer who first expresses a concern about their child. When it is suspected that a child is having problems, staff need to make focused observations of the child to see if they can identify specific difficulties. These observations should be recorded. As previously mentioned, childcare workers often first notice that a child is experiencing a difficulty when they make observations to monitor children's learning and development. They will then plan activities and support to help the child progress.

The SEN Code explains that practitioners will have cause for concern when, despite receiving appropriate early education experiences, one or a combination of the following criteria applies to a child:

- makes little or no progress, even when staff have used approaches targeted to improve the child's identified area of weakness

- continues working at levels significantly below those expected for children of a similar age in certain areas

- presents persistent emotional and/or behavioural difficulties that are not managed by the setting's general behaviour management strategies

- has sensory or physical problems and continues to make little or no progress despite the provision of personal aids and equipment

- has communication and/or interaction difficulties, and requires specific individual interventions (one-to-one attention) to learn.

Once it has been established that a child meets one or more of the above criteria, practitioners should:

- arrange a time to meet with parents or carers to discuss the concerns and to involve them as partners in supporting the child's learning. A childcare worker (usually the child's key worker) should explain the role of the setting's SENCO, and discuss the involvement of the SENCO with the parents or carers. Staff should ask the parents and carers for their own observations of their child's learning and, if appropriate, for information about health or physical problems, or the previous involvement of any outside professionals, such as speech therapists. Parents are the first and best source of information in many cases

- meet with the SENCO. Staff should make available as much helpful information as possible, i.e. observations, assessments, health details

- with the SENCO work together with the parents and carers to decide on the action needed to help the child progress. The SEN Code states that action should 'enable the very young child with special educational needs to learn and progress to the maximum possible'. The diagram below gives examples of strategies (actions) that may be used

- devise an **Individual Education Plan (IEP)** for the child. This should record three or four short-term targets set for them, and detail the strategies that will be put in place to help them work towards the targets. The IEP should only record that which is additional to or different from the general curriculum plan of the setting (see Unit 14 for details of curricula). The IEP should be discussed with the family and the child concerned.

Individual Education Plan (IEP) = a document that records short-term targets for an individual child; it includes details of the strategies that will be put in place to help them work towards the targets

IEPs should be working documents, which means they will be amended over time. Regular reviews should take place in consultation with families to check on how effective the strategies implemented are, and the progress made towards targets. The SEN Code states that reviews need not be 'unduly formal', but a record of them must be kept in the IEP. New targets and strategies decided on at review must also be recorded. There should be a review at least every three months.

Your setting will have adopted a set of record-keeping documents to complete throughout the stages of Early Years Action and Early Years Action Plus. The blank documents may have been bought or the SENCO may have devised them.

Early Years Action Plus

The decision to implement Early Years Action Plus (that is, to involve outside support services and professionals) is generally taken in consultation with a family at a meeting to review a child's IEP. The SEN Code identifies that the implementation of Early Years Action Plus is likely to be triggered when, despite receiving support tailored to their needs, a child:

- continues to make little or no progress in specific areas over a long period
- continues working at a level substantially below that expected of children of a similar age
- has emotional difficulties which substantially interfere with the child's own learning or that of the group, despite an individual behaviour management programme
- has sensory or physical needs and requires additional equipment or regular specialist support

- has ongoing communication or interaction difficulties that are a barrier to learning and social relationships.

The type of support services and professionals available to settings at this stage varies according to local policy. But there will be support available.

To find out about the provision made in your local area by your Local Education Authority (LEA) you can:

- contact your LEA (you may find relevant information on the LEA's website)
- ask the SENCO at your setting
- ask your tutor.

Your LEA's support services or local health or medical services may be able to provide support and help with:

- assessment
- advice on IEPs
- strategies
- activities
- equipment
- specialist support for children during some activities.

At the Early Years Action Plus stage, outside specialists should be consulted as part of the review process while they are involved with the child.

Although the procedures of Early Years Action and Early Years Action Plus apply to schools and settings offering the Early Years Foundation Stage, they can be effectively used by practitioners working with younger children.

Statutory assessment

In some cases, children do not make the expected progress despite the intervention of Early Years Action Plus. At this stage, the family, childcare worker, SENCO and outside professionals meet to discuss if a referral should be made to the LEA requesting a statutory assessment of the child. If agreed, an application for assessment is made.

The LEA asks for all relevant records including observations, IEPs and assessments. These are considered and the LEA decides (within 26 weeks) if the child should be made the subject of a Statement of Special Educational Needs. The statement is legally binding. It sets out a child's needs and outlines what special educational provision must be made to meet them. The LEA must then provide this for the child by law. This applies to all LEAs in England. The nature of the provision made by the LEA will depend on the child's need. Examples of provision include:

- a transfer to a specialist setting
- a place at a mainstream setting with additional one-to-one support
- a place at a mainstream setting with additional resources and equipment
- support of an educational or clinical psychologist
- a home-based programme, such as Portage. This is a programme of activities tailored to suit individual children; parents and carers carry out the activities with the child at home. A Portage worker will support the family.

Statements for children under the age of 5 must be reviewed by the LEA every 6 months. Because of the time it takes to go through the stages of intervention, most children are not referred for statutory assessment until they are over the age of 5 – by which time they will have started school.

Sharing assessment findings with families

Practitioners should share the findings of their assessments with parents and carers. Informing them about their child's progress is a crucial part of working in partnership. Many settings do this effectively by arranging a time for parents and carers to meet privately with their child's key worker. At the meeting, the key worker talks about the assessment methods that were used and the outcome of the assessment. They will summarise the progress that has been made and establish what children are expected to learn next, drawing attention to any areas that may need particular attention. Parents and carers are often keen to know how they can support their child's learning at home, so it is advisable to think this through before the meeting. For instance, the key worker may suggest parents give their child plenty of opportunities to mark make at home by providing pencils, crayons and paper.

▲ Sharing assessment findings with a parent

The key worker should summarise carefully. If a child has not been progressing as expected this will of course need to be discussed. The matter should be handled openly but sensitively. The key worker should ensure that they focus on what children can do and the achievements they have made too, as this will give parents and carers a balanced report. Practitioners, including the SENCO, will want to work in partnership with parents and carers with regard to what should happen next, and to decide if outside support is needed. However, parents and carers may not know about the options open to them. Practitioners should be ready with information about the support available and should have strategies in mind to help the child progress, so that they can end the meeting looking ahead positively. Families may want to think about what has been said and to meet again for further discussion on the way ahead.

Sharing assessment findings with colleagues

Practitioners should share their assessment findings with appropriate colleagues. This ensures that everyone working with a group of children understands how individual children are progressing, what children are expected to learn next and how this will be achieved. This informs practitioners' practical work with the children – they know how to support them effectively to encourage and extend their learning and developmental progress. Many settings share the planning of activities. It is essential that those involved in planning are clear about the findings of individual children's assessments. Only then can the assessment inform the planning, ensuring that appropriate activities are planned to meet the needs of all the children in the group.

Improvement of provision and staff development

Assessments can reveal not only just how well an individual child is learning and progressing but also how well the provision is meeting children's learning and development needs.

Looking at a number of assessments allows practitioners to evaluate the bigger picture. If children are generally not progressing well in one or more particular areas, it may be necessary to improve the way the setting works in that area. Practitioners should discuss this to pinpoint what action can be taken. In some regions an Advisory Teacher may be able to offer support. For instance, it may be that more activities are needed to promote the learning of certain concepts that have not been given due attention. Or perhaps there is a lack of equipment to support specific types of play and learning. Sometimes staff lack confidence in a certain area or have gaps in their knowledge, which impacts on children's progress. In this case, staff development or training is needed. Identifying these issues is a positive step – once the issues are identified they can be addressed and rectified.

▲ Sharing assessment findings with colleagues

Practical example

Nina's review

Nina has been reviewing assessments at her setting. She has noticed that several 3- and 4-year-olds are not making good progress with their mark-making and early writing skills. She raises this with her colleagues in a meeting. It is concluded that while mark-making activities are available on the table at every session, not all of the children choose to participate. So some children actually have very little experience of making marks and practising early writing.

The staff decide to provide children with opportunities to mark make in different areas of the setting. They introduce new strategies, including the provision of paper and pencils to the role-play area – children can now make shopping lists and so on. They also take chalk outside so children can make marks on the ground. They plan to purchase some new and interesting mark-making materials, as supplies are old and have started to dwindle.

(1) *How can Nina and her colleagues monitor the impact of their new strategies over time?*

(2) *What can Nina and her colleagues try next if there's little improvement?*

✔ Progress check

1. What is the purpose of observation?
2. What does the term 'baseline assessment' mean?
3. What are the advantages of being a 'non-participant observer'?
4. What are the advantages of being a 'participant observer'?
5. How should you store completed observations?

Learning Outcome ③

The planning cycle

Assessment is part of a constant cycle of planning for learning and development. Once initial baseline assessment has been carried out, the planning cycle begins. It is the job of childcare workers to plan activities that are appropriate to the child's stage of development. The activities should help children to reach learning/development milestones, goals or objectives. If your setting follows a curriculum framework such as the Early Years Foundation Stage, this will also influence your planning and you should refer to curriculum guidance to assist you. You will learn more about this in Unit 7.

The next stage in the cycle is to carry out the planned activities. The last stage in the cycle is to assess children's progress again. This will reveal what ongoing support children need and/or what they should learn next. These things must be planned for, and so the cycle begins again.

Many practitioners call this the 'plan, do, review cycle,' as this is easy to remember.

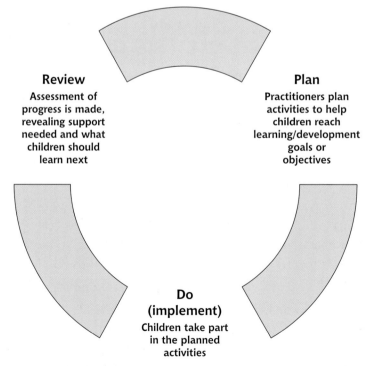

Review
Assessment of progress is made, revealing support needed and what children should learn next

Plan
Practitioners plan activities to help children reach learning/development goals or objectives

Do (implement)
Children take part in the planned activities

▲ The plan, do, review cycle

The key question to ask when starting to plan is: 'In light of the conclusions drawn from my observations, what should I plan to do to support this child's future progress and learning?'

For example, if children are having difficulties learning a particular skill and/or understanding a certain concept, extra support or learning opportunities may be planned to help them. For instance, children may need more opportunities to use scissors because they are having difficulties mastering this skill. Or they may find it difficult to follow stories and have little idea of how to handle books – they would benefit from opportunities to share books on a one-to-one basis with an adult.

If children have particular, persistent difficulties in one or more areas of their learning or development, further consideration is needed to plan the next step. Sometimes difficulties are expected, for example when a child has a special educational need, when they have missed learning opportunities due to a period of illness, or because they are bilingual or multilingual and learning the home language of the setting. In these cases practitioners may already be receiving support from outside professionals and agencies, and an Individual Education Plan (IEP) may already be in place. If so, practitioners should consider the child's progress towards curriculum requirements and their IEP since the last assessment. This would usually be done in consultation with the setting's SENCO.

If progress is being made, practitioners should consider what children should learn next in light of their current development. If sufficient progress is not being made, practitioners can, in consultation with families, refer back to outside professionals and agencies for advice and support.

If those difficulties are unexpected, practitioners should work in consultation with colleagues, the SENCO, families and, where appropriate, children to try to identify the cause. Then children can be given the right support.

Where children are progressing well, practitioners should plan for continued progress.

Practitioners should consider what the child should learn next. What is the next step of their development? What opportunities should be provided for them? What support may they need to continue their progress?

In consultation with the SENCO, parents, carers and children (where appropriate), specialist support and advice can be sought from many professionals who focus on particular areas. These professionals may include:

- educational psychologists – focusing on behaviour and learning
- child psychiatrists – focusing on thoughts and emotions
- play therapists – focusing on dealing with emotions through play
- paediatricians – focusing on health and development
- health visitors – focusing on development of under-5s
- physiotherapists – focusing on the function of the body
- speech therapists – focusing on speech and language
- advisory teachers – focusing on learning and progress towards the national or local curriculum.

It is important to remember that outside professionals working within families can also contribute to the assessment process by sharing observations and insights.

Receiving information from others

Within group settings, key workers will usually know their key children best. But colleagues will also be able to contribute useful information to the observation process. Discussion between practitioners can help to build up a well-rounded picture of a child, which aids the assessment of their development. As well as passing on information about the things they have noticed, colleagues can help at the interpretation stage by sharing their insights. The same applies when outside professionals (such as a speech therapist or social worker) are working within a family.

FAST FACT

Many settings arrange for more than one practitioner to carry out observations on each child over time as this helps to ensure validity (see page 68).

GOOD PRACTICE

It is good practice to share information about the development and progress of a child with their parents or carers. This should be done in an open, positive way – key workers often arrange a meeting with families for this purpose. The information given by the practitioner should be used as a starting point for discussion. It is important to remember that the parents are generally a child's primary carers and that they will know their child best. Families also have much to contribute to a discussion about the progress of their child and this information should be valued. It should be documented in the child's records.

Progress check

1. What are the stages of the planning cycle?
2. With whom can you share and receive information about children?
3. Why is this process helpful?
4. If you find a child is experiencing difficulties, how can your SENCO help?

 **Weblinks**

- www.ntc.org.uk
  The website of the National Childbirth Trust with information on conception, pregnancy and birth

- www.childdevelopmentinfo.com
  The website of the Child Development Institute

- www.chomsky.info
  The website of theorist Chomsky

- http://starfsfolk.khi.is/solrunb/vygotsky.htm
  For information about theorist Vygotsky

- www.freud.org.uk
  For information about theorist Freud from the Freud Museum in London

- www.psy.pdx.edu/PsiCafe/KeyTheorists/Skinner.htm
  For information about theorist Skinner

- www.piaget.org/students.html
  The student page of the Jean Piaget Society

unit 3

Supporting children

This unit studies how childcare workers can support children through understanding of relevant legislation and by following policies and procedures that safeguard children. You will gain understanding of how to empower children and how to support them during transitions. This unit also looks at the causes and effects of discrimination in society.

Learning Outcomes

In this unit you will learn about:

1. the implications of relevant legislation on working practices with children

2. how to recognise strategies, which are fair, just and inclusive, and know how to promote them

3. where to access the policies of the setting and how to follow the procedures for safeguarding children

4. how to empower children to develop self-confidence and self-esteem and self-reliance

5. how to support children to prepare for transfer or transition

6. the causes and effects of discrimination in society.

Learning Outcome 1

FOCUS ON...

the implications of relevant legislation on working practices with children

Further information about legislation, including the rights of children, can be found in Units 1 and 5, and legislation relating to disability and special educational needs is contained in Unit 14 of this book.

This links to assessment criteria **1.1** and **1.2**

Legislation and regulations are in place to provide a positive and acceptable framework of practice. There are many laws and regulations which exist and are intended to protect the children and families you work with, you and your colleagues. These laws outline rights and responsibilities and tell you what is expected of you and how you should behave.

The legislation which relates to the four countries of the United Kingdom (England, Wales, Scotland and Northern Ireland) includes some differences. It is important that practitioners know and understand the regulations that apply to the area where they work. It is important to remember that legislation linked to working with children and young people is vast and often subject to review and amendments; it is therefore part of the professional practice of childcare workers to ensure that they keep up to date with legislation and the implications to practice.

Health and safety legislation

Further information about keeping children safe can be found in Unit 4 of this book.

Health and Safety at Work Act 1974

The Health and Safety at Work Act 1974 is the main piece of legislation in this area, and gives general guidance about health and safety. Since the 1974 Act, several regulations have been passed that give more detail about particular situations. Some of these regulations have been introduced to bring UK health and safety law into line with European laws.

Under the 1974 Act both employers and employees have duties:

- Employers must produce a written policy explaining how they will ensure the health, safety and welfare of all people who use the premises.
- Employees must cooperate with these arrangements and take reasonable care of themselves and others.
- Employers have a duty to display a health and safety law poster.

Health and Safety (Young Persons) Regulations 1997

Employers need to complete risk assessments for people under 18 years of age. Childcare settings are often used for trainees, students and work experience placements. Employers have to consider hazards, such as exposure to chemicals, and specify any supervision or training that a young person may need in relation to such hazards. Risk assessments for manual handling must also be carried out.

See Unit 4 pages 148–149 for further information on risk assessments.

Control of Substances Hazardous to Health Regulations (COSHH) 1994

Substances which pose hazards to health should be risk assessed and stored appropriately in line with COSHH regulations. Such substances in childcare settings will include dishwasher detergent and cleaning solutions. All staff should be made aware of safe storage and safe use of such materials.

Reporting of Injuries, Diseases and Dangerous Occurrences Regulations (RIDDOR) 1995

All accidents and 'near misses' must be recorded. If a staff member is involved in an incident which is serious enough to keep them off work for three days or more, employers need to complete the relevant documents and send a report to the Health and Safety Executive. An investigation may follow. Examples of reportable occurrences include serious illnesses, such as meningitis, and accidents such as those resulting in amputated or broken limbs. Such accidents and occurrences are fully explained on the Health and Safety Executive website listed at the end of this unit.

Implications for good practice – health and safety

As you will already be aware, health and safety is given a very high priority in all that we do. In the first instance, you should be able to locate the Health and Safety at Work Act 1974 poster. Every setting has a duty to comply with health and safety legislation and regulations. Practice in settings reflects this legislation by ensuring that policies and procedures are in place and that everyone at the setting understands their role, responsibilities and the implications for the wellbeing of themselves and others if procedures are not followed. You should be able to locate prompts and reminders about health and safety around the setting: for example, slippery surface signs, reminders about hand washing, mind the step and other signs.

Fire Precautions (Workplace) Regulations 1997

Premises must be checked by fire officers when the premises are registered; they will advise on how to make the workplace as safe as possible. All adults should know the procedures for safe evacuation and these should be rehearsed regularly. Evacuations should be practised at different times to ensure that all users can evacuate the building as safely and quickly as possible. All designated fire exits must be kept clear and unlocked. Fire extinguishers should be checked regularly and placed as advised. A fire blanket should be located in the kitchen.

Implications for good practice – fire

In practice, within every setting that you enter you should always be able to quickly locate and follow an evacuation procedure, with fire exits labelled and

▲ You should always be able to find the fire notice easily

exits kept clear. You should expect to be involved in evacuation practices and the person in charge of the setting will have a record of these.

Health and Safety (First Aid) Regulations 1981

At each session, the employer should ensure that there is at least one person who holds a first aid qualification and is therefore the appointed first aider. In childcare settings at least one person should have been trained in paediatric first aid, as some of the procedures for dealing with children will be different from those for dealing with children.

Implications for good practice – first aid

You should be able to locate well-stocked first aid boxes, find out who is responsible for checking these, who is permitted to administer first aid and how to complete the recording documents for accidents and

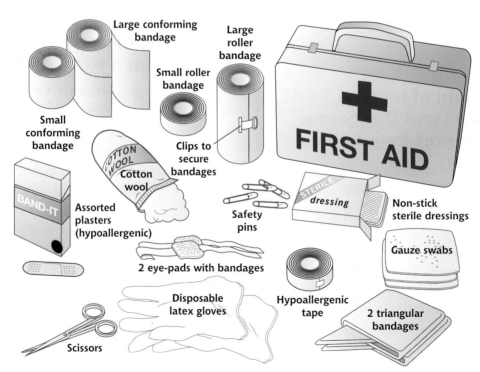

▲ The first aid box must always be kept well stocked and up to date

injuries at any setting. It is important that you ensure that you maintain a high level of good practice when dealing with accidents, ensuring that any blood waste is managed and disposed of in line with procedures.

Food Handling Regulations 1997

Anyone preparing food needs to ensure that they comply with the Food Handling Regulations. This includes hand washing, food handling and storage.

▲ Food safety is a priority when working with children

Implications for good practice – food handling

Within the food handling and preparation areas of the setting you should be able to locate advice about safe practice. Staff in any setting should be aware of expected practice and adhere to these expectations when handling any food.

Personal Protective Equipment at Work Act 1992

Employees who may be exposed to health and safety risks should be provided with the necessary protective clothing by their employer. For example, in childcare settings, workers are exposed to body waste and body fluids whilst dealing with accidents and changing nappies, and so should be provided with protective gloves.

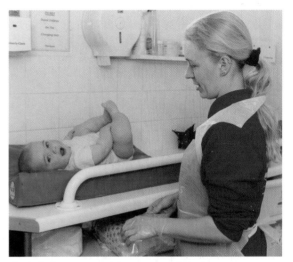

▲ It is important to remember to use protective clothing

Implications for good practice – personal protective equipment

All settings should have a good stock of protective gloves for staff to use for any first aid treatment, nappy changing and toileting, and so that they can deal with any body waste in a safe and hygienic manner. All staff have a responsibility to use what has been provided and to dispose of soiled items in a safe manner in line with practice. In some settings, aprons and specific bags are provided for the disposal of body waste. Gloves should also be provided for staff to use when they are cleaning.

GO☺D PRACTICE ·······

When removing gloves, in order to protect yourself from contamination, gloves should be removed from the wrist thus turning them inside out. This way, the gloves can be disposed of immediately and any contaminated matter will remain inside.

Care Standards Act 2000

This sets out the 14 minimum standards for childcare settings:

1 suitable person
2 organisation
3 care, learning and play
4 physical environment
5 equipment
6 safety
7 health
8 food and drink
9 equal opportunities
10 special needs (including special educational needs and disabilities)
11 behaviour
12 working in partnership with parents and carers
13 child protection
14 documentation.

Implications for practice – care standards

Currently, settings are inspected in line with the care standards and the employer needs to ensure that the setting complies with the standards. The standards and guidance to the standards are published for the variety of settings, for example full day care, childminders. The guidance to the 14 standards describes what the setting is expected to do: for example, behaviour management procedures and ratios. Full details of the standards can be located at the setting.

Data Protection Act 1998

Settings that hold information about individuals are expected to comply with the Data Protection Act 1998. This includes both electronic and paper-based records. Individuals should be made aware of the reasons why the data are kept. For example, children's details and contact information are collected and kept in order to meet the needs of children and to ensure that parents can be contacted. Settings should be able ensure safe storage of information, such as by having locked filing cabinets and password-protected databases.

✔ Progress check

1 Locate and summarise the key health and safety policies for your current setting. Check these with a friend to ensure that you both understand how to put these policies into practice.

2 Who is responsible for health and safety in the workplace?

3 Why is it necessary to wear the protective clothing that is provided in childcare settings?

Learning Outcome 2

FOCUS ON...

how to recognise strategies, which are fair, just and inclusive, and know how to promote them

 This links to assessment criteria **2.1** and **6.1**

 Further information can be found in Units 1, 6, 8 and 14 of this book.

Legal responsibilities in relation to equality, diversity and discrimination

Equal opportunities

Equality can be promoted at government level through laws, at an organisational level through **equal opportunities policies** and procedures and on a personal level through increased awareness and exploration of personal attitudes. Understanding and accepting diversity is essential for all practitioners. We can all benefit from an environment that embraces cultural and linguistic diversity.

The table on page 90 provides a brief overview of legislation.

Fair, just and inclusive strategies

 Further information about **inclusive** practice and special needs can be found in Unit 14 of this book. Further information about children's rights can be found in Unit 6 of this book.

The role of attitudes, values and stereotyped views in influencing behaviour

Attitudes and discrimination

It is important that childcare workers demonstrate positive attitudes towards the children and families that they work with. Children and their families need to feel that they are valued for themselves, for who they are. Negative attitudes on the part of the childcare worker can lead to discriminatory practice, which affects feelings of self-worth. **Discrimination** may result in children failing to achieve their potential in later life and in families becoming disaffected with the childcare centre and its workers.

Positive and negative attitudes

Attitudes reflect our opinions. These can be both positive and negative. Our attitudes to people affect the way we act and behave towards them. If we demonstrate a positive attitude towards someone, it enables that person to feel good, to know that they are valued and have high **self-esteem**. A negative attitude towards a person is likely to lower

---

Equal opportunities policies = policies designed to provide opportunities for all people to achieve according to efforts and abilities

Inclusive = organised in a way that enables all to take a full and active part: meeting the needs of all children

Discrimination = behaviour based on prejudice which results in someone being treated unfairly

Self-esteem = liking and valuing oneself, also referred to as self-respect

▼ UK legislation

LEGISLATION	BRIEF OVERVIEW OF REQUIREMENTS
Disability Discrimination Act 1995	Requires any services offered to the public to be accessible to people with disabilities. This is supported by the Disability Rights Commission, which will support legal action in cases of discrimination against disabled people
Special Needs and Disability Act 2001	Requires LEAs to provide parents of children with special needs with advice and information. It strengthens the rights of children with special educational needs to be educated in mainstream schools
Education Reform Act 1996	Requires LEAs to provide access to the National Curriculum for all children, including those with special needs
Equal Pay Act 1984	Gives women the right to equal pay for equal work
Sex Discrimination Act 1975 & 1986	Makes it illegal to discriminate against someone because of their gender. It also protects people against sexual harassment
The Children Act 1989	Defines the services that should be provided for children. LEAs must consider the race, culture, religion and language when making decisions
The Race Relations Act 1976	Makes it unlawful to discriminate against people because of their race, colour, and nationality, ethnic or national origin. The Commission for Racial Equality researches and investigates cases of alleged racial discrimination

their self-esteem and to make them feel worthless and rejected.

Labelling and stereotyping

Stereotyping contributes to the development of negative attitudes. It involves making assumptions about people, without any evidence or proof, because, for example, they are of a particular race, gender or social origin. Stereotypes are harmful because they perpetuate negative, unthinking attitudes: they are limiting because they influence expectations.

We give specific names to some negative attitudes:

- Racism describes when people of one race or culture believe that they are superior to another.

- Sexism is the term used when people of one gender believe that they are superior to another.

- Stereotypical assumptions are often made about people with disabilities, those in the lower **socio-economic groups**, gay men and lesbian women, and other minority groups.

Where one group in society is powerful and holds stereotyped views about other groups, discrimination and **oppression** are likely to occur. This can reduce the choices,

---

Stereotyping = when people think that all the individual members of the group have the same characteristics as each other: often applied on the basis of race, gender or disability
Socio-economic group = grouping people according to their status in society, based on their occupation which is closely related to their wealth and income
Oppression = using power to dominate and restrict other people

chances and, ultimately, the achievements, of that group.

Institutional discrimination

Discrimination can occur even when individual workers have positive attitudes. If the organisation or institution does not consider and meet the needs of everyone involved in it, and makes assumptions based on one set of values/stereotyped views, institutional discrimination can occur. This can happen when, for example:

- children with disabilities are not given access to the full curriculum
- the meals service does not meet the dietary requirements of certain religious groups
- a uniform code does not consider the cultural traditions of certain groups concerning dress.

Childcare workers are often not aware of how powerful the culture and institutionalised practices of their organisations are in discriminating against certain groups of children or their families. Institutional discrimination is not necessarily a conscious policy on the part of the organisation; more often it occurs because of a failure to consider the diversity of the community. Whether conscious or unconscious, institutional discrimination is a powerful and damaging force.

Effects of discrimination and discriminatory practices on children's development

Children may suffer the effects of stereotyping and discrimination in a number of ways:

- Research by Milner (1983) shows that children as young as 3 attach value to skin colour, with both black and white children perceiving white skin as 'better' than black. This indicates that children absorb messages about racial stereotyping from a very early age. These messages are very demanding to the self-esteem of black children and may result in a failure to achieve their potential. Harm is done to white children too, and to society in general, unless this perception of racial superiority is confronted and challenged effectively. These findings underline the need for all settings, including those in all-white areas, to provide a positive approach that challenges stereotyping.

- Even very young children can hold fixed ideas about what boys can do and what girls can do. Observation of children's play shows that some activities are avoided because of perceptions of what is appropriate for girls and boys. This can result in boys and girls having a very limited view of the choices available to males and females in our society. This is particularly significant when, despite advances in recent years, many women still underachieve.

- Children with disabilities and their families are subject to many forms of discrimination. Even a caring environment may neglect the ordinary needs of the disabled child out of concern to meet their special needs. This may mean that the disability is seen first, rather than the child, and that the child's development is affected because of limited opportunities and low expectations.

Promoting effective equal opportunities, anti-discriminatory and anti-bias practice

Polices and procedures

Many organisations have developed and adopted their own equal opportunities policies, which they apply to matters involving both staff and clients. Operating against policy will often have serious disciplinary implications for staff involved.

GOOD PRACTICE

As with all policies, equal opportunities policies are only effective in promoting their aims if staff are committed to implementing them, if they are properly resourced and if they are regularly evaluated, reviewed and updated.

The role of the individual

As individuals, people contribute to promoting effective equal opportunities, anti-discriminatory and anti-bias practice by:

- examining their own attitudes and values – this can sometimes be a difficult and disturbing experience
- challenging behaviour and language that is abusive or offensive
- increasing their knowledge and understanding of people who are different from themselves
- undertaking training to increase their ability to provide for the needs of all.

Valuing diversity

The first step in implementing anti-discriminatory and anti-bias practice is to recognise the diversity of our society and to value this diversity as a positive rather than a negative factor.

Activities and experiences provided for children can be a powerful tool in promoting equal opportunities. Childcare workers have a responsibility to present activities and experiences in a way that includes and enables all children to participate if they choose to. These activities should reflect the experiences of all sections of society. The planning and delivery of the activities and experiences must provide equality of opportunity, irrespective of race and culture, gender, socio-economic background or disability. Planning and activities must also consider how best to develop the potential of children who are more timid or aggressive or more confident than might be expected of the group. Treating all children the same will not provide for equality of opportunity.

We need to recognise that some children in our society are more likely to experience disadvantage than others and that some positive action might be necessary to enable them to succeed. This is an important consideration when planning the curriculum.

Activities and experiences transmit not just skills and knowledge, but attitudes and values too. The early years are crucial in the formation of children's attitudes about themselves and about the world in which they live. Activities that promote equality of opportunity will enable children to feel positively about themselves and their achievements, to avoid the limitations of stereotyping and to value diversity.

▲ Multicultural activities help all children to value diversity

The hidden curriculum

What else do children learn from activities and experiences provided for them?

Perhaps even more important than the 'official' curriculum in promoting equal opportunities can be the attitudes and values of those who work with children and deliver the curriculum. This is sometimes known as the hidden curriculum and is communicated to children in the way that we talk to them and in the expectations that we have of them.

Here are some examples of ways in which the hidden curriculum can operate against equal opportunities:

- an expectation and acceptance that boys' play is rougher that girls
- giving more time to boys (many studies have shown this to be the case)
- having low expectations of the behaviour and achievement of children from minority groups
- seeing particular games and activities as sex-appropriate
- overprotecting children with disabilities
- making comments such as 'boys don't cry', 'the girls will like this', 'I need two strong boys to move this table'.

Children absorb these messages and they can affect the children's view of themselves. The attitudes and values of the staff, as well as the content of the curriculum, need to address the issues of equal opportunities.

GOOD PRACTICE

Childcare workers are very influential in the formation of children's attitudes and values. Children will take their cue from adult responses and reactions. Because of their powerful role, it is important that staff take issues of equality seriously and do not ignore them.

Codes of conduct in the workplace

When working with children and young people, all practitioners are expected to ensure that they work in line with the requirements of the law and the expectations of the setting. A code of practice is a way of ensuring that everyone knows what is expected of them. At a local level, you should be able to locate a code of practice, policies and procedures, a staff handbook or manual.

Practical example

Valuing diversity

Karen felt the children in the small, all-white, rural playgroup she ran had a very limited experience of cultures other than their own. As part of their regular listening to music sessions, she played some Indian music to the children. Karen had planned the session carefully and had borrowed a box of Indian instruments from a nearby resource centre. After playing the tape a couple of times, she showed the children the instruments and demonstrated the sounds that they made, passing them round so that the children could try them out for themselves. As she played the tape through again, the children were able to recognise some of the instruments as they appeared in the piece. Once the children had become familiar with the instruments and had been shown how to use them, the instruments were placed alongside the other equipment in the music corner so that the children could use them in their own play. Indian music was introduced as part of the playgroup's regular dance sessions and, later on that term, Karen was able to organise a visit to the playgroup by a group of Indian dancers, based at a nearby community arts group.

1. Why was this a valuable experience for the children?

2. How did Karen ensure that this activity would be successful?

3. Think of other, meaningful ways in which the children's experience of cultural diversity could be extended.

Valuing a variety of child-rearing practices

In order to be able to do this, childcare workers will need to adopt an approach that is non-judgemental when working with families. This means that differences in family style, beliefs, traditions and, in particular, ways of caring for children should not be judged as being better or worse but should be respected. Different families will provide for their children in a number of different ways and childcare practice that is anti-discriminatory will seek to meet the needs of all families within a framework that respects their individuality.

The worker's role in recognising discrimination and discriminatory practices

The clearest indication that childcare workers value diversity will be through a positive environment provided for the care and education of children. Good practice suggests that the environment comprises the attitudes and behaviour of everyone associated with the centre, as well as the physical environment of buildings, displays and equipment, and the day-to-day implementation of care and the curriculum. An approach that values diversity enriches the experience of all children and prepares them for adult life in today's society.

The following should be considered:

- demonstrating, through a positive approach, that you value families and children for themselves

- providing resources, including books and displays, that present **positive images**, particularly of under-represented groups

- ensuring that the environment and activities presented are accessible to all children in the group, including those with disabilities

- giving consideration to the wishes and customs of parents concerning the care of their children. This may include preferences concerning diet or dress or any other matter

- having an equal opportunities perspective as an integral element of curriculum planning

- encouraging all children to participate in a full range of activities that avoid gender and cultural bias

- taking positive action when one child or group of children seems to be at a disadvantage. Intervention and another approach will often solve the problem

- encouraging staff to question their own attitudes and values. Is rough play more readily accepted from boys than from girls? Do staff have lower expectations of children from some socio-economic groups, of children from ethnic minority groups or of children with disabilities?

- showing a commitment to monitoring and evaluating provision to ensure it meets the needs of all groups.

The worker's role in confronting and combating discrimination and discriminatory practices

There are occasions when, despite taking the positive steps outlined above, childcare workers will have to deal with instances of discrimination; this is likely to be a difficult and challenging experience.

It may be helpful to consider some strategies in advance. These may include the following:

▲ Appropriate resources enable all children to participate

Positive images = images that challenge stereotypes and that extend and increase expectations

- Challenge abusive behaviour or language. This could be a sexist joke you overhear in the lift or the racist remark someone makes in the staff room. If you allow the incident to go unchallenged, you will appear to be condoning it. If this occurs at work, you may need to discuss the incident with your manager.

- Take seriously any incidence of name calling or bullying. It is not enough to comfort the victim: the behaviour must be challenged and be seen to be unacceptable.

- Remember that language has a powerful influence in shaping children's self-esteem and identity. Be aware of the terms that you use. Sexist comments about strong boys and pretty girls reinforce stereotypes. Avoid terms that associate black with negative connotations, such as 'black mood', 'black magic', 'accident black-spot'; use should be neutral such as 'black paint', 'black coffee'. Challenge abusive words such as 'spastic' when you hear them used by children and adults; use the appropriate term in response, such as 'a child with a disability', 'a child with cerebral palsy'. In doing so you will be giving the speaker the appropriate terminology to use in the future.

Practical example

Responding to discriminatory behaviour

Luke and Callum both attended a busy inner-city nursery. They lived on the same street and were often dropped off at nursery together. The nursery staff were puzzled when they stopped playing together and, in fact, began to avoid one another. One afternoon it became clear what had happened. At home time, their mothers started arguing outside the nursery entrance. They had fallen out about one of them playing loud music late at night and disturbing the neighbours. The argument became very heated, culminating in Callum's mother shouting abuse and calling Luke and his mother a pair of 'black bastards'. The nursery staff heard what was going on and tried to calm things down by separating them and taking them into other rooms, away from the children. The teacher asked them both to come and see her the next day. When she spoke with Callum's mother, she made it clear to her why her remarks were unacceptable and asked for an assurance that it would not happen again or she would not be welcome on nursery premises in future.

1. Why was this a difficult situation for the nursery staff to deal with?

2. How did they manage to defuse the situation?

3. What would the needs of the children be in this situation?

GO☺☺D PRACTICE

Everyone who works with children is very influential in the formation of their attitudes and values. Children will take their cue from adult responses and reactions, and it is therefore important that staff take seriously all issues of equality.

✓ Progress check

1. Why is it important to value diversity?
2. How can childcare workers show their commitment to promoting diversity?
3. What can childcare workers do to oppose discrimination?
4. Why is language an important aspect of anti-discriminatory practice?
5. Why should you always take a stand when you witness abusive or discriminatory behaviour?
6. Copy the following table. Map the CACHE statement of values and any relevant legislation to the policies listed.

▼ Mapping CACHE statement of values and legislation

POLICY/PROCEDURE	CACHE STATEMENT OF VALUES	LEGISLATION
Equal opportunities policy		
Admissions procedure		
Health and safety policies and procedures		
Child protection policies and procedures		
Partnership with parents		
Managing behaviour		
Record keeping		
Emergency procedures		

Learning Outcome 3

FOCUS ON...

where to access the policies of the setting and how to follow the procedures for safeguarding children

This links to assessment criteria **3.1** and **3.2**

Children of all ages, male and female, from all cultures and socio-economic groups are the victims of abuse. History reveals that it is not a new phenomenon; however, our awareness and understanding of child abuse and the need to safeguard children within society has increased and developed in recent decades.

Recognising abuse when working with children

All those working with children have a unique opportunity and responsibility to:

- recognise indicators of abuse
- know how to record and report their concerns and follow the correct procedures if they suspect abuse
- listen to children, to deal with disclosure
- work to support abused children and their families. All workers have a responsibility to empower children, enabling them to develop the skills needed for self-protection
- be aware that abuse may be perpetrated within the institution in which they work and know the policies and procedures to follow to deal with this.

The needs, rights and views of young children

The view by any society of what constitutes child abuse within that society varies both between societies and within them at different stages of their history. In 19th- and 20th-century Britain, views of child abuse changed considerably, together with ideas about the needs and rights which children have as individuals and the responsibilities of parents towards them. In order to understand child abuse, and the way to best protect children in the 21st century, we need to understand the current thresholds of what is considered to be abusive, and what leads to abuse.

The rights of children – the historical perspective

The unkind treatment by some adults of children has occurred throughout history. The novels of Charles Dickens paint a vivid picture of the lives of some children in 19th-century Britain. In *Oliver Twist*, for example, Dickens shows how cruelty and harsh punishment were both common and acceptable. Many children had to work long hours; they were often beaten and neglected.

The Earl of Shaftsbury was one of the people in the 19th century who initiated a series of social reforms to improve the lives of children. However, the amount of abuse that occurs in society depends firstly on the view which that society has of what child maltreatment is, and this in turn determines the threshold at which society will take action against perpetrators. The 19th-century reformers would have had difficulty in recognising some 20th-century definitions of abuse, and when the state believes interventions to be appropriate. Laws passed since the 19th century have increasingly recognised the rights of children to be protected and to have their basic needs met, and the responsibilities of parents to protect children and meet their needs. The most recent major child protection law to be passed was the Children Act 1989 and 2004.

The Children Act 1989

The Children Act 1989 is a major piece of legislation. Previous laws, passed during the 19th and 20th centuries, overlapped and were sometimes inconsistent. This caused confusion and difficulties for those interpreting the laws. The Children Act aims to provide a consistent approach to child protection both by bringing together and changing previous laws.

There was also a concern that recent law, passed before the Children Act, could be used too easily to take rights and responsibilities away from parents. This was thought to be neither in the interests of children nor of parents. One of the main aims of the 1989 Act was therefore to balance the needs and rights of children and the responsibilities and rights of parents.

The needs of children

The Children Act 1989 recognises, however, that all children have certain needs that are universal. These basic developmental needs are the need for:

- physical care and protection
- intellectual stimulation and play
- emotional love and security
- positive social contact and relationships.

The rights of children

All children have certain rights. These include the right to:

- have their needs met and safeguarded
- be protected from neglect, abuse and exploitation
- be brought up in their family of birth wherever possible
- be considered as an individual, to be listened to and have their wishes and feelings taken into account when any decisions are made concerning their welfare.

Cultural differences in child-rearing practices

The way that children are brought up varies a great deal between different social groups and different cultures. Families have different customs involving children. For example, some groups are traditionally more indulgent towards children, while others are stricter. Some use physical punishment more readily; others are more likely to use emotional forms of control. The Children Act 1989 acknowledges differences and values many of them. It recognises that a positive attitude to working in partnership with parents and understanding their perspective must underpin any action when working with families.

The Children Act 2004

The Children Act 2004 was introduced after inquiries into child protection. The tragic death of Victoria Climbié resulted in an independent inquiry; this inquiry into the death of a child, as with many others over the years, criticised the protection of children in our society. This resulted in the introduction of the government's Green Paper, *Every Child Matters*. The Children Act 2004 requires professionals to work together to benefit children and their families; it is essential that every practitioner knows and understands the contents of this Act.

In brief, there are five outcomes and four key themes which must be considered when working with children.

 Further information about *Every Child Matters* can be found on page 29.

The five outcomes are:

1 Be healthy
2 Stay safe
3 Enjoy and achieve
4 Make a positive contribution
5 Achieve economic wellbeing.

The four key themes are:

1 Supporting parents and carers
2 Early intervention and effective protection
3 Accountability and integration – locally, regionally and nationally
4 Workforce reforms.

The Childcare Act 2006

The needs of children and their families are central to this Act. Local authorities acting as champions for children and their families must ensure that their views are heard in the planning and delivering of services, thus reflecting the needs of families.

Key points of the Childcare Act 2006 include the following:

● Local authorities are required to improve outcomes for children under 5 and to close gaps between those with the poorest outcomes and the rest, through ensuring integrated childhood services which are proactive and accessible.

● Local authorities are given the lead role in facilitating the childcare market, ensuring that it meets the needs of working parents, those with low incomes and parents of children with disabilities.

● Access to a full range of information for parents' needs must be provided.

● The Early Years Foundation Stage is introduced.

● There should be reformation and simplification of the childcare and early years regulation framework to focus on raising the quality.

Children (Northern Ireland) Order 1995

This came into force in October 1996 and bears close similarities to the Children Act 1989 but there are some differences. The Children (Northern Ireland) Order 1995:

● expects providers of day care and childminding for children under 12 to be registered

● does not provide for fees to be imposed on providers of childminding and day care services

● requires all children's homes to register, regardless of numbers of children

● removes most of the legal disadvantages of illegitimacy.

The Children (Scotland) Act 1995

This Act contains three child-centred principles, similar to the Children Act 1989:

1 The welfare of the child is paramount – the interests of the child are the most important factor and will be the deciding factor in any legal decision.

2 The views of the child must be taken into account – courts must take into account the child's views. The child has the right to attend their own hearing.

3 'No order' principle – children's hearings and courts must be convinced that making an order is better than not making an order.

The Framework for the Assessment of Children in Need and their Parents (2000)

The framework for assessment is for all professionals working in child protection issues. Usually social services will carry out assessments and the framework clearly lays out the roles and responsibilities for all agencies to make sure there is a common approach. The framework is based on a triangular approach:

- Child's development needs – i.e. how is the child developing, how is their health and education?

- Family and environmental needs – i.e. what is the family income, what is the history of the family and how it functions?

- Parenting capacity – how does the parent offer basic care, safety, warmth, stability?

Procedures for the protection of children

Child abuse is a social and health problem that occurs amongst people of all social backgrounds, cultures and races. It affects both disabled and non-disabled children. It can take place in a variety of settings. Legislation recognises the need and right

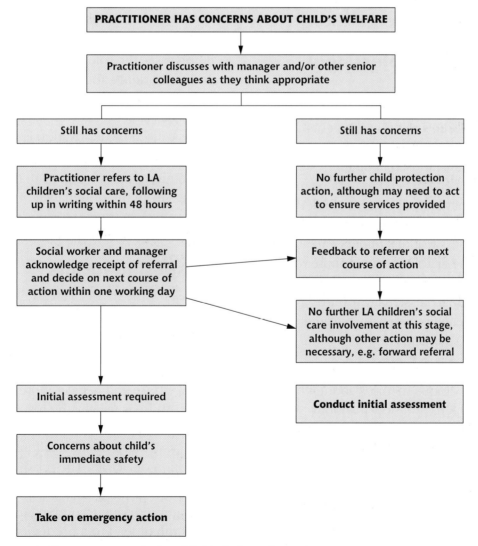

▲ What to do if you are worried a child is being abused

of children from every background and in every setting to be protected from abuse. Section 11 of the Children Act 2004 places a statutory duty on key people and bodies to make arrangements to safeguard and promote the welfare of children. There are recommendations about what should be done. One of these recommendations is the organisation of Local Safeguarding Children Boards.

Local Safeguarding Children Boards have a core membership which includes local authorities, health bodies, the police and others. The objective of the board is to coordinate and ensure that member agencies are effective in safeguarding and promoting the welfare of children.

Adopting a professional approach

Despite the passing of legislation that makes children's rights and parents' responsibilities clear, children are still neglected and abused in different ways. Childcare workers need to understand why this may happen in order to develop a professional approach to parents and carers. Unless workers understand at least some of the factors that contribute to a case of child abuse, they may be in danger of behaving unprofessionally towards a carer and not treating them with consideration.

Theories of abuse

There are various theories about why abuse happens and how it should be viewed. A combination of these perspectives is probably of the most use in understanding abuse:

- A medical model tends to look at the signs of abuse and concentrate on recognising these, distinguishing them from accidental injuries or medical

conditions. A concentration on this, rather than looking at the wider circumstances, occurred in the Victoria Climbié case in 2000 and was one of the factors that contributed to her death.

- A physiological approach concentrates on the failure of attachments between carers and the children they injure. Many children who die are in fact killed by 'stepfathers', who have not been present to build up an early attachment to the child; but this does not give a complete explanation. A physiological approach emphasises the interaction between individuals and their social environments when looking for explanations of abuse.

- A social theory of child abuse emphasises the role of social problems and social deprivation as a cause, but it is known that child abuse happens in all social classes and groups. However, stress caused by deprivation is a recognised factor in many cases.

- A feminist approach argues that abuse springs from the dominance of men in society and their need to assert their power over women and children.

Predisposing factors

Regardless of the theory, research shows that abuse does not occur entirely at random; it is more likely to happen in some situations than others. There is a wide variety of predisposing factors that can make abuse and neglect more likely to occur. Abuse is usually the result of a number of these factors occurring together. In each case, there will be a different combination of factors. The relative importance of each of them will also vary.

The danger in trying to understand abuse is that it might lead to a prediction that, if certain characteristics are present, abuse will happen; or that all people with those characteristics will become abusers. This is definitely not so. However, it is possible to look at certain factors and find that a combination of them is usually present in many cases of abuse. These factors enable us to recognise, understand and work with families where there is a higher risk of abuse.

Researchers have identified five family types that illustrate a range of background characteristics to be borne in mind when abuse is suspected. These family types are: multi-problem families, specific problem families, acutely distressed families, those with perpetrators from outside the family and those with perpetrators from inside the family.

Predisposing factors in many cases of abuse may include:

- factors in the adult's background and personality
- the presence of some kind of difficulty and stress in the adult's life or environment
- factors relating to the child.

Factors in the adult's background and personality

A combination of some of the following characteristics has been noticed in abusing parents (but remember that non-abusing parents may also have some of these characteristics).

Immaturity – some people have not developed a mature level of self-control in their reactions to life and its problems. Faced with stressful situations, an adult may lack self-control and react strongly just as a young child might do, in a temper or with aggression.

Low self-esteem – some people have a very poor self-image; they have not experienced being valued and loved themselves. If they are struggling to care for a child, they may feel inadequate and blame the child for making them feel worse about themselves because they are finding it difficult.

An unhappy childhood where they never learnt to trust others – parents who have experienced unhappiness in childhood may be less likely to appreciate the happiness that children can bring to their lives. They have not had a good role model to create a happy and caring environment for their children.

Difficulty in experiencing pleasure – an inability to enjoy life and have fun may be a sign of stress and anxiety. This person may also have problems in coping with the stress of parenting and gain little pleasure from it.

Unsatisfactory relationships – when parents are experiencing difficulties in relationships, whether sexual or other difficulties, this can make for an underlying base of stress and unhappiness in their lives. There may also be a general background of neglect or family violence within which there is little respect for any individual.

Being prone to violence when frustrated – the damaging effects of long-term family violence on children has been recognised. Research shows that children who regularly see their mothers beaten can suffer as much as if they had been frequently hit themselves.

Being socially isolated – parents who have no friends or family nearby have little or no support at times of need; they have no one to share their anxieties with, or to call on for practical help.

Adults whose responses are low on warmth and high on criticism – in such families, children can easily feel unloved and negative incidents can build up into violence.

A fear of spoiling the child and a belief in the value of punishment – some people have little understanding of the value of rewards in dealing with children's behaviour; they think children should be punished to understand what is right; they think that responding to a child's needs will inevitably 'spoil' the child. They are more likely to leave a baby to cry and not to be warm and spontaneous in their reactions to them.

A belief in the value of strict discipline – there are many variations in parenting styles, family structures and relationships; these are not necessarily better or worse than each other. They meet the needs of children in different ways. Some styles of discipline use punishment (both physical and emotional), rather than reward. This is more likely, however, to lead to abuse when other stressful factors are present.

An inability to control children – parents under pressure seldom have much time for their children and risk lashing out at their children in a rage at the frustrations of everyday interactions.

Not seeing children realistically – this involves having little or no understanding of child development and the normal behaviour of children at different stages; such adults are more likely to react negatively to behaviour that causes them difficulty, rather than accepting it as normal. They may punish a young child inappropriately for crying, wetting, having tantrums or making a mess.

An inability to empathise with the needs of a child and to respond appropriately – some people have difficulty in understanding the needs of children; they may react negatively when children make their needs known and demand attention.

Having been abused themselves as children – these parents may have a number of unmet needs themselves and are therefore less likely to be able to meet the needs of a dependent child; they have also had a poor role model for parenting and family life.

Difficulties during pregnancy and/or birth, or separation from their child following birth – research shows that difficulties during pregnancy and childbirth, or early separation of the mother from her child, can result in a parent being less positive towards a child. Faced with a child's demands, they may be less able to cope. They may lose their temper more quickly and resort to violence more easily.

Adult stress and difficulties

Stress of some kind is found in many cases of abuse or neglect. Stress may be short or long term (sometimes referred to as acute or chronic). It may have many causes, such as:

- social isolation – few friends/no family
- chaotic lifestyles
- domestic violence, usually of a man towards a woman
- loss of relationships, especially through desertion
- mental illness or chronic unhappiness
- physical ill health
- misuse of alcohol and/or drugs
- high levels of pressure in everyday life
- poor environmental conditions

- poor housing
- poverty/unemployment
- debt and money worries
- criminal behaviour within the family
- the experience of discrimination
- bereavement.

The experience of stress drains people's energy and leaves them with fewer resources to cope with meeting the demands of children. The experience of multiple stresses can weaken a person's ability to cope, although it does not necessarily mean that they are irresponsible or lack affection for their children. It can, however, affect the capability of a person to care for their children.

People who have constant worries and who have to endure long-term difficulties probably experience more stress than those without such worries. This can provide a background of unhappiness that may be significant if it is experienced in combination with other factors outlined in this section.

It does not necessarily follow that people who lack the resources to cope with difficult situation will abuse or neglect their children. In the majority of families they do not. The factors outlined above

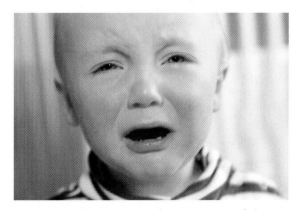

▲ Constant crying can be very stressful

can, however, help us to understand the different types of stress that may be present in any parent's life and may contribute to abusive situations.

Factors relating to the child

In addition to the factors mentioned above, some things about a child can make them less easy to love by some parents or carers. This does not mean that the child deserves ill treatment but, combined with other factors, it can be significant.

The significant factors about a particular child may include the following:

- A crying child – most people can sympathise with the stress created by a child who cries a lot; when a carer is tired, and other factors are present, the stress brought about by constant crying can make a child vulnerable to a violent response.

- Interference in early bonding or attachment between carer and child – there is a wealth of research from Bowlby onwards of the possible ill effects of early separation of parent and child. Early separation can result in poor attachment of parent and child. There is evidence that a carer is more likely to abuse a child when the attachment is weak rather than strong; it is for this reason that modern antenatal and postnatal care aims to keep parents with their newborn babies and encourages the development of a strong bond between parent and child.

- Children who are felt by their carers to be more difficult to care for at a specific stage of development – some people find babies particularly demanding and difficult; others have more difficulty caring for 'stroppy' toddlers or older children.

- Children who 'invite' abuse – these children have learned that the only attention they get is abusive; they learn to bring about certain negative reactions in their carers because this is preferable to having no attention at all.

In conclusion, there are many factors that can contribute to the abuse or neglect of children. An awareness of these can help professionals in their work with families and avoid judgemental attitudes. Such knowledge can also help workers' efforts to make the best possible decisions for a child in partnership with their parents.

A first step in protecting children from abuse involves workers facing up to the fact that it does happen, and then understanding the nature and types of abuse, and the signs and symptoms that may be present. Knowledge of the adverse effects of abuse on children serves to emphasise the duty of workers to make its prevention and diagnosis a key priority in their work.

The effects of abuse

The prolonged abuse or neglect of children can adversely affect all aspects of their development, their health and their feeling of wellbeing. It may be impossible for them to develop a positive self-image and healthy self-esteem, which can continue to affect their adult lives. Children may find it difficult to form and sustain relationships, to work or to be a good parent. The effects of abuse can be influenced for better or worse by the child's ability to cope and adapt their previous experiences of family life, by the support the child subsequently receives within the family and in the community, and by the way that professionals respond.

The impact on the family and community

The child's whole family may be adversely affected by the abuse of a child in its midst; even if most of its members are innocent of abuse they may feel guilty for not having recognised the abuse and for failing to protect the child. If a case is handled sensitively, the outcome for the child and the possibility of remaining with their family is more likely to be positive.

There is recent evidence, highlighted in the media, that the presence of an abuser in a community can cause concern, particularly if the person has been convicted and imprisoned for sexual abuse. It can destabilise relationships in the community and lead to innocent people being mistakenly targeted for further punishment.

Types of abuse

Although the types of abuse are here identified separately, children may be the victims of more than one type of abuse.

The four different types of abuse are:

- physical abuse and injury
- neglect
- emotional abuse
- sexual abuse.

Physical abuse and injury
What is physical abuse and injury?

Physical abuse involves someone deliberately harming or hurting a child. It covers a range of unacceptable behaviour, including what some may describe as physical punishment. It can involve hitting, shaking, throwing, biting, squeezing, burning, scalding, attempted suffocation, drowning and giving poisonous substances, inappropriate drugs or alcohol. It includes the use of excessive force when carrying out tasks like feeding or nappy changing.

Indicators of physical abuse

Early years workers may be in a unique position to notice the signs and symptoms of abuse, which are also referred to as the indicators of child abuse. These include the following:

Bruises

Seventy per cent of abused children suffer soft tissue injury, such as bruises, **lacerations** or **weals**. The position of the bruising is important: bruises on cheeks, bruised eyes without other injuries and bruises on front and back of the shoulders are less likely to occur accidentally, as are **diffuse bruising**, **pinpoint haemorrhages** and fingertip bruises. Bruises occurring frequently or re-bruising in a similar position to old or faded bruising may also be indicators of abuse.

The pattern of bruises may also be an indicator: bruises reflecting the cause, for example fingertip-, fist- or hand-shaped bruising. Bruises incurred accidentally do not form a pattern.

It is very important that mongolian spots are not confused with bruises or arouse suspicion of abuse. Mongolian spots are smooth, bluish-grey-to-purple skin patches, often quite large, consisting of an excess of pigmented cells (**melanocytes**). They are sometimes seen across the base of the spine (**sacrum**) or buttocks of infants or young children of Asian, Southern European and African descent. They often disappear at school age.

Diagnosis of child abuse is by professionals joining together to share information. It is rarely made on the basis of physical indicators alone.

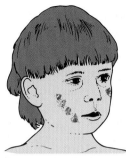

▲ What might you think if you saw this pattern of bruising on a young child's face?

Burns and scalds

Around 10 per cent of abused children suffer burns. These may be cigarette burns, especially when the burn marks are clear and round and there is more than one, and burns reflecting the instrument used, for example made by placing a heated metal object such as an iron on the skin.

The pattern and position of scalds can be significant, showing whether hot water has been thrown deliberately or pulled down accidentally by the child. A child with scalds (on the feet) that are shaped like socks would imply that the child was placed in hot water and held there.

Fractures

In diagnosing non-accidental injury the following would be significant:

- the age of the child – immobile babies seldom sustain accidental fractures
- X-rays revealing previous healed fractures of differing ages

---

Lacerations = tears in the skin
Weals = streaks left on the flesh
Diffuse bruising = bruising that is spread out
Pinpoint haemorrhages = small areas of bleeding under the surface
Melanocytes = pigmented cells
Sacrum = base of the spine

- the presence of other injuries
- the explanation given by child or carer (see Additional indicators of physical abuse, opposite).

Head, brain and eye injuries

Head, brain or eye injuries may indicate that a child has been swung, shaken, received a blow or been hit against a hard surface. A child's skull can be fractured and the brain damaged. Shaking a child or injuring the head can result in bleeding into the brain (a **subdural haematoma**). A child with even a small outward sign of head injury that is accompanied by irritability, drowsiness, headache, vomiting or head enlargement should receive medical attention urgently, as the outcomes can include brain damage, blindness, coma and death.

Internal damage

Internal damage, caused by blows, is a common cause of death in abused children.

Poisoning

Any occurrence of poisoning with drugs or liquids needs to be investigated.

Other marks

Other indicators of abuse may include bites, outlines of weapons, bizarre markings, nail marks, scratches and abrasions. A torn **frenulum** in a young child (the web of skin joining the gum and the lip) usually results from something being forcibly pushed into the mouth, such as a spoon, bottle or dummy. It hardly ever occurs in ordinary accidents.

Behavioural indicators of physical abuse

As with any trauma, children's reactions to abuse may vary. Being subjected to abuse can affect all aspects of children's development: physical, intellectual and linguistic and emotional and social. Perhaps the most significant effect of abuse is the long-term damage to a child's self-esteem, or self-respect, damage which may persist into adult life. To be abused is to be made to feel worthless, misused, guilty and betrayed. Children's feelings may be translated into observable behaviour patterns.

This behaviour should be recorded in order to consider it alongside physical and additional indicators. It may help in diagnosis, but does not alone prove the existence of abuse. This behaviour can include:

- fear and apprehension – professionals working with abused children have described a particular attitude or facial expression adopted by abused children and labelled it **frozen awareness** or **frozen watchfulness**. This describes a child whose eyes are constantly alert and aware (vigilant), while remaining physically inactive (passive), demonstrating a lack of trust in adults but a desire not to provoke attention
- inappropriately clinging to, or cowering from, the carer
- unusually withdrawn or aggressive behaviour (a sudden change in the way a child behaves may be particularly significant)
- the child's behaviour in role-play situations, including their explanation of how the injury occurred.

Martin and Beezley (1977) drew up a list of characteristic behaviour of abused children, based on a study of 50 abused children. The behaviour patterns may be regarded as indicators of abuse:

Subdural haematoma = bleeding into the brain

Frenulum = the web of skin joining the gum to the lip

Frozen awareness/watchfulness = constantly looking around, alert and aware (vigilant) while remaining physically inactive (passive), demonstrating a lack of trust in adults

- *impaired capacity to enjoy life* – abused children often appear sad, pre-occupied and listless
- *stress symptoms*, for example, bed wetting, tantrums, bizarre behaviour, eating problems
- *low self-esteem* – children who have been abused often think they must be worthless to deserve such treatment
- *withdrawal* – many abused children withdraw from relationships with other children and become isolated and depressed
- *learning difficulties*, such as lack of concentration
- *opposition or defiance* – a generally negative, uncooperative attitude
- *hypervigilance*, or frozen awareness or watchful expression
- *compulsivity* – abused children sometimes feel or think they must carry out certain activities or rituals (sets of activities) repeatedly
- *pseudo-mature behaviour* – a false appearance of independence or being excessively 'good' all the time, or offering indiscriminate affection to any adult who takes an interest.

Children's reactions can be summarised as either 'fight or flight'. They may respond by becoming aggressive and anti-social (fight), or by becoming withdrawn and over-compliant (flight).

Additional indicators of physical abuse

Physical and behavioural indicators alone may be insufficient to diagnose child abuse. They should, therefore, always be considered alongside other factors.

The presence of the following additional indicators increases the likelihood that injuries were sustained non-accidentally; they should be recorded alongside the physical indicators. Some of these additional indicators highlight the need to keep accurate, up-to-date records:

- an explanation by the parent or carer that is inadequate, unsatisfactory or vague, inconsistent with the nature of the injury, considering the age or stage of development of the child
- an unexplained delay in seeking medical attention, or seeking treatment only when prompted by others
- a series of minor injuries to a child, which may in themselves have satisfactory explanations
- a history of child abuse or neglect of this or other children in the family
- the existence of certain parental attitudes, such as a lack of concern, remorse or guilt over an accident, blaming others or the child for the injury, denying there is anything wrong or self-righteously justifying the infliction of injury during punishment. An example might be if a child aged 3 was found to have belt marks on his buttocks and lower back, and on being questioned the carer said, 'He deserved it. I warned him if he was cheeky once more I'd thrash him. Smacking does no good at all these days.'

FAST FACT

An average of more than two children call ChildLine each hour. In 2006, 17,956 children spoke to someone at ChildLine about the physical abuse they were suffering

Practical example

Dealing with possible physical abuse

A 2-year-old child often comes to the day nursery with fresh bruises on his arms and upper body. His mother explains these are the result of minor accidents while playing.

1. *What might lead you to suspect that the child was being non-accidentally injured?*

2. *Explain how you would respond to the mother immediately.*

3. *Describe the procedure you would work through within the establishment, including how and what you would record.*

The effects of physical abuse

Physical abuse can lead to physical injuries, neurological damage, disability and death. Children's development can be affected by the context of violence, aggression and conflict within which it takes place. It has been linked to aggressive behaviour, emotional and behavioural problems and educational difficulties.

Neglect

What is neglect?

Neglect involves persistently failing to meet the basic essential needs of a child, and/or failing to safeguard their health, safety and wellbeing.

Neglect involves acts of **omission**, i.e. not doing those things that should be done, such as not meeting a child's developmental needs or not protecting children from harm. This contrasts with other types of abuse that involve acts of **commission**, i.e. doing those things that should not be done, for example beating children.

Types of neglect

These areas will often overlap.

Physical neglect

Physical neglect involves not meeting children's need for adequate food, clothing, warmth, medical care, hygiene, sleep, rest, fresh air and exercise. It also includes failing to protect, for example leaving young children alone and unsupervised.

Emotional neglect

Emotional neglect includes refusing or failing to give children adequate love, affection, security, stability, praise, encouragement, recognition and reasonable guidelines for behaviour.

Intellectual neglect

Intellectual neglect includes refusing or failing to give children adequate stimulation, new experiences, appropriate responsibility, encouragement and opportunities for independence.

Indicators of neglect

The following signs and symptoms may be observed and should be recorded accurately and dated:

- constant hunger, voracious appetite, large abdomen, emaciation, stunted growth, obesity, failure to thrive (see page 112)

Omission = not doing those things that should be done, such as protecting children from harm
Commission = doing those things that should not be done, for example beating children

✏ Practical example

Indicators of neglect

Rachel, aged 2, has just begun to attend an expensive private day nursery. Her parents, both solicitors, drop her off at 8am, Monday to Friday, and are usually the last to pick her up when the nursery closes at 6pm. On a number of occasions they have been as late as 7pm. Rachel is underweight for her age and unable to manage solid food, preferring a bottle. She takes little interest in the activities of the nursery, preferring to sit alone – sucking a toy and rocking rhythmically.

Her mother explains that Rachel was premature, and has never put on much weight, and that relations on her husband's side of the family are all small anyway. Both parents resent being questioned about their child and offer extra payment, to cover the staff's inconvenience, when they are late to collect Rachel.

① Write a list of the indicators of neglect described.

② Describe the kind of ongoing records that should be available to confirm each indicator of neglect in this case.

③ Write a description of a child you have known to be physically neglected.

④ Why may the carers of the child you have described be neglecting their child's needs?

- inadequate, inappropriate clothing for the weather; very dirty, seldom laundered clothing
- constant ill health, untreated medical conditions, for example extensive persistent nappy rash, repeated stomach upsets, chronic diarrhoea
- unkempt appearance, poor personal hygiene, dull matted hair, wrinkled skin, skin folds
- constant tiredness or lethargy
- repeated accidental injury
- frequent lateness or non-attendance at school
- low self-esteem
- compulsive stealing or scavenging
- learning difficulties
- aggression or withdrawal
- poor social relationships.

It is important to remember, however, that behavioural indicators may be due to causes other than neglect. Possible medical conditions that may account for the physical indicators observed will need to be ruled out. For this reason, workers need to be aware of the background of children in their care.

⟩⟩⟩ FAST FACT

A study of 3,000 young people aged 18–24 years was carried out by the NSPCC in 2000. The study found, amongst other things, that 6 per cent of children experienced serious absence of care during childhood. This included regularly having to look after themselves because parents were away or had problems with alcohol or drugs.

(Source: Cawson, 2002. NSPCC Inform, www.nspcc.org.uk)

Failure to thrive

The term 'failure to thrive' describes children who fail to grow normally. This can be for a variety of reasons. Some children are small because their parents are small. Others have a medical condition causing lack of growth. Children may be referred to paediatricians because of concern about growth. Growth charts (**percentile charts**) are used in the assessment of such children.

As a rough guide, any child falling below the bottom line on the graph (the third percentile) may be admitted to hospital for investigation. Most children admitted to hospital for medical reasons tend to continue to lose weight. If in hospital, with no specific treatment, the child gains weight at more than 50g a day, the failure to thrive is likely to be the result of neglect, in particular that the child has been given insufficient food.

The effects of neglect

Severe neglect is linked to major impairment of physical growth and intellectual development. If it persists it can lead to ill health and delayed development. Children may find social relationships difficult and their educational progress can be limited. In extremes it can result in death. Children who are neglected are more likely to be victims of other forms of abuse, such as emotional, sexual or physical abuse.

Emotional abuse

What is emotional abuse?

Failing (omitting) to meet the needs of children emotionally will damage children's development. In addition, some adults commit acts of emotional abuse, such as harming children by using constant threats, verbal attacks, taunting or shouting. This category is usually used in diagnosis where it is the only or main form of abuse.

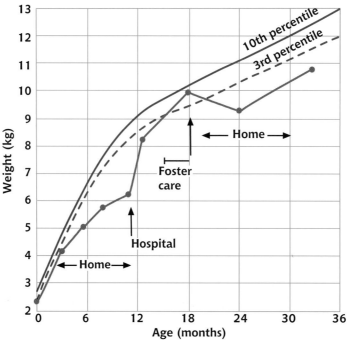

▲ Graph showing a child's weight changes during stays in hospital, foster care and home

---

Percentile charts/centile charts = specially prepared charts that are used to record measurements of a child's growth. There are centile charts for weight, height and head circumference

Practical example

Indicators of emotional abuse and neglect

The Wilson family live in a well-maintained detached house in an expensive suburb. They have two children: James aged 6 and Sarah who is 4. Sarah is small for her age, with a thin, pale face. She looks sad and is wary of adults.

The nursery staff are concerned about Sarah, who seems to be failing to thrive and lacks confidence. Since starting nursery some 3 months earlier, she has been reluctant to join in structured activities and tells nursery staff that she is no good at anything.

When nursery staff invite the family in for an informal chat, Mrs Wilson constantly compares Sarah unfavourably with her brother, who looks on smugly and agrees with everything his mother says. Mr Wilson doesn't speak directly to Sarah at all, treating her as if she does not exist. In conversation with the staff he refers to her as 'just like her mother'.

The story unfolds that Sarah was premature, difficult to feed, did not put on weight, was slow to learn and was happy to be left alone to lie in her cot. Mrs Wilson often left her there as James was a rewarding child and demanded a lot of attention. Mr Wilson was away a great deal when Sarah was a baby.

Mrs Wilson made no effort to protect Sarah from the negative comments she was making, and said repeatedly to her that she was useless and hopeless, compared with her brother. James referred to Sarah as 'the dummy'. Mr Wilson said he couldn't understand what all the fuss was about, as she was only a girl.

1. Write down the indicators of neglect in this case.

2. Describe how Sarah was being emotionally abused.

3. Describe the possible short-term and long-term effects on each aspect of Sarah's development.

4. How could staff in the nursery help to alleviate the effects of neglect or abuse?

5. How might the family be encouraged to adopt a different attitude towards Sarah?

6. Describe the roles of other professionals who may become involved with this family.

Emotional abuse includes the adverse effect on children's behaviour and emotional development as a result of a parent or carer's behaviour, including their neglect and/or rejection of the child. Domestic violence, adult mental health problems and parental substance misuse may be features in families where children are exposed to such abuse.

The effects of emotional abuse

There is increasing evidence of the adverse long-term consequences for children's development where they have been subject to sustained emotional abuse (*Working Together to Safeguard Children*, Department of Health, 1999). Emotional abuse affects children's developing mental health, behaviour and self-esteem, and can be especially damaging to very young children. As an underlying factor its effects on a child may be as important as the other, more visible signs of abuse. Children may fail to thrive as a result of emotional neglect or abuse, as well as physical neglect.

Sexual abuse
What is sexual abuse?

Sexual abuse is 'the involvement of dependent, developmentally immature children and adolescents in sexual activities that they do not fully comprehend and are unable to give informed consent to, or that violate the social taboos of family roles' (Kempe, 1978). An example of a social taboo of family roles is incest.

Victims of sexual abuse include children who have been the subject of unlawful sexual activity or whose parents or carers have failed to protect them from unlawful sexual activity, and children abused by other children. Sexual abuse covers a range of abusive behaviour not necessarily involving direct physical contact. It often starts at the lower end of the spectrum, for example exposure and self-masturbation by the abuser, and continues through actual body contact, such as fondling, to some form of penetration.

Who are the victims of sexual abuse?

Child sexual abuse is a universal phenomenon. It is found in all cultures and socio-economic groups. It happens to children in all kinds of families and communities. It is untrue that it is only found in isolated rural communities.

Both boys and girls experience sexual abuse. As far as we know, many more girls are abused than boys. There have been reported incidents of children as young as 4 months old being sexually abused.

Both men and women sexually abuse children. It has become clear that the majority of children who are sexually abused know the identity of the abuser, who is either a member of the child's family, a family friend or a person the child knows in a position of trust, for example a teacher or a carer.

How widespread is sexual abuse?

The prevalence of sexual abuse is largely unknown as it is under-reported and we are dependent on estimates. In a study of college students, 19 per cent of women and 9 per cent of men reported having been sexually abused as a child. Out of 3,000 respondents to a recent survey by a teenage magazine, 36 per cent said they had been subjected to a sexually abusive experience as a child.

Indicators of sexual abuse

Early recognition of the indicators of sexual abuse may prevent progression, by the abuser, from less to more abusive acts. If sexual abuse is not recognised in the early stages, it may persist undiscovered for many years.

Physical indicators

The following are physical indicators of sexual abuse:

- bruises or scratches to the **genitals** and the anal areas, chest or abdomen
- bites
- blood stains on underwear
- sexually transmitted diseases
- semen on skin, clothes or in the vagina or anus
- internal small cuts (lesions) in the vagina or anus
- abnormal swelling out (dilation) of the vagina or anus
- itchiness or discomfort in the genital or anal areas.

In addition, there are signs that are specific to either boys or girls:

In boys:	In girls:
– pain on urination	– vaginal discharge
– penile swelling	– urethral inflammation, urinary tract infections
– penile discharge.	– lymph gland inflammation
	– pregnancy.

Behavioural indicators

There may be no obvious physical indicators of sexual abuse, so particular attention should be paid to behavioural indicators. The following should be recorded accurately and discussed with the **designated person** in your establishment or a senior member of staff:

- what the child says or reveals through play with dolls with sexual characteristics, genitals, etc.
- over-sexualised behaviour that is inappropriate for the age of the child; being obsessed with sexual matters; playing out sexual acts in too knowledgeable a way, with dolls or other children; producing drawings of sex organs such as erect penises; excessive masturbation
- sudden inexplicable changes in behaviour, becoming aggressive or withdrawn
- showing behaviour appropriate to an earlier stage of development
- having eating or sleeping problems
- signs of social relationships being affected, for example becoming inappropriately clingy to carers; showing extreme fear of, or refusing to see, certain adults for no apparent reason; ceasing to enjoy activities with other children
- saying repeatedly that they are bad, dirty or wicked (having a poor self-image)
- acting in a way that they think will please and prevent the adult from hurting them (placatory), or in an inappropriately adult way (pseudo-mature behaviour).

The effects of sexual abuse

Sexual abuse can lead to disturbed behaviour, inappropriate sexualised behaviour, sadness, depression and loss of self-esteem. The longer and more extensive the experience of abuse is, and the older the child, the more severe the

Genitals = sexual organs
Designated person = the person identified in an establishment to whom allegations or suspicions of child abuse should be reported

impact is likely to be. Its effects can last into adult life. The child's ability to cope with the experience can be strengthened by the support of a non-abusive adult carer who believes the child, helps the child to understand, and offers help and protection. However, only a minority of children who are sexually abused go on to become abusers themselves.

Bullying

Bullying is another form of abuse.

Bullying can take a number of forms and can have serious effects on the wellbeing of the victim. We live in modern times, so the suggestion that victims are free from bullies when they are away from them, i.e at home, is no longer the case. Bullying can occur face to face and this can include name calling and intimidation, excluding the individual and physical acts. However, bullying can also occur using the range of technology available to children and young people. Bullies:

- use text messaging
- make nuisance calls on mobile phones
- use e-mails and personal websites to intimidate and humiliate others.

It is therefore essential that children and people are encouraged to speak to others about what is happening to them. Schools and organisations often provide mediation and support systems such as buddy benches, counselling and worry boxes. There are also some websites listed at the end of this unit.

Vulnerable children and abuse

All that has already been written about abuse applies also to children with disabilities and those with special needs and learning difficulties. These children are particularly vulnerable to all forms of abuse and have special need for protection.

Why are children with disabilities more vulnerable?

Some offenders abuse children because they are particularly attracted to their dependency. This, combined with society's negative attitude to disabled people, may increase the risk of disabled children, and those with learning difficulties, being abused. In addition, children with disabilities:

- receive less information on abuse and may be less likely to understand the inappropriateness of abuse
- are often more dependent on physical care for longer and from different people – this increases their vulnerability
- may receive less affection from family and friends and so be more accepting of sexual attention
- may be less likely to tell what has happened (disclose) because of communication difficulties, fewer social contacts, isolation and the fact that they are generally less likely to be believed
- may have an increased desire to please because of negative responses generally, including rejection and isolation
- may lack assertiveness, vocabulary or skills to complain appropriately
- may find it difficult to distinguish between good and bad touches
- are likely to have low self-esteem and feel less in control
- are likely to have less choice generally, and therefore less opportunity to learn whether to choose to accept or reject sexual advances.

Practical example

Indicators of sexual abuse?

Claire: During play in the nursery, Claire, aged 3 years 6 months, is observed to be preoccupied with bedtimes and bathtimes. She places dolls, a teddy and herself into these situations again and again over a period of two weeks. She also acts out being smacked in the bath.

Rangit: When a group is asked to draw themselves for a display, Rangit draws himself with a huge penis and testicles, stating 'Boys have willies; girls have holes instead'.

Helen: Helen indicates that she is sore in the vaginal area. She has spent the previous weekend with her grandfather. Her grandfather was convicted of sexual abuse of the child's mother years ago.

Raymond: Raymond has been displaying over-sexualised play with other children. One 3-year-old boy states he is frightened of Raymond because he keeps asking him to hide and play 'sucking willies'.

Kearan and Liam: Kearan and Liam were playing together in water; both were lying naked on their stomachs. A staff member heard a lot of giggling and saw the boys doing press-ups in the water. When asked what they were doing, one boy said, 'We're growing our tails.' Both boys had erections.

(**1**) *For each of the cases above, decide whether the behaviour may be an indicator of sexual abuse or not.*

(**2**) *Explain what influenced your decisions in each case.*

Abuse by a childcare worker

Experience has shown that children can be abused in any and every setting by those who work with them. There should be clear written procedures in place in all settings to deal with such allegations, and these should be supported by the training and supervision of staff. All allegations of abuse should be taken seriously and the local child protection procedures should be used to investigate them. It is essential that all allegations are examined objectively by staff who are independent of the institution. (*Working Together to Safeguard Children*, Department of Health, 1999.)

The Protection of Children Act 1999 requires childcare organisations proposing to employ someone in a childcare position to ensure that individuals are checked against a new Protection of Children Act List and List 99 (DfCSF) to ensure that they are not 'persons considered to be unsuitable to work with children'. It also enables the Criminal Records Bureau to disclose information about people who are included on the list along with their criminal records.

Institutional and organised abuse

Institutional, organised or multiple abuse, including that which takes place across a family or community, involves one or more abusers and a number of related or non-related children or young people. The abusers may be acting together or in isolation, or may be using an institutional framework or position of authority to recruit children for abuse. There have been cases in recent years of this occurring in nurseries, residential homes and schools. It

 Practical example

A disabled child and abuse

Wayne Steadman, 7, has learning difficulties. He is looked after regularly by Philip, a long-standing friend of Mr and Mrs Steadman. They believe it is good for Wayne to meet older people and are glad of a break when Philip has Wayne to stay at his flat or minds him at home while the Steadmans go out.

Philip has been sexually abusing Wayne for a year. It started with Philip asking Wayne to show him his penis but has now progressed to mutual masturbation and oral sex. Philip gives Wayne sweets and tells him not to tell his parents or else he won't let Wayne stay up to watch TV with him.

Wayne tells a friend at school that he gets sweets from Philip and is allowed to stay up late watching TV if he lets Philip play with his 'willy'. Wayne's friend doesn't understand and asks Wayne to show him what Philip does. The boys are discovered in the library corner at school and asked to explain what they are doing. Wayne explains but asks the staff not to tell his mother because she will be cross with him for staying up late.

1. Describe how Wayne was being abused.

2. What indicators of sexual abuse may have been evident in this case?

3. Describe the possible short-term and long-term effects on Wayne of this abuse.

4. How could staff in school help to alleviate the effects of abuse?

5. Why was Wayne particularly vulnerable to abuse?

6. Suggest how Wayne could have been helped to protect himself and how the abuse could have been prevented.

includes the growing use of the internet by paedophile rings. Its investigation by police and social work staff is often very complex and difficult.

The effects of institutional abuse

This abuse is profoundly traumatic for children and its effects are very disturbing. This is not least because when children are abused in institutional settings it is usually by the people they rightly expect to be there to care for and protect them. Children in foster homes and residential institutions may have been placed there to protect them from the abuse they have previously experienced at home. To be abused in these settings is a double trauma for such children, leaving them with the belief that they can trust no one and thinking that they have no one to turn to.

The responsibilities of child protection agencies

▲ The logo of the NSPCC

Making enquiries

The only agencies with the legal (statutory) power to make enquiries and intervene if abuse is suspected are the social services department, the police, the National Society for the Prevention of Cruelty to

Children (NSPCC) and the Royal Scottish Society for the Prevention of Cruelty to Children (RSSPCC). The basis for an effective child protection service must be that all professionals and agencies:

- work cooperatively on a multi-disciplinary basis
- understand and share aims and objectives, and agree about how individual cases should be handled
- are sensitive to issues associated with gender, race, culture and disability.

Promoting equality of opportunity

This section also links to assessment criteria **6.1**.

The Children Act 1989 makes it very clear that although discrimination of all kinds is a reality, every effort must be made to ensure that agencies do not use discriminatory practices or reinforce them. All people have a right to good, non-discriminatory services and equality of opportunity, and in some cases workers may need to take advice about how to achieve this. Childcare workers must take account of gender, race, culture, linguistic background and special needs throughout their working practices. In the opening stages especially, workers involved in child protection must keep an open mind about whether abuse has or has not taken place and avoid making any stereotypical assumptions about people.

Here are some ways to increase equality of opportunity:

- Anyone who interviews a child or parent needs to use appropriate language and listening skills.
- It may help when black families are being investigated to involve a black worker,

or at least someone with appropriate cultural knowledge and experience.

- It may be necessary to make arrangements for children and parents to be interviewed in their home language.

- If a parent or child has communication difficulties, for example a hearing impairment, assistance must be given during interviews.

- Remember that children and parents with disabilities have the same rights as any other person.

- The gender of those being interviewed needs be taken into account: it may be better to involve a worker of the same gender. This is especially true in cases where the victim of suspected sexual abuse is female and the alleged perpetrator is male.

The social services department

Prevention

Social services departments have a wide range of statutory duties and responsibilities to provide services for individuals and families. The child protection work of social services departments is only a part of its childcare services. Social workers are also involved in prevention of abuse, by providing services such as referral for day care, and giving advice, guidance and support to families with children and other client groups. They have a broad awareness of the facilities that are available to help and support all families and prevent neglect and abuse.

Making enquiries following a referral

Local authorities, through their social services departments, have a statutory duty under the Children Act 1989 to investigate any referral of a situation where there is reasonable cause to suspect that a child is suffering or is likely to suffer significant harm. They take the leading role both in enquiries, in child protection conferences, and keeping the child protection register (all described in more detail below). To fulfill this role, some social services departments have appointed social work specialists to advise and support other social workers in child protection work.

Social services departments also have a system for people to refer their concerns about individual children to them. They provide a telephone number for the public and children to contact them.

Working in partnership with parents

Local authorities must now involve parents throughout the child protection process, providing this is consistent with the welfare and protection of the child. They must:

- give parents full information about what is happening

- enable parents to share concerns openly about their children's welfare

- show respect and consideration for parents' views

- involve parents in planning, decision-making and review.

The NSPCC (RSSPCC in Scotland)

The National Society for the Prevention of Cruelty to Children is the only voluntary organisation with statutory powers to investigate and to apply for court orders to protect children. To do this, it has teams of qualified social workers, called child protection officers. The society works in close liaison with the social services departments in the areas in which it is active.

The NSPCC is involved in the prevention of abuse, working with vulnerable children and their families, and in research and publication.

The police

Police officers have a duty to investigate cases of suspected child abuse that are referred to them. Their focus is to determine and decide whether:

- a criminal offence has taken place
- to follow criminal proceedings if there is sufficient evidence
- to prosecute if that is in the best interests of the child and the public
- to consider the best way to protect a child victim.

The police share their information with other agencies at child protection conferences. Cooperation and understanding at this level are essential.

The police also have a unique emergency power to enter and search premises and to detain a child in a place of protection for 72 hours, without application to a court.

The role of other workers in child protection

Guardian ad litem

The Children Act 1989 recognises that children can find it difficult both to speak for themselves in court and to understand the decision-making process. A **guardian ad litem** will help with both of these.

Guardians are people appointed by the courts to safeguard and promote the interests and welfare of children during court proceedings. The guardian is an independent person, usually with training in social work. They have a number of powers, including being able to instruct a solicitor to legally represent a child in court if necessary. They also provide a valuable second opinion in court about what outcome is likely to be in the best interests of a child.

The probation service

Probation officers have responsibility for the supervision of offenders. Through this, they may become involved in cases of child abuse; for example if an offender is released from prison. They will inform social services if they are concerned about the safety of a child who is in the same household as an offender.

The health service

All health service workers are committed to the protection of children. They play an important role in supporting the social services department and provide ongoing support for children and their families. General practitioners and community health workers play an effective part in the protection of children. They identify stresses in a family and signs that a child is being harmed; they may make an initial referral and attend a child protection conference. Health visitors and school nurses record and monitor children's growth and development. They are in a good position to identify children who are being neglected and harmed or who may be at risk.

Treatment and examination

Where a child's health is the immediate issue, in an emergency the first duty of a doctor is to give treatment to the child as a patient. However, in situations where abuse is alleged or suspected, but there

---

Guardian ad litem = person appointed by the courts to safeguard and promote the interests and welfare of children during court proceedings

is no immediate medical emergency, a doctor's role is to examine a child who has been referred and record evidence that may be used in any legal proceedings. This is a skilled task and best undertaken by a designated doctor with specialist knowledge of child abuse. Parents may try to prevent such an examination; if they do, steps can be taken to protect the child, for example by calling on the police to use their powers.

The education service

Schools may also be involved in prevention of abuse through a personal and social education programme. They can help children to increase their personal safety by developing assertiveness skills, raising their self-esteem and giving them an understanding of unacceptable adult behaviour.

Observation and referral

Teachers and other staff in schools have daily contact with children. They are therefore in a good position to observe both physical and behavioural signs of abuse. The education service is not an investigative agency; it must refer any suspicions to the social services department. All school staff need to know the **referral** procedures within their setting. Each school should have a trained senior member of staff who is given specific responsibility for referral and liaison with social services. This person is called the designated teacher.

Schools should be notified of any child whose name is on the child protection register (see page 129). This alerts them to observe the child's attendance, development and behaviour.

Educational welfare officers and educational psychologists also have important roles to play. They help and support the child in the school and home environment. They may contribute at child protection conferences.

There is a wide range of national and local voluntary organisations which provide services to support children and their families. National voluntary organisations such as Barnado's, the Children's Society and NCH Action for Children all provide and run family support centres. Parentline and ChildLine provide telephone counselling and support services for parents and children.

There are many voluntary organisations that are locally based. Some of these specifically support families and children from ethnic minority groups.

Referrals of suspected abuse

Referrals

Referral is the process by which suspected abuse is reported by one person to someone who can take action if necessary.

Referrals of suspected abuse come from two main sources:

- members of the public, including family members – just over 51 per cent of all enquiries begin by someone, usually the child or member of the family, disclosing their concerns to a professional
- the identification by professionals who work with children in a range of settings – about 39 per cent of enquiries begin in this way.

Referral = the process by which suspected abuse is reported by one person to someone who can take action if necessary

The remaining 10 per cent of enquiries are suggested during unrelated events, such as home visits or arrests.

Referrals by members of the public

Members of the public are entitled to have their referrals investigated. If any person either knows or suspects that a child is being abused or is at risk of harm, that person should inform one of the agencies with a statutory duty to intervene (that is the police, social services department or the NSPCC/RSSPCC).

Referrals by professionals

Professionals including childcare and education workers have a duty to refer any case of suspected abuse. In order to be able to respond to signs of abuse and make referrals, professionals need:

- appropriate training to recognise the signs of abuse and neglect
- to know the procedures for the setting in which they work, including their own role, how to respond and their responsibility for referral, also whether it is appropriate either to report this to a designated person or to refer it themselves
- to be aware of the local procedures that will follow a referral of suspected abuse
- to be able to recognise and evaluate the difference between different sources of evidence, and the relative value of these, including directly observed evidence (i.e. evidence they see or hear themselves), evidence from reliable sources (i.e. the evidence of other professional colleagues), opinion (i.e. what people think, which must be used very cautiously), hearsay (i.e. evidence that is second hand or more and may have been changed when passed between people).

The role of the childcare and education worker in recording the indicators of abuse

If a childcare worker notices any indicators of abuse, their responsibility will include describing and recording these indicators. The record may be used for referral to, and liaison with, appropriate professionals. Records should be accurate and dated and should clearly distinguish between direct observation and hearsay. The position of the injury, including any pattern, should be recorded as well as the nature of the injury. Physical indicators may be recorded on to a diagram of a child's body to make the position clear and accurate and to avoid misunderstanding.

All staff in an establishment must use similar methods of recording and have to share the responsibility of this task. Workers are in a good position to notice possible indicators of abuse; they must know who to report to in the establishment, i.e. the designated member of staff. They, or a senior colleague, should always be informed immediately in an appropriate way.

Workers must be clear about the rules in their establishment concerning information sharing and confidentiality, and the circumstances under which these may be breached. If they are unsure about something they see or hear, they should discuss it with the designated person or a senior member of staff and not keep it to themselves.

Practical example

Working in a children's centre

Jaswinder is a childcare worker in a busy family and nursery centre. Leanne, a 3-year-old child in her group, is giving cause for concern, partly because of her irregular attendance.

Leanne's young mother, Carly, has been attending the centre and until recently staff had been pleased with the gradual maturing of her parenting skills. However, recently she started bringing Leanne late or not at all. She has also begun to make excuses about why she cannot stay on the mornings there are parenting classes. Jaswinder observes and records that Leanne now seems very hungry at mealtimes; she eats quickly and wants more; she falls asleep sometimes while playing and is wearing small summer dresses into the late autumn. The manager of the centre has already contacted the child's health visitor who is concerned about Leanne's recent weight loss.

One morning Carly arrives late with Leanne and obviously has a bruised eye herself. Leanne clings to her and cries, but Carly leaves her, quickly saying she bumped into a cupboard. Another mother, Marie, is in the room at the time. She tells Jaswinder that Carly has a new boyfriend and that the whole street knows about him because he plays loud music late into the night and is abusive to anyone who complains. She says that apparently he was in prison until earlier this year and neighbours say it was for assault. She says she thinks he is knocking Carly around and taking her money.

Jaswinder makes a full record of all she has seen and heard and signs and dates it. She reports all her evidence and concerns to the manager.

(**1**) *What are the main causes for concern in this case?*

(**2**) *Why is it important that the childcare worker signs and dates her report?*

(**3**) *Give an illustrated example from this case study of observed evidence, evidence from a reliable source, opinion and hearsay evidence.*

Dealing with disclosure

What is disclosure?

In any day care setting, it is possible that children will tell a worker that they are being abused. In other words, they will disclose. This could either happen in a full and open way, or through hinted words or behaviour. **Disclosure** may be partial, indirect or hidden. It may happen at inappropriate or pressured times and in awkward situations. Adults need to be prepared to respond sensitively and appropriately, both immediately, at initial disclosure, and later on. This section deals with the initial response.

Disclosure (of abuse) = when a child tells someone they have been abused

The role of the childcare worker in responding to disclosure

It is not possible to say exactly what a child-care worker should say when children tell them they have been, or are being, abused. Workers will need to draw on their communication skills and adapt their approach according to the age and stage of development of the child. The points below are only guidelines:

- Listen and be prepared to spend time and not hurry the child. Use active listening skills. Do not interrogate them and avoid using questions beginning Why? How? When? Where? or Who?
- Do not ask leading questions, putting words into children's mouths, for example, 'This person abused you, then?'
- Reassure them truthfully. Tell them they are not odd or unique; you believe them; you are glad they told you; it is not their fault; they were brave to tell; you are sorry it happened.
- Find out what they are afraid of, so you know how best to help. They may have been threatened about telling.
- Be prepared to record what the child tells you, as soon as possible (within 24 hours), comprehensively, accurately and legibly, with the date of the disclosure.
- Let the child know why you are going to tell someone else.
- Consult your senior (designated person), your agency's guidelines or an appropriate professional you think will be able to help. If you are working in isolation, for example as a nanny, this may be a social worker, a health visitor, a police officer, or an NSPCC child protection officer. If you are a childminder, you might first speak to an under 8's officer.
- Seek out support for your personal emotional reactions and needs from an appropriate colleague or professional.

Do not attempt to deal with the issue by yourself. Disclosure is a beginning but by itself will not prevent further abuse.

The possible path of child protection procedures
Medical emergencies

Any member of staff who discovers that a child has an injury, whatever its cause, should first decide whether the injury requires immediate medical treatment or not. If it does, the child must be taken to the accident and emergency department of the local hospital. It is better to have parental permission and involvement, although it may be appropriate in child protection cases to consult social services about gaining this.

Procedures for the investigation of suspected abuse

The procedures for the investigation of suspected abuse involve a series of steps, as outlined below.

The first enquiry – consultation

Following a referral and according to whom the referral was made, the social services department, the NSPCC and the police will consult one another. Records are checked, other agencies and professionals involved with the family are contacted, and the register will be checked. Those involved at this stage will decide whether there are grounds for further investigation and agree their respective roles in any subsequent enquiry. This first enquiry may be undertaken without the knowledge of the parents.

Enquiry

The Framework for the Assessment of Children in Need and their Parents (2000)

The framework for assessment is for all professionals working in child protection issues. Usually social services will carry out assessments and the framework clearly lays out the roles and responsibilities for all agencies to make sure there is a common approach. The framework is based on a triangular approach:

- Child's development needs – i.e. how are they developing, how is their health and education?
- Family and environmental needs – i.e. what is the family income, what is the history of the family and how it functions?
- Parenting capacity – how does the parent offer basic care, safety, warmth, stability?

Following a referral and consultation, if there are reasonable grounds to suspect that a child is suffering or is likely to suffer significant harm, a local authority has a duty to carry out an enquiry.

The aims of the enquiry are to:

- establish the facts
- decide if there are grounds for concern

- find out the source of the risk and assess how great it is
- decide what action, if any, to take to protect the child.

The enquiry must establish in particular whether there is an emergency and whether the police or the authority needs to exercise any of its powers under the Children Act to protect the child from any person or situation.

In order to establish the facts, social workers will make a home visit.

Social workers will interview the child, the parent(s), carers, anyone who has a personal interest in the child and any appropriate agencies and professionals. This may include a medical examination by a designated doctor. This is when the enquiry becomes public and the effect of this on a family can be devastating. Parents can be shocked, scared, and confused. Real care needs to be taken to work in partnership with them. Accurate recordings of any interviews are made. As with any records, the difference between fact, hearsay and opinion must be very clear. New provisions under the Criminal Justice Act 1991 allow a video recording of an interview with a child to be used as that child's main evidence in criminal proceedings.

If cause for concern is established during an enquiry, an initial child protection conference will be held. This should take place within eight days of the initial referral, but in practice may not happen for a month.

Police protection

If it is considered that there is an emergency, the police can take a child into police protection. They can remove a child to suitable accommodation (for example, foster care or a community home), or ensure that the child remains in a safe place (for example, a hospital).

Police protection cannot last for longer than 72 hours. During this time, an officer who has special training (a designated officer) will enquire into the case. The officer must inform the child, those with parental responsibility, and the local authority of the steps taken. An appropriate court order (for example, an Emergency Protection Order, see below) must be obtained if the child continues to need protection.

Emergency Protection Order

If it is decided that a child needs further protection during an enquiry, the police or the local authority can apply for an Emergency Protection Order. To make this order, a court must be satisfied that:

- the order is in the child's best interests
- the child is likely to suffer significant harm if not removed from their present accommodation.

This order enables a child to be removed to safe accommodation or kept in a safe place. The court can also say who is allowed to have contact with the child while the order is in force.

An Emergency Protection Order lasts for a maximum of eight days. An authority can ask a court to extend the order for a further seven days if it needs more time to investigate. If the parents of a child were not in court when the order was made, they can, after 72 hours, put their own point of view to the court and apply

for the Emergency Protection Order to be removed. The court may appoint a guardian ad litem to protect a child's interests during this period. In 1992 (the last year for which official figures are available), approximately 1,500 emergency separations were made.

Child Assessment Order

If during the investigation a child is not considered to be in immediate danger, but the authority wishes to make an assessment of the child's health, development, or the way the child has been treated, the authority can apply to the court for a Child Assessment Order, providing that:

- the parents or carers of a child are uncooperative during the investigation
- there is sufficient concern about the child
- the authority believes that the child may suffer significant harm if an assessment is not made.

The authority has to convince the court that it has made reasonable efforts to persuade parents or carers to cooperate with an assessment.

A Child Assessment Order has to say on which date the assessment will begin. It will then last for a maximum of seven days. The court may appoint a guardian ad litem to protect the child's interests during the period of the order. Children can refuse to undergo any assessment or examination (providing they have sufficient understanding to make an informed decision about this).

The initial child protection conference

Following an enquiry, if there is enough cause for concern, an initial child protection conference is called. The

127

Practical example

The home visit

Aneka attends her local infants' school. Her teacher is concerned about a recent decline in her general appearance. Her clothes and her body are frequently unwashed. At milk time she seems very hungry and asks for biscuits. Her mother's neighbour has recently been bringing her to school and implies that all is not well in the family.

The class teacher discusses Aneka with the designated teacher who decides to refer their concerns to social services. Social workers make an initial enquiry and establish that staff are also concerned at the school attended by Aneka's older sisters. They decide to proceed with the enquiry and to visit the family. A social worker makes a home visit and tells Aneka's mother of the referral. She learns that Aneka is one of three young sisters who live with their mother; the father has recently left the family home. Aneka's mother is a shy woman, slow to tell anyone about her difficulties, but since the loss of her partner she has found it hard to cope, and this has led to some neglect of the children's physical needs. A decision is made not to refer the family to a case conference, but the social worker is able to suggest some services that will offer them help and support.

(1) *Why were staff at the school concerned about Aneka?*

(2) *What were the causes of the problems?*

(3) *Why do you think that social services decided not to refer the case to a conference?*

Guidance to the Children Act 1989 says that this should be held within 8 working days, and must be held within 15 days. However, research shows that the average interval between referral and conference is 34 days.

The initial child protection conference brings together the family, professionals concerned with child protection (social services, health, the police, schools, probation), and other specialists who can give advice (psychiatrists, psychologists, lawyers). It enables them to:

- exchange information in a context within which sensitive information can be shared
- make decisions about the level of risk
- decide whether the child needs to be registered and how best to protect the child
- agree a child protection plan for the future and ensure that vulnerable children are subject to regular monitoring and review.

One of the ways that childcare workers may contribute to the protection of children is by providing information to other professionals at a child protection conference. This may take the form of a general report about a child's development, or a more specific report of something you have observed or witnessed.

Working with parents

The principle of working in partnership with parents must form the basis of the child protection conference. Parents and carers will, as a matter of principle, be included in conferences. There may, however, be occasions when parental involvement may not promote the welfare of the child and they will be excluded from all or part of the proceedings. Research shows that in practice nearly a third of parents do not attend or are not invited to attend a conference. Children are encouraged to attend conferences if they have sufficient understanding. They can take a friend to support them.

The conference must assess risk and decide whether a child is suffering or likely to suffer significant harm. The conference may decide to register the child. It will appoint and name a key worker and also recommend a core group of professionals to be involved in a child protection plan. The key worker will be from the social services department or the NSPCC. However, it may agree that other workers from the core group will have more day-to-day contact with the child and family.

FAST FACT

Of the 40,000 cases that went to a conference in 1992, 25,000 were placed on the child protection register. In 96 out of 100 cases the children remained at home with relatives.

The child protection register

The child protection register lists all the children in an area who are considered to be at risk. A child's name is only registered following agreement at a child protection conference. The register must be kept in each social services area office.

The four main categories of registration are:

- neglect
- physical injury
- sexual abuse
- emotional abuse.

But other labels are also used, including:

- failure to thrive
- a child living in the household of a previous abuser.

Following a decision to register, a child's name will be put on a central child protection register. Professionals see the register as an essential tool that gives a case conference a focus and encourages cooperation between agencies. The registration of a child means:

- the protection plan for the child will be formally reviewed at least every 5 months
- that if a concerned professional believes a child is not being adequately protected, or that the plan needs to be changed, they can ask the social services department (or the NSPCC) to call a child protection review
- any professional who is worried about a child can quickly refer to the register to see if the child is registered and therefore considered to be at risk, and if there is a protection plan in force.

Initial child protection plan

The initial child protection plan that is made by the core group of professionals after the conference will:

129

Practical example

Reporting to a case conference

Jackie is 3 years old and attends a local children's centre. Her grandmother has made a referral to social services claiming that Jackie's mother's partner shouts at her a lot and that he makes her spend long periods locked in her room. An enquiry has resulted in a decision to call an initial child protection case conference. Marcia, her key worker at the centre, has been asked to present a written factual report about Jackie to the conference. The manager of the centre will be giving an overview report of the child, including facts about the family. Marcia is told that her factual report should be based primarily on her recorded observations of the child's development, and that it should also include:

- how long the child has been with her
- how often the child is with her during the week
- a description of the child when she arrives and leaves the nursery, including her physical and emotional state
- how the child responds when leaving and greeting her mother
- the stage of the child's physical, intellectual, language, emotional and social development
- the nature of Marcia's contact with the child's parents or carers
- whether she works alongside the parents in the nursery
- any special cultural, gender, physical or educational needs of the child.

(1) *Why has Marcia been asked to write this report?*

(2) *What will she base her report on the child's development on?*

(3) *Why should she be able to describe accurately how the child responds to her mother, and what will she base this on?*

(4) *What should she avoid including in her report?*

- include a comprehensive assessment of the child and the family situation
- form the basis for future plans of work with the child and family.

Care Order

If a conference concludes that a child is at risk, the social services department may apply to a court for a Care Order. If made, this places the child in the care of the local authority. It also gives the authority parental responsibility, in addition to that of the parents. A Care Order gives the local authority the power both to care for the child and to determine the extent that parents can be involved with their child.

Practical example

The child protection register

As an early years worker in a day nursery, you have observed a child being reluctant to go home with her mother. She clings to you at home time, and you hear her mother speaking aggressively to her when leaving the nursery. A few weeks later you notice the child sitting astride a broom handle and rubbing herself and also touching herself inside her pants. You record these incidents and discuss them with colleagues. The next day you notice some fingertip bruising on the child's upper arms. You know that they were not there the day before. You report the matter to your officer-in-charge. She tells you that she will follow the child protection procedures and refer the matter to the social services department. She instructs you to write a factual report about everything you have heard and seen, and to draw on a diagram where the bruises are. Following an enquiry, the child is referred to a case conference. Investigations and discussions reveal that the mother has had a succession of male partners and has poor parenting skills. The child is placed on the child protection register and an initial child protection plan is agreed.

(**1**) What were the signs that made the staff of the nursery concerned?

(**2**) Why do you think the officer-in-charge decided to refer the matter to the social services department?

(**3**) Why was the child placed on the child protection register?

A child may either be placed in the care of foster parents or in a children's home.

Interim Care Order

If assessments are not complete enough to decide on making a full Care Order, the court may make an Interim Care Order. This cannot last initially for more than eight weeks; a subsequent order can only last for four weeks to avoid extending the decision-making process.

Supervision Order

If it is considered that a Care Order is not necessary, the court may make a Supervision Order. This gives the local authority the right to supervise, advise, befriend and direct the care of a child who remains at home. It is effective for a year.

A child protection review

To ensure that registered children continue to be protected from abuse, and that their needs are met, a review of the child protection plan by those involved must be held regularly, at least every six months.

De-registration

De-registration (the removal of a child's name from the child protection register) should be considered at every child protection review. Alternatively, a conference can be called by any agency to consider de-registration. The grounds for de-registration are:

- the original factors that led to registration no longer apply: the home situation may have improved or the abuser has no further contact with the child
- the child and family have moved to another area (when this happens the other area will have to accept the responsibility for the case)
- the child is no longer a child in the eyes of the law: this follows an 18th birthday or marriage before this age
- the child dies.

The procedures for reporting and investigating institutional abuse

Where allegations of abuse are made against a staff member or volunteer, the procedures listed below should be followed.

1 The matter should be referred to the social services department. Social services should always discuss the case with the police at the first possible opportunity if a criminal offence may have been committed against a child.

   Any investigation may have three strands:

   - child protection enquiries related to the safety and welfare of the child
   - a police investigation into a possible offence
   - disciplinary procedures in the setting.

2 The risk of harm to children should be evaluated and managed.

3 The person involved should be supported and treated fairly and honestly and kept informed.

4 Affected parents should be given information about the concerns and informed of the outcomes.

5 The investigation must be open to looking at patterns that suggest it might be more widespread than at first reported.

6 If an allegation is substantiated, the lessons learned should be used to guide future practice.

Investigations of organised, institutional or multiple abuse

Each investigation of institutional abuse will be different, but all will require good planning, inter-agency working and attention to the welfare and needs of the child.

In addition to the guidance above it is important that local procedures reflect the need to bring together a trusted and vetted team of police and social workers to conduct major investigations, and that any investigation involves senior mangers using appropriate resources. As with all cases, records must be safely and securely stored. Workers and the investigating team may need support and counselling.

Ways that childcare workers can protect themselves from allegations of abuse

There may be times when childcare workers are themselves accused of abuse. Sadly, although rare, there are occasions when these allegations are founded. All those who work directly with children need to consider how to avoid unfounded allegations. There may already be guidelines in the establishment in which you work. If so, you should ensure that you know what they are and follow them. If not, the following common-sense ideas, from *The Kidscape Training Guide* may be used to help you to draw up guidelines for your own workplace:

- In the event of any injury to a child, accidental or otherwise, ensure that it is recorded and witnessed by another adult.
- Keep records of any false allegations a child makes against you. Record dates and times.
- Get another adult to witness the allegation, if possible.
- If a child touches you in an inappropriate place, record what happened and ensure that another adult knows (do not make the child feel like a criminal).
- On school trips, always have at least two members of staff.
- Do not place yourself in a position where you are spending excessive amounts of time alone with one child, away from other people.
- In residential settings, never take a child into your bedroom.

- Do not take children in your car by yourself.
- If you are involved in a care situation, try to have someone with you when changing nappies, clothing or bathing a child.
- Never do something of a personal nature for children that they can do for themselves, for example wiping bottoms.
- Avoid going on your own to the toilet with children.
- Be mindful of how and where you touch a child. Consider using a lap cushion with young or disabled children who may need to sit on your knee.
- Be careful of extended hugs and kisses on the mouth from children. This may be particularly relevant to those working with children with learning difficulties.
- Always tell someone if you suspect a colleague of abuse.

✔ Progress check

1. What is physical abuse? What does it include?
2. Describe some possible effects of physical abuse.
3. What is neglect? What does it include?
4. Describe three types of child neglect.
5. What does emotional abuse include?
6. What are some of the possible effects of emotional abuse?
7. Explain the link between emotional abuse and all other forms of abuse.
8. According to Kempe's definition, what is sexual abuse?
9. What are the possible physical and behavioural indicators of sexual abuse?
10. Why is early recognition of the indicators of sexual abuse so important?
11. Why are disabled children more likely to be abused?
12. What is institutional abuse?

▶▶

✔ Progress check

(13) Why is abuse in institutions potentially so damaging?

(14) Which three agencies have the power to make child protection enquiries?

(15) What important role do childcare workers in schools have?

(16) What is a designated teacher responsible for?

(17) What do professionals have a duty to know and do in any case of suspected abuse?

(18) What should a member of staff who discovers that a child has an injury first decide?

(19) What are some of the important things to remember when communicating with children who tell you they have been abused?

(20) What takes place at the initial enquiry stage?

(21) What is a case conference?

(22) What is the child protection register?

(23) What are some of the main ways that workers can protect themselves from unfounded allegations of child abuse?

Learning Outcome (4)

how to empower children to develop self-confidence and self-esteem and self-reliance

This links to assessment criteria **4.1** and **4.2**

Children's needs and rights

Children have many emotional needs, for example:

- affection – the feeling of being loved by parents, carers, family, friends and the wider social community
- belonging – the feeling of being wanted by a group
- consistency – the feeling that things are predictable
- independence – the feeling of managing and directing your own life
- achievement – the feeling of satisfaction gained from success
- social-approval – the feeling that others approve of your conduct and efforts
- self-esteem – the feeling of liking and valuing oneself.

If these needs are not met, it may lead to unacceptable behaviour as children struggle to get what they need. There are likely to be times in all children's lives where they experience short-term stress because some of their emotional needs are not being met, for example, moving school, or a new baby in the family. If these situations are handled sensitively any difficulties are not likely to be long term.

However, when children's emotional needs are not met for a substantial period of time their behaviour can be severely affected.

Self-esteem

This is an important element in emotional and social development, relating to the individual's assessment of their own worth. Self-esteem can be encouraged in a number of ways:

- by providing tasks and activities that are pitched at an appropriate level for the child, challenging but offering an opportunity for success
- by, in your interactions with children, showing that you respect and value them for themselves, through praising their efforts and achievements and through sensitive interventions that allow children to succeed
- by encouraging children to be independent, **self-reliant** and to use initiative, for example being able to select and extend an activity and then be responsible for clearing it away
- by providing positive images for all children with regard to gender, ethnicity and disability, thus encouraging children to value their own cultural background and identity

---

Self-reliance = the ability to depend on oneself to manage

in the daily routine and the way that the setting is organised. A regular routine enables children to predict what is likely to happen and this consistency will foster feelings of security and confidence. An environment where resources are stored at child level and are accessible to children will allow children to be independent in their choices and use of equipment.

Interpersonal skills

Interpersonal skills enable us to get along with other people. Young children find it difficult to see the world from another's point of view and need to be given opportunities to develop social empathy, that is to be able to tune into other people's viewpoints and act accordingly. They need to develop skills in:

● forming and maintaining friendships

● sharing and taking turns

● responding appropriately to others

● being sensitive to other people's feelings

● expressing their own feelings appropriately

● understanding appropriate behaviour.

Childcare workers can help children to develop these skills through the range of experiences and activities they provide, but also through the ways that they interact with children and positively encourage their social behaviour.

Moral development

This is concerned with developing an understanding of right and wrong. Young children cannot be expected to consider their actions and attitudes and their impact on others in the same way that older children do; but by the pre-school years, children are beginning to become aware that their actions and attitudes affect other people and that the rules governing and shaping behaviour have to be kept. Initially, children will accept rules; for example, you cannot snatch the doll away from another child, because someone powerful and significant is enforcing the rule. However,

▲ Encourage children to take turns; adults must be good role models

GOOD PRACTICE

Examples of good practice include the following:

- being a good role model. Children model their behaviour on what they experience and should see their childcare workers demonstrating respect for and sensitivity to others
- planning activities that require children to cooperate and share, such as mural painting, large jigsaws and games and interacting with the children to support this
- encouraging children to share and take turns and monitoring that this happens, for example with popular items of equipment
- providing activities, such as role play and small-world play, that give children the opportunity to begin to experience the world from another perspective
- allowing children opportunities to express their feelings in appropriate ways. A child may wish to stretch and punch at clay to get rid of angry feelings, or curl up in a corner with a blanket if sad or overwhelmed. The death of a nursery pet will provoke sadness and an opportunity to grieve
- supporting children's developing social skills by praising those who cooperate and show consideration for others, providing a model for other children.

eventually the child will understand the reasons why the rule exists and begin to internalise them as moral values.

Even quite small children can begin to understand about rules if they:

- are few in number and are easily recalled
- express the values, ethos and expectations of the setting
- are understood by everyone in the establishment, including parents

- are consistently applied
- are modelled by staff members.

The right to be safe

Children need to understand that they have a basic human right to be safe and to be protected from danger. They can learn that adults have a responsibility to protect them and keep them safe. The NSPCC suggests various activities to emphasise the idea, including some that increase children's understanding of who keeps them safe, how to play safely and what to do if something worrying happens. Kidscape has compiled an advice list for children's personal safety that includes not answering the door if at home alone, not telling anyone they are alone if they answer the phone, always telling carers where they are going, going to a safe place if lost or frightened, running away if attacked, knowing their phone number, and never going anywhere with a stranger – even if they tell a believable story.

An awareness of their bodies and their rights over them

Children can develop an awareness of their own body through curriculum activities. They need to be able to name their body parts and understand their functions at a level that is appropriate to their development. Focus activities such as 'all about me' can help children to understand their own growth and development. Activities about 'me' can help them to explore ideas about different rates of development and the relationships between people's size and their power. An activity about 'me and my body' can be used to develop their understanding that their bodies are their own, that they have the right to say what touches are acceptable and unacceptable, that no one should touch them inappropriately or against their wishes. Children can think and talk about touches that feel good, safe and comfortable, and touches that feel bad, unsafe and are secretive. This also links to the idea of good and bad secrets for children.

Learning to recognise, trust and accept their own feelings

Children can explore feelings and thoughts about a variety of experiences; this may include feelings about anything, including things they don't like. They can learn to talk about 'yes' and 'no' feelings. This will help them to recognise and learn to trust their own feelings.

 Practical example

Establishing the rules

As part of a topic on 'Ourselves', the role-play area was presented as a doctor's surgery. The children had helped to collect the resources for the area and were looking forward to playing in it. On the first morning that it was available, many children wanted to play in it and this resulted in it being too full. At circle time, the childcare worker discussed this with the children and they all agreed that it was unsatisfactory. The problem was that there were too many children playing at the same time. After some discussion, they decided that the problem would be solved if they limited the number of children who could play in the area at one time. They also decided that they needed a sign to show that only four children could be in the area at any one time. The following day some of the children made a sign showing four people. They showed it to the other children and then hung it up at the entrance to the surgery.

A few days later, at circle time, they talked about how well the rule was working and decided that it was now easier to play in the doctor's surgery and so the rule was better for everyone.

This collaborative way of establishing a rule demonstrated to the children the necessity of rules. Their involvement meant that they could see the problem and help to identify a solution. In this way, they could start to understand the reason for rules.

1. *Identify the ways in which the childcare worker helped the children to establish this rule.*

2. *Why is it important that the children were involved?*

3. *How could the staff involve children in establishing other necessary rules?*

Promoting children's self-confidence, assertive skills and body awareness

In order to promote children's assertive skills it is important to enhance their feelings of self-esteem and self-worth.

Adults working with children also need to:

- contradict the usual messages they give children about always listening to adults and behaving in the ways that adults request, so that they learn that there are times when the rules of being polite do not apply

- help children to learn how to say 'no', practising doing this in an assertive way through role play and simulations

- teach children that in some circumstances they may even need to say no to someone they love, but that if it is not possible to say no, because of fear or the threat of violence, other caring adults will understand and support them

- ensure they know the difference between safe secrets and unsafe secrets, and understand the difference between presents and bribes

- show them how to get help and adult assistance when someone tries to take away their rights, for example through abuse or bullying, and differentiate between telling tales to get someone into trouble and getting help when someone is threatening their safety.

Sometimes childcare workers have to deal with anti-social and difficult behaviour from children who have been hurt or abused. The way you respond to difficult behaviour will affect children's self-image and self-esteem. The table on page 140 summarises the underlying principles for managing difficult behaviour. They may be hard to carry out but it is important to set high standards. Remember that we all respond more to praise and encouragement than to punishment. If punishment cannot be avoided, keep it as low key as possible. Try to make punishment a removal of attention from the child, rather than a drama that they will want to repeat because it brings them attention. A child's feelings of anger, frustration or distress can lead to aggressive behaviour. It is not helpful for children to bottle up their feelings, or to be told they are naughty and be punished for them. They have to learn to direct their aggression in a way that gives them some relief without harming themselves or others: for example, playing with malleable and natural materials such as dough, clay, sand and paint.

Play therapy

Some children, particularly those who have had a traumatic experience, will need expert professional counselling or play therapy in order to alleviate the effects of the traumatic experience. This may be with a child psychologist, a psychiatrist, a counsellor or a play therapist. You may be involved in liaising with these professionals. Under their direction you may be involved in the use of specialist resources and equipment (for example **anatomically correct dolls**) with children who have experienced sexual abuse.

Use of such dolls can be helpful because they:

- ease the anxiety involved in discussing sexual matters for adults as well as children

- act as an ice-breaker to get a discussion going, possibly by establishing names and describing the sexual organs and characteristics

---

Anatomically correct dolls = dolls with accurately reproduced body parts including sexual organs

▼ Practical points for managing anger and difficult behaviour

DO	DON'T
• Reward positive or acceptable behaviour	• Punish aggressive behaviour with violence
• Routinely give praise, time and attention	• Presume that a child's behaviour is aimed at you personally
• Remain calm and in control of your feelings	• Pretend that everything is all right if it is not
• Respect the child	• Presume that you are always right
• Reassure the child that you will go on loving them	• Promise what you cannot do
• Recognise how the child's behaviour makes you feel	
• Restrain the child gently if necessary	
• Reason with the child	
• Respond consistently to similar events	

- appeal to a wide age range of children
- maintain a child-oriented atmosphere
- give the child permission to discuss sexual matters and understand what is natural.

The dolls can be used to:

- give children the opportunity to act out, through the dolls, their feelings about what happened to them

- educate children about sexual matters generally
- describe and demonstrate the events involved in the abuse
- facilitate group or individual play therapy sessions, involving other family members.

Such dolls may also be used to encourage and enable disclosure in the investigation of suspected abuse and to obtain evidence of actual abuse. In these contexts their use may be videoed.

✓ **Progress check**

1. Why is praise more effective than punishment?
2. What activities can help children to express strong feelings safely?

Learning Outcome 5

FOCUS ON...
how to support children to prepare for transfer or transition

This links to assessment criteria **5.1**

Transitions

A **transition**, in the context of childcare, refers to the movement of a child from one care situation to another. This usually involves a change of physical environment and a change in carers for all or part of the day. Transitions involve change and loss of attachment figures, both of which are potentially threatening to children's feelings of trust and security.

Transitions are experienced across a range of situations. These include a child going to a childminder, day nursery, crèche or playgroup, nursery school or school. Transition situations can also include moving house, the arrival of a new sibling in the family (either through birth or adoption) or the death of a parent or other family member, such as a grandparent.

Helping children to cope with transitions

Young children need stability and security in their environment and because of this they need help to cope with any transition they have to make. Significantly, they need preparation, good substitutes and help when being reunited.

The research that has been carried out into the effects of separation and loss had a direct effect on the way that children are both prepared for transitions and cared for when separated from their carers in day care, **residential care** or hospital.

Preparation

Children's reactions to separation can be affected by the way they are prepared for change. In the past, there was little or no awareness of the value of preparation. Children were taken to school or hospital and left to cope with the experience. Good preparation has become part of the policy of most institutions, including nurseries, schools and hospitals.

Preparation is often built into the procedures of a day care setting or school. People dealing with children at times of change need to understand and be sensitive to children's needs. The following guidelines for preparation can be applied to a variety of settings.

Before a transition, prepare children by:

- talking to them and explaining honestly what is about to happen
- listening to and reassuring them
- providing experiences for imaginative and expressive play which will help children to express their feelings

---

Transition = the movement of a child from one care situation to another
Residential care = provision of care both during the day and at night outside the child's home with people other than close relatives

▲ Going to a new nursery does not have to be a frightening experience

- arranging introductory visits for them and their carers, when information and experiences can be given both at their own and the adult's level
- making sure that any relevant personal information about the child's likes, dislikes, and cultural background, are available to the substitute carer.

There are many resources available to support children in transitions; these include books, games, video and DVD recordings. It is also helpful to use photographs of the people and places that the child will be experiencing. It can be a great idea to make a personalised transition book for the child.

Caring for children during separation and transition

Workers should assess children's behaviour during separation, recognise if there are any issues for concern and discuss these with parents and colleagues as necessary. Strategies for separation need to be discussed and agreed with parents and carers, as this preparation will serve to alleviate some of the stress that all parties might be feeling. Parents should also be able to give you information about settling and calming strategies and objects that the child uses for comfort or transition. Ensure

that any strategy includes 'goodbyes'; it is only fair to the child that the adults say goodbye openly and let the child know when they will be returning.

Here are a few points to consider when supporting transitions:

- Children under 3 years benefit from a one-to-one relationship with a specific person.
- The particular needs and background of the child need to be known.
- Children's comfort objects should be readily available to them.
- Children should be provided with activities appropriate to their developmental age and stage, especially play that encourages expression of feelings.
- Honest reassurance should be given.
- Children's parents should have access to them if appropriate, whenever possible.
- Children should have reminders of their parents and carers, such as photographs, when they are apart.
- Positive images of parents and reminders of home culture should be promoted.

Reuniting children with their main carers

Children who have been prepared for separation and cared for appropriately will find it easier to be reunited with their carers and to readjust to their home environment. This can apply as much to children starting school as to children who are returning home from full-time care. Children can be helped with being reunited if carers remember to:

- be honest about when they will be reunited
- allow them to talk and express their feelings through play
- advise the parent(s) to expect and accept some disturbance in their child's feelings and possibly some **regressive** behaviour.

Transitions to school

Most children go to school. Some may start by attending a nursery school, others start when they are the statutory school age. Whatever their age, children may experience anxiety and stress when they start school.

Possible sources of anxiety when starting nursery or school are:

- separation from their carer
- being among a large unfamiliar group of children who may already be established in friendship groups
- the day may seem very long
- they may be unfamiliar with the predominant culture and language of the school
- the routines will be unfamiliar and they may have a fear of doing something wrong
- different activities such as PE, playtime, milk and dinner time can feel strange to them
- the scale and unfamiliarity of the buildings may be frightening; using the toilets can be a big source of worry
- being directed and having to concentrate for longer than they are used to.

Ways of supporting transition are illustrated in the following diagram.

Frequent transitions

Those children whose admission to school is handled sensitively, with attention to the

POLICIES
School policies can include:
- an appropriate admission programme
- an admission policy that staggers the intake of children
- a helpful and informative brochure, provided in the home languages of parents and children
- appropriate classrooms and stuff
- good liaison with parents
- a welcoming environment.

Strategies to help children when starting school

STAFF
Staff (teachers, nursery nurses, classroom asssistants, etc.) can provide:
- a relaxed classroom routine
- appropriate activities and expectations
- individual attention
- observation and monitoring of new children
- an awareness of cultural and language differences
- a welcome to parents to participate.

PARENTS
Parents and carers can help by:
- encouraging independence skills, e.g. dressing, washing, eating
- giving children some experience of separation before they start school
- being there for the child when they need reassurance
- having a positive attitude towards school
- reading books about starting school and encouraging realistic expectations
- establishing routines (e.g. bedtime) that will fit in with school
- providing the appropriate equipment (e.g. lunch box, PE kit).

▲ Strategies to help children when they start school

Regressive = going back to an earlier developmental stage

Practical example

Starting school

Marcus started in the reception class at his local infants school the week after his 5th birthday. This was the school policy for all admissions. Previously, he went to a private day nursery full time for four years while his mother and father worked. His parents were given a helpful information brochure about the school and attended a meeting held for parents of all new children. Marcus attended pre-school sessions with other new children during the term before he started. These were held in one of the school classrooms on one afternoon a week, with the reception teacher.

(1) *How was Marcus prepared for the reception class?*

(2) *How could Marcus's parents use the information they were given about school?*

(3) *How well do you think Marcus settled into school and why do you think this?*

(4) *Why might Marcus not have settled without this preparation?*

points already considered in this section, usually cope with attending school each day. Children can also be helped to adjust to frequent hospital admissions if necessary.

Some children also have to cope with movement between their family home and residential accommodation or foster care. This may be because of family difficulties: parents may be unable to care for them because they are experiencing problems. Sometimes, if a child has a disability, a period of respite care in a community respite unit enables the child to receive support and sometimes additional services such as training or assessment. This allows the family rest time. If handled well, a child can adjust to periodic changes of residence of this kind.

Multiple transitions

Some children, however, experience frequent moves. This may be because

of constant and unpredictable family breakdown. Such children may become distrustful of adults. They become accustomed to change but are increasingly unable to relate closely to any carers. Their emotional and social development may be disturbed and this makes them difficult to care for. It is for this reason that frequent changes of environment for young children are avoided if at all possible. Social workers try to make long-term permanent plans for children. These may involve placing children with adopters or long-term foster parents.

✓ Progress check

(1) What is a key worker?

(2) What is transition?

(3) When might children experience separation from their main carers?

(4) What can significantly affect children's reactions to transitions?

Learning Outcome 6

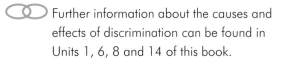

FOCUS ON...
the causes and effects of discrimination in society

This links to assessment criteria **6.1**

Issues relating to this subject area have already been explored in this unit and links have been signposted.

Further information about the causes and effects of discrimination can be found in Units 1, 6, 8 and 14 of this book.

Weblinks

- www.dcsf.gov.uk
  The Department for Children, Schools and Families website has a range of information about services, provision and the children's care, learning and development sector

- www.ofsted.gov.uk
  Information about conditions of registration and legislation

- www.hse.gov.uk
  Information about health and safety, and links to health and safety advice

- www.capt.org.uk
  The website of the Child Accident Prevention Trust, a national charity committed to reducing the number of children and young people who are killed, disabled or seriously injured as a result of accidents

- www.sja.org.uk
  The website of the St John Ambulance has information about first aid and training

- www.redcross.org.uk
  The website of the Red Cross has information about first aid and training

- www.nhsdirect.gov.uk
  Information about medical issues

- www.bbc.org.uk/parenting
  Information about all areas of children's development

- www.parentscentre.gov.uk
  Information on many aspects of children's care, learning and development

- www.teachernet.gov.uk
  Has information on a range of issues relating to the sector including transitions, good practice issues and child protection

- www.nspcc.org.uk
  The National Society for the Prevention of Cruelty to Children aims to protect children from cruelty, raise awareness of abuse and campaign for changes in the law

- www.kidscape.org.uk
  Child protection information and resources

- www.opsi.gov.uk
  The website of the Office of Public Sector Information

- www.childline.org.uk
  This website provides information and advice for children and young people about personal protection and abuse. There are information sheets and case studies on the site

- www.parentlineplus.org.uk
  This website provides telephone counselling and support

unit 4

Keeping children safe

Practitioners need to plan and create an environment that is caring, stimulating and safe. The resources and equipment provided should be suitable for the age of the child and the stage of development. You should be aware of possible dangers and always ensure the safety of the children. You must know about and follow the procedures of your setting when dealing with accidents, emergencies and illness. A valid first aid qualification is an important addition to your training. Practitioners must be aware of the child protection procedures of their setting and be able to recognise and report any issues that give cause for concern to their line manager/supervisor. Practitioners should encourage children's positive behaviour and know how to develop routines, which enable children to learn to care for themselves.

Learning Outcomes

In this unit you will learn about:

1. how to identify and develop strategies to establish and maintain healthy, safe and secure environments

2. the procedures for dealing with accidents, illnesses and other emergencies

3. how to plan and provide an enabling physical environment for children

4. how to develop age-appropriate routines which encourage children to care for themselves.

Learning Outcome 1

The learning environment

A rich, varied and safe environment supports children's learning and their development. An enabling environment will give children the confidence to explore and learn in a safe and secure environment both indoors and outside. While supporting the children's safety, the environment must also present them with challenges to foster their developing skills.

Health and safety requirements

The Health and Safety at Work Act 1974 is the main law that regulates health and safety in the workplace. There have been additions to this **safety legislation**. Similar legislation is in force in Wales, Scotland and Northern Ireland.

The Health and Safety Executive (HSE) reports to the Health and Safety Commission and was created as a result of the Health and Safety at Work Act.

Note: legal information must be used with caution. Although an Act may still be in force, parts may have been superseded by later legislation.

The statutory framework for the Early Years Foundation Stage (2007)

This sets the standards for learning, development and care for children from birth to 5 years. The Childcare Act 2006 provides the context for the delivery of the Early Years Foundation Stage (EYFS).

From September 2008 the EYFS will be mandatory for all schools and early years providers in Ofsted-registered settings attended by young children.

Recent years have seen significant developments in the early years curriculum and standards. The EYFS builds on these, including the Curriculum Guidance for the Foundation Stage, the Birth to Three Matters framework and the National Standards for Under Eights Daycare and Childminding. These three frameworks are replaced by the EYFS.

Risk assessment

Outdoor spaces, furniture, equipment and toys must be safe and suitable for their purpose.

Safety legislation = laws that are created to prevent accidents and to promote safety

Specific legal requirements

A risk assessment must be conducted and reviewed regularly. The risk assessment should identify aspects of the environment that need to be checked on a regular basis and a record must be kept of when and by whom they have been checked. All reasonable steps must be taken to ensure that all hazards – indoor and outdoor – are kept to a minimum. A health and safety policy should be in place.

You will need to risk assess both indoors and outdoors and if you plan to take children on an outing you must risk assess the trip.

There are key assessment steps to follow:

- Identify any hazards.
- Decide on the level of risk posed by the hazard – low, medium or high. The risk is the likelihood of the hazard causing harm.
- Evaluate the risk. What measures should be taken to minimise or remove the risk? Are any safety measures already in place? Are they effective? Is the risk acceptable given the ages, needs and abilities of the children involved? Consider the benefits of the activity against the potential for harm. Decide if the risk can be taken.
- Take any measures needed to remove or minimise the risk.
- Record the assessment. Sign and date the assessment
- Review the risk assessment at an identified later date. Review assessments should evaluate the effectiveness of the action taken. Reassess in the light of any significant changes that influence the original assessment.

There is currently a debate about risk and challenge in settings, particularly the outdoor area. Some professionals and others feel that children are not being challenged enough and are in fact over-protected. Many children do not play outside their homes and are taken to pre-school or school by car, so they have no real experience of assessing risk themselves and have limited opportunities to practise keeping themselves safe. This has led to initiatives like the 'walking bus' and to people being alerted to the demise of school playing fields. With the increasing numbers of obese children, there is now a move by the government to ensure that children in schools do get sufficient opportunities to exercise. See later in this unit for more about some of the current initiatives.

Health and safety policies

Your setting will have a health and safety policy. It is most important that you know about it as you will need to follow this policy in your day-to-day work.

All childcare settings must have a health and safety policy that includes:

- clear safety rules for children's behaviour
- policies for the supervision of children
- provision of safety equipment, for example safety catches on doors and windows, non-slip surfaces, safety glass, safe gym equipment
- procedures for using equipment
- policies for dealing with spills of bodily fluids
- procedures for staff to report potential hazards

- clear rules to ensure that staff work safely, for example closing and fastening safety gates, reporting any damaged or defective equipment, keeping hot drinks away from children
- policies for collecting children
- policies when taking children out of the setting
- child protection policies.

Safeguarding the children

Health and safety policies are there for the protection of the children and the staff. It is very important that these policies are made available to all staff. Policies and procedures must always be followed. There may be a temptation by some workers to cut corners or to ignore safety policies. This is a serious matter. It is important that you do not allow your own standards to be compromised. If you are worried by unsafe practices you may be able to speak directly to the person concerned and tell them why you are worried. If this does not work then you should consult a more senior member of your team. There may be a member of your team who is responsible for health and safety and you should speak to them.

Potential hazards

Many **potential hazards** are a normal part of the everyday environment. It is up to the practitioner to be aware of things that might be a danger to children and know how to deal with them. Examples of potential hazards include electric sockets and cleaning fluids. You should use socket covers and keep cleaning fluids well out of the children's reach, in a high or locked cupboard. Practitioners need to create a safe environment for children. They should identify potential hazards and take action to prevent accidents.

Checking the environment

There may be times when hazards have to be reported to a supervisor or the health and safety officer. Unsafe or broken equipment should be immediately removed. Children should also be removed from a dangerous situation.

It is important to check areas that are going to be used by the children for any hazards, especially the outdoor play space. This is an area that may be used by other people who may create hazards for the children. For example, a playgroup or out-of-school club may use premises that are used by other people.

Check the following before using the outdoor play space:

- Are the gates securely locked, and the boundary fences secure?
- Can strangers come into contact with the children?
- Are there any litterbins and are they properly covered?
- Is the area clear of rubbish, any items thrown into the area from outside, poisonous plants, broken glass, and dog or cat faeces?
- Is there any risk from water?
- Are there any items of equipment left about that could cause accidents?
- Is the play equipment properly assembled according to the manufacturer's instructions and checked for defects?
- Are the surfaces suitable for the play equipment?
- Is the number of staff supervising the children adequate?

Potential hazards = possible dangers and threats to the children's safety

Safety equipment

The use of safety equipment can help to avoid some common hazards. Accidents often happen because simple safety precautions were ignored or the safety equipment was not used properly. Any safety equipment used should be fit for its purpose. It is possible to find this out by checking that safety equipment has a **safety mark** on the label. The labels should show that toys and other equipment such as prams, high chairs and cots are safe and that they are suitable for the age group shown. It is very important

▲ Safety marks

▼ Safety equipment and its uses

SAFETY EQUIPMENT	USE
Harnesses, reins	To prevent falls from prams, pushchairs and high chairs. To stop children running into the road. Harnesses and reins should be purchased with the pram, etc.
Safety gates	To prevent access to kitchens, stairways, outside. Always guard the top and bottom of stairways
Locks for cupboards and windows	To prevent children getting hold of dangerous substances or falling from windows
Safety glass/safety film	To prevent glass from breaking into pieces that would cause injuries
Socket covers	To prevent children poking their fingers or other objects into electric sockets
Play pens	To create a safe area for babies
Smoke alarm	To detect smoke and sound the alarm
Cooker guard	To prevents children pulling pans from the cooker
Corner covers	To protect children from sharp edges on furniture
Firefighting equipment, such as a fire extinguisher, fire blanket	May be used to tackle *minor* fires

Safety mark = shows that equipment has complied with certain guidelines during manufacture

to check for the safety mark before buying equipment or toys. Safety marks do not mean that a piece of equipment or toy is completely without risk. But it indicates that manufacturers have complied with certain guidelines during manufacture. Risk assessment and good supervision are still essential.

Adapting the environment

Ensuring accessibility

All activities and areas of the setting must be accessible to all children, although there will always be some areas where the children are not allowed, such as the kitchen.

Children with a physical disability may need wider doorways, ramps, and a larger toilet area.

There should be sufficient space between furniture and activities to allow free movement around the classroom.

Children with a sensory impairment may need additional equipment. For example, a deaf child may need a hearing aid or a practitioner who can use **British Sign Language**.

Children with a visual impairment will need the reading area to be well lit. Natural light is best but if the area does not get enough daylight then extra lights will be needed. Books with large print and clear pictures will be helpful. There should be extra space to help movement around classroom furniture. The floor must be kept clear of obstacles. Any changes to the physical environment should be planned and explained to the child in advance.

Lifting and carrying

You should follow the policies and practices of your setting when lifting children and equipment. It is easy to injure yourself if you attempt to lift anything that is too heavy. Lifting incorrectly can also result in injury. If you are lifting children or equipment you should always:

- get a firm grip on whatever it is that you are lifting
- bend your knees as you lift, *not* your back
- plan your lifting. For example, consider whether the child could stand up before you lift, so that you do not have to bend down so far
- get help if the equipment is too heavy or too awkward for one person to lift.

Remember, you should never attempt to lift anything that is too heavy for you.

Safety equipment can be a useful and practical aid to ensuring children's safety. However, this is no substitute for close supervision. It is always important to know where children are and what they are doing.

Have a go!

- Find out how and when risk assessments were carried out in your setting and read a current one.
- Carry out a risk assessment in your area of work.
- Identify any examples of risk.
- What would you do to address this risk?

▲ Always check the apparatus and supervise the children

Preventing infection

Personal hygiene

It is important to encourage children to develop good personal hygiene practices as this will help to prevent infections like coughs, colds and tummy upsets which can easily be passed from one person to another. This is very likely to happen in places where children are cared for in groups where they have close contact with each other. Teach children the basic rules of hygiene like washing their hands thoroughly after using the toilet, playing in the sand or water and before eating. This will help to prevent germs being spread.

Practitioners should provide the children with a good role model and use opportunities to discuss why there are hygiene rules.

Providing a hygienic environment

Children are very vulnerable to infection and diseases can spread extremely quickly in a childcare setting. Infection can be transmitted between adults and children and also between the children themselves. Basic workplace routines can prevent the spread of diseases if they are carried out efficiently, thoroughly and regularly. Three important areas of routine hygiene in childcare settings are:

- personal hygiene
- environmental hygiene
- disposing of waste materials.

Hand washing is especially important because it is the single most effective means of preventing the spread of infection.

You should make sure to:

- wash your hands often throughout the day. Always wash your hands after going to the toilet, cleaning up after accidents and before handling food
- use warm water and a mild liquid soap; rub hands on both sides and rinse thoroughly
- dry hands thoroughly using a paper towel or hand drier. If this is not possible, towels should be washed at least daily and kept as dry as possible
- keep nails short and free of nail varnish. Bacteria grow where the varnish is chipped
- disinfect nail-brushes
- cover any cuts or abrasions with a waterproof plaster
- wear latex gloves when changing nappies or dealing with blood or any

other body fluids. Take off used gloves by peeling them back from the wrist to turn them inside out. Dispose of them in a specified bin that does not allow access for children to put their hands in. Even if you wear gloves you must still wash your hands after you take them off.

- keep hair clean, brushed often and tied back. Check regularly for head lice.

Good hygiene practices

A clean childcare setting is not only more welcoming but also less likely to contain harmful germs. Spread of infection can be prevented by:

- ensuring good ventilation
- supervising children when they use the lavatory and making sure that they wash and dry their hands properly afterwards
- avoiding overcrowding. The EYFS stipulates how much space is required
- providing separate rooms for babies and toddlers
- using protective clothing such as plastic aprons and gloves when handling bodily fluids such as, urine, blood, vomit or faeces
- keeping laundry facilities separate from food preparation areas
- cleaning toys and play equipment regularly. Toys should be cleaned daily, more often if used by babies
- using separate cloths and mops for different areas, for example one floor mop for the toilet area and a different mop for the playroom. Floor mops and cloths should be washed in hot water and detergent, rinsed and allowed to dry
- regular checking of the toilet/bathroom area. Hand washbasins should not be used as a source of drinking water

- using paper towels and tissues
- using covered bins with a foot pedal for disposal
- washing and sieving the sand regularly
- ensuring that any pets are kept clean and well cared for
- encouraging parents and carers to keep children at home if they are unwell; including this in the written policies may prevent misunderstandings
- observing strict hygiene procedures in the food preparation areas
- checking the outside area for animal excrement or other hazards, like broken glass or refuse.

Have a go!

Observe the children as they use the toilet area:

- How well do the children complete the hand washing and drying?
- Would this be effective in preventing cross-infection?
- Would you make any changes in this hygiene routine?

Disposing of waste materials

All childcare settings should have a health and safety policy that covers the disposal of hazardous waste. Care must be taken with all bodily waste (blood, faeces, urine, saliva) to prevent the transmission of diseases. Infections can be present without showing signs so the policy must be strictly maintained.

The following guidelines should be implemented when handling and disposing of waste materials:

- Cover any cuts or grazes with a waterproof dressing.
- Wear disposable latex gloves and plastic aprons when dealing with bodily waste.
- Cover bodily waste with a 1 per cent hypochlorite solution (such as bleach) before wiping up.
- Wash hands with an antiseptic soap.
- Dispose of nappies, dressings and used gloves and aprons in a sealed bag and place in a covered bin for disposal. Take off used gloves by peeling them back from the wrist to turn them inside out.
- Provide areas with covered bins with foot pedals for different types of waste.

Cleaning

Cleaning toys and equipment is important to ensure good standards of hygiene and to prevent the spread of infection. Feeding equipment and toys used by babies should be cleaned each time they are used. Any toys that are regularly handled should be cleaned using soapy water or a disinfectant solution. This will also provide an opportunity to check toys and equipment for wear or damage. Surfaces also need to be cleaned, at least daily, using hot soapy water or a suitable anti-bacterial cleaner.

Most settings will have a routine for cleaning. This will include washing floors, bathrooms and toilets, kitchens, and vacuuming and cleaning carpets.

Safe storage

All the cleaning materials and other items such as medicines, food items and waste must be stored safely. Locked storage for these items will make sure that they are kept away from the children. Practitioners also need to be very careful when they are using these items. Make sure the children cannot get hold of them while they are in use. Check carefully that the items have been replaced in the locked storage after use. Be very aware that common household items, like washing-up liquid and washing powder, are also potentially dangerous and need to be kept well out of the reach of children. Children should be kept out of the kitchen and laundry areas at all times.

Supervising children

The number of adults required to care for children in day care is regulated. There are specific legal requirements for ratios of adults to children. These are set out in the standards for the Early Years Foundation Stage in the Appendix. Ratios will vary for the different types of group settings.

These numbers are the minimum requirements. You would expect to have fewer children per adult if some of the children had special needs. Children also need to get out and about to enjoy local outings to the shops or park. You would need more adults in these circumstances.

The adult:child ratios relate to staff available to work directly with the children. Suitable arrangements must be made to cover unexpected emergencies and staff absences. There should be sufficient staff to cover breaks, holidays and time spent with parents. All this will need careful planning by the management to make sure that the ratios are kept up and the children's safety ensured.

Encouraging children to be aware of personal safety

Providing a good role model

Children are great imitators but they will learn and copy both good and poor behaviour. It is very important that adults always follow the safety rules and never compromise their own safety. This is especially important where road safety is involved. Always set a good example. Talk to children about road safety and use the Green Cross Code yourself. If there is a controlled crossing, use it and don't be tempted to cross at a red light even if the road is clear.

The adult role and risk assessment

It is important to have the correct number of adults within a setting, but this is only the beginning of good supervision. Adults must be alert and aware of what the children are doing. Good supervision of children means that the children remain safe, but also allows them to try out new and more challenging activities.

Practitioners must always be aware of potential hazards. Then they can see any possible dangers for the children, before there is an accident, and take action to stop this happening. However, children do need to learn to do new things and to become more independent so it is important not to limit the children to activities that are too easy. They will need to do more challenging things so, think about what simple measures will reduce the risk. For example, you may need to supervise a child more closely if they are trying out their climbing skills on more difficult climbing apparatus or using the woodwork tools.

Children and safety rules

All settings will have safety rules and the adults must make sure that children follow the rules. However, it is also very important to explain to the children why there are rules and how the rules will help to keep them safe as they play and learn. Help the children to understand about risk and

▲ Playground rules

staying safe. For example, practitioners can explain the safety rules to the children before they use the apparatus. They must also explain the rules again during the activities if the children are not playing safely. Always explain why the child is in danger or putting others in danger.

Children will be able to play safely as they begin to understand about the dangers that are around them. However, this awareness takes time to develop and all children will always need supervising as they play. Younger children and babies, because of their stage of development, will be less aware of dangers and will require greater supervision.

Children and adults can make a list of the safety rules together. This can give the children a chance to talk about what is safe behaviour and what is not. Make sure the list is not too long and that it includes the most important points. Examples that the children might suggest could be:

- no running indoors
- no pushing, shouting or fighting
- no walking around with scissors.

Aim to include some positive rules like:

- let everyone take a turn
- always fetch an adult if some one is hurt or crying
- sit down when having a drink.

Safety and security procedures

Childcare settings need to have strict security measures. These are likely to include the following:

- Doors and gates that lead to the outside or to areas where children are not allowed must have a suitable lock. The lock must be well out of the reach of the children. All the adults in the setting must make sure that the locks are used at all times.
- Fire exits must be checked to see that they are not locked or blocked with equipment.
- Window locks must be fitted and used.
- Name badges must be worn by all staff and students.
- Door entry phones and bells will give the staff the opportunity to enquire about the nature of the business of any visitors before letting them enter the building.
- Outdoor play times must always be supervised.

At the start of the day/session

All settings will have a procedure for receiving children at the beginning of a session. Babies, young children and their parents will be welcomed directly by their key worker. Older children may be brought into the pre-school, nursery or classroom by their parent. There will be a method of registering each child's arrival. It is very important that a register of all the children present is taken at the very beginning of the day/session. This register must be updated if a child leaves early. It is a legal requirement that a register is kept. The register is most important. For example, if there is a fire it can be used to ensure that all the children have left the building safely. The start of the day is a very busy time. Practitioners will need to be watchful. You must make sure that children are properly supervised to ensure that children do not go back outside when parents leave.

Home times

Practitioners must ensure children's safety at home times. Most settings have a policy that only allows children to be collected by a named adult. Parents should inform staff about who will be collecting the child if they cannot do so themselves. Every setting should have a procedure for collecting children. Student practitioners must not take messages about the children; always direct the parent or carer to the relevant member of staff.

Taking children out of the setting

Outings with children

Children enjoy going on outings and these have many benefits. They can be short trips to the shops or to post a letter, or longer outings to farms or parks. All will provide valuable learning opportunities. The amount of preparation needed depends on the scale of the outing. If you plan to take children on an outing you must risk assess the trip. This will require a prior visit by a childcare worker to consider the venue and the movement and transport of the children on the outing.

Practical example

Collecting Laurie

Laurie's mum, Wendy, came to the nursery to collect him as usual. She asked to speak to Janice, who is in charge, and explained that she would not be able to collect Laurie herself the next week, as she would be delayed at work. She said that Laurie's granny would come to fetch him. Janice explained that there would be several things that Wendy needed to do to make sure that the staff at the nursery could be certain that it was his granny collecting Laurie.

(1) *Consider what arrangements you think Janice could make with Wendy to ensure that Laurie was safely collected.*

Whenever you are taking children outside the setting there will be local regulations that must be followed. Always make sure that you know about the regulations and follow them carefully.

You should consider these factors when planning to take children on an outing:

- safety
- permissions
- the place
- supervision
- transport
- food
- clothing
- cost.

The age and stage of development of the children

There are differences in the physical capabilities of children. Very young children will be restricted to areas where you can push a buggy. Children will vary in their ability to concentrate and sit still. Choosing a destination that meets the needs of all the age groups you are taking is important. It may be necessary to put children into groups. Each group can then do different things. For example, during a visit to a park the younger children will enjoy feeding the ducks. The older ones will also wish to play ball games, or follow the nature trails.

The distance of the destination from the setting will decide whether the trip will last for a morning, afternoon or whole day. Younger children do not like spending a long time travelling. This should be considered when choosing where to visit.

▲ Outings with young children should be educational and fun

Permissions

Permission to take children outside the setting must always be obtained from the person in charge of the setting. This person will be responsible for carrying out a risk assessment. The risk assessment will reflect the kind of outing planned. A short local visit will need less planning than a longer visit to a place that is further away. It is important to inform parents about the outing and get their written permission for children to take part

Adult help/supervision

It is essential to arrange to have a higher adult:child ratio on any outing away from the setting. This will depend on the risk assessment.

There will be regulations that apply to your setting. Find out about these. Remember that it is always a good idea to have extra adults to help cover any emergencies.

Cost

If there is an entry fee or travelling costs, some families may not be able to afford to pay. Check whether there is enough funding to cater for all the children.

Transport

Is the place within walking distance or will transport be required? If arranging transport with an outside organisation, make sure that:

- it is insured
- the vehicle is large enough to seat everyone – adults and children
- there are sufficient child restraints, booster seats and seat belts
- the vehicles are safe and well maintained.

Records must be kept about vehicles in which children are to be transported. This will include:

- insurance details
- a list of named drivers.

Drivers using their own vehicle to carry any children must have insurance cover.

Avoid travelling during rush hours. When walking, plan to use the safest route, keeping to footpaths and using safe crossing places.

Stages in the planning process

1 Check the national and local authority regulations that apply to your setting that cover outings. Any arrangements must comply with these regulations.

2 Find out about the destination, for example travel routes, opening times and accessibility for children, toilet facilities, picnic areas, refreshments, first aid provision. It should be possible to visit to find out before you go.

3 Prepare a timetable for the day. Everyone will need to know times of departure and arrival. Ensure that your programme is practical and there is enough time to do everything that you have planned for.

4 Plan to take all the necessary equipment with you, for example:
- first aid kit
- emergency contact phone numbers and a mobile phone (check the battery)
- registers
- any medicines and inhalers
- camera
- money

- audio tapes for the journey
- worksheets and bags for collecting items of interest
- packed lunches
- wet-weather wear
- sun cream, sun hats
- spare clothes (and a sick bucket and plastic bags!)
- younger children may need pushchairs, nappies, and harnesses.

5 Consult parents. It is necessary to get written consent from parents for any trip away from the setting. They will need to know about the cost, the day's programme, transport, special requirements – lunch, clothing, etc. A letter home with a consent slip is the best way to achieve this, perhaps combined with posters or notices displayed in the setting.

6 Prepare the children for the outing. Discuss the outing and explain what will be happening, talk about safety issues such as, staying with adults, not speaking to strangers. Discuss any activities related to the outing. Make sure the children know what to do if they become separated from the group (e.g. not to wander about but to stay in the same place). Older children may be shown a central meeting point or the ticket office. Show children the staff uniform or name badges so they know who to ask for help.

Name badges for children are not used nowadays, as they enable strangers to find out the child's name. You could use a system of number badges that link to the register.

7 Brief all the adults who are helping on the outing. They will need to have all the information about the outing, who is in charge and has the registers and the contact numbers. They must also have a list of all the children and know which children they are responsible for. Make sure adults know what to do in an emergency.

8 Plan to meet up and have regular head counts and register checks.

9 Consider the 'what ifs'. Planning includes taking proper safety precautions, supervising the children carefully and preparing for the unexpected. However, unexpected events may still happen during an outing. It is important to think about what might happen beforehand. You can then think about how you would cope to make sure that the children are safe. You should explain any safety rules. Help them as they attempt more difficult things, perhaps in their physical play, while still making sure that they are safe. Check carefully when children come into the setting and when they go home. Make sure that you know about, and follow the procedures of your setting. You will need to show that you know about any regulations, local and national, that are concerned with the safety of the children in your setting.

✓ Progress check

1. Why is it important to teach the children about safety?
2. What do you understand by risk assessment?
3. What are the benefits of taking children on outings?
4. How could outings and visits be used to enhance the curriculum?
5. What are the stages in the planning process for an outing?
6. Consider the safety issues involved when arranging transport.
7. Consider the current disquiet about risk and challenge. How does your present setting approach this?

Learning Outcome 2

FOCUS ON...
the procedures for dealing with accidents, illnesses and other emergencies

This links to assessment criteria **2.1**

All establishments should have:

- written emergency procedures
- staff who have been trained in first aid
- first aid equipment
- an accident book for accurate recording of all incidents requiring first aid
- regular reviews of incidents of accidents to highlight areas of concern.

Emergency procedures

Evacuation and fire procedures

Evacuation and fire procedures must be clearly displayed and pointed out to anyone who comes into the building. The law requires regular practices. All staff must be familiar with evacuation procedures. A fire officer will make regular checks.

Part of the introduction to your setting will include an explanation of the emergency procedures. Any visitors to the setting, such as parents staying with their children, will be shown the procedure for evacuating the setting if there is a fire or other emergency. These procedures should be displayed in every room where everyone can see and read them. They should be simple and easy to follow. A plan will show more clearly where the fire exits are positioned.

GOOD PRACTICE

Fire exits must never be locked or blocked by furniture or any other equipment.

Other emergencies

Other types of emergencies could involve a gas escape, electricity failure or leaking water. There might also be a security incident, such as a bomb threat or intruder alert, which would require staff to use the emergency procedures.

Important factors

Important things that must be included in emergency procedures are:

- a reminder that the alarm should be sounded
- a clear statement or plan to show where the assembly points and fire exits are located
- the route to follow to get out of the building
- how to call for help, e.g. where the nearest telephone outside the building is located
- a reminder *not* to go back into the building
- the name of the person responsible for the procedure and for collecting the registers and parents' contact numbers.

Children should leave the building by the quickest route. This will be shown on the evacuation procedure. It is important that someone is responsible for taking a register outside. An accurate count can then be done as soon as the children and staff get to the assembly point. The first thing the emergency services will want to know when they arrive is if anyone is still in the building. As well as the register it is important to have a record of the parents' contact numbers. These need to be kept close to the register or actually written in the register. Parents will need to be contacted and kept informed about what is happening.

Missing children or persons

If children or other individuals are thought to be missing, it is important to check the register and the records of staff and visitors that are present. If you find that someone is missing, report this to the person in charge immediately so that all the other registers and records can be checked. In the case of a fire evacuation, the fire officer in charge should be told immediately if someone is missing.

Firefighting equipment

It is a legal requirement that all settings will have firefighting equipment. It is important to know where any fireblankets, fire extinguishers and other equipment are kept and that you know how to use them safely. It is important that you have been fully informed about the firefighting equipment before you attempt to use it. Never put yourself at risk by attempting to put out a fire. It is much better to sound the fire alarm and evacuate the building safely.

There are different types of fire extinguishers. It is important that you know what type of fire they can be used

▲ Firefighting equipment

for. For example, fire extinguishers containing water must not be used on fires involving electrical equipment. There are special extinguishers that can be used for these fires. Suitable firefighting equipment should be placed near any potential fire hazard. For example, a fire blanket is necessary in a kitchen.

Practising the evacuation procedure

Regular practices of the evacuation procedure should be carried out to make sure that all staff and children know how to leave the building quickly and safely.

If you work in a home setting, you will be required to work out an evacuation procedure for each room in your home and practise leaving the building.

A record must be kept of each practice and the staff should discuss how well the practice went. Changes should be made to the procedure if there are any difficulties, or if staff can see how to make the procedure work better to ensure the children's safety. It is also very important to have practices that take place without any prior warning. Staff and children can then respond as they would in a real emergency.

Discussing the evacuation procedure and explaining what will happen will help to make the practice go more smoothly. The children will also need time to talk about the practice afterwards. Parents need to be aware of any fire practices. They can also talk this over with their children at home. Stories about firefighters and fire engines will help the children to talk about any worries they may have. Successful practices that have gone smoothly will mean that there is a good chance that all will be well in a real emergency.

Responding in a calm and reassuring way

A real emergency that leads to an evacuation of the setting will be a worrying and frightening experience for the adults and children. However, it is important to stay calm and to reassure the children by talking to them, while carrying out the evacuation procedure as quickly and safely as possible. Give clear and positive instructions in a clear calm voice. It will help if you and the children have practised what you need to do.

Coping with accidents and injuries to children

What follows is an outline of basic first aid for children. It is not intended to replace a recognised training in first aid. It is important that all practitioners undertake recognised training in first aid so that they can act confidently and safely in the event of an accident. The British Red Cross and St John Ambulance run recognised first aid courses in most areas.

First aid box

All settings should have a first aid box. The first aid box should be clearly labelled and put in dry place, where the children cannot reach it. All the staff should know where the first aid box is kept and it should be in a place where it can be easily and quickly reached in an emergency. The first aid box may contain all the items shown in the illustration opposite. There should be a list of the contents kept in the box.

It is very important that the contents of the first aid box are checked. Things that have been used must be replaced at once, as people using the first aid box will be relying on everything being there. Most settings will have a designated member of staff responsible for first aid. There should be a foolproof system for checking and replacing first aid items as they are used.

The contents of first aid boxes may vary. Have a look to see what is in your setting's box.

First aid in emergencies

It is important to remain calm in any emergency situation. If you are the first person on the scene you should:

- *assess the situation*: find out how many children are injured and whether there is any continuing danger.
  Are there any other adults who can help? Is an ambulance required?
- *put safety first*: include the safety of all children and adults, including your own. Remove any dangerous hazards; move the injured child only if it absolutely essential

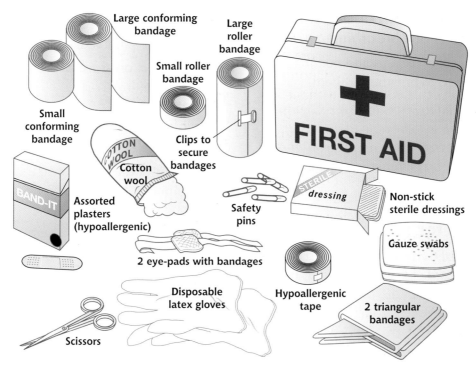

▲ The contents of a first aid box

- *prioritise*: treat the most serious injuries first. Concentrate on the most immediately life-threatening conditions, i.e. children who are *not* breathing or who have severe bleeding
- *get help*: shout for help or ask others to get help and call an ambulance.

If you are not trained to give emergency aid you should concentrate on getting help as quickly as possible. When the trained first aider arrives he or she will take charge, so follow instructions carefully.

If you are told to telephone for an ambulance:

- dial 999
- ask for the ambulance service
- answer the questions that you will be asked accurately and clearly
- know the telephone number from which you are calling
- know the exact place of the accident
- give the details of the accident and what you know about any injuries
- do not put the phone down until you have given all the information requested.

Examining a casualty

Find out if the child is *conscious* or *unconscious*:

- Check for response – call the child's name, pinch the skin.
- Open the airway and check for breathing.
- Check the pulse.

How to manage an unconscious child who is breathing

An unconscious child who is breathing and has a pulse should be put into the recovery position. This will keep the airway clear. Keep checking the airway and pulse until medical help arrives.

How to manage an unconscious child who is not breathing

If a child is unconscious and *not breathing* you will need to breathe for them.

You will need to have done a recognised first aid course to be able to do this. If you are not trained to do this you must concentrate on getting qualified help as quickly as possible.

First aid for minor injuries

It is essential to remain calm when dealing with an injured child. They need to be reassured that they are in safe hands and everything will be all right.

Minor burns and scalds

Immerse the burnt area in cold water for at least ten minutes. Avoid touching the burn or any blisters. Cover with a clean smooth cloth, such as a clean tea towel, and seek medical aid. For all but the most minor burns you should get medical aid as quickly as possible.

Bleeding

Wounds with minor bleeding should be cleaned and covered with a dressing.

Major bleeds must be stopped:

- Send for help immediately.
- Apply direct pressure to the wound and raise the injured part.

Nose bleeds

Sit the child leaning forwards and pinch the soft part of the nose above the nostrils for ten minutes. If the bleeding continues, seek medical aid.

GOOD PRACTICE

Remember that you should always wear gloves when dealing with blood or any other body fluids; this will protect you from infection.

Splinters

Children may get splinters of wood from rough wooden objects so check equipment carefully.

If the splinter is sticking out from the skin, it may be possible to remove it using a pair of tweezers. The wound should be cleaned carefully. If the splinter is deeply embedded, medical aid will be needed.

▲ The recovery position

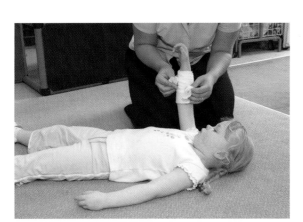

▲ Dealing with bleeding

Check to make sure the child's tetanus immunisation is up to date.

Sprains

Raise and support the injured limb to minimise swelling. Remove shoe and sock if it is a sprained ankle. Apply a cold compress – a polythene bag of ice or a pack of frozen peas would do. Keep the limb raised until you can get medical aid. The ankle should be checked to ensure that nothing is broken.

▲ Managing a nosebleed

▲ A sprained ankle

Objects in noses or ears

Children who have poked anything into their nose or ears should be taken to the nearest accident and emergency department. The object will be safely removed.

Choking

This is potentially a very serious situation. Send for help immediately. If you are dealing with a young child, put the child over your knee, head down:

- Then slap sharply between the shoulder blades up to five times.
- Check to see if the object has become dislodged and is in the mouth.
- If the object has not been dislodged, *call for urgent medical aid* – take the child to the phone with you if you are alone.

Try the back slaps again until help arrives or the object can be removed.

Poisoning

If a child eats poisonous plants or medicines, or swallows bleach or cleaning fluids, these are all serious situations. You should:

- send for help immediately
- check to see if the child is breathing and conscious
- put into the recovery position if unconscious
- take any samples of what has been eaten or drunk to the hospital with the child.

Asthma

Asthma attacks are very frightening for children. The airways go into spasm, making breathing difficult. This could be a serious situation.

Management of an asthma attack:

- reassure the child
- give the child their inhaler
- send for help
- sit the child upright and leaning forward in a comfortable position
- stay with the child
- continue to comfort and reassure the child.

If this is the first attack or if the condition persists, call for an ambulance and contact parents.

Call an ambulance immediately if the above steps have been taken and there is no improvement in 3–5 minutes.

Cuts and grazes

Any cut or graze that breaks the skin will mean that there is a risk of infection. Sit the child down and comfort them. Then explain what you are going to do. You should:

- wash your hands
- put on protective gloves
- gently clean the graze or cut using clean water and a gauze pad (do not use cotton wool or any fluffy material that could stick to the wound)

- cover the cut or graze with a pad and a light bandage
- put all the soiled material and gloves into a sealed bag for disposal
- wash your hands thoroughly.

Some settings may use plasters but this is risky as many children are allergic to them. It is best to use special plasters (hypo-allergenic) that are specially made to avoid allergic reactions.

Head injury

If a child has bumped their head, sit them down and treat any minor wound or bruise with a cold compress. Watch for signs of abnormal behaviour. If the child does not recover within a few minutes it will be important to get medical aid fast.

Concussion

All bumps on the head have the potential to have serious consequences. When the head is bumped the brain may be shaken, causing concussion.

If the child has been unconscious, even briefly, you must call an ambulance.

If the child remains unconscious, you must call an ambulance and follow the procedure for dealing with an unconscious person (see above).

Skull fracture

Fractures of the skull are potentially very serious injuries and require urgent medical attention. Signs you may observe include:

- a wound or bruise on the head
- a soft area on the scalp
- impaired consciousness
- deterioration in the level of response
- clear fluid from the nose or ear

- blood showing in the white of the eye
- distortion of head or face.

In all cases of bumps on the head watch the child carefully for any signs of abnormal behaviour. If in doubt always seek medical aid. There may be a serious reaction to a head injury hours or even days later.

Anaphylactic shock

Anaphylactic shock is a severe reaction to a substance, for example peanuts or a bee sting.

The child will be very anxious and distressed. There is severe difficulty in breathing; the pulse may be rapid and the face will be red with swelling and redness. Call an ambulance immediately. Meanwhile move the child into a position that will help them to breathe more easily.

Note: some children with a known allergy may have an EpiPen that contains the drug adrenaline to be used in the event of an attack. They may be able to use this themselves, or a member of staff may be trained to use it. If so, it should be given without delay.

Maintaining standards of hygiene when dealing with accidents and emergencies

When dealing with accidents and injuries it is important to make sure that you protect yourself and the injured child from infection. Infections such as hepatitis can be transmitted via an open cut or graze.

You should always:

- wear protective clothing, such as gloves and aprons
- wash your hands before and after attending to an injury, even if you wear gloves

---

Anaphylactic shock = a severe and extreme reaction to a substance, such as peanuts or a bee sting

- make sure that anyone helping you also wears protective clothing and washes their hands
- avoid touching the cut or graze or the dressing that will touch the cut. Don't let the child or anyone else touch either
- explain to the children that you are taking these precautions to protect them from infection
- avoid coughing or sneezing over the injury and do not let anyone else do so
- clean up carefully and get rid of any dirty dressings or other material by sealing in a marked plastic bag for disposal, preferably by burning
- clean up spills of blood, urine or other bodily waste, carefully. Always wear gloves and use a solution of bleach (one teaspoon to a half a litre of water) to clean surfaces. Dispose of the waste as described above.

Recording accidents, injuries and other incidents

All settings will have a way of recording any accidents, injuries and other incidents. This is often a special book – the accident book. All accidents, injuries and incidents, however seemingly small or minor, must be recorded as soon as possible. This information should be shared with parents so that they are fully aware of what has happened. It may be that a child who has had a minor accident at nursery, and seems fine, will become ill later in the day, or during the night.

The records should include:

- the full name of the child
- the date and time of the accident
- the exact details of the accident and any injury
- who was involved
- what treatment was given
- who was informed
- what action was taken
- the signature of the member of staff dealing with the accident.

Accident books should be kept for at least three years.

Settings should always ask the parents to sign the book to show that they have read the details

Informing parents

If an accident is serious, the parents should be contacted immediately. This is the responsibility of the senior member of staff or person in charge. Parents should be given the facts. If the child has to go to hospital then the parent will need to go with them, or meet the ambulance there if this is a quicker option. Parents will need to be involved in any decision about their child's treatment so it very important to be able to contact parents as quickly as possible. Parents' contact telephone numbers must be kept up to date.

More minor accidents are usually reported to parents when they collect their children at the end of the session. Again this is the responsibility of a senior member of staff. Parents may well be upset about accidents, however minor. It is very important to keep accurate records so that you can give parents clear information about what has happened and what was done. Parents will need time to talk about this, perhaps more than once. They may need to talk over their worries about what has happened with the person in charge.

Children's reactions to accidents and emergencies

After any accident children may be upset and crying. This is often because they have been frightened by what has happened. They may have injuries that need treatment and it is important to get help and to treat any injuries. However, it is also very important to comfort and reassure children after an accident.

Take care not to blame children for any accident that has happened. It is possible that children were acting in a dangerous way, but save the discussions about this for later. The important thing to do immediately is to sit with the child and talk to them while they recover. Children may want a particular comfort object, such as a toy. Try to fetch this or ask someone else to get it for the child as soon as you can. Children may also ask for their parents. The decision to send for a parent will depend on what has happened and how the child recovers.

Other children, who were not directly involved in the accident, may also be upset. They may be worried about a friend who has been hurt. Try to give simple explanations about what has happened and help the children to settle back into their normal activities. There should be a time later for the children and adults to talk about what has happened.

Allergies

Children may be allergic to some foods, for example nuts or milk. It is very important that staff members are fully informed about any allergies that children may have. *You should always check before giving food and drinks to babies and children.* If children are not allowed certain foods or drinks this should be made clear to all staff. (This is particularly important if you have agency staff or new staff members.) Record allergies in the children's records; notices in the kitchen and the room where children are cared for should also clearly display this information.

Information about children's allergies to food and drink must be regularly updated. This should be discussed with the parents when a child is admitted. The staff must be told about any changes. Practitioners must be aware that some foods could contain quite small quantities of substances that will cause a reaction. In some cases, if children are very allergic, this may only need the food to have been in contact with the ingredient that causes the allergic reaction. Many foods have a warning on the label about this.

Symptoms of food allergy may include:

- vomiting
- diarrhoea
- skin rashes
- wheezing and difficulty in breathing
- convulsions.

Recognising when children are ill

It is very important to know about diseases that are common in childhood and to be able to recognise the signs that tell you a child is ill. Many illnesses begin with the same general signs and need the same general care.

The general signs of illness are:

- a raised temperature
- sore throat
- pale, flushed face, feeling hot to the touch

- headache
- loss of appetite
- upset sleep patterns
- rashes on the skin.

Causes of disease

Diseases are caused by pathogens. The common name for **pathogens** is germs.

The most important pathogens are:

- bacteria
- viruses
- fungi.

Once pathogens enter the body they multiply very rapidly. This period of time is called the incubation period and it can last for a few days or weeks, depending on the type of disease. Although the child is infectious during the incubation period they only begin to feel ill and show signs of the illness at the end of the incubation period.

How diseases are spread

The table below shows some common forms of diseases and their methods of spread.

▼ How diseases are spread

Common childhood illnesses
Colds

Viruses cause colds (so antibiotics will not help). There are things you can do to help the child breathe more easily: keep the nose clear. Make sure the child has plenty to drink, and give light, easily swallowed food. Don't fuss if a child does not want to eat for a while, just give plenty to drink – squash, diluted fruit juice or water will be better than milk.

Coughs

A virus causes most coughs, like colds. If a cough persists or the chest sounds congested, a doctor should be consulted.

Diarrhoea

Young babies' **stools** are normally soft and yellow, and some babies will soil nearly every nappy. If you notice the stools becoming very watery and frequent, and there are other signs of illness, consult the doctor. In the meantime, give as much cooled, boiled water as you can.

METHOD OF SPREAD	EXAMPLE OF DISEASE
Droplet infection: the pathogens are contained in the droplets of moisture in the breath and are breathed out	Colds, coughs, measles, chickenpox
Touching infected people or material	Impetigo, athlete's foot, thrush, coughs and colds
Drinking infected water	Food poisoning, gastroenteritis, polio
Eating infected food	Food poisoning, gastroenteritis, diarrhoea, typhoid
Pathogens entering through a cut or graze	Tetanus, hepatitis, HIV/Aids

Ear infections

Ear infections often follow a cold. The child may be generally unwell, pull or rub the ears or there may be a discharge from the ear. There may be a raised temperature. The child may complain of pain, but small babies will just cry and seem unwell or uncomfortable. If you suspect an ear infection, it is important that it is treated promptly.

Bronchitis

Infection and inflammation of the main airway cause bronchitis (chest infection). The child will have a persistent chesty cough and may cough up green or yellow phlegm. There may be noisy breathing, a raised temperature and the child feels very unwell. Consult the doctor as soon as possible. Meanwhile, allow the child to rest quietly. Sitting well propped up will help breathing.

Raised temperature

Children, especially babies, can develop high temperatures very quickly. If a baby has a raised temperature and/or other signs of illness, always consult the doctor as soon as possible. It is important to bring the temperature down to avoid any complications. Do not wrap a baby up; take off a layer of clothing and let older children wear light clothes. Keep the room cool and give plenty of cool drinks, little and often.

Febrile convulsions

Febrile convulsions are fits that occur as the direct result of a raised temperature. They usually occur in babies and younger children between the ages of 6 months and 5 years. Febrile convulsions are relatively common in childhood and are *not* an indication of epilepsy in later life.

If a child in your care has a febrile convulsion it is important to act effectively and quickly:

- Stay with the child and protect them from injury or falling.
- Get medical aid.
- Put the child in the recovery position when the convulsions have stopped.
- Take the measures described above to bring down the temperature.

Thrush

Thrush is a fungal infection that forms white patches in the mouth, usually on the tongue and the inside of the cheeks and lips. A baby may also have a sore bottom because the thrush has infected the skin in the nappy area. Consult the doctor who will give the specific anti-fungal treatment to clear up the infection.

Vomiting

All babies will bring up some milk from time to time. If the baby is vomiting often or violently and/or there are other signs of illness, contact the doctor. Babies can lose a lot of fluid if they vomit frequently; keep up the intake of fluids – cooled boiled water may be best.

The table on pages 174–176 lists the infectious childhood illnesses you need to know about. It outlines the signs to look for and the specific care needed.

Asthma

Asthma is a condition in which the airways in the lungs become narrowed. Allergy to substances such as pollen, dust and pet hair causes the airways to swell. Spasms of the airways may cause further narrowing, making breathing difficult. The child

---

Stools = the solid products of digestion passed out from the baby's bowel
Febrile convulsions = fits that occur as the direct result of a raised temperature

wheezes and becomes breathless. Attacks vary in severity, but a bad attack can be very frightening. Severe asthma attacks are serious and require prompt medical aid.

▼ Infectious childhood illnesses

DISEASE	INCUBATION	SYMPTOMS	CARE
Chickenpox	14–16 days	Spots on chest and back, red at first, becoming blisters, then forming a dry scab. Spots come in successive crops and are very itchy	Discourage scratching and ease the itching by keeping the child cool and applying lotion such as calamine
Coughs and colds	2–10 days	General signs of illness, nasal congestion, cough	General care, but monitor coughs carefully in case the chest becomes infected. Watch carefully in case other symptoms develop, which would indicate a more serious illness. Consult doctor if unsure, especially with a baby
Diarrhoea (caused by infected food or water)	2–7 days	Loose, frequent, watery stools, pains in the stomach	Give plenty of fluid to avoid dehydration. Consult a doctor for a baby, or if the diarrhoea persists, or the child shows signs of dehydration or other illness
Diphtheria	2–6 days	Difficulty in breathing. White membrane forms in the throat	Medical aid and hospital treatment is needed. Immunisation available
Ear infections	Variable	Pain, discharge from the ear, high temperature	Medical aid, antibiotics and pain relief may be prescribed by a doctor
Gastroenteritis (caused by infected food or dirty water)	1–14 days	Severe and persistent vomiting and diarrhoea	Medical aid and hospital care may be needed. Give plenty of fluids. Oral rehydration solutions may be given

DISEASE	INCUBATION	SYMPTOMS	CARE
Measles	7–14 days	Raised temperature, sore eyes, Koplik's spots in the mouth, red blotchy rash that quickly spreads over the whole body	Medical aid. Eyes and ears may need special attention as complications include sensitivity to light and ear infections. Immunisation is available
Meningitis	2–10 days	Symptoms include high temperature, headache, irritability, vomiting, rash, pain and stiffness in the neck, and sensitivity to light	Get medical aid. Early hospital treatment will be needed. It is very important to recognise meningitis early as the progress of this illness is very rapid and serious. Immunisation is available for some types of meningitis
Mumps	14–21 days	Pain, tenderness and swelling around the jaw and ear, usually on one side of the face, then the other	Doctor may advise pain relief. A rare complication in boys is inflammation of the testes. Immunisation is available
Poliomyelitis (water-borne infection)	5–21 days	Headache, stiffness in neck and back, loss of movement and paralysis	Hospital care. Immunisation is available
Rubella	14–21 days	Mild general symptoms, rash lasting for about 24 hours	General care. Keep the child away from any women who may be pregnant as the rubella virus can damage the foetus. Immunisation is available
Scarlet fever	2–6 days	Red tongue, sore throat, rash on face and body	Medical aid. Doctor may prescribe antibiotics
Tetanus	4–21 days	Painful muscle spasms in neck and jaw	Hospital treatment required. Keep immunisation up to date
Thrush (fungal infection)	Variable	White patches in the mouth, usually on the tongue and inside the cheeks. A baby may have a sore bottom	Consult the doctor who will prescribe a specific treatment. Check that all feeding equipment is sterilised

DISEASE	INCUBATION	SYMPTOMS	CARE
Tuberculosis	28–42 days	Cough, weight loss, investigation shows lung damage	Medical aid. Specific antibiotics are given. Immunisation is available
Whooping cough	7–14 days	Long bouts of coughing and choking, difficulty in breathing during the coughing, whooping noise as the child draws in breath. Vomiting during coughing bouts	Medical aid. Support during coughing bouts, and give reassurance. Give food after coughing if vomiting is a problem. Possible complications are permanent lung damage, brain damage, ear infections and bronchitis. Immunisation is available

Inhalers help to get medication into the lungs and relieve the affected airways. These medicines are called **bronchodilators** and help to reduce swelling and spasm in the airways at the time of an attack. Other medicines given by regular use of inhalers help to prevent attacks occurring. There are different types of inhaler, which children can learn to use. It is very important that a child's inhaler is immediately available.

If a child in your care has an asthma attack, follow the procedure described in the first aid section (see pages 168).

Infestations

Parasites obtain their food from humans and may affect children. Common parasites include the following:

- Fleas: these small insects feed on human blood and live in clothing next to the skin. The bites can be seen as red spots.

- Head lice: these insects live in human hair close to the scalp, where they can easily bite the skin and feed on blood.

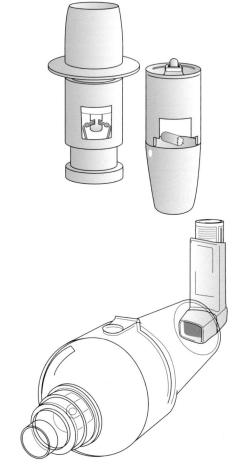

▲ **Different types of inhaler**

Bronchodilators = medicines that are breathed into the lungs by using an inhaler. Bronchodilators help to reduce swelling and narrowing in the airways

176

Parasites = small organisms which live on humans and obtain their food from them

You may see the lice or more likely nits. Nits are the empty white egg cases that are left stuck onto the hair after the louse has hatched.

- Ringworm: this fungal infection is seen on the skin as a raised red circle with a white scaly middle.
- Threadworms: these small thread-like worms are found in the bowel. They cause a very itchy bottom. You may see the worms around the bottom.
- Scabies: these are tiny mites that burrow under the skin causing itching and raised red spots.

Each of these infestations has a specific treatment. The child's doctor should be consulted.

Caring for sick children in the work setting

When a child is ill outside the home environment it is important to report any concerns. At school or nursery this will be to a senior member of staff, who will decide when to contact the child's parent. A childminder or nanny should contact the parents direct.

It is important to keep a record of the child's symptoms and how they change, as you may need to explain this to a parent or doctor. Information should be kept so that contact can be made in an emergency.

Giving medicines

These are the important points to remember when giving medicines to any child in a childcare setting:

- Follow the policy of your setting.
- Get the parents' or carers' written consent.

- Only give medicines advised or prescribed by the child's GP or hospital doctor.
- Follow the instructions for dosage and frequency carefully.
- Store medicine safely in a locked cupboard.
- Keep a record of all the medicines given, including the date, time and dose.

Personal hygiene

Personal hygiene is all about keeping clean and includes washing, bathing, hair washing and teeth cleaning. All children need adult help and supervision as they learn to keep themselves clean. Good standards of hygiene in childhood and beyond are important life skills because they help to:

- prevent disease and the spread of infection
- prepare children for life by teaching them how to care for themselves and become independent.

Personal care

The skin is a first defence against infection and has the following functions:

- protects the body by preventing pathogens (germs) entering the body
- feels sensations of hot, cold, soft, hard
- secretes an oily substance called sebum that keeps the skin supple and waterproof
- makes vitamin D when exposed to sunlight (vitamin D helps to make strong bones)
- makes sweat; sweating helps to regulate the temperature when the body is hot.

Caring for the skin properly helps the skin to perform these functions efficiently.

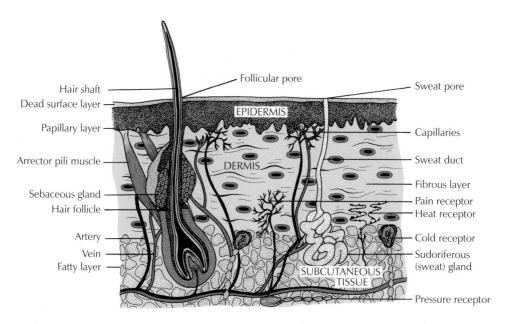

▲ The structure of the skin

 Practical example

Feeling ill at nursery

Leroy is 3 years old and comes to the nursery on 3 days each week while his parents are working. He has been coming to nursery for 2 months now and has settled in happily. He is very sociable and loves to play with the other children. Leroy came into nursery this morning and was his usual bright cheerful self. As the morning went on Sandra, the worker in charge of his group noticed that he was sitting alone looking miserable. She tried to involve him in the activities, but he was reluctant to join in and became tearful. When Sandra went to comfort him, she noticed he was hot and decided to take his temperature. Leroy's temperature was raised and Sandra noticed that he had a flat, red rash on his face and body.

1 *What should Sandra do now?*

2 *What information should Sandra record?*

Importance of personal hygiene

Practitioners should know how to care for a child and promote the child's understanding of the importance of good personal hygiene. Childcare workers may not have full care of a child and so may be more involved in promoting good hygiene practices with the children and their parents and carers.

Guidelines for good personal hygiene

● Wash the hands and face first thing in the morning.

- Wash hands after going to the toilet and after messy play.
- Wash hands before eating and drinking or helping to prepare food and drink.
- Keep finger nails short by cutting them straight across. This will prevent dirt collecting under the nails.
- A daily bath or shower may be necessary for young children who play outside and become dirty, hot and sweaty. Dry the skin thoroughly, especially between the toes and in the skin creases to prevent soreness and cracking.
- Observe the skin for rashes and soreness.
- Black skin and other dry skin types need moisturising. Putting oil in the bath water and massaging oil or moisturisers into the skin afterwards helps to prevent dryness.
- If a daily bath is not possible, a thorough wash is good enough. Remember to encourage children to wash their bottoms after the face, neck, hands and feet.
- Hair usually needs to be washed two or three times a week; more often if parents wish. Rinse shampoo out thoroughly in clean water. Conditioners may be useful for hair that is difficult to comb.
- Black curly hair may need hair oil applying daily to prevent dryness and hair breakage. Use a wide-toothed comb with rounded ends on the teeth. Take care to comb carefully without pulling.
- All skin types need protecting from the sun. Use a sun block or high-factor sun cream and keep a close eye on the length of time children spend in the sun. Make sure that children wear a sun hat.

Helping children to become independent and to care for themselves will establish important life skills. Older children will need time in the bathroom to be able to care for themselves in private.

Normal development of bowel and bladder control

Babies do not have control over their **bladder** or **bowels** and will just wet or dirty their nappies at any time, often after they have been fed. The ability to control the bladder and bowels so that children become clean and dry will develop as the messages received by the brain that the bladder or bowel is full can be understood. Most children will usually be reliably clean and dry by the age of about 3 years, but the age at which this happens will vary. There does not seem to be any point in rushing this. It is much easier if any 'training' is left until the child is at least 2 years old and is able to understand what is needed.

There are some general guidelines for deciding when a child is ready to be clean and dry. These include the following:

- Wait until the child is ready; they may tell you they do not want to wear a nappy or might be interested in other children using the potty or the toilet.
- The child must be aware of the need to use the toilet or potty and be able to tell that the bowel or bladder is full by recognising the feeling.
- Children must be able to tell their carer, verbally or with actions, that they need to go to the toilet.

How to help children become dry and clean

The following guidelines may help when 'training' children to become clean and dry:

- Be relaxed and give praise for success. As children become successful they

---

Bladder = the bladder is situated in the lower abdomen and stores urine
Bowel = the lower end of the intestines

will be more independent and they will feel pleased about their achievements, increasing their self-esteem. Do not show displeasure or disapproval about 'accidents'; just accept these. Do any cleaning and provide clean clothes without any fuss.

- Provide good role models. Seeing other children without nappies and being clean and dry will help children to understand the process.
- Children need to be given the opportunity to visit the toilet or use the potty regularly. They may need reminding if they are playing.
- Avoid sitting children on the potty for long periods of time.
- Remember that parents may have their own ideas about toileting. It is important that this is discussed so that you can follow a similar routine to the home one.

As children get older they will need to be able to use the lavatory in private. They will also need to recognise that opening the bowels at a regular time each day (preferably first thing in the morning) will allow them to use the lavatory at home, ensuring their privacy. Many older children dislike using the toilets at school, so getting into the habit of going before they leave home will help.

Teeth

Teeth may appear at any time during the first two years of life. It is usually expected that they will begin to appear during the first year. They usually come through in the same order as shown in the illustration, but this may vary. The first 20 teeth are often called the milk teeth, and they will usually be complete by the age of 3 years. From 5 to 6 years, these teeth begin to fall out as the adult (permanent) teeth come through. There are 32 permanent teeth, and the care

they are given in childhood will help them to last a lifetime.

Practical example

Toilet training Terry

Cheryl is a nanny and cares for Terry, who is just 2 years old, while his parents are working. Terry is a happy little boy who is still wearing disposable nappies all the time. Terry's mother is very keen that he should become toilet trained and has asked Cheryl for her advice and help.

1. *How will Cheryl know if Terry is ready to be trained?*

2. *How should she suggest that she and Terry's mother go about this?*

Care of the teeth

Parents should be encouraged to provide a soft toothbrush for a baby to use and become familiar with. Babies should have the opportunity to watch adults and other children clean their teeth. When the first tooth does appear, it should be cleaned gently with a small, soft brush. Parents should ensure that cleaning the teeth becomes a habit: in the morning after breakfast and after the last drink or snack before bed. Cleaning the teeth after meals should be encouraged, but this may not always be possible. Children will need help to clean their teeth for quite a while, as it is important to make sure they do it properly. However, as they grow up children will

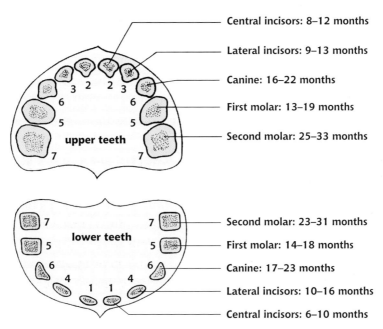

Central incisors: 8–12 months

Lateral incisors: 9–13 months

Canine: 16–22 months

First molar: 13–19 months

Second molar: 25–33 months

upper teeth

Second molar: 23–31 months

First molar: 14–18 months

Canine: 17–23 months

Lateral incisors: 10–16 months

Central incisors: 6–10 months

lower teeth

▲ The first teeth normally come through in this order

become more independent. A two-minute 'egg timer' will help to ensure that they brush for the right length of time.

Encourage healthy teeth and prevent tooth decay by providing a healthy diet that is high in calcium and vitamins and low in sugar. Avoid giving sweet drinks to babies and children, especially in a bottle, as this coats the gums and teeth in sugar and encourages decay. Sugar can also get into the gum and cause decay before the teeth come through. If you need to feed a child between meals, avoid sugary snacks. Provide food that needs to be chewed and improves the health of the gums and teeth, like apples, carrots and bread.

Encourage the parent and child to visit the dentist regularly. A child who attends with an adult, and then has their own appointments, will feel more confident about this. Prepare children for their dental appointments by explaining what will happen and introducing play visits to the dentist. Never pass on any adult feelings of anxiety about the dentist.

▲ Ensure that cleaning the teeth becomes a daily habit

Encouraging independence in hygiene

Children need to be able to learn to keep themselves clean. There are several ways in which carers can encourage a child to develop independence in personal hygiene. Provide a good example yourself.

You should:

- have routines that encourage cleanliness from early babyhood
- make bathtime fun: use toys in the bath, cups and containers, sinkers and floaters
- provide children with their own flannel, toothbrush, hairbrush, etc. that they have chosen themselves
- encourage children to wash themselves and participate at bath time. Let them brush their hair with a soft brush and a comb with rounded teeth
- provide a step so that they can reach the basin to wash and clean teeth
- allow time for the children to complete the tasks without rushing.

▲ Encourage independence in hygiene

Health education

Children need to learn about their bodies and why it is important to be clean and healthy. Children will need help as they carry out personal hygiene routines like bathing, hand washing, teeth cleaning. This gives you time to discuss why these activities are important to keep children healthy and safe from infection. This is also a good opportunity to talk about parts of the body and bodily functions with the children. How much you can talk about will depend on the age and development of the children.

Observation

Supporting children's personal hygiene routines will also give childcare workers opportunities to observe the children for any signs of infection or abuse. Any sign of infection or injury, such as rashes, sore patches, bruising, blood in children's pants or knickers, should be reported promptly to your senior staff member. The accident/incident book should be completed promptly and accurately.

'Accidents'

It is not unusual for small children to wet or soil their pants. They have probably only learned to control their bladder and bowels not long before starting nursery or playgroup. Children will sometimes forget to go to the toilet or wait too long because they are really interested in what they are doing. The important thing is that this is dealt with quickly and without any fuss. Reassure the child and ensure that washing and changing takes place in private.

Preserving a child's or young adult's dignity is very important. If a young child has an accident and needs changing then ensure that you go to the bathroom and shut the door while you make the child clean and comfortable again.

It may be that older children who have a worry will wish to speak to you privately; try to read the signs that this is what is required. If in doubt, ask if they wish to withdraw to a private place.

Be careful when pointing out a child's mistakes, a public 'telling off' is humiliating.

Health and safety

In the bathroom/toilet area

All childcare settings should have a procedure for ensuring health and safety in the toilet/bathroom area. Make sure that:

- children are always supervised and help is given when needed
- the water in the hot tap is not too hot to be used safely
- steps are provided to help children reach the sink
- each child has sufficient time and privacy to use the toilet
- hand washing and drying is done thoroughly
- the area is checked regularly for cleanliness and to ensure that there is a supply of soap and towels or that hand dryers are in working order
- all waste is placed in a bin with a well-fitting lid
- protective clothing for the staff (e.g. aprons, gloves) is available.

Disposing of waste materials

All childcare settings should have a health and safety policy that covers the disposal of hazardous waste. Care must be taken with all bodily waste (blood, faeces, urine, and saliva) to prevent the spread of diseases.

When handling and disposing of waste materials:

- cover any cuts or grazes with a waterproof dressing
- wear disposable latex gloves when dealing with bodily waste
- cover blood with a 1 per cent hypochlorite solution (such as bleach) before wiping up
- wash hands with an antiseptic soap
- dispose of nappies, dressings and used gloves in a sealed bag and place in a sealed bin for disposal
- provide designated areas with covered bins for different types of waste.

Food hygiene

Food must be handled and prepared hygienically to prevent any cross-infection. Follow these guidelines:

- Wash your hands well before touching food.
- Cover any cuts with a waterproof dressing.
- Wear an apron and tie hair back when preparing food.
- Avoid touching your nose and mouth, or coughing and sneezing in the food-preparation area.
- Kitchen cloths and sponges should be disinfected and replaced often.
- Disinfect all work surfaces regularly and especially before preparing food.
- Teach children these food safety rules.

There is more about safe food handling, food and nutrition in Unit 12.

✓ Progress check

(1) Consider why it is important to have emergency procedures. Find out more about these procedures and how they are implemented in your setting.

(2) Find out how your setting manages children who use an inhaler for their asthma.

(3) Who is the trained first aider in your setting? Find out about and evaluate the procedures.

(4) How does your setting inform parents and carers about any accidents involving their child?

(5) Find out about getting first aid training.

(6) What are the rules in your setting that make sure that practitioners and the children handle food safely?

(7) What general and specific signs of illness have you observed in your setting? What action was taken?

(8) What is the policy in your setting for dealing with bodily fluids and waste?

Learning Outcome 3

FOCUS ON...

how to plan and provide an enabling physical environment for children

This links to assessment criteria **3.1**, **3.2** and **3.3**

Children need to have the opportunity to exercise regularly each day. This may be planned exercise, such as physical activities at school or nursery, or naturally occurring opportunities, such as walking to nursery or school.

Current initiatives

Early Years Foundation Stage

Every Child Matters is a major government initiative for children. It has now been become part of the Early Years Foundation Stage (EYFS). Enabling Environments is one of the six key themes of the EYFS. It states that 'The environment plays a key role in supporting and extending children's development and learning.'

The commitments are focused around observation and planning; support for every child; the learning environment; and the wider context – transitions; continuity and multi-agency working.

The Children's Plan

The Department for Children, Schools and Families leads work across the government to ensure that children stay safe and healthy. The Children's Plan (launched in December 2007) is a wide-ranging ten-year strategy for education welfare and play. The plan draws together the government's proposals to improve children's learning and wellbeing by 2020. The wide-ranging plan promises more safe places for children to play – with £225m for upgrading 3,500 playgrounds and the creation of an extra 30 supervised adventure playgrounds.

Getting Serious about Play

In January 2004, 'Getting Serious about Play' a review of children's play opportunities was undertaken by Frank Dobson MP. The formal government response to this was published in January 2005 in *The Children's Play Report*.

Physical Activity Through Childhood

This study by Sport England looked at issues, trends and opportunities for physical activity. Part of the study focused on the early years and school years. These are the study's findings:

- People's attitudes and behaviour with reference to physical activity are often set in early life.

- Tackling health inequalities in childhood is the most cost-effective intervention for reducing health inequalities.

- If we take no action now, it is estimated that a third of girls and a fifth of boys will be obese by 2020.

Reggio Emilia approach

The Reggio Emilia approach is a philosophy focused on pre-school and primary education. The organisation of the physical environment is crucial to Reggio Emilia's approach to early childhood programme and is often referred to as the 'third teacher'.

See also Unit 7.

Forest Education

The Forest Education Initiative aims to increases the understanding and appreciation among young people of the environmental, social and economic potential of trees and woodlands and forests and of the link between trees and everyday wood products.

There may be initiatives in your local area. For example, Nottinghamshire has a pre-school that regularly uses the outdoor area for the whole of some sessions. Additionally, there is a school that encourages children to make their own risk assessments.

Physical development

Physical development is about the growth, development and control of the movement of the body. The physical development of babies and young children should be encouraged through the provision of opportunities for them to be active and interactive. Children should be helped to improve their skills of coordination, manipulation and movement.

Physical development includes two areas:

● gross motor skills: the use of the limbs and the whole body that enables skills such as running, walking and climbing

● fine motor skills: the use of the hands in coordination with the eyes that allows humans to perform very delicate procedures with their fingers such as writing, threading and grasping.

There is more information about this in Unit 2.

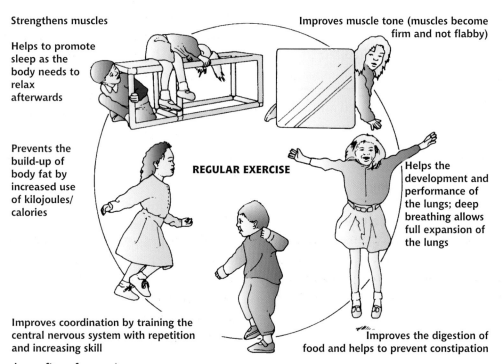

Strengthens muscles

Improves muscle tone (muscles become firm and not flabby)

Helps to promote sleep as the body needs to relax afterwards

Prevents the build-up of body fat by increased use of kilojoules/calories

REGULAR EXERCISE

Helps the development and performance of the lungs; deep breathing allows full expansion of the lungs

Improves coordination by training the central nervous system with repetition and increasing skill

Improves the digestion of food and helps to prevent constipation

▲ The benefits of exercise

Many babies are mobile by the time they reach their first birthday. Babies have no idea of danger and need a watchful adult to ensure their safety until they can anticipate dangers. They need to explore and investigate the world in a safe environment. As the child gets older and their development progresses, they can run easily, sometimes falling, but less often now. Climbing stairs, jumping, riding a tricycle and gradually beginning to use the pedals are among their achievements.

The physical skills learned in the first two years will gradually be perfected and adults need to make sure that children are given opportunities to practise. For example, children move from riding a tricycle by propelling it with the feet, to riding a bicycle without stabilisers, manoeuvring it around obstacles and using the brakes safely. When the child has achieved the basic skills of walking, running and climbing, their future physical development will depend on the opportunities they are given to practise and perfect these skills.

Physical development at nursery and infant school

All childcare settings provide opportunities for physical exercise and activities. It is important that these are planned with the child's age, stage of development and safety in mind.

At nursery, outdoor play with tricycles, prams, trolleys, large building blocks, dens, tyres and climbing frames may create an environment for imaginative physical activity. Using music to encourage movement by using the body to interpret the sounds will improve coordination and balance. Group activities may encourage children who lack confidence.

At infant school, opportunities for exercise could include using the apparatus, dance, music and movement, football, team games, throwing and catching activities, and swimming.

Children will sometimes have separate clothing to wear when doing physical activities. However, during outdoor play at nursery the children will be wearing their own outdoor clothes. It is important to make sure that clothing does not get in the way or make play dangerous. It may be necessary to adjust long skirts or tie up trailing scarves to avoid accidents. Some children may need to keep their limbs and bodies covered for cultural reasons, so it is important to be aware of this and enable the child to take part in activities safely.

Providing for learning outdoors

Being and playing outdoors has a positive impact on the children's wellbeing and helps and influences all aspects of children's development. Being outdoors gives children an opportunity to do things in different ways and on a different scale than when inside; for example, it gives children first-hand experience of the differing seasons and weather. Well-planned outdoor environments should offer children space to run around, freedom to explore, use their senses and be physically active.

Fresh air

All children need regular exposure to fresh air and preferably an opportunity to play outside. The indoor play area should be well ventilated to provide fresh air. Fresh air provides oxygen and helps to prevent infections being spread.

Supporting children's exercise

Children's gross motor skills will be developed through exercise and play.

Physical play on large equipment helps children to develop:

- agility
- coordination
- balance
- confidence.

It allows them to get rid of surplus energy and to make noise. This is particularly important for children who spend a lot of time in smaller spaces. It is also important for children who are learning how to behave in a quiet, controlled indoor environment such as nursery or school.

The equipment provided should give opportunities for children to:

- climb
- slide
- bounce
- swing
- crawl
- move around freely.

Climbing

It can be useful to match the size of equipment to the size of the children. Climbing up is often easier than climbing down – climbing frames with slides attached give children a safe way down.

Safety

- Climbing should always be closely supervised.
- Safety surfaces underneath the equipment are important – mats inside, safety surfaces outside.
- Equipment should be regularly checked for strength of joints, bolts, etc.
- Care should be taken when moving large equipment – you could injure yourself or the children.

Sliding and bouncing

There is a huge range of slides in different materials and sizes. Before buying or using a slide, think about who will be using it and where it will be put.

Bouncing equipment includes trampolines, hoppers, bouncy castles, etc.

▲ Climbing equipment

Safety

- Children need to be taught basic safety rules when using this equipment, for example only one child at a time on the slide or trampoline.

- These activities should be supervised at all times. Children will be excited, which is good, but when they are excited they may need gently reminding about how to use the equipment safely.

Swings

There is a wide range available – what is used or bought needs to be matched to the physical development of the children in the group. Home-made swings are popular with older children, for example a tyre, a piece of wood on a rope, a large knot in a rope.

Safety

- Walking in front of swings is very dangerous. Children need to be taught about this danger and reminded to be careful before playing outside.

Crawling

There are different ways to provide crawling opportunities:

- Rigid concrete tunnels can be installed outside.

- Collapsible plastic tunnels can be used outside and inside.

- Other equipment, such as climbing frames, can be used for crawling through, under and over.

Safety

- Make sure that outside tunnels are kept clean; dogs and cats must be kept out as making a mess can be a problem.

- Ensure that the children know the rules about using the tunnels: for example,

no jumping on to collapsible tunnels or rolling them around the floor.

▲ Tunnels can be used outside

Moving around freely

A variety of bikes, cars, trucks, trikes, carts and trailers will be needed to meet the wide range of children's abilities and needs.

Safety

- Wheeled toys need plenty of space to avoid collisions. It is sensible for these toys to be used in an area set aside for their use.

- Regular maintenance will be necessary.

▲ Wheeled toys need plenty of space

Avoiding stereotyping in physical play

It is important to make sure that all children can use the equipment. The activities provided should be suitable for the range of abilities in the group and be managed by the staff to ensure that all children can join in. Activities should not be taken over by children who are physically very able. It may, therefore, be necessary to limit time on popular toys or at popular activities to make sure that everyone can have a go.

Adults should challenge any stereotyping linked to physical play; comments such as 'Girls can't run fast' or 'Cars are for boys' are unacceptable. These comments are likely to limit what children will try to do or play with. All children will then not have an equal opportunity to develop good physical skills.

Adults must also be aware of their own language and attitudes when supervising physical play. Comments or worries about whether certain children, for example girls or children with special educational needs, are capable of boisterous physical play are likely to limit their physical play. Similar comments or a negative attitude towards less physically capable boys is not acceptable.

Manipulative play

Manipulative play involves children using their hands. They need to develop both fine manipulative and gross motor skills:

- fine manipulative skills – using and developing finger control, using the pincer grip (from about 12 months)
- gross motor skills – using large movements alongside the fine movements, for example pushing pieces of a construction set together to join them.

Children need a lot of practice to develop these skills. The range of activities and experiences offered should enable children to work at different levels and provide opportunity for increasingly effective use of tools and equipment.

Activities should provide opportunities for practising and refining these skills at all levels. For example, within a group of children there may be some who cannot yet build a tower of bricks, while others may be building complex structures. Any activity will need to provide an opportunity for practice whilst also providing an appropriate level of challenge.

Activities for developing manipulative skills include:

- threading
- jigsaws and puzzles
- large and small construction
- mark making
- painting
- using malleable materials such as clay and dough
- dressing and undressing (dolls and themselves).

Equipment

It is important to choose materials and activities that are appropriate for the stage of development of the children. If the activities are too difficult the children will become frustrated and discouraged, but too simple and they will quickly become disinterested. Remember, for manipulative play, the smaller the hands the bigger the pieces need to be!

Practical example

Outside play at the nursery

Staff had noticed that a number of children were reluctant to go outside to play. They decided to observe the play over a week to see how they could improve provision, so all children could take part happily in outdoor play. Each day, a member of staff was given time to observe the play outside and to record what they saw. At the next staff meeting the childcare workers were informed of the results of these observations. The staff had observed that a small group of boisterous children were taking over the space. They enjoyed playing on the bikes and would use the whole of the playground area in their game. This meant that the other children played at the edges of the playground and would sometimes be anxious about crossing the playground. Also, the boisterous children used the bikes all the time. They were the first children outside and raced to get to the bikes. Other children didn't get a chance to play on the bikes.

The staff discussed how they could improve the outdoor play. They decided to create areas in the playground for different activities. Their plans included:

● marking out a section of the playground for the bikes with chalk-marked roads and junctions
● sometimes selecting the quieter children to go on the bikes first
● creating an area with hoops, skipping ropes, juggling balls and stilts
● creating an area with large construction activities
● creating a pretend play area
● looking into acquiring or buying small benches and tables for table-top activities.

The staff's observations and the changes that they made ensured that all the children were able to participate in all activities. It meant that all children had an equal opportunity to develop the necessary skills and concepts. The boisterous children became involved in a wider range of activities and the other children were able to use the bikes and to play outside happily.

① *Why did the staff decide to observe the outdoor play before making changes?*

② *Why was it important to allow the quieter children sometimes to go on the bikes first?*

③ *Why was it important to have a range of boisterous and quieter activities planned for outdoors?*

Guidelines when providing manipulative play materials

- Make sure that there is enough equipment for all the children to participate successfully.
- Ensure that you provide activities that are challenging and accessible to all children in the group, including those with special needs.
- Think carefully about where the equipment is placed – table tops or carpet according to the type of play; this will mean that all children will be able to participate.
- Make sure that you provide sufficient challenge in the activities for the range of abilities in the group.
- Store equipment separately in labelled boxes. This will ensure that equipment is not lost and that children can quickly and easily put equipment away.
- Monitor all equipment regularly for hygiene, safety and completeness.
- Think about how children can record some of their work; ideas could include drawings, photographs or video recording, written instructions or descriptions.

Suitable materials and activities for different age groups

Under 12 months

Activities such as rattles, activity centres and mats. Safe everyday objects will also provide sensory stimulation. Babies will explore these through sucking, banging, rubbing, poking and dropping.

1 to 2 years

Suitable activities include:

- simple cups/shapes that fit inside one another
- simple posting boxes

- building blocks
- interlocking bricks – larger, simpler versions of construction equipment
- large crayons or pencils to experiment with mark marking.

2 to 3 years

Simple construction kits e.g. Duplo, Sticklebrix, etc. are popular now. (But remember safety – children of this age may still put things in their mouths and small pieces can be dangerous.)

3 to 5 years

Provide equipment such as:

- train sets, farms garages, etc.
- construction toys such as Meccano and tool sets
- miniature play equipment (small-world play) such as Playmobil, dinosaurs
- jigsaw puzzles – match level of difficulty to child's ability.

GOOD PRACTICE

As part of their ongoing observation and assessment of children, staff in the nursery noticed that the children in the group needed to work on their fine motor skills. The staff decided to work towards doing some sewing on fabric with each child. They planned a series of activities, linked to sewing, to develop the children's manipulative skills and their hand–eye coordination. Over a term, alongside all the other activities, the children were encouraged to:

- play with lacing boards and tiles
- thread beads, cotton reels and buttons
- play with peg boards
- do some weaving
- complete simple sewing boards, with laces and bodkin needles
- finally, when the staff felt that they were likely to succeed, each child was introduced to sewing on fabric.

Children with disabilities

When caring for children with disabilities, it is important to remember that every child is an individual with specific needs. Some children may not achieve the level of physical ability expected for their age group, so they may need an individual programme that will help them to progress at their own pace. They may spend longer at each stage of development before moving on to the next. Special/individual needs should be viewed positively and each achievement should be encouraged and praised.

Rest and sleep

Many children now have very busy lives and their days are filled with activity. However, although children will be able to join in with stimulating activities for a period of time, they must be allowed to rest. Whether the rest periods involve sleeping, or just more restful and less demanding, quieter activities will depend on the age and stage of development of the child. It may also be important to take into account the parents' wishes, especially where daytime sleeping is concerned. Remember that many young children who have a daytime sleep also tend to sleep better at night. Childcare workers should always provide opportunities for rest and/or sleep as part of the routine of the day.

Restful activities

Restful activities should be planned and a suitable area chosen where the children can relax. Quiet activities could include:

- story time in a suitable area perhaps in a curtained-off area of a bigger nursery or playgroup with some soft cushions to sit on
- a quiet time to look at books

- quiet conversation
- listening to suitable music in a quiet area
- play with small-world toys in a quiet area.

Children do not have to be stimulated all the time; it is sometimes useful for them to be given toys or activities that are relaxing and relatively easy to do.

Sleep routines

We all need sleep but everyone has different requirements. Children will require different amounts of sleep, depending on their age and stage of development, and the amount of exercise taken.

Babies and toddlers need varying amounts of sleep. Some babies may just sleep and feed for the first few months, while others sleep very little. Some toddlers will need a nap morning and afternoon; others might need just one of these or neither.

Some children wake often at night, even after settling late. There is little that can be done apart from following a sensible routine:

- Be patient.
- Plan a sensible 'winding down' bedtime routine and stick to it.
- Don't stimulate the child just before bedtime.
- Encourage daily exercise.
- Reduce stress or worries.
- Ensure that the bedroom is comfortable and quiet.
- Avoid loud noises.

Daytime sleeping

Younger children may need a daytime sleep. It is very important to discuss this with the child's parents so that you are following their home routine and their wishes. If children are sleeping at nursery, it is important to provide a safe place for them to sleep. Cots, mats or beanbags may be provided. If children do not have their own cot to sleep in then any sheets and covers should be changed for each child. The room should be properly ventilated and the temperature controlled so that the children do not become over-heated. Dimming the lights will also help to provide a restful environment. Children should always be supervised when they are sleeping so a member of staff should be with them all the time.

To prevent cot deaths, current research recommends that all babies should sleep:

- on their backs
- without a pillow
- with feet against the bottom of the cot
- using sheets and blankets not a duvet
- in a room temperature of 18 °C/68 °F.

There is more information about practical routines related to babies in Unit 18.

✔ Progress check

1. Evaluate some of the current initiatives influencing early years practice.
2. Look at the outdoor provision in your setting. What aspects of the children's physical development does it promote?
3. How does your setting ensure that the outside environment is safe for the children?
4. Study the long-term planning for your setting. How will the progression of the children's physical development be ensured?
5. Consider the daily plan of activities in your setting. How does it provide a balance of activity with rest and/or sleep?
6. What support is provided for practioners in your setting?

Learning Outcome (4)

FOCUS ON...
how to develop age-appropriate routines which
encourage children to care for themselves

This links to assessment criteria **4.1** and **4.2**

The emotional environment

All those who use the setting help to create the ethos or atmosphere of the learning environment. Children will take their lead from the adults who take part in the running of the environment and caring for the children. Other adults who come into the environment, such as parents, carers and other professionals, will also make their contribution. Therefore it is up to the adults, and particularly the trained childcare workers, to create a warm and accepting emotional environment. To do this the adults have to be capable of empathising with the children and supporting their emotions. This applies to all childcare environments, whatever the age group of the children/young adults.

When children feel confident in the environment they will be more willing to try things out and 'have a go', knowing that the effort they make is valued. In the same way, when children know their feelings are accepted they will be willing to learn to express them, confident in the belief that the adults will respond and help them with how they are feeling. The effective practitioner will understand that some children may need extra support in order to express their feelings and to come to terms with them.

Effective practice in encouraging children to care for themselves

It is important for children to learn to care for themselves and to contribute to do other daily tasks in the setting. Workers should encourage children to help plan the layout of the environment and to keep it tidy and attractive. This will assist in encouraging children to take part in different activities. Young children like to help, but only if they can see that their contribution is a valid one and not just paying 'lip service' to helping.

Adults often think it is quicker to do things themselves – especially if they are busy. However, it is important to resist this urge and make time for children to help; gradually children will become more skilful. You should make time to support the children's understanding of how exercise, eating, sleeping and habits of personal hygiene promote good health. Allow babies and children to do the things they can manage; help them with the things they can't manage without taking over. It is important that practitioners demonstrate clear and consistent boundaries and are reasonable with expectations. It is equally important that children realise that boundaries are set for the protection and comfort of everyone in the setting and understand the reasons why they may not do something. Listen to what children tell you and learn to recognise the non-verbal signals.

Helping children to manage for themselves

It is often helpful to break down a task into different parts, for example getting ready to put on a coat to go outside. A small child may be able to recognise their coat and bring it but may need some help with the fastenings. With cooperation the task can be accomplished together and the child will feel that they have made a valid contribution and will eventually move on to complete the task with little or no help as the skills of independence are learned. Many of the essential care routines can be tackled in this way, such as:

- hand washing
- brushing and combing the hair
- eating
- drinking
- teeth cleaning
- going to the toilet.

Impact on practitioners of meeting the care needs of children

In most childcare settings practitioners will work with colleagues as part of a team. A good team will work well and provide the best possible environment for the children in their care. Working as a qualified childcare practitioner is hard work physically and will also make demands upon you emotionally. You may also be privy to certain sensitive information that is extremely confidential. All this may contribute to a feeling of pressure and worry at work – it may even spill over into your personal life.

A good team will support its members and it may be that this is all that is required. However, there should be clear lines of communication to follow if an individual team member needs more support. It is often the case that settings will put aside time for individual team members to meet with another, more senior, member of the team as a matter of course to discuss issues. This is often called a personal development review. This is usually a two-way process and will often focus on a practitioner's professional development. In this case, you will know whom to approach in the first instance. If there are no clear lines of communication then it is best to approach a senior member of staff.

It could be that your setting will provide other professional help, such as counselling, if required.

▲ A personal development review

✓ Progress check

① Explain the importance of creating an enabling care environment.

② What do you see as your role in fostering children's independence?

③ Investigate what support is given to practitioners in your setting.

④ What advice would you give to a colleague who seemed stressed?

 Weblinks

- www.ncb.org.uk
  Founded in 1963, NCB is a charitable organisation that acts as an umbrella body for organisations working with children and young people, aiming to improve their lives

- www.everychildmatters.gov.uk
  For information about the Every Child Matters framework and extensive links to a range of relevant issues

- www.dcsf.gov.uk
  The Department for Children, Schools and Families leads work across government to ensure that all children and young people:
  - stay healthy and safe
  - secure an excellent education and the highest possible standards of achievement
  - enjoy their childhood
  - make a positive contribution to society and the economy
  - have lives full of opportunity, free from the effects of poverty

- www.culture.gov.uk
  The Department for Culture, Media and Sport has information on children in sport and outdoor leisure activities

- www.foresteducation.org
  The Forest Education Initiative provides learning resources about trees, forests and forest products

- www.reggioemiliaapproach.net
  The Italian Reggio Emilia approach is a philosophy focused on pre-school and primary education

- www.hse.gov.uk
  Information on health and safety advice and legislation

- www.thinkroadsafety.gov.uk
  Road safety website with information on the latest campaigns and road safety advice

- www.hedgehogs.gov.uk
  Road safety website for children with quizzes, games and information on cycling, walking and using the roads and outdoor spaces safely

unit 5

The principles underpinning the role of the practitioner working with children

This unit will help you to develop your knowledge and understanding about the underpinning principles of the role of the practitioner in working with children. These principles shape and support everything that you do. All those working with children recognise that good relationships between all parties – practitioners, other professionals, children and parents – are very important and benefit everyone. This unit looks at maintaining professional relationships with children and adults and understanding current national and local initiatives that influence childcare practice. In addition to this, it will consider the skills of reflective practice and show you how to improve your own learning and performance.

Learning Outcomes

In this unit you will learn about:

1. how to maintain professional relationships with children and adults

2. the skills needed to become a reflective practitioner

3. differing principles and practices that underpin working with children of different ages

4. current national and local initiatives and issues relevant to the sector.

Learning Outcome 1

FOCUS ON...
how to maintain professional relationships with children and adults

This links to assessment criteria **1.1** and **1.2**

Role and responsibilities

The role of the professional childcare worker involves the following commitments:

- putting the needs and rights of children and their families first
- respecting the choices and freedoms of others
- respecting the principles of confidentiality
- demonstrating responsibility, reliability and accountability
- being willing to plan, do, record and review
- working in partnership with parents and carers
- commitment to continued professional development and training.

Putting children first

Within your role you will need to meet the individual needs of the children, irrespective of your personal preferences or prejudices. This will involve recognising the value and dignity of every human being, irrespective of their social and economic group, ethnic origin, gender, marital status, religion or disability. This is particularly important with young children who may be unable to understand or express their own needs and rights.

Working with young children may give you a deep sense of satisfaction, but remember that children are not there to provide this for you; you are there to provide for their needs.

In order to function effectively within any organisation, to ensure that you do your best for the children and their families, you need to be aware of the roles, responsibilities, reliability and accountability – including line management. Effective organisations have clear principles and expectations and these are communicated to everyone within the organisation.

Maintaining professional relationships

In order to maintain positive relationships, it is important to have an understanding of group dynamics and the contributions that all members of the team can make.

Working in groups

It is expected that groups of people within any childcare organisation will have a common core of aspirations and expectations. Clearly the principles and values of the sector will also contribute to this.

The following are some of the many other factors which contribute to and can change the dynamic of any group.

- Clarity of roles and responsibilities – is everyone clear about what is expected of them? Do they know who to ask if they are unsure? Do they function within their role? Do roles overlap? Is there confusion and a lack of clarity?

- Levels of knowledge and experience – do people feel valued? Are they willing and able to share their skills and knowledge? Do they do this in a positive way? Are they learning and contributing to the learning and development of others?

- Aspirations and expectations – does the group have a common purpose? Are there shared goals and targets? Is everyone making a positive contribution? Is there progress?

- Openness – is there a culture of confidence within the group? Do people feel safe and able to contribute without concern? Do people feel respected and valued?

- Communication – are there clear methods of communication in place? Does the group function effectively? Can others engage in group activities easily? Are there processes in place to check back on agreed tasks and activities?

- Collaboration and willingness to share – are people working collaboratively rather than following the direction of a hierarchy? Can colleagues share their thoughts and ideas?

- Leadership and management styles – are leaders and managers effective? Is there a positive culture within the organisation? Are the leaders and managers supportive? Do they get the best out of people?

- Willingness to change and develop – is the organisation flexible? Does it adapt and embrace change or is change a threat?

▲ **Many factors contribute to effective group dynamics**

GOOD PRACTICE · · · · · · ·

In order for any relationship to be maintained, all parties need to play their part and make a positive contribution.

 Have a go!

Look at the list of factors that affect group dynamics and apply it to a working relationship that you have. Is it a positive relationship? If you think that it is, can you list some reasons why? If you feel that it is not, consider the reasons for this.

Working as part of a team

In the work setting, childcare workers usually work with colleagues as part of a team. This may be a multi-professional team, with representatives from a number of other professional groups and organisations; for example, teachers, social workers, area special educational needs coordinators, educational psychologists.

Lone workers such as nannies and childminders may consider themselves as part of a team with the child's family.

Advantages of teamwork

These are potential advantages:

- Individual staff weaknesses are balanced by other people's strengths.
- Members stimulate, motivate, encourage and support one another.
- The skills of all members are used to arrive at the best solutions.
- A more consistent approach to the task of caring for children and their families is possible.
- Individual staff feel a sense of belonging and can share problems, difficulties and successes.
- Responsibility as well as insight is shared.
- Individuals often become willing to adopt new ways of thinking and working.
- Team membership satisfies a need to belong and be respected, and have ideals and aims that are confirmed and shared by others.
- Children and their families see benefits of people working together and cooperating with each other.

Leadership and management

Organisations benefit and develop if teams are well led and effectively managed. Styles of management can vary from one organisation to another and it has to be said that this can be quite challenging from the perspective of the employee. We can get very used to the way that an organisation operates and, when we move to another setting, we may need to adapt and learn to understand the management style in place.

Leaders should be able to motivate and influence the practice and behaviour of others. You may experience a range of leadership styles:

- A leader who tells others what to do, rewards good performance but penalises or applies sanctions to poor performance and maintains formal and strict control of the team would be employing an *autocratic style*.
- A group where communication is good and everyone's contributions are recognised and where members contribute to and shape the decisions of the 'leader' would be employing a *democratic style*.

There are advantages and disadvantages to both styles and some of these have been listed in the opposite table.

Lines of management and reporting

In order to function effectively within an organisation you need to be aware of the people who work there, their role, responsibilities and accountability including their line management. You need to be clear about your own role, responsibilities and accountability.

Responsibility, reliability and accountability

Showing responsibility and accountability involves doing willingly what you have been asked to do, if this is in your area of responsibility. You may need to write down instructions to make sure that you are able to follow them accurately. You can then carry out the tasks to the required standard, and in the allocated time, making sure that you are aware of the policies and procedures of the workplace.

▼ Different leadership styles

STYLE	ADVANTAGES	DISADVANTAGES
Autocratic	Clarity – everyone knows what is expected of them	Limits the development of the employee
	Good time management	Stifles creativity and initiative
	Clear and quick decision-making	Team is reliant on leader and therefore may not achieve if the leader is not there
Democratic	Contented team	May limit achievement and attainment
	Recognition of potential and contributions	Flexible approach may isolate members of the team who would benefit for clarity and direction
	Group ownership of targets facilitates achievement	

You may need to ask your line manager or someone in a supervisory role if you do not understand what to do, or if you think the task is not your responsibility. It is possible that you may even need to refuse to do some tasks until you have been shown how to do them by a senior member of staff who has been appropriately trained. Taking this course of action may be difficult; however, it shows that you understand your responsibilities and that you are accountable for your actions.

If you have any suggestions for changing things, make them to the appropriate person rather than grumbling or gossiping with others. As already mentioned in this unit, open communication is an essential factor when maintaining professional relationships. It is important to contribute to the development of the organisation and essential that this is done in a positive and professional manner with the best interests of the children, their families and the organisation in mind.

Principles of confidentiality

Sensitive information concerning the children and families should be given to you only if you need it in order to effectively meet the needs of the child and family concerned. It should not be given or received to satisfy your own curiosity or to make you feel superior or in control.

GOOD PRACTICE

Although the principles of confidentiality may be easy to understand, the practice can be complex and will require self-control and commitment to the welfare of children and their families. Principles of confidentiality also apply to information about colleagues and the organisation. Consider this when you next engage in a conversation.

Practical example

Hazel and Becky

Hazel and Becky work for a company which owns a group of nurseries. Hazel works in 'Happy Feet' and Becky in 'Tapping Toes'. Hazel helped Becky to get her job and they are friends outside work.

On Tuesday they went out for the evening and chatted about work. Hazel told Becky that one of the children from her nursery would be moving across to Becky's setting because there had been a row between the mother and the manager of Happy Feet. Hazel said that the row had been about the child's father and that the staff had all been talking about how 'friendly' he was with the manager. She said that the child's father had given the manager a lift home on many occasions. Hazel also said that the staff make a special effort to give the child lots of attention on the days when his dad is collecting him.

Becky was delighted with this 'gem of gossip' as she called it; she couldn't wait to get back to the setting the next day and spread the word. Hazel asked her not to as she realised she should not have mentioned it. She said that, as Becky was her friend, she trusted her not to say anything. However, Hazel also mentioned that the family used to have an au pair, but she had left at short notice and the child had increased his sessions at nursery.

(1) *How do you feel about the conversation Hazel and Becky had?*

(2) *Do you think their actions are in the best interests of the child and their family?*

(3) *What effect will the information that Becky intends to share with her colleagues have on their relationships with the child and their family when they join the setting?*

(4) *What effect could it have on the other children and their families?*

(5) *What advice would you give Hazel and Becky about confidentiality?*

Participating in team meetings and groups

Within the work setting there will be many groups meeting formally and informally: staff team meetings, groups of parents/carers, children and other professionals.

Groups can work very effectively by:

- stimulating new ideas (for example, through thoughtstorming)
- managing projects
- making decisions
- monitoring and reviewing progress
- supporting group members.

Behaviour and characteristics of teams

Positive behaviour

Examples include:

- initiating – starting and keeping things going
- informing – volunteering information, ideas, facts, feelings views or opinions
- clarifying, summarising or paraphrasing – helping the group to sort things out, bring things together or round things off
- confronting – an important function if groups are to be effective, but requiring some skill and concern for the feelings of others
- harmonising – working to reconcile disagreements, to relieve tension, and helping to explore differences
- encouraging
- compromising – admitting an error or modifying a view or position
- time-keeping – ensuring the group keeps to time.

Negative behaviour

Examples include:

- behaving aggressively – attacking others, belittling their contribution or putting them down
- blocking – preventing the group from getting on with the task
- dominating – interrupting, asserting authority or interfering with the rights of others to participate
- avoiding – preventing the group from facing the issue
- withdrawing – displaying a lack of involvement.

▲ Displaying a lack of involvement has a negative effect on the team

Effective, well-led teams will be involved in a range of interactions with each other, parents and carers and other professionals, as already stated; these interactions may be formal and informal.

GOOD PRACTICE

Any formal activity such as meetings and reviews will follow an agenda and be recorded in the minutes of the meeting. This contributes to the professional practice of the organisation and to maintaining positive relationships. This is because the agenda maintains the purpose and the focus of the interaction and the minutes provide a written record of what happened and what is expected of the attendees before the group reconvenes.

Working in partnership with parents

Clearly all aspects of this unit contribute to your professional practice and relationships, including your relationships with children, their parents and carers. Professionals recognise the importance of partnership with parents or carers. To carry out your duties in a professional way, you will need to show that you understand the importance of working with parents and carers, respecting their views and wishes, and recognising that, in many instances, they are the ones who know their own children best. In order to do this it is essential to understand and value individual children's cultural background and take account of their **customs**, **values** and **spiritual beliefs**.

If you have any religious or cultural issues which may affect your work or professional relationships, you will need to discuss them with your line manager. An example might be if you are unwilling to work on particular days because of your religious practices.

Communication skills

Effective communication is at the heart of good working practice. There are many ways in which we communicate at work, through conversations, discussions and presentations. These may involve colleagues, managers, children, parents and carers, other professionals and people in the wider working community. Communication can be direct or face to face, over the telephone, by fax, letter or e-mail. Whatever form the communication takes, when you are caring for children, what you say and how it is interpreted or understood can have a serious impact on the wellbeing of the children, the organisation and also on yourself.

Communication includes the following areas:

- taking part in discussions
- producing written material
- face-to-face communication.

Childcare workers need to be able to listen carefully and speak clearly. In any discussion it is helpful to:

- keep to the subject
- express yourself clearly
- keep the discussion moving forward.

Discussions take many forms:

- informal conversations with colleagues
- formal meetings
- planned presentations
- telephone conversations.

Producing written material

The benefit of written communication is that the opportunity for misunderstanding may be reduced and accurate records are kept. Information can also be shared between several people when direct contact is not possible. Once something is written down, however, it is more difficult to amend. Written information must be accurate, legible, easy to understand and in a suitable format. Correct spelling, grammar and punctuation are essential as your document will be read by other people such as parents or other professionals. Make sure that you ask a colleague to take time to read what you have written and that you make the necessary changes before submitting or circulating the document.

Customs = the way of life, the language and the behaviour that are followed by particular groups of people

Values = beliefs that certain things are important and to be valued, for example a person's right to their own belongings

Spiritual beliefs = what a person believes about the non-material world

There are many circumstances in which written material may be necessary. You may have to complete a child's records, send a letter to parents, produce a report for your manager, apply for a job, complete a survey or questionnaire, or send an e-mail to express an interest in a training activity. Spelling, grammar and punctuation should always be checked to ensure accuracy.

Face-to-face communication

Whenever you communicate face to face with someone else, whether this is an adult or child, parent or professional, it is important to consider how you are communicating with them. Remember that communication is not just about what you say – it is how you say it.

GOOD PRACTICE

When you write and send an e-mail you should also consider how it will be received. Remember, the reader cannot judge your mood, intention or tone; similarly you cannot affect how the reader reacts or interprets your e-mail. Also, you have no assurances that the content of your message will only be viewed by the recipient. The same consideration should be taken into account if you are sending a fax, particularly if the fax contains sensitive or confidential information. It is good practice to check with a supervisor or senior colleague.

▼ Aspects of communication skills

YOUR ACTION	INTERPRETATION
Eye contact	Take care not to stare or be overbearing
Interrupting the speaker	You are not listening; you do not value their point of view or opinion
Do you sit/stand/crouch to the level of the other person?	Positioning yourself at a higher level can be dominating. Children may not realise that you are communicating with them if you are not prepared to put yourself at the same level in order to gain eye contact; your listener will benefit from seeing your facial expressions too
Personal space	If you are too close you may be crowding/unnerving the listener, too distant you may be showing a lack of interest
Using jargon, acronyms, sector-specific language	You may be isolating the listener – you may be causing them to feel anxious, confused or inferior
Do you speak quickly?	You are in a hurry and the interaction is not important to you
You speak with your hands	Your gestures are distracting and confusing – your listener may have stopped listening!
Do you ask for the opinion/ view of the listener?	You are concerned and interested – your listener feels valued and respected
Your tone of voice – too loud, aggressive, passive or difficult to hear	Your listener may be overwhelmed, feel that you are taking the issue too seriously or not taking it seriously

Have a go!

● Use the table on page 207 to consider your own communication skills. This is not a definitive list but some points to think about.

● Once you have read the information, think about a time when you have communicated effectively. What made it positive? In contrast think of a negative experience – what made it negative?

✓ Progress check

(1) What makes a good team? Try to write your own motivational team phrase. Begin with:

'We are a great team because we ...'

(2) Using the advice supplied in this section about effective communication, write and review the following piece of written communication. Highlight the points that are unclear and then rewrite the information so that it is clear for the reader.

> Dear Parents
>
> On Friday we will be having a QA visit from the local EYDCP. The purpose of their visit is to look at all aspects of the nursery and to check our understanding and preparation for the new EYFS. Morag will not be here as she will be visiting Happy Grove to look at the SALT provision for the children there. If you need to speak to Morag, you can leave a message for her.
>
> Many thanks
>
> The Team

Learning Outcome ②

What does the term 'reflective practitioner' mean?

To progress in your career you will need to find ways to develop and extend your skills, knowledge and understanding. You will also need to identify what you enjoy doing and what you prefer not to do; you will need to know and understand your own strengths and weaknesses. You will need to reflect. A **reflective practitioner** learns from their own experiences, is self-aware, and adopts the practice of critical analysis.

Reflection is not always something that we find easy. It may help you to develop if you:

- think about what you have done
- review and consider your actions
- plan ahead.

Reflection and evaluation

Help and feedback from others is also very important as this will enable you to get a clear and balanced picture of your practice. However, before asking for feedback, it will help if you have already taken the time to reflect upon what you do well and on the things that you feel you do not do well. We all find it difficult to evaluate our own performance and

practice. To evaluate means to try to understand how good or bad we are at something, the factors which have affected or influenced our practice and what our strengths and weaknesses are.

To work out your strengths and weaknesses, to reflect upon and evaluate your professional performance and to improve your skills, you must:

- take responsibility
- identify your needs
- be objective
- be realistic
- move forward in your development, learning and professional practice
- ask for and accept feedback.

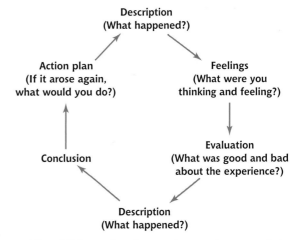

▲ The Gibbs reflective cycle can be a useful evaluation tool (Gibbs, 1998)

Reflective practitioner = a worker who thinks about what they have done/said with a view to improving practice

Solving problems

You will encounter a range of different problems at work. The way that you choose to solve the problem will depend greatly on what the problem is, who is involved and the impact that the problem has or will have on others.

There are many ways to interpret and solve problems and there are a range of models to support and enable you to do this.

Firstly, consider that solving problems involves working through a process. You will need to be objective and able to set goals and targets.

When faced with a problem it is important to use skills of *analysis*. You need to be objective as you are aiming to be part of the solution – not part of the problem.

You will need to ensure that you have gathered all of the information that you need to be able to tackle the issue – this uses skills of *investigation* and *interpretation*.

Next you will need to decide on the appropriate course of action in order to solve the problem.

Once there is a satisfactory *outcome*, as a reflective practitioner you now need to evaluate your actions and decide on a course of action for the future.

 Have a go!

Consider the problem in the next example and apply a problem-solving strategy. Alternatively, consider a real problem you have experienced and use the process. Did you solve your problem?

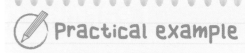 **Practical example**

Lunchtime problems

Maria is a nursery leader; the setting she manages has 52 places for children between the ages of 3 months and 5 years. During the staff appraisal process, a few of the room leaders told her that there were issues with lateness of staff returning from lunch breaks and this was impacting on the care of the children and the afternoon activities. Maria was surprised that this was the first time she had been made aware of this problem, but she assured the room leaders that she would look into the problem and endeavour to reach a satisfactory solution. One of the room leaders did suggest that sometimes the lunch was late and that this had an impact on the staff breaks.

(1) *Consider how you would advise Maria to approach this situation and solve the staff lunch break problem at her setting.*

Improving your own learning and performance

We all have strengths and weaknesses, and to improve our own learning and performance it is important to that we can identify them. Setting targets and reviewing progress will help you to focus more clearly on what you need to do. Improving your own learning and performance includes feedback and appraisal.

Appraisal

Appraisal is often used in the world of work as a vehicle to enable staff to improve and develop within their role and the wider professional community.

The system and format and terminology may vary. A basic appraisal structure is outlined below:

1 An appointment for your appraisal should be made.

2 There will be an opportunity for you to reflect upon and evaluate your own performance and practice prior to the meeting – you might be given a pro-forma to complete.

3 At the meeting, your practice and performance will be reviewed.

4 There will be an opportunity to discuss development and training.

5 Action points and target(s) will be set and a timescale agreed.

6 A record of the meeting and outcomes will be kept on file and reviewed (you should also be given a copy).

▲ Feedback should enable the individual to develop

Receiving feedback

It is important that feedback is constructive and that the development of the individual remains the focus of the discussion. Good supervisors will be effective in facilitating the process and enabling the individual to accept any feedback as positive to their development.

It is therefore very important that the individual is prepared to listen to feedback and is able, through prior reflection, to move forward in their practice.

Identifying targets

You should be able to identify your strengths and weaknesses and provide evidence to support what you say. You will also need to be able to help in setting short-term targets for your own improvement, in conjunction with your teacher, assessor or workplace supervisor. When targets have been set, make sure that you understand what is required of you.

Be SMART!

In order to ensure that you set yourself appropriate targets, that you are able to meet to the satisfaction of all concerned, try to apply the SMART model to any target setting that you do.

In order to ensure targets are SMART check to make sure that the targets are:

Specific
Measurable
Achievable
Relevant
Time-bound.

You can use this approach when setting targets as part of a team and also when you are aiming to achieve a personal goal or study target.

Practical example

Juan and Louisa

Juan had a meeting with his manager and he was asked to develop the imaginative activities provided in his room. His supervisor asked him to come back to her at the end of the month to feedback on his progress.

Louisa has been on holiday and has returned to college to discover that she has an assignment deadline looming. She meets with her tutor to decide on a way to achieve this. Louisa and her tutor agree that they will meet at 2pm every Wednesday for the next three weeks. At the first meeting, Louisa must present a plan for the assignment; at the second meeting she must bring her draft, and at the third she needs to present the final version.

1 Has Juan agreed to a SMART target?

2 Has Louisa agreed to SMART targets?

Timing

Once your targets for improvement have been agreed, you should be able to follow them without close supervision, within the specified timescale. You will, of course, receive support in your work and you should know how to put this support to good use in improving your work and meeting your targets.

✔ Progress check

1 What are the characteristics of a reflective practitioner?

2 Consider your own developmental needs. Write three SMART targets that will support you and enable you to meet your objectives.

Learning Outcome 3

FOCUS ON...
differing principles and practices that underpin working with children of different ages

This links to assessment criteria **3.2**

Principles and values

All settings and childcare workers should be clear about and work in line with the desired **principles** and values. The Early Years Foundation Stage encompasses the Birth to Three Matters Framework, Curriculum Guidance for the Foundation Stage and the National Standards for Under 8s Day care and Childminding. KEEP (Key Elements in Effective Practice) are the principles and values which relate to the EYFS commitment cards, Principles in Practice. KEEP is for local authority staff to use in their work with all government-funded settings.

What are the key elements in effective practice?

Effective practice in the early years requires committed, enthusiastic and reflective practitioners with a breadth of knowledge, skills and understanding.

Effective practitioners use their own learning to improve their work with young children and their families in ways which are sensitive, positive and non-judgemental.

Therefore, through initial and ongoing training and development, practitioners need to develop, demonstrate and continuously improve their:

- relationships with both children and adults
- understanding of the individual and diverse ways that children develop and learn
- knowledge and understanding in order to actively support and extend children's learning in and across all areas and aspects of learning
- practice in meeting all children's needs, learning styles and interests
- work with parents, carers and the wider community
- work with other professionals within and beyond the setting.

(From *Key Elements in Effective Practice* www.standards.dcsf.gov.uk)

CACHE statement of values

You must ensure that you:

1 Put children first by:
   - ensuring the child's welfare and safety
   - showing compassion and sensitivity
   - respecting the child as an individual
   - upholding the child's rights and dignity
   - enabling the child to achieve their full learning potential.

2 Never use physical punishment.

Principles = basic truths, which underpin activities

3 Respect the parent as the primary carer and educator of the child.

4 Respect the contribution and expertise of staff in the care and education field, and other professionals with whom they may be involved.

5 Respect the customs, values and spiritual beliefs of the child and their family.

6 Uphold the Council's Equality of Opportunity Policy.

7 Honour the confidentiality of information relating to the child and their family, unless its disclosure is required by law or is in the best interests of the child.

(From www.cache.org.uk)

Child-centred versus adult-led practice

This links to assessment criteria 3.1.

Studies of the way that children learn, and research by Piaget in particular, indicate that concepts are best understood through actual experiences: in effect, that children learn by doing. These theories have had a significant influence on the way that we organise our provision. Such research has led to an approach to learning that takes into account the child's individual learning capabilities and interests and which holds that learning is achieved through experience. Piaget's work provides a rationale for play as an appropriate medium for young children's learning, because it provides appropriate opportunities for children to develop understanding through first-hand experiences.

Child-centred practice ensures that the focus is on outcomes for children, where children's wellbeing and interests are at the centre of practice, where children are recognised as individuals and where children are encouraged to reach their full potential.

Child-centred practice can be advantageous to both adults and children. It means that adults gain extensive knowledge about the child and their interests and preferences, therefore enabling adults to work more effectively with the child. The result of this is that children build strong relationships with those around them. Children also benefit from increased self-confidence and self-esteem as they are able to instigate their own learning, share their thoughts and ideas.

In contrast, adult-led practice is planned and initiated by the adult. There will always be some aspects of the provision in which adults will need to take the lead, for example story activities, cooking and outings. Adult-led practice provides purposeful activities which meet the requirements of the curriculum whilst providing opportunities for observation and monitoring of children's learning and development. However, practitioners are encouraged to balance adult-led and child-initiated activity. This approach is a skill, as we need to be flexible and ensure that we are embracing all aspects of the child's involvement in the activity.

▲ Child-centred practice can be advantageous for both children and adults

Child-centred = with the child at the centre, taking into account the perspective of the child

▲ Adult-led practice is planned and initiated by the adult

Practical example

The red treasure hunt

A member of staff has planned an outdoor treasure hunt for some of the children. The staff member has hidden a range of red items for the children to locate and has made a large map of the outdoor space as a guide. He talks to the children before they go outside and, when they are all ready, they go out to the garden.

One of the children spots a red car in the car park and calls out to the staff member. He gets no response and runs over to the gate to see if there are any more red vehicles; the postman has arrived on his red bicycle. The member of staff calls the child back to the group as he wants to get on with the treasure hunt.

1 *How do you feel about the scenario; do you think there was room for adult-led and child-initiated learning here?*

2 *What could the member of staff have done differently to capture the learning and follow the treasure hunt activity?*

GOOD PRACTICE ·······

Clearly there are benefits to both approaches and there is a need for balance and a thoughtful approach to practice. Within any setting, it is very important to ensure that your approaches to children are enabling and empowering, that you use a vocabulary which encourages children to express themselves and will extend their learning.

Providing an environment for children that facilitates independence in learning

If we consider everything that has already been covered in this chapter, then we should be ready to explore the issues relating to the provision of environments that facilitate **independence** in learning.

Independence is a key issue in relation to children's learning and development. Childcare workers should ensure that the environments that are provided reflect the needs of the children and provide opportunities for challenge. A positive environment is not just about the physical provision, i.e. the furniture, layout and equipment: the people who work there are crucially important to fulfilling the needs of the children. Environments where staff have a sound knowledge of children's development, understand children and are aware of how children learn will be able to facilitate children's independence in learning.

There is not a definitive list which captures all aspects of provision in such environments; but listed below are some key points and suggestions.

An environment that facilitates independence in children's learning does so by:

- providing interesting and challenging activities, experiences and extended learning environments – both indoors and out

- ensuring that children are enabled and supported to be active learners

- enabling children to explore, investigate, discover and solve problems

- encouraging children to express their thoughts and ideas

- ensuring that the adults are enthusiastic supporters and facilitators of children's learning

- encouraging adults to affirm and value children's previous experiences, knowledge and interests and to promote extension and expansion of learning

- embracing all learning opportunities

- encouraging adults to reflect on their practice and to develop their skills.

▲ Child-accessible resources help to facilitate children's learning

Valuing children's interests and experiences

⊂⊃ This links to assessment criteria **3.1**.

Professional childcare practitioners and workplaces aim for all children to be included, feel valued and to make a positive contribution. Working in partnership with parents enables staff to draw on the child's interests and experiences when away from the setting. Open communication and positive relationships are essential to this partnership. Such an approach will also enhance relationships with parents and extend the learning and experiences of the child whilst they are at the setting. Workers are then in an informed position and this enables them to further engage children in conversations, provide for the child's preferences and facilitate activities and experiences for the child.

✓ **Progress check**

(1) What are the differences between child-initiated and adult-led activity? What are the benefits of each approach?

(2) How can practitioners ensure that they value the interests and experiences of individual children?

Learning Outcome 4

FOCUS ON...

current national and local initiatives and issues relevant to the sector

 This links to assessment criteria **4.1** and **4.2**

You will be aware that there have been extensive developments in the childcare and education sector – both nationally and locally – in recent years. For ease of presentation, these have been presented in the form of reference tables.

 Further information can be found in Unit 1 of this book.

Research and literature

Professional literature can be accessed in a variety of ways and can be used for the purpose of analysis and research. Journals, articles and other publications as well as websites can be used to support your professional development through research. Individuals can sign up for

▼ National initiatives in childcare and education

NATIONALLY	KEY POINT	PURPOSE OF INITIATIVE	WHERE CAN I FIND MORE INFORMATION?
The Children's Workforce Strategy (2006)	Common core of skills and knowledge for the children's workforce	In time, everyone working with children and young people will be able to demonstrate a basic level of competence in the six areas of the common core. Common core will form part of qualifications	Children's Workforce Development Council (CWDC) www.cwdc.org.uk
The Common Assessment Framework for Children and Young People (CAF)	A shared assessment tool which will be used across all children's services in England	To help early identification of need and promote coordinated provision for children and young people A common recording structure to record and share information between practitioners	Children's Workforce Development Council (CWDC) www.cwdc.org.uk

▼ Local initiatives in childcare and education

LOCALLY	KEY POINTS	WHERE CAN I FIND MORE INFORMATION?
Sure Start	Local authorities must publish plans on early years and childcare and work with the early years development and childcare partnership (EYDCP) Ensure nursery provision for 3- and 4-year-olds Support providers by giving advice and information Children's information service Provide an annual review of childcare in the area	Sure Start www.surestart.gov.uk Individual local authority
Positive Activities for Young People	Part of the Every Child Matters: Change for Children strategy aimed at 8–19-year-olds at risk of social exclusion and crime	www.everychildmatters. gov.uk
Children's Trusts	A partnership framework aiming to achieve better outcomes for children	www.everychildmatters. gov.uk
Youth Matters (2005)	Sets out proposals to improve outcomes for young people aged 13 to 19 years, including having more to do in their local area, opportunities to volunteer, information advice and guidance about issues that are important to them	www.everychildmatters. gov.uk
Community activities	Within every local community there are a variety of initiatives and activities in support of the needs of children and young people Some examples include voluntary groups and organisations	Look in your local directories, library or search local websites

electronic alerts when new research is published; this is an effective way of ensuring that you are up to date with initiatives and sector-specific issues.

How you access such information is entirely up to you; what you do with this information will depend upon your professional development needs and study requirements.

The following are key points to consider:

● Take time to think about what you want to find out as this will influence your approach and the literature that you read. You should have clear intentions and any reading you do should in turn support, dispel and or modify your concerns.

- It is important to keep a record and where possible, copies of what you read, as you may choose to review these documents in the future or share them with others.

- Ensure that quotes and references are recorded in the accepted format; make sure that you apply electronic referencing protocol. Noting down page numbers will help as this enables you to refer back to specific sections of reading which influenced your research.

- Ensure that you read a broad range of publications in relation to your subject.

- Employ a critical and analytical approach; authors may only view a subject or issue from a single viewpoint and it is acceptable to disagree

✓ Progress check

1. Find out about and list childcare practice initiatives across all providers in your local area.

2. What are the key points to remember when preparing to undertake research?

 weblinks

- www.cache.org.uk
  Information on CACHE and its standards

- www.standards.dcsf.gov.uk
  The Department for Children, Schools and Families has information on all government initiatives

- www.everychildmatters.gov.uk
  For information relating to the Every Child Matters framework

- www.cwdc.org.uk
  Provides up-to-date information about issues relating to the sector including research

- www.surestart.org.uk
  Information about Sure Start initiatives and projects

Unit 6

Promoting a healthy environment for children

Promoting healthy environments for children is also about choices and making appropriate decisions. Within any setting, there are policies and procedures in place to support practitioners to ensure that a healthy environment is provided. Environments are checked for safety and suitability which in turn promotes the health and wellbeing of children. Other aspects that contribute to a healthy environment include security practices and positive role models. Healthy environments mean that children are valued and supported through close positive relationships with informed and caring adults. However, beyond the setting, practitioners have no control over the home environments of children. Some children are not living in healthy environments; they may be living in poor housing which puts their health at risk, unsafe environments or environments where the lifestyles of adults expose children to a range of risks.

Learning Outcomes

In this unit you will learn about:

1. the principles underpinning the rights of children to a healthy lifestyle and environment

2. the factors that affect the health of children

3. how to plan and implement routines and activities for children.

Learning Outcome ①

FOCUS ON...
the principles underpinning the rights of children to a healthy lifestyle and environment

This links to assessment criteria **1.1** and **1.2**

Introduction
Defining health

Health is a difficult concept to define because it means different things to different people. Some may consider themselves to be healthy because they do not smoke; others because they have not been ill recently. Being healthy involves more than the physical condition and may include being fit, not being ill and living to a very old age.

The World Health Organization (WHO) defines health as 'a state of complete physical mental and social well-being and not merely the absence of disease or infirmity'. This definition recognises that there are three aspects to health – physical, mental and social – that will affect overall health. However, this definition has been criticised as being too idealistic as it makes healthy status out of the reach of a large proportion of the world's population. Poverty or disability may affect health, but need not imply that poor health is inevitable.

The World Health Organization also states that 'The enjoyment of the highest attainable standard of health is one of the fundamental rights of every human being without distinction of race, religion, political belief, economic or social condition.'

One of the main issues in health is the person's capacity to make their own choices. The choices are based on:

- traditions of the cultural group
- the family
- self-awareness
- knowledge.

Adults make choices for themselves and their children. Examples include when to wean their babies, which foods to give their children, whether to immunise and raising awareness of safety. It is important that choices made by parents and childcare workers should be informed choices. The Department of Health and health professionals seek to inform the population in the UK so that they can make their own informed choices.

Health education

The main objective of health education is to improve the general health of the population. It enables people to take responsibility for their own and their children's health by:

- changing behaviour or attitudes
- providing knowledge and raising awareness
- empowering people to choose their own lifestyle and to be aware of the implications of their choices

- promoting the interest of a particular group
- meeting local and national targets in health, e.g. promotion of self-examination to detect breast cancer.

Legislation and initiatives

Every Child Matters

Every Child Matters is the government's vision for children's services and was published in September 2003. It proposed reshaping children's services to help achieve the outcomes children and young people said were key to wellbeing in childhood and later life.

The table on page 232 gives details of the five outcomes. They are part of the Every Child Matters: Change for Children Outcomes Framework used by children's services inspectorates to shape the criteria for Joint Area Views of local areas.

The UN Convention on the Rights of the Child

Children's rights are most fully described in the United Nations Convention on the Rights of the Child. Created over a period of ten years, with the input of representatives from different societies, religions and culture, the Convention was adopted as an international human rights treaty in 1989.

It came into force in September 1990 and contains a comprehensive array of rights, bringing together civil and political, economic, social and cultural rights, as well as humanitarian rights, for the first time in one international instrument. Overall, the convention serves as a landmark in the promotion of the **rights of children**, placing them alongside other population groups whose rights necessitate protection by way of an international treaty.

It is based on the belief that all children are born with fundamental freedoms and the inherent rights of all human beings. This is the basic premise of the Convention on the Rights of the Child: an international human rights treaty that is transforming the lives of children and their families around the globe. People in every country and of every culture and religion are working to ensure that each of the two billion children in the world enjoys

- the rights of survival
- health and education
- a caring family environment
- play and culture
- protection from exploitation and abuse of all kinds
- freedom to have their voice heard and opinions taken into account on significant issues.

Drugs and alcohol

There are laws in place to protect children and young people from the use and effects of drugs and alcohol. So it is illegal to give alcohol to children under 5 years old; children aged 14 and under cannot go to the bar in a public house unless the pub has permission by way of a condition on the licence which permits children to access areas of the pub, and a children's certificate is required. Children under 18 may not buy alcohol from licensed premises.

Under the Misuse of Drugs Act 1971, illegal drugs are categorised in three classes:

- Class A such as heroin, cocaine and crack cocaine
- Class B such as amphetamines
- Class C such as steroids and cannabis.

It is illegal to possess, import and cultivate, possess with intent to supply and to supply drugs.

Rights of children = the expectations that all children should have regarding how they are treated within their families and in society

▼ Every Child Matters: Change for Children Outcomes Framework

OUTCOMES	AIMS
Be Healthy	Physically healthy Mentally and emotionally healthy Sexually healthy Healthy lifestyles Choose not to take illegal drugs Parents, carers and families promote healthy choices
Stay Safe	Safe from maltreatment, neglect, violence and sexual exploitation Safe from accidental injury and death Safe from bullying and discrimination Safe from crime and anti-social behaviour in and out of school Have security, stability and are cared for Parents/carers and families provide safe homes and stability
Enjoy and Achieve	Ready for school Attend and enjoy school Achieve stretching national educational standards at primary school Achieve personal and social development and enjoy recreation Achieve stretching national educational standards at secondary school Parents, carers and families support learning
Make a Positive Contribution	Engage in decision-making and support the community and environment Engage in law-abiding and positive behaviour in and out of school Develop positive relationships and choose not to bully and discriminate Develop self-confidence and successfully deal with significant life changes and challenges Develop enterprising behaviour Parents, carers and families promote positive behaviour
Achieve Economic Well-being	Engage in further education, employment or training on leaving school Ready for employment Live in decent homes in sustainable communities Access to transport and material goods Live in households free from low income Parents, carers and families are supported to be economically active

(From *Every Child Matters: Change for Children in Schools*, DfES/1089/2004)

Smoking

Children under the age of 18 years are not permitted to buy cigarettes in England, Scotland and Wales. Selling cigarettes to children could mean that shop owners could lose their licence. Smoking has also been banned in enclosed public places and a requirement of this ban is that every public building must display a sign stating that it is illegal to smoke.

▲ 'No smoking' sign

Statutory provision

 You will find more information about health services in Unit 1.

Child health surveillance

Child health surveillance is a system of reviewing a child's progress. These reviews are carried out at certain ages in a child's life. Programmes with regular reviews at fixed ages are intended to safeguard children and stop them from 'slipping through the net', especially when families move home frequently and change doctors and health visitors. In many areas of the UK the child health record is held by the main

carer of the child in the form of a book. Parents and professionals contribute to the record. Professionals include:

- health visitors
- family doctors
- child health clinic staff
- hospital emergency staff
- school health team
- outpatients staff
- dentists.

In this way, the information can be shared and is easily available to all those caring for the child. Parents and carers have an ongoing record to which they can refer.

Principles of child health surveillance

There are certain principles that underpin the effective use of a child health surveillance programme. Child health surveillance should be:

- carried out in partnership with the parents and carers – they are the experts and the best people to identify health, developmental and behavioural problems in their own children
- a positive experience for parents and carers
- a learning experience for the parents and carers, the child and the health professional – it should involve exchanging information
- an opportunity to provide guidance on child health topics and health promotion
- a continuous and flexible process – as well as fixed assessment there should be opportunities for other reviews as required by each child

- carried out by observation and talking with the parents or carers; tests and examinations should complement the process
- based on good communication and teamwork.

Most child health surveillance is carried out in the child's own home or at the child health clinic. Clinics are held in health centres, GP surgeries or other local convenient places such as children's centres, community centres or village halls. The professionals most concerned with child health surveillance are health visitors and doctors. Health visitors are trained nurses who undertake further training in midwifery and health visiting. Each professional is responsible for part of the child health surveillance programme; they work as a team with the parents and carers. The general practitioner and health visitor are part of the **primary health care team** and are involved with **primary health care**.

School health service

The school health service carries out a range of services and activities for children. These include:

- routine tests for vision and hearing
- school nurses – measure height and weight
  - support and advise on health conditions
  - administer immunisations
  - support and advise parents and may provide health promotion workshops
  - liaise with school doctors.
- speech and language therapist

▲ Child health surveillance is often carried out at school

- school doctor
- providing parents with health and wellbeing questionnaires.

Health promotion and education

Campaigns and initiatives which affect and promote the health and wellbeing of children and young people include the following:

- *Birth to Five* – a guide distributed to all new mothers in England which explores parenting and the first five years of life
- School Fruit and Vegetable Scheme – this is part of the '5-a-day' campaign whereby all children aged 4 to 6 years in LEA schools and special schools are entitled to a piece of fruit or vegetable in school
- 'Water is Cool in School' – improving access to and consumption of fresh water during the school day

---

Primary health care team = professionals who are concerned with the delivery of the first-line health care and health promotion

Primary health care = first-line health care and health promotion

- 'Sun aware' and care initiatives are promoted in school, often through skin cancer awareness programmes; children are reminded to cover up and use sun care products
- drug awareness, smoking cessation and sexual health are also supported in school through curriculum activities, guest speakers and road shows.

▲ Learning about the harmful effects of the sun is very important for young children

Parent and carer events are also promoted to encourage participation and further promotion of the health of children and young people. Obviously where issues and subject matter are age and preference specific, permission is sought from parents and carers. For example, when sex education is part of the curriculum, the school nurse may be involved and parents are informed in advance. They are asked if they give permission for their child to participate in lessons; communication of concerns or questions is encouraged and in some settings an information session may be offered. This is another example of partnership.

✔ Progress check

(1) Find out about current national and local initiatives and campaigns which promote drug, alcohol and smoking awareness.

(2) How can you contribute to planning a sun awareness activity for young children? Make a list of ideas.

Learning Outcome ②

FOCUS ON...
the factors that affect the health of children

This links to assessment criteria **2.1**, **2.2** and **2.3**

The growth and development of children and young people can be affected by a range of factors; these include:

- social disadvantage and poverty
- diet and nutrition
- infection
- housing
- accidents
- illness
- emotional and social factors
- lifestyle
- environmental issues.

Social pressures and disadvantages

Personal and social pressures and problems

All adults are likely to face some kind of difficulty, problem or pressure in their lifetime. If they are parents, their children will probably be affected in some way by the experience.

Some problems can be referred to more accurately as 'personal', others as 'social'. The source of personal problems lies very close to the circumstances of the individual person's life. Examples include difficulties with or loss of relationships, bereavement, mental and physical ill health. Other problems are usually referred to as 'social' when their source is mainly in the way the social and physical environment is organised. Examples of 'social problems' are urban decay, housing or rural decline, racial and social discrimination, poverty, unemployment, poor housing and homelessness. Many families are multiply disadvantaged and the term 'social exclusion' is used to describe this disadvantage.

There are often close links between personal and social problems; the experience of social problems often causes personal problems. For example, the experience of long-term poverty can cause stress, anxiety and feelings of uselessness; social problems can then lead to anxiety, depression and ill health or domestic violence, drug or alcohol misuse.

Sources of social disadvantage and pressure

People can be described as disadvantaged if they do not have an equal opportunity to achieve what other people in society regard as 'the norm'. This may be because they are experiencing poverty, unemployment, inadequate housing, homelessness, racial discrimination, an impoverished environment, are sick or disabled or are lone parents.

Poverty

Lack of money and the long-term experience of poverty is often experienced as a major problem for families. A family is considered to be living in poverty if their income is less than half the national average weekly wage. This is called the poverty line.

Poverty is now usually described as being relative in the UK. This means that people are considered to be poor 'if their resources fall seriously short of the resources commanded by the average individual or family in the community' (Peter Townsend, *Poverty in the United Kingdom*, 1979). In past centuries in the UK there were many people living in absolute poverty, that is, they did not have 'enough provision to maintain their health and working efficiency' (Seebohm Rowntree, *Studies of Poverty in the City of York*, 1899).

Causes of poverty

The main causes of poverty are low wages or living on state or social security benefits. The people who are most likely to be poor are those who are:

- unemployed
- members of lone parent families
- members of minority groups
- sick or incapacitated
- elderly
- low paid
- poorly educated.

Effects of poverty on the family

Poverty can affect every area of a family's life. There may not be enough money for a nutritious varied diet, adequate housing, transport, household equipment, leisure activities or toys. It can cause stress, anxiety, unhappiness and lead to poor physical and mental health. People are limited in their ability to go out, to entertain others and to have outings or holidays. Family relationships can become strained.

Nowadays people are very aware through the media – especially television – that others have a much higher standard of living. All of this can result in a feeling of hopelessness and of being outside (excluded from) the mainstream society.

Some sociologists refer to people living in extreme and continuous poverty as the 'underclass' – a group of people who feel they have no hope of improving their situation. The Social Exclusion Unit works at the centre of government to bring those who are marginalised and socially excluded back into society.

Many people experience the **poverty trap** if they are receiving state benefits. They find that, by earning a small additional amount, they lose most of their benefits and become worse off. They are trapped in their position. This is of great concern to the government, which now aims to get people out of this trap through welfare reforms that enable people to keep more of any increase in earnings they achieve.

'Poverty can have a profound impact on the child, their family, and the rest of society. It often sets in motion a deepening spiral of social exclusion, creating problems in education, employment, mental and physical health and social interaction.' (From www.endchildpoverty.org.uk)

Poverty trap = situation experienced by people if they are receiving state benefits and they find that, by earning small amounts more, they lose most of their benefits and become worse off

Family health and lifestyle

Nutrition

In infancy, milk is the food that babies need. Breast milk is the best thing for babies but some mothers prefer to bottle feed. Guidelines for safe sterilisation, preparation and feeding of formula milk must be adhered to in order to prevent illness or infection. Breastfeeding mothers who wish to store expressed breast milk also need to ensure that they do so in a safe manner. Health visitors are able to advise parents about feeding issues and concerns about feeding babies.

A balanced diet involves an intake of food that provides the nutrients the body needs in the right quantities. Research has shown that food is one of the first items that people cut back on when they are short of money. This can have a serious effect on the nutritional health of families managing on a low income.

There may be other problems that contribute to this. Cooking facilities may be limited, or impossible if, for example, the family live in bed and breakfast accommodation and much of the family diet has to be brought in ready cooked. Fuel costs for cooking will also be an important consideration if money is tight. Shopping around for food to get the best bargain or selection may not be possible if bus fares are needed or food has to be carried a long way. Many supermarkets with the widest range of groceries and the best prices are only accessible to those with their own transport and the money to take advantage of special multi-buy offers.

In these circumstances, knowing about food and the nutrients that are essential to provide an adequate diet is very important. Help needs to be concentrated on achieving an adequate diet within the budget and ability of the family. Knowing which cheaper foods contain the essential nutrients will enable sensible advice to be offered.

Alongside the provision of a healthy diet is the need for food safety and hygiene. Food is essential to good health and survival but has to be stored correctly to avoid contamination with harmful bacteria that could cause food poisoning. Once food has been purchased, it needs to be stored and prepared safely. Children are particularly vulnerable to infection, so it is important that food is prepared and handled safely. It is also important for children to learn about basic food hygiene and how to handle food safely. Food safety education and guidance is often available through the media as well as local authorities and food suppliers such as supermarkets.

See also Unit 12.

Preconceptual care

Preconception is the term used to describe the time between a couple deciding they would like to have a baby and when the baby is conceived. For the first few weeks of the pregnancy a woman may not realise that conception and implantation has taken place. This is a time when future parents can make sure they are in the best of health so that their child has the best chance of growing and developing.

Preconceptual care also means that future parents take steps to reduce the known risks before conception. Known risks include:

- drugs – any substance taken for its effect on the working of the body is a drug. Alcohol is a drug; so is nicotine, which is present in tobacco: these and medicines prescribed by a doctor or purchased

Preconception = the time between a couple deciding they want to have a baby and when the baby is conceived

over the counter without a prescription, or drugs acquired illegally, may all cross the placenta and affect the **foetus**

- smoking – it is much better for both parents to stop smoking before conception takes place. Smoking can lead to higher risk of miscarriage, premature birth, low birth weight, stillbirth, sudden infant death syndrome (SIDS). It can also affect the male sperm, causing problems with conception

- alcohol – evidence suggests that moderate and high levels of alcohol consumption during pregnancy affect foetal growth and development. Excessive alcohol consumption in men can cause infertility and abnormalities in the sperm

- medicines – only medicines prescribed by a doctor should be taken and only after a doctor has confirmed that they do not damage the foetus

- illegal drugs – all drugs are potentially dangerous substances. They are not only dangerous for a woman to take but could risk the life of a baby

- use of substances – inhalation of fumes from aerosols and glue.

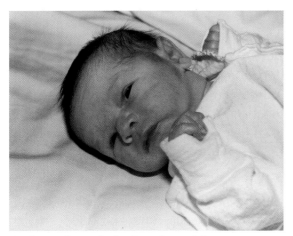

▲ A newborn baby is vulnerable to many outside influences

Clearly, further engagement in the lifestyle choices explained above is going to have an ongoing effect on babies, children and young people. Exposure to drugs, smoking and alcohol will all have a negative effect on children's health and wellbeing in the long term.

Drug and substance use

Children with parents who use drugs may be affected through emotional and physical neglect; exposure to substances such as aerosols, glue, drugs and drug paraphernalia can put children at risk. As a consequence of drug or substance misuse, parents may not be able to meet the needs of the child and this may result in children being at risk of harm. Drug or substance misuse may also be associated with factors such as deprivation, poverty, debt and criminal activity. Although it is important not to generalise, there are a number of risks to the health and wellbeing of children when parents use drugs. These risks include:

- living conditions – the living environment may pose health and wellbeing risks as children may be in contact with a range of unfamiliar adults; the drugs themselves may be accessible; children may be left unattended, not get regular meals and may be exposed to inappropriate adult behaviour as a result of the adult taking drugs

- parental behaviour – this may be unpredictable as a result of the use of drugs; children may be exposed to unpredictable behaviour and the behaviour of adults withdrawing or craving drugs

- poor parenting – sometimes the use of drugs is associated with a lack of parenting skills. This can affect children in a number of ways: physical and

Foetus = term used to describe the baby from the eighth week after conception until birth emotional neglect, not meeting basic care needs of children, higher risks of accidents and injuries due to lack of care or supervision. The effects of this can be varied and may include poor nutrition, failure to thrive, poor relationships, lack of attachment, social stigma and social exclusion.

Children of all ages can be affected in different ways. Very young children and babies may lack stimulation; children at school may feel isolated as they become aware of the difference between their own lifestyles and those of others; older children may become 'carers' in environments where the adults in the parental role are reliant on substances and neglect to meet their own needs and the needs of their children.

Passive smoking

Exposure to cigarette smoke can pose risks to the health and wellbeing of children, including heightened risk of:

- chest infections
- asthma
- colds and coughs
- loss of sense of smell
- low birth weight
- cot death
- absence from school due to ill health.

Health professionals and government advice suggest that parents who choose to smoke should do so away from children – preferably outside the house.

National campaigns to support smokers in giving up are well publicised and supported through local health authorities, schools and workplaces. Further information can be found through local 'stop smoking' services/groups.

Infections and diseases

Children have illnesses and infections that are passed very easily from one child to another.

Disease is a condition that arises when something goes wrong with the normal working of the body. As a result the child becomes ill. Signs that a child is ill and has a disease or infection include:

- raised temperature
- headache
- sore throat
- rashes on the skin
- diarrhoea.

Other possible signs include: crying, being irritable, behaviour that is unusual for the child. Possible signs of illness can be more worrying and significant in a baby or very young child.

Organisms that cause disease are called **pathogens**. The most important pathogens are bacteria, viruses and some fungi. The everyday name for pathogens is germs. Pathogens get into the body mainly through the mouth and nose, and sometimes through cuts in the skin. Once they are inside the body, they multiply very rapidly. This is called the **incubation period** and it can last for days or weeks, depending on the type of pathogen. Although the person is infected during the incubation period, they only begin to feel ill and have signs of the infection towards the end of the incubation period.

Pathogens work in different ways when they infect the body. Some attack and destroy body cells; others produce poisonous substances in the bloodstream called toxins. The intense activity of the

Pathogens = germs such as bacteria and viruses which cause illness
Incubation period = the time from when pathogens enter the body until the first signs of infection appear

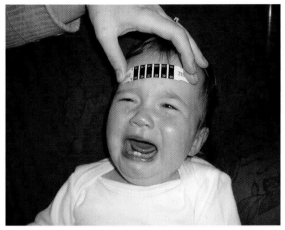

▲ You can spot certain signs and symptoms in a child who is unwell

pathogens produces a lot of heat, so one of the signs of infection by pathogens is that the child's temperature goes up.

How diseases spread

Diseases are spread by:

- droplets of moisture in the air
- touch
- food and water
- animals
- cuts and scratches.

Droplets in the air

When you cough, sneeze, talk and sing, tiny droplets of moisture come out of your nose or mouth. If you have a disease, these droplets will be warming with pathogens. If these infected droplets are breathed in by another person, the disease can be spread to them. Colds (caused by viruses) spread rapidly in this way.

Touch

It is possible to catch some diseases by touching an infected person, or by touching towels or other things used by that person.

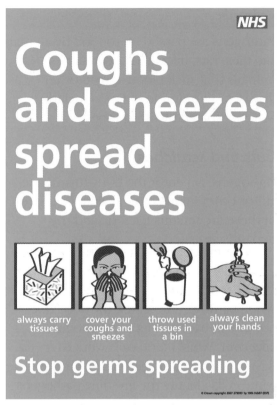

▲ It is true that coughs and sneezes spread diseases

The skin disease impetigo (caused by bacteria) is spread in this way. Another skin disease, athlete's foot (caused by a fungus), can be picked up from the floors of public changing rooms and showers.

Food and water

The urine and faeces of an infected person will contain pathogens. Drinking water may be contaminated if sewage gets into it. Food and drinks can be contaminated if they are prepared or handled by a person with dirty hands, or if the preparation area is dirty. This is why washing hands after visiting the lavatory and before handling food is so important. Food poisoning (caused by bacteria) easily spreads in this way, especially in places where lots of children play and eat together.

Animals

Pathogens are passed on to food by animals like flies, rats, mice and cockroaches. Animals that suck blood spread other diseases; an example of this is malaria, which is spread by mosquitoes.

Cuts and scratches

Pathogens can enter the body through a cut or other injuries to the skin. Examples of these are tetanus bacteria and the hepatitis virus.

Immunity

When pathogens do enter, the body does not just sit back and let the pathogens take over. White blood cells work to try to destroy the invading bacteria or viruses. The white cells identify the invading pathogens as a foreign substance and begin to make **antibodies**. Antibodies make the pathogens clump together so that the white blood cells can destroy them by absorbing them – this process is called **phagocytosis**.

It will take a while for the white cells to make enough antibodies. This may give the pathogen enough time to multiply so that the child shows signs of having the disease. Eventually, however, the white cells make enough antibodies to destroy the pathogens and the child recovers from the illness. If the same pathogen attacks again some time later, the white cells recognise it and can quickly make large quantities of antibody so that the pathogen is destroyed before it has a chance to multiply – **immunity** has been created; the child is now immune to that pathogen and the disease it causes.

Active immunity

One way of becoming immune to a disease is to have a disease and recover from it is. This is called **active immunity**, because the white cells make the antibodies against the pathogens causing the disease. Active immunity is also acquired by having an immunisation with a **vaccine**. Vaccines contain killed or weakened forms of the

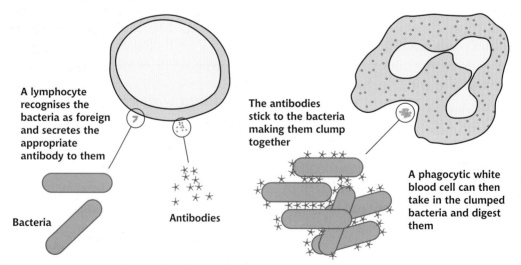

A lymphocyte recognises the bacteria as foreign and secretes the appropriate antibody to them

Bacteria

Antibodies

The antibodies stick to the bacteria making them clump together

A phagocytic white blood cell can then take in the clumped bacteria and digest them

▲ Phagocytosis: how white cells destroy bacteria

Antibodies = made by white cells to attack pathogens
Phagocytosis = process by which white cells absorb pathogens and destroy them
Immunity = the presence of antibodies that protect the body against infectious disease
Active immunity = the body's ability to resist a disease that has been acquired by having the disease or by having a specific immunisation
Vaccine = a preparation used to stimulate the production of antibodies and provide immunity against one or several diseases

pathogens that cause the particular disease. The BCG vaccine for tuberculosis, for example, contains bacteria that have been weakened. When they are injected into the body, they are too weak to multiply; but the white cells can identify them as foreign cells and begin to make antibodies to overcome them. Immunity to the disease is then acquired because the body has learnt to recognise that pathogen and can make the antibody required to combat it.

The immunisation programme

Immunisation (see table on page 236) protects children from serious diseases. It also protects children by preventing diseases from being passed on.

Advice and guidance on immunisation is part of the child health promotion programme. Doctors and health visitors will advise parents or carers about immunisations and discuss any worries they may have about their child.

Effects of problems on child health

Sources of pressure which can have a negative affect on children's development and health include misuse of drugs and alcohol by carers; these areas have already been described in this unit. In addition, there are the problems caused by domestic violence and mental illness, unemployment, housing and homelessness and environmental factors; these are described below.

Domestic violence

This can affect children in many ways and prolonged exposure can affect a child's development in every area, but particularly emotionally and physically. They may become caught up in the violence directed at their parent and emotionally suffer great distress in witnessing this. Their parent's ability to care for them may be profoundly affected by their experiences, particularly where violence is combined with the misuse of drugs or alcohol. Prolonged exposure to parental conflict can have a serious effect on children's wellbeing, even when not combined with physical violence.

Mental illness of the carer

This does not necessarily have an adverse effect, especially if the illness is short term and mild and does not lead to parental conflict. It can, however, have an impact on a child's experiences. Mental and physical illness may restrict a child's activities and may put the child in a caring role at too young an age. In some cases a child's needs may be neglected.

Unemployment

Unemployment rates have always varied. Unemployment was high in the 1980s and since then it has fallen, risen and fallen again. While full employment is unlikely to be achieved, if only half a million unemployed people are registered in Britain at any one time, this is considered very low unemployment. Unemployment has affected every section of the population, but some people are more vulnerable to it than others. These are:

- people without skills or qualifications
- manual workers
- young people and old people
- women
- people who generally suffer discrimination in society – these include people from ethnic minority groups and people who have disabilities, people who have suffered mental illness or have been in prison.

235

▼ The immunisation programme

AGE	VACCINE	METHOD
2 months	● Diphtheria, tetanus, pertussis (whooping cough) (DTP), polio, Hib ● Meningitis C	● One injection ● One injection
3 months	● Diphtheria, tetanus, pertussis (whooping cough) (DTP), polio, Hib ● Meningitis C	● One injection ● One injection
4 months	● Diphtheria, tetanus, pertussis (whooping cough) (DTP), polio, Hib ● Meningitis C	● One injection ● One injection
12–15 months	● Measles, mumps and rubella (MMR)	● One injection
3–5 years (before starting school)	● DTP booster ● MMR booster ● Polio booster	● One injection ● One injection ● By mouth
10–14 years	● Tuberculosis (BCG) for children to be shown at risk after a skin test	● One injection
13–18 years (before leaving school)	● Diphtheria and tetanus booster ● Polio booster	● One injection ● By mouth

Unemployment can have a profound effect on the families and individuals. Those experiencing long-term unemployment are more likely to be living in poverty and suffering the ill effects. They may also have feelings of shame, uselessness, boredom and frustration that can affect their mental and physical health. Family relationships can become strained and provide an unhappy or even violent environment for children. Whole communities can become demoralised and run down.

Inadequate housing

Despite the fact that there has been a massive slum clearance and rebuilding programme since the 1950s, many people still live in accommodation which is damp, overcrowded or unsuitable for children. Some high-rise flats that were built to re-house people in the 1950s and 1960s were very poorly built. They contribute to a wide range of personal and social problems. Some of the accommodation has since been demolished or redesigned, although examples still remain in some urban areas.

Damp, inadequate and dangerous housing can lead to bad health, illness and accidents, the spread of infection and poor hygiene. It is difficult to improve broken-down houses or keep them clean. Adults are likely to feel stressed, may blame each other or feel depressed and worried. This, linked with lack of play space, creates an unsuitable environment for children to grow up in.

Homelessness

There is a national shortage of accommodation at affordable prices. This was a result in part, in the 1980s, of the Conservative government's policy of giving council tenants the right to buy their houses, while not allowing councils to use the money from sales to build more houses. Private owners have been reluctant to rent accommodation to families because legislation makes it difficult subsequently to evict them.

There is a growing number of homeless people; they mainly become homeless when:

- their relatives are unwilling or unable to continue to provide them with accommodation
- they are evicted for mortgage or rent arrears
- their marriage or partnership breaks down.

The local authority has a legal duty to accommodate homeless families but the shortage of accommodation means that an increasing number are placed in bed and breakfast accommodation.

The conditions for families in bed and breakfast hotels are totally unsuitable. The accommodation can often be overcrowded, dangerous and unhygienic. There is usually a lack of cooking facilities, washing and other basic amenities. There is little privacy or play space. People often suffer isolation from family and friends. In addition, their access to education, health and other services is disrupted. Families can spend several years in this type of accommodation. Obviously this type of lifestyle will have a very negative impact on the health of children.

Living in cramped and unsatisfactory conditions for long periods of time can have a very bad effect on the relationships within the family. Parents who experience this degree of stress in their everyday existence may have little energy to provide more than the basic necessities for children. It is often difficult for people to maintain standards of hygiene and the provision of nutritious food can be a problem if there are little or no cooking facilities. The lack of play space can lead to children being under-stimulated and having little access to fresh air and exercise. Every aspect of their development can therefore be affected.

Environmental issues

The urban environment

Many inner-city areas in the UK are characterised by environmental pollution and decay, lack of play space and higher crime rates. They have attracted a lot of publicity in recent years. This has resulted in a number of government-funded and voluntary-funded schemes aimed at improving the environment and the quality of people's lives. The success of these initiatives is varied, partly because of the difficulty of knowing exactly what the problems are.

The UK's inner cities have suffered a loss of population in recent years. Many people have chosen to move from urban centres to the suburbs to have gardens and cleaner air. This was made possible by the development of public and private transport. There has also been a loss of industry and employment opportunities in inner cities, and poor planning has contributed to impersonal environments and decay.

In most cases, therefore, with the exception of some 'sought-after' city-centre areas, people who have material resources choose not to settle in the centre of towns but to live on the outskirts. This leaves a concentration of people in inner cities who have fewer resources, including people experiencing:

- poverty, unemployment and housing stress
- physical and mental illness
- discrimination because of ethnicity or disability
- social isolation, such as being members of one-parent families
- family problems, including violence and abuse.

There are also more people involved in crime, drug abuse and prostitution in inner-city areas. In addition, demands on health and social services tend to be higher, and because of this the quality of these services tends to be poorer.

One way of understanding inner-city problems, therefore, is through the idea of **multiple disadvantage**, which emphasises the fact that urban deprivation is not a single problem, but a number of problems concentrated in one area.

Effects on the family

It is important to remember that an urban environment is not necessarily a negative experience for all residents. There are many people who live happy and fulfilled lives and who rear children successfully in cities and towns. Disadvantage is, however, more common than in suburban areas. The lives of some children and their development may be adversely affected in a variety of ways by living in such an environment.

Rural environmental problems

Much less publicity is given to the problems faced by families living in rural areas. The UK has a proportionally smaller rural population than many European countries. Some people who live in rural areas are supported by a high income and this buys them desirable housing, land and private transport. Others, for example farm workers, have incomes well below the national average. They may suffer from poverty, unemployment and all the effects that this can bring. Housing and transport can be expensive and very difficult to obtain. Their housing may be tied to their job so they could lose both at the same time.

Families living in a rural environment can be subject to similar pressures to those of an urban family if they have low incomes. The lack of public transport, and distance from support and advice services may further exacerbate their experiences.

Diet and exercise

Children are growing and developing all the time, so they need large amounts of protein to help the formation of bone and muscle. They are also using lots of energy, so they need carbohydrate in the form of starches

Multiple disadvantage = the concentration of social problems in one area

that they can use during the day to sustain their activities. In addition, they will need adequate supplies of vitamins and minerals.

Exercise is a necessary and natural part of life for everyone. It is especially important for young children who need to develop and perfect physical skills. All physical exercise strengthens muscles, from a young baby kicking on the floor to a 7-year-old playing football. Encouraging exercise from an early age will lay the foundations for a life-long exercise habit. It is generally believed that children who do not get enough exercise will be at increased risk of heart disease and other health problems in later life.

As with many aspects of children's care and development, positive role models must provide children with positive messages about diet and exercise. The increase in numbers of overweight and obese children has been widely publicised. It is therefore important that professionals support messages of healthy eating and attitudes towards foods, cooking methods and the importance of exercise and a range of physical activities. Children and young people need to be encouraged and empowered to make healthy choices which will benefit them throughout life.

Illness and disability

It is expected that children and young people will experience a range of common minor illnesses throughout their lives. In contrast, some children will suffer from chronic and major illnesses and conditions which are long term and have a huge impact on their life, their family and all-round development.

Long-term effects may include:

- difficulties in learning due to absence from school
- depression
- difficulties in maintaining friendships and relationships if they are unable to spend time with peers.

Children with disabilities are discussed in Unit 14 of this book.

✔ Progress check

1. What is an antibody?
2. Which cells in the body destroy pathogens?
3. What is phagocytosis?
4. How is active immunity acquired?
5. Why is it important for children to be immunised?
6. How can unemployment affect people?
7. Why is it difficult for people to bring children up in bed and breakfast accommodation?
8. What multiple disadvantages can be experienced by people living in inner cities?

FOCUS ON...
how to plan and implement routines and activities for children

This links to assessment criteria **3.1** and **3.2**

Health promotion and education

Daily routines

As already considered in this unit, there are many important factors involved in maintaining children's health and keeping them safe from illness. Childcare workers have an impact on the health of children in their care by providing routines, activities and education that increase adults' and children's awareness of the importance of good health and ways of keeping healthy.

It is important that health topics and activities are part of the planned programme for children. It is often possible to link these successfully with other areas of the curriculum.

Health issues should be part of the daily routines and reminders and explanations about health and hygiene will reinforce healthy life skills. Childcare workers should practise in a way that reinforces and builds on children's self-esteem so that they can feel good about themselves, develop independence and form positive relationships. This will have a positive effect on children's health and wellbeing.

Childcare workers should provide role models. For example, children who see their carers smoke are more likely to go on and smoke themselves.

The childcare setting must be safe. This is a legal requirement. Both staff and children should be aware of safety issues and the implications of their actions. Staff should use every opportunity to raise children's awareness of their own safety and the safety of others.

Routine activities throughout the day can be used to support a healthy lifestyle for children and young people. A balanced routine is a routine which encourages children to eat well, have periods of exercise and to rest and sleep when they need to.

Children and young people require differing amounts of calories and sleep as they grow and develop and these needs should be supported by caring adults. As already stated in this unit, a lack of play and support and the housing/living arrangements of some families will mean that children will not always be able to access and experience the food and activities that we know will benefit their growth and development. Therefore, practitioners should use the activities and experiences provided at their setting to promote wellbeing.

Food and nutrition

Creative planning for menus and cooking activities with children can promote healthy eating experiences and messages. Using

▲ Children need access to outdoor play and activities in order to thrive

simple recipes which encourage children to try a range of fruit and vegetables and to become more adventurous in their food choices can be extremely exciting. These recipes may not necessarily require much cooking and can be easy to prepare.

GOOD PRACTICE

Good role models join children for meals; they are positive about food thereby igniting an enthusiasm for food in the children.

Outdoor play and garden activities

It may help to consider the use of the outdoor space. Some children may not have access to outdoor play space at home. Sometimes the decision to use the outdoor space is shaped by adults and the weather; however, the outdoor environment is, as we know, an invaluable resource for children's development and learning. It is therefore essential that the adults behave in an enthusiastic manner.

GOOD PRACTICE

Accessing and enjoying the outdoor environment is not only about attitudes, but it is also about adults ensuring that they have the appropriate clothing and footwear to enable them to support children out of doors in all weathers!

Once the adults are equipped for outdoor activities, consider how they are engaged in physical activities: what do the children see? If the adults are standing around getting cold, they might choose to go inside when they wish to rather than when the children choose to.

Being positive about exercise

There are concerns that some children and young people do not currently get as much exercise as they should. Part of this issue could be related to the environment where children live; however, there is also the suggestion that children and young people spend too much time watching television, sitting at computers or playing with electronic games. This will have implications for their health and wellbeing in later life.

It is therefore very important that childcare workers have a positive attitude to exercise and that this message is communicated to the children and young people. Engaging children and young people in exercise activities could include arranging team games and training sessions, for example football, netball or basketball.

▲ Splash and dash – exercise can be fun!

GOOD PRACTICE · · · · · · ·

Exercise could also be introduced through activities such as line dancing and aerobics, using music and actions. However, if older children are reluctant to engage in such activities it may be necessary to take a creative approach such as adding an activity floor mat to an electronic game which will encourage the user to exercise their limbs and have fun at the same time.

Sleep and rest

We all need to sleep but everyone has different requirements. The sleep needs of children will depend on their age and stage of development, the amount of exercise taken and also their personal needs.

Sleep is a special kind of rest, which allows the body to recuperate physically and mentally. Social and cultural expectations of children may include letting them stay up later at night. Some children may lack role models that set expectations for bedtime routines and this may impact on learning and interaction. Disturbed sleep could also be the result of parental lifestyles, noise and disturbances or situations where children are living in temporary accommodation. A small child who is attending a day nursery may be able to compensate for a bad night during the day at the setting. However, this is not the case for older children attending school; lack of regular sleep may affect their ability to concentrate during lessons.

✔ Progress check

Consider five new activities that you could introduce that will promote a healthy lifestyle for groups of children aged:

a) 1–3 years

b) 3–5 years

c) 5–9 years

d) 9–11 years.

Weblinks

- www.savethechildren.org.uk
  A charity which works to transform attitudes towards children in the UK and 51 other countries around the world

- www.shelter.org.uk
  A charity which focuses on and campaigns on behalf of homeless people in the UK

- www.cpag.org.uk
  CPAG is the leading charity campaigning for the abolition of child poverty in the UK and for a better deal for low-income families and children

- www.jrf.org.uk
  The website of the Joseph Rowntree Foundation – a social policy and research charity

- www.endchildpoverty.org.uk
  Information on the End Child Poverty charity

- www.ich.ucl.ac.uk
  The website of the Institute for Child Health; this is the combined site of University College London and Great Ormond Street Hospital, forming the International Centre of Excellence in treating sick children, teaching and training

- www.nhsdirect.gov.uk
  For information about illnesses; this website also has interactive health promotion activities

- www.who.int/en/
  The website of the World Health Organization

- www.everychildmatters.gov.uk/strategy/uncrc/articles
  For a summary of the main articles of the United Nations Convention on the Rights of the Child

Unit 7

Play and learning in children's education

In this unit you will learn about the theoretical approaches to play and learning. You will also be introduced to pioneers in the field of play and education and will see how they have impacted on current play and learning provision. This will help to inform your own approach to the planning cycle, including the way in which you provide play and learning experiences for children, and the way in which you observe and assess children's learning.

Learning Outcomes

In this unit you will learn about:

1 the relevant theoretical approaches in the field of play and education

2 how to use appropriate tools to assess the learning needs of individual children

3 how to plan and provide learning opportunities in consultation with others

4 how to record and evaluate the planning and assessment cycle.

Learning Outcome (1)

FOCUS ON...

the relevant theoretical approaches in the field of play and education

This links to assessment criteria **1.1**, **1.2** and **1.3**

Why is play important?

Benefits of play

Playing is great fun for children, and it is also the main way in which young children learn. Play has both long-term and short-term benefits for children. The benefits of play were outlined in *Best Play: What play provision should do for children*, published by the National Playing Field Association in 2000. *Best Play* is referred to again in this unit. You can read the whole document online – see the weblinks for details.

Play provides children with the opportunity to interact with both adults and children, at whatever level is appropriate for them. This helps children gain the social skills they need to get on with others and become part of a group. Children learn and practise a wide range of skills when they are playing: such as how to ride a tricycle, for example. They also make discoveries and learn concepts – at the water tray they may learn that pebbles sink, for instance. The activity, game or experience will finish when children stop playing, but the learning will eventually be remembered. These are all long-term benefits of play, which develop over time. Other long-term benefits gained through play include increasing:

- independence
- self-esteem
- knowledge and understanding
- wellbeing, health and development
- creativity
- capacity to learn.

The short-term benefits of play occur at the time a child is playing. They include the opportunity to:

- enjoy freedom
- have fun
- test boundaries
- explore risk
- exercise choice
- exercise control over their bodies
- exercise control over their actions and emotions.

Social skills and relationships

Play acts as a bridge to social skills and relationships. Young children need to gain skills such as:

- sharing
- taking turns
- cooperating
- making and maintaining friendships
- responding to people in an appropriate way.

Listed below are some play activities and experiences that help children to develop these skills. By grouping children thoughtfully, and through being a good social role model, adults can enhance children's learning about how to behave sociably when they play.

Socialising opportunities include:

- circle games
- rhymes and songs
- packing away time, with all children encouraged to participate
- snack and meal times, with children helping to set up, serve and clear away
- pretend play in pairs or groups
- any activity where there are limited resources that the children need to share, for example painting at easels or playing at water and sand trays
- board games and table-top activities.

▲ Sharing resources develops social skills

The pioneers of play and education

Friedrich Froebel (1782–1852)

The work of Froebel has been the most influential of the 20th century. He opened the very first kindergarten in 1837 (although he did not use the term 'kindergarten' until 1840), and he is often referred to as the 'father of kindergarten'. By the time Froebel died in 1852, 31 kindergartens had been opened in German cities.

Froebel had studied in a training institute under Johann Pestalozzi. His teacher's basic ideals promoted a permissive school atmosphere and a focus on nature. Froebel accepted these but felt a 'spiritual mechanism' was missing. He developed a philosophy of education centring on these four principles:

- *Free self expression*: alongside maths and science, Froebel encouraged children to explore expressive arts (drawing, painting, model making, etc.) and literature (listening to, reading and writing stories). He promoted the idea of exposing children to nature and beautiful objects. He taught his students to value children's ideas and feelings.

- *Creativity*: Froebel encouraged imaginary play for children of all ages. He gave us the idea that children think at their highest level when they are at play, and particularly when they play imaginatively. Froebel said this was shown in children's symbolic play – it occurs when a child uses one object to stand in for another object. For instance, a child may pretend a piece of string is a snake, or that a twig is a pen.

- *Social participation*: Froebel emphasised the importance of children learning to have good relationships with adults, but he thought children's relationships with each other were equally important. He recognised that parents were a child's primary educators and so he welcomed them into his centres, as he believed all schools should do.

- *Motor expression*: Froebel believed children learn as well outside in the garden as they do inside the classroom, and he promoted plenty of time to move around freely outside. He encouraged children to dance and do movements he created. Children at his centres dressed in comfortable clothing that allowed them to move about freely. He did not like the idea of children being restricted.

Froebel developed the idea of two key principles. They are:

- the principle of *Unity*: this says that everything in the world is connected and linked in some way.

- the principle of *Opposition*: this says that while everything is linked to everything else, there are still comparisons and contrasts. Froebel believed experiencing these firsthand helped children to think.

As you will have recognised, many of Froebel's philosophies are still at the heart of integrated play and learning today. Unusually for that time, Froebel's institutes welcomed families from all religions (most commonly Jewish and Christian) and of all social classes. Froebel developed special toys (which he called 'Gifts') and made up his own activities (which he called 'Occupations') to promote his principles. You will be familiar with the use of these today. They include:

- beautiful sets of wooden blocks
- wooden rods in different colours and shapes for mathematical discovery (each brown rod is the same length as two purples, etc.)
- songs and rhymes with actions and finger play
- activities with materials that could be manipulated, including paper, clay, sand and string

- movement and dance to music
- observing and caring for plants in the garden
- physical and intellectual games.

Froebel's children did not have to do formal activities given to them by adults, which was unusual in his day. Instead children were encouraged to play and explore the Gifts and Occupations in their own way. This was the introduction of what we now know as 'free-play' (or free-form play). You can see Froebel's Gifts online – see the Weblink section at the end of the unit.

FAST FACT

Froebel invented the word *kindergarten* to describe the learning environments he created. He said, 'Children are like tiny flowers; they are varied and need care, but each is beautiful alone and glorious when seen in the community of peers.'

▲ Foebel encouraged children to care for plants in the garden

Rudolf Steiner (1861–1925)

Steiner developed his ideas when working as a private tutor. He went on to open schools in Germany, where he also trained teachers.

FAST FACT

The last original German Steiner school was closed when the Nazis came to power, not long after Steiner's death. All of the original records were destroyed.

Steiner believed that all children deserve to fulfil their full learning potential. But he did not believe that children should be forced into learning things before they are ready. In particular, he thought it was wrong to push children towards goals which adults think are desirable but which a child may not. He encouraged his students to learn for the pleasure of learning, rather than for tests or exams. He believed children passed through these three phases:

- *the Will* (aged up to 7 years): a deeply spiritual person himself, Steiner said children's spirits and their bodies became one in this phase.
- *the Heart* (aged 7–14 years): Steiner believed that feelings and relationships were paramount in this phase.
- *the Head* (from age 14 years): this was identified as the 'time for thinking'.

Steiner's schools promoted these ideals:

- In the first phase, children should play and spend plenty of time at home. Drawing and storytelling are important. Children should be exposed to nature and natural objects. One teacher should remain with a class throughout the first phase.
- Children should not be taught to write until the second phase. They should learn writing before they learn reading.
- Children should be engaged, so they think enthusiastically about the information taught. Links between art and science are important.
- In the third phase, children should concentrate on one subject at a time. For example, Steiner might have taught literature every morning for a few weeks and then moved on to teach history in the same slot. This allowed children to become immersed in the subjects they studied.

There are private Steiner schools in the UK today, but Steiner's philosophies have not become embedded in the maintained sector.

Margaret McMillan (1860–1931)

An American-born educationalist, McMillan grew up in Scotland and first worked in Bradford. She was a member of the Froebel Society and promoted many of Froebel's ideals. She agreed that children learnt through doing and experiencing things first hand. She felt that their play was crucial to their learning and thought that children could not be 'whole' without opportunities for play. She believed that free-play gave the best opportunities of all for learning and achievement.

McMillan agreed with Froebel's philosophy of welcoming parents into places of education. She liked the idea of both parents and children learning, and promoted sessions for adults where they could learn things such as foreign languages and crafts.

McMillan worked in the inner-city areas of the north at a time when there was widespread poverty. She campaigned tirelessly for children, both for improved health care and nursery education. She made it known that children who were undernourished and those who were in poor health (suffering rickets, or problems with their ears and eyes for instance) could not possibly be expected to learn well. She also campaigned for school dinners.

The traditional British nursery school was first modelled by McMillan. Many believe we have her to thank for many aspects of the nursery provision we have here today: play-based environments with gardens and outside play spaces, which welcome and value parents. She also pushed for high-quality training for staff, recognising the difference this made to the experience children had in nurseries.

McMillan opened the very first open-air nursery with her sister Rachel. In 1917 she said that disadvantaged children could come and enjoy 'Light, air and all that is good.'

Maria Montessori (1870–1952)

As a doctor (and the first woman in Italy to qualify as a physician), Maria Montessori worked with children who had learning difficulties. She observed the children over long periods, and developed her own method of educating them. Montessori first introduced the idea that there are naturally occurring periods of time during children's lives when they are most open and receptive to learning particular skills and understanding certain things. Montessori observed that it was harder for children to acquire these skills once this sensitive period had passed.

Modern research agrees with this, finding that while it may be more difficult for children who have missed sensitive times to learn the things they have missed, it is possible for them to catch up fully. For instance, if a baby has been seriously ill in hospital for several months, they may have missed the sensitive times to learn to crawl, stand and walk. Once they are well, it may take them longer than usual to master these skills, but they should catch up with other children of their age eventually, and should not be at a long-term disadvantage in their gross motor skills.

Montessori went on to work with a group of 50 non-disabled children who were living in poverty in Rome, where she developed the Montessori Teaching Programme. Many of Montessori's ideas are opposed to Froebel's, although she did take some of his work as the inspiration for her own. Montessori's programme was structured, featuring graded learning activities, including many for children to do with their hands. Teachers were the 'keepers of the environment'. This meant they set up the activities as required by the programme, then let children get on with them while they observed, only intervening from the 'edges'. Montessori did not place much value on play. Her programme did not encourage children to express creativity through art, craft or ideas until they had passed through all of her graded learning activities. She famously said, 'First education of the senses, then education of the intellect.'

Montessori thought working alone encouraged children to become independent learners, although she did think it was good for them to be in a social group with children of different ages. She believed that a child was thinking and learning at their highest level when they were silently working alone, completely engaged in their task. She called this the 'polarisation of the attention'.

There are private Montessori classes and schools in the UK today, but Montessori's work has not influenced the majority of private settings or maintained settings in the same way as Froebel's work.

Susan Isaacs (1885-1948)

Isaacs is best known for the work she did in her nursery school in Cambridge. She extensively observed the children, not only when they attended her setting but also after they had left and started infant school. Influenced by Froebel, Isaacs valued play highly, and this was the bedrock of her nursery provision. She was interested in what effect leaving this provision and starting formal schooling had on the children with whom she worked. Her research showed that many children did not fare well when they moved on, and some even regressed (moved backwards).

Isaacs concluded that young children physically need to be able to move around freely. She thought that it was wrong to put children under the age of 7 in classrooms where they are expected to sit and work at a table for much of the day. She thought children should remain in provision modelled on nurseries until this age.

Isaacs also did some interesting work on feelings, particularly fear and anger. She stressed that bottling up these feelings could be damaging. She promoted the expression of all types of feelings through play.

Reggio Emilia

Reggio Emilia is a town in the hills of northern Italy, where a programme of early childhood education was developed. The programme is named after the town. It is based on 'socio-constructivist' theories, including those of Vygotsky, Piaget and Bruner. A group of parents originally founded the schools in 1945 (after the Second World War) because they did not want to send their children to the existing ones which were run strictly by the church. By the end of the 1970s, the Reggio Emilia approach had taken over governing the schools in the area; this is largely credited to a man named Loris Malaguzzi. He believed that, after years of Italy being ruled by the dictator Mussolini, this approach to education would help the region to start afresh and to work towards a better future.

The approach has been given many international awards, and educators from all over the world visit Reggio Emilia to learn about the methods and to see them in action. See the Weblink section at the end of the unit for details of a video showing how two teachers brought the Reggio Emilia approach into UK classrooms, following a visit to Italy.

FAST FACT

The Reggio Emilia approach considers children to be strong and capable learners. The infant-toddler centres and schools treat children's ideas and thinking with great respect.

These are characteristics of the Reggio Emilia programme:

- Teachers work in pairs. This is known as 'co-teaching'. There is no staff structure, i.e. no head teacher; and staff such as cooks and assistants are regarded as equal with teachers.

- To promote a feeling of community, teachers stay with the same class of children for three years.

- The majority of educational activities are done in the mornings when children are at their freshest.

- There is a sleep time after lunch.

- Teachers are encouraged to listen to children on a deep level. This is their way of really getting to know a child's learning processes and how they think and understand.

- Infancy is regarded as a period of curiosity in its own right, not as the preparation or foundation for learning in later childhood.

- Topics and themes are used, sometimes at the children's suggestion.

- Teachers do plan and make preparations, but there is not a strict curriculum or timetable. Teaching and learning is allowed to evolve and unfold at the pace of the children and follows the interests they develop along the way.

- It is believed that approaching things creatively can encourage children to look at the world from a new viewpoint.

- Expressive arts are valued as an excellent way to teach children about themes and the world in general.

- There are many opportunities to participate in music, painting, model making, sculpture, dance, writing, etc. Children draw every day.

FAST FACT

Pioneer Loris Malaguzzi famously said there are 'a hundred languages of children'. He saw the different ways in which children express themselves – through music, dance, art, writing and so on – as different languages used in childhood.

High/Scope

High/Scope is an educational approach founded in America by David Weikart. It developed out of a programme which was originally intended for students who were considered talented. The name came from this – 'high' represents the high aspirations of those involved and 'scope' represents the broadness of the vision the founder hoped to achieve.

The approach is based on a philosophy of 'active participatory learning'. The High/Scope Education Research Foundation (High/Scope ERF) explains this as students having, 'Direct, hands-on experiences with people, objects, events, and ideas'. Again, the 'active learners' theories of Piaget and Vygotsky can be recognised. Children are encouraged to 'construct knowledge' through direct interaction with people and the world in general. Like the Reggio Emilia approach, children make decisions and choices about their learning, and their interests inform the curriculum.

But uniquely, a 'plan, do, review' sequence is at the heart of the programme, and time is dedicated to this each day. Children are encouraged to make plans, and to follow them through. Adults involved in the child's life (including parents and carers) are there to give the child support and access to the materials and interactions that will help them. It is believed that children learn best when they plan their own activities, take part in them and then review them.

The High/Scope goals for young children are:

- to learn through active involvement with people, materials, events, and ideas

- to become independent, responsible, and confident – ready for school and ready for life

- to learn to plan many of their own activities, carry them out, and talk with others about what they have done and what they have learned

- to gain knowledge and skills in important academic, social, and physical areas.

Teachers see themselves as partners in children's activities rather than their superiors, and they seek to share control with the children. They aim to encourage initiative, independence and creativity. They help children to resolve conflicts for themselves, and focus on children's strengths.

In addition to the centres in the US, there are High/Scope Institutes in the UK – see the Weblinks section at the end of the unit. There are also institutes in other countries including Holland, South Africa, Singapore and Korea.

FAST FACT

The High/Scope Education Research Foundation mission is to 'lift lives through education. We envision a world in which all educational settings use active participatory learning so everyone has a chance to succeed in life and contribute to society.'

Parten's five stages of play

In 1932, researcher Mildred Parten was studying the play of children aged between 2 and 5 years. Parten focused on the children's social interactions during their play. She identified five stages of play which children pass through:

- solitary play
- spectator (or 'onlooker') play
- parallel play
- associative play
- cooperative play.

Further details about each of the play types are given below.

FAST FACT

Despite the fact that her research was carried out almost 80 years ago, Mildred Parten's findings are still valid today and are generally accepted by practitioners.

Solitary play

Solitary play occurs when a child plays alone, completely independent of others. Very young children only play alone.

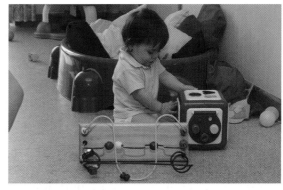

▲ Solitary play

Spectator play

The word 'spectator' means someone who is watching. Spectator play occurs when a child watches another child or children at play but does not join in. The spectator will either not be playing themselves, or will be doing a different activity from the one they are watching. This is sometimes called 'onlooker play'. Toddlers can often be observed watching others from a distance.

▲ Spectator play

Parallel play

This stage occurs from approximately 2 years of age. At this stage the child plays alongside others and may share resources, but they remain engrossed in their own

Practical example

Felix wants to watch

Shobna is a new learner on placement. She is at the water tray with a group of children. She notices 2-year-old Felix watching nearby. She invites Felix to come and play but he does not. Shobna doesn't want to just leave him there. She thinks he must want to join in but is too shy. She tries hard to persuade Felix again but he wanders off.

1 *It was fine for Shobna to invite Felix to play. But what should she have done when he didn't want to join in?*

2 *Give the reason for your answer.*

activity. The child has companionship, but even in the middle of a group, the child remains independent in their play. They do not look at other children.

▲ Parallel play

Associative play

This stage generally occurs from between the ages of 3 and 4 years. During the associative play stage, children share resources and talk to each other. But they each have their own **play agenda** (their own idea of what they want to do). The children do not coordinate their play objectives or interests. This means there will be trouble! Conflicts arise when children have separate ideas that others do not share. Children especially have trouble when trying to play imaginatively together.

▲ Associative play

Cooperative play

The cooperative play stage occurs when children fully interact, and can participate together in play with specific goals in mind. They can play their own imaginary games, organising themselves into roles etc.: for example, 'You be the doctor and I'll be the patient'. The older children in Parten's study were capable of cooperative play from the ages of 4 to 5 years.

▲ Cooperative play

Play agenda = what a child wants to achieve in their play

Although Parten's work was with children aged between 2 and 5 years, you will find you can observe older children playing in the ways she describes. Once children achieve the next stage of play, they will still at times play in the ways they have before. For instance, all children like to have the personal space to play alone sometimes. Most children will also stand back and watch others without joining in at times, especially in new circumstances. Older children will be seen playing alongside each other with little interaction when engrossed in an art or craft activity, such as drawing or making jewellery. Because of this, some people like to think of the stages of play more as 'phases' of play, because children phase in and out of them.

To progress effectively through the stages of play development, children need the opportunity to play with other children, and the support of skilful adults.

Playwork

Learners undertaking a playwork qualification may work in a playwork setting with older children. Playworkers work with children of school age in play settings during the children's leisure time. Examples of playwork settings include before- and after-school clubs, holiday clubs and adventure playgrounds.

The 'Playwork Principles' explain the current values playwork is based on. You should always promote them in your work with older children in play settings. The Principles themselves appear below.

Note: the Playwork Principles were endorsed by Skills Active in 2004 and are being incorporated into the Playwork National Occupational Standards to replace the old Playwork Assumptions and Values.

Playwork Principles

These principles establish the professional and ethical framework for playwork and as such must be regarded as a whole. They describe what is unique about play and playwork, and provide the playwork perspective for working with children and young people. They are based on the recognition that children and young people's capacity for positive development will be enhanced if given access to the broadest range of environments and play opportunities.

1 All children and young people need to play. The impulse to play is innate. Play is a biological, psychological and social necessity, and is fundamental to the healthy development and wellbeing of individuals and communities.

2 Play is a process that is freely chosen, personally directed and intrinsically motivated. That is, children and young people determine and control the content and intent of their play, by following their own instincts, ideas and interests, in their own way for their own reasons.

3 The prime focus and essence of playwork is to support and facilitate the play process and this should inform the development of play policy, strategy, training and education.

4 For playworkers, the play process takes precedence and playworkers act as advocates for play when engaging with adult-led agendas.

5 The role of the playworker is to support all children and young people in the creation of a space in which they can play.

6 The playworker's response to children and young people playing is based on a sound up-to-date knowledge of the play process, and reflective practice.

7 Playworkers recognise their own impact on the play space and also the impact of children and young people's play on the playworker.

8 Playworkers choose an intervention style that enables children and young people to extend their play. All playworker intervention must balance risk with the developmental benefit and wellbeing of children.

Supporting play

This is the practitioner's role:

● Supporting children/young people's play: because of the benefits of free play (including the enjoyment it gives), it is good practice for practitioners to intervene in or interfere with children and young people's play as little as possible, as long as their play remains safe and their behaviour is acceptable. The emphasis is more on supporting children and less on directing them. This approach is sometimes called 'low intervention, high response'. Practitioners remain on hand to join in with play if they are invited to do so.

● Enriching children/young people's play: practitioners can enrich play by providing children and young people with suitable, stimulating environments that give rich opportunities for play of different types (see pages 258–259). This means the provision of appropriate play spaces and a wide variety of resources.

● Effectively managing risk involved in play: practitioners must manage risk by balancing the benefits of activities and experiences with levels of risk during risk assessments. Full details are included on page 156–159.

Practitioners may become 'advocates' for children and young people and their play – that is, people who stand up for children's rights to play in public places such as parks, since play can sometimes be misinterpreted as anti-social behaviour. Practitioners can also be 'custodians' of the play space – the people responsible for securing its use for play.

Using objectives to evaluate play provision

The effectiveness of play provision can be evaluated by considering seven 'play objectives' that have been identified in the *Best Play* publication. These are broad statements that play practitioners can use as indicators of good practice. By comparing the setting's practice against the objectives, practitioners can identify how well the setting is doing in terms of supporting play. Practitioners should consider what evidence they have of the setting's work against each objective. Once complete, the evaluation can be used to develop and improve the setting's practice as areas for development will have been highlighted.

The seven play objectives state that provision should:

● extend the choice and control that children have over their play, the freedom they enjoy and the satisfaction they gain from it

● recognise the child's need to test boundaries and respond positively to that need

● manage the balance between the need to offer risk and the need to keep children safe from harm

● maximise the range of play opportunities

● foster independence and self-esteem

● foster children's respect for others and offer opportunities for social interaction

● foster the child's wellbeing, healthy growth and development, knowledge and understanding, creativity and capacity to learn.

Play types

Play expert Bob Hughes studied children and young people's play extensively. He identified different types of play. He gave each type of play a name and defined the characteristics of each, explaining the role he believed each type of play had in children's development. He called his research findings the 'taxonomy of play types'. It is now widely accepted within the playwork field that practitioners should support children's development within each type of play and provide good opportunities for children and young people to experience them. The table on pages 258–259 gives further details. The information is adapted from Hughes's *Taxonomy of Play Types and Best Play* (1996, Playlink, London).

Hughes has identified criteria which will enrich the play environment and provide opportunities for play of all types. The criteria are outlined below:

- a varied and interesting physical environment: including different play spaces of various sizes; places that inspire imagination, create mystery and allow children to hide; man-made features and natural forms such as bushes and trees
- playing with identity: opportunities to take responsibility and to role play, dress up, enact or perform
- playing with the natural elements – earth, water, fire and air (with appropriate supervision and risk assessment): building campfires, water play, flying kites, digging in earth/sand
- challenge in relation to the physical environment: activities and experiences that allow children to test the limits of their capabilities, e.g. rough-and-tumble games, chasing and running games
- experiencing a range of emotions: opportunities to experience being scared and confident, brave and cowardly, in control and out of control
- movement (such as running, jumping, balancing, etc.): balancing on beams or stilts, riding bicycles, skateboarding, skipping
- stimulation of the five senses (sight, hearing, taste, touch and smell): having quiet places and places where noise (such as shouting) is permitted; listening to music; trying a range of food and drinks; variety of colour, shapes, textures and brightness in resources and play spaces
- experiencing change in the natural and built environment: outdoor access that allows children to experience changes in the weather and the seasons, participation in building or transforming the environment
- manipulating natural and fabricated materials: art and craft resources, tools, materials for building and creating, a broad range of 'bits and pieces'
- social interactions: opportunities to solve own conflicts, to negotiate, co-operate and compete with others of different ages, abilities, ethnicity, culture and gender; also, opportunities to choose when to play alone and when to play with other individuals and groups.

Hughes's research and conclusions are explained fully in the book *Taxonomy of Play Types and Best Play* (Hughes, 1996, Playlink, London).

▼ Play types

PLAY TYPE	CHARACTERISTICS OF PLAY TYPE	EXAMPLES OF HOW THIS PLAY TYPE CAN BE PROVIDED FOR BY PRACTITIONERS
Communication play	This is play that uses words, gestures or nuances, including conversation, debate, jokes, singing, poetry, play acting	Through musical activities, group circle time/debate time, consultation activities, drama games and performances
Creative play	This occurs when children play in a way that allows them to transfer information, respond in new ways and develop an awareness of new connections with an element of surprise. An example of this would be to create a sculpture from clay or to paint a picture, for the sake of creation	Through art and craft activities such drawing, painting, collage, chalking, sculpture with malleable materials and tools. Access to a broad range of materials both natural and synthetic including wool, fabrics, cellophane, tissue paper
Deep play	This play occurs when children participate in experiences that are risky, perhaps even potentially life threatening. It allows children to conquer fear and to develop survival skills. Examples of this play include balancing on a high beam and skateboarding along a wall	Through exhilarating play within adventure setting – using zip wires, climbing trees, caving, mountain biking. Participating in sports/physical activities such as skateboarding, rollerblading or sledging (as always, practitioners must carry out a risk assessment before these activities)
Dramatic play	This occurs when children dramatise events which they do not participate in directly. This includes playing TV shows or games based on cartoons or superheroes, or the enactment of a religious/festive event, perhaps even a funeral	Through time and space for children to develop their own such games and activities. Practitioners can support this play by not interrupting unless play becomes dangerous, and allowing children to use resources and materials freely to develop 'sets' and so on
Exploratory play	This occurs when children gain factual information through manipulation or movement. This can include handling objects in a range of ways, such as throwing, banging or mouthing – this allows children to assess the properties of the object and to assess its possibilities. An example of this is the way in which children manipulate recycled objects to make a model	Provide interesting resources for children, and regularly introduce new objects, both synthetic and natural. This could include autumn leaves for example. Allow children to find their own way of using tools and objects as long as this is safe – do not insist on showing them the 'right' or 'proper' way unless children ask for help
Fantasy play	This takes place when children rearrange the world in a way that is unlikely to occur, but that appeals to them. For instance, they may play at owning a zoo, or an expensive car, or play at being a pop star or a pilot	Through allowing children the time and space to develop fantasy play and worlds themselves. Practitioners can support this play by not interrupting unless play becomes dangerous, or they are invited to participate. In this case practitioners should follow the child's lead, and not impose their own ideas on the child's fantasy world
Imaginative play	This occurs when the conventional rules that govern our real physical world have no meaning or do not apply to the world of children's play. For example, children may pretend to be a plant, scarecrow or an aeroplane. Or they may act out pumping petrol from an invisible pump	Through allowing children the time and space to develop their imaginary play. Practitioners can support this play by not interrupting unless play becomes dangerous, or they are invited to participate. In this case practitioners should follow the child's lead and not impose their own ideas or rules on the child's play. Practitioners should accept without question the rules children have devised

PLAY TYPE	CHARACTERISTICS OF PLAY TYPE	EXAMPLES OF HOW THIS PLAY TYPE CAN BE PROVIDED FOR BY PRACTITIONERS
Locomotor play	This occurs when children move around in any and every direction for the sake of doing so. Examples of this include playing playground games such as tag and climbing apparatus and trees	Through allowing plenty of free-play time in large areas, so that children can develop their own games and travel around the play space spontaneously. Practitioners can also organise and join in with playground games such as Sticky Glue (also known as Stuck-in-the-Mud)
Mastery play	This occurs when children's play controls the physical and affective ingredients of the environment. Examples include making fires, building dams, digging holes and creating shelters	Through activities that involve the elements, such as building a camp fire and cooking on it or making and flying windsocks or kites. If necessary (depending on the nature of the play space) practitioners can arrange visits/trips so that children can experience making shelters in the woods or digging trenches in the sand
Object play	This occurs when children handle an object using an interesting sequence of manipulations and movements. This includes examining properties of objects closely, or using items in a new or novel way – using a ruler as a twirling baton for instance	Through providing interesting resources for children and regularly introducing new objects likely to stimulate curiosity and imagination (both synthetic and natural). Allowing children to find their own way of using objects as long as this is safe
Rough and tumble	This occurs when all children involved are obviously unhurt and enjoying themselves while they play chasing, wrestling or playful 'fighting' games. This 'close encounter play' is about discovering physical flexibility, gauging relative strength and the exhilaration of display. It involves safe touching	By not stepping in too soon if children are enjoying rough-and-tumble play – monitoring the play enables practitioners to step in if rough and tumble escalates to play which is outside safe or acceptable limits. Resources such as soft-play equipment and soft-play zones are helpful for facilitating this type of play in otherwise 'formal' areas – within a classroom used for an after-school club for instance
Social play	This occurs when children play together. Rules and criteria for social engagement and interaction between the children can be revealed, explored and amended (changed during play). Examples are activities where children involved are expected to stick to rules or protocols such as in games or conversations	Through allowing children plenty of time and space to develop rules and protocols for themselves. Practitioners should support children when the rules of play and interaction are explored or changed, as long as behaviour does not become unsafe. Team activities and opportunities for children to design their own board games can facilitate this type of play
Socio-dramatic play	This occurs when children act out experiences of an intense personal, social, domestic or interpersonal nature. The experiences acted out may have really happened to children, or they could potentially occur. Examples of this play include playing homes/families, playing shopping and even arguing	Through providing play areas such as home corners and the provision of prop resources such as play money, play telephones and so on. Older child may enjoy role play or moral dilemma games where they act out or describe how they would behave in certain situations – if they missed the last bus home for example
Symbolic play	This occurs when children use an object to symbolise something else: e.g. a piece of wood may become a snake, or a piece of string may be used as a wedding ring. Symbolic play allows control, gradual exploration and increased understanding, without children risking being out of their depth	Through providing interesting resources for children and regularly introducing new objects likely to stimulate curiosity and imagination (both synthetic and natural). Allowing children free access to resources, so they can get out items they want to play with

Stages of development

The stages of child development influence children and young people's play needs and behaviours. Practitioners must remember that all children develop at different rates and so their play needs and behaviours will also vary. For example, children tend to have different interests and be drawn to different types of play as they grow up and develop, and the amount of independence that children are comfortable with increases over time. A good knowledge and understanding of children's development is essential to the provision of good, appropriate play opportunities.

⊂⊃ There is more about this throughout Unit 2.

Barriers to access

Some children and young people may experience barriers that affect their access to play. Practitioners must take action to identify and remove barriers to ensure that all children are given equal opportunities to play.

Adaptations may be made to the way an activity is offered to allow everyone to participate. For instance, other children may play parachute games kneeling down so a child who uses a wheelchair can join in.

Identifying play needs and preferences

It is important for practitioners to identify the play needs and preferences of the children and young people they work with. This enables practitioners to provide play opportunities that will meet the needs of children and young people and promote their development. It also enables practitioners to provide experiences that all will enjoy and will find engaging and interesting. This increases children and young people's motivation to participate in play experiences. Practitioners can collect information on play needs and preferences by using the following methods:

- researching theory and practice
- observing children/young people at play
- interacting with children/young people.

Consultation

Practitioners should consult with children and young people about their play needs and preferences. This becomes increasingly important as children grow up. Through consultation practitioners can interact with children and young people, finding out what they want and need from their play.

Consultation can take place during casual conversation as practitioners interact with children and young people. But planned consultation activities can also take place during:

- meetings
- circle time
- planning sessions
- evaluations and reviews.

It is important to tailor the methods of consultation utilised to the ages and abilities of the children in the group. Many methods can be used to consult, including the following:

- Discussion: practitioners can talk with children and young people individually or in groups about their play needs, preferences and ideas about play experiences and play spaces.
- Questionnaires: these can be written or pictorial, depending on the ages and abilities of the children.

- Interviews: an alternative to questionnaires – an 'interviewer' can verbally ask children/young people questions and record their answers.

- Suggestion boxes: children/young people can write and draw their ideas, thoughts and feelings and put them into a box anonymously. Suggestion video tapes/audio tapes can also work well, although the element of anonymity is lost.

- Voting: a good, quick way of consulting with children/young people – children can vote on the layout of the play space at the start of the session for instance. It can be as simple as a show of hands or can involve a ballot (anonymous paper vote).

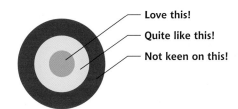

▲ Evaluation target

- Evaluation: involving children/young people in the evaluation of play sessions reveals what they have enjoyed – this can inform future planning. There are several visual ways of recording

evaluations. It is common to ask children to rank, in order of preference, the activities they have participated in. Here are four examples:

– Drawing out a large bull's-eye target and asking each child to place a cross on it to indicate how they felt about a particular experience. The nearer to the bull's-eye the cross is, the better they enjoyed the experience. See the diagram below

– Drawing up a list of play experiences. Children are given a gold, silver and bronze sticker. They are asked to place the stickers next to the experiences on the list awarding them first, second or third in terms of their favourites

– Drawing a list of numbers, perhaps one to five. Next to the relevant numbers the children write or draw on their top five play experiences of the session

– Four corners of the play space are identified as 'really liked it', 'liked it', 'didn't like it', and 'really didn't like it'. Practitioners call out play experiences, and children run to the relevant corner depending how they felt about the experience.

- Thought-storming.

1. What are the long-term benefits of play?
2. What are the short-term benefits of play?
3. What is meant by the term 'pioneers of play and education'?
4. What influence has Froebel's work had on play and education today?
5. Explain the purpose of the Playwork Principles.

Learning Outcome ②

FOCUS ON...
how to use appropriate tools to assess the learning needs of individual children

This links to assessment criteria **2.1**

The relationship between play and learning

As you learnt in section one, children learn through play. Play is an effective vehicle for children's learning because:

- children enjoy playing
- children are intrinsically motivated to play (they are internally driven)
- children can make their own discoveries through play
- children can initiate their own activities and explore their own thoughts and ideas through play
- children can actively learn through play – the learning is a real, vivid experience
- play is necessary for children's wellbeing – under the UN Convention on the Rights of the Child, children have a right to play.

Planning for play through observation and evaluation

You will find that you naturally observe things about individual children's play and learning needs and preferences as you interact and play with children, and as you stand back and supervise. These naturally occurring observations can be informative. Writing them down in a notebook is a helpful way to gather information. Planned observations of children are also valuable.

Information about methods of observation and how to analyse observations is given in Unit 2, section 2.

When planning your work with children, you should always consider the starting point of each individual child – what do they already know and understand? What do they have experience of? This allows you to pitch your activity to the right level for the children. The starting points will differ within any group of children, even those of the same age, so this will require good knowledge of the children and some careful thinking. The practical example on page 278 shows how you can adjust activities to suit individual children.

The observations that you carry out will inform your knowledge of what children already know and understand, making observation central to the planning process.

FAST FACT

Different settings have their own ways of recording activity evaluations, and it is important to follow organisational requirements. Some settings allocate space for evaluation on the activity planning sheet.

Using observations to assess and respond to individual learning needs

Information on using observations to assess and respond to individual learning needs is included within Unit 2, section 2. The details of how to write observation-based individual learning/education plans are also included.

This links to assessment criteria **2.2**.

Information from other services and professionals

Information from other agencies can make an important contribution to the assessment of individual children's learning needs. You need to know how to access and use information from other services and professionals.

Full details are provided within Unit 2, sections 2 and 3.

✓ Progress check

(1) What is the relationship between play and learning?

(2) How can observation inform the planning process?

(3) How can you use observation techniques to assess individual learning needs?

(4) How can you use information from other services/professionals to assess children's learning needs?

Learning Outcome ③

FOCUS ON...
how to plan and provide learning opportunities in consultation with others

This links to assessment criteria **3.1**

The Early Years Foundation Stage

From September 2008 the Early Years Foundation Stage (EYFS) will be mandatory for:

- all schools
- all early years providers in Ofsted-registered settings.

It will apply to children from birth to the end of the academic year in which the child has their fifth birthday.

In the *Statutory Framework for the Early Years Foundation Stage* the Department for Children, Schools and Families tells us that:

> "Every child deserves the best possible start in life and support to fulfil their potential. A child's experience in the early years has a major impact on their future life chances. A secure, safe and happy childhood is important in its own right, and it provides the foundation for children to make the most of their abilities and talents as they grow up. When parents choose to use early years services they want to know that provision will keep their children safe and help them to thrive. The Early Years Foundation Stage (EYFS) is the framework that provides that assurance. The overarching aim of the EYFS is to help young children achieve the five *Every Child Matters* outcomes."

Every Child Matters is the government agenda which focuses on bringing together services to support children and families. It sets out five major outcomes for children:

- being healthy
- staying safe
- enjoying and achieving
- making a positive contribution
- economic wellbeing.

The EYFS aims to meet the Every Child Matters outcomes by:

- *setting standards* for the learning, development and care young children should experience when they attend a setting outside their family home. Every child should make progress, with no children left behind

- *providing equality of opportunity and anti-discriminatory practice*: ensuring that every child is included and not disadvantaged because of ethnicity, culture, religion, home language, family background, learning difficulties or disabilities, gender or ability

- *creating a framework for partnership working between parents and professionals*, and between all the settings that the child attends

- *improving quality and consistency in the early years* through standards that apply to all settings. This provides the basis for the inspection and regulation regime carried out by Ofsted

- *laying a secure foundation for future learning* through learning and development that is planned around the individual needs and interests of the child. This is informed by the use of ongoing observational assessment.

FAST FACT

From September 2008 the EYFS will replace the Curriculum Guidance for the Foundation Stage, the Birth to Three Matters Framework and the National Standards for Under 8s Daycare and Childminding.

Themes, Principles and Commitments

▼ Themes, Principles and Commitments

The EYFS is based around four *Themes*. Each theme is linked to a *Principle*. Each Principle is supported by four *Commitments*. The Commitments describe how their Principle can be put into action. The Themes, Principles and Commitments are shown in the table below.

Additional statements are provided within the EYFS to explain each Commitment in more detail. You can see these on the Department for Education and Skills' 'Principles into Practice' poster, an extract of which is reproduced on page 266.

Areas of Learning and Development

Theme 4, Learning and development, also contains six *Areas of Learning and Development*. These are shown on the diagram on page 266.

THEME	PRINCIPLE	COMMITMENTS
1 A unique child	Every child is a competent learner from birth who can be resilient, capable, confident and self-assured	1.1 Child development 1.2 Inclusive practice 1.3 Keeping safe 1.4 Health and wellbeing
2 Positive relationships	Children learn to be strong and independent from a base of loving and secure relationships with parents and/or a key person	2.1 Respecting each other 2.2 Parents as partners 2.3 Supporting learning 2.4 Key person
3 Enabling environments	The environment plays a key role in supporting and extending children's development and learning	3.1 Observation, assessment and planning 3.2 Supporting every child 3.3 The learning environment 3.4 The wider context
4 Learning and development	Children develop and learn in different ways and at different rates. All areas of learning and development are equally important and interconnected	4.1 Play and exploration 4.2 Active learning 4.3 Creativity and critical thinking 4.4 Areas of learning and development

The Early Years Foundation Stage: Themes and Commitments

A Unique Child	Positive Relationships	Enabling Environments	Learning and Development
1.1 Child Development Babies and children develop in individual ways and at varying rates. Every area of development – physical, cognitive, linguistic, spiritual, social and emotional – is equally important.	**2.1 Respecting Each Other** Every interaction is based on caring professional relationships and respectful acknowledgement of the feelings of children and their families.	**3.1 Observation, Assessment and Planning** Babies and young children are individuals first, each with a unique profile of abilities. Schedules and routines should flow with the child's needs. All planning starts with observing children in order to understand and consider their current interests, development and learning.	**4.1 Play and Exploration** Children's play reflects their wide ranging and varied interests and preoccupations. In their play children learn at their highest level. Play with peers is important for children's development.
1.2 Inclusive Practice The diversity of individuals and communities is valued and respected. No child or family is discriminated against.	**2.2 Parents as Partners** Parents are children's first and most enduring educators. When parents and practitioners work together in early years settings, the results have a positive impact on children's development and learning.	**3.2 Supporting Every Child** The environment supports every child's learning through planned experiences and activities that are challenging but achievable.	**4.2 Active Learning** Children learn best through physical and mental challenges. Active learning involves other people, objects, ideas and events that engage and involve children for sustained periods.
1.3 Keeping Safe Young children are vulnerable. They develop resilience when their physical and psychological well-being is protected by adults.	**2.3 Supporting Learning** Warm, trusting relationships with knowledgeable adults support children's learning more effectively than any amount of resources.	**3.3 The Learning Environment** A rich and varied environment supports children's learning and development. It gives them the confidence to explore and learn in secure and safe, yet challenging, indoor and outdoor spaces.	**4.3 Creativity and Critical Thinking** When children have opportunities to play with ideas in different situations and with a variety of resources, they discover connections and come to new and better understandings and ways of doing things. Adult support in this process enhances their ability to think critically and ask questions.
1.4 Health and Well-being Children's health is an integral part of their emotional, mental, social, environmental and spiritual well-being and is supported by attention to these aspects.	**2.4 Key Person** A key person has special responsibilities for working with a small number of children, giving them the reassurance to feel safe and cared for and building relationships with their parents.	**3.4 The Wider Context** Working in partnership with other settings, other professionals and with individuals and groups in the community supports children's development and progress towards the outcomes of *Every Child Matters*: being healthy, staying safe, enjoying and achieving, making a positive contribution and economic well-being.	**4.4 Areas of Learning and Development** The Early Years Foundation Stage (EYFS) is made up of six areas of Learning and Development. All areas of Learning and Development are connected to one another and are equally important. All areas of Learning and Development are underpinned by the Principles of the EYFS.

department for education and skills   ISBN 978-1-84478-886-6   00012-2007DOM-EN © Crown copyright 2007

ST IVES DIRECT 02-2007

recycle   80% recycled

▲ Extract from 'Principles into Practice' (DfES)

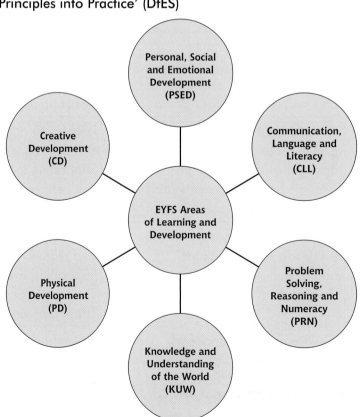

▲ EYFS Areas of Learning and Development

Each Area of Learning and Development is divided up into Aspects. You can see these on the Department for Children, Schools and Families' Learning and Development card, reproduced below. Together, the six areas of Learning and Development make up the skills, knowledge and experiences appropriate for babies and children as they grow, learn and develop. Although these are presented as separate areas, it is important to remember that for children everything links and nothing is compartmentalised.

FAST FACT

All Areas of Learning and Development are connected to one another and are equally important. They are underpinned by the principles of the EYFS.

So what does all this mean?

Childcarers working in settings following the EYFS need to meet the standards for learning, development and care. Their responsibilities include:

- planning a range of play and learning experiences that promote all of the Aspects within all of the Areas of Learning

- assessing and monitoring individual children's progress through observational assessments

- using the findings of observational assessments to inform the planning of play and learning experiences

- ensuring that children's individual interests and abilities are promoted within the play and learning experiences.

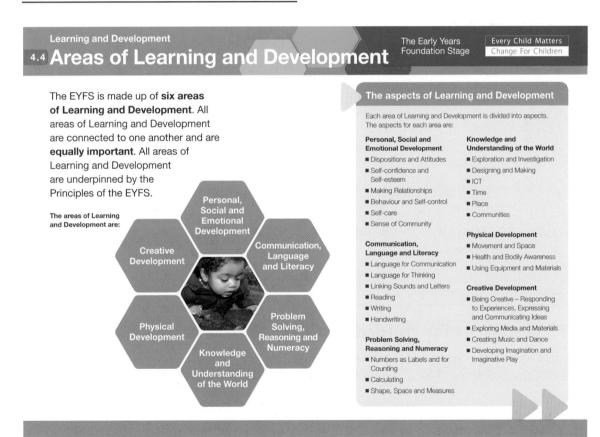

▲ Learning and Development card extract (DfCSF)

Crown Copyright © 2008

In their *Key Elements of Effective Practice* (KEEP) the Department for Children, Schools and Families tells us that:

> "Effective practice in the early years requires committed, enthusiastic and reflective practitioners with a breadth and depth of knowledge, skills and understanding. Effective practitioners use their own learning to improve their work with young children and their families in ways which are sensitive, positive and non-judgemental.
>
> "Therefore through initial and ongoing training and development practitioners need to develop, demonstrate and continuously improve their:
>
> - relationships with both children and adults
> - understanding of the individual and diverse ways that children learn and develop
> - knowledge and understanding in order to actively support and extend children's learning in and across all areas and aspects of Learning and Development
> - practice in meeting all children's needs, learning styles and interests
> - work with parents, carers and the wider community
> - work with other professionals within and beyond the setting"

EYFS resources for childcarers

The EYFS pack of resources for providers includes the following:

The Statutory Framework for the Early Years Foundation Stage

This booklet sets out:

- the welfare requirements
- the learning and development requirements, which set out providers' duties under each of the six areas of Learning and Development.

Practice Guidance for the Early Years Foundation Stage

This booklet provides further guidance on:

- legal requirements
- the areas of Learning and Development
- the EYFS principles
- assessment.

24 cards

These give the Principles and Commitments at a glance, with guidance on putting the principles into practice. They include an overview of child development.

CD-ROM

This contains all the information from the booklets and cards. It includes information on effective practice, research and resources. This can also be accessed via a website – see the Weblink section at the end of the unit.

 Have a go!

Using the Weblink at the end of the unit, visit the EYFS website. Now:

- take the overview tour to familiarise yourself with the site
- follow the links to the Areas of Learning, and read more about the Aspects
- follow the links to the Principles in Practice for examples of how practitioners following the EYFS work with children within their settings.

The National Curriculum

The English National Curriculum (National Curriculum) sets out the minimum curriculum requirements for all maintained schools, including:

- the subjects taught
- the knowledge, skills and understanding required in each subject
- attainment targets in each subject
- how children's progress is assessed and reported.

Within the framework of the National Curriculum, schools are free to plan and organise teaching and learning themselves. Many schools choose to use Schemes of Works from the Qualifications and Curriculum Authority. These help to translate the National Curriculum's objectives into teaching and learning activities for children.

Key stages

The National Curriculum is divided into four *key stages* that children pass through as they move up through the school system. These stages are in addition to the Early Years Foundation Stage described earlier:

- Year 1 and Year 2 of primary school are known as Key Stage 1.
- Years 3 to 6 of primary school are known as Key Stage 2.
- Years 7 to 9 of secondary school are known as Key Stage 3.
- Years 10 to 11 of secondary school are known as Key Stage 4.

Subjects at Key Stage 1 and 2

The compulsory National Curriculum subjects for Key Stages 1 and 2 are:

- English
- maths

- science
- design and technology
- information and communication technology (ICT)
- history
- geography
- art and design
- music
- physical education.

Schools also have to teach:

- religious education: parents have the right to withdraw children from the religious education curriculum if they choose.

Schools are advised to teach:

- personal, social and health education (PSHE)
- citizenship
- one or more modern foreign language.

There are attainment targets and a programme of study for each subject. Programmes of study describe the subject knowledge, skills and understanding pupils are expected to develop during each key stage.

FAST FACT

It is acceptable for schools to use different names for the subjects, as long as they are covering the National Curriculum.

Levels and formal teacher assessments

Attainment targets are split into levels.

Teachers carry out regular checks on children's progress in each subject. There will also be formal teacher assessment at the end of Key Stages 1–3. (Pupils will usually take GCSE/equivalent exams at the end of Key Stage 4.) This indicates which National Curriculum level best describes individual children's performance in each subject. Schools send parents a report telling them what National Curriculum levels their child has reached in formal assessments.

Subjects at Key Stage 3 and 4

Key Stage 3 compulsory National Curriculum subjects are:

- English
- maths
- science
- design and technology
- information and communication technology (ICT)
- history
- geography
- modern foreign languages
- art and design
- music
- citizenship
- physical education.

Schools also have to provide:

- careers education and guidance (during Year 9)
- sex and relationship education (SRE)
- religious education

Note: parents can choose to withdraw their child from the religious education curriculum.

In Year 9 (at the end of Key Stage 3), children do national tests and choose what to study at Key Stage 4, when they will study both compulsory and optional subjects. Most pupils work towards national qualifications. Pupils are advised to choose a balance of options to give them

more choice when deciding on courses and jobs later on. Pupils may also choose from a growing range of vocational qualifications. The compulsory Key Stage 4 subjects are:

- English
- maths
- science
- information and communication technology (ICT)
- physical education
- citizenship.

Schools must also provide:

- careers education
- work-related learning
- religious education
- sex and relationship education (SRE)
- one subject from each of the four 'entitlement' areas.

The entitlement areas are:

- arts subjects
- design and technology
- humanities
- modern foreign languages.

Note: parents can choose to withdraw their child from religious education.

Review of the curriculum

A new secondary curriculum was published in September 2007. Its aims include cutting back on compulsory subject content and developing pupils' personal attributes and practical life skills. The Department for Children, Schools and Families tells us that:

"The new Key Stage 3 curriculum will be brought in over a three year period. It becomes compulsory for Year 7 pupils in September 2008. From September 2009, it will apply to all Year 7 and Year 8 pupils, and from September 2010 it will apply across Years 7, 8 and 9. Changes to the Key Stage 4 curriculum will be brought in from September 2009."

"As part of changes to the curriculum for 14 to 19 year olds, from September 2008 a new Diploma qualification will be introduced alongside GCSEs and A levels in selected schools and colleges."

 Have a go!

For more information about the new secondary curriculum, visit the Qualifications and Curriculum Authority website. The address is given in the Weblinks section at the end of the unit.

The Children's Plan

In 2007, the government published the *Children's Plan* which sets out ambitious new goals for 2020. The Plan is intended to:

- strengthen support for all families during the formative early years of their children's lives
- take the next steps in achieving world-class schools and an excellent education for every child
- involve parents fully in their children's learning
- help to make sure that young people have interesting and exciting things to do outside of school
- provide more places for children to play safely.

The Government says that the Children's Plan:

"also means a new leadership role for Children's Trusts in every area, a new role for schools as the centre of their communities, and more effective links between schools, the NHS and other children's services so that together they can engage parents and tackle all the barriers to the learning, health and happiness of every child."

There will be regular reports on the progress the government is making. For more information, see the Weblinks section at the end of the unit.

Learning styles

All people (both adults and children) have different preferred styles of learning, that is, ways of learning that are particularly effective for them. The styles are known as:

- visual
- auditory
- kinaesthetic.

There are some differing theories about these, but essentially styles of learning are about the way people:

- perceive information: the way they learn information
- process information: the way they think and interpret
- organise and present information: how they retain and pass on information.

People generally employ all of their senses to perceive, process, organise and present information, but they tend to employ one of the senses more than the others.

Visual learners prefer to learn by seeing. They may:

- often prefer an orderly environment
- become distracted by untidiness or movement
- be good at imagining
- be good at reading (may have good early literacy skills, such as letter recognition)
- particularly enjoy looking at pictures.

Auditory learners prefer to learn by hearing. They may:

- learn things well through discussion
- think things through well when asked questions
- enjoy listening to stories
- like reciting information
- be good at remembering what they are told.

Kinaesthetic learners learn through doing, movement and action. They may:

- learn well when they are moving around
- learn best when they have the opportunity to do a task rather than listen to theory
- be good at constructing things
- use expressive movements
- become distracted by activities around them
- prefer to jump right in rather than being shown what to do
- prefer action stories.

When you are planning activities you should take the different learning styles into consideration so that you provide a balance of activities that are likely to be beneficial for the different styles of learner. However, you should remember that young children are only just establishing their styles, and you should be wary of labelling them as solely a particular type of learner. Even if you recognise yourself as a particular type of learner, you probably have several traits that will fit into the other styles.

 This links with the information given on page 31.

Curriculum planning

Practitioners must plan how they will provide activities and experiences that will promote children's learning and development and help them to progress, in line with any learning frameworks that apply to the setting. Planning allows practitioners to ensure that the learning environment is:

- purposeful: play and activities should benefit children in terms of learning and experience (don't forget that having fun is an experience!)
- supportive: activities and play are planned with regard to the support that individual children may need. They are also devised with children's sense of confidence, self-esteem and general wellbeing in mind
- challenging: opportunities that challenge children are offered as well as those that consolidate learning. This encourages motivation and progression in terms of learning
- varied: there should be planned adult-led activities as well as free-play and child-initiated activities. Learning should take place both indoors and outside. A range of physically active pursuits should be offered as well as those that require quiet concentration
- balanced: opportunities should be provided to stimulate children's learning

in all areas of their development and learning, and they should appeal to different styles of learner (see page 271).

- vibrant and exciting: interesting, exciting activities motivate children, helping to foster a love of learning and discovery.

Practitioners make plans to show how learning will take place in the:

- short term
- medium term
- long term.

Most practitioners approach this by planning for the long term first, then the medium term and lastly the short term.

Making and recording plans

There are many good ways to make and record plans. Examples are given on pages 274, 275 and 276, but it is important that you follow your setting's requirements when drawing up your own plans.

The short-term planning example shows that a theme has been selected. While it's generally agreed that themes are not beneficial for younger children under two and a half years, many settings do find them effective for older children. They can be a good way to link activities and play experiences, making them purposeful and progressive. The table on page 277 shows how a group of practitioners may plan a theme together for a setting following the Early Years Foundation Stage.

An integrated approach to planning

It is important to develop an integrated approach to planning. To do this you must recognise that the activities and experiences you provide for children will generally promote more than one area of their development, since children's learning is not compartmentalised. For instance, children playing with ride-on toys in the playground could be simultaneously learning and consolidating in many ways. They could be:

- cooperating and taking turns (Personal, Social and Emotional Development)
- using pedals, steering, changing direction (Physical Development)
- pretending they are going to the garage for petrol (Creative Development).

By pulling together different areas of learning into activities and experiences when you are planning, you can maximise the potential learning opportunity for children. It is not necessary to mould every activity to fit every area – this would probably make your activity so broad that it would lack purpose – but it is effective to integrate those that are a natural fit.

For example, if you were planning to plant sunflower seeds with the children, you could cover the following:

- reading about seeds and how they grow, and discussing things already growing in the environment (communication, language and literacy)
- handling seeds, looking at them closely (knowledge and understanding of the world)
- counting the seeds and sharing them out (problem solving, reasoning and numeracy)
- planting the seeds gently, thinking about how to care for them (physical development, knowledge and understanding of the world)
- pretending to be seeds unfurling and growing to music (creative development).

▶ Long-term planning

	SEPT	OCT	NOV	DEC	JAN	FEB	MARCH	APRIL	MAY	JUNE	JULY	AUG
Theme	Autumn	Animals	Light	Patterns	Winter	Storytime	Health	Spring in the garden	Carnival	Summer holidays	Sport	Our homes
Special events and activities	Trip to country park	Visits to children's farm	Diwali visit to Hindu temple	Visit by artist Christmas	Parents' evening	Visit from an African story teller	Visits from a dentist and a doctor	Trip to garden centre	Fancy dress party	Picnic by the sea	Sports open day	Family barbecue
PSED												
CLL												
PRN												
KUW												
PD												
CD												

The aspects of Learning and Development to be promoted are entered here. Settings often number the bullet points of the aspects so that they can be identified easily on the plans, e.g. if ICT is being promoted, practitioners may enter 'KUW 3'.

▶ Short-term planning

THEME: 'All About Me'				DATE: 10–14 September	
	WHAT DO WE WANT THE CHILDREN TO LEARN?		HOW WILL WE ENABLE THIS LEARNING TO TAKE PLACE?	HOW WILL WE KNOW WHO HAS LEARNED WHAT?	WHAT NEXT?
	LEARNING INTENTIONS BASED ON THE ASPECTS OF LEARNING AND DEVELOPMENT	VOCABULARY	ACTIVITIES/ ROUTINES	ASSESSMENT	NOTES ON HOW ASSESSMENTS MADE WILL INFORM FUTURE PLANS
					[This column will be filled as assessments are made.]
Personal, social and emotional development	Separate from family with support	Greetings in various languages	Self-registration Selecting activities Changing books	Note which children are finding it hard to separate	
Communication, language and literacy	Talk about home/community. Listen to others Enjoy rhymes Show awareness of rhymes Use talk to connect ideas Listen with enjoyment and respond to stories, songs and other music, rhymes and poems and make up their own stories, rhymes and poems	Names of body parts Names for family Alliteration in rhymes	Circle time focus Make a class book about the children Sing and recite favourite nursery rhymes	Collect examples of stages in drawing and mark making Record significant comments made by the children	

THEME: 'All About Me'				DATE: 10–14 September
WHAT DO WE WANT THE CHILDREN TO LEARN?		**HOW WILL WE ENABLE THIS LEARNING TO TAKE PLACE?**	**HOW WILL WE KNOW WHO HAS LEARNED WHAT?**	**WHAT NEXT?**
LEARNING INTENTIONS BASED ON THE ASPECTS OF LEARNING AND DEVELOPMENT	VOCABULARY	ACTIVITIES/ ROUTINES	ASSESSMENT	NOTES ON HOW ASSESSMENTS MADE WILL INFORM FUTURE PLANS
Problem solving, reasoning and numeracy Numbers connected with home Numbers in games Show an interest in numbers and counting Use number names Begin to understand and use numbers	Counting numbers more/less	Workshop – making house fronts Counting games in garden	List children who know and can use numbers 1–5 List children who are aware of larger numbers	
Knowledge and understanding of the world The 'Now' and 'Me' in the past Show interest in the lives of people familiar to them Begin to understand past	Family name Home Work Body parts	Circle time focus Collect baby photos Take photos Class book (graphic)	Checklist of the names of the parts of the body	
Physical development Use space safely Show increasing control in using equipment Use tools appropriately Understand equipment and tools have to be used safely	Climb, jump, scramble swing Cut, stick	Garden – climbing equipment, etc. Workshop and graphics	Record children who use/do not use equipment Note on their ability to cut with scissors Record right- and left-handed children	
Creative development Use bodies to investigate colours and textures	Feel hard, soft, rough smooth	Creative area Finger painting Materials for collages	Keep selection of items for 'me' booklet	

▼ Theme planning process

STEP ONE
Take a theme and set a timescale, e.g. Gardening, two weeks (This may be informed by the long-term plan.) Let parents and carers know the theme and encourage them to become involved – with planning ideas, or collecting resources perhaps
STEP TWO
Divide the theme into subcategories, identifying a logical order for progressive learning, e.g. Planting, Growing, etc.
STEP THREE
Referring to the Aspects within the Area of learning, plan activities and play for children's learning, related to the theme. Take account of individual children's needs, play plans and individual learning styles. Plan a balance of activities and play across the curriculum, for all areas of learning
STEP FOUR
Take the activities and play opportunities identified, and fit them into a timetable for each week, around the normal routines such as circle time and snack time. Ensure variation between the types of activities to keep children interested and to give time for being active as well as time for them to rest and recharge their batteries, taking children's attendance patterns into consideration
STEP FIVE
Identify the roles of adults. Who will do what, and how should children be generally supported? What resources/equipment are needed, and who will organise them?
STEP SIX
Identify opportunities for assessment/observation and plan for them
STEP SEVEN
Identify how the plan will be monitored/evaluated
It is important to note that everything does not need to be themed, and that a theme need not cover all aspects of learning – in fact, this could be rather overwhelming. Routine activities such as news time or pouring out drinks should still be recognised as learning opportunities although they are not theme related. Free-play and child-initiated activities should not be replaced with themed activities

Consider the best way to group children for activities, and what the role of adults will be in terms of supporting children's learning. For instance, through effective deployment of adults and thoughtful grouping of children, it is possible to plan activities that operate on more than one level. This meets the needs of different children working on the same activity.

Practical example

Lisa's games

Nursery worker Lisa is planning some table-top games for her group. She decides to split the group into three subgroups for the activity. One group of mainly 4-year-olds will play a game of sound lotto. An adult will be on hand, but they will be encouraged to manage the game themselves, and to operate the tape recorder. A group of mainly 3-year-olds are going to play a sequencing lotto game. An adult will work with them, encouraging them to talk about what is happening in the pictures, and the order in which the pictures should go. A third group of mainly $2\frac{1}{2}$-year-olds will play a game of picture lotto with two adults. They will focus on sharing out the cards, taking turns, naming the pictures and matching.

1 *Why has Lisa decided to split the group?*

2 *Why is she planning three groups in total?*

3 *Why is the focus of the game different, despite the fact that all groups are playing lotto games?*

Encouraging participation

Children need to engage with activities and experiences in order to learn effectively. Practitioners sometimes make the mistake of thinking that children have experienced or learnt all of the things that the setting offered that day, or that week or month. But children may have benefited little or not at all if they have not actually participated actively themselves. You can promote participation by providing:

- activities that meet the needs of the children
- a balance of activities across the areas of development and any curriculum framework that applies to your setting
- activities that are fun and playful, and present them to children in a playful or engaging manner
- a balance of structured activities and free-play
- a balance of adult-directed and child-initiated activities
- a balance of activities for all styles of learning
- a balance of indoor and outdoor activities
- appropriate groups for children
- appropriate adult support
- and participating at the start of an activity by working alongside the children.

 Have a go!

Try an experiment to see what effect it has on the children when you initiate an activity by participating yourself. Choose an activity relevant to the age group you are working with, and just start doing it. For instance, if working in a nursery you might try going into the dressing-up corner alone and trying on hats. You're likely to have company very soon!

Inclusion and anti-discriminatory practice

You must ensure that you provide inclusive activities that are suitable for all of the children in the group, regardless of their age, gender, culture and ethnicity, needs, abilities and learning styles.

When children need additional support or have particular learning needs or disabilities, practitioners should focus on removing barriers where they exist, and on preventing them from developing, so that children can fully participate within the setting.

G☺☺D PRACTICE · · · · · · ·

It is good practice to note on your plans any special support, adaptation, resources or equipment that may be required to facilitate a child's participation. You must make the necessary arrangements as part of your preparation.

Where children have individual education plans (IEPs) or play plans, you should incorporate the goals contained within them into the overall planning, indicating them on your plan. For instance, a child who lacks confidence when speaking within the group may be identified within the plan as in need of support during circle time, when they may feel under pressure.

See Unit 2, section 2, for information about IEPs.

Remember that you must always promote anti-discriminatory practice, and this should be included in your planning. For instance, you should promote positive images of people and include cultural activities within the programme.

Consolidating, extending and challenging

It is generally accepted that children need a variety of activities and experiences appropriate to their age and abilities that will allow them to:

● consolidate

● extend

● be challenged.

Consolidation is when children have opportunities to repeat activities and experiences, confirming their previous learning, practising skills and perhaps developing a deeper understanding. Children are naturally drawn to consolidating in their play, for example a child may frequently build the same house or aeroplane from small interlocking bricks.

Extension occurs when children's existing learning is moved forward in a new way, perhaps by applying consolidated learning and skills to a new situation. For example, a child who has learnt to use a sewing machine may learn to hem a garment. We can link activities to encourage this (see the Practical example on page 280). Extension activities are particularly helpful when you are working with groups of children with different levels of development. For instance, you can plan a core activity for all of the children and follow this up with an extension activity for the children who are ready for it.

Children are *challenged* when they are introduced to new activities and experiences that are just beyond their current competence, for example a child who has learnt to jump is introduced to the skill of hopping on one leg.

These strategies promote learning and development.

Practical example

Antonio extends learning

Key Stage 1 teacher Antonio has planned to read a story about a bird that drops pebbles into a bottle of water to make the water level rise. The bird can then take a drink from the bottle. Afterwards, the children retell the story themselves using props – a bird puppet, pebbles, water and a bottle. They measure the water level and record how much it rises when they drop in the pebbles.

1. *How did the extension activity extend the children's learning?*

2. *Suggest another way in which Antonio could extend children's learning?*

GOOD PRACTICE

Look out for naturally occurring opportunities to support and extend children's learning.

It may be appropriate to offer your support if children:

- could be encouraged to think or discuss further if they were asked a question
- need a suggestion to initiate an activity or experience
- show signs that their play/learning is flagging, and new input is needed
- are becoming frustrated or struggling
- seem nervous, reluctant or unsure

- need a demonstration of a skill, e.g. how to hold scissors or how to add fractions
- are not understanding something
- are beginning to behave inappropriately or have given up.

Supporting development of skills

You should have high expectations of children and commitment to supporting the development of their skills. Some studies within schools have found that the attitudes of teachers can influence how well children actually achieve. In one study, teachers were told completely at random that certain children were high achievers. With their teachers believing in them, many of the children actually performed better than they had before.

You should base your expectations on a realistic appraisal of what children's current capabilities are, and what they might achieve next. But always aim to let children know that you believe they are good at learning, and remember to praise them for both achieving and trying their best. Key skills that help children to become effective learners are shown on the diagram on page 281.

Determination and motivation

You need to encourage children to persevere when they cannot get something right at first. Motivation and determination are linked, because a child who is motivated to achieve a goal grows in determination. You can motivate children by celebrating their achievements and praising them for trying. A small reward to look forward to often helps to motivate older children; it may be something as simple as saying to them, 'When you've finished your

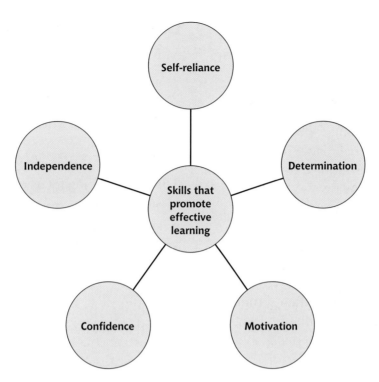

▲ Skills to help children become effective learners

assignment, why don't we hire that film you wanted to see?' But the best motivation of all is the desire to learn. That is why it is so important to foster a love of learning and an interest and curiosity about the world when children are young.

Confidence

Children who feel nurtured (cared for) and respected for who they are as an individual are likely to develop confidence. Children develop confidence when they take emotional risks successfully (see page 195). Experiencing physical risk and taking on challenges in a supporting environment also helps (see page 257). Teamwork activities can help to give confidence a boost as well.

Independence

Confidence breeds independence. Children experience a desire to do things for themselves and in their own way from an early age. Most of us will have experienced a frustrated 2-year-old who cannot quite manage a task such as putting on shoes themselves but definitely doesn't want our help! It is important to encourage independence as appropriate to children's age and abilities from early on. This helps children to become increasingly independent as they grow up. Adults won't always be with children in the older age range, so independence is a very important life skill. Also see page 309.

Self-reliance

Independence breeds self-reliance. Self-reliant learners trust themselves to pick up the knowledge and skills they need. This helps children to feel relaxed, which makes it easier for them to concentrate and participate in activities and experiences. In turn, this helps them to learn. You can also help by reminding children of their past learning successes.

Everyday routines

Everyday routines are essential to the care of children, and they also provide them with a sense of security and structure to their day. But they should not be overlooked as learning experiences. Settings can plan to enhance learning through everyday routines. For instance, in a pre-school you could:

- promote children's understanding of healthy foods through discussion at snack times and mealtimes
- promote good manners at the table
- make sets and groups when setting the table (i.e. putting in order the things that belong together) and talk about position, for example 'The fork goes opposite the knife'
- count out how many cups and plates are needed
- encourage children to pour their own drinks
- encourage children to put on and fasten their own outdoor clothes
- talk about hygiene with children when washing hands and toileting
- discuss respect for the environment when tidying up
- use name-recognition opportunities when marking the register
- allow children to see you writing when you make notes.

 Have a go!

Make a list of five everyday routines that exist within your setting. Now think about each routine in turn. Try to come up with at least one new way to use each routine as a learning opportunity with the children.

Different types of activity

Activities may be:

- adult directed: when an adult tells children what to do
- child initiated: when an activity is a child's idea
- structured: when an activity is planned with a learning focus or objective – see Unit 8
- spontaneous: when children spontaneously start an activity (free play).

Children learn best from a range of activity types. The table on page 284 gives examples of different types of activities that may be offered to children aged up to 16 years.

Consultation

It is important to consult children when supporting their learning, as appropriate to their abilities. This promotes the theory of 'active learning' you learnt about in Section 2. It also helps you to plan activities that meet children's needs, and to work with children in the ways that suit them best. Babies and very young children are unable to tell you what they want verbally. But by being a responsive carer, you can notice what they want and how they want to do things. Think of it as a kind of 'silent consultation'.

Sources of planning support

You can access sources of support in planning and development to help you to draw on best practice. Curriculum documents relevant to your home country will provide helpful guidance, supporting and underpinning your work. Extra support may also be available online. For instance, the Early Years Foundation Stage website holds very useful information. See the Weblinks section at the end of the unit.

▼ Age-appropriate activities

AGE	ADULT-DIRECTED ACTIVITY	CHILD-INITIATED ACTIVITY	STRUCTURED ACTIVITY	SPONTANEOUS ACTIVITY
3–5	Setting the table	Sinking boats in the water tray	Clapping out the rhythm of a nursery rhyme	Jumping from one paving stone to the next
5–8	Preparing food for snack time	Imaginary games	Putting objects into sets (i.e. all the red buttons together, all the hexagons together)	Telling a joke
8–12	Rehearsing a play	Making a birthday card for a friend	Visiting a museum	Singing along to background music
12–16	Writing about a personal experience	Setting out a skating area with ramps, jumps, etc.	Doing science experiments	Dancing with a friend

Training on curriculum frameworks may be offered in your region. You can also access support from relevant membership organisations, such the National Day Nursery Association, or the Pre-School Learning Alliance, and statutory organisations such as Sure Start.

Appropriate resources

It takes a wide range of equipment and materials to support a diverse range of activities and experiences. The list is extensive, but the table on pages 284–285 has a few examples for each area of learning in the Early Years Foundation Stage.

⊂◯◯ This links to assessment criteria **3.3**.

Flexibility and adaptations

It is important to remember that plans should be regarded as guidance. They should be flexible, a work in progress. You should be prepared to adapt them when appropriate – some practitioners find this difficult to accept after they have spent time on the planning stage. However, it is necessary to remain flexible so that your plan fits changing circumstances, meets the needs of the children and makes the most of opportunities that arise unexpectedly. For instance, you may need to adapt your plan if:

● you were unaware which children you would have in when the plan was designed. It may need to be altered to reflect individual children's needs, abilities and stages of development

● you did not know how many adults would be available to support activities – perhaps no volunteers are available, so an activity that required extra adult support will have to be adapted or postponed

▼ **Resources**

AREA OF LEARNING	RESOURCES/EQUIPMENT	ACTIVITIES
Personal, social and emotional development	Puppets, dolls and soft toys (with expressions for exploring feelings), table-top games, dressing-up clothes, cultural artefacts, a range of dolls showing a representation of people in the world (in terms of ethnicity, age, gender, ability), well-resourced imaginary areas including a home corner, comfortable quiet areas for resting and talking	New activities to build confidence, excitement, motivation to learn: leaves in the water tray, or earth to dig instead of sand, games for rules and turn taking, celebrating festivals for awareness and respect of the wider world, handling living things for sensitivity, pouring drinks for independence, circle time for talking about home
Communication, language and literacy	Varied range of mark-making materials and paper, letter frieze, letter cards/tiles/magnetic letters, comfortable book area/corner, books, pictures, poetry, fiction and non-fiction, story tapes, talking books, word processor, musical recordings, communication boards, signs, notices, labels, lists, sequencing cards/pictures	Story time, children retelling stories with props for understanding elements of stories, feely bags to promote descriptive language, role play for negotiation, mark-making opportunities in role-play area for writing with purpose, participating in and making up stories, rhymes, songs and poems, opportunities to write alongside adults
Problem solving, reasoning and numeracy	Counting beads, sorting trays, diverse objects to sort, scales, weights, rulers, measures, height chart, number cards/tiles/magnetic numbers, number and shape friezes/posters, number line, number signs/notices/symbols and labels, shape sorters, shape puzzles, different shaped construction resources, clocks, cash till, money	Counting how many we need (cups, for example), sharing out for calculating, singing number songs/rhymes for number operations (e.g. 'How many speckled frogs are left now?'), tidying up for sorting objects/positioning (e.g. 'That goes on the shelf'), finding numbers on our doors for number recognition, weighing cooking ingredients

▶▶

AREA OF LEARNING	RESOURCES/EQUIPMENT	ACTIVITIES
Knowledge and understanding of the world	ICT resources (e.g. computers, programmable toys, tape recorders), magnifying glasses, binoculars, money, books and CD-ROMs, water and sand tray/water and sand resources (e.g. funnels, wheels, rakes) living plants, manufactured construction materials (e.g. interlocking bricks), natural resources (e.g. fir cones, wooden logs)	Bark rubbings for observing closely, looking up information for asking questions and investigation, growing plants from seeds for observing change, patterns, similarities and differences, going for a walk and discussing ICT, e.g. traffic lights to identify technology, making recycled models from junk for building and joining
Physical development	Tools – scissors, brushes, rolling pins, cutters, computer mouse, etc. – threading beads, play dough/cornflour paste/jelly, different sized balls, hoops and quoits, large wheeled toys (ride-on toys), tunnels, carts to push and pull, low stilts, skittles, hoopla, bats, parachutes, slide, climbing frame, balance beam, swing, stepping stones	Playground games, e.g. 'What's the time Mr Wolf?' for movement – creeping, running etc., negotiating a chalk-drawn 'road' on wheeled toys for awareness of space (themselves and others), obstacle courses for travelling around, under, over and through, pretending to go 'on a bear hunt' for moving with confidence/imagination
Creative development	Diverse range of art and craft resources including different colours and textures, e.g. paper, card, tissue, cellophane, paint, glue, felt tips, crayons, craft feathers, lollipop sticks, sequins, buttons, pipe cleaners, etc., musical recordings, musical instruments, equipped role-play areas, dolls	Painting anywhere outside with water and large brushes for expression and imagination, making tactile collages for responding to what they see, touch and feel, music and movement for using imagination in movement and dance, singing time with musical instruments for play with expression
Remember: children's learning is not compartmentalised – all of these activities and resources can be used in many ways to promote different aspects/areas of learning, even at the same time	

- a natural event such as snow or hail occurs, and you decide to make the most of the experience and postpone other planned activities
- a key piece of equipment is broken or, alternatively, suddenly becomes unexpectedly unavailable
- an activity does not interest or engage the children as expected, and you decide to cut it short
- the children are so interested or engaged in an activity or experience that you decide to extend it.

Providing a stimulating environment

By carefully planning the environment, practitioners can make effective use of space both indoors and outdoors, and create a stimulating and enjoyable place for children and adults. When planning the layout of both indoor and outdoor areas, there are some important considerations. Room layout can affect:

- atmosphere
- mood of children and adults
- how children participate in activities
- how children play
- what children learn
- whether children rest
- whether children play indoors and/or outdoors.

Records

You should keep appropriate records about the implementation of plans. Your records may include:

- details of any changes or adaptations made to the curriculum plan
- which activities children participated in

- observations/assessments made
- progress made by children
- new learning achieved by children
- evaluation of session
- evaluation of own performance.

Records should be:

- dated
- stored carefully with regard to confidentiality as appropriate.

Sharing information with families and other professionals

The table on page 290 refers to consultation. It is good practice to involve parents, carers and families in the planning of provision and assessment, regardless of whether a theme is used. Familiarity with the setting's plans can help parents and carers to understand how curriculum frameworks operate and how their children are learning.

You may have parents and carers who would like to join in and suggest ideas, which is to be encouraged. However, many parents and carers may be willing to participate in other ways. For instance, they can help to collect resources (such as yoghurt pots to plant seeds in), or they might like to volunteer practical help during a session. A parent or carer may be able to visit the group to share something with the children – perhaps to show them their family's new pet kitten, or to demonstrate a hobby or a skill they use in their job.

It is also important that colleagues plan together where possible, or make other arrangements for consulting each other on planning matters. This allows for a melting pot of ideas, and it also shares the workload. It is an effective way to make sure that everyone understands their roles and responsibilities during a session (that includes volunteer helpers and students) so that the children can be supported effectively, and the activities are carried out as intended. If roles and responsibilities are not clearly defined, the implementation of the plan may well be adversely affected.

Outside professionals may also contribute to plans when appropriate – a speech therapist may suggest ideas for the support of a child with communication difficulties for instance. Children themselves can be involved in planning too. For example, they can suggest ideas, talk about their preferences and initiate their own activities spontaneously.

Details of how to access information from other services/professionals to aid the assessment of learning needs is included in section 2. Details about sharing the information you gather during assessment is included in section 4.

✓ Progress check

(1) What is the purpose of observational assessment in the Early Years Foundation Stage?

(2) Which key stages of the National Curriculum will children follow in primary school?

(3) What does 'consolidating learning' mean?

(4) What does 'extending learning' mean?

(5) How can you involve families in assessment and planning?

Learning Outcome 4

FOCUS ON...
how to record and evaluate the planning and assessment cycle

This links to assessment criteria **4.1**

The purpose of assessment

Through initial and ongoing assessment (**formative assessment**) of children's learning and development, practitioners can monitor children's progress. By summarising findings and drawing overall conclusions (**summative assessment**), practitioners can see what children should be learning next, and they can provide the appropriate learning opportunities. This is how assessment informs the planning process. Assessment also helps practitioners to identify areas where children need specific support.

See Unit 2, section 3, for full details of the planning cycle.

FAST FACT

Effective practitioners plan assessment. They make and record their assessments with care, and use them to inform their planning. With regard to confidentiality, they share their findings only with those who need the information.

Learning and stages of development

Children's learning is generally accepted to be strongly linked to their stage of development. You can start to understand child development through studying key theories of learning. Secure knowledge of the stages of child development enables practitioners to assess a child's capabilities. This is explained in more detail in Unit 2, section 1.

The assessment process

There are various methods of assessment, which we will look at below; but essentially, practitioners make observations of the children they work with, noticing the things they can do. Some of the observations:

- will be mental notes, part of what the practitioner knows about individual children
- are likely to be written down because they have been made at a planned time which the practitioner dedicated to observing that child's behaviour.

See Unit 2, section 2, for full details of how to observe children.

In addition, some knowledge may have been gained from seeing children's work, or through conversation with parents, carers, colleagues or other professionals. All of these things provide evidence of a child's achievements, and knowledge of them is collected over time.

Formative assessment = the first assessment of a child's knowledge and understanding or development
Summative assessment = the summarised findings of assessments

Assessing within curriculum frameworks

Practitioners carry out specific assessments to check children's progress against the curriculum framework they are following. Settings generally use an assessment form for this, which prompts practitioners to make judgements about children's achievements. Now all the accumulated knowledge the practitioner has gathered is used formally, and the judgements based on it are recorded.

G☺☺D PRACTICE

It is important to remember that each assessment is only a snapshot of the child's learning and development at that time, since children are constantly mastering new skills, learning new concepts and making new discoveries.

Assessment forms are helpful because they ensure practitioners remember to consider every aspect of development and learning included in the curriculum framework. They also ensure that the picture of progress built is based on assessment in the same areas – otherwise progress could not be accurately tracked over time.

FAST FACT

At the end of the Early Years Foundation Stage, practitioners are required to complete an 'Early Years Foundation Stage Profile' for each child. This is an assessment document that takes the form of a book, and records both formative and summative assessment. Many settings are now modelling the assessments they do throughout the EYFS on this style of assessment document.

G☺☺D PRACTICE

Practitioners must comply with all the curriculum framework requirements that apply to their setting, including those concerned with the way assessments are planned, conducted, recorded, shared, acted upon and stored. The timing and frequency of assessments must also meet these requirements.

Safeguards and objectivity

There are many advantages to knowing a child well when it comes to assessment. However, when assessing children's learning and development, it is important to remain objective – and the better you know a child the harder this can be. You should record facts based on evidence rather than simply on your opinion or what you believe to be true. Because they acknowledge this is difficult, practitioners often build safeguards into the assessment process to ensure accuracy.

The following strategies are safeguards:

- drawing on evidence from a variety of sources, including everyday observation, assessment and knowledge of individual children and information given by the child concerned

- consulting with colleagues who have also worked with individual children, and their parents and carers, and outside agencies or professionals so that evidence comes from different people

- asking colleagues who do not know individual children very well to contribute to the process of gathering evidence for formative and summative assessment, as they are likely to have the most objective view.

Consultation

It is important to conduct assessments in consultation with the relevant adults. The following table explains which people are likely to be involved in assessment and their roles.

▼ People involved in assessment and their roles

PEOPLE INVOLVED IN ASSESSMENT	ROLE IN ASSESSMENT PROCESS
Key worker	Usually the key worker is selected (as the practitioner who knows the most about an individual child) to plan and implement assessment. They must ensure there are adequate resources to carry out assessment, i.e. sufficient human and material resources to assess children's progress (ensuring there are enough observation forms available for instance). They must ensure those involved are confident, well informed, clear about assessment methods, requirements and the importance of making judgements based on a variety of sources
Other practitioners within setting	Colleagues of the key worker who work with the child are likely be required to contribute evidence and assist with making a summative assessment. All those who plan and support the child's learning and development will need to know the findings so that planning and practical work is informed. Anyone present at the time of assessment should be informed of the setting's process, and if appropriate their role
The child themselves	The child can be involved in talking about and celebrating their achievements, as well as expressing their opinions, preferences, knowledge and feelings
Parents, carers (and the wider family)	As the people who know the most about their child, parents and carers should be asked to contribute to the formative and summative assessment. They should also receive information about their child's progress and the learning and development planned for the future
Outside professionals	Any outside professional who will be asked to contribute to the assessment through the provision or consideration of evidence will be able to offer expert/specialist knowledge

Planning for assessment

Whatever method is of assessment is used, organisation and planning are important. You can ensure you have prepared thoroughly for assessment by checking that the considerations shown below have been addressed.

See page 286 for information about reporting/sharing assessment findings.

This links to assessment criteria **4.2**.

Children's achievements

When children have achieved something you should sensitively acknowledge, praise and celebrate their achievement. If you involve children in the assessment of their progress, milestones can be recorded together. It is important to look out for such achievements not only in order to mark them, but in order to recognise when children are ready to move on in terms of what they are ready to learn and experience next. When you decide what children should learn from activities, consider how you will know and recognise when they have learnt it – this will help you to notice new learning.

Moving on in this way keeps children motivated and keen to learn and participate. Children will not thrive in terms of their learning if they are made to carry out activities they have already mastered. However, children should be given sufficient opportunity to consolidate their learning (see page 279) and to choose their own direction via free-play and child-initiated activities.

For information about devising individual education/learning plans, see Unit 2, section 3.

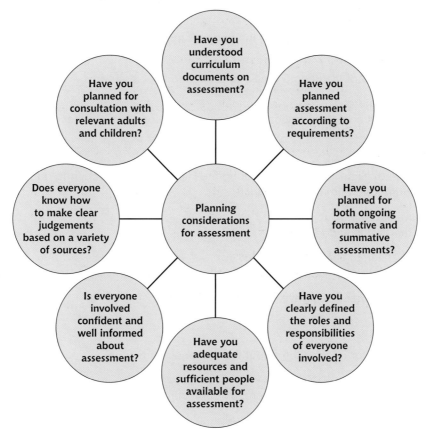

▲ Planning considerations for assessment

Reflection and evaluation

The process of reflecting on your own practice is central to a good assessment process. Reflection time should be built into each part of the planning cycle, including observation, planning and reporting. This will help you to do a thorough job, and to identify goals for your own self-development.

⚬⚬ Refer to Unit 5, page 209 for details of how to be a reflective practitioner.

✓ Progress check

(1) What is 'formative assessment'?

(2) What is 'summative assessment'?

(3) What are the stages of the planning cycle?

(4) What strategies can you use to ensure your assessments are objective?

(5) What are the benefits of building reflection into each stage of the planning cycle?

Weblinks

- www.friedrichfroebel.com
  A website created by the Froebel family

- www.reggioinspired.com/main.htm
  For a slideshow presentation about the Reggio Emilia approach

- www.teachers.tv/video/213
  To watch a video of the Reggio Emilia approach in UK classrooms

- www.highscope.org
  An independent non-profit research, curriculum development, teacher training, and public advocacy organisation

- www.high-scope.org.uk
  The Mission of High/Scope UK is to bring the High/Scope Approach to adults working with children from birth to adolescence

- www.playlink.org.uk/publications
  To view the *Best Play* document

- www.everychildmatters.gov.uk
  For further information about Every Child Matters

- www.standards.dcsf.gov.uk/eyfs
  The EYFS site

- www.direct.gov.uk
  Follow the links for information about the National Curriculum

- www.qca.org.uk/qca_13575.aspx
  For information about the new secondary curriculum

- www.dcsf.gov.uk/publications/childrensplan
  For details of the Children's Plan

Unit 8

Caring for children

Issues relating to caring for children are explored and examined in this unit. Provision for children's care and development is broad and varied. Within any setting, childcare workers recognise that each child is different and that meeting individual needs is the basis of providing for equality of opportunity. The diverse care needs of children must be supported by adults with a good understanding of the promotion of care and the need for future independence. Practitioners are in essence supporting the development of life skills and encouraging such skills is of the highest importance. It is important to remember that children's needs are not met just by one individual but that many people contribute to the care of children; in addition to the parents, these people will include the core adults at the setting and a range of professionals.

Learning Outcomes

In this unit you will learn about:

1. the range of settings that provide care for children

2. the diverse care needs of children

3. how to work effectively in multi-professional teams to support the care of children.

Learning Outcome 1

FOCUS ON...
the range of settings that provide care for children

This links to assessment criteria **1.1**, **1.2** and **1.3**

Care of children within the family and in society

What is a family?

It is surprisingly difficult to define what a family is, but it can be said that:

- all families have things in common
- all families are different!

One all-purpose definition is: 'a group of related people who support each other in a variety of ways, emotionally, socially and/or economically'.

Family life in some form is basic to the experiences of most children. The family has a strong influence on every aspect of a child's life and development. For this reason, childcare workers need to:

- understand the importance of the family to children's development
- know the particular family background of the children in their care
- understand the possible influences and effects of different family circumstances on children.

 Practical example

Different families

In a busy nursery class the teacher is aware of the personal details of some the children who attend. Anna lives with her grandmother, her mother is dead and her father is unknown. Royston and his half-sister live with his mother, who is a lone primary carer. Jamil lives with his grandparents, parents, uncle, aunt and cousins. Jasmin lives with her mother and her mother's female partner. Tom lives with his father, his father's new partner and her older daughter.

1. According to the definition above, which of these children are living in a 'family'?

2. Are there any reasons that some people might say that any of these children are not living in a family?

Functions of the family and similarities between families

The functions of the family are the things the family does for its members. Families all perform similar functions to a lesser or greater extent. These functions include:

- socialisation
- practical care and protection
- emotional and social support
- economic support.

Families do, however, have different traditions, customs and ways of carrying out these functions.

Socialisation

Families provide the basic and most important environment where children learn the **culture** of society of which they are a part. The family consciously and unconsciously teaches children the main aspects of any culture. These are shared **values**, **norms** and a language.

The peer group, schools and the media have a strong influence as children grow older; but children learn the foundations of culture within the family.

Practical care and protection

The family is generally very effective in providing practical day-to-day care of its dependent members – children, those who are sick or have disabling conditions and those who are old. Outside carers may sometimes have to be used, but this can cost a lot of money and may be a less effective form of care.

Emotional and social support

Families perform a very important role. They give a baby a name and initial position in society. (For example, when we hear about an abandoned baby, we immediately wonder who the child is and where the child comes from.) The family gives a child an identity, a sense of belonging and a feeling of being valued.

A child's family is able to provide a positive feeling of worth that is fundamental (i.e. basic and very important) to healthy emotional development. It meets the essential need for love and affection, company and security. In a busy and crowded life, people are less likely to find this support outside their family where contacts are more impersonal. Foster care, or adoption (that is, a substitute family), is now the usual provision in the UK – rather than residential care – for children who lose their families. This is because the experience of family life is regarded as very important for emotional and social wellbeing.

Economic support

The extent of economic support that families provide varies between cultures. The family is still an economic unit in many ways. However, in the UK and other European countries, family members are no longer totally dependent on each other for survival. The state now provides an economic safety net, through, for example, social security benefits, which prevents the starvation and destitution that people experienced in the past when they were totally dependent on their families.

Culture = the way of life, the language and the behaviour that are followed by particular groups of people

Values = beliefs that certain things are important and to be valued, for example a person's right to their own belongings

Norms = behaviours and beliefs accepted by a group

Structure of the family

Although there are many similarities between families, there are many variations in their structure and size. These differences can significantly affect the way the families carry out their functions and, therefore, the lives of children.

The nuclear family with two parents

The **nuclear family** is a family grouping where parents live with their children and form a small group. They have no other relatives living with them or near by. This type of family has become increasingly common in modern societies like that of the UK, where many people move for work or education and leave their family of origin (that is, the one a person is born into).

In countries where there is an agricultural economy and people work on the land, they are much more likely to remain near their **family of origin**.

Social and cultural variations in nuclear families

Nuclear families are more common in higher **socio-economic groups**, that is, among those employed in managerial, administrative and professional jobs (such as business managers, doctors, teachers or lawyers). These families are more likely to move around geographically in order to obtain education and employment. The fact that they may then earn higher incomes make it both possible and worth doing. In some nuclear families, parents have developed a system of sharing family responsibilities. This is called a democratic

▲ The nuclear family is often portrayed as the 'traditional' family in the media

system, because each partner shares earning money, childcare and domestic jobs.

Life in a nuclear family

Children who grow up in a nuclear family may:

- experience close relationships within the family
- receive a lot of individual attention
- have more space and privacy.

They may, however:

- feel a sense of isolation
- experience intensity of attention from parents
- have fewer people to turn to in times of stress
- suffer if their parents have no support system to care for them at times of illness or need.

Nuclear family = a family grouping where parents live with their children and form a small group with no other family members living near them

Family of origin = the family a child is born into

Socio-economic group = grouping people according to their status in society, based on their occupation which is closely related to their wealth and income

The nuclear family with a lone parent

The terms 'one-parent family' or 'lone-parent family' are also used to describe families with dependent children which are headed by a lone primary carer; of these, roughly 10 per cent are headed by men and 90 per cent by women. Of the women, about 60 per cent are divorced or separated, 23 per cent are single and 7 per cent widowed.

Social and cultural variations in lone-parent families

FAST FACT

An increasing number of children in the UK (one in every eight) are born to women who are not married and do not live with the father of the child.

The incomes of most lone parents are lower than those of most two-parent families. Many receive state benefits and their lifestyle is affected, as there is little spare money for luxuries. Both lone parents and their children are also vulnerable at times to difficulty, such as illness, if they do not have an extended family nearby to support them. The publicity given to the Child Support Agency focused attention on the government's attempts to make fathers more financially responsible for their families following separation.

Only a small minority of lone parents are well off economically and receive incomes that enable them to work and to afford day care for their younger children. Most lone mothers are less likely to work than those who have partners. However, the government now has a clear policy, Every Child Matters, to support them with their childcare costs, and to encourage them not to be dependent on welfare benefits. Most lone parents are divorced or separated; a small number are single parents. A high proportion is in the lower socio-economic group. The government does encourage absent fathers to contribute to their child's welfare.

Although there are many married couples in the African-Caribbean community, there is also a tradition of single parenthood. This was one of the outcomes of slavery in the Caribbean, where the nurturing of children by their fathers was forbidden. Subsequent high employment rates, both in the West Indies and in the UK, have perpetuated this tradition of low involvement by some fathers. Many African-Caribbean families, therefore, tend to be **matriarchal**, where women are important and dominant.

Life in a lone-parent family

Children who grow up in a lone-parent family may:

- establish a close, mutually supportive relationship with the parent they live with
- maintain a close relationship with their other parent and his or her family.

However they may:

- have experienced a period of grief and loss when their parents separated
- lose contact with their other parent resulting in loss of contact with the extended family
- experience lower material standards than children from a two-parent family
- receive less adult attention at times when their parent is coping with practical and emotional difficulties.

Matriarchal family = a family in which women are important and dominant

Extended family

An **extended family** extends beyond parent(s) and children to include other family members, for example grandparents, aunts and uncles. A family is usually referred to as extended when its members:

- live either together or very close to each other
- are in frequent contact with each other.

Many people who live at a distance from their relatives gain a great deal of emotional support from them, but distance makes the practical support offered by a close extended family difficult. When an extended family includes only two generations of relatives such as uncles, aunts and cousins, it is referred to as a joint family.

Social and cultural variations in extended families

People in lower socio-economic groups involved in semi-skilled or manual jobs are less likely to move from their locality for work or education. This means that they are more likely to be part of a long-established extended family system. This is evident in white, working-class families, where there is a tradition of women staying close to their mothers and a matriarchal system is common. Roles within the family are likely to be divided, with men traditionally the breadwinners and women in charge domestically, although they may also work part time or full time outside the home.

Families who came originally from India, Pakistan and Bangladesh have maintained a tradition of living in close extended families. Many came from rural areas where this was traditional. Their cultural and religious background also places a strong emphasis on the duty and responsibility to care for all generations of the family. These extended families are usually **patriarchal**, where men are dominant and make the important decisions. On marriage, a woman becomes a part of her husband's family and usually lives with or near them.

▲ An extended family can offer practical and emotional support to its members

---

Extended family = a family grouping that includes other family members who either live together, or very close to each other, and are in frequent contact with each other

Patriarchal family = a family in which men are dominant and make the important decisions

Families whose origins are in the Mediterranean countries, such as Cyprus and Italy, also tend to have strong extended family traditions. Family members frequently meet together for celebrations. Daughters tend to stay close to their mothers on marriage, but the man has considerable authority in the family.

Life in an extended family

Children who experience life within an extended family:

- have the opportunity to develop and experience a wide variety of caring relationships
- are surrounded by a network of practical and emotional support.

However they may:

- have little personal space or privacy
- feel they are being observed by and have to please a large number of people
- have less opportunity to use their individual initiative and action.

Reconstructed family

The reconstructed family, or reorganised family, is an increasingly common family system, since an increasing number of parents divorce and remarry. A reconstructed family contains adults and children who have previously been part of a different family. The children of the original partnership usually live with one parent and become the stepchildren of the new partner and stepsiblings of the new partner's children. Children born to the new partnership are half-siblings. Such families vary in their size and structure and may be quite complicated!

Social and cultural variations in reconstructed families

Reconstructed families are more common among people who accept divorce. This could include people who have no religious beliefs and Protestant Christians. Muslims do not forbid divorce but are committed to family life and divorce is less common.

Reconstructed families are less common among people who have a strong belief in the family and who disapprove of divorce, usually because their religious doctrines are against it. These include Hindus, Sikhs and Roman Catholics for whom marriage is sacred and should not be dissolved.

Life in a reconstructed family

This can be a positive experience for a child because:

- their parent may be happier, more secure and have greater financial resources
- the child gains a parent and possibly an extended family.

However, they may:

- have difficulty relating to a step-parent and stepbrothers and sisters
- have to compete for attention with children of their own age
- feel a loss of attention because they have to share their parent
- have to accept the birth of children from the parent's new relationship.

Partnership arrangements

Adults have a wide variety of arrangements for the way they form partnerships. These provide different care environments for children. Such partnership arrangements include the following:

- *Monogamy* – the marriage between heterosexual partners (one partner of each gender); this is still popular in the UK, although the rate of marriage has declined since the 1960s.

- *Polygamy* – the marriage of a person of one gender (usually a man) to a number of others (usually women) at the same time; it is illegal to enter into this arrangement in the UK, where it is called bigamy. It has been very common in other countries, especially those with Muslim cultures.

- *Serial monogamy* – this term is used to describe one person of either gender having one partner followed by another over a period of time, each followed by separation or divorce.

- *Cohabitation* – partners live together without getting married; this is increasingly common in the UK, where about 30 per cent of partners cohabit.

- *Homosexual partnerships* – especially between women – are increasingly viewed as an acceptable base for the rearing of children. As recently as the early 1980s, women who left their husbands to live with a woman often lost the custody of their children; such an arrangement was thought unsuitable.

FAST FACT

In June 1994, two women from Manchester became the first lesbian couple to be made joint legal parents of the child of one of them. This was made possible by the Children Act 1989 because it enables parental responsibility to be shared by a range of people. All the research carried out since the 1960s shows no differences in the social and emotional development of children of lesbian and heterosexual partnerships, or changes to their gender orientation.

Practical example

Family life

Mr and Mrs Jameson were married 26 years ago. They have three children, Sylvia, Roy and Belinda. Sylvia divorced her husband and now lives with her new partner in a house in the same road as her parents and sees them frequently. She has two daughters and he has a son, all of whom live with her. Sylvia's ex-husband has remarried and now has a baby son. Roy is also married, to a woman who has a child but was never married; they have one son, but live many miles away. Belinda lives locally with her female partner and their two daughters, each from previous relationships that have ended in divorce.

1. Which family members are monogamously married?

2. How many of their original marriages ended in divorce?

3. Which people are living as part of an extended family?

4. Are any people in this case study not living in a family?

5. Draw a family tree and try to include all these people.

Family life, care and protection: the alternatives

The family, both in the past and present, is by far the most common environment for bringing up children, both in the UK and other countries. The family is probably the most common arrangement for childcare because it is the most practical way to meet the needs of both the child and the parents. However, there are circumstances and places where alternatives to family life have been either necessary or thought to be preferable. Some examples of such alternatives are children's homes, communes and kibbutzim.

Changing patterns of family life and roles

Family size and family roles

The average number of dependent children per family in the UK is now a little under two children. This has gradually fallen since the middle of the 19th century when it was about six children. The most significant reason for this change is:

- increased availability of contraception and legal abortion
- a rise in the standard of living, together with the fact that children are costly to support and they start work later than in the past
- changes in women's roles, attitudes and expectations; many women regard child-rearing as only a *part* of their lives and want to do other things as well.

Although the average family has two children, there are of course larger families. Children from large families have some differences in their life experiences.

Research shows that on average their life chances are not as good as children from small families.

Many children grow up in families where they are the only child. These children may be more successful, but there are possible disadvantages for them.

Changing gender roles within the family

There is evidence that, in families across a range of social and cultural groups in the UK, the traditional roles of male as 'provider and breadwinner' and female as 'carer and homemaker' have changed. Men are increasingly involved in the care of their young children, and women are more likely to work outside the home. Research shows, however, that women still have the majority of responsibility for either doing or organising the domestic work, whatever their social or cultural background.

Women and employment

FAST FACT

Nearly half of the workforce in the UK is female.

Although an increasing number of women with dependent children work outside the home, the younger their children are, the less likely they are to work either full time or part time. The growth of affordable childcare provision for young children is leading to an ever-increasing number of working mothers, and the government is encouraging this trend by supporting the expansion of childcare. In some European countries, there is a much higher level of provision and a much higher proportion of mothers working outside the home.

▲ It has become more common in recent years for dads to look after the children at home while the mums go out to work

make arrangements for the care of their children. An increasing choice of day care alternatives is now available – partly as a response to this demand and also in response to government initiatives. Research shows that children's needs can be met satisfactorily if they are provided with good day care.

The outside world

Beyond the core care within the family, children are cared for and educated in a variety of ways across a range of settings. These settings may be statutory, private or voluntary.

⚭ Details of the range of settings across the sector can be found in Unit 1 of this book. Details of relevant legislation can be found in Units 1, 3, 6, and 14.

Working parents

When both parents of young children work outside the home, they have to

✎ Practical example

Changing family roles

Wendy is married to John and they have a baby, Chloë, who is 9 months old. Chloë has attended a day nursery for 5 days a week since she was 6 months old, when her mother returned to work full time as a pharmacist. Wendy and John share all household tasks, including looking after Chloë, shopping and cooking. John's mother, Mary, sometimes visits and helps them out, but she has worked full time for the past 10 years so gets little spare time even for her own household tasks, although she does have a cleaner. She is a little concerned about her son and daughter-in-law's lifestyle and often reminds them of how different things were when they were children. Wendy gets a bit annoyed when Mary reminds them of how she gave up work when her children were young and only returned part time when they went to school. Wendy's grandfather, however, expresses very strong feelings about his granddaughter's lifestyle. He remembers the time when his wife gave up work and became a housewife as soon as they were married. When Wendy, in her annoyance, once said to him, 'What for?', he replied, 'To look after me, that's what for. I went out early and she needed to be there to cook my breakfast.' Wendy decided not to respond to this, as it was so different from her own experiences!

① *What are the major changes in childcare practice that can be seen over these three generations?*

② *How do these three generations reveal the changing role of women and paid work?*

③ *What changes can you see in men's and women's domestic roles?*

④ *Why do you think Wendy decided not to respond to her grandfather's statement?*

✓ Progress check

① What is the average number of dependent children per family in the UK?

② What are the most significant reasons for reduction in family size?

③ Why do an increasing number of mothers work?

Learning Outcome 2

FOCUS ON...
the diverse care needs of children

This links to assessment criteria **2.1** and **2.2**

Development needs

Social and emotional development

All children are individuals and, as such, grow and develop at different rates and have varying needs. Children's needs differ as they grow and change. Emotional development is the growth of a child's ability to feel and express an increasing range of emotions appropriately. It includes the development of feelings about and for other people, and the ability to express them appropriately and with self-control. Social development is the growth of the child's ability to relate to others appropriately, and become independent, within a social framework. It includes the development of social skills and independence.

An important strand of social and emotional development is the development of self-concept and self-image. This is the picture we have of ourselves and the way in which we think other people see us. Self-identity includes the characteristics that make us separate and different from others. This could also be referred to as personality.

Clearly, all of these issues relate to development of children; however, they shape and affect us as we grow and become adults. It is therefore very important that children are supported as they grow and develop, and that they are supported by knowledgeable adults who have their best interests at heart and are aware of their role and their limits.

The stages and sequences of all areas of children's development can be found in Unit 2 of this book.

Some general principles of development

It is important to remember the following:

- Development is a holistic process: all areas of development are integrated and interact with each other; they mix together and are affected by each other.

- The interaction of different factors results in an individual pattern of development that varies from one child to another.

- Development is usually made up of a period of rapid growth followed by a period of relative calm. During a period of calm, the previous growth is consolidated. This means that it becomes a definite and practised part of the child's being. One development area may be relatively calm while there is more rapid growth in another.

- The path of development moves from complete immaturity and dependence towards social and emotional maturity.

- Children do not develop in isolation; they develop within family systems. Families have individual characteristics that influence each child differently.

- A child's family exists within a wide-ranging cultural system. The experience of this cultural environment has a profound effect both on the family and on the child's behaviour.

- Family and cultural environments interact with and affect children's developing skills, their awareness of themselves and their relationships with others.

The role of the adult

The role of adults in children's development should be seen as a role of the highest order and one to be taken very seriously. Children view adults as role models and take their cues from the ways that adults behave and interact around them and with them.

Key workers

The key-worker system in many centres is where a named person takes responsibility for groups of children. This enables the member of staff and the child to form close relationships. The adult is responsible for getting to know each child's abilities, needs and preferences and then planning appropriately to support the child. Key workers also liaise with parents and carers and, where appropriate, with other agencies involved with the child. This system ensures that the parents and carers have someone with whom they can talk who knows the child very well.

GOOD PRACTICE

When planning activities and routines the adult's role is vital and needs careful consideration. Clearly, with routines and the physical care of children, hygiene and safety are the adult's responsibility. Why this is important and what the adult needs to do to ensure a clean and safe environment should be included in the plans and discussed with children and other adults.

Promoting social and emotional development

It is obvious that, in this area of development, children are fundamentally affected by the thoughts and actions of others. The guidelines on page 306 summarise, in a practical way, some of the principles involved in encouraging a positive self-image and self-concept, and healthy social and emotional development.

In order to apply the golden rules and to ensure that adults fulfil their role, it is important to understand how behaviour is learned.

There are several different ways that encourage children to learn about the behaviour that is expected of them.

Rewards and punishments

Adults encourage acceptable behaviour in children by rewarding it. A reward can be a very simple thing like a smile, saying thank you, giving praise or a hug; it also includes giving children things such as toys, food or a treat. Children can also

G😊😊D PRACTICE

20 golden rules:

1. From the earliest age, demonstrate love and give children affection, as well as meeting their all-round developmental needs.

2. Provide babies with opportunities to explore using their five senses.

3. Encourage children to be self-dependent and responsible.

4. Explain why rules exist and why children should do what you are asking. Use 'do' rather than 'don't' and emphasise what you want the child to do rather than what is not acceptable. When children misbehave, explain to them why it is wrong.

5. Encourage children to value their own cultural background.

6. Encourage children to do as much for themselves as they can, to be responsible and to follow through activities to completion.

7. Do not use 'put-downs' or sarcasm.

8. Give children activities that are a manageable challenge. If a child is doing nothing, ask questions to find out why. Remember that they may need time alone to work things out.

9. Give appropriate praise for effort, more than for achievement.

10. Demonstrate that you value children's work.

11. Provide opportunities for children to develop their memory skills.

12. Encourage children to use language to express their own feelings and thoughts and how to think on their feet.

13. Provide children with their own things, labelled with their name.

14. Provide opportunities for role play.

15. Give children the opportunity to experiment with different roles, for example leader, follower.

16. Provide good flexible role models with regard to gender, ethnicity and disability.

17. Stay on the child's side! Assume they mean to do right rather than wrong. Do not presume on your authority with instructions such as 'You must do this because I am the teacher and I tell you to', unless the child is in danger.

18. Be interested in what children say; be an active listener. Give complete attention when you can and do not laugh at a child's response, unless of course the response is supposed to be funny.

19. Avoid having favourites or victims.

20. Stimulate children with interesting questions that make them think.

Remember: Every Child Matters.

feel rewarded by the good feeling they get when they please adults. Children want rewards to be repeated, and this encourages them to repeat the behaviour that brought the reward.

Adults discourage behaviour by punishing or ignoring it. Punishments, like rewards, can take a variety of forms; they include telling children they are wrong, physically or emotionally hurting them, depriving them of something they want, ignoring or isolating them. Children usually enjoy adults' attention and do not like to be ignored. There are many different views about the relative effectiveness of rewards and punishments in changing behaviour.

Copying and imitating

Children learn how to behave by copying people in different roles. They use people as role models. For example, children copy what their mothers or fathers do and learn a lot about the roles of men and women. The idea that children develop partly by copying behaviour has implications for childcare workers, since children will also use them as role models.

Role play

Children enjoy pretending to be someone or something else. In their play they sometimes act as if they are another person; this is called *role play*. They often copy the adults who are close to them, or the ones they see on television. When they do this, they may not be able to tell whether or not the adults' behaviour is socially acceptable. This may happen, for example, when children copy violent parents in their play or general behaviour.

▲ Peer group pressure becomes increasingly strong as children get older

Peer group pressure

Peers (other children) can exert very strong pressure on children to behave in certain ways. Children change their behaviour when they are with their peer group, and may sometimes behave in ways that they know are unacceptable to adults. A peer group can punish a child who does not conform to their expectations by excluding the child from the group or by making the child feel different. The fear of exclusion from the group can be stronger to some children than fear of adult punishment. This peer group pressure can become a form of bullying. There is an increasing awareness of the different forms bullying can take, and a greater commitment to combating bullying.

⊂⊃ Unit 6 of this book examines health and wellbeing in further detail.

Activities which support and maintain the daily life of children

⊂⊃ This section links to assessment criteria **2.2** and **2.3**.

There are a range of activities that are considered necessary for daily living. Discussing this subject with others would enable us to draw up a list of **independent life skills** based on our own experiences. If we were to pose the question, 'What do I need to be able to do to get through the day?' we would probably create a personalised list based on our knowledge and experiences.

Activities for Daily Living can be described as the things we do in normal everyday living, which include self-care. The medical model for Activities for Daily Living is used by health professionals to measure the functional status of a person. This model considers all or some of the 12 activities of living drawn up by Nancy Roper in the 1970s.

Practical example

Promoting healthy development – using praise

Jo attends a nursery school. She is a lively and responsive 4-year-old child who uses the nursery resources enthusiastically. One morning Jo is sitting in the book area looking at different books, she asks a childcare and education worker who is standing near the area if she can read a book to the worker. The worker knows that Jo can read very few words but willingly agrees, knowing that the policy of the school is to encourage free reading in this way. Jo turns the pages of the book and mainly uses the pictures to tell the story; she also reads a few words correctly and the worker helps her with a few others. The worker says, 'I think you are very clever, well done! Would you like to read another book to me?'

(1) Why would this response encourage Jo to want to go on reading books?

(2) If the worker had said to Jo, 'That wasn't very good; you didn't know many words', what effect could this have on the child's behaviour in future?

(3) What knowledge about children's social and emotional development and their behaviour is the worker basing her responses on?

(4) List some other rewards that can be used in a school to foster healthy social and emotional development and encourage acceptable behaviour.

The 12 activities are:

- maintaining a safe environment
- communicating
- breathing
- eating and drinking
- eliminating
- personal care – grooming and dressing
- controlling body temperature
- mobilising
- working and playing
- expressing sexuality
- sleeping
- dying.

In relation to the needs of the developing child, and in the context of the role of the childcare worker in promoting and supporting children's independence and self-care, it is appropriate to consider some of the activities listed above. Childcare workers support children by:

- maintaining a safe environment
- communicating
- providing for and supporting the nutritional needs of children
- supporting children to develop self-help skills for their personal care and hygiene practices
- supporting the development of mobility

Independent life skills = skills needed to live and care for oneself

- supporting play and learning
- encouraging and supporting sleep and rest.

▲ At 2 years 6 months children can dress with supervision

Dependence to independence

It is fair to say that there is some distance to travel from **dependence** to achieving total **independence**: consider the new born baby, dependent on carers for it's every need. As they mature, children are seen to develop independence in a range of skills and daily activities. It is also fair to say that adults, as role models, can have a huge impact on the development of independence.

▲ At 3 years children can toilet themselves and wash hands

Have a go!

We have all seen children manage a morning at the setting, pouring their own drinks, using the toilet and putting on their own coat. But can we say that they did this completely independently or were there aspects of these tasks that were prompted and facilitated by adults?

- Next time that you are in a setting, observe a range of children when they participate in the following daily activities:
    - pouring drinks
    - using the toilet area
    - putting on their coats.
- Note the role of the adult and try to decide whether the children completed the tasks independently or if they were dependent on the adults to prompt them.

Promoting and encouraging independence and self-care

There are several ways in which carers can encourage a child to develop independence in personal hygiene. These include the following:

- provide positive role models
- establish care routines that encourage cleanliness from early babyhood
- make hygiene fun – use toys, games and books
- encourage the child to choose and use their own items such as toothbrush and toothpaste
- allow children to participate, to wash themselves during bath-time, to brush their own hair and teeth

---

Dependence = relying on another for support
Independence = the emotional need to feel you are managing and directing your own life

- ensure that sinks and toilet facilities are accessible to all children

- make sure that the supporting adults have time to complete the activities with the child

- make sure that the adults are realistic and that they provide manageable challenges for children, which are achievable and support the development of independence and self-esteem.

Encouraging children to make choices and decisions and promoting some form of responsibility will also contribute to developing independence. As children grow and develop, they will benefit from opportunities to choose their own clothes, make decisions about portions of food at mealtimes, and have the chance to have some form of responsibility such as carrying their own items to nursery in their own bag.

The following table illustrates some of the self-care skills that you might notice in children of different ages.

The ability to develop self-care skills and independence may be affected by special

> ### G☺☺D PRACTICE
>
> Effective and supportive adults should:
> - be aware of the development stage of the child and support this
> - be patient and resist the temptation to complete tasks for children
> - allow time for children to fulfil tasks
> - be patient
> - be ready to praise effort as well as achievement and to share this good news with parents and carers
> - support the child by creating manageable and realistic opportunities.

needs or disabilities. As stated in Unit 14 of this book, it is important to have realistic and well-informed expectations of children and young people. It may be necessary to teach and support skills at a pace and in a manner that suits the individual child. It is also important to remember that all children should be treated with respect; their privacy and dignity must be considered when supporting their needs. Any issues that arise should be discussed and clarified with senior colleagues and supervisors.

▼ Children's self-care skills

AGE	ACTIVITY
Under 1 year	Babies start to learn to drink out of a cup and hold out limbs when they are being dressed; may brush hair with a hair brush
1–4 years	Get undressed, brush teeth, wash hands, use the toilet, imitate self-care tasks on toys, for example feeding teddy and wiping its face
4–8 years	Use a knife and fork when eating, dress and undress, wash and use the toilet – may need some prompts to complete the whole task
8–12years	Should be fulfilling self-care routines – but may need gentle reminders

✔ Progress check

1. List five of the golden rules
2. What is role play? What are the benefits of role play activities?
3. What effect can peer pressure have on children and young people?
4. What is the difference between the terms 'dependence' and 'independence'?
5. List five ways that childcare workers can contribute to the development of daily living skills in children.
6. Look again at the development table on page 310 and consider ways of supporting these skills for children in their development.

Learning Outcome 3

FOCUS ON...

how to work effectively in multi-professional teams to support the care of children

⬭⬭ This links to assessment criteria **3.1**

⬭⬭ The roles and responsibilities of a range of professionals are described in Unit 14 of this book.

GOOD PRACTICE

What makes the team effective? Look at the table on page 313.

Effective teams

In most work settings, people work as part of a team. To be effective, any professional team should have:

- clearly defined aims and objectives that all members can put into words and agree to put into practice
- effective leaders who manage the work of the team, encourage and value individual contributions and deal with conflict
- team members who are:
  - building and maintaining good working relationships
  - demonstrating effective communication skills
  - expressing their views assertively rather than aggressively
  - understanding, recognising and valuing the contributions of others
  - carrying out their expected role.

Teamwork is most effective when members understand their role and to whom they are accountable.

Working with colleagues in multi-professional teams

Within a childcare setting, teams of professionals may be required to work together for a variety of reasons. If children at the setting are being assessed because they may have learning difficulties, behavioural difficulties or special needs, other professionals will be required to engage with the children, carry out assessments and observations and liaise with staff. Professionals may be working to develop particular interventions or strategies to support the care and learning needs of a child.

⬭⬭ Further information about such situations can be found in Unit 14 of this book.

Special programmes for children

Childcare workers may be asked to complete child observations, share their knowledge and experience of the child and support and implement programmes

▼ Characteristics of effective teams

CHARACTERISTIC	BENEFIT
Cooperation	The children see the benefits of people working together and cooperating with each other
Consistency	All team members adopt the same approach to the task of caring for children and working with their families
Encouragement	Members of the team stimulate, motivate, praise, encourage and support one another
Respect	Team membership satisfies the need to belong and to be respected and to have ideals and aims confirmed and shared by others
Efficiency	The skills of all members are used to arrive at the best solutions
Belonging	Individuals feel a sense of belonging and can share problems, difficulties and success
Sharing	Responsibility and insight is shared by all
Innovation	Individuals become more willing to adopt new ways of thinking and working
Balance	The strengths and weaknesses of one person are balanced by the strengths and weaknesses of others

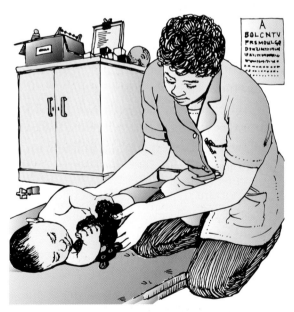

▲ Other professionals may be working to develop particular strategies or interventions

▲ In most settings, people work as part of a team

which have been developed and agreed. Such programmes may include:

- programmes for personal care
- feeding
- play and learning
- behaviour support
- speech and language therapy
- physiotherapy.

Programmes will be individualised and personal to the child in question. As part of the multi-professional team, the childcare worker will also be expected to keep records of such interventions and programmes. These records will serve to form part of any review or evaluation of programmes and it is therefore essential that the records are accurate, legible, and up to date and recorded in the required format.

At this stage of multi-professional working, it is important to put into practice everything that you have learned about observing children, such as the following key points:

- confidentiality
- objectivity
- ensuring the rights of children and their families
- contextualising the observation.

Working with other professionals

It is fair to suggest that because childcare workers are generally in day-to-day contact with individual children and their families, they have a broad knowledge and understanding of that child. It can therefore be difficult to accept that others, such as visiting professionals, may be more able to assess and judge what is best for the child at certain times. At this point, it is therefore important to remember

that other professionals have undertaken training in their area of expertise and they are therefore in a position to guide and inform others using their professional skills and knowledge.

Supporting parents

Parents can find the multi-professional approach quite daunting and childcare professionals who have day-to-day contact with them are in a position to support, interpret and keep them up to date with any developments. However, it is essential that such engagement is left to or referred to senior staff or supervisors, as this will ensure that everyone is operating within their expected role and the limitations of such roles. If a supervisor, is unable to answer parents' questions, they will be in a better position to put the parent in contact with the appropriate person or agency.

Confidentiality

One of the ways that we show respect for the rights of children is in maintaining confidentiality. Confidentiality requirements are laid down in the procedures and policies at the setting; local authorities will have procedures to follow which will have been devised in line with current legislation.

It is important that the needs of children are not discussed beyond the multi-professional team, that the expected methods of communication are adhered to and that documentation is kept in line with procedures. The parents of the child will already be part of this process and their needs and rights must also be considered. Parents may choose to discuss issues about their child with other people and this is their choice. It is not acceptable for any childcare worker to discuss children or their families with other parents under any circumstances. If you are asked for information, for example a telephone number or address, you must not give it; you may find it easier to refer the enquiry to a senior colleague or the manager of the setting.

It is also important to ensure confidentiality of information that you have been asked to send to other professionals. It is best to take advice locally about the best way to do this.

Further information about confidentiality can be found in Unit 5 of this book.

✓ Progress check

① List five characteristics of effective team work.

② Why is it important to ensure that teams communicate effectively?

③ Which other professionals might be involved at your setting?

Weblinks

- www.everychildmatters.gov.uk
  For current information and guidance about professional practice

- www.cwdc.org.uk
  The Children's Workforce Development Council, for information specific to the sector

- www.ofsted.gov.uk
  For information about the Early Years Foundation Stage

- www.parentscentre.gov.uk
  For information about supporting children's development

- www.homestart.org.uk
  Offers support and information for families with young children

- www.cpcs.org.uk
  The Centre for Parent and Child Support – offers information, advice and training as well as sources of current research

unit 9

Development of professional skills within children's education

Professional skills are the expected standards of the sector. Practitioners need to be aware of these expectations and ensure that they behave appropriately. Professional standards include how you present yourself and dress, the policies and procedures that you need to be aware of in relation to your role, the way that you communicate with others, timekeeping and attendance. Professional standards are set out in most settings through a code of practice for staff. Practical placements are a key feature of this unit.

This unit links very closely to a range of other units within this book and a table of links has been included at the end.

Learning Outcomes

In this unit you will learn about:

1 the professional standards expected of the practitioner

2 how to apply theoretical knowledge to the professional setting

3 how the planning cycle is used in various practical settings.

4 how to meet the needs of individual children and groups of children in a variety of settings

5 how professional practice is linked to legislation, policies and procedures

Learning Outcome ① 1

FOCUS ON...
the professional standards expected of the practitioner

This links to assessment criteria **1.1, 1.2** and **1.3**

Professional standards

The professional standards expected of the practitioner include:

- timekeeping
- regular attendance
- appropriate dress code
- communication skills
- personal hygiene
- smoking
- role models.

Timekeeping

Timekeeping is an essential standard which the practitioners are expected to meet. Keeping to the expected time for attendance at a setting, college or the workplace reflects well on the individual. Lateness has an impact on everyone who is relying on you to arrive or do things on time. If you are late for college, for example, it will be disruptive for the tutor and other students and will also affect your own learning. Within the setting, lateness may suggest a lack of interest or commitment of the individual. Similarly, when you have been on a break during the day, a late return may mean that others are then late taking their break and therefore this will impact on the routine and planned activities later in the day.

Regular attendance

Attending placements and college on a regular basis is a core requirement of any programme. It is the responsibility of every individual to attend when they are expected to and to have everything with them that they need to fulfil their responsibilities and to get the most out of the experience.

When you are expected at a setting, lateness or non-attendance can have an impact on the day and the people and children who were expecting you. For example, children may feel let down and disappointed that you are not there to fulfil a commitment that you had made to play with them or help with a task. Some children and parents may have come to rely on you to follow their individualised settling-in strategy. Similarly, other adults may be expecting you to carry out a specific task or activity. Whatever the situation, it is important that any unavoidable absence is communicated as early as possible as this will enable the setting to make alternative arrangements if necessary.

Appropriate dress code

Within the world of work, there will be an expectation that individuals present themselves in an appropriate manner. The way that you present yourself will serve to shape the opinion others form about you. It is therefore very important that your clothes and personal appearance are appropriate and acceptable for the job. You must present yourself in a manner that suggests that you respect the importance of your contact with children and young people, that you are ready to fulfil the role that is expected of you and that you have self-respect.

Part of this expectation is the dress code for the setting or organisation. Anyone working with children needs to be dressed according to the requirements. Some settings provide uniforms; others provide a tabard, and there are settings where individuals can choose what they wish to wear. This last point is a responsibility in itself and you will need to make appropriate choices. As part of any dress code in a childcare setting, the appropriate style of jewellery, footwear, accessories, finger nails, make-up and hair style should also be explained. There is a tendency to want to follow trends and fashions but this is not necessarily what is best for you or the children that you work with. All workwear must be appropriate to the setting, adhere to the health and safety requirements and set positive role models for children; all items should be clean and in good repair.

Some settings might suggest suitable clothing for children to wear; in the school environment; it is common to expect children to wear uniform and there will also be restrictions on jewellery and footwear for health, hygiene and, of course, safety reasons.

Communication skills

Communication skills are an essential part of professional practice within children's

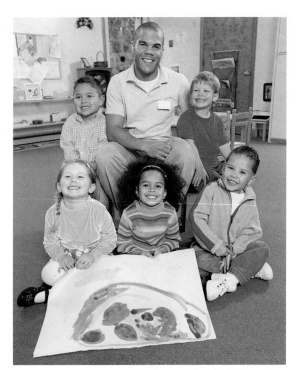

▲ Personal presentation is important at all times

education. It is essential that everyone is aware of the methods for communicating within the organisation amongst the staff team and beyond the setting to parents, carers and other professionals.

Communication is covered in more detail in Unit 1 of this book.

Personal hygiene

Personal hygiene is very important in your work and contact with children and young people. Practitioners should ensure that they present themselves well in clean clothes and that they have attended to personal hygiene needs. During the day, hand washing and cleaning of spills on your own clothes is essential, not just for hygiene reasons but so that you are a good role model for the children. It is also a good idea to have some spare clothes with you just in case!

Smoking

In line with government regulations, smoking is not permitted inside public buildings and this rule applies to you and your setting. Workers who do choose to smoke should only ever smoke off site and out of the view of children and their parents. Many settings now insist that staff who smoke on breaks change out of their work clothes or uniform before doing so, because the smell of smoke tends to stay on clothes. Smokers should consider the implications for the health and wellbeing of the children and themselves. Government health promotion supports 'stop smoking' groups through most local health authorities and GP surgeries.

Role models

All of the points above contribute to the practitioner being a good role model for children and young people.

 Have a go!

What not to wear!

Look at the following statements and offer what you consider to be good practice advice; discuss your advice with a colleague:

- It's a hot summer and the staff at the nursery are complaining that the uniform trousers and shoes that they have to wear are causing them to overheat. What do you think they should do? What alternatives would be appropriate?

- Natasha is going on holiday on Friday night, but the only appointment that she can get to get her nail extensions done is on Wednesday. What do you think she should do?

- Rochelle has a tongue piercing. At lunchtime, the children notice it and ask her about it; one child says that she would like to get her tongue pierced. How do you think Rochelle should deal with this situation? What advice would you give to someone who was working with children who was considering a piercing like this?

Learning Outcome 2

FOCUS ON...
how to apply theoretical knowledge to the professional setting

This links to assessment criteria **2.1**

CACHE statement of values

You must ensure that you;

1 Put children first by:
   - ensuring the child's welfare and safety
   - showing compassion and sensitivity
   - respecting the child as an individual
   - upholding the child's rights and dignity
   - enabling the child to achieve their full learning potential.

2 Never use physical punishment.

3 Respect the parent as the primary carer and educator of the child.

4 Respect the contribution and expertise of staff in the care and education field, and other professionals with whom they may be involved.

5 Respect the customs, values and spiritual beliefs of the child and their family.

6 Uphold the Council's Equality of Opportunity Policy.

7 Honour the confidentiality of information relating to the child and their family, unless its disclosure is required by law or is in the best interests of the child.

(From: www.cache.org.uk)

In order to uphold the CACHE statement of values, childcare workers need to be able to apply the values to their own practice.

Each work setting is likely to have its own specified aims and objectives to influence and inform its practice. These, together with supporting policies and procedures, should be underpinned by the rights and needs of children.

Have a go!

Consider the table of policies and procedures below and see if you can relate each point to one or more of the points in the CACHE statement of values.

POLICY/PROCEDURE	CACHE STATEMENT OF VALUES
Equal opportunities policy	
Admissions procedure	
Health and safety policies and procedures	
Child protection policies and procedures	
Partnership with parents	
Managing behaviour	
Record keeping	
Emergency procedures	

Signposting to other units for content requirements of Unit 9

LEARNING OUTCOME	ASSESSMENT CRITERIA	UNIT LINK
1 The professional standards expected of the practitioner	1.1	Unit 1 and this unit
	1.2	Unit 1 and this unit
	1.3	Unit 1 and this unit
2 How to apply theoretical knowledge to the professional setting	2.1	Units 1, 2, 3, 5, 6 and 14
	2.2	Units 2 and 7
3 How the planning cycle is used in various practical settings	3.1	Units 2 and 7
4 How to meet the needs of individual children and groups of children in a variety of settings	4.1	Units 1, 2, 3, 5, 6, 7, 8 and 14
5 How professional practice is linked to legislation, policies and procedures	5.1	Units 1, 3, 5, 6, 8 and 14
	5.2	Unit 1 and this unit

 Weblinks

- www.cwdc.org.uk
  This is the website of the Children's Workforce Development Council and contains information about current issues relating to professional practice

- www.ndna.org.uk
  The National Day Nurseries Association aims to enhance the development and education of children in their early years through the provision of support services to members

- www.pat.org.uk
  This is the website of the Professional Association of Teachers – here you can find information about practice and issues relating to support staff

- www.ofsted.gov.uk
  This is the website of the Office for Standards in Education

unit 12

Nutrition and healthy food for children

This unit will provide you with knowledge of the principles of nutrition and how to provide a healthy diet for children. This will include baby and infant feeding, influences on food and diet, safe food preparation and disorders that may need a special diet. The social and educational role of food and the role of the practitioner in encouraging healthy eating is considered.

Learning Outcomes

In this unit you will learn about:

1. the essential food groups and a balanced diet for children

2. nutrition and the growing child

3. influences on food and diet

4. disorders requiring special diets

5. safe food preparation.

Learning Outcome ①

Good nutrition is essential for general good health and wellbeing. We need food for four main reasons:

- to provide energy and warmth
- to enable growth, repair and replacement of tissues
- to help fight disease
- to maintain the proper functioning of body systems.

The food we eat each day makes up our diet and should contain the nutrients we need. Before these nutrients can be used, food must be digested. Digestion is the process that breaks down food into smaller components that the body can absorb and use.

Inadequate dietary intake is still the most common cause of failure to thrive. Good eating habits begin at an early age and practitioners need to ensure that children establish healthy eating patterns that will promote normal growth and development.

Digestion

Digestion of food takes place in the alimentary canal. This is a long muscular tube made up of the:

- mouth
- **oesophagus**
- stomach
- small intestine
- large intestine
- rectum
- anus.

The process of digestion

In the mouth

The food is chewed to break it up into small pieces. At the same time it is mixed with saliva. **Enzymes** in the saliva start to work on the food. The food is then swallowed and passes down the oesophagus into the stomach.

In the stomach

Food is churned up and mixed with the gastric juices that continue the process of changing and digesting the food.

In the small intestine

Digestive juices containing enzymes from the pancreas, gall bladder and intestine are mixed with the food and further digestion takes place. The components of the digested food are absorbed into the body through the walls of the small intestine.

In the large intestine

Materials remaining after absorption in the small intestine are mainly water and fibre. Water is absorbed in the large intestine, and the remaining fibre, bacteria and some water form the waste products that pass into the rectum and out of the body via the rectum and anus.

326

Oesophagus = the top of the digestive tract, leading from the mouth to the stomach
Enzyme = a substance that helps to digest food

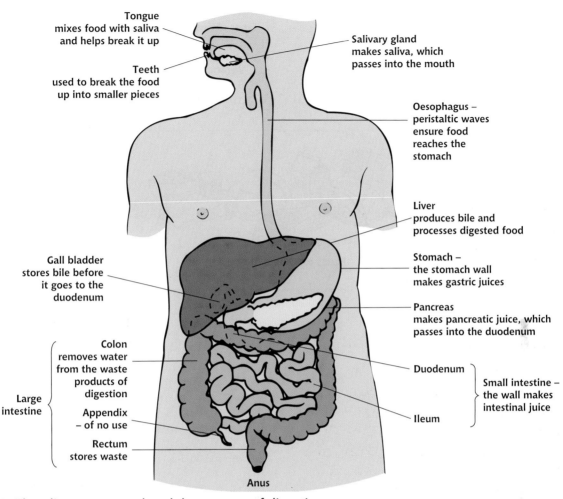

Tongue
mixes food with saliva
and helps break it up

Teeth
used to break the food
up into smaller pieces

Salivary gland
makes saliva, which
passes into the mouth

Oesophagus –
peristaltic waves
ensure food
reaches the
stomach

Liver
produces bile and
processes digested food

Gall bladder
stores bile before
it goes to the
duodenum

Stomach –
the stomach wall
makes gastric juices

Pancreas
makes pancreatic juice, which
passes into the duodenum

Colon
removes water
from the waste
products of
digestion

Large
intestine

Appendix
– of no use

Rectum
stores waste

Duodenum

Small intestine –
the wall makes
intestinal juice

Ileum

Anus

▲ The alimentary canal and the process of digestion

The nutrients in food and drink

To be healthy, the body needs a combination of different **nutrients**. These nutrients are:

- protein
- carbohydrate
- fats
- vitamins
- minerals.

Water and fibre are not nutrients, but are essential for a healthy diet.

Protein, fat, carbohydrates and water are present in the foods we eat and drink in large quantities. Vitamins and minerals are only present in small quantities, so it is much more common for these to be lacking in a child's diet.

Protein

Protein foods are made up of **amino acids**. There are 10 essential amino acids. **Complete protein** foods contain all of them; **incomplete protein** foods contain some. If protein in the diet is wholly restricted to vegetable sources, care will need to be taken that a variety of vegetable proteins are used. This will ensure that all 10 essential amino acids are included in the diet.

Nutrient = a substance that provides essential nourishment
Amino acid = part of protein
Complete proteins = proteins containing all the essential amino acids
Incomplete proteins = proteins containing some essential amino acids

Proteins provide material for:

- growth of the body
- repair of the body

Types of proteins:

- **Animal** – first-class or complete proteins, supply all 10 of the essential amino acids
- **Vegetable** – second-class or incomplete proteins, supply some of the 10 essential amino acids

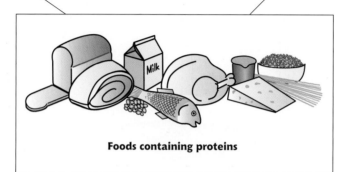

Foods containing proteins

Examples of protein foods include:

- **Animal proteins** – meat, fish, chicken, eggs, dairy foods
- **Vegetable proteins** – nuts, seeds pulses, cereals

Protein foods are made up of amino acids. There are 10 essential amino acids

▲ Foods containing protein

Carbohydrates

Carbohydrates provide:

- energy
- warmth

Types of carbohydrates:

- sugars
- starches

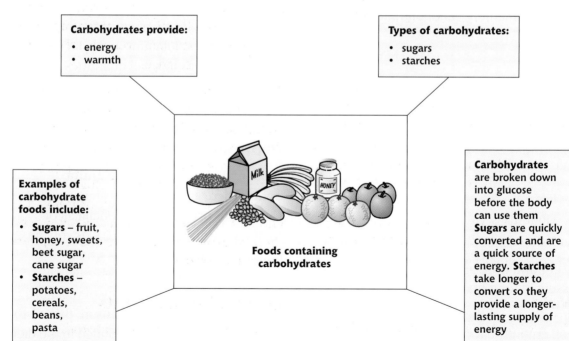

Foods containing carbohydrates

Examples of carbohydrate foods include:

- **Sugars** – fruit, honey, sweets, beet sugar, cane sugar
- **Starches** – potatoes, cereals, beans, pasta

Carbohydrates are broken down into glucose before the body can use them **Sugars** are quickly converted and are a quick source of energy. **Starches** take longer to convert so they provide a longer-lasting supply of energy

▲ Foods containing carbohydrates

Fats

Fats:		Types of fats:

Fats:
- provide energy and warmth
- store fat-soluble vitamins
- make food pleasant to eat

Types of fats:
- saturated
- unsaturated
- polyunsaturates

Examples of foods containing fat include:
- **Saturated** – butter, cheese, meat, palm oil.
- **Unsaturated** – olive oil, peanut oil
- **Polyunsaturated** – oily fish, corn oil, sunflower oil

Foods containing fat

Saturated fats are solid at room temperature and come mainly from animal fats
Unsaturated and polyunsaturated fats are liquid at room temperature and come mainly from vegetable and fish oils

▲ Foods containing fats

Vitamins and minerals

Vitamins and minerals are only present in small quantities in the foods we eat, but they are essential for growth, development and normal functioning of the body.

The tables below show the main vitamins and minerals, which foods contain them and their main functions in the body.

Fibre

Fibre, while not a nutrient, is an essential part of a healthy diet. Fibre is found in the fibrous part of plants in the form of cellulose. It provides the body with bulk or roughage. Fibre has no nutritional value, as it cannot be broken down and used by the body. Fibre adds bulk to food and stimulates the muscles of the intestine, encouraging the body to eliminate the waste products left after the digestion of food.

Water

Water, while not a nutrient, is an essential component of the diet. It contains some minerals, but its role in maintaining a healthy fluid balance in the cells and blood stream is crucial to survival.

A balanced diet

A well-balanced diet ensures that the food eaten provides all the nutrients that the body needs in the right quantities. There are nutrients that the body is able to store (**fat-soluble vitamins** are an example), so nutrients can be taken over several days to form the right balance.

A diet that includes a selection of foods is likely to be nutritious. Different combinations of vitamins are found in different foods, so a varied selection of foods will ensure an adequate supply of all the vitamins needed. Offering a variety of foods gives children an opportunity to choose foods they like. It also encourages them to explore other tastes and to try new foods and recipes.

Combining nutrients

There are some nutrients that work together and are more effective if the foods, which contain them, are combined.

Fat-soluble vitamin = a vitamin that can be stored by the body, so it need not be included in the diet every day

▼ The main vitamins

VITAMIN	FOOD SOURCE	FUNCTION	NOTES
A	Butter, cheese, eggs, carrots, tomatoes	Promotes healthy skin and good vision	Fat-soluble; can be stored in the liver Deficiency causes skin infections, problems with vision Avoid excess intake during pregnancy
B	Fish, meat, liver, green vegetables, beans, eggs	Healthy working of muscles and nerves Active in haemoglobin formation	Water-soluble, not stored in the body so a regular supply is needed Deficiency results in muscle wasting, anaemia
C	Fruits and fruit juices (especially orange and blackcurrant), green vegetables	Promotes healthy skin and tissue Aids healing processes	Water-soluble, daily supply needed Deficiency means less resistance to infection; extreme deficiency results in scurvy
D	Oily fish, cod liver oil, egg yolk; added to margarines and to milk	Aids growth and maintenance of strong bones and teeth	Fat-soluble; can be stored by the body. Can be produced by the body by the action of sunlight on skin Deficiency results in bones failing to harden and dental decay
E	Vegetable oils, cereals, egg yolk, nuts and seeds	Promotes healing, aids blood clotting and fat metabolism	Fat-soluble; can be stored by the body
K	Green vegetables, liver, whole grains	Needed for normal blood clotting, aids healing	Fat-soluble; can be stored by the body Deficiency may result in delayed clotting, excessive bleeding

Calcium and vitamin D

The body only absorbs calcium if it is taken with vitamin D. If growing children do not have sufficient calcium and vitamin D in the diet there is a risk that they will develop rickets, which is a condition that affects the formation and the strength of the developing bones.

Iron and vitamin C

Iron, which is important for the formation of the red blood cells, is absorbed more effectively if food or drinks containing vitamin C are taken together with those containing iron.

▼ The main minerals

MINERAL	FOOD SOURCE	FUNCTION	NOTES
Calcium	Cheese, eggs, fish, pulses	Essential for growth of bones and teeth	Works with Vitamin D. Deficiency means that bones fail to harden (rickets) and leads to dental decay.
Fluoride	Occurs naturally in water or may be added to water, toothpaste, drops and tablets	Makes tooth enamel more resistant to decay	There are arguments for an against adding fluoride to the water supply
Iodine	Water, seafoods, vegetables, added to salt	Needed for proper working of the thyroid gland	Deficiency results in disturbance in the function of the thyroid gland
Iron	Meat, green vegetables, eggs, liver, dried fruit, (esp. apricots, prunes, raisins)	Needed for the formation of haemoglobin in red blood cells	Vitamin C helps the absorption of iron. Deficiency results in anaemia, causing lack of energy.
Phosphorus	Fish, meat, eggs, fruit and vegetables	Formation of bones and teeth, helps absorption of carbohydrate	High intake is harmful to babies.
Potassium	Meat, milk, cereals, fruit and vegetables	Helps to maintain fluid balance	Deficiency is rare as potassium is found in a wide range of foods.
Sodium chloride	Table salt, fish, meat, bread, processed foods	Needed for fluid balance, fomation of cell fluids, blood, sweat, tears	Salt should not be added to food prepared for babies and young children.

Vegetable proteins

Vegetable proteins do not contain all the 10 amino acids that are essential so a combination of vegetables containing protein should be eaten. To ensure effective absorption, a mix of vegetables should be eaten.

Progress check

1. What foods are commonly sources of protein?
2. Amino acids make up two kinds of protein. What are they and why is it important to know about this when planning meals for children?
3. Why are starches a more valuable source of carbohydrate than sugars?
4. Consider the role that vitamins and minerals play in children's diets. How can practitioners ensure that children get all the vitamins and minerals they require?
5. Why is excess salt harmful in a child's diet?
6. Explain why water and fibre, while not nutrients, are essential for a healthy diet.

Learning Outcome 2

FOCUS ON...
nutrition and the growing child

This links to assessment criteria **2.1**

Nutritional needs of babies

Breast milk feeding

The guidance on infant feeding from the Department of Health recommends that:

- breast milk is the best form of nutrition for babies
- babies should be fed on milk only for the first 6 months (26 weeks) of a baby's life
- 6 months is the recommended age for the introduction of solid foods for babies
- breastfeeding and/or breast milk substitutes should continue beyond the first 6 months, along with appropriate types and amounts of solid food.

The decision to breast- or bottle-feed is a very personal one. Most women have an idea of how they will feed their babies before they become pregnant. This may be influenced by how their mother fed them or how their friends feed their babies.

Breast milk is the natural milk for babies. It provides all the nutrients a baby needs for the first 6 months of life and should continue to be an important part of a baby's diet for the first year of life.

Practitioners should be aware that mothers who are breastfeeding their babies will wish to leave expressed breast milk for their infant. This will be given in a bottle or a cup depending upon the mother's wishes. It is very important that strict hygiene procedures are observed when storing and handling expressed milk. You should follow the same procedures for storing, handling and feeding as described below for formula feeding.

Bottle-feeding (formula feeding)

Most modern infant formulas (modified baby milks) are based on cows' milk. However some are derived from soya beans, for babies who cannot tolerate cows' milk. Manufacturers try to make these milks as close to human breast milk as possible. All modified milks must meet the standards issued by the Department of Health. There are basic differences between breast and modified milks. Unmodified cows' milk can be difficult to digest as it has more protein and fat than breast milk. Unmodified cows' milk also has a higher salt content. Salt is dangerous for babies as their kidneys are not mature enough to excrete it. Making feeds that are too strong or giving unmodified cows' milk can be very dangerous as it may cause damage to the baby's kidneys and brain.

Cleaning and sterilising equipment for feeding

All equipment for bottle-feeding or feeding expressed breast milk must be thoroughly cleaned and sterilised. Equipment that is used to feed small babies, under 1 year of age, needs to be sterilised to kill germs that are not removed using normal washing and drying methods. This includes feeding bottles, teats, teat caps, plastic spoons, bowels and feeding cups. Equipment can be sterilised using cold-water sterilising solutions. These come in tablet or liquid form. A more common method now is to use a steam steriliser.

Equipment must be washed and rinsed before it is sterilised. Do not use salt to clean teats, as this will increase the salt intake of the baby if the salt is not rinsed off properly. Use a proper teat cleaner, which is like a small bottle-brush. When it has been thoroughly washed the equipment is ready to be sterilised. Follow the manufacturer's instructions on the sterilising solution bottle, packet or steam steriliser.

Making a formula (bottle) feed

Feeds should be made up according to the guidelines on the milk container. The following equipment will be needed:

- bottles (some have disposable plastic liners)
- teats
- bottle-covers
- bottle brush
- teat cleaner
- plastic knife
- plastic jug
- sterilising tank, sterilising fluid or tablets, or steam steriliser.

These are the important points to remember:

- Always wash your hands before and after making up feeds or weaning foods.
- Wipe down the work surface before preparing feeds, using hot soapy water or anti-bacterial spray.
- Rinse the feeding equipment with boiled water after it comes out of the sterilising fluid.

When making up a feed

Always:

- use the same brand of baby milk; do not change without the advice or recommendation of the health visitor or doctor
- put the water into the bottle or jug *before* the milk powder
- use cooled boiled water to make up feeds.

Rinse the equipment with cold water, then wash in cold water and detergent. Use a bottle brush for the inside of bottle and treat cleaner for teats

Rinse everything thoroughly in clean water. Check that the holes in the teats are clear by squeezing water through them. Fill the steriliser with clean, cold water and the tablets or solution. Follow manufacturer's instructions

Place the equipment into the solution and ensure that everything is completely covered and there are no air bubbles. Do not put metal equipment into the solution. Cover and leave for the stated time.

▲ Cleaning and sterilising feeding equipment

Never:

- add an extra scoop of powder for any reason
- pack the powder too tightly into the scoop
- use heaped scoops.

These actions would result in the feed being too strong. This is dangerous for the baby.

Feeds should be made up for each baby as it is required. If a feed or expressed breast milk is taken from the fridge it should be used immediately; any milk that is left should be discarded straight away. The teat should always be covered when not in use.

How much milk?

Bottle-fed babies should also be fed on demand and they usually settle into their own individual routine. New babies will require about eight feeds a day – approximately every three to four hours – but there will be some variations. A general guide to how much to offer babies is 150 ml per kg of body weight per day (24 hours). For example, a 3 kg baby will require 450 ml over 24 hours.

Divide the daily amount by the number of feeds a day to work out how much milk to offer the infant at each feed. When a baby finishes each bottle offer more milk.

Choice of milks

There are many different kinds of formula milk available. Parents choose the type of milk for their baby and this should be continued when the baby is being cared for at nursery or in other situations. A decision to change the type of milk used may be made for medical or other reasons. Some babies have difficulty in digesting cows'

milk products so the baby's doctor may advise soya-based milk. There are some medical conditions such as phenylketonuria (PKU) that require the baby to be fed with very special formula milk.

GOOD PRACTICE

Always check that you are giving the correct feed.

When feeding babies

- Check the feed chart to make sure that you prepare the correct amount of feed and that you are aware of any special requirements for the baby's feed.

- *Some babies are allergic to milk protein and other ingredients in baby milks and weaning foods. It is very important to be sure that you have checked that the feed you are preparing to give the baby is the correct one. Never give milk or food to a baby without checking first.*

- Ensure that you have everything ready before beginning to feed the baby.

- You should allow plenty of time to feed the baby without rushing.

- Wash your hands.

- Make sure that you are comfortably seated and that you are holding the baby securely.

- Fasten the baby's bib to protect her clothes.

- This is an ideal time to develop a close and loving relationship with the baby. Use this time throughout the feed to make eye contact with the baby and to talk to them. Make this a relaxed and enjoyable time. Feeding should never be rushed.

1 Check that the formula has not passed its sell-by date. Read the instructions on the tin. Ensure the tin has been kept in a cool, dry cupboard.

2 Boil some fresh water and allow to cool.

3 Wash hands and nails thoroughly.

4 Take required equipment from sterilising tank and rinse with cool, boiled water.

5 Fill bottle, or a sterilised jug if making a large quantity, to the required level with water.

6 Measure the <u>exact</u> amount of powder using the scoop provided. Level with a knife. Do not pack down.

7 Add the powder to the measured water in the bottle or jug.

8 Screw cap on bottle and shake, or mix well in the jug and pour into sterilised bottles.

9 Cool and use as soon as possible. Test the temperature on the inside of your wrist.

10 Babies will take cold milk but they prefer warm food (as from the breast). If you wish to warm the milk, place bottle in a jug of hot water. <u>Never keep feeds warm for longer than 45 minutes</u>, to reduce the chance of bacteria breeding.

▲ Preparing a feed

- Test the temperature of the milk. An easy way to do this is to drop some milk on to the inside of your wrist. It should feel just warm.

- Check the size of the hole in the teat: tilt the bottle to allow the milk to flow. It should come out of the teat in steady drops. If the hole is too small the baby will take in air as they suck hard to get the milk. This will cause wind; if the teat is too large the feed will be taken too quickly and the baby may choke.

- Make sure that the bottle is held at an angle, so that the baby cannot take in air as they are fed.

- Wind the baby once or twice during a feed and at the end of the feed. To do this sit the baby upright on your lap; you may like to gently stroke or rub their back. This should help the air in the baby's stomach to be brought up. The baby may also bring up a very small amount of the feed during this so have a tissue or bib ready.

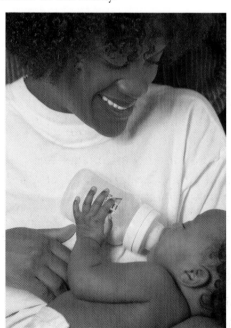

▲ Feeding a baby

- Settle the baby, clean and wash the baby's face; change the nappy if necessary.

- Wash your hands.

- Clear away. Wash and re-sterilise feeding equipment.

- Record information about the amount taken and any other relevant points on the baby's feed chart so that you can give information to the parents at the end of the day.

- Ensure that any other information about any feeding difficulties is passed on to the relevant member of staff.

Special equipment for feeding babies

Some babies may need adaptations to the feeding equipment or specialised equipment for feeding. For example, some babies may require a larger or smaller hole in the teat or a softer or harder teat. In more specialised cases, such as babies with a cleft lip and palate, a special teat or spoon may be used and the baby may need to be fed in an upright position. These requirements should be clearly recorded on the baby's feed chart so that practitioners can follow parental and medical advice consistently.

Colic

Whether breast- or bottle-fed, some babies may experience colic, which is caused by air taken in during feeding or crying. This wind passes through the stomach and becomes trapped in the small intestines resulting in painful contractions of the intestines.

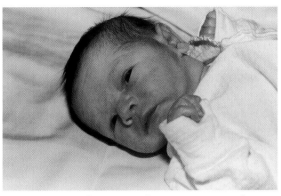

▲ Colic usually occurs between 2 weeks and 3 months of age

Signs of colic

The signs of colic are the baby crying, a reddened face, drawing knees up and appearing to be in pain. It is common for this to happen in the evenings in babies. However, some babies are affected by colic in the day and night. Any concerns should be discussed with the parent who may consult the health visitor or doctor.

Care of a baby with colic

- Comfort the baby.
- Lying the baby on the tummy on the carer's lap and rubbing the back will help.
- Rocking movements may also help to relieve the pain.
- Some doctors advise breastfeeding mothers to monitor their diet to avoid certain foods which may cause colic.
- Bottle-fed babies should be winded regularly; check the teats for hole size and flow of milk.
- The GP may prescribe medicinal drops to be taken before a feed.

Weaning (introducing solid food)

Current advice from the Department of Health is that exclusive breastfeeding until a baby is 6 months old provides the best nutrition for babies. Six months is the recommended age to introduce solid food for all healthy infants, whether they are breastfed or bottle-fed. However, there may be individual circumstances when this might vary. You should always follow the advice given to the parents by their health visitor or doctor.

FAST FACT

The Department of Health produces a pack entitled Infant Feeding and Nutrition.

Why is weaning necessary?

Milk alone is not enough for a baby over the age of 6 months. The baby has used the iron which was stored during pregnancy and must begin to take iron in the diet. Starch and fibre are also necessary for healthy growth and development. Weaning also introduces the baby to new tastes and textures of food.

Weaning and development

Babies at around 6 months can actively spoon feed with the upper lip moving down to clean the spoon. They chew and use the tongue to move food from the front to the back of the mouth. This muscular movement helps the development of the mouth and jaw, and also the development of speech. At 6 months a baby can also have finger foods and this helps to develop their hand–eye coordination. Babies at 6 months will be curious about other tastes and textures.

Mealtimes are sociable occasions and babies need to join in with this. As weaning progresses, they learn how to use a spoon, fork, feeding beaker and cup. They also begin to learn the social rules in their cultural background associated with eating. To do this they need good role models. Rules may include using feeding utensils, chewing with the mouth closed or sitting at the table until everyone has finished eating.

How to wean

Once the baby can sit with support it will be easier if the baby is in a high chair at mealtimes. There should be a relaxed atmosphere and no distractions. The practitioner should sit with the baby throughout the feed. It may take a few days of trying for the baby to take food from the spoon successfully.

Guidelines for weaning

- Try different tastes and textures gradually – one at a time. This gives the baby the chance to become accustomed to one new food before another is offered. If a baby dislikes a food, do not force them to eat it. Simply try it again in a few days' time. Babies of 6 months will be taking an interest in what others are eating, they will want to pick up and taste finger foods, and this should be encouraged.

- Gradually increase the amount of solids to a little at breakfast, lunch and tea. Try to use family foods so that the baby experiences foods from their own culture. Offer lumpier, thicker foods to encourage chewing. The baby may be offered food to hold and chew, such as a piece of toast or apple. A cup may be introduced. Three regular meals should be taken as well as breast or formula milk each day.

- As the baby becomes used to eating solid food they should be having three minced or chopped meals each day plus breast or formula milk as the main drink.

Babies who do not eat meat or fish should have two servings of split pulses such as red lentils, beans, chickpeas or tofu. This will ensure that they get the nutrients they need.

- Milk will still form the largest part of a baby's diet during the first year of life – around 500–600 ml each day

- Water may be offered in a feeding cup.

▲ There should be a relaxed atmosphere with no distractions

Cows' milk

Babies should *not* be offered unmodified cow's milk as a drink until they are over 1 year old. Milk drinks should continue to be formula milk or breast milk.

Young children over 1 year can be given cows' milk to drink. Semi-skimmed milk should not be given until a child is 3. Skimmed milk is not suitable for children.

Iron

By the age of 6 months, the baby's iron stores are low, so foods containing iron must be given. These include:

- liver
- lamb
- beans
- dahl
- green vegetables
- wholemeal bread
- cereals containing iron.

Note: do not add salt to any food, as babies' kidneys cannot cope with it. Avoid adding sugar to food or drink as this can lead to tooth decay.

Healthy eating

The government has introduced a number of initiatives to encourage healthy eating and to limit the advertising of unhealthy foods and drinks. There have been debates about this in both the House of Commons and the House of Lords as a result of the government's White Paper *Our Healthier Nation*.

The Food Standards Agency is a government body whose role is to give authoritative advice and information about food so that people can make informed choices.

From January 1 2006 New European Union (EU) food hygiene legislation has applied throughout the United Kingdom (UK).

More information about relevant legislation can be found in the Weblinks section at the end of this unit.

Proportions of nutrients

Children are growing all the time, so they need relatively large amounts of protein to help the formation of bone and muscle. They are also using a lot of energy, so they need carbohydrate in the form of starches that they can use during the day to sustain their activities. In addition, they will need adequate supplies of vitamins and minerals.

Suggested daily intakes are as follows:

- two portions (helpings) of meat, fish or other vegetable protein foods, such as nuts and pulses
- two portions of protein from dairy products such as milk cheese, yogurt (for vegans substitute two other protein foods from plant sources)
- four portions of starchy carbohydrate foods, such as bread, pasta, potatoes, sweet potatoes, cereal foods
- five portions of fruit and vegetables
- six drinks of fluid, especially water.

Begin with small portions. The size of the portion will increase as the child grows and can eat more.

Select the best-quality food that you can find and afford. For example, choose wholemeal bread rather than white and select the best fresh fruit and vegetables. Use whole unprocessed foods as much as you can. Never add salt to food that you prepare for babies and children and use sugar sparingly.

Although children are small in size they need sufficient food to satisfy their hunger and provide the **calories** they need. The table below shows the number of calories recommended for children and adults. The energy value of food is measured in calories: a medium egg, for example, is about 75 calories. Comparing the requirements of children and adults gives some idea of portion size. A child of 2 or 3 needs roughly half the amount of food, in terms of calories, as an adult.

▼ The required number of calories for children and adults

AGE RANGE	ENERGY REQUIREMENTS IN CALORIES
0–1 year	800
1–2 years	800
2–3 years	1,400
3–5 years	1,600
5–7 years	1,800
7–9 years	2,100
Women	2,200–2,500
Men	2,600–3,600

Water

Drinking water is essential and is thought to be important for efficient functioning of the brain. It is important that younger children are given regular drinks of water and older children have access to drinking water throughout the day. However, it is important to ensure that supplies of water are fresh and that good hygiene is maintained.

Older children often carry around bottles of water that they fill up from the tap. Practitioners should make them aware that these bottles should be thoroughly washed and dried at the end of each day to avoid bacterial growth and the risk of infection.

 Have a go!

Devise a survey among the children in your setting to find out what children know about eating fruit and vegetables. Find out how many portions of fruit and vegetables the children are actually having. You could link this to a display or activity.

Healthy snacks

Young children eat smaller amounts because they have smaller stomachs than adults. This means that they will often be hungry between meals. In addition to their three main meals most children will need a snack in the middle of the morning and afternoon.

Healthy snacks are nutritious and lay the foundations for good eating habits. They include:

- slices of fruit and vegetables
- cheese
- yoghurts
- dried fruit such as apricots.

Drinks should be water and milk.

Avoid:

- crisps
- chocolate
- sweets
- chikki (Indian dessert)
- sweet biscuits
- sugary drinks
- undiluted fruit juice
- fatty foods, or foods that are cooked in fat or ghee.

✓ Progress check

(1) Consider how a child's diet may change as they move towards independence.

(2) What important factors will influence practitioners as they work with different age groups?

(3) What is the recommended age for a baby to begin weaning?

(4) Why is weaning necessary?

(5) Why is breastfeeding recommended as the best way to feed a baby?

(6) Why is it important to check carefully before giving babies and children any food or drink?

Learning Outcome 3

FOCUS ON...
influences on food and diet

This links to assessment criteria **3.1**

Diets of different groups

Each region or country has developed its own local diet over many years. Diets have evolved based on available foods, which in turn depend on climate, geography and agricultural patterns, as well as social factors such as religion, culture, class and lifestyle. Each diet contains a balance of essential nutrients.

When people migrate, they take their diet with them and generally wish to recreate it as a familiar feature of their way of life.

Religious aspects of food

For some people, food has a spiritual significance. Certain foods may be prohibited and these prohibitions form a part of people's daily lives. Adhering to religious food restrictions should not be taken as being difficult about food. Respecting an individual's culture and religious choices is part of respecting that individual as a whole. It is important that practitioners talk to parents and carers about food requirements, especially when caring for a child from a cultural or religious background different from their own.

Religious restrictions may affect the diets of Hindus, Sikhs, Muslims, Jews, Rastafarians and Seventh Day Adventists. Members of other groups may also have dietary restrictions.

People are individuals and will vary in what they eat and what restrictions they observe; you should be aware of this when discussing diet with parents or carers.

Note: it is not possible to make blanket statements about the diets of different groups, only to suggest possibilities and factors that may be important.

Other dietary restrictions

- Vegetarians do not eat meat and restrict their intake of other animal products in different ways. They may eat dairy products such as eggs and milk.

- Vegans do not eat any animal products at all, so it is important to be aware of any components of food that are of animal origin such as gelatine. A vegan diet needs careful balancing if it is to be followed by children, to ensure that they get the right nutrients to sustain normal growth.

It is very important to take account of these points when preparing activities involving food. If you are setting up a baking activity, for example, it would be best to make sure that you use vegetable fats, as these are generally more acceptable. Many more people today are moving towards a vegetarian diet or a diet that restricts the intake of animal products.

▼ Dietary principles of different groups

GROUP	PRINCIPLES
Jews	May not eat pork or shellfish. May not cook or eat milk and meat products together. May use a different set of utensils and dishes and pans for milk and meat. May only eat meat and poultry prepared by a kosher butcher. May fast at Yom Kippur (the Day of Atonement)
Rastafarians	May be vegetarian. May not eat fruit from the vine. May only eat foods in their natural state. May not eat processed or preserved foods
Muslims	May not eat pork or pork products. Meat and fish must be halal. May fast during Ramadan from sunrise until sunset, although there may be some exceptions, e.g. young children. May not drink alcohol
Sikhs	May be vegetarian but some may eat lamb and chicken. May fast regularly
Hindus	May eat no beef or they may be completely vegetarian. May observe other principles during festivals. May not drink alcohol
Christians	May not eat meat on a Friday. May give up certain foods during Lent. Some may fast before taking Holy Communion

Social and educational role of food

Children like to take part in cooking and food preparation at home and in nurseries. These activities can create learning opportunities and enhance developmental skills.

Physical development

Gross motor skills are developed through mixing and beating. Manipulative skills are improved by cutting and stirring. Hand–eye coordination is improved by pouring, spooning out and weighing ingredients.

Cognitive development

Scientific concepts are learnt by seeing the effects of heat and cold on food. Mathematical skills are developed by counting, sorting and grading utensils, laying the table for the correct number of people and weighing and measuring the

▲ Activities can create learning opportunities

ingredients. Children can be encouraged to plan and make decisions about what they will eat.

Language development

Conversation and discussion can be encouraged at mealtimes. Adult interaction will promote and extend vocabulary.

Children and adults can share their ideas and experiences of the day.

Emotional development

Eating food is often a comfort, and sharing and preparing food for others provides pleasure. Helping to prepare a meal for themselves and others will give children a sense of achievement.

Social development

Children can learn the skills of feeding independently. They can share with others and learn about appropriate behaviour at mealtimes. Mealtimes are a good opportunity for families and other groups to exchange their news and ideas.

▲ Younger children need to practise the manipulative skills by feeding themselves

Problems with food

Food intolerance

Food intolerance is a condition in which there are specific adverse effects after eating a certain food; this may be caused by an allergic response or an enzyme deficiency. The removal of foods from a child's diet must be carried out with medical supervision. If the suspected food source is a major source of nutrients, for example milk, then alternatives must be included to make good any deficiency. Conditions such as phenylketonuria (PKU) and coeliac disease require very specialised diets. There is more information about the coeliac condition later in this unit.

Food refusal

Refusing to eat food provided and making a fuss about food at mealtimes is common among young children, especially the under 5s; it is most common around 2 years of age. Refusing food, or adopting a diet that is restrictive or unusual, can occur at any age. It is important to check that the child is growing as expected. Checking the weight and height over time will show that a child is following the expected pattern consistent with their birth weight and length. It is important that a doctor has identified no medical condition in the child, as losing weight or failing to grow may be consistent with an underlying condition.

It is not unusual for children to lose their appetite and refuse food if they are ill. This should be expected as it is one of the general symptoms of illness in children and in adults. In these circumstances it is always good practice to encourage the child to drink while waiting for a doctor to diagnose the illness.

GOOD PRACTICE

Ensuring that a sick child of any age has plenty to drink is essential. Thinking about food and tempting the child to eat can come a little later.

If children of any age are faced with changing circumstances or are worrying about something, they will experience a loss of appetite. So it follows that children starting at a new school or nursery may not eat well until they have settled in. If older children are anxious they will need to be able to talk about their problems and get support before their appetite returns.

Children will need to adapt to the routines and the requirements of their new nursery or school. It may be that mealtimes are handled differently from home. Older children may have to choose their food, handle dinner money, join a queue and then find somewhere to sit.

Young children may be faced with different eating utensils from those used at home. Some children may not be used to sitting up at a table; they may be more used to eating from their lap while watching television. Some children will cope with this well; others may find mealtimes difficult and may choose not to eat.

If older children do refuse food, or adopt a very unusual diet, they should be seen by their doctor as this could point to the onset of a more serious condition, such as anorexia, where specialist help may be needed. Very often the parents may not have noticed what is happening, especially if the onset has been gradual.

Managing children under 5 who refuse to eat

Mealtimes should not become a battle ground so practitioners should:

- offer food at mealtimes only
- offer small portions attractively served
- encourage children to take part in family and group mealtimes
- allow the child to eat independently
- not fuss about any mess when children are learning to eat independently
- remove any remaining or rejected food without fuss
- make mealtimes a pleasant experience for all.

▲ Allow children to eat independently

Practical example

Food refusal

Joanna is a nanny who looks after Joshua, who is 2 years 6 months old, and Anna, who is 6 months old, while their parents are at work. Joshua is a lively, happy little boy who knows Joanna well, as she was his nanny before Anna was born.

Joanna has continued to care for him and also his sister when their mother returned to work four weeks ago. Joshua seems well and healthy, but for the last week or two he has been refusing to eat his meals. He has become very upset and on one occasion threw his plate on to the floor when Joanna insisted that he eat his dinner. As his nanny, Joanna has decided that she must take some action.

(1) *What should Joanna do first?*

(2) *What steps should Joanna then take to try to re-establish Joshua's previous good eating patterns?*

Food additives

Additives are included in food to:

- preserve it for longer
- prevent contamination
- aid processing
- enhance colour and flavour
- replace nutrients lost in processing.

Care should be taken with additives in children's diets because:

- chidren often eat more foods with additives, for example drinks and sweets
- children are smaller and the amount they take is, therefore, greater in proportion to their size.

To reduce additives in the diet, you can:

- use fresh foods as often as you can
- make your own pies, cakes, soups, etc.
- avoid highly processed foods
- look at the labels the ingredients are listed.

E numbers

Permitted food additives are given a number. If the number has been approved by the European Union (EU), as well as the UK, there is an E in front of the number – an E number. A category name such as 'preservative' must come before the additive number to tell you why it has been included, for example preservative E200.

Allergies, food additives and behaviour

An increasing number of allergies now affect babies, young children and young adults. Food allergies in babies can be detected most easily if a baby is introduced to new foods one at a time. Practitioners should be aware of any allergies experienced by the children in their care.

Practical example

Marian looks after Laurie and Anna. She needs to give the children lunch and, as she hasn't got time to shop, she will be using food from the fridge and freezer. Laurie's family is vegetarian and Anna is allergic to food colourings. Marian finds some fish fingers in the freezer and some chocolate puddings in the fridge. This is what the labels say:

Fishfingers

Nutritional information:

Protein	3.9 g
Carbohydrate	4.0 g
Fat	2.2 g
Fibre	0.3 g

No artificial colouring or flavouring

Chocolate pudding

Ingredients:

Skimmed milk

Sugar

Chocolate

Vegetable oil

Beef gelatine.

1. Will Marian be able to give the food to Laurie? Explain the reason for your answer.

2. Will Marian be able to give the food to Anna? Explain the reason for your answer.

Allergic reactions may include:

- vomiting
- diarrhoea
- skin rashes

- wheezing
- severe reactions such as convulsions, difficulty in breathing, swelling of the mouth and throat.

Peanut and nut allergy is increasing among young children; for this reason nuts should not be given to children.

Some children may have erratic behaviour after having, for example, orange squash or coloured sweets, and behaviour improves when these colourings are avoided. Avoiding additives need not affect the nutritional value of the diet, but any regime that leads to a nutritionally inadequate diet should not be followed. Hyperactivity as a medical condition will be diagnosed by a paediatrician (a doctor who specialises in caring for children). Dietary manipulation, for example elimination diets, must be prescribed by a paediatrician and supervised by a dietician. Behaviour and hyperactivity problems are, however, rarely caused solely by food additives and, there are, usually, other contributing factors.

Always check before you give babies or children any food or drink to make sure it is safe to do so.

If you are caring for a baby or young child with a known allergy there should be a procedure in place to ensure that proper checks are carried out before any food or drink is given. *If in doubt – double-check.* These procedures will apply not just to food and drink that is part of meals or snacks but also to any food used in activities such as cooking or colourings added to the water play. Make sure that the children don't share their food with other children.

Food and poverty

Research has shown that food is one of the first things people cut back on when they are short of money. This can have a serious effect on the nutritional quality of the diet of families managing on a low income.

 See Unit 6 pages 230–231.

School meals

All food provided by local authorities must meet national nutritional standards. These ensure that children are provided with a healthy balanced diet. The new standards introduced in 2006 set out what schools should provide.

- High-quality meat, poultry or oily fish should be regularly available.
- There should be at least two portions of fruit and vegetables with every meal.
- Bread, other cereals and potatoes should be regularly available.

There are controls on the following foods:

- deep-fried food to be limited to no more than two portions per week
- fizzy drinks, crisps, chocolate and other sweets to be removed from school meals and vending machines.

Some children qualify for free lunches or milk or to be given free fruit and vegetables at school.

Milk

Local authorities are not obliged to provide milk for pupils, but if they do so it must be free to pupils qualifying for free school meals. Under-5s are eligible for free school milk.

Free fruit and vegetables in schools

The school fruit and vegetable scheme is a government programme which gives all children aged 4 to 6 in infant, primary and special schools a free piece of fruit or vegetable each school day.

You can visit the websites of Foods
Standard Agency (FSA) and the School
Food Trust for more information.

> ✓ **Progress check**
>
> (1) Explain why additives are put into foods and the strategies you can use to ensure
>   that these are kept to a minimum in children's meals.
>
> (2) How are schools and nurseries tackling the problem of poor-quality food and the
>   lack of fresh food in school meals? Why is this important?
>
> (3) Investigate how your setting takes account of the cultural and health needs of the
>   children with reference to their diet.
>
> (4) What is the procedure in your setting for making all the practitioners aware of any
>   important information about children's diets?
>
> (5) Consider the significant influences on the diets of children. How may this affect
>   professional practice?
>
> (6) Consider the influence that poverty may have on children's diet.

Learning Outcome 4

FOCUS ON...
disorders requiring special diets

> This links to assessment criteria **4.1**

Disorders experienced by children

Some children will experience conditions that mean they require special diets. These include:

- obesity
- coeliac condition
- **cystic fibrosis**
- **diabetes**.

Obesity

Being seriously overweight – to the extent that it affects the health of an individual – is described as obesity.

Obesity is caused by:

- an unhealthy diet. This is usually a diet that contain too much sugar and fat. Sugar and fat both contain a high level of calories in small quantities of food. This means that high numbers of calories are consumed quickly even though the portions may be relatively small
- not taking enough exercise to burn off the calories consumed
- some rare conditions such as Prader-Willi syndrome and hypothyroidism.

Obesity affects children in a variety of ways. There may be problems with the bones and joints, such as bow legs. Other problems include gall bladder disease, high blood pressure and diabetes (see below).

More and more children are becoming obese. Around 27 per cent of children are now overweight. The main problem is a continual reduction in the amount of exercise taken. Many overweight children have overweight parents so it can be a matter of family lifestyle.

Obesity is clinically diagnosed by measuring the body mass index (BMI). Specific age-adjusted charts are used when calculating the BMI of children.

When treating obesity the emphasis will be on making long-term changes to healthy eating for the whole family and involving the child in sport or other forms of exercise, such as walking to and from school if this possible.

Aggressive dieting should be avoided. It is better to aim at increasing the child's intake of fruit and vegetables and reducing the intake of fat and sugar. Help should be sought from the family doctor who can involve a dietician.

Coeliac condition

The coeliac condition is a metabolic disorder involving a sensitivity to gluten (a protein found in wheat, rye, barley and oats), which leads to difficulty in

---

Cystic fibrosis = hereditary, life-threatening condition affecting the lungs and digestive tract
Diabetes = a condition in which the body cannot metabolise carbohydrates, resulting in high levels of sugar in the blood and urine

Do some research in your school or nursery.

- Add up the amount of time in the timetable that is allocated to structured physical activity and to informal activity such as play times.

- Go out into the playground to observe the children. Note how they occupy their time. How much vigorous exercise do the children participate in? How much time do they spend standing around, chatting or playing more static games? What influences what the children do?

digesting food. There is thought to be a familial tendency to the disease. The lining of the small intestine is sensitive to gluten and the resulting damage to the walls of the intestine reduces the ability to absorb nutrients from the food broken down by the digestive process.

Characteristics

The child exhibits signs of malnutrition and does not gain weight and grow normally.

Diagnosis

Diagnosis in children is made by observation of the failure to grow and gain weight satisfactorily, particularly after weaning on to foods containing gluten. Diagnosis can also be made by examination of tissue taken from the small intestine.

Treatment and progress

A diet free from gluten must be followed. Gluten is found in many foods. However, foods like meat, fish, and fruit and vegetables are gluten free. Any food containing wheat, rye, barley and oats in any form, e.g. bread, cake and cereals, will contain gluten. It is also possible to obtain gluten-free foods on prescription.

The intestine then begins to recover and as long as the diet is followed the child will be able to grow normally.

Cystic fibrosis (CF)

Cystic fibrosis is a hereditary and life-threatening condition that affects the lungs and the digestive system. It is a recessively inherited condition. For the child to be affected both parents must carry the CF gene.

Characteristics

Mucus throughout the body is thick and sticky and the airways in the lungs become clogged. This leads to breathing difficulties, coughing and repeated chest infections. The **pancreas** fails to develop properly and mucus clogs the ducts, affecting the flow of enzymes into the digestive tract. Food is not digested and absorbed properly. The child fails to gain weight and grow satisfactorily.

Diagnosis

Family history and genetic counselling may mean that prenatal diagnosis is possible. A blood test is carried out on the sixth day after the birth as part of routine screening. Later, diagnosis is by observation of the baby's symptoms, followed by a sweat test and/or a blood test.

Treatment and progress

The treatment is aimed at:

- keeping the lungs free from infection, with antibiotic therapy and physiotherapy

- respiratory education and therapy to expel mucus and keep the lungs clear
- pancreatic enzymes taken with every meal; a high-protein diet with vitamin and mineral supplements is prescribed.

Treatment is time consuming, but children gradually become more independent and are able to manage and understand their condition.

The Cystic Fibrosis Trust has an informative website.

Diabetes

Diabetes occurs when the pancreas gland produces insufficient amounts of **insulin** or none at all, resulting in abnormally high levels of sugar (glucose) in the blood and urine. Insulin controls the amount of glucose in the body by moving it from the blood into the cells, where it is broken down and used to create energy.

There are two types of diabetes:

- Type 1, insulin dependent, usually starts before 40 years of age and requires insulin injections.
- Type 2, non-insulin dependent, is common in older people and is controlled with diet and medication.

Characteristics

Early symptoms of diabetes are excessive thirst, frequent passing of urine; children may lose weight. Complications include visual impairment, kidney damage and problems with the circulation.

Diagnosis

Diagnosis is by observation of the child's symptoms, and by testing the blood and/or urine for sugar.

Treatment and progress

For children, treatment is by injections of insulin together with a carefully controlled diet that restricts the amount of carbohydrate that can be eaten. Children quickly learn how to test their own blood and/or urine and keep a record of the results. They also learn how to give their own insulin. Keeping healthy requires regular meals, regular insulin, regular exercise and regular medical supervision. Once the child and family have adjusted to the need for regular treatment and diet, a full and active life is possible.

One of the possible complications that may occur when a child is in your care is **hypoglycaemia** – low levels of glucose in the blood.

Signs of hypoglycaemia include:

- irritability
- confusion, loss of coordination and concentration
- rapid breathing
- sweating
- dizziness.

When managing of a hypoglycaemic attack:

- stay with the child
- give glucose to drink if the child is conscious and able to swallow
- if the child is unconscious, put them in the recovery position (see Unit 4) and get someone to call an ambulance. Stay with the child.

Insulin = a hormone produced in the pancreas to metabolise carbohydrate in the bloodstream and regulate glucose
Hypoglycaemia = low levels of glucose in the blood

 Practical example

Recognising signs and symptoms of diabetes

Ben is 5 years old and has just started at his local infants school. He had not been going to school long before his mother became worried about him. She came into school to discuss the situation with the class teacher and the teaching assistant. Ben's mum had noticed that he was always tired these days, having previously been a really lively boy. He had lost his appetite but seemed to need a lot more to drink. His mum wondered if this was why he had wet the bed a few times. Ben's class teacher and nursery nurse had noticed that Ben seemed to be unable to concentrate; he also seemed to be drowsy and sweaty at times. Ben's mum was taking him to the family doctor that evening.

(1) List Ben's symptoms.

(2) What do you think might be wrong with Ben?

(3) How will a diagnosis of Ben's condition be made?

(4) What is the likely treatment for Ben's condition?

✔ Progress check

(1) Consider a child who is obese. What factors do you think may have contributed to this situation?

(2) What problems do you think a child who has been diagnosed as having coeliac disease may experience?

(3) How do you think having cystic fibrosis will affect a child's everyday life?

(4) How will having diabetes affect a child who is a keen footballer?

Learning Outcome (5)

safe food preparation

This links to assessment criteria **5.1** and **5.2**

Food safety

Food is essential to good health and survival, but it has to be looked after to avoid contamination with harmful bacteria that could cause food poisoning. Since January 1991 there have been stricter laws about storage and handling of food in shops and restaurants. These laws help to keep food safer and cleaner. Once food has been purchased, it must be stored safely and prepared hygienically in order to prevent food poisoning.

Buying food

- Check the 'use by' dates.
- Take chilled and frozen food straight home and use an insulated bag.
- Make sure you buy from a shop where cooked and raw foods are kept and handled separately.

Storage at home

- Put chilled and frozen foods into the fridge or freezer as quickly as possible.
- The coldest part of the fridge must be between 0 and 5 °C, and the freezer temperature below 18 °C: use a fridge thermometer to check the temperature.
- Keep raw meat and fish in separate containers in the fridge and store them carefully on the bottom shelf so that they do not touch or drip on to other food.

In the kitchen

- Always wash your hands well before touching food. Hand washing is the single most effective measure in preventing infection.
- Cover any cuts with a waterproof dressing.
- Wear an apron and tie hair back when preparing food.

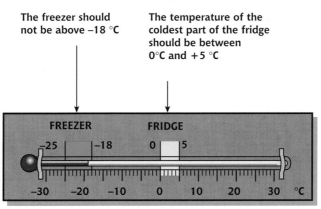

The freezer should not be above −18 °C

The temperature of the coldest part of the fridge should be between 0 °C and +5 °C

▲ Temperatures for home storage in the fridge or freezer

- Avoid touching your nose and mouth, or coughing and sneezing in the food-preparation area.
- Kitchen cloths and sponges should be disinfected and renewed frequently.
- Disinfect all work surfaces regularly and especially before preparing food.

Separate raw meat and ready-to-eat meat

- Raw meat contains harmful bacteria that can spread easily to anything it touches.
- Do not let raw meat touch other foods.
- Never prepare ready-to-eat foods with a knife that has been used to prepare raw foods, unless the knife has been very thoroughly washed first.
- Wash your hands thoroughly after touching raw meat, poultry or fish.
- Always cover raw meat and fish and store it on the bottom shelf of the fridge where it cannot touch or drip on other foods. The bottom of the fridge is also the coldest part.

▲ Store raw meat and fish on the bottom shelf of the fridge

Cooking

The following guidelines should always be followed when preparing and cooking food:

- Defrost food thoroughly before cooking.
- Make sure all food is thoroughly cooked – chicken and meat need special care and must be cooked thoroughly through to the centre.
- Prepare raw meat separately – use a separate board and knife.
- Cooked food should be cooled quickly and then refrigerated or frozen.
- Cover any food standing in the kitchen.
- Eggs should be thoroughly cooked before eating. For babies and small children, cook eggs until the white and yolk are solid.
- Cooked food should only be reheated once – reheat until piping hot all the way through.
- Reheat all cooked chilled meals thoroughly.
- Pregnant women, and anyone with a low resistance to infection, should not eat pâté or soft cheeses of the Brie or Camembert type. These cheeses have usually been made with unpasturised milk and contain live organisms.

Implications for children

Children are particularly vulnerable to infection, so it is important to make sure that food is prepared and handled safely. It is also vital that children learn the basic rules about handling food. Always make sure that they wash their hands before eating. If children prepare food as part of a learning activity, the food safety rules should always be followed. Children need to understand why this is important, so that they develop important life skills.

The responsibilities of practitioners

Specific legal requirements

'Where children are provided with meals, snacks and drinks, these must be healthy, balanced and nutritious. Those responsible for the preparation and handling of food must be competent to do so.' (*The Early Years Foundation Stage*, 2007)

New legislation that will come into force from September 2008 will be mandatory for all schools and early years providers in Ofsted-registered settings.

Other provisions under this legislation include:

- providing fresh drinking water at all times
- notifying Ofsted if two or more children are affected by food poisoning
- providing healthy meals, snacks and drinks
- recording and acting on information about child's dietary needs
- registering with the local authority environmental health department
- providing food hygiene training as part of induction for all staff
- provide safe and hygienic storage for packed lunches.

Registration with the local authority

Registering with the local authority means that environmental health officers will visit each year to inspect the premises and to give advice. Suitable food premises should:

- be clean and in good repair
- be designed to permit good hygiene practices
- supply drinking water at all times
- have suitable natural or artificial light
- be protected against pests
- be well ventilated
- provide clean lavatories
- have proper facilities for hand washing
- have adequate drainage.

Implications for children

Practitioners have a responsibility to comply with food-handling regulations to ensure the safety of the children in their care. It is also essential that practitioners ensure that the children are aware of the important things that they must do to safeguard their health. Practitioners can never stress too strongly the importance of hand washing before handling or eating food. It is up to practitioners to teach the children how to wash their hands properly. A useful observation is to watch the children as they wash their hands. How many of them do this adequately without adult intervention? This is the time for some relevant health education. Encourage the children to make the links between good hygiene and good health.

✔ Progress check

1. In what part of the fridge would you store raw meat and fish?
2. Give reasons for your answers to question 1.
3. Which bodies are responsible for monitoring food safety in childcare settings?
4. Why is eating certain foods not advised for those who are vulnerable to infection?
5. What is the single most effective measure that can be taken to avoid food becoming contaminated?
6. Why is it important to have separate utensils when preparing raw and cooked food?

Weblinks

- www.dh.gov.uk
  The Department of Health provides information on health issues and policy, including feeding babies and healthy eating guidelines

- www.foodinschools.org
  Information on school meals and eating and drinking while at school

- www.nutrition.org.uk
  The website of the British Nutrition Foundation provides information on and resources for healthy eating

- www.foodstandards.gov.uk
  Offers information and advice on safe food and healthy eating for all

- www.coeliac.co.uk
  The Coeliac Society provides information and support for families

- www.ctrust.org.uk
  The Cystic Fibrosis Trust is the national charity in the UK that funds research and provides information and support for families

- www.diabetes.org.uk
  Diabetes UK works for people with diabetes

Working with children with special needs

Understanding the needs of children with special needs requires a thorough knowledge of child development and professional practice. Information in this unit cannot cover every aspect of special needs; however, there are many condition- and/or impairment-specific organisations working with particular groups of people with special needs that produce a range of useful information and training.

Learning Outcomes

In this unit you will learn about:

1. the concept of special needs and current attitudes and values

2. the range of factors affecting children's ability to learn

3. the provision for children with special educational needs

4. the roles and responsibilities of professionals working with children with special educational needs.

Learning Outcome 1

FOCUS ON...

the concept of special needs and current attitudes and values

This links to assessment criteria **1.1**

Concept of special needs

Role of attitudes, values and stereotyped views in influencing behaviour

Disability is generally seen as an undesirable condition experienced by other people which individuals hope will never happen to them. Disability in children is often regarded as a tragedy, eliciting pity for the 'victim' and their family. These and other attitudes, together with the environment, for example physical access to buildings, often cause unnecessary disability. Ignorance and fear can lead to separation, exclusion, prejudice and discrimination against people with disabilities. It is therefore important to provide information that informs and affects the attitudes of others and to increase their knowledge. Working with children and young people provides an ideal opportunity to influence attitudes. Children do not exclude or devalue each other until they are taught to do so by the unconscious or uninformed behaviour of adults.

Implications of history

During the Industrial Revolution in Britain there was a move away from small, family-based cottage industry to employment in large factories. This served to discriminate against people with disabilities because they were no longer able to control their own surroundings, nor their pace of work. People with disabilities were forced into dependency and poverty, losing the status that comes with employment.

At about the same time, the influence of the medical profession was increasing. Doctors sought to treat people and cure their **impairments** so that they could fit into society. If this was not possible, people with disabilities were hidden away in hospitals and long-stay institutions out of sight; there was little contact with the outside world.

Models of disability
Medical model

The legacy of the past is that society has become conditioned to treat people with disabilities according to the **medical**

Disability = disadvantage or restriction of activity caused by society that takes little or no account of people who have physical or mental impairments and thus excludes them from the mainstream of social activities. According to the social model, disability is defined as 'socially imposed restriction' (Oliver, 1981)

Impairment = lacking all or part of a limb, or having altered or reduced function in a limb, organ or mechanism of the body. According to the social model, impairment is defined as 'individual limitation' (Oliver, 1981)

Medical model = view of disability as requiring medical intervention

model (also known as the personal tragedy model). Society separates and excludes incurably disabled people as if they are somehow not quite human. Disability is viewed predominantly as a personal tragedy needing medical intervention. This encourages a negative view, focusing on what a person cannot do – rather than what they can do. Disability is seen as a problem to be solved or cured, rather than as a difference to be accepted. It is all too easy, within this medical model, to see disabled people as problem individuals who should adapt themselves to fit into society.

Social model

People with disabilities, however, are no longer prepared to accept the medical model of disability. Through organisations such as the Disability Movement, people with disabilities are campaigning for acceptance of the **social model** of disability. They want people to see impairment (the medically defined **condition**) as a challenge, and to change society to include people with disabilities whether or not they are cured. This will involve responding to their true needs.

The social model defines disability as a problem within society rather than within people with disabilities. It maintains that many of the difficulties faced by people with disabilities could be eliminated by changes in people's attitudes and in the environment. According to the social model, a mobility problem, for example, is seen to be caused by the presence of steps rather than by the individual's inability to walk; when a person who is deaf has difficulty accessing information, this is seen to be caused by people's lack of skill in sign language rather than the individual's hearing loss.

People with disabilities have taken the social model a stage further and defined disability as a **social creation**, a problem created by the institutions, organisations and processes that make up society. This model of disability has led to people with disabilities coming together to campaign for their rights, for social change and to fight against **institutional oppression**.

The importance of terminology

Terminology reflects and influences the way that disability is viewed by society, including people with disabilities themselves. It also influences people's perceptions and attitudes, which subsequently affect the provision of resources and services.

Over the years, people with disabilities have been referred to and labelled using many different terms, usually conferred on them by non-disabled professionals. These have included general classifications that dehumanise, like 'the infirm' and 'the handicapped', or even 'the disabled'.

In addition, people have been referred to in such a way that they become their impairment: 'John is epileptic', 'the autistic boy'. Many of these terms are patronising and contemptuous of people with disabilities. Other terms are used as a form of abuse amongst non-disabled people.

There are many different conditions or impairments; when the condition or impairment is known, the correct name should be used. This is particularly true

---

Social model = a view of disability as a problem within society
Condition = medically defined illness
Social creation – brought about by society
Institutional oppression = the power of organisations brought to bear on an individual to keep them in their place

of children with disabilities, who are often denied accurate information about themselves.

G☺☺D PRACTICE · · · · · · · ·

Explaining terminology to young children provides opportunities to teach basic information about such topics as health, the body and illness. This is not a taboo topic for young children who need and like to know the truth. It also provides an opportunity to dispel some of the myths and fears surrounding disability, and to influence attitudes at a formative stage.

▲ Children do not exclude or devalue each other until they are taught to do so by the behaviour of others

Definitions of disability

The definitions used in this book seek to respect the views of people with disabilities and promote good practice in the use of terminology. They were devised by the Union of the Physically Impaired Against Segregation in 1976. They are widely accepted by the Disability Movement and those working on disability issues.

Impairment may be described as lacking part of a limb, or having altered or reduced function of a limb, organ or mechanism of the body. Oliver (1981) defines impairment as 'individual limitation'.

Disability may be described as the disadvantage or restriction of activity caused by contemporary social organisation (society), which takes little or no account of people who have physical or mental impairments and thus excludes them from the mainstream of social activities. Oliver defines disability as 'socially imposed restrictions'.

It follows from the above definitions that people may have physical impairments, sensory impairments and/or learning impairments. There may, however, be preferences for other terms within these groups. For example, some adults who have lost their hearing later in life may refer to themselves as 'hard of hearing'. People born with a hearing loss may refer to themselves as 'partially deaf'. Some people with learning impairments prefer to be referred to as 'having learning difficulties'.

Children with special needs

The term 'special needs' (in full – **special educational needs**) is now in common usage, especially in educational settings, in relation to children. The 1981 Education Act introduced the concept of special educational needs. Children with special needs include those whose learning difficulties call for special educational provision to be made. The Act states that children have learning difficulties if they have:

- significantly greater difficulty in learning than the majority of children their age, or

- a disability that prevents or hinders them from making use of educational facilities of a kind generally provided in school, for children of their age, within the local authority concerned.

In the past children with special needs may have been categorised as 'handicapped' or 'subnormal'. Individual children may have been labelled as 'physically handicapped', 'visually handicapped' or 'mentally subnormal'.

Those who advocate use of the term 'special needs' suggest that these other labels are unsatisfactory because they:

- focus on weaknesses, not strengths
- do not indicate the practical difficulty and thus the measures that may support the child
- suggest that all 'handicapped' or 'subnormal' children are the same and need the same kind of support
- encourage people to focus on the condition and view children with particular difficulties in stereotypical ways: for example, children with Downs Syndrome are seen as sweet and lovable
- imply a clear-cut division between 'handicapped' and 'subnormal' children and other children.

Supporters of the term 'special needs' seek to emphasise the similarities between children with special needs and children who are developing according to the norm. They hope that the change in terminology from 'handicap' to 'needs' will encourage the treatment of each child as a unique individual with their own personality, ideas, sense of humour and level of ability. However, the term 'special needs' does still conform to the medical model of disability.

The range of special educational needs

Within the term 'special educational needs', children can be considered to have:

- moderate to severe learning difficulties
- sensory impairment, that is hearing and/ or visual impairment

- physical or neurological (linked to the function of the brain) impairment
- speech and language difficulties
- emotional or behavioural difficulties
- **specific learning difficulties** – this term is used to describe children's difficulties in learning to read, write, spell or in doing mathematics. Such children do not have difficulty learning other skills.

Factors leading to delayed development, physical or sensory impairment or learning difficulties

Before, during or after birth

As already detailed in Unit 6, preconceptual care and parents' lifestyle and choices during pregnancy are very important factors in the health, development and wellbeing of the unborn child.

Some tests can be carried out during pregnancy to check for specific conditions. Some tests are offered to all women; others are offered to mothers considered to be in 'at risk' categories. These tests include tests for spina bifida, Down's syndrome, sickle cell disease and thalassaemia.

Other common tests and investigations include:

- ultrasound scans – which can be used to check the size and position of the foetus in the uterus, diagnose some foetal abnormalities and detect and confirm multiple pregnancies
- placental function tests – a healthy placenta is essential for a foetus to grow and develop. It is possible to test the health and strength of the placenta by checking the amount of pregnancy hormones produced

---

Specific learning difficulties = difficulties in learning to read, write or spell or in doing mathematics, not related to generalised learning difficulties

- amniocentesis – amniocentesis involves the removal of a small sample of amniotic fluid from the uterus, via the abdominal wall. It may be performed after the 16th week of pregnancy, when it is possible to check that the chromosomes, including the sex chromosomes, are normal. Amniocentesis may be offered to women who have a history of chromosomal abnormalities, such as Down's syndrome, and women over the age of 35 years as the risk of chromosomal abnormalities increases with age.

Some conditions are inherited and are carried by the chromosomes and genes – see the table below.

Premature babies

Pre-term or premature babies are immature and are not yet ready to survive alone outside the womb. Complications that might arise for a pre-term baby are:

- birth asphyxia – pre-term babies may be slow to breathe at birth due to an immature respiratory centre in the brain
- respiratory problems – immaturity of the lungs may make breathing difficult
- intracranial haemorrhage (bleeding in the brain) – fragile blood vessels in the brain may bleed easily. This may cause long-term damage.

The care of premature babies is a highly specialised field; they are prone to many difficulties. For example, like all babies they cannot control their temperature, but the smaller the baby, the greater the risk of hypothermia. They are more likely to be jaundiced or anaemic and are vulnerable to infections. Some pre-term babies do survive and develop well, but some suffer long-term damage as a direct result of their prematurity.

Possible effects on development are:

- generalised developmental delay – this 'global' delay may affect all areas of development, with milestones being achieved at a much later age, if at all

▼ Genetic and chromosomal conditions

CONDITION	CHARACTERISTICS
Recessive inheritance	Both parents carry a defective gene for a particular conditions or illness, for example cystic fibrosis or sickle cell disease. There is a one-in-four chance of the disorder being passed on with each pregnancy
Dominant inheritance	One parent carries a dominant gene for a particular condition, for example Huntington's chorea. There is a one-in-two chance of this being passed on with each pregnancy
Sex-linked inheritance or X-linked	Conditions are passed from mothers to their sons, for example haemophilia and Duchene muscular dystrophy. With each pregnancy, mothers who carry an affected gene on their X chromosome have a one-in-two chance of each boy being affected and a one-in-two chance of each girl being a carrier
Chromosomal abnormalities	Conditions that result from defects in the chromosomes have characteristic patterns. Down's syndrome is a well-known chromosomal abnormality

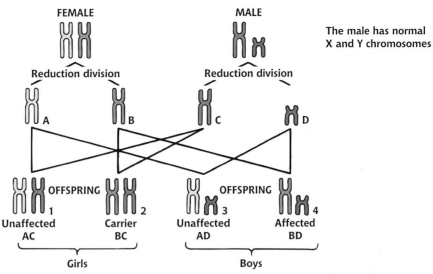

The abnormal gene is present in the shaded female (X) chromosome

The male has normal X and Y chromosomes

If the baby is a boy, there is a 1:2 chance of him being affected. If the baby is a girl, there is a 1:2 chance of her being a carrier.

▲ Recessive inheritance

The chromosome pattern of a male infant with Down's syndrome. Note the presence of the extra number 21 chromosome, Trisomy 21.

▲ Dominant inheritance

- specific developmental difficulties – there may be a particular problem with one area of development, such as motor or communication skills

- sensory loss – blindness and deafness are much more common in children who have been born very early.

Characteristics of common conditions and impairments

You should already be aware that there are a large number of disabilities and special educational needs. It is not possible to give details of them all. It is very important that, as a practitioner, you are aware of the needs of any child with whom you are working. You will be able to find information, locally both in your setting and beyond the setting through local authority support, training, and research with national organisations.

The table below shows details of some common conditions and impairments.

▼ Some common conditions and impairments

CONDITION/ IMPAIRMENT	FACT	CAUSES	SOME CHARACTERISTICS	SOURCES OF INFORMATION
Autism	A child with autism has difficulty in relating to other people and making sense of the social world	The primary cause is unknown Autism occurs in all parts of the world and usually begins from birth	Lack of awareness of others Communication difficulties May lack imagination	Autism Independent UK www.autismuk.com
Cerebral palsy	A disorder of movement and posture; the part of the brain that controls movement and posture is damaged or fails to develop	There are many causes that may occur before, during or after birth; these include: mother catching rubella during pregnancy, lack of oxygen to the brain before or during birth, rhesus incompatibility, pre-eclampsia, birth injury, accidents or infections after birth	The term covers a wide range of impairment. There are three main types: spasticity – where movements are stiff, muscles tight, limbs held tight and turned in towards the body athetosis – when limbs are floppy, movements frequent and involuntary ataxia – where there is a lack of balance and poor coordination	Scope www.scope.org.uk
Diabetes mellitus	A condition in which the body cannot metabolise carbohydrates, resulting in high levels of sugar in the blood and urine	The pancreas gland produces insufficient amounts of insulin resulting in high levels of sugar in the blood Type 1 usually starts before 30 years of age, requiring insulin injections Type 2 is common in older people and controlled with diet and medication	Early symptoms are excessive thirst frequent passing of urine Children may lose weight Complications include visual impairment, kidney damage and problems with circulation	Diabetes UK www.diabetes.org.uk

CONDITION/ IMPAIRMENT	FACT	CAUSES	SOME CHARACTERISTICS	SOURCES OF INFORMATION
Dyslexia	Dyslexia is a specific learning difficulty Dyslexia is neurobiological in origin		Difficulties with phonological processing, rapid naming, working memory; child therefore may have difficulties with reading, sequencing and organising thoughts	Dyslexia Action www.dyslexiaaction. org.uk
Dyspraxia	Symptoms evident from an early age; many children with dyspraxia don't go through the crawling stage of development		Children with dyspraxia may demonstrate a range of behaviours such as high levels of motor activity, high levels of excitability, may constantly bump into things and fall over	The Dyspraxia Foundation www.dyspraxia foundation.org.uk
Hearing impairment	Either conductive deafness or nerve deafness; ranges from slight hearing difficulty to profound deafness	Causes include heredity congenital defects, head injury, infection of the middle ear, impairment of the cochlea nerve	There is a wide range of impairment affecting a substantial number of people in the UK Diagnosis is by hearing test	The National Deaf Children's Society www.ndcs.org.uk
Visual impairment	May be present at birth (congenital) or may occur later	Causes of congenital blindness include infections in pregnancy (such as rubella and syphilis), optic nerve atrophy or tumour Causes after birth include cataract, glaucoma, infections such as measles, injury	Three main categories: blind partially sighted – entitled to services for blind people partially sighted. Parents and carers may notice a lack of response to visual stimuli	The National Blind Children's Society www.nbcs.org.uk

CONDITION/ IMPAIRMENT	FACT	CAUSES	SOME CHARACTERISTICS	SOURCES OF INFORMATION
Epilepsy	A condition in which there are recurrent attacks of temporary disturbance of brain functions	It may occur spontaneously or be triggered by stimuli such as stroke, severe injury, fever or drugs There may be a familial tendency towards this condition	Diagnosis takes many different forms The condition is different for each child and ranges from disturbances in consciousness that are barely noticeable, such as mild sensations and lapses of concentration, to severe seizures with convulsions	Epilepsy Action www.epilepsy.org.uk

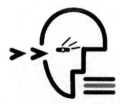

Time to get equal

sc⊖pe

About cerebral palsy.
For disabled people achieving equality.

DYSPRAXIA
FOUNDATION
recognising developmental
co-ordination disorders

epilepsy *action*

Dyslexia Action

Assessment · Education · Training

ndcs

every deaf child

Diabetes
UK

▲ These national health organisations are good sources of information

GOOD PRACTICE · · · · · · ·

It is very important for childcare workers to find out about the needs, abilities and characteristics of each individual child and not to pre-judge the child based on common characteristics and information. Remember – every child is a unique individual.

✓ Progress check

1. Describe the medical model of disability.
2. Describe the social model of disability.
3. Choose five conditions/impairments and use the website to carry out some further research.

Learning Outcome ②

FOCUS ON...
the range of factors affecting children's ability to learn

This links to assessment criteria **2.1**

It is important to remember that it is not possible to provide definitive information within this section; it is therefore essential to extend your reading and knowledge by accessing a range of additional material which is specific to the individual needs of children.

▲ **The individual needs of a child must always be met**

Different events in children's lives

Events and experiences in the lives of children and young people can have a variety of effects on their ability to learn. Some children will be affected by:

- loss and separation
- abuse
- deprivation
- drugs and related medical treatments.

Childcare workers must ensure that they always strive to meet the individual needs of each child; they must never expect specific issues relating children to be managed in the same way. When children are experiencing some form of social or emotional difficulty, it is fair to say that their ability to learn can be affected. Professional advice beyond the setting should be sought to enable practitioners to support the individual needs of the child. There are many organisations which are able to provide advice and support; such organisations can be found locally and nationally.

Effects on learning

During times of stress and upset, children may:

- regress in areas of their development
- find it difficult to concentrate
- experience and exhibit strong emotions and changes in mood
- become emotionally reliant on key adults
- reject emotional support and physical contact
- not want to interact with peers and adults
- find it difficult to remember and recall previously learned information.

Loss and separation

Issues relating to children's emotional development have been covered in Unit 2 of this book where further information can be found.

In times of loss, adults should attempt to meet the needs of the individual child in the best way they can. This could include providing physical comfort, time and attention, patience and reassurance. Allowances may need to be made for regressive behaviour and appropriate play provided so that the child can express their feelings safely.

Adults should recognise that they must be less demanding and help the child to reorganise gradually, helping the child to participate in activities when they are ready. They should also give time throughout to listen to the child, care for them and promote their welfare.

During any separation, workers should assess children's behaviour and respond appropriately.

Drugs and medical treatment

Issues relating to illness and medical conditions have been covered in Unit 4 of this book where further information can be found.

When children and young people are using drugs or medical treatments, it is important to remember that there are often related side effects and effects on their ability to learn. Some treatments may cause, for example, pain, discomfort, drowsiness, inability to concentrate and difficulties with memory.

Sensitive support of the needs of the child or young person is needed; sometimes this will be short term, but in other circumstances

GOOD PRACTICE

When caring for children, the following points are relevant:

- Children under 3 years benefit from one-to-one relationships with a specific person.
- The particular needs and background of children need to be known.
- Children's comfort objects should be readily available to them.
- Children should be provided with activities appropriate to their developmental age and stage, especially play encouraging them to express their feelings.
- Honest reassurance should be given.
- Children's parents should be involved and informed about progress or changes in behaviour.
- Children should have reminders of the family, parents or carers, such as photographs.

this support may be needed over a long period of time. It is therefore important to have realistic expectations and to ensure that you access advice and guidance.

Abuse

Issues relating to child abuse have been covered in Unit 3 of this book where further information can be found.

As with any trauma, children's reactions to abuse vary. Being subjected to abuse can affect all aspects of children's development. Some children may find social relationships difficult and their educational progress may be limited. Some children may experience erratic attendance at the setting and therefore this factor alone may affect their learning.

Deprivation

Issues relating to deprivation have been covered in Unit 6 of this book where further information can be found.

Some children may experience a home life and environment that impact on their ability to learn. Children living in overcrowded homes may find it difficult to complete homework tasks and extension activities that they have been set. Diet and the quality of sleep can also affect children's ability to learn and participate in learning activities. If families are unable to provide the resources and equipment that enable the child to engage in some activities, such as clothing for physical education or boots for outdoor learning, this can be an issue – not only for learning but also for the self-esteem of the child. It is therefore important that settings take these issues into consideration and do not put unnecessary pressures and strains on the resources that families have. Similarly, practitioners should never make assumptions about children and their families.

Effects of illness on children's learning

Sick children need play and learning opportunities, but they may not make the effort or have the ability to create suitable activities for themselves. Therefore, it is important that childcare workers encourage and support play and learning in a manner that is appropriate to the needs of the child and at a pace that suits their medical and physical needs. Such activities should build on the familiar, fit the child's ability and stimulate their interests.

It is also important to remember that a child who experiences long periods of absence from the learning environment may experience a lack of confidence and anxiety about returning to the setting. They may feel that their friends and peers have moved on and they have been left behind; it may take them some time to rebuild these relationships. Children may feel negative about their abilities because they have missed out. Sensitive adults will need to be prepared to support the individual and should consider strategies to do so and ways of preparing others for the return of the child.

Children who need to stay in bed because they are ill, or because their treatment means that they cannot get up, will need appropriate activities that will interest them. These could include reading, tape-recorded activities, computer-based activities and board games. Variety is essential as children who are ill often have short attention spans. Specific medical advice from other professionals should be available to the setting.

Progress check

1. Briefly describe five factors which might affect children's ability to learn.
2. How can a setting support a child who has been absent for a long period due to illness?

U14

LO3

Learning Outcome 3

FOCUS ON...

This links to assessment criteria **3.1**

Laws on disability and special educational needs

Legislation concerning the care and education of children with disabilities is regularly changed and updated. This section aims to explain the underlying principles contained in current legislation. You will need, however, to refer to the legislation itself in more detail, and to update yourself regularly on any changes.

Education Act 1944

This was the first piece of legislation to describe and define special educational needs and provision. Doctors were central to the process, and children were assessed as having one of 11 'disorders' before being placed in a specialist school.

At this time, children with severe learning difficulties were not thought to be able to benefit from education and were looked after in junior training centres by local authorities.

The Warnock Report 1978

This report reviewed the provision that was available to all children with special needs. The Warnock Report was very important because it informed the Education Act 1981.

Education Reform Act 1988

The 1988 Act requires all maintained schools, including special schools, to provide the National Curriculum. For a child with a statement, it is not necessary to modify or exempt the child from the requirements of the National Curriculum; but it is possible if modification is in the child's best interests. The 1988 Act encourages inclusion, rather than exclusion, of children with special needs in the National Curriculum. Most importantly, it states that all children with special educational needs have the right to a broad and well-balanced education. This includes as much access as possible to the National Curriculum.

The Children Act 1989

This brings together most public and private laws relating to children. It includes the functions of social services departments in relation to disabled children. Disabled children are treated in the Act in the same way as all other children.

The Act defines a category of 'children in need' for whom the social services department should provide services. Disabled children are included in this category. The Children Act defines disability as follows: ' A child is disabled if he is blind, deaf or dumb or suffers from mental disorder of any kind or is substantially or permanently handicapped by illness, injury or cognitive deformity or such other disability as may be prescribed'.

Duties of local authorities

The Act places a general duty on the local authority to provide an appropriate range and level of services to safeguard and promote the welfare of 'children in need'. This is to be done in a way that promotes the upbringing of such children within their families.

Underlying principles

The Children Act outlines the following principles for work with disabled children:

- the welfare of the child should be safeguarded and promoted by those providing services
- a primary aim should be to promote access for all children to the same range of services
- the need to remember that disabled children are children first, not disabled people
- the importance in children's lives of parents and families
- partnership between parents and local authorities and other agencies
- the views of children and parents should be sought and taken into account.

The Education Act 1993

This builds upon and largely replaces the Education Act 1981. It includes the Code of Practice giving practical guidance on how to identify and assess special educational needs. There are sections which relate to disabled people and these adapt and supplement conditions published in the

Disability Discrimination Act 1995. The Education Act 1996 imposes duties on schools and LEAs to identify, assess and meet children's special educational needs.

The Education Act 1996

This covers the roles and responsibilities of all aspects of education and covers every phase of education from early years to higher education. It also places a **statutory duty** on local authorities and health authorities to support and assist when a child has special educational needs. Part of the Education Act 1996 has been revised and is now the Special Educational Needs and Disabilities Act 2001.

The Special Needs and Disability Act 2001

This Act requires LEAs to provide parents of children with special needs with advice and information. It strengthens the rights of children with special educational needs to be educated in mainstream schools.

Special Education Needs Code of Practice 2001

The Code of Practice 1993 for children with special educational needs revised the Education Act 1981. Some terms from the old legislation, such as Statements of Special Educational Need, were retained.

The code of practice is a guide for schools and LEAs about the practical help they can give to children with special educational needs. Since 1 September 1994, all state schools should identify children's needs and take action to meet those needs as early as possible, working with parents.

The code is a large and very detailed document; every setting should have a copy of the *Special Education Needs Code*

Statutory duty = duty required by law

Special Educational Needs

Code of Practice

LEAs, Head Teachers and Governors of Schools, early education practitioners and other interested parties.

Date of Issue: November 2001
Ref: DfES/581/2001
Related Documents:
The Education Act 1996

department for
education and skills
creating opportunity, releasing potential, achieving excellence

Crown Copyright © 2008

▲ Special Education Needs Code of Practice

of Practice. The code states that children have special educational needs if they have a learning difficulty which calls for special educational provision to be made for them.

The code defines children as having a learning difficulty if they:

a) have a significantly greater difficulty in learning than the majority of children of the same age; or

b) have a disability which prevents or hinders them from making use of the educational facilities of a kind generally provided for children of the same age in schools within the local authority

c) are under compulsory school age and fall within the definition at (a) or (b) above or would do so if special educational provision was not made for them.

The code of practice also states that children must not be regarded as having a learning difficulty solely because the language or form of language of their home is different from the language in which they are taught.

Special educational provision means:

a) for children aged 2 or over, educational provision additional to, or otherwise different from, the educational provision made generally for children of their age in schools maintained by the local education authority, other than special schools, in the area

b) for children under 2, educational provision of any kind.

The Special Education Needs Code of Practice sets out fundamental principles which serve to inform the code. These principles are:

- a child with special needs should have their needs met

- the special educational needs of children will normally be met in mainstream schools or settings

- the views of the child should be sought and taken into account

- parents have a vital role to play in supporting their child's education

- children with special educational needs should be offered full access to a broad, balanced and relevant education, including an appropriate curriculum for the Foundation Stage and National Curriculum.

Critical success factors

Within the code, there is a list of critical success factors which are based around the needs, rights and provision for the children. These factors encourage:

- provision for all children's needs
- collaborative working between LEAs, schools and settings to ensure early identification of any child's special educational needs
- best practice of LEAs, schools and settings when interventions are designed
- the wishes of the child to be taken into account by those responsible for special educational provision
- partnership with parents
- professionals to take parents' views into account in respect of their child's needs
- regular reviews with contributions from the child, their teachers and their parents
- issues to be resolved by cooperation between all agencies – a multi-disciplinary approach
- set time limits for assessment to be adhered to by LEAs
- a statement determined by the LEA to be clear, detailed, made in line with set time limits, stating how the statement will be monitored and that the statement is annually reviewed.

The Statutory Assessment of Special Educational Needs

The code of practice states that the special educational needs of the majority of children should be met in mainstream settings as follows:

- *Early Years Action* – this is when practitioners or the SENCO who have day-to-day contact with a child identify special educational needs and they work in collaboration to provide strategies that are in addition to, or different from, those usually provided in the curriculum. They will usually provide an **Individual Education Plan (IEP)**.
- *Early Years Action Plus* – this is when practitioners who have day-to-day contact with a child and the SENCO are given advice and support by specialists in order to provide alternative interventions which are in addition to, or different from, those interventions identified in Early Years Action. A new IEP will usually be provided.
- *School Action* – this is when special educational needs are identified by a teacher and interventions additional to or different from those provided by the usual differentiated curriculum are put in place. An IEP is usually provided.
- *School Action Plus* – this is when the teacher and SENCO are given advice and support by specialists in order to provide interventions for the child that are in addition to, or different from, those identified in School Action. A new IEP is usually provided and the SENCO supports the teacher and takes the lead role.

The statutory assessment process is carried out because a referral has been made to the LEA. A request for assessment may be made by a parent, a school or setting or another agency such as health authorities or social services.

Individual Education Plan (IEP) = a document which sets out short-term targets that are in addition to or different from those set out in the curriculum for the individual child

The body or person making the referral will be expected to support the request with reasons and a range of evidence such as IEPs, progress records and information from parents.

Full details of the types of evidence to be submitted and statutory assessment process are described in detail within the code of practice.

Statements of Special Educational Needs

As a result of the statutory assessment procedures it is sometimes necessary for the LEA to provide a **Statement of Special Educational Needs**. This statement describes in detail a child's needs and the resources that should be made available to meet these needs.

Every statement should be in five parts:

- Part 1, introductory page, including factual information such as name, address, age, etc.
- Part 2, the child's special educational needs as identified during the statutory assessment
- Part 3, special educational provision considered necessary to meet the child's special educational needs, specifying objectives, provision and how progress will be monitored
- Part 4, the type and name of school or establishment thought to be appropriate for the child or the arrangements that the LEA will make for provision other than in school
- Part 5, information about non-educational needs as agreed between LEA and health services, social services or other agencies
- Part 6, non-educational provision to meet the non-educational needs of the child as agreed.

The final statement should be sent to the parents, with an explanation of their right to appeal and the time limits that apply to this process. The confidentiality of the statements is crucial. In most circumstances, no disclosure from the statement can be made without the parents' consent. The statement is usually kept in the administrative offices of the local authority.

The progress of children who are the subject of a Statement of Special Educational Needs must be reviewed at least once every 12 months. This is called the Annual Review. Children, parents, professionals and all other interested parties are given the opportunity to contribute to these reviews. The review should consider any progress made and set new aims and targets for the coming year.

GOOD PRACTICE

You should be able to locate a copy of the *Special Education Needs Code of Practice 2001* and the toolkit which has been provided to support this in every setting that you attend.

School policies and procedures

Schools must consider what the Code of Practice says when drawing up their policies for children with special educational needs. The school's policy will outline:

- the name of the teacher who is responsible for children with special educational needs (often called the school's SENCO)
- the school's arrangements for deciding which children need special help, stage by stage

Statement of Special Educational Needs = a written report setting out a child's needs and the resources required to meet these needs

• how the school plans to work closely with parents and the child. Records of interventions, progress reports and assessments are all important aspects of the effectiveness of the IEP and the provision at the setting.

Access to learning experiences for all children

⊂⊃ Links to assessment criteria **3.2**.

It is essential to ensure that children's special needs do not override their ordinary needs. Following the medical model of disability, the implication is that there is something wrong, and that the child's efforts should be directed to **specific therapeutic goals**. This attitude may be encouraged through special programmes such as conductive education.

Children who have disabilities may need physiotherapy, speech therapy or special learning programmes, but these should not always override their ordinary needs. All children need periods of self-directed play. Children with disabilities need adults who will facilitate, rather than direct, their activities.

Each child is an individual with unique gifts and needs. In order to meet these needs, some knowledge of the causes and medical implications of their specific impairment or condition will be helpful.

This knowledge will be most helpful when combined with a positive attitude and a willingness to learn how to maximise the potential of individual children. You can support your knowledge by further reading or talking to professionals, but remember that the full-time carer of each child will often be the best source of information and guidance.

In order to meet the individual needs of the child, attitudes and assumptions about disability need to be examined.

For an establishment to include all children, including those with special educational needs, certain aspects need to be considered. Detailed information and training about inclusion is available from a range of sources, including local authority support teams and condition-specific organisations, some examples of which can be found in the table on pages 374–375. Inclusive practice does not mean making special or different provision for children. It is important that the children at the setting are supported as individuals at all times. However, it is also important that supportive adults answer any questions and avoid using language that suggests difference: for example, 'Please don't sit there; that's Mica's "special" chair.'

▲ Settings should be accessible for all children

Practice issues

Images

Everything learned about images of other marginalised or minority groups applies to children with disabilities. In the past,

---

Specific therapeutic goal = identifies objectives to counteract the effects of the condition or impairment

GOOD PRACTICE

Establishments should provide:

- equipment that all children can use – much equipment produced for the specific needs of children is generally inclusive: ramps, lifts, adjustable tables, automatic doors, long-handled taps, touch-sensitive controls, large print and grab rails can be used by all children
- a range of options such as tapes, Braille and print versions of documents
- a range of seat and table sizes and shapes
- empty floor space that is kept uncluttered
- flexible, adjustable equipment, for example a sand tray that comes off the stand, high chairs with removable trays
- a range of scissors, knives and other implements
- soft-play areas for activities such as crawling, jumping and climbing
- some equipment for individual children to facilitate integration – there should be discussions with the child and the full-time carers about what to buy before expensive purchases are made
- private toilet and changing facilities
- training for staff.

Activities

Organised, directed activities should always seek to be inclusive. The needs of children with disabilities should be considered at the planning stage and in line with the Early Years Foundation Stage. The learning environment which enables the child to learn and develop needs to be reviewed to ensure accessibility and freedom of choice which promotes child-initiated activity.

In educational establishments, teachers aim to use differentiation in the tasks set. This means that individual or groups of children are given 'manageable challenges'. This involves careful planning to ensure that children with disabilities are not segregated. Special needs support assistants may be involved in this process, ideally at the planning stage. This will enable the support staff to implement effective activities.

Role models

The involvement of a range of adults, including adults with disabilities, can provide positive role models for all children. These role models can also support the development of disability awareness at the setting.

Access for children with visual and aural impairments

Children with impaired sight

The following aspects need to be considered in order to include blind and partially sighted children. Establishments will need to provide:

- Opportunities to explore the environment and people, using taste, touch, smell, hearing and any residual sight
- The opportunity for children to orientate themselves physically (this

nearly all images of people with disabilities were produced by people who did not have disabilities – often on behalf of charities. Their aim was to evoke sympathy, pity or guilt. This was justified as necessary to raise money for people with disabilities. It is very difficult to find positive images of children with disabilities. Children's books generally have few disabled characters. The books available often focus entirely on the impairment. Rarely are people with disabilities portrayed as ordinary. However, this situation is improving and this is something to be celebrated as these texts are developing positive images.

may involve visiting the setting when few people are present)

- Stability and order, a place for specific items and activities; someone should ensure that the child is informed of any changes
- Plenty of light
- A hazard-free environment, or an indication of hazardous things such as steps or sharp corners
- Information about other children's needs; for example a child with a hearing loss might not respond to them
- Some specific items, such as books in Braille, toys or board games which are designed to be inclusive.

Children with hearing impairment

The following points need to be considered by an establishment including deaf and hearing-impaired children:

- Hearing impairment is largely invisible; even if a mild hearing loss is significant in a noisy, crowded room.
- A child with impaired hearing cannot tell you what they have missed.
- Hearing aids are not a replacement for hearing and may be of little or no use to some children.
- Deaf children's greatest special need is access to language and communication; complete access can only come about through universal use of language

▲ Braille books are needed for children with impaired sight

and communication accessible to deaf children. This will often mean sign language, which will need to be used accurately by everyone at the setting.

- Deaf children need to communicate with other children as well as adults.
- Deaf children have a range of intellectual ability as all children do; if we deny them access to language we create a learning difficulty for them.

GOOD PRACTICE

It is clearly good practice to ensure that what you do is in line with the required provision for the individual child. An IEP for the child will advise on ways of working. It is essential that a good practitioner ensures that they fulfil the role they have been given, provides feedback when required and raises issues which are of concern to the appropriate person at the appropriate time.

Practical example

Inclusive education

'Lake View Primary School's brochure states that they provide education for all children in the locality aged 3–7 years. I don't think they realised what a challenge it would be when they offered my daughter, Emily, a place in the nursery.

'Before Emily started, we went to visit for a session. The other children were curious and asked me why Emily had a funny face and couldn't talk properly. After our visit, the staff decided to prepare the children before Emily started properly. They had to search hard for suitable books to read to the children, but finally found Letterbox Library. The staff were willing to learn; they asked me questions about Emily and had a couple of sessions with a disability equality trainer.

'Emily was very clingy and demanding at first. Staff couldn't manage her with 35 other children, so the school employed a special needs support assistant for part of the time, to help Emily integrate with the other children. They approached the local college and a student with learning difficulties came to the school on work placement. Emily latched on to him and it seemed to increase his self-confidence, as well as Emily's.

'Whenever the children ask what is wrong with Emily, staff explain that she has Down's syndrome. They always answer the children's questions honestly, even when they are funny, like "Is it catching?"

'The nursery staff say they have learned so much from having Emily and now do some things differently for all the children.'

(1) Why did Emily's parents want her to go to the local school?

(2) How did the nursery staff prepare for Emily's admission?

(3) Why did staff explain Emily's condition using the proper name?

(4) Why did staff seek out a student with learning difficulties to help in the nursery?

Progress check

1. Draw a flow chart to show the staged process laid down by the Special Education Needs Code of Practice.
2. What should be included in a statement of special educational needs?
3. What is the purpose of the annual review?
4. How can parents appeal against the assessment process or provision made by the LEA?
5. List five ways to promote inclusive practice.
6. What does the term 'differentiation' mean?
7. How can involving disabled adults benefit any educational setting?

FOCUS ON...
the roles and responsibilities of professionals working with children with special educational needs

⊙⊙ This links to assessment criteria **4.1**

Professionals and organisations working with children with special needs

There may seem to be a baffling array of professionals involved with children and their families. Their titles change from time to time. It is important to have an understanding of the statutory, voluntary and private sectors, and to know that some adults act as a signpost for children and their families. You will need a basic knowledge and understanding of the roles of significant professionals.

For simplicity, the professionals described in this section have been identified as working in the areas of health, education, social services or voluntary organisations. Of course, some may work for more than one. In some areas, a service that is provided by, for example, social services will, in another area, be provided by a voluntary organisation, on behalf of social services.

Health service professionals
Paediatricians

Paediatricians are doctors specialising in the diagnosis of conditions and impairments in children, and the medical care of children with these conditions

▲ Health service professionals may work here

and impairments. They may be the first health service professional to become involved with a child with a disability in the maternity unit, the children's ward or outpatient department.

Health visitors

Every child under the age of 5 has a health visitor. Health visitors are qualified nurses with additional training. They work in the community, attached to a clinic or general practice, and usually undertake the routine development checks. The health visitor is often the health-care professional most closely involved with the family at home. They are able to provide a link with, and between, other professionals and services.

Physiotherapists

Physiotherapists assess children's motor development and skills, and assess how well they can move and balance. They may work in schools as well as hospital clinics. They may demonstrate exercises and activities that carers will carry out themselves with their children. Physiotherapists may visit children at settings and provide training for childcare workers.

Occupational therapists

Occupational therapists seek to encourage independent life skills, such as eating and moving around independently. For example, they may assess a child's fine motor skills. They can advise about any specific equipment that may be helpful and arrange for it to be supplied. This may be done in the community as well as in hospital clinics.

Speech and language therapists

Speech and language therapists seek to develop all aspects of children's expressive and receptive communication skills and language development. As well as assessing speech, they also assess tongue and mouth movements, and their effects on eating and swallowing. Speech therapists will work out programmes of activities and exercises to help children to acquire language, understand concepts and use speech. Parents or carers may be involved in carrying out programmes. Speech therapists may be based in schools, hospitals or the community.

Clinical psychologists

Clinical psychologists are mainly concerned with children's emotional, social and intellectual development. Their assessment of children covers all aspects of their circumstances. They will have discussions with families and other carers, as well as making direct observations of children's behaviour.

School nurses

School nurses often check children's weight, height, eyesight and hearing in school. They may pick up difficulties in any of these areas. They may be based full time in special schools where they supervise the routine medical care of the children

Play therapists

Play therapists use play to help children to handle particular feelings or experiences that may be hindering their development. Play therapists need to have been specially trained for and supported in this task, as they are likely to be dealing with powerful emotions.

Playworkers

Playworkers are usually trained nursery nurses, employed in some hospitals to play with children, both those visiting clinics and those admitted to the wards. They represent a non-threatening adult in a setting that may provoke anxiety for children. They may be involved in raising awareness and preparing children for a stay in hospital and will use play to help a child to understand medical procedures.

Education service professionals

Educational psychologists

Educational psychologists advise the local education authority about the education of individual children. They will be involved in the educational assessment of children with disabilities, including the assessment that may lead to a Statement of Special Educational Needs. They may advise the professionals who are working directly with the child about learning and behavioural modification programmes.

Special needs support teachers

Special needs support teachers, sometimes called specialist teachers or support teachers, are teachers who often have additional training and experience; they are often **peripatetic** and visit children with disabilities in different schools. They may specialise in one particular impairment, for example hearing loss or visual impairment. They are involved in the direct teaching of individual children, as well as in advising staff and parents of ways to maximise children's potential.

Pre-school support teachers

These are special needs support teachers who work with children and their families before the child starts school. They visit children in their own homes and devise small steps teaching programmes for parents and carers to follow with their child.

Special needs support assistants

Special needs support assistants may have many different titles, for example special assistants, education care officers, classroom assistants or special needs nursery nurses.

They adopt a variety of different roles, depending on the school or nursery and the needs of the children whom they are employed to support. Some work with individual children who have a Statement of Special Educational Needs; others with groups of children with a variety of additional needs. The main focus of their work may be involved in learning support. They may be observing and monitoring children, liaising with other professionals and working under their direction. They may have regular contact with parents and carers.

Special needs advisers

Special needs advisers focus on the curriculum, teaching methods, materials, schemes and equipment used in schools. They have a role as inspectors to ensure provision of the National Curriculum.

Education welfare officers

Education welfare officers undertake welfare duties on behalf of children and their parents or carers. They will be involved with children whose attendance is irregular. They may arrange transport for children to school.

Social services professionals
Social workers

Social workers may be based in hospitals or in local authority offices. Their work with children with disabilities includes statutory child protection duties. They may advise on the availability of all services in the area, such as health, education, welfare benefits or care; or they may put families in touch with appropriate agencies.

They may advocate on behalf of children, for example enabling them to obtain services to which they are entitled. Social workers may be involved in assessment for referral to day care or respite care and for home helps and other domiciliary care, under the heading of family aids.

Specialist social workers and technical officers

Specialist social workers and technical officers may have additional training and experience to work with children with particular conditions or impairments, for example deaf or blind children.

Peripatetic = travelling (to see those they work with)

Nursery officers

Nursery officers work in day nurseries, family centres and children's centres. They may also visit family homes to liaise between the home and the setting.

Family aids/visitors

Family aids or visitors provide practical support for families in the families' own homes. The helpers may be involved in domestic duties, childcare and other family needs.

Residential childcare workers

Residential childcare workers may work in long-stay or short-stay residential accommodation for children with disabilities. The worker may be a key worker for a specific child accommodated away from home by the local authority.

Jobcentre Plus

The main role of Jobcentre Plus is to deal with customer work searches and benefit needs. There is a range of benefits available to children with disabilities and their families. These are frequently subject to change. The Citizens' Advice Bureau provides up-to-date advice and information about welfare benefits.

Voluntary organisations

Collectively, voluntary organisations provide every conceivable type of support for children with disabilities and their families. Some are national organisations and others local. It is beyond the scope of this book to provide information about the services they offer, but much information is available at local libraries and on the internet.

In recent years, there has been an increase in the role and extent of involvement by

▲ Social service professionals may work here

voluntary organisations in the lives of children with disabilities. Many of these organisations work in a highly professional and pioneering way. Much of the innovative work with and on behalf of people with disabilities is done through voluntary organisations and self-help groups.

This work includes learning and therapy programmes such as those described below.

Portage home teaching scheme

The Portage Guide to Early Education was originally developed in a rural area centred on the town of Portage in Wisconsin in the US. The schemes devised are used with children with moderate and severe learning difficulties, behaviour problems and developmental delay. Weekly home visits of one to two hours are made by a Portage home visitor. Home visitors come from a range of professions.

Most approaches have found that a short training programme is all that is initially required. The purpose of each visit is to help the parent or carer to select and set short-term goals for the child, expected to be achieved in one or two weeks, and to devise an appropriate way for the parent or carer to teach these.

As well as short-term goals, each Portage home visitor sets, with the parent or carer, long-term goals for the child to work towards, so that the weekly visits and short-term goals can be seen as steps in a general progression towards the desired objective.

Workers are trained to use development checklists, which covers development from birth to 6 years, in the areas of socialisation and language, cognitive, self-help and motor skills.

One of the aims of Portage is that parents and carers will become sufficiently skilled to enable the role of the Portage home visitor to change to consultant and supporter. The Portage method aims to enable parents and carers to become independent of the home visitors eventually, and to become the main worker with the child.

Bobath technique

The Bobath technique is a form of physiotherapy developed by Professor Bobath and his wife, aimed at enabling the best possible posture and mobility for children with cerebral palsy. It is important that skills are transferred from the therapist to the parents or carers and from them to anyone caring for the child. Treatment begins with an initial assessment at the Bobath centre in London.

Doman-Delacato therapy (patterning)

Doman-Delacato therapy claims that it is possible to treat the brain itself. The theory is that undamaged portions of the brain are taught to take over the function of the damaged part. The basic assumption behind the therapy is that mobility can be achieved through movement. This movement cannot occur spontaneously and must be initiated from the outside by other people.

Movement must be frequent, intense and repetitive. Teams of volunteers put the child through set movements for between three and eight hours a day. Not surprisingly, the child often protests at this and Doman-Delacato is consequently a controversial therapy.

Conductive education

According to Dr Mari Hari, a leading supporter of conductive education, this is 'a method of enabling "the **motor impaired**" to function in society without requiring special apparatus such as wheelchairs, ramps or other artificial aids'. It is based on the theory that, under the right conditions, the central nervous system will restructure itself.

Conductors (therapists) use **orthofunction**, a teaching method that involves the whole person physically and mentally and 'instils in children the ability to function as members of society, and to participate in normal social settings appropriate to their age'.

Conductive education offers a positive approach to a clear set of goals. It has produced results beyond the expectations of professionals and parents of children with cerebral palsy and spina bifida. It should be remembered, however, that the treatment places emphasis on adapting individuals rather than environments. It follows a medical, not a social, model of disability.

Motor impaired = having an impairment of a function of movement
Orthofunction = a teaching method that involves the whole person physically and mentally, and 'instils in children the ability to function as members of society, and to participate in normal social settings appropriate to their age'

Need for professional and personal support

⬭⬭ This section links to assessment criteria **4.1**.

Support available to practitioners

Work with children who have disabilities or special educational needs is important and such a role can be very rewarding. However, the challenges of the role can at times be overwhelming and individuals are encouraged to find strategies and support to help them to deal with these feelings.

It is fair to suggest that working to support children's needs and to facilitate engagement in activities can be exhausting and intense. Practitioners should endeavour to fulfil the requirements of any role to the best of their ability. A practitioner supporting a child with a disability or special needs may find that their role involves:

- personal care
- behaviour
- engagement in activities
- close and intense levels of engagement
- feeding routines
- medical issues
- manoeuvring individuals
- using specialist equipment.

As already stated within this unit, anyone working in this role will need to be supported by senior staff, supervisors, parents and professionals who have been involved in devising and agreeing specific plans, interventions and strategies for the child.

▲ It is important that childcare practioners are offered support

There should be clear guidelines about interventions and accepted practice when:

- managing behaviour
- lifting, moving and handling
- feeding and meeting care needs.

Childcare workers may find that their work is draining both physically and mentally. It is therefore very important to ensure that breaks are taken. It is also best to let other people know if you are finding it very difficult to support the child or if you feel that the child is not benefiting from your support. As stated many times, all children are individuals; children with learning difficulties or special needs react and respond differently to others and you may find that some children will respond well to you but not to others and vice versa.

Practical issues

Practical activities with children who have mobility difficulties, for example, may involve a large amount of moving and handling. We know that back care is very important, but we also want to do what is best for the children in our care. It is therefore very important to ask for additional help if you are unable to move or lift a child safely. Settings should also have a range of specialist support equipment available for use with particular children.

Emotional needs

Your own emotional needs must also be considered; practical engagement with children with disabilities or special needs can be repetitive and progress may be limited. This can be quite challenging from the point of view of the practitioner. It is easy to feel like a failure and lack motivation because you are putting in so much effort and seeming to get little back in return. It is important to ensure that you have done your research in advance as you will have already been aware that this would be the case. However, if you are feeling despondent it is best to speak to someone about it.

Challenging behaviour

Another reason why practitioners may find their role emotionally challenging is because some children with disabilities or special needs may also present a range of challenging behaviours. Such behaviours may be physical or verbal; they may be directed at themselves, others or key carers. Often these behaviours are not deliberate or personal; they may be part of a condition or specific difficulty. Some children will harm themselves and this can be very distressing for others to witness.

It is understood that constant physical or verbal behaviour can be exhausting. It is essential that support is sought in such situations; colleagues should be able to allow you time out and other professionals may be able to suggest coping mechanisms that you could employ which will help you to deal with the situation.

✓ Progress check

1. Choose one of health, education or social services. Outline the roles and responsibilities of three professionals in that service.

2. What advice would you give a childcare worker who found their role in supporting a child with a disability difficult?

3. Where can you find information about specific difficulties and impairments?

4. What are the implications for the practitioner who works with children with particularly challenging behaviour?

Weblinks

- www.dcsf.gov.uk
  The Department for Children, Schools and Families aims to improve outcomes for children in all areas of life

- www.ofsted.gov.uk
  Office for Standards in Education: 'We inspect and regulate to achieve excellence in the care of children and young people, and in education and skills for learners of all ages.'

- www.talkingpoint.org.uk
  For information about speech, language and communication difficulties; there are pages for professionals and parents

- www.bcodp.org.uk
  The website of the British Council of Disabled People (BCODP) has information and advice about inclusion, discrimination and legislation

- www.earlysupport.org.uk
  Provides information about early support programmes, training and current issues relating to supporting young children with special needs and their families, including multi-professional partnership approaches

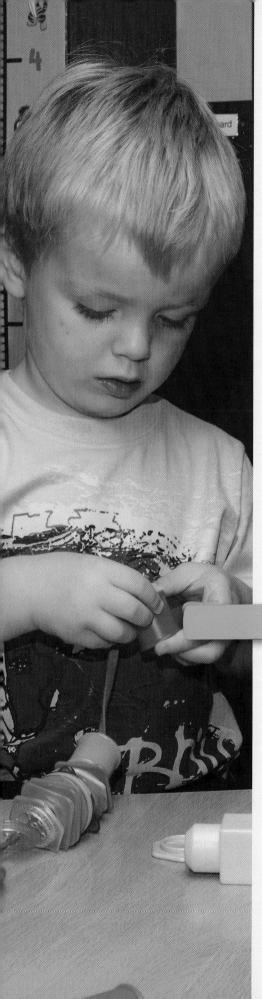

Unit 15

Developing children's (3–8 years) mathematical skills

In this unit you will learn about curriculum frameworks and the different mathematical areas children need to learn. There is information on how to provide appropriate activities within a supportive learning environment. You will also learn how to contribute to planning and the importance of reflective practice and positive working relationships between practitioners and families.

Learning Outcomes

In this unit you will learn about:

1 the stages of development of mathematical skills in children from 3 to 8 years

2 how to help children develop their understanding and use of mathematics

3 the role of the adult in supporting children's understanding and development.

Learning Outcome 1

This links to assessment criteria **1.1** and **1.2**

FOCUS ON...
the stages of development of mathematical skills in children from 3 to 8 years

Stages of development of mathematical skills in young children

Many adults throw up their hands in despair at the thought of using mathematics, because they consider that they are 'no good at it'. A very negative mindset has developed in many people and, as early years practitioners, it is important to help children develop an 'I can do it' approach, rather than an 'I *can't* do it' approach to using number and developing mathematical skills. It is also important to remember that many aspects of mathematics are about solving problems, and that we all have our preferred, and often differing, approaches to doing this. It reminds us that there is no one fixed way of doing something and that we each have our own learning styles.

Early development

From birth, infants begin to develop the sense of interest and enquiry needed for their mathematical development:

- Immediately after birth, babies look around them and respond to events, e.g. smell mother's breast, start rooting for a feed – this is an example of early cause and effect.

- In the early weeks their feet kick and their fists wave, occasionally touching an item that brings a reward: e.g. a cot mobile moves; the teddy swings; a bell jingles, etc. Again, this is cause and effect.

- In time babies become eager to hold an object, temporarily experiencing its properties (hard/soft, big/small, etc.).

- Then, as their hands gain strength, they take each object to their mouth, exploring it orally. This is soon followed by passing objects from hand to hand, and then eventually purposefully releasing them.

- Parents and carers use mathematical vocabulary during domestic routines: 'one arm, two arms', 'one sock, two socks', 'what a big boy', 'up you come', 'one more spoonful', 'all gone', 'down you go', etc. These everyday vocalisations help introduce and reinforce the early concept of one-to-one correspondence, the familiarity of the terms and numbers paving the way for the infant to respond to and use them themselves later on.

- The various toys and household objects babies come into contact with help them explore size, shape, texture and surface temperature.

- When crawling begins, infants start to experience distance, and once able to stand they can be seen trying to gauge how far it is to the next solid furniture item, as they take their first steps.

- As toddlers, they learn to master push-a-long toys, initially bashing into door frames and other objects, but eventually gaining an understanding of space, direction and orientation.

- Early water play sees children simply splashing, filling and tipping (all useful learning experiences), but this soon turns into more purposeful experimenting, with the child trying out different-sized containers (size, measure and early conservation experience), using pumps (the concepts of pressure and force).

- As children are introduced to rhymes and stories involving number, they begin to make sense of what actually is meant by the number one, what actually is two, etc. They need plenty of practice and reinforcement – through the repetition of singing old favourites like 'five currant buns', through regular stories using number, and through practical activities involving the grouping of numbers, adding one more, taking away, etc. – as their understanding develops.

- As a child moves on in their thinking, they gradually develop an understanding of more abstract concepts.

GOOD PRACTICE

It should, be remembered that children do not follow a neatly set pathway in their learning and much will be based on the experiences they receive.

Theories of mathematical development

In order to understand numeracy and the development of mathematical understanding, it is important to consider the thinking regarding cognition of some of the most well-known theorists. These include Jean Piaget, Lev Vygotsky, Jerome Bruner, Tina Bruce and Chris Athey. The following summaries will help you in understanding how children learn generally, which in turn will help you understand how mathematical skills develop.

Jean Piaget

Jean Piaget has been an important theorist in helping adults to focus on the minds of children and how their understanding develops, but in more recent times some of his findings have been challenged. Piaget considered that children's thinking moves through four main stages, each stage building on the one before:

- Sensorimotor stage (0–2 years)
- Preoperational stage (2–7 years) divided into
  - Pre-conceptual stage (2–4 years)
  - Intuitive stage (5–7 years)
- Concrete operational stage (7–11 years)
- Formal operational stage (from around 12 years).

Refer to Unit 2 page 57, for an explanation of each of these stages.

Piaget believed that children develop knowledge concepts by using and building on previous experiences. Initially children will represent their thinking physically in their actions, moving on to symbolic representations.

He considered that they gradually adapt these concepts, which he called *schemas*, to establish new understanding. An example would be a child initially seeing a coin and understanding it is a one pence piece because it is round, made of metal and brown. Typically the child would use the term 'money'. This experience, reinforced over time, will eventually move them on to understanding that other coins are also round, made of metal and that they can be either brown or silver. They are, however, all referred to as money. The child will learn that a coin is part of the money system and gradually understand that there are other forms of money (notes, cheques and credit/debit cards, all used as payment for Mummy and Daddy's shopping). Piaget called this process *assimilation* and *accommodation*.

Piaget considered children to be active learners who learn best through doing (discovery learning). He felt it was important that they had access to a range of materials and resources to help them experiment and find out for themselves. A child's learning about money will therefore be supported by role-play activities involving shops, tills and going shopping. Using coins for counting, adding and taking away will also help reinforce both use of money and its value.

In Example A, the child was shown two identical rows of pennies and was asked if they were the same. The pennies in the second row were then spaced apart and the child was asked if there were still the same number of pennies. If the child was able to conserve, they would answer that there were the same number. If the child could not conserve, they would answer that there were more pennies in the longer row. In Example B, the child was shown two identical beakers of water and asked if they contained the same amount. After watching the adult pour the water from one beaker into a taller beaker, the child was asked if the amount of water in the beakers was still the same. If the child could conserve, they would answer that the amount of water remained the same. If they could not conserve, they would state that the amount of water was different – that there was

Preoperational children say that the two rows have the same number of pennies.

Preoperational children say there are more pennies in the longer, fourth row.

▲ Conservation – Example A

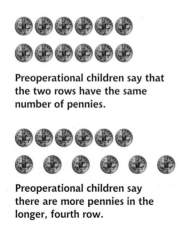

250 cc   250 cc

250 cc   250 cc

▲ Conservation – Example B

more water in the taller beaker. In a further example, the child was shown two identical balls of play dough and asked if they were the same amount. Having seen the adult roll one ball into a sausage shape, the child was asked if the amount of play dough was still the same. If the child could conserve, they would answer that the balls of play dough were still both the same size. If they could not conserve, they would think that the sausage shape was made from a greater amount of play dough.

▲ Donaldson found that young children can conserve – an important contradiction of Piaget's work

Piaget is also well known for his thinking on conservation. He believed that children in the preoperational stage were unable to conserve, and cited the outcomes of several 'experiments' to support this. The examples on page 402 show his findings.

Lev Vygotsky

Like Piaget, Lev Vygotsky believed that children learn best by doing. The main difference between their thinking was Vygotsky's belief in the importance of social interaction between a child and an adult or more able peer. Vygotsky believed that discussion, sensitive questioning and guidance from a more able 'other' could help a child reach a higher level of

understanding than they are likely to have reached on their own. He called this their 'zone of proximal development' (ZPD).

⚭ More on Vygotsky can be found in Unit 2 pages 57–58.

Jerome Bruner

Jerome Bruner describes a child's development of thinking in what he terms 'three modes'. These are:

- the enactive mode, where the child learns through first-hand experiences (like Piaget's discovery learning)
- the iconic mode, where the child is able to form mental images and use memory
- the symbolic mode, where the child expresses their understanding through a range of media.

Bruner's thinking about a child's learning builds on the work of Vygotsky. He uses the term 'scaffolding' to describe how an adult can support a child, offering support to help them move to the next stage in their understanding, and then gradually removing the support structure, leaving them more able than they were beforehand.

⚭ See Unit 2, page 58, for more on Bruner.

Chris Athey and the development of schema

Chris Athey has built upon Piaget's thinking about schemas. Her observations and research have shown that children spend specific passages of time focusing on a particular area of interest and learning, practising and exploring a concept from all angles. This exploration builds upon their understanding, moving them on to the next stage in their learning. Examples would include a child who repeatedly lines up objects (e.g. dolls and teddies, cars and other vehicles, their cutlery at lunchtime, their items of clothing along the sofa in the morning). It may also be seen in their paintings or drawings, with the creation of rows of splodges, dots, lines, etc.

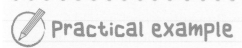

Practical example

Jasmine

Jasmine, aged 2 years 9 months, showed a fascination with shapes. She delighted in people helping her make circles, squares and 'tangles' (rectangles) with any items she could find. Jasmine demonstrated a clear enclosure schema, wrapping up herself, her dolls, and other items such as crayons, bricks and empty cups. She also liked to surround things with a circle of bricks.

1 *What other activities would you expect Jasmine to enjoy, linked to this schema?*

2 *What activities would you offer Jasmine?*

Practitioners working with young children agree that learning opportunities are at their best when provided within a well-planned play environment. Tina Bruce (1991) refers to the Plowden Report of 1967 and how it gave play 'central status' in the education of young children. This 'central status' was also upheld by the Rumbold committee report of 1990 (section 89) which read:

"Young children learn effectively in a number of ways, including exploring, observing and listening. Playing and talking are, for young children, two principal means of bringing together a range of these activities. We believe that effective curriculum implementation requires careful attention to be given to providing fully for these."

The report goes on to say (section 91) that:

"Play that is well planned and pleasurable helps children to think, to increase their understanding and to improve their language competence. It allows children to be creative, to explore and investigate materials, to experiment and to draw and test their conclusion. Such experience is important in catching and sustaining children's interests and motivating their learning as individuals and in co-operation with others."

This promotion of play has continued with successive governments and through to the development of the present frameworks, which guide and support early years practitioners in their work.

Tina Bruce

Tina Bruce has been an important contemporary influence on the promotion of play. She uses the terms 'free-flow' or 'ludic' to describe what she considers to be the only true concept of play – a form of play that allows children to learn by discovery.

'Games help children to understand external pressures and constraints; free-

| Free-flow play | = | Wallowing in ideas, feelings and relationships | + | Application of competence and technical prowess that has already been developed |

▲ Free-flow play

flow play helps children to see the function of rules for themselves.' (Bruce, 1991)

Bruce illustrates her definition of free-flow play as follows:

Bruce's 12 features of free-flow play are summarised as follows:

- It is an active process without a product.
- It is intrinsically motivated.
- There is no external pressure to conform.
- It is about lifting the 'players' to their highest levels of functioning, involving creativity and imagination.
- It involves reflection, the wallowing in ideas.
- It actively uses previous first-hand experiences.
- It is sustained and helps us to function ahead of our real-life ability levels.
- It allows control, using competence previously attained.
- It can be initiated by child or adult, but adults need to be aware of not imposing rules, or directing activity.
- It can be a solitary experience.
- It can be in partnership with others.
- It brings together what we learn, feel and understand (Bruce, 1991).

Janet Moyles

Another important contributor to the thinking on play is Janet Moyles. She developed the idea of the play spiral. This

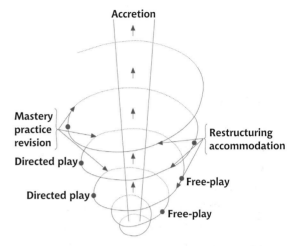

▲ The play spiral

spiral clearly shows how children move in and out of different modes of play (directed and free-play) each stage building on the one previous as their learning develops.

Refer to pages 408–411 for more general information on play, its importance in a child's learning process and examples of activities to support numeracy and mathematical development.

G☺☺D PRACTICE

Providing resources to support understanding of mathematical concepts that can be freely accessed by children around the setting or classroom will help ensure that they have plenty of opportunities to consolidate previous learning, to experiment, and to reinforce understanding of new concepts.

Have a go!

Imagine you have been asked to talk to a group of parents at your placement about the ways in which their children are developing mathematical understanding. Produce two information cards, one for each of two different types of mathematical activities of your choice. Give a clear explanation of relevant theory, and provide examples for the parents of how each theory is supported by the activity.

National frameworks for mathematical skills

Legislation and guidance

There is a variety of relevant legislation and curriculum guidance to support the development of children's numeracy skills, either directly or indirectly. This includes:

- the Children Act 1989 and 2004
- the Childcare Act 2006
- the Children's Plan (December 2007)
- Continuing the Learning Journey (2005)
- Every Child Matters
- Early Years Foundation Stage (mandatory from September 2008, supporting children from 0 to 5 years)
- the National Curriculum
- The Primary Framework for Literacy and Mathematics, part of the National Curriculum
- the Warnock Report 1978 – this can be found on page 427
- the Code of Practice 2001 – this can be found on page 428.

The Children Act 1989 and 2004

The Children Act 1989 and its update of 2004 legislates for the all-round health, development and safe living of young children. It sets out minimum requirements for staffing numbers, staffing qualifications, the state of and resources within the care and learning environment, and how children's needs should be met. The regulatory body Ofsted oversees the maintenance of standards of both care and learning, and has the powers to act if these standards are not met. Ofsted inspection teams ensure that all areas of care, stimulation and learning, as set out by the Early Years Foundation Stage, are fully met. Mathematics and general numeracy skills are significant aspects of these.

The Childcare Act 2006

The Childcare Act 2006 includes specific updates on the Children Act 2004. It asks for local authorities and their local partners to reduce inequalities for young children in their areas by providing an integrated service for children and their families, part of the ethos of Sure Start. Each local area should have sufficient provision for care and learning for all the children aged 3 and 4 of parents who wish to take it up. A free minimum amount of provision for all 3- and 4-year-olds is set out.

Section 12 of the Act highlights the newly extended age range (now up to age 20 years) for which parents have a right to obtain information for their child. This includes language skills and the use of advocates and interpreters where appropriate.

Sections 39–48 of the Act introduce the Early Years Foundation Stage (EYFS), and explain how it builds on previous documents such as *Birth to Three Matters*, the *Foundation Stage Curriculum*, and the *National Standards for Under 8s Day Care and Childminding*. The Act explains how the new EYFS will support an integrated provision for children from birth through to five years, and makes reference to the adjusted Ofsted Childcare Register standards.

The Children's Plan 2007

The aims of the Children's Plan are that it will:

- strengthen support for all families during the formative early years of their children's lives
- take the next steps in achieving world-class schools and an excellent education for every child
- involve parents fully in their children's learning
- help to make sure that young people have interesting and exciting things to do outside of school
- provide more places for children to play safety.

It also means a new leadership role for Children's Trusts in every area, a new role for schools as the centre of their communities, and more effective links between schools, the NHS and other children's services so that together they can engage parents and tackle all the barriers to the learning, health and happiness of every child.

Continuing the Learning Journey (2005)

This was a package of in-service training (inset) materials to support practitioners in successfully helping children make the transition between the Foundation Stage and Key Stage 1.

The package aimed to:

- 'Establish an understanding of the principles of the foundation stage
- Show how these principles can be used to ensure an effective transition into key stage 1
- Promote continuity in learning by ensuring that year 1 teachers are aware of children's achievements and can implement the next stage in their learning
- Show how information from the foundation stage profile can be used to support school development.'

GOOD PRACTICE

Continuous Professional Development (CPD) is important to all teachers and practitioners. There are various inset packages and training sessions available. The example above is just one of many. There will be others within your local area, and also within each setting where you work. Undertaking CPD throughout your career will keep you up to date with new thinking and ensure that your practice remains appropriate and meets the needs of all the children you work with.

Every Child Matters

Curriculum guidance and frameworks to support all-round health, education and wellbeing are provided for all-children – both before and throughout compulsory schooling. The EYFS framework aims to support children in achieving the five main outcomes of Every Child Matters: staying safe, being healthy, enjoying and achieving, making a positive contribution, and achieving economic wellbeing. All children attending any care or education setting that meets the criteria to receive government funding will be supported through government strategy or curriculum guidelines. i.e.:

- the Early Years Foundation Stage (EYFS) (this brings together the Curriculum Guidance for the Foundation Stage, Birth to Three Matters, and also the National Standards for Under 8s Day Care and Childminding)
- the National Curriculum
- the Primary Framework for Literacy and Mathematics (a framework from the EYFS through to Year 6/7).

Early Years Foundation Stage (EYFS)

The EYFS principles which guide the work of all practitioners are grouped into four distinct but complementary themes:

- A Unique Child
- Positive Relationships
- Enabling Environments
- Learning and Development.

A Unique Child recognises that every child is a competent learner from birth who can be resilient, capable, confident and self-assured. The commitments are focused around development, inclusion, safety, and health and wellbeing.

Positive relationships describes how children learn to be strong and independent from a base of loving and secure relationships with parents and/or a key person. The commitments are focused around respect, partnership with parents, supporting learning, and the role of the key person.

Enabling Environments explains that the environment plays a key role in supporting and extending children's development

and learning. The commitments are focused around observation, assessment and planning, support for every child, the learning environment, and the wider context – transitions, continuity, and multi-agency working.

Learning and Development recognises that children develop and learn in different ways and at different rates, and that all areas of learning and development are equally important and inter-connected.

Within Learning and Development there are six areas of learning ultimately leading through to the early learning goals. These are:

- Personal, Social and Emotional Development
- Communication, Language and Literacy
- Problem Solving, Reasoning and Numeracy
- Knowledge and Understanding of the World
- Physical Development
- Creative Development.

Each of these areas must be delivered within a broad range of contexts, through planned purposeful play, with a balance of adult-led and child-initiated activities.

The National Curriculum

The National Curriculum is intended to be a broad and balanced framework to meet the learning needs of all children; its main principles are based on the Education Acts of 1988 and 1996. All state schools must offer the National Curriculum and although schools in the private sector can opt out, few do. It is considered to be a prescriptive curriculum in that it gives precise outcomes to be achieved at certain stages in a child's school career.

Schools are also free to provide extra areas of learning in addition to the National Curriculum to reflect the particular needs and circumstances of the setting.

The National Curriculum is divided into four key stages.

The key stage that follows on from the Foundation Stage is Key Stage 1. You will usually work with children who are following this stage during placement experience in a Year 1 or Year 2 class.

▼ National Curriculum key stages

KEY STAGE	AGE	YEAR GROUPS
Key Stage 1 (KS1)	5–7 years	1–2
Key Stage 2 (KS2)	7–11 years	3–6
Key Stage 3 (KS3)	11–14 years	7–9
Key Stage 4 (KS4)	14–16 years	10–11

(QCA, 2000, pages 74–81)

At the end of each key stage, there are a number of tests known as Standard Attainment Tasks (SATs), which all children must complete. The purpose of SATs is to monitor each individual child's performance as they progress through school.

Primary Framework for Literacy and Mathematics

The Primary Framework for Literacy and Mathematics sets out core learning aims for both literacy and mathematics for children in each year group, from Foundation Stage through to Year 6/7. There are seven strands to the Primary Framework for mathematics. They are:

1 using and applying mathematics
2 counting and understanding number
3 knowing and using number facts
4 calculating
5 understanding shape
6 measuring
7 handling data.

Practical example

Phoebe

Miss Norman sent Phoebe home with a maths game for her to play with her parents and older siblings. It involved a board with numbers randomly sited along a spiral, culminating in a number 20 at the centre. A spinner with numbers 1–10 needed to be spun, and the number the spinner rested upon had to be doubled. The player moved to the next occurrence of this number along the spiral. The winner was the player who reached the centre of the spiral first.

1 Which strand of the Primary Framework for Mathematics do you think this game mostly supports?

2 Which year group might Phoebe be in?

Research the National Primary Framework for Mathematics. Interview at least two practitioners who work with it, and, using their opinions together, with your own findings, reflect on the effectiveness of this framework in the development of children's numeracy and mathematical skills.

Impact of legislation/ guidance on practice

In recent years greater levels of guidance on practice have been drawn up by government and implemented by early years practitioners. Initially, practitioners were concerned at the structure of the curriculum guidance; but thankfully this has been reviewed and redeveloped, and is considered much more acceptable by most practitioners today. There have always been good early years settings, excellent early years settings and settings which needed to improve their provision. There have also always been settings that provided a good range of opportunities for children, but where staff did not always understand the full value of what they were providing, perhaps seeing just the main learning opportunity to be gained from an activity but without realising just how many other aspects of learning were also involved. The structure of strategies such as the Early Years Foundation Stage has enabled more staff to develop their understanding of the value of play to a greater level. This has been beneficial to children, to the staff and to the field of early years generally.

Funded places for children, initially for 4-year-olds, and more recently for three-year-olds as well, have been a massive boost to many families, enabling all parents who wish it to receive an early years placement for their child. For nurseries and other early years settings, there has, however, been some concern about the impact on occupancy levels and about issues of funding not actually covering fees completely, leaving providers losing revenue for their businesses. This problem is ongoing.

The other main impact of recent legislation and practice guidance has been the more stringent inspection procedures. These have been controversial at times, and it took time for practitioners to fully value the process, but, for children, it has meant that, on the whole, most unacceptable provision has been identified and guidance given on how those settings can raise their standards. In some cases low standards have meant the closure of settings which were considered not to meet standards sufficiently. There have been clearer pathways set up for concerns to be raised; and the greater level of policies and procedural paperwork, whilst adding to the workload of those who write them and need regularly to review them, has helped to support safe working practice for all.

The introduction of (initially) Early Excellence centres, and more recently Sure Start centres around the country has been welcomed by the majority as a move forward in providing extended care, learning and support for both children and their families, incorporating health, education and adult learning. There have, however, been concerns regarding funding and the impact some of these centres have had on other provision in the area.

Policies and procedures supporting the development of numeracy skills

Schools and early years settings will each have written information for parents on how their child's learning will be supported in each main area of learning. This may include material provided through printed sheets, grids, assessment booklets and observation files, through the use of posters and noticeboard information, talks and open days for parents/carers, and through individual discussion. Staff will use planning documents, selected by the setting, and profile documents, either DfES produced, or their own.

G☺☺D PRACTICE · · · · · · · ·

As you move from placement to placement it will be useful for you to familiarise yourself with the differing ways each setting sets out its information, planning, assessments and feedback. There is no one correct way for practitioners to work, and as with all aspects of learning, people work best through a variety of contexts and approaches.

Have a go!

Working as a group, collect together examples of policies and procedures to support numeracy from a range of early years providers and primary schools. Consider the similarities and differences between them. Note ideas from them and obtain permission to keep them in your file for future reference and personal use.

Obtaining information about individual children's progress and planning appropriate activities

Observation and assessment

Using a range of observation methods, individual children's progress should be followed and recorded according to the setting's procedural practice. This helps progress to be monitored and the identification of any specific areas of need, for example any areas of numeracy in which they are less able (if any), and also their preferred learning style. In early years settings this will usually be carried out by a child's key worker, using the benchmarks of the appropriate curriculum or guidance structure, for example the Early Years Foundation Stage. In school this would usually be done by the class teacher, but it could also be carried out by the classroom assistant, with assessment linked to the Primary Framework for Mathematics and the National Curriculum as appropriate.

Types of planning – individual, long-term, medium-term, short-term

Planning for the long term provides practitioners with a broad overview of the main themes they wish to cover. This type of planning is not usually followed rigidly; it is flexible according to need and circumstance. Written long-term plans are useful as a basis for all staff to refer back to, reminding them of how the period of time (e.g. a school year) is intended to be approached. In the Early Years Foundation Stage, long-term planning ensures that all six areas of learning are given sufficient attention both in allocated time, and in regularity, in order for children to have meaningful learning experiences and for them to make progress appropriately.

Short-term planning is more likely to focus on day-to-day planning or weekly plans, or as a block of two to three weeks, as often used in the Primary Framework for Mathematics. Short-term planning should take into account the observations and informal assessments made of children during previous activities and use them to inform the next stage of the planning.

Medium-term planning is used by some, but not all practitioners. It provides a secure link between the long-term and the short-term plans, for example:

- long-term planning may cover a whole academic year in a school, e.g. divided into the five main blocks of the National Primary Framework for Mathematics

- medium-term planning may be linked to each of the terms within the school year, or to each of the five main teaching blocks

- short-term plans will refer to the weekly and daily planning of each unit of each main teaching block.

 Refer to page 401 for an outline of the National Primary Framework for Mathematics.

GOOD PRACTICE

One of the most important aspects of planning is to ensure that intended activities gradually introduce new concepts and build upon prior learning. In many nursery and pre-school settings, long-term plans may simply cover the main 'terms' of autumn, spring and summer, with short-term planning covering small topics within each season.

There is no hard-and-fast rule regarding written planning, but each school or early years setting will have its preferred 'in-house' method. Be sure to check the requirements of each setting where you are on placement, or in which you work.

 Examples of planning sheets are set out on page 404–405, to accompany the overview of the National Primary Framework for Mathematics.

Five blocks for planning

Planning for mathematics within the Primary Framework is through organising learning into five main blocks. The structure for each year group is the same. Each block incorporates objectives from the 'Using and applying mathematics' strand, together with two or three of the other core strands. The blocks are as follows:

- Block A: Counting, partitioning and calculating

- Block B: Securing number facts, understanding shape

- Block C: Handling data and measures

- Block D: Calculating, measuring and understanding shape
- Block E: Securing number facts, relationships and calculating

Each block is made up of three units and teaching each unit lasts two to three weeks.

The following example is taken from the government website.

Each plan follows the same format:

- What we want the children to learn (Development matters)
- Related Early Learning Goals (showing the interdependency of all six areas of learning)
- Possible contexts (contexts for the learning to take place)
- Example of adult-led activities (this gives an example learning context with ideas for the role of the adult)
- Opportunities for children to explore and apply (this gives learning contexts for children's spontaneous play and ideas for the role of the adult)
- Look, listen and note (examples to support observation for assessment)
- Assessment opportunities (examples to support observation for assessment)
- Related Scale Points (Foundation Stage Profile scale points that these learning contexts might support).

Example of mathematics planning and resourcing

What we want the children to learn (Development matters)

(The objectives in italics refer to Early Learning Goals.)

Mathematics objectives

- Estimate how many objects they can see and check by counting.
- *Count reliably up to 10 everyday objects.*

Using and applying mathematics

- *Use developing mathematical ideas and methods to solve practical problems.*

Related Early Learning Goals

- Respond in a variety of ways to what they see, hear, smell, touch and feel (CD).

Possible contexts

- Use collections of rhymes, songs, storybooks and props.
- Provide a variety of objects and collections for children to sort, match and incorporate into play.
- Use clipboards inside and outside in the learning environment and encourage children's mark making of numbers of objects.
- Use washing lines to match objects, and encourage children to find collections of objects to set their own challenges.
- Engage in games and small-world play throughout the day and challenge children to estimate quantities and check the number by counting, for example the number of children on the climbing frame, the number of apples in the fruit box, the number of pens in the pot.

- Develop interactive displays of objects with number cards for matching, moving and reordering.
- When tidying up, pay attention to numbers of objects, for example cutlery, construction equipment and garden tools.

Example of adult-led activity

Context: Using a storybook

Read the story with the children, for example *Handa's Surprise*. Have a basket of the fruit, count them in the basket and illustrate the story as each one is taken.

Provide opportunities for the children to retell the story, for example children telling each other from the book, using toy animals and fruit to act out the story, or scan the pages of the story into interactive whiteboard software or into Powerpoint as an electronic book.

Tell the children they can use the fruit to make fruit kebabs. (There are eight types of fruits and animals in *Handa's Surprise*. Add two to reinforce counting up to 10.) Say that the kebabs can have one piece of each kind of fruit. If they don't like some of the types of fruit, they can swap them for ones they do like but they mustn't have more than the number of types of fruit available (10). Encourage their methods in problem solving to work out how many pieces of each fruit they are putting on their kebab when they are leaving some kinds out.

Welcome the children's different ways of recording their recipes for their own kebabs. Share with them how they have represented their different types of fruit and how many they had of each. Count together and see that each kebab was made up of 10 pieces of fruit.

Make a pictogram (could use 2count from the simple 2simple Infant Video Toolbox) to find out which was the favourite and which was the least favourite fruit.

Adult role

- Model counting in everyday experiences.
- Use a puppet to count wrongly and encourage the children to correct.
- Demonstrate counting accurately during group activities: for example, how many cups do we need? 1, 2. 3…
- Scaffold children's learning by helping them to count accurately in their own play.
- Participate in all areas of children's experience and model counting for a purpose: for example, how many wheels are we going to need on this car?
- Encourage children to make guesses about numbers and then check: for example, 'let's guess how many objects there are in this box'.

Opportunities for children to explore and apply

- In construction and small-world play, provide plans for models using photographs or children's own models showing number of objects, for example 4 wheels or 10 pieces of straight track.
- Use photographs of numbers of objects and their numerals in the learning environment for children to collect and match when tidying, for example numbers of items of cutlery, cups or plates or construction tools.
- Provide clipboards inside and outside in the learning environment and model uses for shopping lists, recording

measurements of, for example, sunflowers growing, turn taking and children waiting, planning picnics/ parties, numbers of skips or jumps or other achievements.

- Provide a collection of counting rhymes, songs and storybooks and tapes or CD-ROMs with props. Encourage children to make their own. Model uses and encourage children to share in similar ways with each other.

- Use interactive whiteboard software to re-create stories using numbers of objects, for example 'Goldilocks and the three bears'.

- Make a wide variety of collections available for children to sort, match and incorporate into play, and to hide and find.

- Model games for them, for example dropping objects into a tin and guessing their number by listening to the sounds or asking how many of each object will fit into a matchbox.

- Use dice and domino numbers to help with the visual pattern of numbers. Children begin, for example, to see patterns of four as two twos, and six as two threes.

Adult role

- Model counting in everyday experiences.

- Use a 'silly puppet' to count wrongly and encourage the children to correct.

- Demonstrate counting accurately.

- Scaffold children's learning by helping them to count accurately.

- Participate in all areas of children's experience and model counting for a purpose; for example, how many wheels are we going to need on this car?'

- Encourage children to make guesses about numbers and then check: for example 'let's guess how many objects there are in this box.'

Look, listen and note

- Observe how children count an irregular arrangement of up to 10 objects: for example, as Zara dropped pennies noisily into the tin, she said, 'Listen for how many.'

- Note how children count out up to six objects from a larger group: for example, when a group of children were doing a jigsaw together, they shared out the pieces and counted to check everyone has the same number.

- Notice how children represent numbers using fingers, marks on paper or pictures: for example, Kim and Edward made a number track to 10. They then added numbers to 17 when they realised they could throw the beanbag further than they had expected.

Assessment opportunities

- Encourage children to join in rhymes and songs and notice how they are able to count: for example, five little ducks, ten green bottles, five little speckled frogs, five currant buns. Use a puppet to 'speak' and get numbers wrong, encouraging children to correct the puppet.

- Use collections of objects and everyday materials to count, for example when tidying things back into containers or baskets.

Related Scale Points

NLC 5, 6, 7

▼ Examples of planning sheets: (a) planning a unit in mathematics; (b) teaching and learning focus chart; (c) medium-term plan

(a) Planning a unit in mathematics

UNIT:		CURRICULUM LINKS:
Learning objectives and *Children's learning outcomes* Most children will learn to:	Vocabulary	Building on prior learning and intervention materials Check that children can already:

(b) Teaching and learning focus chart

TEACHING AND LEARNING FOCUS	LESSONS	LEARNING FOCUS, TEACHING NOTES AND RESOURCES	ASSESSMENT FOR LEARNING QUESTIONS AND SUCCESS CRITERIA
Introductory *teachingto assess and review learning*	Day(s)		
Direct *teaching of new knowledge, skills and concepts, with opportunities to practise and apply learning*	Day(s)		
	Day(s)		
Interactive *whole class teaching*	Day(s)		
Consolidation *and further practice*			
Interim review *of achievement and progress*	Day(s)		
Intervention *support with groups*	Day(s)		
Enquiry, *extension enrichment work, problem solving, reasoning*	Day(s)		
Summary *assessment of progress over the unit with children*	Day(s)		

(c) Medium-term plan

YEAR:			TERM:		
	Unit (weeks)	Learning objectives	Children's targets	Successful criteria	Focus and use of application
1					
2					
3					
4					
5					
Notes:					

The areas of mathematics you will support

At every level of learning there should be opportunities for children to develop an understanding of:

- counting
- working with measures, shapes and space
- problem solving and reasoning
- sorting and matching
- making connections and seeking patterns
- data representation through graphs, diagrams and tables
- calculation
- use of calculators.

Counting

Counting can be incorporated into almost any activity you can think of, for example counting children, resources, the times something occurs. Initially, counting will simply be in numerical order, but gradually this will develop into counting in twos, then threes and so on as skills develop.

▲ Finger rhymes are a useful way of learning to count

Working with measures, shapes and space

Measurements involve length, width, weight, height, and distance. They can involve people, plants, toys, etc., and also distances walked, jumped, etc., or measurements of fixed items such as furniture, size of carpet area, playground and so on. Weighing can be of people, cooking ingredients, or simply small items being weighed against each other for children to estimate how many? How many more?

Problem solving and reasoning

Children are solving problems whenever they are thinking about options, 'weighing up' ideas, and finding solutions to achieve a specified outcome.

Sorting and matching

There is a myriad variety of resources in which to sort small items, for example trays, boards, insets. Similarly there is an almost never-ending array of matching activities available commercially, and many simple ideas that you can put together yourself with the use of readily available items such as pencils, rubbers, clothes pegs, counting blocks, etc.

▬▬ FAST FACT

An enormous range of suggestions can be found in any commercial catalogue of resources for primary schools and early years.

Making connections and seeking patterns

Shape work, tessellation and symmetry can easily be supported through creative activities, such as those involving repetition and printing. Again, there are many commercial resources available.

G☺☺D PRACTICE · · · · · ·

Ask to look at the range of resources available at your current placement. Do the same at each placement you visit, and consider the differences and similarities between them and how they are used with the differing aged children.

Data representation through graphs, diagrams and tables

Children love 'doing surveys', particularly when they involve themselves and their friends. Simple opportunities to plot data representations would be through comparing ages, birthday months, height order, favourite foods or games, etc.

Calculation and use of calculators

Calculation can be through mental maths, or through practical activities. Early calculations will be made with the use of counters, rods, tiles, miniature animals and so on, helping children to add and take away, to count in twos, threes, etc. and to group according to one or more features. Much later on the use of simple calculators will be introduced, initially to check mental outcomes. Calculators are not likely to be introduced before Year 4.

Refer also to examples of activities to support the understanding of concepts and early practical mathematics skills starting on pages 408 and 411–416.

Have a go!

- Draw up planning for two different activities to promote children's number skills. You may wish to use the example shown on page 404 as a guide. Remember to consider resources, environment, adult input and assessment opportunities, as well as stating clearly what your learning objectives are and where they fit into the relevant curriculum.

- Carry out at least one of the activities with children in your placement, recording the outcomes clearly.

✓ **Progress check**

1. Explain Lev Vygotsky's ZPD theory, and give an example of how you have seen this theory support mathematical learning.

2. What are Jerome Bruner's three modes of thinking? Describe 'scaffolding' and its links to the work of Lev Vygotsky.

3. Explain Janet Moyles's play spiral and give an example of this in relation to mathematical understanding.

4. Explain the main areas of learning for Problem Solving, Reasoning and Numeracy development within the Early Years Foundation Stage.

5. Explain the main elements of the seven strands of the Primary Framework for Mathematics.

Learning Outcome 2

FOCUS ON...

how to help children to develop their understanding and use of mathematics

This links to assessment criteria **2.1** and **2.2**

The context in which children can explore, enjoy, learn, practise and talk about their understanding

The following extract is based on material taken from the *Practice Guidance for the Early Years Foundation Stage*, and is referring to its four main themes:

- Babies' and children's mathematical development occurs as they seek patterns, make connections and recognise relationships through finding out about and working with numbers and counting, with sorting and matching and with shape, space and measure.

- Children use their knowledge and skills in these areas to solve problems, generate new questions and make connections across other areas of learning and development.

- Re: Positive Relationships
  - Children need sufficient time, space and encouragement to discover and use new words and mathematical ideas, concepts and language during their own play.
  - They need to have opportunities to explore real-life problems, to make patterns and to count and match up items.

  - Children who are not learning English as a first means of communication need support in developing understanding in their most familiar communication system.

  - Adults need to show children that both their graphic and practical explorations are valued.

- Re: Enabling Environments
  - Adults need to actively promote the use of the outdoor environment to enable children to discover shape, distance and measure through physical activity.

  - Within the indoor environment the full potential should be exploited, e.g. through enabling children to use numbers, counting and calculating through practical situations, such as finding out how many children use the music area in one day, or look at a particular book, etc.

(Based on DfES, 2007)

Develop understanding through play across the curriculum

Understanding can be developed through, for example, stories, songs, games and imaginative play. A range of popular activities have been included in the following section. You will have the opportunity to plan, implement and reflect upon many of them during your placement experience. There are of course, many more that could have been included.

GOOD PRACTICE

It can be helpful to keep a file of ideas and how to carry them out, with the information obtained from placement. These will help you in your planning for the future.

As you read through this section, refer also to Unit 16 page 458. Links to literacy within some of the same activities have been included.

Board and boxed games

Board games, such as snakes and ladders, and boxed games, such as picture lotto, all involve numeracy. Snakes and ladders involves terminology linked to position, for example climbing up the ladder, slithering along or down the snake, overtaking X, and Y, being X places ahead, X places behind, etc. Picture lotto encourages children to count how many pictures, they still need to get, who has the most/least or same number of pictures, etc. Both games involve the use of dice, counting or recognising the numbers of spots etc. and picture lotto also involves early matching skills.

Role play

Role play can provide children with opportunities to group and match objects, for example cups and saucers, knives and forks. They use practical counting skills in providing appropriate numbers of resources, for however many people are sitting at the table. They develop estimating and matching skills as they dress large dolls in large clothes, and small dolls in smaller clothes, and they can learn to use money and write numerals as they go shopping, play at being shopkeeper, café owner, post office worker, etc.

Role play gives children opportunities to use both verbal and written numeracy. There will be opportunities for example, for:

- labelling and putting up notices as their role-play area becomes a shop, the post office, a bank and so on
- writing lists and prices as they make up menus for their café, takeaway or restaurant
- noting down orders from customers, writing cheques at the bank, writing receipts at the petrol station, etc.
- writing reference numbers as they make luggage labels, tickets and boarding passes to get on their aeroplane
- using mark making to indicate temperatures on a chart during hospital play, plotting the weight of a baby during baby clinic play.

Note: This is not an exhaustive list.

FAST FACT

You may find it interesting to also look at Green, S (2006) *Role Play* (David Fulton Publishers, London).

Books

Books can be both for pleasure and for information. In our modern-day world, strongly influenced by technology, it is important to help children value the use of books as a tool of reference. Linking books to displays and interest tables is an easy way to help children make this link. Even with the youngest toddlers and babies we use books to help children focus on a specific aspect of mathematical understanding, for example opposites such as big/small, short/tall, high/low, heavy/light, thick/thin, etc. We can use maps to locate places which children know or have been to, referring to direction, reference numbers, etc. This all helps to support a child's understanding of numeracy in its widest contexts and also how book use is still important in our technology-led world.

▲ In the age of the internet, books are still essential both for pleasure and as a source of reference

Storytelling

Stories provide both pleasure and information. Stories can be either written or oral and can provide opportunities to count, order, describe actions and position, and will often include repetition too. Great examples would include *1 Hunter* by Pat Hutchins, a fun book of lovely pictures for children to count in sequence, and also *Going on a Bear Hunt* by Michael Rosen and Helen Oxenbury. In this story (full of fun and lots of repetition), each time the children reach a new obstacle in their path, they find that they 'can't go over it, can't go under it, they have to go through it', and when they run from the bear, and get home they have to 'run up the stairs, down again to shut the door, and then get under the covers'.

You can probably think of many more examples.

Music and dance

The use of music and dance can easily support the understanding of position, orientation, grouping, sequencing and ordering. Through movement and the instructions given by the supervising adult, children will learn positional terms such as behind, next to, opposite, step forward, jump backwards. They will learn to form a circle, square and so on, to group themselves by specified numbers, to add one more on, or take one off a line of children. Terms linked to symmetry will be learned through actions copying another child, such as mirroring, copying, being the same as, matching, and also terms to describe the opposite effect, for example different from, unlike, reverse. These are just a few examples. Again, you can probably think of others.

The use of rhythm is important too, as language is full of rhythm, and listening to and being able to identify and replicate rhythm can help general speech and language development as well as aiding numeracy skills.

Drama

Numeracy can be supported through drama as children respond to and act out stories well known to them, for example 'Three Little Pigs', 'Three Billy Goats Gruff', 'Three Bears', etc. They can count to three, taking on the roles of biggest, middle-sized and smallest, speaking their 'lines' and following the story structure from its beginning, through its main sections and on to the climax. It also supports understanding of one-to-one correspondence.

Practical example

The Three Billy Goat's Gruff drama

Class One had enjoyed re-enacting the timeless classic of the 'Three Billy Goats Gruff'. It was part of a focused topic on positional language. Their teacher was following up the drama session with a discussion. She began by asking the children to think about the movements they had made during the drama e.g. across the river, over the bridge, through the meadow, etc.

(1) What other aspects of discussion could she introduce relevant to numeracy and mathematical development?

(2) What mathematical terminology would you link to the 'Three Billy Goats Gruff'?

(3) What opportunities for written numerical work could you bring to this project?

GOOD PRACTICE

You can develop the story further yourself with the help of the children – counting hooves, predicting and comparing size of horns, adding in fences for goats to climb over (and count), estimating distance to the meadow, etc.

Small-world play

Small-world play is play with resources such as farms, zoos, roadways, doll's houses, etc. It is basically playing out 'life' in miniature. It is favoured mostly by children of pre-school ages who tend to speak to themselves in a monologue as they play. This gives great opportunities for mathematical thinking as children:

- name positions of objects, e.g. the car is behind the bus but in front of the tractor; the cows are standing next to each other, etc.

- label actions, e.g. going upstairs, moving along the road, going in, coming out, going through the tunnel

- vocalise intentions regarding positions, e.g. I am putting my car in front of, behind, on top of, underneath, beside, inside, outside, etc.

- line objects up by size (sequencing), grouping them by colour or type

- make patterns, e.g. horse/cow/sheep, horse/cow/sheep, horse/cow/sheep.

Activities for developing mathematical understanding

Learning the use of number names

Suggestions to ensure that children learn number names include:

- counting games and rhymes

- matching numbers of children to the written number

- grouping small objects into numbered hoops

- hopping 5 times, 10 times, 100 times.

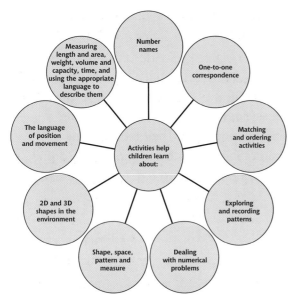

▲ The range of activities that you provide help children to develop mathematical understanding

Learning one-to-one correspondence

Suggestions for helping children learn one-to-one correspondence include:

- laying the table in the role-play area to seat a specified number of 'guests'
- matching up sets of objects, e.g. in hoops
- counting games and rhymes
- buying and selling items, 1 pence per item initially, building up as understanding develops.

Learning about matching and ordering

Suggestions for matching and ordering activities include:

- threading large beads in a repeated order, e.g. by colour or shape
- children sorting themselves into order of height

- making a display, setting objects out by size, e.g. a row of different-sized teddy bears
- matching socks into pairs on a washing line.

Learning to explore and record patterns

Suggestions for exploring and recording patterns include:

- making a class/group chart to show numbers of something, e.g. how many red bricks compared with blue, green or brown bricks
- grouping objects (e.g. teddy bears) into small, medium and large
- tessellating patterns using colour
- printing activities with intended outcomes.

▲ Learning to put colours in order is early maths

Learning about numerical problems

Suggestions for numerical problems include:

- counting games, songs and rhymes, e.g. 5 currant buns, 5 speckled frogs on a speckled log, 10 green bottles
- number puzzles and games
- number lines on wall, referred to as a whole group, or individual number lines for use in counting activities, adding on and taking one away
- sharing out resources, cakes, fruit pieces, etc.

Learning about shape, space, pattern and measure

Suggestions to ensure children learn about shape, space, pattern and measure include:

- sand and water play, having a range of utensils to experiment with
- cooking activities, weighing, noting scientific changes, etc.
- play with a variety of shaped objects, e.g. exploration of a range of fruit, vegetables, seeds, etc.
- finding items around the classroom or at home that are 'longer than my pencil', 'shorter than my arm', 'same height as me', etc.

Learning to recognise 2D and 3D shapes

Suggestions to help children recognise 2D and 3D shapes in the environment include:

- whole group discussions thinking of items (large or small) that are square, e.g. a window; round e.g. a hoop; rectangle e.g. a door, or that are a cube,

e.g. a softplay block; a sphere, e.g. a football; a cylinder, e.g. a drainpipe; etc.

- home activity to identify and draw objects of a certain shape from around the home, e.g. 'What can you find that is round?'
- using shaped backgrounds to displays made with the children, e.g. a large circle of card as the background for a display of circular paintings or drawings, or pictures of round items collected by the children, consolidating their recognition of various shapes and their names
- using a 'feely bag' of 3D shapes, and asking children to find a cube, a sphere and so on without looking.

Learning to use position and movement language

Suggestions to help children use the language of position and movement include:

- jigsaw puzzles, from the easiest play-tray puzzles through to more complex designs, for table or floor, big or small pieces. All puzzles help children to learn about shape and making sense of spaces, linking shapes to gaps, estimating and trying to position the pieces and developing the understanding of how to manoeuvre them
- dance activities involving sequences of movement (could sometimes be designed by the children), helping them to follow the required pattern
- using programmable toys, learning to control and operate them to follow a trail, and to instruct others in their movements
- playing 'follow the leader'-type games, being trains, caterpillars, etc.

Learning about measuring

Suggestions for measuring length and area, weight, volume and capacity, time, and the associated appropriate language include:

- sand play, with children filling and transporting containers, matching, comparing, weighing and measuring
- water play, with children using small containers to fill larger containers, encouraging them to estimate and predict, count and reflect
- making timelines, for example of people: baby/toddler/child/teenager/ parent/grandparent, or of the children's usual day, for example getting out of bed/breakfast/getting dressed/school/ lunchtime/school/teatime/story time/ bath-time/bedtime
- introducing children to terms such as 'volume, capacity, level, equal'.

 Have a go!

Take an example of mathematical learning you have seen used in your placement. Describe in detail where it fits into the curriculum guidance for the age range of the children in your example. How do you consider the relevant curriculum guidance has influenced or impacted this type of learning experience?

Support strategies to scaffold children's learning

When developing activities for whole class, group and individual work, it is important to take into account the resources you are providing, where the activity will be taking place within the room, the grouping of the children, and the environment in general. Each of these affects the success of an activity and getting it wrong can have a negative impact on learning. You will need to consider the following.

 Have a go!

- Draw up planning for two different activities to promote children's understanding of shape, space and/ or measure. You may wish to use the example shown on pages 401–403 as a guide. Remember to consider resources, environment, adult input and assessment opportunities, as well as stating clearly what your learning objectives are and where they fit into the relevant curriculum.

- Carry out at least one of the activities with children in your placement, recording the outcomes clearly and noting specific support strategies you have used.

Other ideas

Consider also the following 'hints':

- Provide a wide variety of materials and resources for mathematical experiences, including:
  - ensuring that there are sufficient resources and space available to provide each child with a meaningful and satisfactory experience
  - remembering that children differ in their interests, and in their learning styles. It is important to have a range of resources that support both interest and learning style.

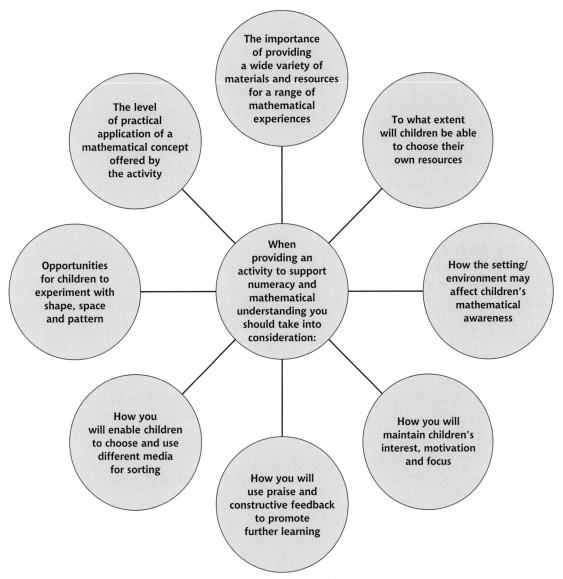

▲ Considerations when providing an activity to support numeracy

● Enable children to choose their own resources, including:

– ensuring that resources are easily accessible, e.g. through child-friendly storage units

– clearly labelling all resources, with visual labels (illustrations of the resource) to support the independence of younger children and those with limited literacy skills.

● Enable children to choose and use different media for sorting, including:

– providing natural items such as leaves, cones, pebble and seeds, or commercial items such as 'compare bears', elephants, beads, counting cubes

– opportunities to sort and group small-world items, e.g. zoo animals, farm animals, small vehicles.

- Experiment with shape, space and pattern, including:
  - learning to fold paper equally and then discuss shape, size, shapes within shapes, etc
  - tessellation activities, experimenting with different shapes to see which can tessellate and which cannot.

- Provide opportunities to use and apply mathematics in practical tasks, including:
  - counting and grouping children in everyday situations, encouraging children to suggest, estimate, count and reflect on accuracy
  - charting the weather each day and noting temperature.

- Encourage children to explain their thinking to support the development of their reasoning, including:
  - building children's sense of self-worth and self-esteem to give them the confidence to speak out in a group, to ask and answer questions, and to initiate ideas
  - the use of careful and sensitive questioning, ensuring that questions are clear, at the appropriate level and are not ambiguous.

Refer back to page 390 and re-read Piaget's conservation research and the issues raised by others regarding how his questions were phrased and the impact this might have had. You may also like to refer to Unit 3 page 135 where self-esteem is discussed.

The effect of the environment on children's mathematical awareness

The setting or environment can affect children's awareness in the following ways:

- Ensure that displays make maximum use of all aspects of mathematics, e.g. use of shape, pattern, grouping and making links, highlighting opposites, contrasts and symmetry.

- The number of children in any one teaching group will be determined by staffing, the overall class size, the range of learning styles within the class and the ability levels of the children. It will also be influenced by how much individual input each child is likely to need. Whenever practicable, work with children in small numbers, or one to one. Some children will be able to learn from their peers, and so a well-thought-through pairing can be a good strategy.

Refer to page 391 and also to Unit 2 pages 57–58 for information on Lev Vygotsky and his theory of the zone of proximal development, and also Jerome Bruner's thinking on scaffolding.

Child-centred activities

It is important to plan activities for children that build on previous experience and are child centred.

Mathematical concepts build upon each other. For example, children need to know the number names and understand the 'two-ness' of the number two, before they are able to make a collection of objects, e.g. two of each colour brick, bear, etc. Similarly, they need to understand two-dimensional shapes before they are expected to work with three-dimensional shapes.

The introduction of puzzles with graded levels of difficulty is a good example of how the same activity progresses based on previous learning. Initially the youngest infants may be given a two- or three-piece wooden shape that fits together and comes apart again. Next, play-tray-type puzzles with pieces to lift out and replace help develop shape discrimination, together with hand–eye coordination and fine motor skills. Once a child has mastered this stage they move on to understand the concept of the puzzle making an overall picture. The number of pieces and the complexity of the portrayed image can now be increased.

Many children learn best through a hands-on approach (kinaesthetic learning), therefore, the more opportunities there are for children to 'do' rather than simply 'see' or 'hear', the more successful the learning will be.

GOOD PRACTICE

It is important to speak clearly at all times.

Have a go!

- Reflect upon two activities you have implemented in your placement.
- What aspect of the relevant curriculum framework were you aiming to support?
- Evaluate how effective each activity has been in meeting your learning objectives for the children.

Make clear what was successful in each case, and what could have been better, and note the changes you would make another time. How were the children building on previous learning? If you have written feedback from your placement supervisor, include this also, and use it to support your reflection.

Awareness of diversity and cultural need

Some children will be learning English as an additional language. Again, it will be important in helping them to understand and consolidate their learning of numeracy to introduce and embed mathematical language within appropriate contexts. The use of both two-dimensional and three-dimensional visual images will be helpful, providing concrete examples to help them.

FAST FACT

Posters and number lines are available in dual languages. These can help non-English-speaking parents to support their child's learning and show that a family's heritage language is valued by the school or setting.

When asking questions, an action or display of objects to accompany your words will usually be helpful, for example:

- holding up a handful of coins during shop play when asking 'How much will we need to pay?'
- drawing a shape in the air with your finger when stating its name.
- pointing to the cutlery at snack time, and then at each member of the group whilst asking 'How many knives and forks will we need?'
- using gesture to confirm position when using terms such as 'behind', 'in front of', 'next to'.

FAST FACT

Children who are learning more than one language at a time are usually slower in their general language development. This is likely to impact on their verbal numeracy too, but, as with all language development, children can normally understand more than they can vocalise.

GOOD PRACTICE · · · · · · · ·

Asking a child's parents to help the whole class or group learn to count in their heritage language can also be beneficial, and fun for all.

Children need to have plenty of opportunities to listen to the mathematical vocabulary. Useful activities include whole group times (where children are grouped or divided up into certain numbers), the regular inclusion of number rhymes and counting games such as 'Five speckled frogs sitting on a speckled log'. These all help to consolidate learning.

⟫ FAST FACT

Many languages do not follow the left-to-right convention, as found in written English. This applies both to letters and numbers, so this is an additional concept for a child to learn.

Conditions needing specific support strategies

Additional support is needed for many different reasons; for example, if a child is born with a congenital condition, e.g. Down's syndrome, and some forms of cerebral palsy, sensory loss, e.g. blindness or vision impairment, profound deafness or hearing loss. It can also be due to less 'obvious' problems such as dyslexia, dysgraphia or dyscalculia. Such children can be helped to reach their full potential through a carefully planned programme of activities designed to stimulate and compensate for any known sensory loss, and by providing resources, approaches and timescales that enable children to learn more easily, more successfully and more satisfactorily (to the child themselves).

Sensory loss – vision

Children who are blind or are visually impaired can be helped by:

- tactile experiences to help them develop understanding through touch
- an environment that enriches all their senses
- a rich spoken environment, with adults talking to them throughout each activity, domestic routine or experience, naming, describing, explaining, etc.
- rhymes and songs, musical boxes, musical instruments and listening to music
- mathematical vocabulary used within context, e.g. counting when doing up buttons
- listening to stories, enjoying repetition and familiarity, and learning to predict, to anticipate, to understand the process of stories told either orally or through auditory media such as tapes/CDs
- input from Portage workers in the earliest years.

Sensory loss – hearing

Children who are deaf or have a hearing impairment can be helped by:

- a rich visual environment which encourages them to look carefully and with pleasure
- an environment that enriches all of their senses
- an environment where written text and numerals are used widely, labelling items all around them, helping them make links between spoken (or signed) numbers and printed numerals
- learning sign language or a signing system such as Makaton

- the use of sorting trays to help them group items into 2s, 5s, etc. for themselves
- books of all types, picture books in both colour and black and white, to help them count, group and grade items by size, length and height
- input from Portage workers in the earliest years.

 Refer also to Unit 18 page 484, for a list of indicative signs regarding sensory loss.

Dyslexia

Dyslexia is a neurological disorder caused by a slight impairment to sensory pathways. It affects reading, both its fluency and its accuracy, and has an impact on numeracy skills too as it can also affect writing and both number recognition and formation. Children who are dyslexic have normal levels of intelligence. Their difficulties with reading, writing, etc. often appear as an inconsistency in a child who is otherwise bright, inquisitive and able. Dyslexia is a lifelong disorder, but children can be taught strategies to help them deal with it and overcome any limitations it may have posed to people in the past.

Children with dyslexia can be helped by:

- patience and plenty of time to complete work and activities
- visual or oral clues alongside written text where appropriate
- one-to-one guidance from practitioners on developing organisations skills
- an environment with minimal distractions to help concentration
- the use of overlays, usually in yellow, which help them in reading the written text, and instructions for problem solving and numeracy activities

- opportunities to use alternative ways to provide answers or express themselves
- additional use of concrete objects within activities
- specific work on sequencing
- input from an educational psychologist.

Dyscalculia

Dyscalculia is often found alongside dyslexia. It is a lifelong condition but can be managed quite well with appropriate support. Children who have dyscalculia have problems with sequencing, both in number use and in time (past and present events). They have difficulty in understanding concepts, order and rules. They find dealing with money challenging and also, as they get older, have difficulty grasping the concepts of music, such as sight reading, and the fingering layouts for playing a musical instrument.

Physically, children with dyscalculia have poor coordination and struggle with quick physical changes in direction as in dance, movement and exercise classes. Memory is often poor, with children frequently seeming absent-minded, losing or mislaying items, having difficulty in remembering the rules of a game or managing to keep score. It can also be hard for them to remember the sequence of steps in a dance or movement routine.

Children with dyscalculia can be helped by:

- patience and plenty of time to complete work and activities
- visual or oral clues alongside written text where appropriate
- one-to-one guidance from practitioners on developing organisational skills
- an environment with minimal distractions to help concentration

- returning to foundations of learning to remind, support and consolidate understanding
- additional use of concrete objects within activities
- numeracy and mathematical activities being as practical as possible
- specific work on sequencing and timeframes
- using calculators to check own calculations
- using commercial learning aids
- input from an educational psychologist.

FAST FACT

Dysgraphia can also be an associated difficulty for children with dyscalculia.

Refer to Unit 16, page 446, for information on dysgraphia.

Dealing with difficulties to maintain the child's confidence

All children need to feel good about themselves in order to achieve their potential. A child's difficulty or disability should not overshadow who they are as an individual. It is important to see them as a child first and foremost, and then as a child with X, Y or Z as an additional need. Sometimes adults make assumptions about a child's ability, based on what they can or cannot do in another aspect of their learning. This can be dangerous. In making an assumption, rather than observing and assessing ability, you may plan inappropriately for a child's needs, either providing them with challenges that are too great, potentially knocking their confidence as they struggle to cope, to keep up with peers or to achieve; or, conversely, assuming that a child will not be able to do something so leaving them under-challenged, unstimulated and bored, potentially leading to an unmotivated child who lacks enthusiasm for new experiences.

FAST FACT

The manner in which children are paired up or grouped for tasks can help or hinder progress. Again, this should be linked to levels of challenge, but also take regard of issues of personality, age, learning styles and interests.

GOOD PRACTICE

Sometimes simple aids can help a child. For example, having access to counting blocks, number rods, etc. will help a child practically as they will achieve more easily, but, also, this will help them mentally, boosting their self-esteem as they manage more successfully to 'keep up' with their peers.

✓ Progress check

1. Provide examples of how the curriculum guidance is planned and implemented within your placement setting, explaining their use and reflecting on their success.

2. Give at least five examples of how role play supports mathematical development.

3. Explain how small-world play helps a child in their mathematical development.

4. Give five examples of activities that support the understanding of one-to-one correspondence.

5. Give five examples of activities that support the understanding of matching and ordering.

6. Give five examples of activities that support the understanding of shape.

Learning Outcome 3

FOCUS ON...
the role of the adult in supporting children's understanding and development

This links to assessment criteria **3.1** and **3.2**

Planning, monitoring and supporting mathematics

When planning, monitoring and supporting mathematics it is important to work effectively with colleagues. Staff or team meetings provide important opportunities for practitioners to:

- share ideas, both in general, and as contributions to forward planning
- seek advice and guidance about working practice
- discuss good practice and particularly successful activities
- reflect upon activities that were less successful than planned, discussing what went wrong and how this could be rectified another time
- contribute ideas when developing plans for the setting
- share skills. The most successful teams utilise the strengths of each team member to provide the strongest approach to each task
- share any concerns regarding practice
- share any concerns regarding children's learning or development
- discuss strategies to support particular needs (e.g. visual learners, kinaesthetic learners), sharing previous experiences and ideas

- share observations and learning assessments, always maintaining appropriate levels regarding confidentiality.

Many settings will have a mentoring scheme in which a senior or more experienced staff member will support a new or less experienced colleague. The mentor will often be first port of call for advice or guidance. They will often supervise the initial planning of a less experienced colleague and guide them in developing support strategies and in how to group children together effectively.

Refer also to pages 401–403 for examples of planning, and an overview of observation.

Praise and encouragement

As with all activities, praise and encouragement are a vital part of the learning process. If a child knows that they have adult approval they will usually work to ensure it continues. Children need praise and encouragement for effort, not just for success. There is nothing more demoralising than trying very hard at something and then receiving a limited response from a parent, significant adult, peer or colleague. If a child does not feel that their efforts are valued, they are likely to lose confidence in their abilities and in themselves in general. Lack of, or loss, of confidence can have a direct impact on learning. This is particularly important for those children learning English as an additional language. Practitioners need to encourage children to make attempts at both verbal and written responses to questions and practical problems and activities. Gaining self-confidence in this way will help them continue to try in other situations too.

G☺☺D PRACTICE

Practitioners should give one-to-one attention whenever possible, particularly if a child is known to find concentration difficult.

Refer to Unit 3 to remind yourself about self-esteem and positive reinforcement.

Maintaining interest, motivation and focus in the children

Children are mostly curious, interested and motivated to learn and find out more, but this can be lost if adults do not respond appropriately or provide a suitable (enabling) environment. The awe and wonder shown by children regarding new experiences, and the enthusiasm to 'have a go' is, for most of us, one of the greatest pleasures to see.

However, as adults we need to be aware that poor concentration and lack of focus can result from distraction, boredom and lack of confidence. Adults should ensure that children are not distracted by unsuitable seating or work areas which can take their attention away from a task. It is also important to reduce noise levels. Many children find listening to instructions and concentration very hard to sustain, so it is important that unnecessary noise is kept to a minimum.

It should be remembered that a child who has a good understanding of the concept required for an activity, but who finds writing difficult, may be 'put off' if set tasks that involve too much written evidence. It is important to accommodate differing learning styles, e.g. providing opportunities for practically based evidence wherever possible.

 Practical example

Ashie

Ashie is 5 and has a lively personality. He needs clear boundaries and a strong focus, to keep him 'on task'. At one end of his classroom, windows open on to the school hall where parents are currently hanging large drapes and setting up scenery for the end-of-year performance. Ashie is far more interested in what is going on there, than working with his tessellation activity.

How could Ashie's teacher have helped keep Ashie more focused on his work?

Refer to page 418 for strategies to support children with a range of difficulties, and to pages 442–443 for information on differing learning styles.

Working to overcome barriers to providing support

Building up relationships with children and their families is a fundamental part of the role of every teacher and early years practitioner. If an adult has a secure and positive relationship with a child, then it is likely that the child will feel able to ask questions, express their worries, and feel able to 'try' without fearing making mistakes. An adult who upholds confidentiality and is known to do this will also receive the trust of parents. This effective relationship enables practitioners to have a better understanding of:

- when and how to intervene in the learning of each individual child
- the inclusive needs of individual children
- how they can address each child's specific needs.

It will also enable them to raise concerns with parents about a child's progress, knowing that the parent will usually trust them and their judgement and be willing to explore options and take advice from other professionals, understanding that it will be carried out within a framework of confidentiality and professionalism.

Practitioners need to find the appropriate way in which to build a trusting relationship and also how best to communicate with a new child and their parents. Different people need different approaches. This may involve considering issues of temperament, personality and confidence, and also how easy it is to communicate with the child or adult

initially. This may involve both verbal and body language, and also consideration of any barriers that may prevent or impact upon the success of any communication.

Refer to Unit 16, page 495, for an overview of barriers to communication.

Planning learning activities and outcomes that reflect curriculum frameworks

Within the EYFS learning area of Problem Solving, Reasoning and Numeracy, guidance is divided up into:

- numbers as labels and for counting
- calculating
- shape, space and measure.

Within the Primary Framework for Mathematics, guidance is divided up into:

- using and applying mathematics
- counting and understanding number
- knowing and using number facts
- calculating
- understanding shape
- measuring
- handling data.

 Have a go!

Using a planning sheet in the style preferred by your current placement, plan activities for the age range you are working with, to support two of the main aspects of the relevant curriculum guidance i.e. EYFS or Primary Framework for Mathematics.

Planning and provision of opportunities

The role of the adult in providing an appropriate context in which children can learn

Using the spidergram as a guide, write a description of three occasions on which you have personally supported the development of mathematical learning during your placement experience. Try to include an example from three different age ranges and/or three types of settings, e.g. nursery, school, childminder.

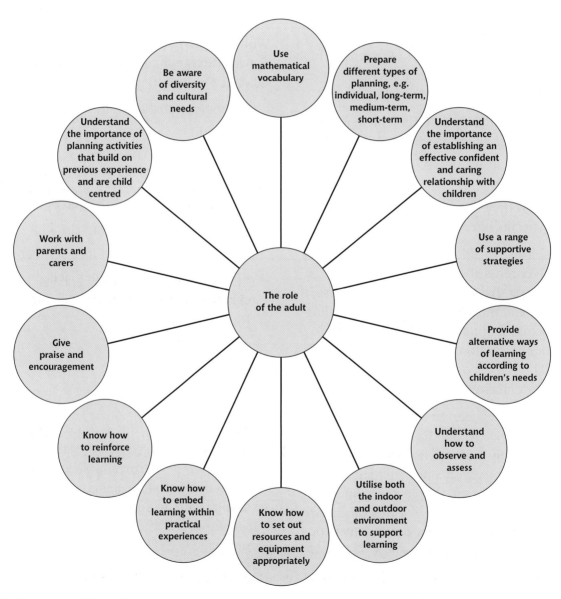

▲ The role of the adult

Reinforcement

Children need practice in using numbers, both their names and order as in counting, and in their use, for example one-to-one correspondence. Both aspects are fundamental to all mathematical learning. An environment in which children are regularly exposed to the use of mathematical vocabulary in context will support and reinforce this learning.

Some children naturally develop understanding of new concepts quicker than others, and some need more experience-related examples to help them. This was clearly seen in the differing findings of Jean Piaget and Margaret Donaldson, regarding ages at which understanding takes place. Piaget's initial experiments in conservation found children to be unable tested by conserve until much later than those tested by Donaldson, who phrased her questions to relate directly to the children's current levels of understanding.

Have a go!

Ask your placement supervisor if you can look through a catalogue of resources for early years and primary teaching. This will extend your understanding of what resources are available.

▲ Practice and consolidation reinforces learning

FAST FACT

Reinforcement is about repeating elements of learning to help consolidate them for the child or group.

G☺☺D PRACTICE

It is important that a group of children are not simply taught through one learning style.

Have a go!

As you visit schools, nurseries, etc., and spend lengths of time in placement, make a note of the different resources for consolidating and extending learning.

These are likely to include:

- board games for matching, bingo, fractions and other concepts
- games using dice and number tops
- fraction tiles, boards, construction kits and puzzles.

You will almost certainly find many more examples to support all areas of mathematical learning.

The importance of using mathematical language

Most activities involve numeracy and/or mathematical understanding in some way. This may simply be through counting with or by the adult, grouping objects or children by a specific factor, such as height, date of birth, etc., or within the instruction given, for example, get into groups of three, stand behind/in front of/opposite a partner. It may be that the planned activity involves the scribing of or demonstration of a specific number or group of numbers.

Children will only build up an understanding of number use and mathematical terminology if they are exposed to it, preferably within the context of everyday actions. This practical application of numeracy consolidates their learning and helps them develop the confidence to try to work out answers and solve mathematical problems mentally. It is therefore important that early years practitioners use a wide and varied mathematical vocabulary with all the children they work with. This means, for example, thinking about how you describe and discuss position, quantity, size and measurement, introducing new terminology whenever possible, encouraging children to think, to predict, to reflect and evaluate, and to ask themselves and others questions – for example, How many? How far? How long? How heavy? – and to make comparisons.

Each of us uses mathematical language everyday as we discuss and describe amounts, measurements, position and shape, and as we order, shop, cook and work. When working with children the use of these terms in context reinforces their learning, helping them associate meaning with actions. The simple habit of vocalising what is happening within the setting provides children with additional and important opportunities to consolidate and further develop their understanding: for example, 'We are all sitting in a lovely circle', 'What a lot of hoops; let's count them', 'The largest is on the bottom and the smallest is on the top', 'Everyone turn to the right', etc.

 Refer to pages 401–403 for activities and ideas on supporting children's understanding and use of number.

The role of parents in supporting mathematics

In schools, teachers have limited time to spend with each child on an individual basis and for a child who takes a little more time than others to grasp a concept, or consolidate new learning, additional time spent on mathematics outside the classroom can be invaluable. Good links with parents help to actively encourage them to help their own child reach their potential. Giving even very young children 'homework' is now commonplace and most children enjoy sharing these experiences with their family. Examples could include:

- playing a numeracy-based game, loaned by the school
- children being asked to find as many things at home as possible that are the same length as, for example, their hand or a pencil
- children identifying objects of a specific shape from around their home environment
- being asked to write family names in order of height, for example shortest first
- writing a timeline of 'My day'.

Many parents will not automatically recognise that numerical learning is taking place within certain activities. It is important that they are given appropriate information to help them see when and how mathematics and problem solving are being developed. For example, this might include:

- a clear label above the car mat explaining that cars are currently being driven in traffic jams of 6 cars, 10 cars and so on
- a visual and written sign encouraging children to make the train track into a circle
- regularly updated noticeboards explaining which songs and rhymes are currently supporting numeracy for example 5 currant buns, 10 green bottles, 12 days of Christmas, etc.
- encouraging children to bring in their doll or teddy and displaying them in size order
- displaying objects in groups, again labelling them clearly to show what is being learned and where the numeracy is to be found.

Supporting individual needs

The Warnock Report 1978

In 1978 Mary Warnock headed the first enquiry for almost 90 years into the 'education of handicapped children and young people'. The focus of the enquiry was on the children's rights to an education, whatever their disability, and the importance of seeing the child as a child first and foremost, and as a child with a disability second.

The report concluded that although around 20 per cent of children might have a special educational need (SEN), either ongoing or temporary, many of this group of children could be successfully educated in a mainstream setting. It concluded that it was inappropriate to place all children with an SEN in a 'special' school or unit. Each child's needs would be assessed individually in conjunction with the child's parents.

Much of the 'old' terminology (e.g. 'remedial', 'sub-normal', etc.) was discontinued following the Warnock Report, with terms such as 'mild', 'moderate' or 'severe' learning difficulties, and 'children with specific learning difficulties' being the favoured terms. It proposed that labelling should be avoided whenever possible and also that children should not be categorised as either having or not having a handicap or disability as this causes an unnecessary division.

The term 'specific learning difficulties' would often be used to describe the needs of children with conditions such as dyslexia, dysgraphia, or visual or auditory loss. These children have an identified specific need that can be targeted specifically with appropriate strategies. The report recommended that relevant resources and equipment should be included in the classrooms for children with specific learning difficulties, for example, hearing aids and tactile learning materials.

The term 'Special Educational Need (SEN)' came into use following the report along with the five-stage process of assessment. The report also highlighted the importance of early years provision for all children, again whenever practical, within a mainstream setting.

There have been many more legislative papers and Acts since the Warnock Report in 1978. Each paper has attempted to build on the foundations laid by Mary Warnock and her enquiry team.

Code of Practice 2001

The Code of Practice 2001 was a response to the Education Act 1996, providing teachers, teaching assistants and all other early years practitioners with practical guidance on how to meet the needs of children considered to have an SEN. Regarding the support and development of numeracy skills, the following paragraphs (summarised below) of the Code of Practice are particularly relevant:

Provision in the early years:

- 4.8 Children making slower progress may include those who are learning English as an additional language or who have particular learning difficulties. It should not be assumed that children who are making slower progress must, therefore, have special educational needs. But such children will need carefully differentiated learning opportunities to help them progress and regular and frequent careful monitoring of their progress.

Statements for children under 2 states that:

- 4.48 It is rare for a child under the age of two to be given a statement, but Portage, and/or specific peripatetic services should be made available for children identified as being blind or deaf, or having either a visual or auditory impairment.

Moving to primary school:

- 4.54, 4.55 The needs of a child who enters school, having had a considerable level of support (e.g. from Portage or similar) but without a statement, should be carefully considered, in both the context of their current learning and in the wider context of the home environment and circumstances to establish if their difficulty is linked to any family issue. A record of their progress and needs should be passed on to the school, with agreement of their parents. The school will then be alerted to potential support needs for that child.

Communication and interaction:

- 7.55, 7.56, 7.57 These paragraphs raise the point that children with SENs are more able in some areas than in others, and that their communication needs may be 'both diverse and complex'. It should be remembered that communication can impact directly on numeracy skills development. The Code of Practice states that children may require some or all of the following:
  - flexible teaching arrangements
  - help in acquiring, comprehending and using language
  - help in articulation
  - help in acquiring literacy skills
  - help in using augmentative and alternative means of communication
  - help to use different means of communication confidently and competently for a range of purposes, including formal situations
  - help in organising and coordinating oral and written language
  - support to compensate for the impact of a communication difficulty or learning in English as an additional language
  - help in expressing, comprehending and using their own language, where English is not the first language.

Children may be supported through School Action Plus, or, if acceptable progress has not been made following receipt of this support over a period of time, statutory assessment will be considered.

⊙⊙ School Action Plus is explained in Unit 14 page 373.

Cognition and learning:

- 7.58, 7.59 This section refers to severe and profound difficulties, and also to specific learning difficulties such as dyslexia, which is often found alongside dyscalculia. It states that these children may require:
  - flexible teaching arrangements
  - help with processing language, memory and reasoning skills
  - help and support in acquiring literacy skills
  - help in organising and coordination of spoken and written word to aid cognition
  - help with sequencing and organisational skills
  - help with problem solving and developing concepts
  - programmes to aid improvement of fine and motor competencies
  - support in the use of technical terms and abstract ideas
  - help in understanding ideas, concepts and experiences when information cannot be gained through first-hand sensory or physical experiences.

LEA support services:

- 10.7 The Code of Practice describes how local education authorities (LEAs) can provide advice on teaching techniques, classroom management and appropriate resources and materials; also direct teaching or practical support for teachers, specialist teaching assistants and specialist help.

(Based on *Special Educational Needs Code of Practice*, DfES, 2001)

FAST FACT

Most college libraries will have a copy of the Code of Practice. You may find it helpful to look at it in more detail.

Specific needs

Meeting children's individual learning needs involves a careful assessment of the ways in which they learn best, what aspects of learning they find difficult, and why that might be. Sometimes parents and practitioners have 'advance warning' that a child may face difficulties, for example if a specific condition or chronic illness has already been identified and a known pattern regarding learning and development is usual. Examples that affect numeracy include developmental delay, congenital conditions and illness such as hearing and sight loss, dyscalculia and dyslexia. Practitioners need to know where they can obtain information on conditions they meet for the first time. This ensures that they meet a child's needs from the outset of their involvement in their care and education.

Developmental delay

Developmental delay is the term used whenever an infant or child is consistently behind in meeting the normal developmental milestones. This may be due to congenital conditions, illness or poor nutrition and/or the effects of drugs, tobacco or alcohol whilst still within the womb. Occasionally, an infant is simply small in size and develops very slowly.

Developmental delay can be due to sensory, physical, genetically inherited, social or environmental reasons.

All children showing signs of developmental delay will be closely monitored by health professionals and appropriate interventions made where it is considered necessary.

When and how to access help

A child may benefit from an assessment by another professional if their progress slows down and seems to stop, if they are making only minimal progress despite already having a programme of learning specifically set up for them by current staff, or if they are working at a level considerably below that of their peers. The Special Educational Needs Co-ordinator (SENCO) is always the first port of call. It is their role to make appropriate contacts, and, along with parents, help develop a programme of intervention for any child who needs it. Help may come from a key worker, speech therapist, curriculum advisor or health visitor.

Refer to Unit 14, page 374, for more information on meeting additional needs and the role of SENCOs.

✓ Progress check

1) Give 10 examples of how you use mathematical vocabulary in your day-to-day work with children.

2) Give five examples of how children can consolidate their mathematical development at home.

3) Explain how dyslexia and dyscalculia can affect numeracy skills.

4) Explain why a good working relationship with parents supports a child's mathematical learning.

5) Give an overview of three different strategies for supporting learning.

Weblinks

- Each part of the UK has its own framework for supporting early development through to adulthood. These can be accessed at:

    – England www.dcsf.gov.uk

    – Wales www.learning.wales.gov.uk

    – Scotland www.scotland.gov.uk

    – Northern Ireland www.ccea.org.uk

- www.qca.org.uk
  For details of the Early Years Foundation Stage and other curriculum matters

- www.standards.dfes.gov.uk/primaryframeworks
  For details of the five blocks for planning mathematics

unit 16

Developing children's (3–8 years) communication, language and literacy skills

This unit provides an overview of a variety of differing theories of how language and language use develops, with reference to some of the main theorists. It explains the usual sequence of development, setting it out in stages. It should of course always be remembered that, as with all aspects of development, each child reaches each stage in their own time. Guidance on planning and meeting additional needs is given, using a variety of activities as examples, together with references to relevant curriculum frameworks, and legislation, and the contexts within which children learn best.

Learning Outcomes

In this unit you will learn about:

1. the stages of development of children's communication, language and literacy aged from 3 to 8 years

2. how to help children develop their communication, language and literacy

3. the role of the adult in supporting communication, language and literacy.

FOCUS ON...

the stages of development of children's communication, language and literacy aged from 3 to 8 years

This links to assessment criteria **1.1** and **1.2**

Main characteristics of the stages of development of communication, language and literacy

Theories of language development

There are different theories regarding how language develops. Some are based on the theory of innate learning and some are based more on the influences of environment and experience. Those theorists specifically recognised for their thinking on language development are:

- Burrhus F. Skinner
- Noam Chomsky
- Eric Lenneberg
- Jean Piaget
- Lev Vygotsky
- Jerome Bruner.

The following theories offer some very different ideas about how language develops. As you read them, consider which you could accept and which seem less likely.

Theories of language development include:

- association theory
- behaviourist theory
- language acquisition device theory
- maturational theory
- interactionist theory.

Association theory

The theory of learning by association proposes that a child gradually builds their language by associating words with what they see. This theory works well up to a point, but does not take into account all aspects of language, for example those used to describe feelings or emotions.

Behaviourist theory

Theorists such as Skinner proposed that a child's language is shaped by the responses given to them by their parents or main carers (operant conditioning); the positive reinforcement of vocalisations encourages the child to repeat a specific sound over and over again. For example, Daniel is an infant of 6 months whose babbling sounds have become 'dadadada'. Daniel's mother greets this with delight and encouragement, stating that 'Dada' will be home soon.

Skinner believed that the continuous positive reinforcement of 'correct' speech sounds, and the lack of positive response to sounds or (eventually) sentence structure that is not 'correct', will mould a child's language formation. For example, if Daniel's babbling sounded like 'bibibibibi', his mother is less likely to have reinforced it, as she would not have recognised it as a 'word' and therefore would not have used it when speaking back to him.

Skinner's theory would indicate that children have to go through a trial-and-error process for every aspect of speech, but this is obviously not the case, although it is accepted that infants are encouraged by the positive reactions of adults. It does not take into account how quickly children can pick up language, which clearly is not learnt simply through regular reinforcement.

Skinner's theory was challenged by many psychologists and consequently the nativist theories set out below became an inviting alternative.

FAST FACT

The principles of social learning theory can also be applied to language; i.e. that humans repeat behaviour which they see being rewarded. If, for example, a child sees an older brother or sister being rewarded for speech, the younger child may try to imitate that behaviour.

Language acquisition device (LAD) theory

Noam Chomsky (a *nativist*) believed in the biologically based theory that infants are born with a predisposition for language. He suggested that infants have a language acquisition device (LAD). He considered that this LAD enables children to absorb the language that they hear, to decode it and then develop an understanding of its rules and grammatical structure. It has been shown that children of all cultures develop language at much the same time and this gave support to the theories of Chomsky and others like him.

However, other researchers have shown that simply hearing language is not

sufficient for full speech development. Children need to interact with others, to converse, in order to fully develop their spoken language skills.

It is interesting that research carried out with hearing children born to deaf parents has shown that, while a child may learn words from what they hear around them (radio, television, videos, and so on), they need to be actively involved in conversation in order to develop their understanding and use of grammar. In the cases of some children, speech therapy resulted in a sudden improvement in their language structure which soon brought them up to the expected level of language development for their age. This indicated that they had previously been ready to learn the grammatical rules associated with their culture, but needed the active involvement with others in order to facilitate it.

Maturational theory

Eric Lenneberg, like Chomsky, considered that, as long as children were exposed to language, they would simply pick it up as their development progressed in other ways too. (This should not be confused with Gesell's maturational theory which is concerned with other aspects of maturation.) Lenneberg considered that there is a critical period in which children need to be exposed to language. He considered that it is linked to brain development and how in the earlier years there is less defined use of each side of the brain. There have been cases where brain damage has occurred to the left side of a child's brain (normally associated with language). The older the child is at the time of the accident, the less likely they are to have a full recovery. Conversely, there have also been cases where children have had extensive periods without hearing language early in life, but they have been able to develop some form of communication, even if not full speech.

Interactionist theory

The basis of the interactionist theory is that the schemas which children develop subsequently facilitate language development: children first experience and then talk about their experiences. Therefore, this theory sees language as a reflection of cognitive development. Piaget, Vygotsky and Bruner took this interactionist approach to their thinking on language and its development.

Jean Piaget considered that cognitive development starts during what he called the sensorimotor period, and that children's language follows these sensory experiences and that their early words are often linked to symbolic play. Piaget did not place any particular significance on social interaction and its impact on language development.

Lev Vygotsky considered that language and thought initially developed separately, with early language developing simply as a means of communication. He considered that gradually children internalise language to help their thinking, 'thinking aloud' at times when faced with a significant challenge. Vygotsky put considerable emphasis on the importance of social interaction in language development. This is the main difference between the thinking of Piaget and Vygotsky.

Jerome Bruner considered that a child's language was very dependent on their interactions with their primary carers and other familiar adults, with the adults helping the child to make sense of the vocalisations he hears around him. According to Bruner, there is a language acquisition support system (LASS).

Refer to Unit 2, pages 55–58, for more on the work and thinking of Jean Piaget, Vygotsky and Bruner.

Development of speaking and listening skills

Language is the main way in which humans communicate with one another. It involves facial expressions, tone of voice, body posture and expression of meaning through the use of words or symbols.

Language is:

- rule-governed – grammatical rules are present in each language (syntax)
- structured – the sound system that makes up the speech sounds (phonology)
- symbolic – words have meanings, building into phrases, and so on (semantics)
- generative – it is the basis of the sharing of knowledge (pragmatics).

Pre-requisites for language

The normal, unimpeded development of language is affected by other areas of development. For example, socially and cognitively an awareness of the need to interact as a means of communication is imperative, as are the physical abilities of vision, hearing and speech. Children learn the basis of their culture through communication (socialisation theory), and develop an understanding of themselves and how they fit within their peer and social groups (goodness of fit). As discussed above, some psychologists believe that language plays an important part in all aspects of human development, with some theorists arguing that language is the basis of learning. An important debate involves the questions:

- Is language dependent on thought?
- Or is thought dependent on language?

You may find it helpful to consider what your first thoughts are on this language versus thought debate. Do you think understanding is needed in order to develop linguistically? Or do you think that language enables understanding to develop? Come back to these questions again once you have completed this unit.

Stages of language development

As with every aspect of development, children develop language at differing rates within what is considered to be the 'normal' range. This process of language development can be divided into 10 basic stages:

1 Non-verbal communication/expression
2 Speech-like noises
3 Controlling sounds, using mouth and tongue
4 Imitating sounds
5 First words
6 Development of vocabulary (50 words is usual at 2 years)
7 Putting words together to form simple phrases and sentences
8 Use of grammar
9 Use of meaning
10 Using language to develop other skills, for example early literacy.

These 10 stages can be linked to approximate ages as shown in the table on page 436.

GOOD PRACTICE

As you move through the various placements that will make up your professional practice experience, observe and note the differences in speech intonation, questioning and grammar of children at different ages and stages.

The development of speech sounds in the English language

Up until around 7 or 8 months, the babbling of babies is universal. But, from this age onwards, their speech sounds begin to take on the speech sounds of the languages that surround them, i.e. their heritage language. The following section describes the usual pattern in spoken English. You will see how complex it can be to articulate clearly and will hopefully build on your understanding of how difficult some children find it, and why that might be.

Speech sounds are made up of consonants, vowels, syllables and words.

Consonants

Consonants are 'closed' sounds. This means that, for a consonant sound to be produced, the airflow is obstructed by parts of the mouth coming into contact with each other or almost contacting. For example, try saying the word 'book'. To pronounce the *b* in book, the lips need to come into contact. To pronounce the *s* in the word 'sand', the tip of the tongue touches the ridge just behind the top front teeth.

GOOD PRACTICE

How we pronounce sounds is quite complex. It is, however, a useful exercise for early years workers to explore their own pronunciation to gain a better understanding of how the parts of the mouth work together and how each sound is subsequently produced. This helps with understanding the difficulties faced by some children in developing their speech sounds.

▼ Stages of language development

AGE	UNDERSTANDING	NO. OF WORDS	TYPE OF WORDS	AVERAGE LENGTH OF SENTENCE
3 months	Soothed by sound	0	Cooing and gurgling	0
6 months	Responds to voice tones	0	Babble	0
1 year	Knows own name and a few others	1	Noun (naming word)	1 word
18 months	Understands simple commands	6–20	Nouns + gobbledegook	1 word
2 years	Understands much more than they can say	50+	Verbs and pronouns (action + name)	1–2 word phrases
2½ years	Enjoys simple and familiar stories	200+	Pronouns I, me, you; questions what, where	2–3 word phrases
3 years	Carries out complex commands	500–1,000	Plurals; Verbs in present tense; questions who	3–4 word phrases
4 years	Listens to long stories	1,000–1,500	Verbs in past tense; questions why, where, how	4–5 word phrases
5 years	Developing the ability to reason	1,500–2,000	Complex sentences with adult forms of grammar	5–6 word phrases

▼ The approximate sequential development of consonants in the English language

AGE	CONSONANTS
2 years	m, n, p, b, t, d, w
2½ years	k, g, ng (as in sing), h
2½ to 3 years	f, s, l, y
3½ to 4 years	v, z, ch, j, sh
4½ years onwards	th (as in thin), th (as in the), r
Double consonants such as sp, tr and fl, and also the sounds r and th, can develop as late as 6½ years in some children.	

Vowels

The basic vowel sounds are *a*, *e*, *i*, *o* and *u*, but there are other vowel sounds too. These include the double sounds such as *ee*, *oo*, and so on. Vowels are 'open' sounds. There is no obstruction to the airflow during pronunciation and each sound differs according to the position of the mouth:

- If the lips are spread widely, the sound *ee* is produced.
- If the lips are rounded, the sound *oo* is produced.
- Vowels can be long sounds as in the word 'more'. They can also be short sounds as in the word 'pack'.
- There are simple vowels such as *o* as in 'pot', *u* as in 'put', *a* as in 'pat'. They are simple because once the mouth is set in position it does not need to alter in order to produce the sound.
- There are also more complex vowel sounds such as *oy* as in 'boy' and *ow* as in 'cow'. With these sounds, you need to change the mouth and/or tongue position for the full sound to be made.
- All vowels in English are 'voiced'. This means that they involve the vibration of the vocal chords.

Syllables

Speech sounds combine together to form syllables. A syllable is made up of a combination of consonants (c) and at least one vowel (v). There can be up to three consonants before a vowel and up to four consonants after a vowel in the English language.

Examples of syllables:

- be = cv (1 consonant and 1 vowel)
- and = vcc (1 vowel and 2 consonants), and so on

- plot = ccvc
- strip = cccvc
- tempts = cvcccc.

The more consonants in a syllable, the harder it will be for a child to pronounce, because it requires a greater ability to coordinate the articulators.

Words

Syllables, in turn, combine together to form words. Some words have just one syllable, for example 'cat', 'dog' and 'hen'. These are called monosyllabic words. All other words have more than one syllable and are known as polysyllabic words.

Even in adulthood, some people have difficulty in pronouncing some polysyllabic words. For example, common difficulties are found in pronouncing:

- laboratory (often mispronounced as 'labroratrory')
- certificates (often mispronounced as 'cerstificates').

National and local frameworks and policies

Legislation and guidance

There is a range of relevant legislation and curriculum guidance to support the development of children's literacy skills either directly or indirectly. This includes:

- the Children Act 1989 and 2004
- the Children's Plan 2007
- the Childcare Act 2006
- Continuing the Learning Journey (2005)
- Every Child Matters
- Early Years Foundation Stage
- the National Curriculum

- the Primary Framework for Literacy and Mathematics, part of the National Curriculum
- the Warnock Report 1978 – refer to page 427
- the Code of Practice 2001 – refer to pages 428–429.

Refer to pages 406–408 for more information.

Primary Framework for Literacy and Mathematics

The framework sets out core leraning aims for both literacy and numeracy for children in each year group, from Foundation Stage through to Year 6/7. There are 12 strands for literacy.

Speak and listen for a wide range of purposes in different contexts

1. Speaking

- Speak competently and creatively for different purposes and audiences, reflecting on impact and response
- Explore, develop and sustain ideas through talk

2. Listening and responding

- Understand, recall and respond to speakers' implicit and explicit meanings
- Explain and comment on speakers' use of language, including vocabulary, grammar and non-verbal features

3. Group discussion and interaction

- Take different roles in groups to develop thinking and complete tasks
- Participate in conversations, making appropriate contribution building on others' suggestions and responses

4. Drama

- Use dramatic techniques, including work in role to explore ideas and texts
- Create, share and evaluate ideas and understand through drama

Read and write for a range of purposes on paper and on screen

5. Word recognition: decoding (reading) and encoding (spelling)

- Read fluently and automatically by using phonic knowledge of grapheme–phoneme correspondences and the skills of blending as their prime approach for decoding unfamiliar words, and thereby:
  - build up a store of words that are instantly recognised and understood on sight
  - segment words into their constituent phonemes and understand that spelling is the reverse of blending phonemes into words for reading

6. Word structure and spelling

- Learn that segmenting words into their constituent phonemes for spelling is the reverse of blending phonemes into words for reading
- Spell words accurately by combining the use of grapheme–phoneme correspondence knowledge as the prime approach, and also morphological knowledge and etymological information
- Use a range of approaches to learn and spell irregular words

7. Understanding and interpreting texts

- Retrieve, select and describe information, events or ideas
- Deduce, infer and interpret information, events or ideas
- Use syntax, context, word structures and origins to develop their understanding of word meanings
- Identify and comment on the structure and organisation of texts
- Explain and comment on writers' use of language, including vocabulary, grammatical and literary features

8. Engaging with and responding to texts

- Read independently and creatively for purpose, pleasure and learning
- Respond imaginatively, using different strategies to engage with texts
- Evaluate writers' purposes and viewpoints, and the overall effect of the text on the reader

9. Creating and shaping texts

- Write independently and creatively for purpose, pleasure and learning
- Use and adapt a range of forms, suited to different purposes and readers
- Make stylistic choices, including vocabulary, literary features and viewpoints or voice
- Use structural and presentational features for meaning and impact

10. Text structure and organisation

- Organise ideas into coherent structure including layout, sections and paragraphs
- Write cohesive paragraphs linking sentences within and between them

11. Sentence structure and punctuation

- Vary and adapt sentence structure for meaning and effect
- Use a range of punctuation correctly to support meaning and emphasis
- Convey meaning through grammatically accurate and correctly punctuated sentences

12. Presentation

- Develop a clear and fluent joined handwriting style
- Use keyboard skills and ICT tools confidently to compose and present work.

Refer to page 398 for information on:
- they impact of legislation/guidance on practice
- policies and procedures supporting on a child's learning
- information about progress and planning appropraite activities
- types of planning.

The areas of language and literacy you will support

At every level of learning there should be opportunities for children to develop understanding and skills for:

- communicating
- listening
- speaking
- reading
- writing.

Stages of development of reading and writing skills

The foundations of reading and writing develop most easily when children have plenty of opportunities to see, hear and replicate language within a range of everyday situations and play experiences. It moves through four main stages prior to being able to scribe clearly understood text. These are:

- mark making
- understanding that the printed word carries meaning

- recognition of, initially, letters, followed by letter combinations, and words
- emergent writing.

 Refer also to the play activities an opportunities set out on pages 456–463. These show how literacy is developed through a range of popular fun experiences.

▼ The development of reading and writing

ASPECT OF LITERACY DEVELOPMENT	KEY CONCEPTS
Mark making	Plenty of early opportunities to make marks in a range of ways – with pencils, pens, felt tips, paint and brushes, printing, finger painting, chalking, tracing marks in the sand, etc. – all help children to learn how to make and control the arm and hand movements necessary for writing, and can help them to learn how to hold mark-making tools. It is helpful to encourage children to make patterns, perhaps by sitting at the painting table and making some yourself
	This also helps children to understand that marks can be used to communicate with other people. Practitioners can comment on children's pictures and patterns to demonstrate this
	Children can make marks from the time they are babies
Understanding that letters and words carry meaning	Sharing stories, books and giving children plenty of opportunities to see adults reading and writing for real purposes, helps children to understand that print carries meaning. For instance, this can be demonstrated by making a list of the drinks that children would like at snack time and giving it to the practitioner who will fetch the drinks. When sharing books on a one-to-one with children, practitioners can run their finger along the sentences as they read, demonstrating that they are following text. In settings that do this, children may be observed 'playing reading', copying the technique when 'reading' to a doll or teddy
Recognising letters and words	Children usually recognise their own name first. You can help by providing children with plenty of opportunities to see and look for their name. For instance, you may have names displayed above the coat pegs or have names written on pieces of paper for the children to find at craft time. You can also provide labels on familiar objects (on your boxes of resources for instance) or in familiar places (such as the book corner). Help children to learn both the names of letters and the sound that they make. This aids learning to read phonetically

▶▶

ASPECT OF LITERACY DEVELOPMENT	KEY CONCEPTS
Emergent writing	When children first attempt to write, they tend to draw rows of patterns and shapes that look similar to letters. They will eventually include some letters amongst the patterns and shapes, although they may be muddled – perhaps back to front. Children benefit from lots of practice at emergent writing, and this can be effectively provided as children play. You can supply envelopes and paper (a good use for junk mail) and encourage children to write 'letters' and post them in an imaginary post office area for instance. You can provide a notepad when the imaginary area is turned into a restaurant, and encourage children to take orders
	Give children opportunities to see words and letters in the areas in which they mark make so that they can try to copy them. For instance, you may place children's name cards on the drawing table and invite children to find their seat. They may then attempted to copy their name since all the materials will be at hand
	When children can write their name and some letters, they can begin copying simple words. Many children learn to do this by writing simple captions for their art work, e.g. a cat, my doll

✓ Progress check

1. Identify the main theorists associated with language development.

2. Explain at least three theories regarding how language develops and state which theorist agrees with which theory.

3. What is syntax?

4. What is phonology?

5. What is semantics?

6. Describe the 10 basic stages of language development and the prerequisites needed for successful development.

Learning Outcome 2

FOCUS ON...
how to help children develop their communication, language and literacy

This links to assessment criteria **2.1** and **2.2**

Using constructive feedback to support children

As with all activities, praise and encouragement are a vital part of the learning process. If a child knows that they have adult approval they will usually work to ensure it continues. Children need praise and encouragement for effort, not just for success. There is nothing more demoralising than trying very hard at something and then receiving a limited response from a parent, significant adult, peer or colleague. If a child does not feel that their efforts are valued they are likely to lose confidence in their abilities and in themselves in general. Lack or loss of confidence can have a direct impact on learning. This is particularly important for those children learning English as an additional language. Practitioners need to encourage children to make attempts at both verbal and written responses to questions and practical problems and activities. Gaining self-confidence in this way will help them continue to try in other situations too.

Refer to Unit 3, page 135, to remind yourself about self-esteem.

GOOD PRACTICE
Practitioners should give one-to-one attention whenever possible, particularly if a child is learning English as an additional language

Barriers to learning how to read and write

For optimum progress in language and literacy development, it is important that any identified barriers are removed or reduced. Examples include:

- ensuring that as far as is practical each child's preferred individual learning style is supported, for example:
  - *visual learners* like uncluttered learning environments which do not easily distract them. They enjoy visual images to support them and are often creative learners who have a good imagination
  - *auditory learners* tend to have good memories, so will be able to cope with references back to previous learning. They learn well through discussion, can think well and benefit from the use of questioning
  - *kinaesthetic learners* like to be active. They will benefit from practical tasks, and hands-on learning

opportunities where they learn through trial and error. They can be easily distracted so benefit from a focused learning environment

- ensuring that there are sufficient resources and space available to provide each child with a meaningful and satisfactory experience
- ensuring that children are not distracted by unsuitable seating or work surfaces, causing discomfort or taking their attention away from where it is meant to be
- reducing noise levels. Many children find listening hard, so it is important that unnecessary noise is kept to a minimum. Having an 'only one person to speak at a time' rule will help children to keep focused
- giving praise and encouragement for effort. This is particularly important for those children learning English as an additional language, to build up children's self-confidence and help them avoid developing low-self-esteem
- giving one-to-one attention whenever possible, particularly if a child is known to find concentration difficult.

Poor concentration can result from distraction, boredom and lack of confidence. The points noted above will help.

Factors impacting on a child's ability to communicate effectively

In order to meet the individual needs of a child, practitioners thus understand the main problems associated with the conditions and disorders they are likely to come across. They also require information

on the less common disorders should they need to support a child who is struggling to communicate. Commonly heard terms linked to additional needs include:

- developmental delay
- congenital conditions and illness, e.g. hearing and sight loss
- dysphasia
- dyslexia
- dyspraxia
- dysgraphia
- disordered or delayed speech
- language disorder.

Developmental delay

Developmental delay can be due to a variety of reasons. Some children will develop slowly because they were born prematurely. These infants may have delayed development for the first few years, with most eventually catching up with their peers.

Some children who have a chronic illness may also suffer delayed development. Many will miss out on schooling, or will regularly be tired, due either to their illness or the effect of medication. Time with friends can also be limited which can impact on children's social development.

Development can be delayed due to sensory disabilities, physical difficulties and genetically inherited disorders. Also there can be the impact of social and environmental factors, such as passive smoking and/or either alcohol or drug intake whilst still in the womb. Poverty, passive smoking, neglect, abuse and a lack of secure attachments can in addition impact on development.

Congenital conditions and illness

A condition already present when a child is born is referred to as being congenital. These conditions are mostly identified at birth, for example, Down's syndrome and some forms of cerebral palsy. But some are identified within the first few weeks or months, for example, blindness or vision impairment, profound deafness or hearing loss, as reactions by the infant differ from what is expected of them. There may be specific testing: the distraction hearing test is carried out at around 8 months, and the otoacoustic emissions test (which has mostly taken over from the distraction hearing test) is carried out before an infant reaches 4 weeks old. Children with congenital problems can be helped to reach their full potential through a carefully planned programme of activities designed to stimulate and compensate for any known sensory loss.

Sight loss

Children who are blind or are visually impaired can be helped by:

- tactile experiences to help them develop understanding through touch
- an environment that enriches all their senses
- a rich spoken environment, with adults talking to them throughout each activity, domestic routine or experience, naming, describing, explaining, etc.
- rhymes and songs, musical boxes, musical instruments and listening to music
- listening to stories, enjoying repetition and familiarity, and learning to predict, to anticipate, to understand the process of stories told either orally or through auditory media such as tapes/CDs.
- input from Portage workers in the earliest years.

Hearing loss

Children who are deaf or have a hearing impairment can be helped by:

- a rich visual environment which encourages them to look carefully and with pleasure
- an environment that enriches all of their senses
- an environment where written text is used widely, labelling items all around them, helping them to make links between spoken (or signed) words and printed text
- learning sign language or a signing system such as Makaton
- the use of puppets, dolls and small-world play to help them re-enact stories for themselves
- books of all types, picture books in both colour and black and white, stories with pictures alongside as cues, illustrated alphabet books, etc.
- input from Portage workers in the earliest years.

Dysphasia, dyslexia, dyspraxia and dysgraphia

Dysphasia, dyslexia, dyspraxia and dysgraphia are specific conditions that can be well supported within mainstream settings. Practitioners need to think creatively regarding what each child needs and how best they learn.

Dysphasia

Dysphasia is the term used for difficulty in expressing thoughts in words. Another term, aphasia, is used if the child is unable to express their thoughts in words.

Children with dysphasia can be helped by:

- opportunities to express themselves through painting and drawing
- opportunities to use a range of creative resources
- modelling of actions and expressions by adults working alongside them
- the use of alternative communication systems
- patience and plenty of time allowed for their communications to take place
- an environment with minimum distractions to help them concentrate
- input from a speech therapist.

Dyslexia

Dyslexia is a neurological disorder caused by a slight impairment to sensory pathways. It affects reading – both its fluency and its accuracy. It can also affect writing and spelling. Children who are dyslexic have normal levels of intelligence. Their difficulties with reading, writing, etc. often appear as an inconsistency in a child who is otherwise bright, inquisitive and able. Dyslexia is a lifelong disorder, but children can be taught strategies to help them deal with it and overcome any limitations it may have posed to people in the past.

Children with dyslexia can be helped by:

- patience and plenty of time to complete work and activities
- visual or oral clues alongside written text where appropriate
- one-to-one guidance from practitioners on developing organisational skills

- an environment with minimal distractions to help concentration
- the use of overlays, usually in yellow, which help them in reading written text
- opportunities to use alternative ways to express themselves
- opportunities to listen to story tapes either alone or in a group
- specific emphasis on phonetic work
- specific work on sequencing
- input from an educational psychologist.

Dyspraxia

Dyspraxia is a sensory disorder affecting the organisation of movement skills. Children tend to be clumsy and uncoordinated, and this impacts on their use of mark-making materials, books and generally in their play and learning. In the earliest months and years it can affect feeding and when the child reaches the expected motor development milestones of walking, etc. As children get older it affects communication, both their own, and their understanding and responses to communication from others. Children with dyspraxia tend to be easily excited, particularly in noisy environments.

Children with dyspraxia can be helped by:

- a calm environment with minimum noise
- one-to-one guidance by their key worker or classroom assistant
- a very structured approach to each task or activity
- patience and plenty of time given to them
- input from an occupational therapist
- input from a physiotherapist
- input from a speech therapist
- input from an educational psychologist.

445

Dysgraphia

Dysgraphia is often linked to dyslexia or dyspraxia. It is a difficulty in controlling a pen or pencil sufficiently to allow the individual to write correctly. It can cause difficulties in letter formation and with consistency of letter size and shape.

Children with dysgraphia can be helped by:

- the use of pencil grips to help them develop a good tripod grasp
- opportunities to use alternative means of expressing themselves
- sensory boards and shapes to help letter formation and writing in lines
- specific work on visual memory skills
- specific work on fine motor skills development
- input from an occupational therapist.

G☺☺D PRACTICE

Practitioners should always keep in mind the differing learning sytles mentioned on pages 442–443, visual, auditory, and kinaesthetic.

Maintaining the child's confidence

Every child needs to feel good about themselves in order to achieve their potential. A child's difficulty or disability should not overshadow who they are as an individual. It is important to see them as a child first and foremost, and then as a child with X, Y or Z as an additional need. Sometimes adults make assumptions about a child's ability, based on what they can or cannot do in another aspect of their learning. This can be dangerous. In making an assumption, rather than observing and assessing ability, you may plan inappropriately for a child's needs, either providing them with challenges that are too great, potentially knocking their confidence as they struggle to cope, to keep up with peers or to achieve; or conversely, assuming that a child will not be able to do something, so leaving them under-challenged, unstimulated and bored, potentially leading to a unmotivated child who lacks enthusiasm for new experiences.

The manner in which children are paired up or grouped for tasks can help or hinder progress. Again, this is linked to levels of challenge, but also to issues of personality, age, learning styles and interests.

G☺☺D PRACTICE

Sometimes simple aids can help a child, e.g. rubber pencil grips will help a child position their fingers and thumb correctly, gradually helping them to favour this grip automatically.

Disordered or delayed speech

Many children have phases of unclear speech, but they do not all need to be seen by a speech therapist.

Dysfluency

Many temporary disorders are due to the child hastening to say something and stumbling over it in their eagerness and excitement. This common occurrence is known as *dysfluency*.

Hesitation occurs as a child tries to express themselves. This type of dysfluency is often associated with their attempting to use more complex language structure. Speech therapists refer to this as normal developmental dysfluency as it does not usually need professional intervention.

When conversing with a dysfluent child, it is important to give them time and attention to minimise the affect of the dysfluency.

G☺☺D PRACTICE

The following checklist should be helpful:

- Do speak steadily and clearly yourself.
- Do give the dysfluent child your full attention.
- Do avoid interrupting the child when ever possible.
- Do focus on what they are saying, and try to ignore the dysfluency.
- Do not ask the child to repeat it or to start again.
- Do not tell the child to 'take a deep breath' before they speak.
- Do not tell the child to slow down.
- Do not ask the child to 'think it through' before they speak.
- Do not allow discussion of their dysfluency in their presence.

If a child's dysfluency continues for more than a short period of time, or if the parents or the child appear to be worried by the dysfluency, a referral to a speech therapist will usually be made. The British Stammering Association has drawn up the following guidelines to help with decision-making regarding referrals. A referral is made if the child has dysfluent speech and one or more of the following factors are present:

- a family history of stammering or speech or language problems
- the child is finding learning to talk difficult in any way
- the child shows signs of frustration or is upset by their speaking
- the child is struggling when talking
- the child is in a dual-language situation and is stammering in their first language

- there is parental concern or uneasiness
- the child's general behaviour is causing concern.

Elision

The term 'elision' refers to when a child regularly misses out part of a speech sound altogether. It is a common occurrence, particularly with the second consonant of a cluster of two, for example:

- the *st* in the word 'postman' would become 'pos'man'
- the *pt* in the word 'slept' would become 'slep'.

In young children this is part of the maturational development of speech patterns. In older children and adults it is usually more likely to be habit!

Language disorders and speech therapy

Concerns regarding language development include:

- lack of communication with parents and carers in early weeks
- significant feeding difficulties (speech therapists are often involved at this early stage)
- lack of vocalisation from 3 months onwards
- no babbling from 8 to 9 months onwards
- lack of verbal responses to play
- vocalisation completely out of line with the developmental 'norms'.

Language disorder can affect other aspects of a child's learning and development. Additional factors that can affect language include medical problems such as glue-

When expressing themselves, language disordered children may:

- have difficulty in finding appropriate words
- display word-order confusion
- have difficulty in giving explanations
- use confused grammar
- omit grammatical word endings
- use confused sounds within individual words.

ear. This is a condition of the middle ear in which sticky mucus is formed which is unable to drain away through the eustachian tubes in the normal way. If severe and left untreated, it can lead to permanent hearing loss.

A cleft lip and palate is another medical and physical problem that can affect speech. A child born with one or both of these physical conditions will automatically be referred to a speech therapist, to ensure

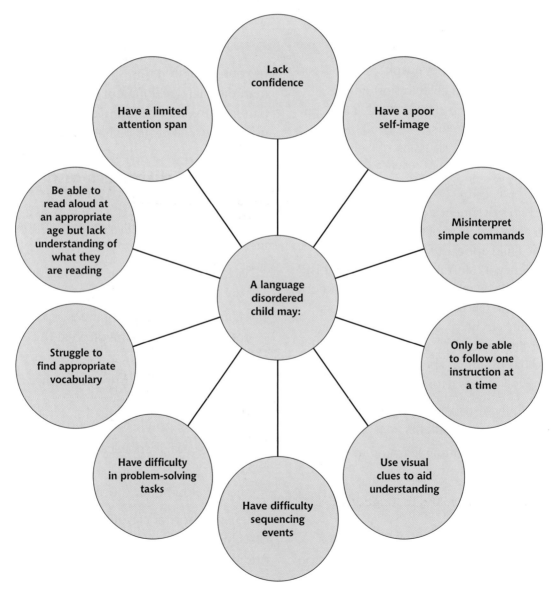

▲ How language disorder may affect the child

that the most appropriate feeding positions are established from birth.

Language delay

As with language disorder, any significant delay in language developing in line with the expected 'norms' is monitored, and a referral made to a speech therapist as appropriate. There are environmental, medical, social, cultural and genetic factors that can affect language development, as summarised in the spidergram below.

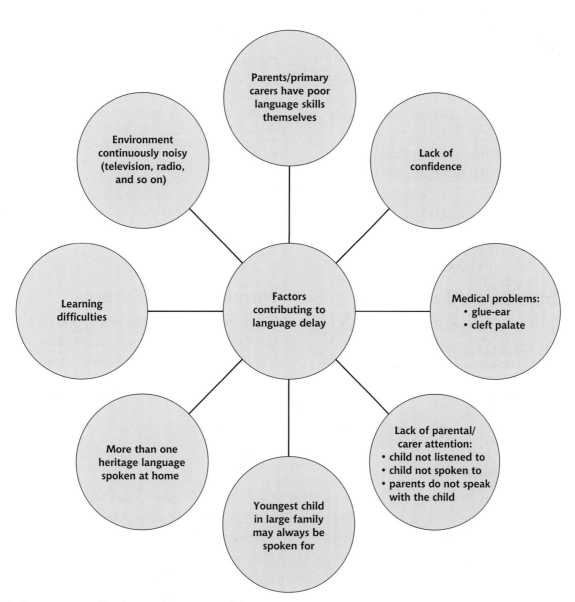

▲ Factors contributing to language delay

When and how to access help

A child may benefit from an assessment by another professional, such as a key worker, speech therapist, curriculum advisor or health visitor, if their progress slows down and seems to stop, if they are making only minimal progress despite already having a programme of learning specifically set up for them by current staff, or if they are working at a level considerably below that of their peers. The (Special Educational Needs Co-ordinator SENCO) is always the first port of call. It is their role to make appropriate contacts, and, along with parents, help develop a programme of intervention for any child who needs it.

 Refer to Unit 14, page 374, for more information on meeting additional needs and the role of SENCOs.

Child-centred activities

It is very important to plan activities that build on previous experience and are child centred.

The more opportunities build on children's current interests, the more successful learning will be for many children, especially those who are kinaesthetic learners.

GOOD PRACTICE

Although there needs to be a planned curriculum and day for children of all ages, as this provides both stability and structure, teachers and early years practitioners should, whenever possible, take up spontaneous learning opportunities too. These 'triggers' will often be initiated by the arrival of an object of interest, such as a sudden downfall of snow or hailstones, or the return of a child or adult from somewhere special, e.g. hospital, holiday, etc. Such opportunities offer rich learning opportunities that may be lost if relegated to a planned 'slot' at a later date.

Numbers of children

The number of children in any one teaching group will be determined by staffing, the overall class size, the range

Practical example

Stella and Max

Max learns best by doing. He is easily distracted from tasks and his key worker, Stella, tries to find him as many hands-on opportunities as she can. Max has recently been building with construction materials. He is very proud of what he has achieved. Stella has made a set of labels for the block shapes he has been using and the colours in the construction kit. She is now helping him to match them to his building.

(1) What else could Stella do to support Max?

(2) Is this child-centred learning do you think?

of learning styles within the class and the ability levels of the children. It will also be influenced by how much individual input each child is likely to need. If you know that a child or group of children is likely to need a higher level of adult guidance or support than 'average', you should whenever practicable, work with these children in smaller numbers, or one to one. Some children will be able to learn from their peers, and so a carefully considered pairing can be a good strategy.

Refer to Unit 2, pages 55–56, and also to Unit 5, page 391 for information on Lev Vygotsky and the zone of proximal development, and also Jerome Bruner's thinking on scaffolding.

The range of needs to be addressed and developed by the activities

Some children will be considered 'able' in some aspects of literacy but may struggle with other areas. These are important aspects to take into account. For example, a child who has a good vocabulary and tries to use it when writing, but who finds letter formation slow and difficult, can be 'put off' if set tasks that are too challenging for them to undertake with some degree of success.

 Practical example

Bryn

Bryn is 6 years old. He uses a range of vocabulary to describe and discuss all that interests him or happens around him, asking relevant questions and listening carefully to the answers. He is a confident speaker, both one to one and in a group. However, Bryn finds writing difficult. He has a clumsy pencil grip and writing is a slow and laborious process. Bryn gets frustrated during written activities and his extensive knowledge and understanding of many different subjects is not evidenced by his writing.

1. What activities could you devise for Bryn to help him improve his pencil skills?

2. What would you encourage Bryn to do to build on his fine motor skills in general?

3. How else could Bryn's knowledge and understanding be evidenced?

4. What might be the outcome of an assessment purely based on Bryn's writing?

Working with children with English as a second language

Some children will be learning English as an additional language. It will be important in helping them to understand and consolidate their learning to introduce and embed language within appropriate contexts. The use of both two-dimensional and three-dimensional visual images will be helpful, showing children an artefact or picture of the object you are talking to them about: for example, having a selection of brushes when discussing personal care, emphasising each name as they are being demonstrated – toothbrush, hairbrush, clothes brush. This helps to introduce the word 'brush', and shows how the same word is used in each action: i.e. 'brush' is the action word, and 'hair, tooth and clothes' are the nouns.

When asking questions, an action to accompany your words may be helpful. For example:

- pointing to the garden whilst asking 'Do you want to go outside?'
- making a drinking motion with your hand whilst asking 'Do you want a drink?'
- dabbing your eyes and pointing to the child to ask 'Are you feeling upset?'
- making an 'open book' action with your hands and pointing back and forth between the child and yourself to indicate' Would you like to share a story with me?'

Children will need to have plenty of opportunities to listen to the new language they are learning being spoken. Examples include group talking times (circle time is ideal), listening to taped stories, songs and rhymes, etc. These will all help familiarise the child with the language sounds. It is important to speak clearly and as normally as possible.

It will also be important to show that a child's heritage language is valued by the setting. This has an additional benefit for English-speaking children as they are introduced to a range of different writing styles and letter formations. Most schools and early years settings have greetings signs or welcome posters in a range of languages, but there is so much more that can be done.

It can be invaluable to have a selection of dual-language books readily available. Practitioners can read to the group using the English, whilst showing the other language alongside. This helps the child understand that their heritage language is valued by the setting. It will also encourage non-English speaking parents to sit and read them with their own child (and others too), enabling all the children to listen to and appreciate the differences in their languages. This helps the whole family feel valued and part of the school or early years setting community, and can also reinforce the message that learning both their heritage language and English is a good thing.

GOOD PRACTICE

Whenever practicable it can be helpful if early years practitioners and teachers learn a few words in each heritage language represented within their group or class. Many parents will be very willing to transcribe greetings, messages, etc. for labelling and display use. They often just need to be asked.

Where practicable, also include artefacts from a child's culture in relevant play situations, e.g. chappati pan, chopsticks, sari, *shalwah kameez* in the role play area.

Children who are learning more than one language at a time are generally slower in their language development in general. It should be recognised that some children will be learning more than one dialect at home, so learning English may well be a third language for them.

Many languages do not follow the left-to-right convention, as found in written English. Activities to encourage left-to-right actions will help children to understand the writing conventions of written English before they are ready to read or write themselves. Pencil skills, weaving, sewing, etc. can all help reinforce this action.

Children learning English as an additional language will build up their skills gradually. They normally understand far more than they can speak in the earliest weeks and months, and they will normally be able to speak far more than they can read or write as time moves on. In this way, language development follows the same sequential pathway as for any child learning their heritage language. You have probably found the same if you have tried to learn another language in the past.

✔ Progress check

1. Explain how children's communication, language and literacy can be supported in each of the following ways: visually, through auditory means, and kinaesthetically.

2. What is meant by the term 'developmental delay'? How might this affect communication, language and literacy?

3. Explain how dyslexia and dysgraphia can affect literacy skills.

4. Explain what is meant by 'dysphasia' and 'dyspraxia'.

5. Give some examples of how children who are learning English as an additional language can be supported in developing their communication, language and literacy.

Learning Outcome (2)

FOCUS ON...

the role of the adult in supporting communication, language and literacy

This links to assessment criteria **3.1** and **3.2**

Working with colleagues, parents and families

Building up relationships with children and their families is a fundamental part of the role of every teacher and early years practitioner. If an adult has a secure and positive relationship with a child, then it is likely that the child will feel able to ask questions, express their worries, and feel able to 'try' without fearing making mistakes. An adult who upholds confidentiality and is known to do this will receive the trust of parents. This effective relationship enables practitioners to have a better understanding of:

- when and how to intervene in the learning of each individual child
- the inclusive needs of individual children
- how they can address each child's specific needs.

It will also enable them to raise concerns with parents about a child's progress, knowing that the parent will usually trust them and their judgement and be willing to explore options and take advice from other professionals, knowing that it will be carried out within a framework of confidentiality and professionalism.

Staff or team meetings provide important opportunities for practitioners to:

- share ideas, both in general, and as contributions to forward planning
- seek advice and guidance about working practices
- discuss good practice and particularly successful activities
- reflect upon activities that were less successful than planned, discussing what went wrong and how this could be rectified another time
- contribute ideas to developing plans for the setting
- share skills; the most successful teams utilise the strengths of each team member to provide the strongest approach to each task
- share any concerns regarding practice
- share any concerns regarding children's learning or development
- discuss strategies to support particular needs (e.g. visual learners, kinaesthetic learners), sharing previous experiences and ideas
- share observations and learning assessments, always maintaining appropriate levels regarding confidentiality.

Many settings will have a mentoring scheme in which a senior or more experienced staff member will support a new or less experienced colleague. The mentor will often be the first port of call for advice or guidance. They will often supervise the initial planning of a less experienced colleague and guide them in developing support strategies and in how to group children together effectively.

The role of the adult

The role of the adult in planning and implementing opportunities to develop reading and writing skills is to:

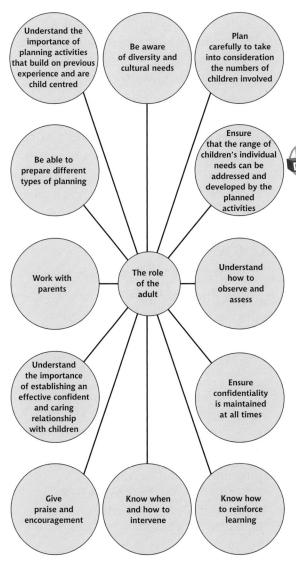

▲ The role of the adult

Working with parents

At times children will need extra practice in order to maintain progress, or to reach their potential. In schools teachers have limited time to spend with each child on an individual basis and if a child takes a little more time than others to grasp a concept, or to consolidate new learning, time spent with the child on these skills outside of the classroom can be invaluable. Having 'homework' is now commonplace and most children enjoy sharing these experiences with their family. Good links with parents enable active encouragement of reading at home. Using either schemed readers or library books, and also word tins/lists etc., parents can help encourage, reinforce and be actively involved with their child's development.

Have a go!

Using the spidergram as a starting point, give a range of examples of how you personally have been involved in supporting the development of literacy skills with children during your placement experience. Remember to include examples from each of the age ranges you have worked with, and each type of setting you have experienced, e.g. nursery, school, childminder, etc.

G☺☺D PRACTICE

As with all activities, praise and encouragement can work wonders. Children need to know that they have adult approval and will continue to work to achieve this further.

Activities to develop and extend language and literacy

Learning through play

Early years professionals have promoted learning through play for decades and, in recent years, government policy groups have voiced their agreement too, although there will probably always be discrepancies between the early years profession and the policy makers in how 'play' is actually thought of and defined. As the process of curriculum and strategy development has evolved (Foundation Stage Curriculum, Birth to Three Matters, Every Child Matters, EYFS and so on) each stage emphasises (just that bit more) how play should be the basis for early learning, raising the status of a play-based curriculum.

Have a go!

Reflect back on activities you have carried out with children, identifying which were play based. For any that you identify as not being play based, think through how they could be made so another time.

Refer to pages 458–463 for ideas on supporting literacy through play. Also, refer to Unit 7, page 263 for ideas on learning through play in general.

Tina Bruce and Janet Moyles are modern-day theorists whose thinking is firmly based in the value of play. Refer to material by either of them to further your understanding.

GOOD PRACTICE

Language involves communicating, thinking, linking sounds to letters, reading and writing. These separate but inter-connected aspects of learning should be kept in mind when planning. Think about them as you read through the following section.

Activities

Every activity will involve language in some way. This may simply be through the adult reading a story or using written instructions on how to do something. It may be that the planned activity involves writing or reading or using a reference source such as a book or information website. Children will only build up a wide vocabulary if they are exposed to one, so it is important that early years practitioners use a wide and varied vocabulary with all the children they work with. This means thinking about how you describe and discuss something, introducing alternative names for objects, using a range of descriptive terms, encouraging children to think, to describe, to ask questions: why? What if? When? How?

Have a look at the following list of activities. Brief examples of how each helps support reading and writing are given. These are just a few to get you started. You will be able to think of many more.

As you read the following section, refer back to Unit 15 for further ideas.

Role play supports the development of reading and writing as children:

- write shopping lists
- take down messages
- 'read' newspapers and magazines.

Sand play supports the development of reading and writing as children:

- develop fine motor skills whilst filling and pouring
- learn to control implements
- use fingers to make patterns and letter shapes.

Painting supports the development of reading and writing as children:

- develop arm and hand control through brush use

- enjoy early mark-making experiences
- create an expression with paint.

Story sacks support the development of reading and writing as children:

- make links between what they hear and the written word
- listen to tapes and CDs
- join in repetition and story format, using the provided props.

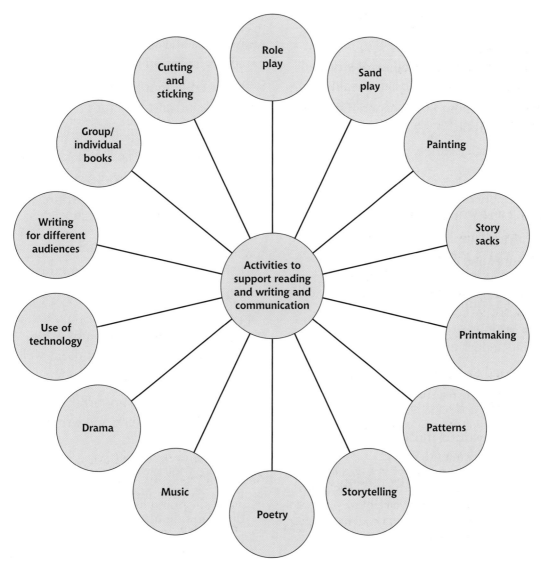

▲ Activities supporting reading, writing and communication

Printmaking supports the development of reading and writing as children:

- make patterns
- learn to work from left to right
- plan, implement and reflect on what they produce.

Patterns support the development of reading and writing as children:

- learn about shape, size and structure
- learn to discriminate and group by function
- identify and learn about order.

Storytelling supports the development of reading and writing as children:

- develop an understanding of story order: beginning, middle, conclusion
- find enjoyment in the experience, wanting more
- experience a variety of story types and genre.

Poetry supports the development of reading and writing as children:

- learn about pattern and rhyme
- identify and enjoy repetition
- experience sounds, and links between similar sounds in a fun way.

Music supports the development of reading and writing as children:

- respond to rhythm
- follow patterns during movement sessions
- observe written music and how it is formed from left to right.

Drama supports the development of reading and writing as children:

- take on roles, responding to the process of familiar stories
- maintain interest in books to support further experiences

- use gesture and develop body control.

Use of technology supports the development of reading and writing as children:

- develop the skills they will need to use online sources of reference for the future
- practise early design and creativity through computer games
- develop keyboard skills alongside early letter recognition.

Writing for different audiences supports the development of reading and writing as children:

- recognise how important written communication is in the world
- try out different forms of writing, expression and structure
- experience the practical application of writing as they use references.

Group and individual books support the development of reading and writing as children:

- experience stories in different formats
- learn alongside others, sometimes supported by those at a more advanced level
- learn to share reading times with parents, siblings and friends, as well as teachers and other practitioners.

Cutting and sticking support the development of reading and writing as children:

- explore their own creativity
- impose order and pattern on their work
- develop fine motor skills as they use small utensils.

A selection of activities has also been set out in more detail in the following section.

Board and boxed games

Board games, such as snakes and ladders, and boxed games, such as picture lotto, all involve verbal interaction. Snakes and ladders involves terminology linked to position, e.g. climbing up the ladder, slithering along or down the snake, overtaking X, and Y, being X places ahead, X places behind, etc. Picture lotto involves the use of description, and the skill of matching words to pictures, e.g. 'Who has the red car?' or 'Who has the teddy with the hat?' etc.

Refer also to Unit 15, page 409, for ideas to promote number skills too throughout each of the following activity areas.

Role play

Role play can involve the child acting out a role, dressing up, being another person, acting out a scenario either imaginary, from previous experience, or something that may be about to happen, or they are worried might happen.

In role-play situations most children will naturally speak within their role, taking on the language of mummy, daddy, baby, shopkeeper, ticket collector, etc. They will use expression and intonation, often mimicking what they have heard at home. They may express concerns, worries and anxiety. Observation, together with sensitive adult input, can help alleviate these fears and anxieties by using books, discussion, etc. at another time to help them work through how they are feeling. These instances show how important having language skills is to a child trying to make themselves understood and communicate their needs, either directly or indirectly. At times undesirable expressions

may be used. These can be left to pass unless use is regular, excessive or causing distress to others; but modelling more appropriate language will be helpful. If, however, what a child says or intimates ever causes you concern regarding their safety or wellbeing, you should speak to your placement supervisor, who will know what (if any) action to take.

In role play children will draw on their own personal experiences and those that they have seen on television, heard about in stories, and discussed with others either formally or informally.

Role play gives children opportunities to use both oral and written language. There will be opportunities, for example, for:

- inviting others to play, and joining in play on request or invitation from others
- using appropriate questions and responses when 'shopping' or in other role-play situations
- using verbal social conventions within context
- labelling and putting up notices as their role-play area becomes a shop, the post office, a bank, etc.
- writing lists as they make up menus for their café, takeaway or restaurant
- noting down orders from customers, writing cheques at the bank, writing receipts at the petrol station and so on
- writing to others as they make party invitations, send letters, Christmas or birthday cards
- writing names as they make luggage labels, tickets and boarding passes to get on their aeroplane
- using mark making to indicate temperatures on a chart during hospital play, plotting the weight of a baby during baby clinic play

- reading newspapers during 'at home' play, magazines at the hairdressers, holiday brochures at the travel agents.

The list can be endless.

Books

Books can be both for pleasure and for information. In our modern world, heavily led by technology, it is important to help children value the use of books as a tool of reference. Linking books to displays and interest tables is an easy way to help children make this link. Using books to help children follow up an idea, an experience or an opportunity will again encourage the habit of book use. Examples would include:

▲ Sharing a story at home with family is important foe development of literacy skills

- using books at the centre of a discussion, or to start off a new topic

- looking at books on birds to support work on flight/feathers/bird feeding

- using maps to help place children's holiday locations

- looking at books on the body following a visit from a doctor, or following a child's stay in hospital for an operation, talking through experiences and discussing 'people who help us' where appropriate.

Reference books can be used to support all areas of the curriculum. This also applies to stories.

Storytelling

Stories provide both pleasure and information. Stories can be either written or oral and can provide either imaginary events, or descriptions of real life, past or present. Children love stories. They usually feel comfortable with them as there is a familiar structure to them. They have a beginning and a clear end, with usually an interesting, and perhaps exciting or funny,

middle. The way the story starts helps children to know and predict what might come next. For example:

- Once upon a time …

- When Jake went to hospital, he …

- In the woods, near the stream …

Each of these beginnings provides the child with a clue as to where the story is set, and what sort of story it is likely to be.

Stories support the development of language and literacy through:

- the introduction of new vocabulary, when and how to use it

- supporting understanding of sentence structure

- supporting children's own initial attempts at constructing stories

- description and alliteration

- the links they can give to current topics and the overall curriculum

- the introduction of alternative cultures, religions and the associated language structures, greetings and social gestures

- helping children find pleasure through listening and concentration, forming good habits for life in general.

Props and story sacks

Using props alongside storytelling can bring an extra dimension to the story, can extend learning and also help children to maintain focus. Fidgety children can be stilled by the encouragement to hold a shell, refer to a puppet or doll, take part in placing a picture on a storyboard, etc. Props can be almost anything linked to the story being told. Story boards can either be produced along the way, with a group of children, or used as a ready-prepared prop. They can easily be made, using simple illustrations, backed with Velcro or something similar, and placed on a textured board or cloth.

G☺☺D PRACTICE

Children love stories with repetition and these opportunities to join in regularly during a story give encouragement to quieter children to contribute verbally, and encouragement to all children to listen carefully, anticipating the next opportunity to join in the 'chant' etc.

Story sacks as a concept have been around for many years; they are in essence a collection of related props, and, as with the storyboards, they can be home made or commercial. As a commercial idea they were set up by Neil Griffiths in the 1990s. A typical story sack includes an illustrated story book, an information book to help extend learning, puppets or toys linked to the story, a recorded version of the story and some associated props, e.g. a simple game, relevant artefacts, etc. The age group the story sack is aimed at is clearly indicated, and there are always instructions for parents on how to use the story sack with their children.

Again, the use of story sacks extends story time and encourages language use through discussion, repetition and the exploration of the accompanying props and artefacts.

FAST FACT

Neil Griffiths provides training in developing story sacks and many schools and early years settings have benefited from this, going on to produce their own library of story sacks.

Music and dance

The use of music and dance helps introduce vocabulary linked to movement and expression in a fun way. Through imitation initially, children will learn terms such as glide, soar, fly, hover, etc. as they move to appropriate music. They will learn, the terms stomp, march, thump, flatten, etc. as they move around as giants, and the terms roar, screech, howl and groan as they play at being monsters. There are many other examples that could be used here.

Similarly, terms linked to position and direction will be learned as children are asked to move to the right, step forward, jump backwards, face a partner. Terms linked to symmetry can be learned through actions copying another child, e.g. mirroring, copying, same as, matching, and also terms to describe the opposite effect, e.g. different from, unlike, reverse.

Once again, you can probably think of many more examples to add to the above.

The use of rhythm is important, as language is full of rhythm, and listening to and being able to identify and replicate rhythm can also help general speech and language development.

Drama

Language and literacy is supported through drama as children reflect on stories well known to them, e.g. the story of the three little pigs, taking on various roles, speaking their 'lines' and following the story structure from its beginning, through its main sections and processes, and on to the climax with the big bad wolf. Re-enacting stories is part of the literacy strategy. It encourages children to listen, to speak and make links with the written word. It can also help develop discussion skills.

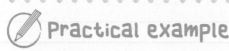

Practical example

The Three Little Pigs drama

Class Two had enjoyed re-enacting the timeless classic – 'The Three Little Pigs'. It was part of a project on homes and buildings. Their teacher was following the drama session up with a discussion about houses. She began by asking the children what sort of building they lived in.

(1) What other aspects of discussion could she introduce?

(2) What examples can you think of to extend children's vocabulary linked to the three little pigs?

(3) What writing opportunities could you bring to the project? How would you set you them up?

Opportunities to share a drama experience as a whole group can be helpful, especially for less confident children, encouraging them to take part, share verbal exchanges and experiences with others, reinforcing for themselves a sequential process. Other examples could be working as a team to be

a large wave in the sea, a huge snake moving around the room, or a volcano exploding.

Story tapes

A range of well-known and much-loved stories, both classic and contemporary, are now available on tapes and CDs. Listening to tapes or CDs will never replace adult reading to a child, which is so important, but they do make an excellent alternative and are an additional way of exposing children to language and literature. Encouraging children to listen to a story in this way in the home, provides a far more focused experience for them than passively watching television or a DVD, and encouraging parents to consider this can also be beneficial to children.

Because story tapes are usually read by professionals, often actors, the use of tone, expression and emphasis is usually extremely good, helping build on children's understanding of language use.

FAST FACT

Parents who are not fluent readers themselves will also benefit from the experience of sharing a story with their child in this way.

Making tapes

Making tapes with or for children can be great fun. Commonly heard sounds are popular. Children will be using auditory discrimination as they listen and identify what they hear. Examples could include:

- household sounds – running water, toilet flushing, doorbell ringing, the telephone, a broom sweeping, spraying from a polish tin, etc.

- street sounds – dog barking, car horn, bus doors closing, siren from an emergency vehicle, birds fluttering

- a walk in the park or woods – the wind in the trees, birds singing, frogs croaking, walking on crunchy leaves, etc.

You could also help children make a recording of them each saying hello, playing it back and identifying the other voices, or taking it in turns to tell a story, a little bit at a time. Children love to hear their own voices, and, again, this focuses their listening and helps them to discriminate sounds.

Circle time

Circle time is a regular time slot in a class or group where either specific topics are discussed, perhaps linked to the PSHE Citizenship strand of the National Curriculum, or where there is simply time for the whole group to gather, to listen to each other's news and ideas and perhaps discuss plans for something specific. Only one person is allowed to speak at any one time, and it is usual with young children for the speaker to hold something special, e.g a large shell, a teddy, or a beautiful artefact of some kind. This reminds the group who they should be focusing on. The 'only one person to speak at a time' rule helps teach the louder and more outgoing children to listen to others, building their listening skills, their concentration and their social skills, and the quieter, less confident children to feel more able to speak within a group setting, helping to build their confidence and self-esteem. This also gives them opportunities to express themselves, and put forward ideas that they might otherwise not feel able to contribute.

Small-world play

Small-world play is play with resources such as farms, zoos, roadways, doll houses, etc. It is basically playing out 'life' in miniature. It is favoured mostly by children of pre-school ages who tend to speak to themselves in a monologue as they play. This gives great opportunities for:

- naming objects, e.g. car, bus, tractor, lorry, table, basin, lamp, cow, horse, bear, lion
- labelling actions, e.g. going upstairs, moving along the road, going in, coming out, going through the tunnel
- vocalising understanding of positions, e.g. in front of, behind, on top of, underneath, beside, inside, outside
- vocalising social greetings and pleasantries as they play, e.g. hello, goodbye, thank you, excuse me.

Materials and sources

Other opportunities to support the development of language and literacy include:

- using puppets – hand puppets, paper puppets, pop-up puppets, etc. (also, life-size puppets and Persona dolls).
- using rhymes and finger rhymes, easily filling any short time gaps with a rhyme to reinforce current learning aims
- giving children instructions and directions, and asking them to do the same for each other. This can be either indoors or outside, involving the children moving physically, or controlling programmable toys, using computer programmes etc.
- setting up discussion tables, and displays, planning with the children what is needed, where objects can be collected from
- labelling any relevant objects or places, notices, signposts and posters. These all reinforce the meaning of printed text

and teach the convention (in English) of reading from left to right, and from top to bottom

- making books with children. This helps introduce them to the construction of a book, e.g. its title page, the introduction, the main body of text, the conclusion

- using stories in the development of listening and comprehension skills, encouraging the skills of recall and summary

- spoken language in any shape or form. Any adult working with children can help their language development simply by conversing with them. If a child is listened to, they will also learn to listen to others

- poetry. Language is often set out at its best within poetry, so regularly enjoying poems with children can help them to learn about timing, rhyme and vocabulary, and also develop an appreciation of the expression and emotions often found within the poem

- using tape recorders and listening centres. These encourage children to focus on listening to something specific, without the distractions of surrounding noise (dulled by the wearing of headphones). They offer opportunities for extension work for children working at the higher levels and focused time for easily distracted children, helping them to keep 'on task' whilst freeing up their teacher to work with others, and are a source of pleasure for all

- dual-language books. It is important that there are appropriate resources for those children for whom English is an additional language. This includes the use of dual-language labelling and notices, and also books wherever possible.

FAST FACT

Some children live in homes where being heard is a challenge above the noise of a busy household. This tends to make them feel they need to shout and talk over others, in order to be heard. Knowing that they will be listened to will help them learn to wait their turn without anxiety.

Methods of teaching reading and writing

As children learn to read, they will be using the experiences they have already had of rhyme, letter recognition, alliteration and phonic sounds. It is an accepted fact that children who are introduced to and surrounded by language in all its forms from birth are likely to be earlier, better and more interested readers at an earlier age than those children who have limited exposure to language or the written word until a later date.

Ideally, children will have an early introduction to stories, finger rhymes, picture books and singing, together with opportunities for discussion and conversation, and looking at alphabets. Also, having their awareness of signs, labels and the use of written language raised by adults for both practical and pleasure purposes will help build an automatic acceptance that using language is a good and necessary part of life.

Phonics

Hearing and learning to identify the sounds of words and the individual parts of words is early *phonology*. The sounds of words are called *phonemes*. As children learn the sounds of letters and words, they are usually introduced to a visual image of them too. The written letter 'sound' is called a *grapheme*. Children need to understand and be able to use both the phoneme and the grapheme in order for them to read and write.

Learning phonics involves more than just learning the 26 letters of the alphabet. It includes all the other letter sounds too, e.g. *ee, oo, ch, ng.*

Children need to learn the association between the sound of a letter or sequence of letters (a blend), and how they are visually presented.

Some teachers teach the phonetic (sound) of the letter linked to an associated action. This aims to help consolidate the letter sound for children. They may, or may not, also teach the visual image alongside this. Teaching by purely phonetic methods is not accepted by all teachers. There are well-known commercial products that support teaching through phonics. You may work with these within your placements.

G☺☺D PRACTICE

Teaching phonics is part of the Primary Framework for Literacy.

Development of mark making leading to emergent writing

As they learn to write, children will be building on the mark-making skills they have developed through the use of paint, crayons, pencils, charcoal, etc. Exposure to these media provides opportunities for them to develop their fine motor skills, and an appropriate tripod grasp needed for concise pencil control. The development of controlled movements of the arm and shoulder through twirling streamers or ribbons, painting on easels or covered wall surfaces, and arm gestures linked to music, movement activities and PE will all be helpful.

All children progress through the same general stages of early mark making and patterning, gradually leading on to what is known as emergent writing. The interest in 'writing' patterns helps consolidate the left-to-right convention (in English), and the skills needed to write in straight lines using consistent letter sizes.

The illustration on page 466 shows how the process of mark-making usually develops. As with all aspects of development, it tends to be sequential and children follow the same pattern – but at their own individual pace.

Fine motor development required for writing

Young children need to have opportunities to develop their fine motor skills through the use of resources such as:

- malleable materials – sand, water, clay
- puzzles
- construction and model making with junk etc
- threading activities, sewing and weaving
- pencils, crayons, pens, paint
- dressing-up clothes
- domestic skills such as dressing and undressing, teeth cleaning, using cutlery.

With access to these everyday play and domestic opportunities children move away from having the clumsy primitive grasp of the youngest toddler as they crayon for the first time, to develop the careful handling of pens and pencils and the desired neat script of the older child. Their fine skills are developed through the actions needed for each activity, e.g. squeezing, rolling, grasping, pummelling, kneading, threading, careful positioning, manoeuvring, connecting, fixing, stacking, holding, and also the manipulation of

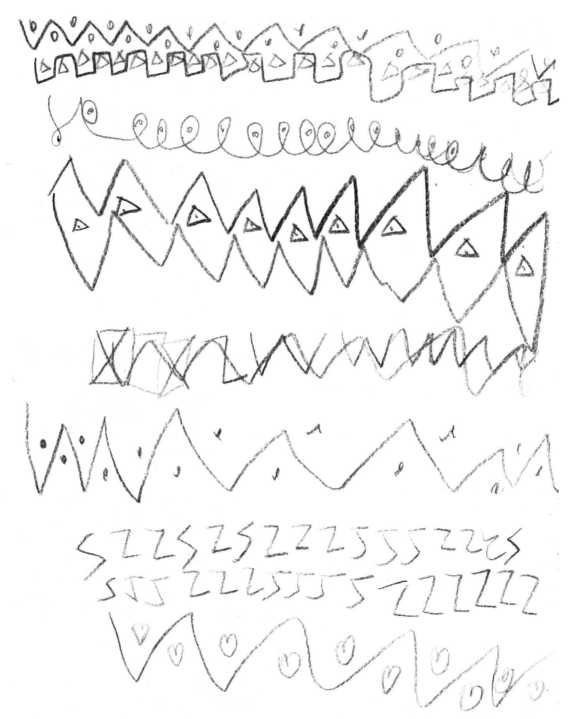

▲ Early pattern practice helps develop letter formation

knives, forks, zips, buttons, toggles, Velcro, hooks, sleeves, gloves, scarves, hats, shawls, etc.

As children master control of their pencil they increasingly develop the skills to follow the letter-formation style taught by most teachers. It is important that they are also taught to hold their pencil correctly. This helps each letter to 'flow' more easily.

Children are encouraged to write freely and often. They are encouraged to 'have a go' at setting down as much of what they want to write as they can, labelling drawings, adding captions, etc. This is referred to as emergent writing. The child uses their phonetic knowledge together with their mastery of the grapheme (written letter) to 'do their own writing'. This is an important stage of literacy development that needs plenty of praise and encouragement.

▲ Children are encouraged to write freely and often

Have a go!

Referring to children from your placement where possible, describe the stages of writing of children at ages 3, 5 and 7. Give some ideas to support further development at each of these ages, again using examples from your placement whenever you can.

G☺☺D PRACTICE · · · · · · · ·

Left-handed children need additional support in developing writing skills. Owing to the classic 'slightly awkward-looking' position of the left-handed child when writing, they often require greater surface space to allow them to position their paper or book at an angle. There are letter-formation charts available that provide instructions for left-handers too.

Development of reading

The Primary Framework for Literacy uses the term 'searchlights' to explain how children learn to read. What they mean by this is that a child uses four main 'pathways' of learning as they read through any written material, constantly cross-referencing between each 'searchlight' to gain and build on their understanding. Understanding of phonics is needed initially in early reading, followed by word recognition, with both supported by context and general knowledge.

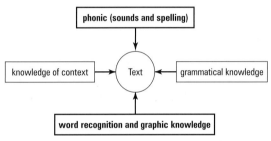

▲ Knowledge and support are provided by these 'searchlights'

As already mentioned children need to understand letter sounds and how these combine together to form blended sounds. As with all areas of learning it is important that the learning styles of all children are taken into account, by having a balance of each style. Remember, the three learning styles.

Visual learners

Visual learners like uncluttered learning environments which do not easily distract them. They enjoy visual images to support them and are often creative learners who have a good imagination.

Auditory learners

Auditory learners tend to have good memories, so will be able to cope with references back to previous learning. They learn well through discussion, can think well and benefit from the use of questioning.

Kinaesthetic learners

Kinaesthetic learners like to be active. They will benefit from practical tasks, and hands-on learning opportunities where they learn through trial and error. They can be easily distracted so benefit from a focused learning environment.

Possible structure of a literacy teaching session

In past years schools were asked to use a framework known as the literacy hour. This was initially set up as a specific time slot allotted each day to focus on literacy skills. The aim of this approach was to raise the standards of literacy everywhere, focusing on the earliest age groups, reducing the numbers of children leaving school with limited reading and/or writing skills. The time-bound structure lacked the flexibility needed by teachers and learners and the guidance for teaching literacy has been changed. The term 'literacy hour' has now been abandoned, along with its set timings, but the basic teaching elements remain. For example, a teacher may use the following structure to a literacy session:

- whole class work, e.g. shared text work – a balance of reading and writing
- whole class work, e.g. focused word work or sentence work
- group and independent work, e.g. independent reading, writing or word work, enabling the teacher to work with specific ability groups on guided text work (reading or writing)

- whole class time, e.g. reviewing, reflecting, consolidating teaching points, and presenting work covered in the lesson.

Shared text work

During this stage of a literacy teaching session the teacher may use written material relevant to all children. This would often be a 'big book'. This stage is likely to involve the following:

- Shared reading as a whole class at KS1 – focusing on comprehension and on specific text features such as word-building, spelling, punctuation and layout of the text for a purpose; this provides a specific context for applying and teaching the use of reading cues to check for meaning, and word level skills.

- Combining shared writing with shared reading helps children develop an understanding of grammar, sentence construction and punctuation.

- At KS2 shared reading extends reading skills and is a context for teaching and reinforcing grammar, punctuation and use of vocabulary.

- Shared reading helps children to work with texts that are beyond their independent reading levels, giving them access to richer and more complex texts than they would be able to access alone, building confidence and building on skills.

- Shared writing provides opportunities for children to learn, apply and reinforce skills with careful teacher guidance.

- Ideally, shared reading and writing will be linked, e.g. firstly through the introduction of a text, secondly through shared reading work, and finally by using the text as a frame or stimulus for writing.

Focused word work

This section needs to provide regular and focused work on the awareness and use of phonics and spelling, using the relevant word level objectives. These objectives can be practised through shared reading, but also need to be specifically taught through structured activities. At KS2 children should be working on sentence level objectives.

Have a go!

You could ask the class teacher at your placement, if you are in a school, if you can look at their copy of the standards for word and sentence objectives.

Group and independent work

This section of a session could have two complementary purposes:

- to enable the teacher to teach at least one group each session, differentiated by ability, for a sustained period through 'guided' reading or writing
- to enable other children to work independently – individually, in pairs or in groups – without recourse to the teacher.

It is an important part of this section of a session for children to learn not to interrupt the teacher.

Guided reading

The aim is for children to become independent readers. Usually children will be in small groups of around the same ability. They will use the same (carefully selected) text and the teacher will focus on independent reading, rather than modelling reading for the child. At KS1 the teacher usually introduces the text and

the general context of the story. They also point out any key words. The children then read the text with the teacher assessing and supporting them individually. At KS2 silent reading is gradually and increasingly encouraged, with progress assessed through questioning and discussion.

Guided writing

The aim is for children to become independent writers. The work covered here will often be linked to whole-class shared writing sessions, again working towards specific objectives.

Whole class work

The final stage of this style of session would bring the class back together to:

- enable the teacher to re-emphasise points, clear up misunderstandings and develop new teaching points
- enable children to reflect upon what they have learned and clarify their thinking
- enable children to revise and practise newly learned skills
- provide feedback, encouragement and constructive criticism
- enable children to present and talk about key issues, and for the teacher to monitor and assess the work of some of the children.

Contexts for reading and comprehension skills

It is important to consider how the context in which children learn affects the learning process. This was referred to on page 468 where a suggested structure for a literacy session was set out, explaining how children benefit from shared and guided opportunities in both reading and writing. It should be remembered that children need:

- shared reading experiences to learn to work with texts that alone they would not be ready to manage
- opportunities to read aloud and alone
- opportunities to read for pleasure, enjoying a wide variety of books of differing styles
- reading to be linked to other activities, to learn how it is used and contextualised within the world they live in
- to listen to and discuss stories and rhymes on a one-to-one, small group or whole class basis. This helps consolidate learning and helps them progress further
- to learn about cues and conventions, e.g. phonics, graphic and contextual cues, the structure of a text and the organisation of texts. Each of these aspects is supported through listening to stories, reading with an adult following the text together, using books for reference and knowing where to look to find what they need, e.g. index, contents list, etc. Rhymes and repetition are also of benefit, as are games involving the sounds of letters, syllables, etc.

Writing forms

Children need to want to write, to have a purpose for writing, and understand the breadth of purposes that written communication can be used for. They need to be able to practise letter formation freely. They need opportunities for letter formation, word development and learning the use and meaning of punctuation from an early age, building on each aspect as they move through school. Active involvement of children in labelling their own work, making choices about greetings and messages when creating 'products' for special occasions, developing signs and indicators within the learning environment and in giving

titles to display work, will increase their ownership of the written word. Also, group and individual opportunities to develop composition work incorporating various forms and genre should be built into planning, taking on children's own ideas as well as those proposed by the adult.

GOOD PRACTICE

Most children are given word lists/tins to take home and share learning with parents and older siblings. They will also be introduced to an appropriate reading scheme and will work through a range of graded books in a sequential order. Books are usually 'tiered' by colour and a child usually consolidates their reading skills by reading across one colour range of books before moving onto the next colour level.

The support of parents reading with their child at home is hugely important, as is the sharing of reading books in general at home.

Reinforcement

Some children will develop the understanding of how letters are linked to individual speech sounds (grapheme – phoneme) quite quickly and be ready to sound out word blends (e.g. d/o/g). The explanation of how vowels and consonants are articulated on pages 457 to 461 demonstrates how difficult this can be for some children and how the greater number of consonants in a word, the more complex the spoken or written format becomes.

It is usual for most children (without any noticeable speech difficulty) to be able to pronounce complex words long before they can write them, although they may make attempts (part of emergent writing).

Reinforcement is about repeating elements of learning to help consolidate them for the child or group. Children need a:

'broad and rich language curriculum that takes full account of developing the four independent strands of language – speaking, listening, reading and writing – and enlarging children's stock of words.'

(DfES, 2006)

Sometimes a different approach will be needed for different children according to preferred learning styles. Sometimes additional practice is appropriate for some children. For most children taking a contextualised approach works best.

FAST FACT

It is important that a group of children are not simply taught through one learning style.

Methods and techniques to support children with speaking and listening

Language as a means of communication

Language is essential to humans in order to communicate our needs, express our feelings and extend our experiences beyond our own environment by interacting with others. These interactions enable us to enhance our thinking and learn new skills. Spoken language is our most important means of communication. It is enhanced by facial expression, tone of voice and body language. Supporting communication is an important aspect of the early years professional.

Refer to Unit 5, pages 206–207, for a discussion of effective communication and how to develop the skills to communicate with both children and adults.

Development of listening skills

If a child does not listen, he will miss out on a range of communication opportunities. Good listening skills ensure that messages are understood and their meanings are clear. Children are more likely to develop good listening skills if they are listened to by significant adults and these adults are good listening role models for them. Palmer and Corbett (2003) state that a good listener:

- looks at the speaker
- tries to keep still
- concentrates on what the speaker is saying
- thinks about what the speaker says
- asks questions if it is not clear
- values what the speaker has to say
- tries to remember what the speaker has said.

Children need a good foundation in listening to enable them to discriminate sounds, a vital part of phonic work. If you look at the aims of the Early Years Foundation Stage Practice Guidance for Communication, Language and Literacy you will see that it includes:

- enjoy listening to and using spoken and written language, and readily turn to it in their play and learning
- sustain attentive listening, responding to what they have heard with relevant comments, questions or actions
- listen with enjoyment, and respond to stories, songs and other music, rhymes and poems and make up their own stories, songs, rhymes and poems
- hear and say sounds in words, in the order in which they occur
- link sounds to letters, naming and sounding the letters of the alphabet

- use their phonic knowledge to write simple regular words and make phonetically plausible attempts at more complex words.

FAST FACT

Books, stories and rhymes are important to support communication, language and listening. They provide children with language set within relevant contexts, clear demonstrations of the power of both written and verbal communicating, and reinforce the rhythm of language through both rhyme and story repetition.

The use of technology to support language and literacy

We live in a society that is technology led. Young children will need to be more technically able than any generation before them. Technology is found within the primary classroom, and many early years settings through:

- computer use
- digital cameras
- scanners and printers
- programmable toys
- calculators
- audio-recorders/players
- listening centres
- video/DVD recorders/players
- voice-operated items such as Dictaphones.

Children learn that each of the above:

- needs information to enable them to be used
- enables information to be obtained by or provided to someone else
- can support fun, learning, and the sharing of information.

▲ ICT helps children in many ways, including communication, language and literacy

How to work with children whose progress may be causing concern

The Warnock Report 1978

Refer to page 427 for information on the Warnock Report 1978.

Code of Practice 2001

The Code of Practice 2001 was a response to the Education Act 1996, providing teachers, teaching assistants and all other early years practitioners with practical guidance on how to meet the needs of children considered to have an SEN. Regarding the support and development of literacy skills, the following paragraphs (summarised below) of the Code of Practice are particularly relevant.

Statements for children under 2:

- 4.48 It is rare for a child under the age of two to be given a statement, but Portage, and/or specific peripatetic services should be made available for children identified as being blind or deaf, or having either a visual or auditory impairment.

Moving to primary school:

4.54, 4.55 The needs of a child who enters school, having had a considerable level of support (e.g. from Portage or similar) but without a statement should be carefully considered, in both the context of their current learning and in the wider context of the home environment and circumstances to establish if their difficulty is linked to any family issue. A record of their progress and needs should be passed on to the school, with agreement of their parents. The school will then be alerted to potential support needs for that child.

Communication and interaction:

7.55, 7.56, 7.57 These paragraphs raise the point that children with SENs are more able in some areas than in others, and that their communication needs may be 'both diverse and complex'. It is stated that children may require some or all of the following:

– flexible teaching arrangements

– help in acquiring, comprehending and using language

– help in articulation

– help in acquiring literacy skills

– help in using augmentative and alternative means of communication

– help to use different means of communication confidently and competently for a range of purposes, including formal situations

– help in organising and coordinating oral and written language

– support to compensate for the impact of a communication difficulty or learning in English as an additional language

– help in expressing, comprehending and using their own language, where English is not the first language.

Children may be supported through School Action Plus, or, if acceptable progress has not been made following receipt of this support over a period of time, statutory assessment will be considered.

Refer to Unit 14 page 373 for more on School Action Plus and supporting the additional needs of children.

Cognition and learning:

7.58, 7.59 This section refers to severe and profound difficulties, and also to specific learning difficulties such as dyslexia. It states that these children may require:

– flexible teaching arrangements

– help with processing language, memory and reasoning skills

– help and support in acquiring literacy skills

– help in organising and coordinating spoken and written word to aid cognition

– help with sequencing and organisational skills

– help with problem solving and developing concepts

– programmes to aid improvement of fine and motor competencies

– support in the use of technical terms and abstract ideas

– help in understanding ideas, concepts and experiences when information cannot be gained through first-hand sensory or physical experiences.

Speech and language therapy:

8.49, 8.50, 8.51, 8.52, 8.53 Speech and language is considered to be so fundamental to learning that 'addressing speech and language impairment should normally be recorded as educational provision unless there are exceptional reasons for not doing so'.

- Speech and language support is usually provided through NHS support. Some children will receive regular support either one to one or in a small group from a speech therapist. In some cases it is felt appropriate for a child's teacher to 'deliver a regular and discreet programme of intervention under the guidance and supervision of a speech and language therapist'. And occasionally children will receive language support as an integral part of their day. This too will be supported and monitored regularly by a speech and language therapist.

LEA support services:

- 10.7 The Code of Practice describes how local education authorities (LEAs) can provide advice on teaching techniques, classroom management and appropriate resources and materials. Also direct teaching or practical support for teachers, specialist teaching assistants and specialist help.

(Based on *Special Educational Needs Code of Practice*, DfES, 2001)

 Have a go!

You may find it useful to read through the Code of Practice in more detail. Most college libraries will have a copy.

How to monitor progress and keep appropriate records

Progress is monitored through observation and assessment and written down in some form of recording system. Assessment can be both formative and summative. Formative assessment is assessment for learning (AfL), whereas summative assessment is the assessment of learning (AoL). Assessment is a key part of the learning process as it provides information and feedback for teachers and early years practitioners to enable them to provide the most appropriate learning opportunities for the children in their care.

Assessment of learning (AoL)

This form of assessment is a snapshot of where a child has reached at a specific point in time. Examples include where the child has reached at the point of transfer from:

- early years setting to primary school
- one year group to another
- one key stage to another.

Assessment for learning (AfL)

This form of assessment should inform the next stage of learning, i.e. activities should be built on the outcomes of assessment, continually helping the child to develop a skill further and further. Regarding the Primary Framework for Literacy the Assessment Reform Group identified five key factors that improve learning through assessment:

- providing effective feedback to children
- actively involving children in their own learning
- adjusting teaching to take account of the results of assessment
- recognising the profound influence assessment has on the motivation and self-esteem of children, both of which are crucial to learning
- considering the need for children to be able to assess themselves and to understand how to improve.

The Assessment Reform Group also identified seven key characteristics which were evident in schools where AfL was effective in promoting learning and in raising standards of attainment.

There is a single assessment strategy for the Early Years Foundation Stage; it is known as the Foundation Stage Profile. Thirteen assessment scales are used to assess the six areas of learning. These are usually completed by the end of the Foundation Stage and observations of a child's progress will be made although the early learning goals are not summatively assessed.

Assessing the Foundation Stage

Assessment for the Foundation Stage will be the most likely assessment process you will be involved in. Progress through the Early Years Foundation Stage (EYFS) is assessed using a booklet for each child called the Early Years Foundation Stage Profile.

From September 2008 a new EYFS booklet will be in use. There will only be minor differences.

Resources to support learning and development

Children need to learn that books are good, useful and play a vital part in life and learning. They need to be inspired by what they see, read and refer to. Adults should regularly review the books on offer in their nursery, pre-school or classroom. Settings should be providing books that:

- are fun
- are visually appealing
- are appropriate to the children's level of understanding and concentration span

- are factual
- are fictional
- are used for reference
- offer repetition and the chance to join in with familiar refrains
- introduce children to poetry and rhymes
- introduce children to new experiences
- help children learn about fears and emotions and how to deal with them
- portray positive images regarding gender and ability
- portray a range of cultures and heritage in positive ways
- show both similarities and differences between cultures, celebrating those differences
- are in more than one language, ideally having a representation of all languages spoken within the setting.

For younger children, books need to:

- be durable
- be easy to handle
- be (mostly, but not exclusively) presented in clear, bold text
- be inviting to look at
- have clear pictures
- offer satisfaction
- be short, with an easy-to-follow content.

For older children, books need to:

- include both classic and contemporary language use
- stretch their concentration spans
- relate to interests and potential risks
- extend learning of health issues, personal safety and care.

Early years settings should be providing free-writing areas at all times. There should be mark-making and writing opportunities alongside all role play, and adults should take all opportunities, planned or spontaneous, to encourage the writing of written records, reflective comments, etc.

Accessing resources

Having easy access to reading materials will encourage children to choose to read during free-learning sessions, or as time-fillers at the end of a session. In early years settings books would normally be set out in book boxes, on shelves and tables, or in racks or storage units (these need to be secure and unable to close or fall).

A comfortable and inviting book area will encourage children to enjoy a quiet time curled up with a book, perhaps alongside a friend, or as a shared experience with an adult.

The labels, notices, posters and signs around the setting will illustrate different writing forms for children. Providing them with relevant materials to choose freely will help them start to develop an understanding of writing contexts.

The learning environment

Throughout your studies for this qualification there will have been many references to the importance of providing a suitable (enabling) environment for children, both in their care and in their learning. Regarding literacy development, the more that language is used around children, in all its forms, the more their respect for it will be

developed and consolidated. A child who is provided with an exciting range of books to choose from, appropriate to their level of ability and to their current interests, will be most likely to develop a love of language and literature for the future.

▲ Books should be easily accessible

Progress check

(1) Explain how the input and approach taken by adults can impact on children's communication and literacy skills development.

(2) Give 10 examples from your placement of activities that support literacy and language development.

(3) How do good listening skills support communication, language and literacy? Give examples of activities to support this.

(4) What are the nine assessment points of the Foundation Stage Profile for Communication, Language and Literacy?

(5) What do you need to take into consideration when choosing books for young children from toddlers through to primary school?

Weblinks

- Each part of the UK has its own framework for supporting early development through to adulthood. These can be accessed at:

  – England www.dcsf.gov.uk

  – Wales www.learning.wales.gov.uk

  – Scotland www.scotland.gov.uk

- Northern Ireland www.ccea.org.uk

- www.standards.dcsf.gov.uk/primaryframework
  This gives the whole Primary Literacy Framework

- www.mantralingua.com and www.milet.com
  These are both good sources of dual-language books

- www.anythingleft-handed.co.uk/letter_formations.html
  Specialists in items to help left-handed children

unit 18

Working with babies from birth to 12 months

This unit covers how to describe and evaluate the normal development of babies and the different influences that may affect developmental progress. You will learn how to provide stimulating play activities, how to use observation and develop an understanding of how reflection on providing play, care routines, the suitability of the environment and using observation each helps promote the overall development of babies from birth to 12 months. You will learn about some of the organisational requirements of working with babies from birth to 12 months and how they have a positive impact on their care, and how they provide support for their families too.

Learning Outcomes

In this unit you will learn about:

1. the progress of development from birth to 12 months

2. the role of the professional in promoting development

3. the roles and responsibilities of professionals working with babies.

FOCUS ON...

the progress of development from birth to 12 months

This links to assessment criteria **1.1**, **1.2** and **1.3**

The patterns and sequence of development of babies from birth to 12 months

During the first year of life the human body develops at an incredible rate. This unit takes you from the helplessness of the newborn baby (the neonate) through to the rapidly developing skills and personality of the 1-year-old. Care routines for feeding, bathing and clothing needs are covered here, together with play and its importance in development. The development of communication is discussed and reference is made to the use and relevance of observation.

In supporting the all-round development of an infant, you will need not only to understand what each of the different areas

of development is, and the maturational pattern of development for each of them, but also you need to be able to see how development areas link together, and how you will be supporting the development of the whole child with most of the activities you prepare, actions you take, and opportunities you provide. It is important to remember that every infant develops at an individual rate and that there are many variations to what is considered normal.

Areas of development are shown below.

Sequence

In this unit development details are initially given for the neonate (the first month), and are then discussed under the areas shown above, dividing physical development into gross and fine skills, combining social and emotional development together, and also combining intellectual development with communication and language development.

You will see how developmental progress is sequential, each stage building on the previous one, as skills are learned, consolidated and then developed further. You will also learn how the physical development of muscle strength etc. affects the development of physical control and how stimulation affects interest, curiosity and therefore learning.

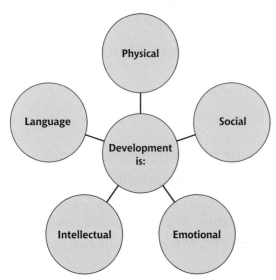

▲ The different areas of development

Refer to pages 40–53 for more information on the stages of development.

Expected pattern of development

Physical development includes the primitive reflexes seen in newborn infants, as set out on pages 552–553. It also involves motor development and manipulation. Motor development can be divided between locomotor skills and non-locomotor skills:

- Locomotor skills involve the body moving forward in some way. Examples of this would be walking, running, hopping.
- Non-locomotor skills comprise the physical movements that take place while stationary. Examples are bending, pulling, pushing.
- Manipulation involves actions using dexterity. Examples are throwing and catching a ball, threading cotton reels and placing one brick on top of another.

Physical skills can be gross (large) or fine. They include movement and balance, and can be either precise or carefree. Movement can involve the whole body or just one part of it.

Development becomes increasingly more complex and more difficult as it progresses. The 'maturational' changes can be described as moving:

- from the simple to the complex – this means that a child learns simple actions, such as learning to stand, before learning the more complex actions of being able to walk
- from cephalo (head) to caudal (tail) – physical control starts at the head and gradually develops down through the body. For example, head control is attained before the spine is strong enough for an infant to sit unsupported, and sitting unsupported is attained before the child is able to stand
- from proximal (near to the body) to distal (the outer reaches of the body) – these terms refer to how a child develops actions near to the body before they develop control of the outer reaches of the body. For example, a child can hug and carry a large teddy bear (arm control) before they can fasten their clothing (finger control)
- from general to specific – for example the more generalised responses of an infant showing excitement when recognising a favourite carer gradually becomes the facial smile of an older child on greeting the same person.

▲ An infant sits unsupported before being able to stand

The normal neonate

The first month of life is known as the neonatal stage, and the infant is referred to as a **neonate**. Most infants are born at full term and thrive well, settling quickly into a routine with their mother and other carers.

This settling-in period involves many new experiences and the starting-up of body processes not previously experienced. In the neonate these include breathing, circulation and digestion of new forms of nutrition (milk). In the mother this includes the onset of **lactation**, healing from the trauma of birth and the resettling of the uterus. Each of these is a normal process, but each can also present problems.

Milestones of physical development up to 12 months

Summary of gross motor skills

- Movements remain jerky and uncontrolled.
- Head lag gradually decreases and head control is usually achieved by 5 months.
- Rolling over is first seen between 4 and 6 months (from back to side), and then from front to back by about 8 months.
- Reaching for objects begins at about 4 months with the ability to pass toys from hand to hand seen from about 7 months.
- At 4 months the infant discovers their own feet and manages to sit with support.
- Sitting alone commences at about 7–8 months, with gradually greater balance developing.
- Crawling can start from 6 months (commando crawling) and traditional crawling from about 8 months. Some infants also bear-walk or bottom-shuffle.

- Some infants miss out the crawling stage, and move straight to pulling themselves up on furniture at around 8–10 months.
- Standing alone can occur any time from 10 months, but is more usual at around a year, when generally balance is more established.
- Walking is normally achieved by 12–16 months.

Summary of fine motor skills

- Hand and finger movements gradually increase, from the grasping of an adult's fingers in the earliest months, through to playing with own fingers and toes, handling and then holding toys and objects from 3–4 months.
- Everything is explored through the mouth.
- At about 7 months, the infant will try to transfer objects from one hand to the other with some success. Pincer grasp (index finger and thumb) is emerging.
- By about 10 months, pincer grasp is developed.
- The infant will pick up small objects.
- Toys are pulled towards the infant.
- Pointing and clapping are deliberate actions for most infants by 10–12 months.
- Controlled efforts when feeding, with some successes.

Milestones of social and emotional development up to 12 months

Summary of social and emotional development

- The first social smile is usually seen by 6 weeks.
- Smiling is first confined to main carers, and is then in response to most contacts.

Neonate = an infant under 1 month old
Lactation = the production of milk by the breasts

▲ Social and emotional development builds through constant contact

- The infant concentrates on the faces of carers.
- Pleasure during handling and caring routines is seen by 8 weeks, through smiles, cooing and a general contentment.
- Expressions of pleasure are clear when gaining attention from about 12 weeks and in response to the voices of main carers.
- Social games, involving handling and cuddles, gain chuckles from 4–5 months onwards.
- Infants enjoy watching other infants.
- Sleep patterns begin to emerge from about 4 months onwards, although these will continue to change.
- From about 9 or 10 months the infant may become distressed when the main carer leaves them, temporarily losing their sense of security and becoming wary of strangers. This is a normal stage in development.

- Playing contentedly alone increases by 1 year, but the reassuring presence of an adult is still needed.

Summary of intellectual development and communication skills

As well as physical growth and development, which can be observed and measured quite easily, babies also develop their knowledge and understanding. This is often referred to as intellectual (or cognitive) development. The development of knowledge and understanding is closely linked with the development of language and communication skills, and it involves the senses too.

At birth, the infant's nervous system is incomplete and understanding their level of sensory awareness is not easy. It has been established that an infant's system for vision is not initially strong and develops considerably in the first few months, whereas an infant's hearing is quite well developed right from birth. The main areas of sensory development studied are vision, hearing and perception.

Milestones of sensory development up to 12 months
Vision and visual perception

From birth, infants will turn to look at sources of light. They show an interest in the human face, and researchers (particularly Robert Fantz in the 1950s) have repeatedly shown that the human face receives a greater response than other similar options, for example a 'head' with facial features muddled up.

Within a few days of birth babies can demonstrate both spontaneous and imitative facial expressions, and the eyes of the newborn infant can at times be seen

---

Perception = the process of interpreting sensory information

to move in the direction of sounds. These early visual interactions (eye contacts) between the infant and their carer strengthen the process of bonding and therefore enhance their emotional security.

▲ An illustration of Fantz's faces

A checklist for visual development

Concerns regarding vision would include:

- lack of eye contact with main carer
- no social smile by six weeks
- lack of visual tracking of carer's face or bright mobile by 2 months
- lack of visual response to breast or bottle feed
- lack of cooperative eye movement after 3 months
- lack of signs that infant reaches out for toys in response to visual stimulus
- lack of mobility or directed attention by 12 months.

Hearing

At birth, the hearing of infants is acute (sharp), as their auditory perception (ability to make sense of what they hear) is not yet cluttered by the sounds of everyday living. They can often be seen responding to sound by blinking and through startled movements (the startle reflex). Newborn infants respond to the sound of their mother or main carer. They also show signs of auditory awareness by turning towards other sounds. Many infants are settled by calming or familiar music, often first heard within the safety of the womb.

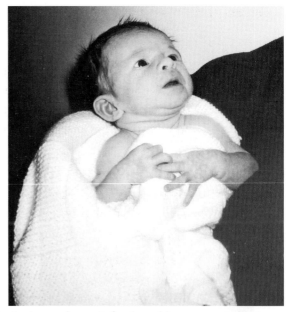

▲ A newborn infant making eye contact

A checklist for auditory development

Concerns regarding hearing would include:

- lack of response to sudden or loud noises in first few months
- lack of response to familiar sounds, either by listening or by being calmed
- no tracking of gentle sounds by 9 months
- no indication of turning to the sound of familiar voice
- limited changes in vocalising from about 6 months
- no obvious response to carers' simple instructions at a year.

From 1 year onwards the development of speech is the greatest indication of how well a child hears, although health problems such as 'glue ear' or repeated ear infections can have an effect on hearing.

Infant perception in general

Perception is the organisation and interpretation of information received from the sensory organs. It helps us to

▼ Stages of visual development

AGE	DEVELOPMENT OF VISION
Birth	Infant turns to the source of light Imitative facial expressions are seen, e.g. poking out the tongue The human face gains the greatest level of an infant's attention An infant's eyes do not at first move cooperatively
1 month	Infant turns to light source Staring at face of an adult carer is usual The eyes are now usually working in cooperation Vision is held by a bright mobile or similar object The infant can visually track their mother's face briefly
3 months	The eyes move in cooperation A defensive blink has been present for some time The infant follows the movement of main carer There is more sustained visual tracking of face or similar Infant may now be demonstrating visual awareness of their own hands
6 months	Infant is visually very alert Infants appear visually insatiable (their eyes fix on anything and everything) Their eyes and head move to track objects of interest
12 months	Hand–eye coordination is seen as small objects are picked up using pincer grasp (index finger and thumb) The infant's eyes follow the correct direction of fallen or dropped objects

Sheridan (1991)

understand all that is happening both to us and around us. Even very young babies can perceive some features of their environment, such as familiar smells and textures, for example their mother's skin. Visual perception and auditory perception are two early indicators that development is progressing as expected. Vision and hearing link directly with language and cognition (understanding), and are both assessed specifically at regular intervals during infancy and early childhood.

Milestones of intellectual development

The text below details the milestones of intellectual development.

Birth to 1 year

- The infant's main source of learning is to explore orally (with their mouth) throughout most of the first year. Jean Piaget (a psychologist) called this the sensorimotor stage.

▼ Stages of auditory development

AGE	DEVELOPMENT OF HEARING
Birth	Startle reactions to sound is normal Blinking is common in response to ongoing gentle sounds The infant turns to sounds, including their mother's voice
1 month	Infant is still startled by sudden noises They stiffen in alarm, extending their limbs They usually turn to sound of a familiar voice Also usually calmed by the sound of a familiar voice
3 months	The infant turns head or eyes towards the source of sounds They often appear to search for location of sounds They listen to musical mobiles and similar sounds
6 months	They now show considerable interest in familiar sounds Infant turns to locate even very gentle sounds Now vocalises deliberately, listening to self Infant vocalises to get attention, listens and then vocalises again Infant can usually imitate sounds in response to carers
12 months	Now responds to own name Infant's behaviour indicates hearing, by appropriate response to carers

Sheridan (1991)

 Practical example

Kos

Kos is 6 months old, and his parents are concerned that he doesn't seem to respond to his environment in the way his older brother did at a similar age.

Kos smiles a lot and visually tracks people, and also toys if shown them first. He makes very little noise apart from crying when his needs are not being met, mostly making cooing sounds.

(1) Do you think Kos's parents are right to be concerned?

(2) If yes, what would concern you about Kos's progress?

(3) How would you expect Kos to be responding at this stage?

- By about 4 months, recognition of an approaching feed is demonstrated by excited actions and squeals.

- By 9–10 months the infant achieves what Piaget called *object permanence*. They know that an object exists even if it has been covered up. For example, they pull a cover off a teddy they have seen hidden to 'find' it again.

- The understanding of simple instructions or statements begins from about 9 months, and this is clearly evident by 1-year-old, for example, 'Wave bye bye to Daddy'.

▲ The infant's main source of learning is to explore orally

Milestones of language development

As with every aspect of development, children develop language at differing rates within what is considered to be the normal range. This process of language development can be divided into 10 basic stages. These stages are as follows:

1 Non-verbal communication/expression
2 Speech-like noises
3 Controlling sounds, using mouth and tongue
4 Imitating sounds
5 First words
6 Development of vocabulary (fifty words is usual at 2 years)
7 Putting words together to form simple phrases and sentences
8 Use of grammar
9 Use of meaning
10 Using language to develop other skills, for example, early literacy.

Speech sounds

Speech sounds in the English language are made up of consonants and vowels. The approximate sequential development of consonants in the English language is as follows:

- At age 2 years – m, n, p, b, t, d, w
- At 2½ years – k, g, ng (as in sing), h
- At 2½–3 years – f, s, l, y
- At 3½–4 years – v, z, ch, j, sh
- At 4½ years onwards – th (as in thin), th (as in the), r.

Double consonants such as sp, tr and fl and also the sounds r and th, can develop as late as 6½ years in some children.

FAST FACT

You will see from the above that the initial sound of the 'first words' a baby most usually hears are the earliest consonant sounds mastered, e.g. mum mum mum, bababa, dadada.

▼ Stages of language development

AGE	UNDERSTANDING	NO. OF WORDS	TYPE OF WORDS	AVERAGE LENGTH OF SENTENCE
3 months	Soothed by sound	0	Cooing and gurgling	0
6 months	Responds to voice tones	0	Babble	0
1 year	Knows own name and a few others	1	Noun (naming word)	1 word
18 months	Understands simple commands	6–20	Nouns + gobbledegook	1 word
2 years	Understands much more than they can say	50+	Verbs and pronouns (action + name)	1–2 word phrases
2½ years	Enjoys simple and familiar stories	200+	Pronouns: I, me, you Questions: What? Where?	2–3 word phrases
3 years	Carries out complex commands	500–1,000	Plurals Verbs in present tense Questions: Who?	3–4 word phrases
4 years	Listens to long stories	1,000–1,500	Verbs in past tense Questions: Why? Where? How?	4–5 word sentences
5 years	Developing the ability to reason	1,500–2,000	Complex sentences with adult forms of grammar	5–6 word phrases

Communicating with babies

It is important to have an understanding of how to communicate with babies in order to interpret their needs and respond to them.

Communication between human beings, whatever their ages involves:

- facial expressions
- tone of voice
- body posture
- expression of meaning through the use of both words and symbols.

Language development is also affected by all other aspects of our development. For example, socially and intellectually, an understanding of the need to interact with others as a means of communication is vital, as are the physical abilities of vision, hearing and speech. Without these, it can be difficult for language to develop normally.

Sequence of communication development

The 10 main stages of language development, through which most infants pass, were set out on page 562, together with a table on page 563 illustrating how and when the first words are produced, the type of words that appear first, i.e. nouns before verbs and pronouns, and how these develop into phrases and the asking of questions. You may find it helpful to remind yourself of these sequences before you read on.

How and why babies communicate from birth

Communication with babies can be both verbal and non-verbal. Pre-verbal communication is a vital part of supporting an infant's future language skills. It is seen as the adult encourages the baby to take a turn in the conversation, asking them questions and supplying them with answers or making reaffirming comments following a pause in which the infant adds their own vocalisations. Welcoming the vocal sounds of babies encourages them to vocalise further.

Babies are born ready to communicate and they respond from birth to both voice and touch, quickly recognising their main carers.

GOOD PRACTICE

Taking time to observe an adult with a young baby will give you an example of how you too can 'converse' with a baby in their earliest weeks.

Pre-verbal stage

When you spend time with a young baby you will find that talking to them and watching them respond to you will automatically encourage and enhance their communication with you. This 'turn-taking' between carer and infant was identified in the 1970s by Stern who put forward the theory that infants learn the basis of their social interactions in this way.

Motherese

The term 'motherese' is given to what we often call 'baby talk'. Motherese speech:

- has a higher pitch than that used with other people
- is slower, with simplified words and phrases usually being employed
- includes frequent pauses, to facilitate the turn-taking
- mostly consists of key words linked to the current situation, for example, naming words if playing jointly with a toy (nouns), or action words (verbs) when moving the infant or referring to a specific action.

Examples could include 'Here is teddy' or 'Up you come for a cuddle'.

Adults communicate with babies in many ways. These are some of the most important ones:

- eye contact during breast or formula feeds
- turn-taking vocally or visually
- initiating 'conversations' with babies as you play
- observing babies' needs through their body language or facial expression
- responding to their cries
- encouraging them to vocalise

- showing appreciation of their vocalising
- giving praise
- calling to them when out of their visual range
- stimulating them aurally
- stimulating them visually.

Responding to pre-verbal speech

Babies may become distressed for many reasons. It might be because they are tired, wet, hungry, uncomfortable, unwell, teething or simply bored. It is not always easy to work out what is the cause of their distress. If a young baby is distressed at the same time of day, every day, it can often be attributed to a condition known as colic. Mostly, when a baby cries, they are trying to tell us something.

G☺☺D PRACTICE · · · · · · ·

Sometimes babies will simply want a drink in the same way as adults and older children do. Small amounts of cooled boiled water can be given to even very young babies, especially in hot weather.
   Babies are best dressed in layers of lightweight clothing that can be taken off or added to as necessary.

FAST FACT

Every baby is different. Each baby has their own individual personality. Some babies cry much more than others. It is possible to overstimulate a baby, tiring them and causing irritability. Illness must never be ruled out, but will usually be considered when other causes have been eliminated unless additional symptoms are present. Offer support to parents of a constantly crying baby as it can be very draining.

✏️ Practical example

Mary

Mary works in the baby room. She is preparing a formula feed for William, who is 6 months old. William is in his chair, and Mary is currently out of his line of vision as she gets his bottle ready. She calls to him in a sing-song voice, pausing to hear him make a noise in response, before calling him again. When she brings his feed to him, Mary takes him out of his chair and cuddles him on her lap while he is fed. He watches her face, and she smiles at him, talking quietly to him all the time.

① Which forms of communication listed above do you consider that Mary used?

② Do you think there were opportunities for any other form of communication to have taken place?

③ What might be the outcome for a baby who does not have opportunities for communication?

G☺☺D PRACTICE · · · · · · ·

It can be useful to find out about support groups such as 'Cry-sis', collecting copies of their information that could be given to parents or carers of a regularly distressed infant.

I'm too hot
A baby who is too hot or too cool may also cry in discomfort. Adjusting the temperature of the room or their clothing will usually help

My tummy hurts
If a baby is distressed at the same time of day every day, it can often be attributed to colic. Colic is a painful condition, common in the first 4 months, in which the baby pulls up their legs indicating abdominal pain and is very difficult to console. There is no known cause for colic and it tends to disappear by itself by the time the baby reaches 4 months old. It is, however, distressing for both baby and carer and advice from a health visitor is advisable. The baby is usually thriving well in spite of the colic and no other symptoms are displayed

I'm tired
Babies become over-tired if they do not have sufficient periods of restful sleep, and a baby who is constantly disturbed may become irritable. It is important to allow babies an extended period of sleep whenever possible

My gums hurt
If a baby is unwell or teething, they may simply want to be cuddled. For a teething baby, a refrigerated teething ring will help cool down their gums and firm flexible teething toys will give them something appropriate to chew hard on. Preparations are available to rub on to the gums to alleviate discomfort of the gums and paediatric paracetamol can be given in times of extreme discomfort

Why is the baby crying?

I want my nappy changed
A wet or soiled nappy is uncomfortable, and most babies prefer to be clean and dry. Regular changing of babies helps prevent the development of nappy rash, as does allowing fresh air to their bottoms by leaving them to kick freely at some point each day

I want my bottle
A hungry or thirsty baby is often the easiest to identify as they tend to root for the breast or bottle when picked up or suck on whatever passes their mouth. In a daycare setting, making a note of the time and amount of feed taken by the baby helps you to anticipate their next feed time and is a general requirement of those caring for babies

I'm so bored
Sometimes, however, babies are simply bored, and so it is important to offer them stimulation. Mobiles over the cot or hanging from the ceiling are ideal visual stimulants and musical toys will stimulate them aurally. Babies also enjoy the company of their carers and will respond with pleasure and recognition from a very early age

Please leave me alone
Sometimes babies become distressed when being handled, but this is usually a stage that passes quickly. Handling should be gentle and kept to a minimum until they find it more pleasurable

▲ Babies become distressed for lots of reasons

Have a go!

Describe three situations you have observed where a baby or young child has been distressed.

- What, if any, signs did they give before hand?
- How was their distress dealt with?
- Would you have done anything different?
- What have you learned from these examples about interpreting and responding to needs?

Remember that:

- By about 4 months recognition of an approaching feed is demonstrated by excited actions and squeals. This is communication.
- Language develops through cooing, gurgling, excited squealing and changing tones of their own voice.
- By five months enjoyment of the infant's own voice is obvious. Chuckles and laughs are evident.
- By about 8 months the infant babbles continuously and tunefully, for example mamamama, babababa.
- First 'words' may be apparent by a year, usually dada, mama, baba.
- Understanding of simple instructions or statements begins from about 9 months, and is clearly evident by a year (see table on page 493).

Communication development through bonding

Forming a bond is a child's secure two-way relationship with a parent or regular carer.

GOOD PRACTICE

During your placement experience you will notice differences in speech, questioning and grammar of children at different ages and stages. You will probably notice that some children will be quite advanced in their speech, but are perhaps less skilled physically, or that a very physical child may communicate less well. This demonstrates how very few children are 'advanced' in all developmental areas.

One very pleasurable way of developing a bond with a baby is through baby massage.

Baby massage

Baby massage is a popular and important means of communication between an adult and a baby, as it enhances the adult's understanding of the baby's needs. Baby massage involves eye contact, touch, smiling and, other pleasurable facial expressions, and, as it involves such close contact, interaction between parent and baby, or carer and baby, is heightened. Baby massage is also used by therapists to help mothers who are suffering from post-natal depression. It strengthens their contact with their baby and encourages the bonding process.

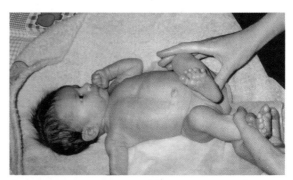

▲ Baby massage provides a means of communication between baby and parent

▼ An example of the language development of an infant

AGE	UNDERSTANDING	NO. OF WORDS	TYPE OF WORDS OR SOUNDS	AVERAGE LENGTH OF SENTENCE
3 months	Calmed by Mummy's voice and by music (e.g. Pachelbel's Canon and Sinead O'Connor)	0	Chuckles , coos and gurgles conversationally, turn-taking with adults	0
6 months	Responds to familiar voices	0	Babbles almost incessantly, mainly using the sounds 'ummm' and 'yi yi yi'	0
12 months	Knows own name and a few others	2	'In air?' (Who's in there? or What's that), 'dor' (dog), 'hooray'	1 word
18 months	Repeats her own new word – 'gollygollygolly' and understands 'car' and 'duck'	8	Nouns plus gobbledegook	1 word
2 years	Understands much of what is said to her. Enjoys simple and familiar stories	Approximately 120, some clear, others less so	Verbs and pronouns, e.g. 'Mummy fine it' (Mummy find it), 'Daddy a gate' (Daddy's opening/shutting the gate'), 'boon in sky' (the hot air balloon is in the sky)	2–3 word phrases, e.g. 'bean a sausee' (beans and sausages), 'cackers a chee' (crackers and cheese), 'socks a pink' (the socks are pink)

Green (2004a)

Baby signing

Baby signing is another form of communication. In some early years settings, signing with babies is a new strategy being developed, but always with the agreement of the babies' parents. There are programmes to help train staff and parents, and the thinking behind it is that, during the pre-verbal stage, the infant can make themselves understood more easily by using a simple sign indicating that they need a drink, or wish to go to sleep, etc. This communication aid may help avoid some of the frustration felt by infants who are unable to make themselves understood.

Signed languages

There are a range of languages using signs and visual aids. These can help build up a channel of communication for babies, children (and adults) of any age who are unable to communicate verbally, or who find verbal communication very difficult. Makaton, Bliss Symbols and the PECs system can be used from a very young age.

Have a go!

Produce a chart to describe the different methods of communicating with babies that you have observed in your placement.

Problems with communication

Barriers to communication can be social, emotional or cultural. You will need to be aware of each of the ones shown on page 570 and how they can potentially prevent communication taking place.

When communication breaks down for a child they will often only be able to express this through actions; the tantrums that are often seen during the toddler stage are linked to the frustrations of not being able to communicate fully. You will need to find appropriate ways of managing undesirable behaviour and encouraging emotional development.

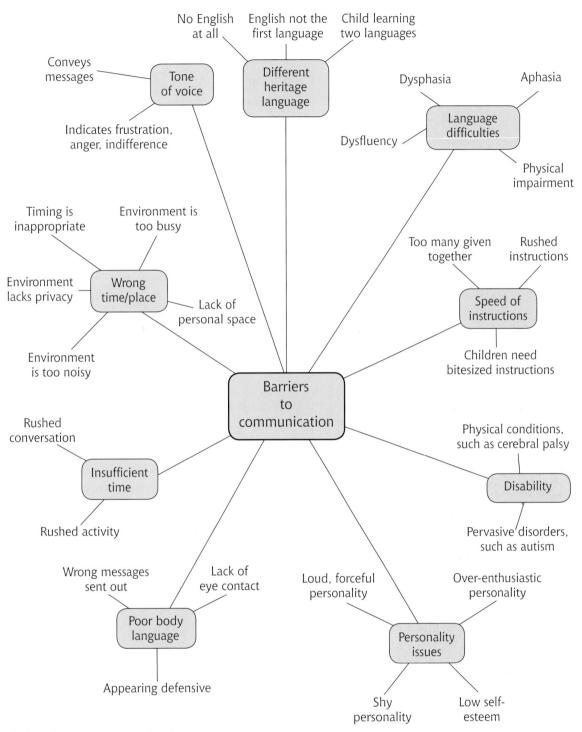

▲ Barriers to communication

Have a go!

Consider the list below of ideas aimed at enhancing communication:

● Which encourage one-to-one communication?

● Which encourage communication with others?

● Which encourage communicating, and which encourage listening?

● How can you identify when understanding has taken place?

- Greet babies as they arrive, and give both a verbal and non-verbal farewell too.
- Read stories and share poems as a group, enjoying excitement and outcomes together. Even quite young babies will enjoy this.
- Sing or say rhymes such as 'heads, shoulders, knees and toes', helping babies to make simple relevant gestures.
- Play rocking games such as 'row, row your boat'.
- Use descriptive terms when eating (yummy), bathing (splish, splash).
- Play music and encourage moving to it.
- Make eye contact, especially during one-to-one activities.
- Talk, smile and use physical contact such as tickling during care routines.
- Whisper during one-to-one times, at the start of story reading or perhaps when putting to bed.
- Join in with games and laughter.
- Describe for babies what they are seeing, hearing or feeling.
- Provide instruments and encourage older babies to make simple differentiated sounds, e.g. loud and soft, short and long.

GOOD PRACTICE

Whenever you are with babies, take as many opportunities as you can to build your communications with them. You will find out more of what they enjoy and will be able to enhance their enjoyment further. The infants will feel valued and wanted, knowing that adults enjoy being with and talking with them. Many children lack opportunities at home simply to chat. Early years settings can help fill that gap for them, building on their confidence as communicators from the earliest ages.

Factors influencing the health of the newborn

Before birth

Any woman planning to have a baby needs to consider the factors that can potentially affect the development of a foetus. These include the following:

● Diet and exercise – the fitter and healthier the mother is, the better it will be for her child.

● The inclusion of supplements in her diet, such as taking folic acid daily – this is recommended before becoming pregnant, and up to 12 weeks into pregnancy to help prevent problems with what is known as neural tube development. The neural tube is divided into three layers:

- the endoderm which provides the lungs, stomach and intestines
- the mesoderm which provides the heart, blood, bones and other 'sinewy' bits
- the ectoderm which provides the skin, the brain and the nerves.

The most well-known neural tube problem is Spina bifida.

The stability of her relationship and social life – a woman struggling to cope on her own or dealing with relationship difficulties is more likely to be stressed, and stress can impact on her health, therefore potentially on her unborn child's health too.

Smoking – all women should give up smoking, ideally before they become pregnant as this can restrict foetal growth and birth weight, and increase the risk of respiratory problems and also learning difficulties.

Alcohol – pregnant women are advised to avoid alcohol as it can affect development, causing developmental delay, deformities and learning difficulties. Foetal alcohol syndrome can result from a mother continuing to drink alcohol throughout her pregnancy.

Drug use – any non-essential drugs should be avoided during pregnancy. Pregnant women should always take advice before taking any medication, even cough and cold remedies. Doctors prescribe medication cautiously, and a woman who takes medication for a life-long condition (e.g for epilepsy) may need to have her medication changed, or the dose altered, during her pregnancy. Illegal drugs such as crack cocaine cause low birth weight, developmental delay, significant distress to infants at birth, and ongoing development problems and, sometimes, epilepsy.

Job role and health – i.e. the likelihood of coming into contact with German measles which can affect the development of a foetus

Age and antenatal status of the mother

A mother over the age of 35 runs a greater risk of having a child with a chromosomal condition such as Down's syndrome.

A range of routine tests are carried out during pregnancy, with additional tests available for older mothers and those considered to be at a higher risk due to previous antenatal history or family history.

These tests are described in Unit 14, pags 361–362.

At times, the number of pregnancies a woman has had can mean that an infant is at greater risk due to 'wear and tear' on her uterine muscles. The number of pregnancies and deliveries a woman has had is usually noted on her ante-natal record.

A woman who experiences problems with blood pressure and oedema (swelling of feet, ankles, etc.) is at risk of developing pre-eclampsia in the later stages of pregnancy. This can be very serious for both mother and infant. The mother is hospitalised and confined to bed, and is monitored carefully.

During birth

Birth is exciting, painful and often exhausting for the mother. It is also likely to be the infant's most dangerous journey. Birth can be either completely natural, with the mother finding the position which is most comfortable for her and managing to deliver her baby without medication, or possibly with just a little gas and air. Contrastingly, medical intervention may be needed to help deliver an infant who gets stuck, turns awkwardly, or when either mother or infant is running out of strength. Interventions include the following:

Epidural – anaesthesia via an injection or through the continuous administration by catheter, usually in the lumbar region of the spine, provides pain relief and can be used for non-emergency caesareans too.

- Forceps delivery – the infant is eased from the womb with a flat tong-shaped tool. This can sometimes leave the infant's face bruised or a little distorted. It will re-shape itself within a few days.

- Ventouse suction delivery – the infant is delivered by the creation of a vacuum through attaching a disc-shaped cup to the infant's skull, and drawing the air out via a pumping action, in time with the mother's contractions. Infants can be left with an elongated head shape and bruising. This settles down and realigns itself within a few days or weeks.

- Caesarean section delivery – the delivery of the infant is through an incision made in the abdominal wall if the infant is considered to be too large for a vaginal delivery, or if there is foetal distress or trauma, or the infant presents awkwardly (e.g. a breech birth). In a planned caesarean trauma is not usual, but in an emergency caesarean delivery, the infant will sometimes need additional care immediately following birth.

After birth

Immediately after birth most infants are checked and attended to according to their Apgar score (see above). Some may need a little oxygen, or are rubbed and massaged to stimulate them. They are also usually given (with parental permission) vitamin K, either orally, or via an injection. Vitamin K helps to prevent a rare, but very dangerous condition called 'neonatal haemorrhage'.

Infants are monitored daily by a midwife, within the hospital, or by a community midwife once mother and infant have returned home. They monitor:

- weight
- muscle tone
- the consistency and colour of the baby's stools

- the passing of urine
- head circumference
- general appearance
- how feeding is progressing.

Before leaving hospital, or being handed over to the care of the community health visitor, the infant will be carefully examined, to check:

- their reflexes
- the heart, to ensure it sounds clear
- the mouth to ensure the palate is intact
- that the hips rotate properly and joints are secure
- that the spine looks healthy and straight
- the abdomen, to ensure that all the internal organs feel appropriate both in size and position.

At around day seven, infants have a blood sample taken from the heel. This is commonly known as the Guthrie test. It checks for a rare inherited disorder called phenylketonuria (PKU) which can be treated if identified early and managed through a very restricted diet. Without treatment, learning difficulties and skin problems occur.

Together with the Guthrie test, blood is also tested for thyroid stimulating hormone (TSH). If the result is positive the infant will need to take a hormone supplement throughout life to manage the TSH levels.

If all is well, the care of the infant is handed over to the community health visitor who provides support and advice for parents throughout early childhood.

Premature and multiple births

Infants born before 37 weeks of pregnancy are considered to be premature or **pre-term**. An infant who is born at the expected time, but is of lower than average weight, is referred to as being 'light for dates'.

The average birth weight in the developed world is 3.175 kg (7 lb) for a girl and 3.4 kg (7½ lb) for a boy.

Multiple births usually occur before full term, and many deliveries are through planned caesareans. Most multiple births are of twins, but since the 1970s there have been higher numbers of triplets due to fertility interventions such as in-vitro fertilisation (IVF).

Twins can be monozygotic (identical) or dizygotic (non-identical). Monozygotic twins share the same placenta. The fertilised egg splits into two and each half becomes a separate baby. Dyzigotic twins result from the fertilisation of two eggs at the same time. They develop as a single infant would, each with their own placenta.

Prematurity is the main problem facing multiples. If they are born too early, their lungs may not be fully functioning, causing breathing and other difficulties. Many multiples need to be cared for initially in the neonatal care unit. There is a higher risk of death in smaller infants, premature infants, and multiple-birth infants.

Infant deaths

Sadly, a small number of infants still die each year despite the advanced levels of medical interventions available. They are recorded according to the stage at which they died:

- Stillbirth: any infant who dies before birth and after the 24th week of pregnancy is termed stillborn.
- Perinatal death: this term is used to describe an infant whose death occurs within one week of birth. It officially includes all infants who have been stillborn.

- Neonatal death: this term is used to describe an infant who has died within the first 28 days following birth.
- Post-neonatal death: this term is used to describe any infant who dies following the 28th day after birth, but before they reach their first birthday.

Factors influencing development in the first year of a child's life

Infections in pregnancy may also affect the developing embryo/foetus and, although some infections cannot be prevented, there are known sources of infection that can be avoided. This is especially relevant to the first trimester of pregnancy when the embryo is particularly vulnerable to infection.

- Rubella (German measles) is the most well-known example and, if transmitted to a nonrubella-immune woman, can result in a baby with sensory impairments and congenital heart disease.
- HIV may be transmitted to the developing baby via the placenta, resulting in HIV-positive status for the newborn and the resulting disease process, although this appears to be more likely if the mother shows signs of Aids during pregnancy.
- Cytomegalovirus is a virus in the herpes group that can lead to severe learning problems, delayed physical and motor skills, and problems with the liver.
- Toxoplasmosis is a parasitic infection which, if contracted in pregnancy, can lead to visual impairment, damage to the central nervous system, seizure disorders and learning difficulties.
- Listeriosis is caused by a pathogen found in food, soil, vegetation and water

and may be present in some packaged and raw foodstuffs. It can be the cause of premature labour.

Genetic effects and genetic disorders

Each chromosome in the human body is made up of thousands of genes, and our genetic inheritance is determined by the influences and combination of the genes present in the chromosomes of our parents. The term 'genotype' is used to describe the complete genetic inheritance of one person, and the term 'phenotype' refers to the visible arrangement of the characteristics the person has inherited.

Genetically inherited disorders can be due to either autosomal recessive, autosomal dominant or X-linked transference. There are many other disorders that occur following conception; these are termed congenital disorders. Congenital disorders differ from genetically inherited disorders in that their origin is not from the gene bank of the parents.

Autosomal recessive disorder

This type of disorder can occur when both parents are carriers of the defective recessive gene. There is a one-in-four chance of offspring being affected, and a two-in-four chance of their being carriers. Disorders include Batten's disease, cystic fibrosis, phenylketonuria (PKU), sickle cell anaemia and thalassaemia.

Autosomal dominant disorder

This disorder occurs when the carrier is also affected by the disorder. If one parent is an affected carrier, there is a two-in-four chance of the offspring also being affected. If both parents are affected carriers, the incidence rises to a three-in-four chance. Disorders include Huntington's chorea,

Marfan's syndrome and osteogenesis imperfect (brittle bones).

X-linked disorders

The X-linked disorders are carried on the X chromosomes of the mother. As the mother has two X chromosomes, the defective X acts in a recessive way in female offspring and in a dominant way in males, making male offspring more likely to be affected than females. X-linked disorders include Duchenne muscular dystrophy, fragile-X syndrome, haemophilia and Lowe's syndrome.

 Refer to Unit 14 for more information about conditions that affect development.

Recognising developmental delay or sensory impairment

The potential for a delay in development or sensory loss may already have been identified through standard antenatal monitoring procedures, following a low Apgar score achieved immediately after birth and any subsequent specialised care needed, or through neonatal screening practices. These infants will automatically be followed up more thoroughly. Growth and weight concerns are identified by the plotting of weight, length and head circumference on percentile charts, usually by a health visitor. Any infant who is found to be measuring outside the parameters within which 80 per cent of infants usually fall will be followed carefully. This also applies to infants whose measurements cross two percentile lines, outside the usual growth patterns. Concerns regarding vision and hearing are important 'triggers' for investigation, as would be an infant who simply fails to respond or has a marked lack of muscle tone.

Refer back to pages 483 and 484 for vision and hearing loss concerns.

Theoretical perspectives on development

Importance of attachment and understanding temperament

The most important theoretical perspectives for you to understand regarding infants of up to 1 year old are those of bonding, attachment and temperament. Attachment and bonding is about the relationship that builds up between an infant and their primary carer or carers as they identify and respond to their needs. Bonding develops during the close physical contact of care routines, play and cuddling, with emotions deepening as the contact progresses.

Some infants will always demonstrate a greater pleasure and need for cuddling and close contact. These infants tend to calm more easily and are therefore 'easier' to respond to and care for. However, if

infants are less responsive to cuddling and close contact, other strategies to calm and respond to them are needed, for example through increased carer vocalisations.

Both an individual infant's temperament and the emotional status of the mother or primary carer can impact on how the infant develops, through:

- the levels of contact between them
- the sensitivity of the mother/primary carer to the infant's needs
- the responsiveness of the infant to care routines and attention.

G☺☺D PRACTICE

It is important to find the best way to interact with each infant as an individual. The way in which you care for and respond to one infant is likely to be quite different from how you behave to the next. Identifying and responding appropriately to these differences is part of your role as a professional.

Refer also to Unit 1, pages 25–27, for a more in-depth coverage of these important theories.

✓ Progress check

1. What primitive reflexes can you name and explain?
2. What is perception?
3. When would you become concerned that a child's hearing might be impaired?
4. When would you become concerned that a child's vision might be impaired?
5. What does the Apgar score measure?
6. Explain these developmental terms: 'simple to complex', 'cephalo to caudal', 'proximal to distal' and 'general to specific'.
7. Which birth mark is only found on dark-skinned infants?
8. Which fontanelle closes by 18 months of age?
9. Why are black infants usually pale at birth?
10. What is meant by the terms 'bonding', 'attachment' and 'temperament'?

FOCUS ON...

the role of the professional in promoting development

This links to assessment criteria **2.1** and **2.2**

Working in partnership with parents/carers and families

Every parent wants to know how well their child is settling into their early years setting. They want to hear how they are developing, what they enjoy doing, who they enjoy being with and also about anything that becomes a problem. Developmental milestones need to be dealt with sensitively. For example, a parent does not wish to hear that they have missed their child's first steps (they will no doubt see this 'miracle' for themselves within a day or so), but will appreciate hearing how responsive the child has been, how they have recognised carers, shown pleasure at routines and activities, mastered control of a toy, or smiled at others, etc.

Each setting needs a procedure for two-way communication between parent and staff. This enables vital information regarding health, dietary needs, routines and any significant event in an infant's life to be shared. The sharing of such information provides the basis for each individual infant's needs to be fully met.

An infant's key worker will be the main person to keep parents informed and updated. It is important that any communication with a parent is kept as positive as possible. If it becomes necessary to discuss distress, or later on there is the difficult issue of managing tantrums or unacceptable behaviour, it is helpful if praise can at first be given for what the child has done well.

It is the responsibility of the setting to arrange regular feedback to parents about their child. For some settings this will take place on a daily basis, usually at collection time. In other settings a home/setting book enables written comments to be added each day, and provides two-way communication with parents, helping them to notify carers of any potential problems (such as with teething, or a family crisis resulting in interrupted sleep), or concerns they may have (e.g. the infant is suddenly very clingy although usually quite sociable).

The role of play in development

Identifying and choosing play activities

Play and learning go hand in hand. Babies and young children learn through exploration, and that exploration is their play. From the moment an infant finds their toes, or waves their fingers in front of their face, they are starting to play. The turn-taking exchanges of vocalising and visual focusing are all early play. The infant explores through each of their senses.

As an early years practitioner you will need to provide a range of stimulating experiences for the babies and toddlers within your care. This does not necessitate expensive toys and resources. Many stimulating opportunities are found within the home or care environment and through the responses of the adults caring for the child. It is important to remember that the adults in a child's life are also a vital resource. They each offer knowledge, skills and experience drawn from their own upbringing, education and general experiences within life.

This part of the unit sets out a range of ideas for stimulating young infants. There are, of course, many, many more, and as your practical experience grows you will build up a mental list, including an assortment of resource ideas and activities; some need forward planning, but many offer spontaneous entertainment and stimulation. Finding new ideas is an area of practice that you will find never ends. Practitioners who have many years' experience still continue to discover fresh ideas or new ways of doing things.

G☺☺D PRACTICE · · · · · · ·

It should be remembered that all activities and resources must meet safety standards and be checked, cared for and replaced according to the practice of the setting. Risk assessment procedures help to identify any potential problems in advance, providing the time to withdraw items or adjust the age group they are offered to. Remember! Items suitable for a 3-year-old child are unlikely to meet safe care practices for a baby.

Refer to Unit 4 page 151, for guidance on safety marks and symbols.

Activities need to be carefully thought through for the baby or child being cared for. As a general guide the selection of activities and/or resources offered should:

- be appropriate for the age and stage of their development
- be stimulating
- hold attention
- provide **challenge**, but with achievable outcomes
- provide opportunities for making choices

As a carer you should:

- plan for each infant and provide suitable resources and activities to meet their needs
- supervise and observe the individual infant's responses to help inform your planning for them for the future
- encourage them to explore new items, and at times present resources in different ways to help the infant explore from a different perspective
- give praise and show delight in their discoveries
- support their development by at times modelling the use of unfamiliar resources or activities.

G☺☺D PRACTICE · · · · · · ·

Children respond well to praise and encouragement, and this applies to babies too. When interacting with babies you can make them feel wanted and valued as people by remembering to:

- give them your full attention
- mimic their actions, showing pleasure
- make eye contact with them
- offer objects to them and accept objects when they offer them to you.

Challenge = experience that will help develop a skill or aspect of learning

Planning a suitable environment

Babies and toddlers need sensory experiences, so it is important to ensure that each sensory area is considered in turn and resourced accordingly. What follows are some suggestions for sensory play.

To encourage *visual* experiences (sight) try providing:

- three-dimensional mobiles
- safety mirrors
- bubble tubes
- bubbles for blowing
- balloons and streamers.

To encourage *tactile* experiences (touch) try providing:

- textured mats and 'surprise' bags
- natural wooden items
- messy play, such as finger-painting
- silk scarves and hankies
- malleable play, such as water, sand and dough
- blocks and cotton reels.

To encourage *auditory* experiences (hearing) try providing:

- wind chimes
- music boxes
- rattles, shakers and bells
- objects to bang (box and spoon)
- music to listen to and bounce, jiggle, clap and wave to.

To encourage *olfactory* experiences (smell) try providing:

- wooden items permeated with smells such as lavender or lemon
- bags of herbs, lavender or flowers
- scented tissues inside a box or cloth bag
- citrus fruit (changed regularly).

To encourage *oral* experiences (taste and touch) try providing:

- hard objects in different shapes
- squashy objects made from various materials
- spoons and cups
- 'feely' books
- textured mats.

▲ Different sensory areas must be considered

Have a go!

Select five play items or experiences each from a baby setting you are familiar with, and consider which senses each item or experience will stimulate.

When planning play for babies and toddlers an important consideration is the positioning of visual stimuli around the room. Because of the different physical stages of a baby's development, they need visual stimulation when they are:

- lying on their backs (supine)
- lying on their tummies (prone)
- sitting, either propped up with cushions or in a chair
- moving around.

Visual stimulation is therefore needed on a range of levels to meet the changing needs of babies and toddlers at different stages in their development. Try lying down on the floor to see the room from the viewpoint of the baby. How good or how limited is your vision?

You could try positioning items of interest:

- at skirting-board level (for example, safety mirrors)
- on windows and on walls (for example, pictures, designs, areas of colour)
- on the wall behind and immediately above a sofa (a great place for a safety mirror)
- as objects hanging from ceilings (mobiles, balloons and wind chimes are favourites)
- as attachments to prams, cots, highchairs, etc. (for example, music boxes, soft toys and wobbly objects).

Providing activities to meet the needs of babies

From around the age of 6 weeks babies benefit from an activity frame or something similar that can be placed above them. This will encourage them to focus visually and aurally on the items hanging in front of them and they can enjoy tactile experiences too, as they come into contact with the items during their natural body movements. Eventually, these movements become more intentional, and repeated actions will be observed, often in response to the 'reward' of a noise or visual 'experience' (movement, reflection or fluttering of material). Bath time or when having their nappy changed gives babies opportunities to play free from the restriction of clothes and with full leg mobility, which should be encouraged whenever possible.

▲ An activity frame encourages babies to focus visually and aurally

Outdoors

Babies enjoy being outside watching the leaves on trees fluttering and taking in the sounds and smells of the garden. Fresh air is good for them, although they should never be left unsupervised. Care should be taken to ensure that prams are not positioned in the sun, as a baby's delicate skin burns extremely easily. Whenever possible allow a baby to lie out of doors in warm weather without a nappy on, as exposure of the nappy area to fresh air is healthy and stimulating for the skin too. Although most professionals agree that taking a baby out each day is a good idea, this does not apply if the weather is particularly cold, or is foggy.

Stimulating play for older babies

As they develop, older babies will be interested in a range of household articles. Sturdy boxes can be handled easily, being passed from hand to hand from about 6 months onwards and knocked together as manipulative control is developed. They will also enjoy banging things in order to make a noise. A useful item for this is a wooden spoon on a saucepan lid or the tray of the high chair. Babies enjoy activities that enable them to explore by themselves through all of their senses. An excellent resource for this is a treasure basket.

Treasure baskets

Infants from about 6 months of age will enjoy exploring a treasure basket. Ideally babies need to be able to sit up securely in order to benefit from the freedom to explore. A treasure basket includes a range of objects that are made of natural materials and can be easily handled by the infant. They should be selected carefully to stimulate all the senses, and they should be completely safe. The infant should be allowed to focus on the objects they are handling without distraction from the adult or older children. Nothing in a treasure basket should be made of plastic or any synthetic materials.

The original treasure basket principle can be extended to providing baskets of items of a particular type. Examples could be shiny objects, furry objects, sparkly objects, metal objects, etc.

Stimulating play for young toddlers

A few infants are already toddling by their first birthday. These early toddlers enjoy a range of play activities, from developing new ways of playing with their 'baby' toys, through to exploring the range of activities also enjoyed by the slightly older toddlers. Early encounters with activities such as sand, paint, model making, clay, construction materials, etc. will often highlight the limitations of their manipulative dexterity, their creativeness, and at times their confidence in trying new experiences, compared with older toddlers. The adult role here is to provide opportunities, encourage the child's participation in their own time at a level they are secure with and, as they get older, to model actions and make successful (and unsuccessful) attempts at achieving voiced intentions for them. As with all aspects of development, children progress at different rates.

Popular activities and resources for toddlers include:

- push along toys, e.g. brick trolley, dog on wheels
- pull along toys, e.g. caterpillar, train
- climbing frames, tunnels and trikes

- resources to support mimicry of real life, such as telephones, tea sets, shopping bags
- dolls, dolls' clothes and bedding
- books
- simple to handle construction materials, e.g. Sticklebricks or Megablocks.

Linking play to development

Understanding which areas of development are supported by which activities comes with experience. Sometimes it is obvious, for example providing creative play with crayons and pencils clearly helps manipulation skills, and encouraging play on climbing frames, through tunnels and generally running around, clearly helps large motor skills to develop: but it is much more complex than that. Most activities offer stimulation and support for more than one development area. Look at the example opposite and consider how many areas of development are involved in this one play experience.

Earliest toys

Early toys include:

- soft toys to cuddle
- soft toys that hang from prams, cots and mobiles
- three-dimensional mobiles
- those that help with teething, e.g. made from rubber or moulded plastic
- sound makers, e.g. toys with rattles, shakers, bells
- textured items, e.g. toys that have parts to scrunch, feel, stroke
- those that offer instant reactions, e.g. rainmakers, wind-up musical toys.

Each of the above items helps to stimulate the senses of an infant.

Practical example

Oomah

Oomah, aged 9 months, loves to play 'peepbo'. He hides his face in cushions, 'popping up' with a big smile; he crawls behind curtains and 'appears' laughing (physical skills), and he hides behind chairs and sofas waiting to be found.

Oomah is using cognitive (intellectual) skills in his understanding of where and how to hide. He is communicating (language development) through smiles, laughs and body language. Oomah's game is social, because he is enjoying responses both to and from others, and these responses boost his feeling of being loved and wanted, i.e. his emotional development and the building of his self-esteem.

1. What other simple games can you think of to clearly demonstrate areas of development and learning?

2. How could you further reinforce Oomah's learning in the above example?

GOOD PRACTICE

Remember that many 'toys' can be found around the home. For example:

- silk scarves and satin ribbons can stimulate the skin if gently stoked across by an adult
- empty cotton reels on a shoe lace provide both visual and auditory stimulation.

Activities to support development as the infant grows

Sometimes it is easy to see the learning value of activities and toys: for example, a push-along dog clearly helps the development of balance and walking in toddlers. Sometimes, however, the learning value is less obvious. The following pages show a few examples of popular activities, noting the support they give to different aspects of children's development.

 Refer also to Unit 7, pages 284–285, for more activities.

The activities here are set out under the following headings:

- social development
- emotional development
- physical development
- intellectual development
- language development.

Construction play

Social development

This is supported by:

- developing confidence in selecting resources
- sharing resources with others
- negotiating exchanges of resources
- asking (or indicating) and responding to requests
- building, using own ideas from observations of their own environment (older toddlers).

Emotional development

This is supported by:

- showing satisfaction with own achievements
- showing frustration and disappointment if their intentions fail.

▲ Construction play and physical development

Physical development

This is supported by:

- handling resources with increasing confidence and skill
- manipulative skills development with smaller construction pieces
- precision and increased ability to place pieces carefully
- large motor skills development when using large boxes, tables, chairs, etc.
- use of senses to explore shape and texture, e.g. Sticklebricks, Megablocks.

Intellectual development

This is supported by:

- increasing ability to understand how pieces fit together
- development of planning and intention
- increasing understanding of stability and strength
- increasing understanding of weight and height
- increasing understanding of the differences between resources

- increasing ability to select and group pieces together by size, shape, colour, etc.
- opportunities to develop sustained concentration.

Language development (older toddlers)

This is supported by:

- development of new words and terminology, e.g. build, together, on top of
- describing intentions e.g. 'there'
- adult and/or infant vocalising ideas and actions.

Sand play

Social development

This is supported by:

- playing alongside or with others
- development of the ability to interact
- imitating the actions of others
- passing and exchanging tools and resources.

Emotional development

- Sand can be a soothing experience.
- Sand can be a very satisfying experience.
- It is a safe, non-fail activity – you cannot play with sand 'wrong'.
- Child develops confidence in interacting with others.

Physical development

This is supported by:

- handling the sand, experiencing the feel and textures of both the sand itself and the various tools that may be provided (sensory experiences)
- manipulative development – the skills needed to use both dry and wet sand
- increasing control over body movements.

Intellectual development

This is supported by:

- understanding about the properties of sand, i.e. dry sand pours; wet sand moulds, etc.
- learning that adding water can alter the sand and the type of play
- increasing understanding of absorbency
- increasing understanding of the effects various sand 'tools' can have
- opportunities to develop sustained concentration.

Language development (older toddlers)

This is supported by:

- development of new words and terminology, e.g. sift, sieve, pour, trickle, mould, pat, shape, etc.
- increased ability to express ideas and put words to intentions.

Water play

Social development

This is supported by:

- playing alongside others
- selecting tools and resources
- sharing and passing tools to others
- swapping and negotiating for tools
- indicating requests for items.

Emotional development

- Water can be a soothing experience.
- Water allows a sense of achievement.
- It is a non-fail activity – you cannot play with water 'wrong'.
- Child displays expressions of pleasure and excitement at new and favourite activities.

Physical development

This is supported by:

- increased manipulative skills
- increased control over body movements
- handling the water, noting the feel, texture, etc.
- physically tipping, pouring from one container to another.

▲ Water play offers both fun and learning

Intellectual development

This is supported by:

- increasing understanding of what water can do
- investigating and trying out ideas
- increasing understanding of full up and empty
- increasing understanding of volume and capacity
- increasing understanding of floating and sinking
- opportunities to develop sustained concentration.

Language development (older toddlers)

This is supported by:

- development of new words and terminology, for example, float, sink, pour, swish, splash, empty, full, more, less, greater than, less than, heavier, lighter.

Activities involving paint

Social developments

This is supported by:

- opportunities to make choices – choosing colours, position of 'creations', etc.
- sharing experiences with others
- using observations as a basis for expression.

Emotional development

- Paint is satisfying.
- There are opportunities to show pleasure and excitement at new and favourite activities.
- Child develops confidence in joining in the 'messiest' activities.

Physical development

This is supported by:

- manipulative skills development when using brushes, rollers, etc.
- increasing control of body movements
- handling paint textures – runny paint, thick paint, etc.
- handling and using the various alternative 'tools', for example, sponges, print blocks, rollers, etc.

Intellectual development

This is supported by:

- developing the ability and confidence to make choices
- mixing colours to make additional colours, initially accidentally (and later on deliberately).
- choosing colours, showing understanding (later on) to illustrate

specific things, for example blue for the sky, green for the grass

- experimenting with new ideas and activities – printing etc.
- developing and identifying patterns in colours, shapes, etc.
- using paint to demonstrate what they have observed (older toddlers).

Language development

This is supported by:

- adults using language to describe colours
- adults using language to describe texture
- adult and/or infant vocalisations of what they have painted or created.

Books and stories

Social development

The activity:

- is usually a shared experience at this age
- can be one-to-one or in a small group, each infant with an adult
- helps to develop observation skills
- often offers opportunities to join in with actions and repetition sounds – to belong.

Emotional development

- Names of familiar objects and experiences are named and repeated.
- The repetition of familiar stories and the repeated sequences in many books is comforting to most children.
- Books and stories offer opportunities to express emotions, for example, worries, laughter, mock 'fear' or 'anger' etc.

Physical development

This is supported by:

- manipulative skills development through handling books appropriately – turning pages, holding books the right way up, holding books still while looking at them
- hand–eye coordination skills in following the text even before they can read
- opportunities for actions alongside stories.

Intellectual development

- Children develop an understanding of how books 'work' – from top to bottom and left to right (in English).
- Children understand that books can be both for pleasure and a source of information.
- Children learn a great deal about their own environment through the stories they hear and the books they look at.
- A child's understanding is consolidated by the repetition of familiar stories.

▲ Enjoying a story

Language development

This is supported by:

- development of new words and terminology:
  - about new objects, new situations, other cultures
  - through joining in with repetition or hearing adults do so
  - through adults (or older toddlers) describing what will happen
  - through adults (or older toddlers) indicating what might happen next .

Musical instruments

Social development

- This is often a joint activity with others.
- Babies and children learn to play cooperatively.
- Children develop an understanding of how to respond to instructions and guidance regarding when to start and when to stop.
- Childrn learn about taking turns to play.

Emotional development

- There can be an emotional release through music.
- Gentle sounds can soothe a distressed child.
- Bold sounds can liven up a sad or unusually quiet child.
- Children learn to enjoy and value the sounds and instruments of their own culture.
- Children learn to enjoy and value the sounds and instruments of other cultures.
- An understanding of the need to consider other people can be learnt through taking turns to listen (older infants).

Physical development

This is supported by:

- manipulative skills development through the use of instruments
- large motor skills development through the opportunities to bounce, sway, balance, dance and march to music (locomotion)
- developing the ability to move rhythmically
- learning to link music to dance and movement
- learning about the different feel of various instruments, for example cymbals – metal, drums – skins, maracas – wooden, shakers – gourds (a hollowed-out fruit).

Intellectual development (the following mostly apply to older toddlers)

This is supported by:

- increased knowledge of the origins of instruments and music
- increased knowledge of the different types of sounds that can be made
- sequencing and patterning within music
- linking music to dance and movement
- understanding the changes in pitch, tempo, etc.
- opportunities to develop sustained concentration.

Language development (again, mostly older infants)

This is supported by:

- increased vocabulary, for example,
  - sound names
  - instrument names
  - rhythmic words: slow, slow, fast, fast, slow

– development of voice pitch and how it can be changed to match different instruments

- increased listening skills.

Puzzles

Social development

- With young toddlers this is usually a shared activity with an adult.
- Floor puzzles are usually enjoyed by older toddlers.
- Pictures often depict objects of situations from children's own environment and experience.

Emotional development

- Confidence increases alongside skill development.
- Satisfaction is experienced when puzzles are completed.
- Children learn to deal with frustration if puzzle becomes difficult to achieve.

▲ Doing a puzzle

Physical development

This is supported by:

- manipulative skills development
- increased ability to handle small pieces
- increased hand–eye coordination.

Intellectual development

This is supported by:

- developing understanding of how to match pieces to gaps, identifying shape, size, etc.
- learning through trial and error in the earliest stages
- demonstrating understanding of processes by matching pieces to accompanying pictures
- opportunities to develop sustained concentration
- eventual development of memory for the completed picture, helping the child to visualise what they are trying to achieve.

Language development

This is supported by:

- adult and infant using language to name objects and talk about the picture
- using language to talk about shapes, size and how to position pieces
- new words, for example place, hold, edges, twist, turn, flat, turn over, etc.

Stacking toys and posting boxes

Social development

- Initially this would be a shared activity with an adult or older sibling.
- Children learn to build jointly with another person.
- Knocking down the tower would be another joint fun action.

513

- Working together, the adult will help the child (perhaps hand over hand) to guide them to success in posting a shape in a post box or shape sorter.
- There are opportunities for child to select which piece to post, or which piece to stack next.

Emotional development

- Satisfaction and pleasure is seen when successful.
- Pleasure and excitement is seen in knocking down the tower.
- Increased confidence is developed in line with increased physical (manipulative) skills.

Physical development

This is supported by:

- manipulative skills development – handling with increasing control
- precision and positioning skills
- hand–eye coordination
- exploration of shapes with both hands and mouths.

Intellectual development

This is supported by:

- learning to stack by size (beakers and rings)
- learning to enclose by size (beakers, 'Russian doll'-style objects)
- matching shapes to correct shape holes
- learning by trial and error
- counting opportunities as stacking and sorting objects occurs
- learning about colours as each colour is stated for them by the adult.

Language development

This is supported by:

- shape names introduced by the adult
- colour names introduced by the adult

- counting
- introduction of vocabulary, such as biggest, smallest, bigger than, etc.

Threading reels and buttons

Social development

This is supported by:

- playing alongside or with others
- making decisions and selecting resources
- asking (or indicating) required resources and responding to requests
- sharing and swapping resources.

Emotional development

- This is a calm, satisfying activity.
- A sense of pleasure is seen in achievement.
- Children enjoy being able to make their own choices and colours.

Physical development

This is supported by:

- manipulative skills development
- hand–eye coordination
- increased control over body movements
- handling the threading of objects with increased ability and precision, often mimicking older siblings or playmates.

Intellectual development

This is supported by:

- developing the ability to sequence by shape, size and colour
- developing the ability to group by shape, size, colours, etc.
- learning to plan and have intentions.

Language development

This is supported by:

- development of words and terminology through hearing:

- colour names
- shape names
- counting
- use of language to ask for and negotiate
- use of language to talk about length, purpose etc.

Early Years Foundation Stage (EYFS)

Early years practitioners need to ensure that the way in which they care for and provide for babies complies with the guidance of the four main principles of the EYFS. These are:

- A Unique Child
- Positive Relationships
- Enabling Environments
- Learning and Development.

This guidance aims to ensure that each child is considered as an individual and that their individual needs are planned for, their learning pace and style is provided for and their sense of self-esteem is promoted and enhanced by the adults in their lives. The need for positive cohesion when adults work together to care for a child is emphasised, with key-worker systems and good communication between practitioners, parents and any other partnerships being of utmost importance.

The suitability of the environment in which care and learning takes place, the type of, care of and number of resources set out for babies and children is highlighted in order to promote, support and extend learning.

The six areas of learning which lead through to the early learning goals for children between 40 and 60+ months are set out, in the Practice Guidance document, in the following ages/stages:

- Birth – 11 months
- 8 – 20 months
- 16 – 26 months
- 22 – 36 months
- 30 – 50 months
- 40 – 60+ months.

As development varies from infant to infant, the first three development stages (as set out above) will be most relevant to this unit.

Using observation methods to assess development

Observation

When working with babies you will need to carry out different types of observations. These will be both formal and informal. Observations are used to note progress, assess needs and to enable accurate feedback to be given to parents and in some cases health care professionals. They also help day care staff to ensure that safe practice is carried out at all times.

When carrying out observations you will need to take into consideration:

- parental permission
- the importance of accuracy
- using both formal and informal observation methods
- how you record your observations
- language and recording formats
- the recording procedures of the setting where you work
- why you are carrying out the observations and what you hope to gain from them.

To refresh your understanding of observing babies and young children, refer back to Unit 2, page 63–71, where the role of observation is discussed together with explanations of how to carry out a range of different observation methods.

GOOD PRACTICE

Observing babies and young children can help to:

- inform future planning
- learn about individual infant's interests and needs
- identify links between circumstances and behaviour
- note changes in behaviour
- get to know an infant better
- identify any safety issues
- gauge the success of activities or resources
- monitor any concerns that may already have been raised
- assess an infant's state of health
- assess an infant's overall stage of development
- assess an infant's progress.

Have a go!

Write a letter to an imaginary parent asking for permission to carry out observations on their baby. Explain how you will carry out your observations and outline what you consider you can learn about a baby through observation. Ensure that you refer to the issue of how confidentiality is upheld.

Planning care and activities to promote development and support the child's welfare

Feeding

Everyone working with young babies must be able to make up a formula feed accurately, and also know how to store breast milk, previously expressed by the mother, to give to the infant during time within their care. Most placements ask parents to bring in their own milk, made up for the day. Supporting the diet and nutrition intake of babies and young children includes encouraging parents to provide healthy balanced foods at home and supporting the feeding choices of new mothers. Having an understanding of food groups and how foods support development will help you plan appropriately to meet children's energy needs as they change according to both growth and activity levels.

Refer also to Unit 12, pages 332–338, for information on breastfeeding, bottlefeeding and weaning.

Nutritional requirements of babies

As with children and adults of all ages, once weaning has started, babies need a well-balanced diet which includes foods from the four main food groups.

A well-balanced diet is one that provides all the nutritional requirements for growth, maintenance and development of the body. What we eat helps us to repair and maintain our body tissues, supports the functioning of muscles and organs and helps to prevent infection. It also supplies us with the energy we need in order to function from day to day.

The four main food groups are:

- proteins, which help growth, development and tissue repair
- carbohydrates, which provide energy
- vitamins, minerals and fibre, for general good health and the prevention of illness
- dairy products, which are high in calcium, enhancing and maintaining bones and teeth.

A fifth food group – fats and oils – contains higher energy-giving foods, which are essential to babies and young children, but should be consumed sparingly by adults.

Refer to Unit 12 for guidance on the weaning process, nutritional requirements of babies and both cultural and medical dietary needs.

Diet and the unwell child

Infants who are unwell are likely to be more selective in what they want to eat, and it is often more appropriate to allow them to eat what they feel like eating, rather than insisting they try something they do not want, which may result in little food being consumed. Again, portion size is important. An unwell child will usually require far less food at each meal than usual. Many infants will return to just wanting milk feeds. This is not a problem in the short term.

Overcoming feeding difficulties and food allergies

At times babies can repeatedly refuse solid foods. It is important during these periods to consider the following questions:

- Is the child unwell?
- Is the child teething?
- Are you giving too many new foods too quickly?
- Are you offering food at the right consistency?
- Are you feeling anxious about the weaning process, and possibly passing your anxiety on to the child?

It is important to make sure that you:

- make mealtimes a pleasure, not a battle
- make gradual changes to the consistency of foods
- only offer one new food or new consistency at a time
- only offer new foods when the infant is well and content
- offer a new food alongside a familiar food, to ensure that at least part of the meal is eaten.

G☺☺D PRACTICE

- When an infant or a child is unwell it is not an appropriate time to introduce new foods to them.
- Processed foods contain many hidden ingredients, such as sugar and salt. Whenever possible, offer infants fresh foods and use fresh ingredients in your cooking.
- Milk remains an important part of the baby's diet until they are at least a year old. The aim of weaning is to introduce babies to a variety of textures, tastes and experiences to integrate them fully into family mealtimes. As the level of solid food intake increases, the milk feeds will decrease until the baby is having sufficient solid food at a 'mealtime' to be satisfied with a drink of water to accompany it.

Babies experimenting with feeding themselves

Babies enjoy trying to feed themselves. They can usually cope with finger foods from 8 months onwards, and suitable foods would include rusks, fingers of soft bread, pieces of pear and slices of banana. When the infant shows an interest in trying to handle the spoon, give them a spare one. You will then remain in control of the feeding process, while satisfying their curiosity and skill development.

GOOD PRACTICE

Feeding can be messy, so feed babies in a suitable environment. Babies need to try to feed themselves in order to learn. Happy mealtimes will encourage a positive attitude to food and eating later on.

Complying with parental wishes relating to feeding babies

When working in care settings you will need to be aware of a variety of dietary needs. There may be:

- medical needs, for chronic conditions such as lactose intolerance, gluten intolerance or food allergy
- cultural needs, heeding the rules about forbidden or restricted foods and food combinations of some cultures
- social needs/family choice, which would include vegetarian or vegan diets.

Parents' wishes about their child's diet must be valued. It is perfectly acceptable to seek their advice regarding meeting their child's needs. Most parents will be pleased that you have shown an interest and taken the time to ensure you are providing for them appropriately.

 Have a go!

Produce two charts, one for a baby, and one for a young toddler, showing a suitable daily care and feeding routine. You may find it helpful to refer back to Unit 12, where diet and nutrition are covered in more detail.

Washing, dressing and nappy changing

Hygiene must always be a top priority when dealing with body fluids of any kind. This includes nappy changes. In day care settings, the use of disposable gloves is now the norm, whereas in a home setting good personal hygiene practice should be sufficient.

Babies are usually topped and tailed in the mornings, and bathed in the evening before being put to bed. Topping and tailing involves washing the face and refreshing the top half of the body, and changing the nappy.

Topping and tailing

Preparation

Get everything ready in advance. You will need:

- towel
- changing mat
- bowl of cool boiled water
- bowl of warm water
- cotton wool
- barrier cream (if using)
- a clean nappy
- a fresh set of clothes
- access to a nappy bucket (for towelling nappies) or a nappy sack (if using disposables)
- access to a laundry basket for clothes.

How to do it

1 Place baby on changing mat and undress them to their vest and nappy.

2 Using the cooled boiled water, wipe each eye from the nose corner outwards, using each piece of cotton wool only once.

3 Repeat two or three times for each eye.

4 Dry gently with the corner of a clean towel.

5 Gently clean ears and around the face using moistened cotton wool, ensuring that you reach all the creases, particularly under the chin and behind the ears. Dry gently.

6 Using a larger piece of moistened cotton wool, freshen up the baby's armpits and hands, removing all fibres collected between the fingers. Dry gently.

7 In newborn babies check that the umbilical stump is clean, but do not clean it unnecessarily. Whenever possible, it should be left alone. (The stump tends to shrivel up and drop off 7 to 10 days after birth.)

8 Remove soiled nappy and place in bucket or nappy sack.

9 Clean the nappy area thoroughly, with warm water (or baby wipes if used), ensuring that you clean all creases, wiping from the front to the back.

10 Put on clean nappy (applying barrier cream if used), dress and have a cuddle!

Changing nappies

Parents and carers today have a vast array of choices regarding the type of nappies they use. Disposable nappies are extremely

GOOD PRACTICE

Cleansing of a girl's nappy area should always be by wiping from the front to the back to avoid any infection from the bowels passing into the vaginal area. Cleansing of a boy's nappy area does not necessitate the pulling back of the foreskin. Excessive cleaning can actually cause irritation and infection, rather than prevent it.

absorbent and can be easy to use, but they are expensive and are a significant environmental concern. Towelling nappies are cheaper to use, but they have to be washed and dried. In many areas there are nappy laundering services. These are expensive to use, but sometimes appeal to the environmentally conscious parent, who does not want to bother themselves with the extra washing. Towelling nappies have been revolutionised. They can be bought ready 'shaped', often used with a waterproof wrap. These nappies are usually secured with a Velcro-type fastening (aplix), poppers or a nappy nipper (a three-pronged rubber grip).

If the infant in your care wears nappies made from folded towelling squares, you will need to know how to fold them. There are a number of ways to do this, as shown on page 520.

There should be separate nappy-changing facilities in every appropriate care setting. The surfaces used should be safe, clean and offer privacy. Each baby or child needs to have their own changing items labelled and stored separately. Creams and lotions should not be shared between children. Staff should follow hygiene protection practices as directed by the policy of the setting.

► Example 1

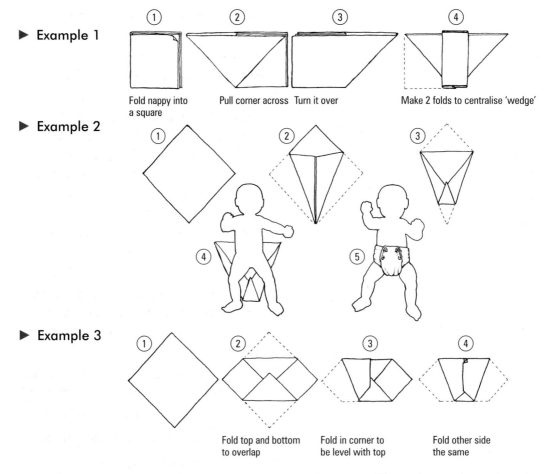

① Fold nappy into a square

② Pull corner across

③ Turn it over

④ Make 2 folds to centralise 'wedge'

► Example 2

① ② ③ ④ ⑤

► Example 3

① ②

③ ④

② Fold top and bottom to overlap

③ Fold in corner to be level with top

④ Fold other side the same

GOOD PRACTICE

A baby or child should never be left alone on a raised changing surface. All resources needed should be gathered in advance.

Bathing

Bathing young babies is usually very pleasurable, and can be carried out by either the 'traditional' method or the 'modern' method. Early years professionals need to be able to carry out both methods, to meet with parental preferences.

Traditional bathing method

Prepare everything in advance, ensuring that the temperature of the room is suitable (at least 20°C/68°F) with no draughts, and that all windows and doors are closed. All that you will need must be to hand, and the bath should be in a safe and secure place. A special bath stand or a firm surface is ideal, but many people choose to place the baby bath in the family bath or on the floor. Any of these options are acceptable.

Preparation

Get everything ready in advance. You will need:

- bath, with water at 37°C – always check this before putting the baby in (using your elbow or preferably a bath thermometer)
- changing mat
- towels
- cotton wool
- bowl of cool boiled water (for the eyes)

- shampoo (if using)
- soap
- barrier cream (if using)
- a clean nappy
- a fresh set of clothes
- access to a nappy bucket (for towelling nappies) or a nappy sack (if using disposables)
- access to a laundry basket for clothes.

How to do it

1 Undress baby to just their nappy and wrap them in the towel with the top corner folded away from you.

2 Wash eyes and face as in topping and tailing guidelines above.

3 Hold baby over the bath (still wrapped in towel) under your arm, resting on your hip.

4 Gently wet their hair all over.

5 Add shampoo or soap and rub in gently but firmly.

6 Rinse their hair by leaning baby backwards over the bath, towel-drying their hair with the folded-over corner of the towel.

7 Lay baby across your lap and remove nappy, cleansing away excess faeces.

8 With your spare hand gently wet and soap baby all over, turning them by pulling them over towards you, holding shoulder and thigh, and on to their tummy. When their back and bottom are also soaped, turn again in the same way (always towards you).

9 Supporting the baby's head and neck with one hand and their bottom with the other, lower them into the bath.

10 Gently rinse baby all over, continually supporting the head and neck with your wrist, and holding their shoulder and arm.

11 When ready to be dried, lift baby on to your lap, wrap in towel and cuddle dry!

12 Apply nappy and clothing as before.

13 Brush or groom hair as appropriate.

14 Trim nails as necessary using blunt baby scissors (with parents' permission).

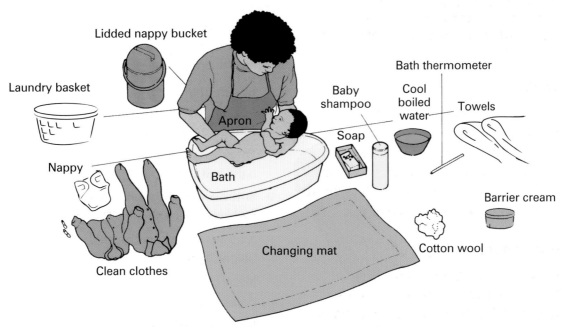

▲ **The traditional method for bathing a baby**

GOOD PRACTICE

Always keep hold of the baby, by firmly holding the arm and shoulder furthest away from you. Even very young babies can move suddenly.

Other points to remember

- Babies usually have a feed after a bath and are then put down to sleep.

- Only use talcum powder if parents insist. (It has been thought that its use may be linked to the development of asthma in early childhood.)

- Cultural practice regarding hair care, use of oils and creams should be adhered to.

- Never poke cotton buds into ears, noses and so on.

- Babies need complete supervision by a responsible adult at all times when being bathed.

Modern bathing method

How to do it

1 Bath water, clothing and so on needs to be prepared in the same way as with the traditional method.

2 A bathing preparation is added to the water.

3 The baby is lowered into the water after the eyes and face have been washed.

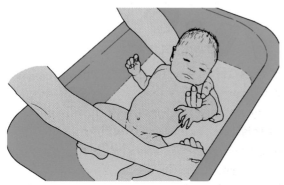

▲ Support the baby's head and neck while holding their shoulder and arm

4 The baby is soaped using the 'bubble bath'.

5 The process then continues as in the traditional method.

GOOD PRACTICE

Using a bathing preparation can make the water (and baby) quite slippery, so particular care is needed in holding the baby securely. If a bathing preparation causes irritation of the baby's skin you should stop using it. Some preparations irritate a baby's skin in the early weeks but can be used without problems later on.

Bathing older babies

From 7 or 8 months onwards, babies can be bathed in the family bath, although some babies will prefer the security of the baby bath for far longer. They are usually much more active by this time and the additional room for splashing is appreciated. They are often able to sit alone quite well, but remember that the water will make them buoyant and you will need to be ready to support them if they slip.

The same precautions are needed regarding temperature, preparation and supervision as with younger babies.

- Ensure that the baby cannot touch the hot tap, which remains hot for some time after use.

- Do not have the water too deep, or the baby will float.

- Sitting on a rubber mat can help them feel more secure.

- A range of containers and bath toys will be enjoyed.

- Many babies enjoy bathing with a parent.

Fearful babies

At times a baby may become fearful of water. This may be due to:

- an incident such as slipping in the bath
- disliking water getting in their eyes
- stinging eyes from soaps or shampoos.

You should ensure that you:

- always hold babies securely when in the bath
- never allow babies to try and stand in the bath
- always use non-stinging products, especially designed for babies' delicate skin
- use a hair ring to keep water out of their eyes, if they dislike the sensation
- do not make a big issue of bathing if it becomes a battle – often if you omit the bath or the hair wash for a couple of days, the issue will go away, as the baby 'forgets' it was a problem.

Although most parents and carers like to freshen their babies at the end of each day with a bath, it is not absolutely essential. A thorough wash using the top and tail method can also maintain good health care.

Clothing for babies

Adults need to take responsibility for what the babies wear while in their care, ensuring that temperature, weather or planned activity is taken into account.

Clothing for babies must:

- be easy to put on and take off
- have room for them to grow
- allow unrestricted movement
- be suitable for the time of year and temperature of the environment they are in

- avoid cramping of their toes (for example in all-in-one suits)
- be free from long ties or ribbons (to avoid choking)
- be free from loose buttons or poppers (another choking hazard)
- be free from looped edgings on seams that may catch their fingers
- avoid lacy designs that may also catch small fingers
- be easy to wash and dry
- be made of natural materials, such as cotton, to allow the baby's skin to breathe
- not involve fluffy materials or wools, such as mohair, as this can irritate noses and get in hands and mouths
- be of a suitable length, e.g. for dresses not to get caught when toddling or crawling
- be washed in non-biological powders to avoid reactions to the harsh detergents in many modern washing agents.

GOOD PRACTICE

It is better for babies to wear several layers of clothes that can be removed or replaced according to temperature, than one warmer layer that offers no opportunity for adjustment, as babies are not able to control their body temperature and could therefore become overheated.

Babies' footcare

Babies' feet are very delicate and their bones are still forming. They should not be given shoes before they are walking, as this can hinder the natural growth and development of their feet, leading to deformity. Socks, all-in-one suits and bootees should all have sufficient room for natural movement and growth.

Caring for a baby's environment

Room temperature and suitable levels of ventilation are an important factor in looking after a baby, and any room where a baby spends much of their time should be a constant 20 °C (68 °F) day and night. A room thermometer should be placed on the wall in the baby room of any early years setting and should be checked regularly, adjusting the heating accordingly.

Overheating of babies is thought to be a contributory factor in sudden infant death syndrome (cot death), and recommendations are that babies should not be piled high with blankets: just a sheet and two layers of blankets will normally be sufficient.

Duvets and baby nests are no longer recommended, as they do not allow for temperature regulation. Cot bumpers are also advised against as they add extra warmth to a baby's cot, as well as having the potential for suffocation.

A well-ventilated room will help to prevent cross-infection and make the working or living environment a more pleasant place to be, both for the baby and for their carers.

FAST FACT

A blanket folded in half counts as two layers.

Checklist

- You can check if a well baby is too warm or too cool by feeling their abdomen. If it feels warm and clammy then they are hotter than necessary. An abdomen that is slightly cool to touch is usual.

- Removing a layer of clothing should be sufficient to keep them at a more comfortable temperature.

- Cool hands and feet do not automatically indicate a 'cold' baby.

- The circulation of young babies is not as fully developed as that of adults and older children, and many babies have cool extremities, especially before they become mobile.

- If you are concerned that a baby is unwell or has a raised temperature, always check with a thermometer and seek medical advice as necessary.

- Normally body temperature is between 36 and 37 °C.

High temperature (pyrexia)

Normal body temperature is between 36 and 37 °C. A temperature above 37.5 °C indicates pyrexia (fever). Young children's temperatures are often a sensitive indicator of the onset of illness and a raised temperature should never be ignored.

Check for overheating in the first instance by:

- removing clothing or a layer of bedding
- reducing the temperature of the room
- sponging the infant with a cool flannel.

If fever is suspected:

- take the infant's temperature and record the outcome
- remove clothing or a layer of bedding

- sponge with a cool flannel
- offer plenty of fluids
- use a fan to circulate cool air around the child
- observe the child carefully, particularly a very young baby.

Febrile convulsions

- Febrile convulsions can occur in some infants when their temperature rises, involving loss of consciousness, flickering of eyes and general jitteriness.
- A child who has one febrile convulsion is more likely to have another. It does not, however, mean that they have developed epilepsy.
- Medical advice should be sought if a febrile convulsion occurs.
- The child should be placed in the recovery position when the convulsion is over while medical advice is sought.
- The child needs reassurance and rest following a febrile convulsion.

GOOD PRACTICE

Parents should always be informed if a child has become unwell, even if the child appears well again by the time they are collected.

Ensuring the environment remains suitable

A baby's environment and care routines must be constantly monitored for their suitability, as they will need to be adjusted as the infant gets older, in order to meet their changing developmental needs. These needs will include:

- sleeping patterns, as the infant gradually has longer periods of wakefulness
- feeding times, incorporating the introduction of weaning

- time spent specifically playing with them
- time for stimulation, involving games, music, outings and so on
- time for rest and relaxation, sleep, cuddles and books.

Babies need a routine that is not rigid but provides continuity and security for them. A secure baby is usually a settled baby. Babies have periods of wakefulness and periods of deep sleep. They can appear very alert and content at times, and restless and irritable at others. A baby's day must include:

- sufficient feeds for their current age, weight and level of development
- sufficient extended periods of sleep
- time for love and cuddles
- stimulation through toys, adult communications and through the general environment
- regular changes of nappies
- opportunities for fresh air.

Care of skin

Care of the skin is important because it is the front-line area of defence for the body as it comes into contact with the environment. It is necessary to protect the skin from short-term problems:

- discomfort
- irritation
- infection.

It is also necessary to protect the skin from long-term problems:

- sunburn
- sun damage (that can lead to skin cancers)
- scarring from repeated irritation or infections.

Babies have sensitive skin and many of our everyday products are far too harsh for them. It is therefore important to use specially prepared baby products suitable for sensitive skins during all care routines.

Skin types

Skin types vary, as do family practices, and it is important that in any early years setting the preferences of parents are taken into account. Most day care settings ask parents to provide their own products and these are clearly labelled and kept solely for the use of their baby.

Practical example

Jerome

Jerome is West Indian and his skin tends to be very dry. His parents rub cocoa butter into his skin after his bath. They also massage his skin with oil, particularly his arms and legs, at each nappy change. They have supplied Jerome's nursery with a bottle of oil, and asked them to continue this practice during the day.

① What precautions, if any, need to be in place here?

② Who should carry out the massage?

FAST FACT

It should be remembered that babies with black skin have a greater tendency to dry skin than those with other skin types.

GOOD PRACTICE

Any oil used on babies and young children should be free of nut traces (almond oil used to be popular but is no longer used), as there is concern about links with the increase in nut allergies in young children. Many specialists recommend the use of organic sunflower oil.

Eczema

A common skin complaint in infants and young children is **eczema**. Children with this condition will need particular support during bad phases. Some will need to have prescribed ointments applied during the day. Staff taking on this role should wear disposable gloves to reduce the risk of passing on any infection to the child, and also to prevent themselves from absorbing the ointments or creams (which often incorporate corticosteroids) into their own skin.

Note: babies may need to wear cotton mittens to prevent scratching. Older children with eczema may need to be encouraged to wear gloves during activities such as sand play to avoid exacerbating their condition. They should be taught to wash and dry their skin carefully and thoroughly.

Skin infestations and conditions

From time to time skin infestations and infectious conditions can occur in early years settings. These can spread very quickly, but preventive measures for cross-infection, which should be standard practice, should help contain them to some extent. There will usually be a policy regarding the admittance of children and babies with an infectious condition. Ask your current placement setting if you can see what is included in their policy. Common skin infestations and infectious conditions include:

- scabies
- impetigo
- hand, foot and mouth disease.

Scabies

Scabies are tiny parasites that burrow into the skin. They are sometimes known as itch mites due to the intense itching they cause, particularly at night. It is an extremely infectious condition, which is passed on by physical contact, either from person to person, or via towels, flannels and bedding.

The scabies mites burrow into the skin, leaving thin track marks under the skin where they have passed through. The itching causes redness and sore patches, which may at times be mistaken for eczema.

Scabies will not disappear without treatment. A special lotion prescribed by the GP is needed, and each individual who has been in contact with the infected child needs to be treated. This usually includes their whole family and the staff in their care setting who have worked closely with them.

Impetigo

Impetigo is an extremely infectious skin condition, which often affects the mouth and nose. It also affects the nappy area of babies. It is caused by bacteria, which enter the body through a break in the skin. As with scabies, it is passed on by physical contact, either from person to person, or via towels, flannels and bedding.

Red skin with tiny blisters is the most noticeable sign of impetigo. The blisters weep and gradually crust over with yellowish scabs.

Antibiotic creams will be needed from the child's GP. It is important to try to avoid cross-infection, and to discourage children from scratching. Babies and toddlers may benefit from wearing cotton gloves at night. Scarring can occur if scratching is intense. Complications are a possibility, causing a general infection of the body, which can affect the child's kidneys.

Hand, foot and mouth disease

Hand, foot and mouth is a mild, but highly infectious condition, which is common in children of pre-school age, but less often seen in babies. It is in no way connected to foot and mouth disease found in cattle and other hoofed animals. It is caused by a viral condition spread by droplet infection. The virus is called coxsackie.

A child's temperature may be raised slightly if they have this condition. They are likely to have very small blisters inside the cheeks, which may ulcerate. About two days after the mouth blisters, blistery spots with a red surrounding edge appear on hands and fingers, and tops of feet.

Paracetamol can be given to reduce the raised temperature. Giving plenty of fluids is important. Avoid giving the child anything that might irritate their sore mouth. Complications are rare, but prolonged mouth blisters may need treatment from the child's GP.

Sun care

We all know how seriously our skin can be damaged by the sun's rays, and children and babies should not be exposed to the sun for more than a very short period of time. Babies should be kept in the shade whenever possible (watch out for the sun moving round if they are in prams or pushchairs) and outdoor play in sunny areas should be restricted, particularly around midday when the sun is at its highest point.

Hats should be worn, and each setting should have a policy regarding the application of suncreams. Sunscreen creams and lotions for children and babies should be of the highest factor, or be a total sun block. Written parental permission should be obtained before staff can apply cream to any child.

Hair care

Hair care is needed to prevent infestation from head lice and to encourage good grooming for the future. Again, cultural practices differ. Muslim babies will have their heads shaved within 40 days of birth as part of cultural tradition, and many Caribbean parents traditionally weave and plait their babies' hair at a very early age.

Washing the hair of babies can at times be traumatic, as not all babies are happy to have water in their eyes. Hair rings can be purchased; these prevent water from

reaching the eyes and can make for a happier bathtime. Hair-washing products should always be 'non-stinging' to the eyes. There are plenty of different products available for babies and children.

Dental care

The brushing of a baby's teeth should commence as soon as the first ones arrive, and definitely when a baby has corresponding teeth top and bottom. Soft baby toothbrushes are specially designed for the delicate gums and first teeth, and their regular use will encourage the baby into a habit of good oral health care for the future. In day care settings each baby and child should have their own toothbrush, which should be labelled and kept separately.

As the toddler phase arrives it is important to teach children the correct amount of toothpaste to use, and to remember that toothpaste should not be swallowed. Cleaning of teeth should be encouraged after eating and before bed.

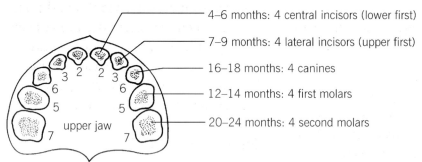

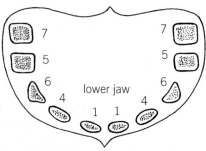

4–6 months: 4 central incisors (lower first)

7–9 months: 4 lateral incisors (upper first)

16–18 months: 4 canines

12–14 months: 4 first molars

20–24 months: 4 second molars

▲ The eruption of milk teeth

Toilet training

Bowel and bladder control cannot be achieved until a child is both physically and emotionally ready. The nervous system must be mature enough for physical control to take place, and a child needs to be both interested in using a potty and willing to sit on it. The age at which control is attained varies enormously, and the development process needs to be child led, not thrust upon them by an adult.

It is useful to have a potty around for a child to become familiar with, with positive comments given when they show interest in it. Generally, potty use should take place in the bathroom of the setting, giving the child privacy and restricting any risk of cross-infection.

G☺☺D PRACTICE

Once a child has started to gain bowel or bladder control it is important that 'accidents' are dealt with in a matter-of-fact way, and the child is not made to feel anxious.

Bowel and bladder problems in children

All infants and young children suffer from minor bowel and bladder problems, such as diarrhoea and constipation, at some point. These are usually due to gastroenteritis, a viral infection (diarrhoea) or changes in the diet (constipation). They are unpleasant conditions, but rarely serious.

Diarrhoea

A child who is suffering from diarrhoea should avoid food and drink plenty of clear fluids; this usually helps to keep the child hydrated until the virus has passed. If, however, a child suffers from vomiting and diarrhoea for a considerable length of time, they may begin to suffer from **dehydration**, particularly babies and toddlers, and medical attention will be important to ensure that their body is rehydrated.

FAST FACT

Young infants should continue with milk feeds, unless directed otherwise by a doctor.

Constipation

Usually, increasing the infant's consumption of roughage (fruits and vegetables in particular) will reduce the problem, and improve their health in general too. If the problem continues, advice from a health professional may be needed.

G☺☺D PRACTICE

Laxatives should never be given to a child without medical advice.

More serious bowel and bladder problems

Children with certain chronic conditions suffer from either intermittent or constant bowel problems. This includes children with cystic fibrosis and coeliac disease. Both of these conditions are regularly diagnosed by the toddler stage.

Cystic fibrosis (CF)

Cystic fibrosis is a condition that is mostly associated with respiratory problems, due to the sticky secretions that build up in the lungs, but it is a serious digestive condition too. The digestive tract is affected due to the pancreas not being able to produce the appropriate enzymes needed to break down the food and absorb it into the body's systems. It is often identified shortly after

---

Dehydration = where the water content of the body falls dangerously low

birth due to a blockage at the opening of the intestine. This is called a meconium ileus.

Infants that are not diagnosed shortly after birth usually fail to thrive during the first few months, due to the malabsorption of food. Their stools will be fatty and have an offensive smell. The sticky lungs are treated with percussion physiotherapy of the chest several times each day to loosen the secretions. Antibiotics are given to treat chest infections. The digestive tract is treated by giving pancreatic enzyme supplements, taken before each meal. These help the body to absorb food.

Children with cystic fibrosis need a diet that is low in fat but high in protein and carbohydrates. It is a life-limiting condition, but current research is moving forward very positively.

Coeliac disease

Coeliac disease is a condition affecting the lining of the small intestine. It is an intolerance of the protein gluten, which is found in wheat, barley, rye and oats. Symptoms indicating coeliac disease begin to show once foods containing gluten are introduced to the infant's diet. Sufferers of this condition fail to thrive in the usual way, they do not put on weight and are continuously low on the percentile growth charts. Children are lethargic and pass pale, unpleasant stools.

The condition can be confirmed through blood tests and/or a biopsy of the jejeunum (part of the small intestine).

The only way to control the symptoms of coeliac disease is to adopt a gluten-free diet. This will be necessary for life. Advice will be given to the family from a dietician, as gluten is found in many everyday foods,

and it can take time to establish what is suitable and what must be avoided.

If coeliac disease remains untreated it can lead to iron-deficiency anaemia and, possibly, long-term problems with bone density. Calcium supplements are often given throughout life.

Illness

Most babies are born with a degree of immunity passed to them from their mother via the placenta. Those who are breastfed continue to benefit from their mother's protection during the early months. Although the common childhood illnesses are mostly seen from the toddler stage onwards, it is possible for young babies also to be affected, as they come into contact with older siblings with an infectious condition or when an infection enters their early years care setting.

Most childhood illnesses last only a short period of time but can be very unpleasant during the process. Others, such as meningitis, are far more serious. Long-term consequences can result from some conditions and the severity of some conditions, such as measles, particularly in children who have not been immunised, should never be underestimated. If you are able to identify some of the common conditions you will be able to help prevent cross-infection of the condition by notifying parents and carers, and arranging to exclude the affected child from the setting.

Common childhood illnesses include:

- chickenpox
- rubella
- measles
- mumps
- coughs and colds
- gastrointestinal problems.

Refer to Unit 4 page 172, for details of common childhood illnesses. See also Unit 12, page 349, for information on disorders requiring special diets.

Appropriate responses to illness

Every early years setting has a policy and procedure for dealing with illness. It is important that you familiarise yourself with these. They will set out who deals with what, where children need to be taken (a separate room or screened area), who telephones a child's parents and when, and who telephones for medical advice or the emergency services. It will also cover the storage and administration of medicines

As an early years practitioner it is inevitable that you will sometimes have to deal with children who are unwell. This covers not only minor colds and sniffles but also the sudden onset of tummy upsets, childhood illnesses and more serious infections. It is important that you are able to recognise signs that may indicate an unwell child.

You may notice an infant or child crying, lying down or sitting quietly without interest in activities and clearly not being their usual self; but other signs of illness include:

- pallor – sickly pale skin tone
- fever – a raised temperature above 37.5 °C
- rashes – spots, blisters and blemishes
- breathlessness – often associated with asthma and allergies.

How to provide a safe, hygienic environment

Safety and hygiene feature strongly in all good provision for babies and toddlers. This ensures a safe working environment for practitioners and clean surfaces on which babies can lie and crawl or move around; this involves stringent efforts to avoid the hazards of cross-infection.

In early years settings:

- carpeted surfaces should be vacuumed regularly
- washable (non-slip) floors should be cleaned with a mop (disinfected)
- all surfaces used for making up, or standing feeds upon, should be thoroughly cleaned with an anti-bacterial product
- all general surfaces should also be kept clean with an anti-bacterial product
- soft toys should be washed regularly
- all toys should be cleaned regularly with an anti-bacterial product
- thermometers must be checked regularly to ensure that rooms are kept at an appropriate temperature (18–20 °C/65–68 °F)
- lighting must be adequate for safe working practice
- good ventilation is important to reduce the risk of cross-infection
- ventilation points need to be kept clean, to avoid a build-up of dirt and bacteria.

Hygiene and protection practices

It is important that all care staff understand the health and safe practice procedures for the setting. This helps to prevent the spread of illness and infection

Safe disposal of waste

Soiled nappies and clothing need to be safely and hygienically dealt with. Every care setting should have a policy regarding:

- the safe disposal of nappies, baby wipes, etc.
- the safe disposal of cleaning materials
- the sending home of soiled clothing.

If the setting washes soiled items on site, these should be sluiced in a sink kept especially for that purpose and washed on the appropriate heat setting of an industrial-strength washing machine. Blood-stained garments are likely to benefit from an initial rinsing on a cold-water cycle.

If garments are sent home with the child, they should be sluiced off to remove excess body fluids, double bagged and tied securely to prevent leakages.

Disposable nappies and any items used during care routines should be securely bagged and disposed of in a waste bin set aside for that purpose.

Safety

Both in the home and in early years settings, appropriate safety equipment is needed which is relevant both to the setting and for the development stages of the babies and children being cared for. In any setting that cares for babies and young toddlers there should be an awareness of safety marks, and the need to buy toys and equipment that have been tested and safety marked whenever possible.

Safety equipment is needed for the different stages of a baby and toddler's development.

For newborn infants

These should be:

- a safe surface on which to change the baby
- a cat/insect net
- a sturdy cot, Moses basket or carry-cot that conforms to current safety standards
- a suitable mattress, again which conforms to current safety standards and is the correct size for the cot
- an appropriate (rear-facing) car seat

Avoid cot bumpers, quilts and duvets, which have been linked to the overheating of young babies that can contribute to cot death.

When the baby sits up

- Be aware of new areas that can be reached by the baby.
- Flexes should be kept out of reach.
- Hot food should not be placed in front of the infant, in case they topple on to it.
- Harnesses are definitely needed in chairs, prams and strollers.
- In home care situations, do not change the baby's car seat round until they reach the correct size or weight (as indicated on the car seat).

When the baby can crawl

- Play pens can be useful.
- Fireguards prevent the baby accessing fires.
- Electric socket covers should be used.
- A video guard can be bought.

- Safety gates should be put at the top and bottom of stairs, and are possibly needed across the kitchen door too.
- Toilet lid catches can be useful.
- Trailing leads must be secured.
- Sharp corners need to be protected with transparent 'corners'.
- Safety glass (or a special safety film) should be placed in all full-length glass doors.
- Remove overhanging tablecloths.
- Keep cleaning fluids up high, preferably shut away out of sight.
- Hot drinks should be kept out of the baby's reach.
- Be aware of pet food and pet water bowls.
- Be aware of loose carpet fibres, which can cause choking if swallowed.
- Strong netting is needed over garden ponds.

When the baby is standing, climbing or toddling

- Cooker bars help to protect from saucepan spills.
- Keep cooking handles turned inwards at all times.
- A fridge lock may be needed.
- Catches are needed on windows, doors and drawers.
- Put safety glass, or safety film on doors, and low windows, and on glass coffee tables.

General safety points

- Smoke alarms should be installed.
- Safety mats in baths are important.

- Anchor points are needed for harnesses in highchairs, prams, buggies, etc.
- Slam stoppers on doors, to prevent fingers being trapped, are extremely useful.
- Razors, chemicals and medicines should be kept locked away securely.
- Cold water should always be added to baths before hot water.
- Toys should be checked regularly to ensure they are whole, undamaged and clean.
- Household plants that can cause irritation to the skin, or are poisonous should be removed.

When buying equipment

- Sturdy pram (or similar) is needed. It should be stable, with good brakes, and be the correct height for the main adult using it.
- Appropriate anchor points are needed for harnesses in all prams, pushchairs, buggies and feeding chairs.
- Cots must conform to safety legislation regarding gaps between bars, the inclusion of childproof safety catches and the avoidance of paint containing lead.
- Mattresses should conform to the latest health and safety standards. They must always fit the cot or carry-cot properly, with no gaps.

Safety marks

All equipment should conform to current safety guidelines.

 Refer to Unit 4 for greater detail on good safety and hygiene practice.

Parenting and child-rearing practices

Social, cultural and religious influences

Demonstrating respect for social, cultural and religious practices regarding baby and toddler care involves ensuring that you practise appropriate feeding and care routines. Some cultures have restrictions on who can visit a newborn infant in the first few days and also specific food rituals for the new mother. This may be particularly relevant if you work with families at home.

Customs vary widely, e.g. Muslim babies often have their heads shaved shortly after birth, whereas many West Indian infants have their hair tightly plaited. Some cultures use oils to cleanse the hair rather than washing hair at bath time.

Parents may be bringing their children up as vegetarians, vegans or organically without the use of chemicals; therefore, respecting their choice of care products will be important and seeking advice on feeding is likely to be necessary too.

Most parents will be happy to provide guidance and advice on how to support their child's needs. They will usually be pleased that you wish to know more.

GOOD PRACTICE

It is good practice for practitioners to research the needs of any child due to come into their care if social, cultural or religious practices are new to them. Food customs are of particular importance.

 Refer to Unit 12, pages 342–343 for more on food customs.

✎ Practical example

Narindar

Narindar is a young mum with a small baby. She has recently returned to work, leaving 3-month-old Vikram in the care of the baby room at her company's workplace nursery. Vikram's key worker is Shumilla who has already built up a good relationship with Narindar and they chat easily each evening when Vikram is collected.
Shumilla is rather concerned that Narindar seems unaware of some of the safety precautions needed when caring for a baby. For example, Narindar has referred to leaving Vikram 'lying happily on the sofa' while she makes tea.

(1) *How could Shumilla raise Narindar's awareness of safety issues further, without causing offence?*

(2) *What are the safety issues regarding caring for a baby of Vikram's age?*

✓ Progress check

1. Why is breast milk best for babies?
2. Why is weaning usually introduced at about 6 months?
3. Give some examples of stimulating activities for a baby.
4. Give some examples of stimulating activities for a toddler.
5. How does observing a baby or young child help you to care for them?
6. Describe a variety of food customs linked to different cultures.
7. Describe ways in which babies and toddlers can be protected from harm.

Learning Outcome 3

FOCUS ON...
the roles and responsibilities of professionals working with babies

This links to assessment criteria **3.1** and **3.2**

The importance of the key-worker system in a variety of settings

Babies and young children develop best within caring, emotionally close relationships. If the bond with their parent or primary carer is strong then they will feel secure and safe. When entering day care their feelings of security can at times become compromised, as they are faced with an unfamiliar environment, and new faces, sounds and equipment. Having a key-worker system enables each infant to form a new regular relationship, being mostly cared for by the same person or persons. This helps to re-establish their sense of security and provides continuity of care to help maintain it.

When infants are cared for in a home environment, by either a childminder or nanny, their surroundings remain much the same, and elements of familiarity from their own home are likely to be present. This is less so in a nursery setting, so greater care is needed to make the surroundings feel cosy and safe as well as stimulating.

As a key worker you will build a close relationship with both 'your' children and their families. To each child you will become a source of comfort, and be the person who makes them feel particularly special. Having such a close link enables you to understand their needs and development just that bit more, enabling you to plan more effectively for them than others might.

With the parents and family of each child, you will, it is to be hoped, develop a trusting relationship so that you can share concerns, celebrate achievements and be a person in whom they feel confident when handing over the wellbeing of their child in their absence.

Being a key worker is demanding, but rewarding. Key-worker systems provide stability and cohesion for day care settings, and help to fully utilise the professional and personal skills of all staff.

The organisation of care in a variety of settings

In most day care settings babies and toddlers are cared for separately within small groups. Each 'age-related' area will be specifically designed to take into account the mobility needs of the age range. For example, the youngest babies need plenty of floor space to roll and crawl, with floor and skirting-board-level stimulation. Early toddlers need space to develop their early walking and tottering movements and to push and pull along wheeled toys. There will always be an area specifically for sleeping, and cots etc. will be set out correctly, with sufficient space between to allow for safe adult movement and good hygiene practice, and positioned appropriately so that they can be well supervised.

A kitchen area with storage for feeds and feeding equipment will be easily accessed by staff, as will a separate changing area. Each infant's feeds, feeding equipment and nappy-changing items will be stored separately and labelled clearly to lessen the risk of cross-contamination.

Staff will draw up feeding and sleeping plans in accordance with each infant's routine. These will be discussed and reviewed with parents as an ongoing process, as the needs and routine of the youngest infants can change quite rapidly.

Key-worker systems are usual in baby and toddler rooms, with each key worker recording details of feeds, nappy changes, sleep, periods of wakefulness and all activities to inform parents on collection.

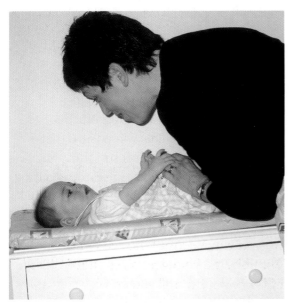

▲ Changing a nappy provides opportunities for playing and communicating

Policies and procedures for the care of babies and legal and ethical responsibilities

All settings must be aware of legal requirements and ensure that they update their records, policies and procedures as and when changes are brought in. Each setting will have a policy for the following:

- registration of children, both initially, and within daily practice
- risk assessment – when, what, how often and who carries it out; also, training of staff in carrying out risk assessments
- health and safety, including equipment and resources, hygiene practices, emergency procedures, first aid and the giving of medicines
- equality of opportunity – gender, ability, race, culture and religion
- child protection
- referrals.

On occasions, it will be necessary to refer a child to another professional. This could be for health, development, care or learning needs. As a student, if you have any concerns about a child for any reason, you should speak to your placement supervisor or to the child's key worker. It is likely that some needs would be managed within the setting, with the staff and resources already available. At other times, additional or one-to-one support will be required and an extra member of staff may be brought in, or the child may have a Portage worker who will give guidance to other carers.

You may find it helpful to refer to Unit 14, for more about the procedures for supporting development.

A child may also have to be referred because of suspected neglect or another form of abuse. Each setting has a member of staff designated to make such referrals to the local child protection team. It is inappropriate for you as a student to make the referral yourself. You must always talk to your placement supervisor.

GOOD PRACTICE

Any concern about a child in your care must always be reported. There are guidelines and legislation regarding reporting, storing and sharing information on children.

Confidentiality

It is expected that you will maintain confidentiality regarding children, families and colleagues. At times you may become privy to information about a child or their family that you will have received for a purpose, and in trust. You will have received it on a 'need to know' basis. Confidentiality forms part of your role as a professional. It also applies when carrying out observations.

Data protection

The Data Protection Act 1998 covers any information kept on paper or on a computer. This Act is relevant to you not only as a student, in relation to the information you use in writing your assignments, observations and recordings, but also as a practitioner, writing observations and maintaining records of babies and children.

Parents should be kept informed of any concerns about their child and should also have access to – and be welcomed to read – their child's file. It is inappropriate, however, for a parent to find out about

observations made of their child, and any concerns staff may have, simply by reading the file. Concerns and notes on development should always be discussed with them.

Safety

It is your responsibility to become informed regarding the health and safety practices in each setting you attend. You are responsible for working safely yourself and you should report any concerns you have regarding the safety of any equipment, resources or working practices that you identify.

Refer also to Unit 4.

Good practice in non-group settings

Non-group settings in this context means working as a nanny, registered childminder or foster carer.

For a nanny, registered childminder or foster carer there is a greater emphasis on 'the family'. A nanny will usually be working within the family home, and may share the care of the child or children with the parent. Respecting family policy and approaches, providing they do not go against good working practice, will be important. This will ensure that the children are not confused through receiving mixed messages regarding eating, sleeping, boundaries, discipline, etc. It will also help prevent conflict between parent and nanny.

Nannies need to take responsibility for keeping themselves updated with current thinking and for ensuring that they are competent to deal with all aspects of looking after young children, for example first aid.

Childminders will be offering a home-based form of care, which is often favoured by parents of very young babies and of children who are considered to be sensitive. The smaller unit of the childminder's home offers secure care without the (sometimes) hurly-burly atmosphere of nursery life.

Both nannies and childminders need to keep clear records of each child in their care, in the same way as in a nursery, with an overview of activities and outings, to keep parents informed about what their child has experienced, what they enjoy or show hesitation about, and how they have reacted in general.

Foster carers will often be working with children who have experienced trauma of some kind. This may be due to the illness of a parent, leaving them unable to cope, or due to difficulties within the family regarding parenting practices etc. At times children will have witnessed or experienced violence or abuse. These children must be made to feel very safe and secure. They often display challenging behaviour initially, and need clear boundaries to help them learn that their new environment is both stable and safe, and that they are both welcomed and wanted.

How to work with other professionals in a multi-agency team

Early years practitioners have to be able to work with other professionals from a range of agencies, such as health, education, social services and youth justice. Examples include:

- health visitors
- speech therapists
- occupational therapists
- physiotherapists
- psychologists
- social workers
- teachers
- family support agents
- interpreters
- advocates.

At times these links will be made within the working environment; on other occasions it may mean attending meetings and case conferences. Clearly presented and accurate records are vital when sharing information with others. Written observations and comments should always be factual and avoid personal interpretations of events. Communication skills will be of utmost importance, as is the ability to work as part of a team, at times working under guidance, and at others, initiating ideas and taking the lead.

As your career progresses, you will develop an understanding of the different protocols and working practices of a range of relevant agencies. You will learn how they provide support for each other and how this links to practical help in getting appropriate support for a specific child.

 Refer to Unit 3, pages 119–133, for information on child protection, and to Unit 5, pages 205–207, for effective communication skills.

Safeguarding and protecting children from harm

Babies are totally reliant on adults for their welfare and protection. This is why each care setting has a policy on who is allowed to handle, change and feed the infants in its care. Procedures for collecting children are strict, with only known adults having an infant handed over to them. As a student you are likely to find that you will not initially be allowed to be alone with an infant, and supervision will be particularly strict regarding nappy changing and all personal care routines. This protects both the infant and you, as your actions will be fully observed.

Any concerns you may have regarding an infant's welfare should be raised with your placement supervisor, or line manager. As a nanny or childminder, any concerns must be raised with the appropriate persons within the local authority children's services team.

 Refer also to Unit 3.

Sources of support for families

All families struggle from time to time, with most managing to cope without any undue distress caused. However, in some families additional support is needed. This may be due to a multiple birth, or siblings born very close together; both these situations being physically and emotionally draining for parents. Alternatively, it may be because an infant cries a great deal, or their temperament leads them to demand a lot of adult time and attention. Sometimes parents have not had good parenting role models themselves, and struggle to develop positive parenting strategies. Lone parents may be struggling with the total responsibility of caring for their children.

It can be helpful to have a list of sources of support on file that can be given to parents when appropriate. Examples would include:

- Cry-sis – support for parents who have an infant that cries a great deal (perhaps from colic)

- TAMBA – twins and Multiple Birth Association
- National Childbirth Trust – support with feeding and early care
- local post-natal support groups
- Gingerbread – a support group for lone parents
- the Council for One Parent Families – again, a support for lone parents
- Families Need Fathers – support for absent fathers
- CAB (Citizens Advice Bureau) – provides legal and financial advice
- Children's Information Service – a government-led support line available for each local authority.

 Have a go!

Find out about the various family support groups and associations in your area, and add the details of each to your file for future reference. Remember to update the details from time to time.

Promoting an inclusive, non-judgemental approach

It is important to promote and maintain a non-judgemental, anti-discriminatory approach when working with babies and toddlers and their families. You will need to consider:

- diversity
- equality of opportunity
- equality of access
- children's rights
- inclusion and special needs
- issues of discrimination.

This will help to ensure that the cultural practices of families are recognised and promoted, that food customs are provided for, and that language and ability needs are supported.

Refer also to Unit 3 page 92 where supporting diversity and inclusion is discussed in detail.

✓ Progress check

1. Explain how a key-worker system supports the care of babies and toddlers.

2. Explain how the key-worker system benefits the parent–practitioner relationship.

3. Describe some of the differences between a day-care setting and care within the home by a nanny or childminder.

4. Provide a list of policies that should be in place at every care setting.

5. Explain confidentiality and why it is so important.

6. List the range of professionals that an early years practitioner may need to work with.

7. Give an overview of the role of at least two other professionals.

8. Explain why key-worker systems are important.

9. Give examples of policies and procedures from your placement experience.

10. Give an example of how professionals work together as a multi-agency team.

11. Explain how multi-agency working can benefit a child.

12. List a range of sources of support that you could give to parents.

13. Give an example of diversity within the care of babies.

Weblinks

- www.babycentre.co.uk
  Offers expert advice, information and parent-to-parent support for pregnant women and those wanting to become pregnant

- www.bounty.com
  Information and features on pregnancy, babies and toddlers from the Bounty Club (which give out promotional 'Bounty packs' to all new mums with free samples, vouchers, etc. for baby products)

- www.nctpregnancyandbabycare.com
  National Childbirth Trust website: information and support on pregnancy, birth and babies and children. NCT is the leading charity for pregnancy, birth and parenting in the UK

- www.sandy-green.com
  Website for early years students, practitioners and parents

IMPORTANT INFORMATION ABOUT NEW LEGISLATION

Every Child Matters

Every Child Matters is a major government initiative which focuses on bringing together services to support children and families. It sets out five major outcomes for children:

- staying safe
- enjoying and achieving
- making a positive contribution
- economic well-being
- being healthy

The Early Years Foundation Stage (EYFS)

As part of the Every Child Matters initiative, the EYFS (a framework for learning) will be mandatory from September 2008 for:

- schools
- early years providers in Ofsted registered settings

It will apply to children from birth to the end of the academic year in which the child has their fifth birthday. The EYFS brings together and replaces the *Curriculum Guidance for the Foundation Stage*, *Birth to Three Matters* and the *National Standards for Under 8s Day Care and Childminding*, which will no longer apply from September 2008.

For more information on The Early Years Foundation Stage (EYFS) please visit: www.standards.dfes.gov.uk/eyfs

Glossary

Active immunity – the body's ability to resist a disease that has been acquired by having the disease or by having a specific immunisation

Amino acid – part of a protein

Anaphylactic shock – a severe and extreme reaction to a substance, such as peanuts or a bee sting

Anatomically correct dolls – dolls with accurately reproduced body parts including sexual organs

Anti-discriminatory practice – practice that encourages a positive view of difference and opposes negative attitudes and practices that lead to unfavourable treatment of people

Antibodies – made by white cells to attack pathogens

Baseline (or formative) assessment – the first assessment of a child's current stage of development

Bladder – the bladder is situated in the lower abdomen and stores urine

Bowel – the lower end of the intestines

British sign language (BSL) – the visual and gestural language of the British deaf community

Brochodilators – medicines which are breathed into the lungs by using an inhaler. Brochodilators help to reduce swelling and narrowing in the airways

Challenge – experience that will help develop a skill or aspect of learning

Child-centred – with the child at the centre, taking into account the perspective of the child

Children in need – a child is 'in need' if they are unlikely to achieve or maintain a reasonable standard of health or development without the provision of services, or if they have a disability

Commission – doing those things that should not be done, for example, beating children

Complete proteins – proteins containing all the essential amino acids

Condition – medically defined illness

Culture – the way of life, the language and the behaviour that are followed by particular groups of people

Customs – special guidelines for behaviour which are followed by particular groups of people

Cystic fibrosis – hereditary, life-threatening condition affecting the lungs and digestive tract

Dehydration – where the water content of the body falls dangerously low

Dependence – relying on another for support

Designated person – person identified in an establishment to whom allegations or suspicions of child abuse should be reported

Diabetes – a condition in which the body cannot metabolise carbohydrates, resulting in high levels of sugar in the blood and urine

Diffuse bruising – bruising that is spread out

Disability – disadvantage or restriction of activity caused by society that takes little or no account of people who have physical or mental impairments and thus excludes them from the mainstream of social activities. According to the social model, disability is defined as 'socially imposed restriction' (Oliver, 1981)

Disclosure (of abuse) – when a child tells someone they have been abused

Discrimination – behaviour based on prejudice which results in someone being treated unfairly

Eczema – a dry, scaly, itchy skin condition

Enzyme – a substance that helps to digest food

Equal opportunities policies – policies designed to provide opportunities for all people to achieve according to efforts and abilities

Expected pattern of development – when children are generally expected to achieve key development milestones. These milestones are sometimes called the 'development norms'

Extended family – a family grouping that includes other family members who either live together, or very close to each other, and are in frequent contact with each other

Family of origin – the family into which a child is born

Fat-soluble vitamin – vitamin that can be stored by the body, so it need not be included in the diet every day

Febrile convulsions – fits that occur as the direct result of a raised temperature

Foetus – term used to describe the baby from the eighth week after conception until birth

Formative assessment – the first assessment of a child's knowledge and understanding or development

Frenulum – the web of skin joining the gum to the lip

Frozen awareness/watchfulness – constantly looking around, alert and aware (vigilant) while remaining physically inactive (passive), demonstrating a lack of trust in adults

Genitals – sexual organs

Guardian ad litem – person appointed by the courts to safeguard and promote the interests and welfare of children during court proceedings

Hypoglycaemia – low levels of glucose in the blood

Immunity – the presence of antibodies that protect the body against infectious disease

Impairment – lacking all or part of a limb, or having altered or reduced function in a limb, organ or mechanism of the body. According to the social model, impairment is defined as 'individual limitation' (Oliver, 1981)

Inclusion – when children with disabilities or special needs are included within settings alongside non-disabled children

Inclusive – organised in a way that enables all to take a full and active part: meeting the needs of all children

Incomplete proteins – proteins containing some essential amino acids

Incubation period – the time from when pathogens enter the body until the first signs of infection appear

Independent life skills – skills needed to live and care for oneself

Individual Education Plan (IEP) – a document that records short-term targets for an individual child; it includes details of the strategies that will be put in place to help them work towards the targets

Individual needs/specific needs – terms used describe how an impairment impacts on the needs of an individual child. This will be specific to them; for example, Emily, a wheelchair user, needs assistance with toileting and dressing but Nina, also a wheelchair user, does not

Institutional oppression – the power of organisations brought to bear on an individual to keep them in their place

Independence – the emotional need to feel you are managing and directing your own life

Insulin – a hormone produced in the pancreas to metabolise carbohydrate in the bloodstream and regulate glucose

Lacerations – tears in the skin

Lactation – the production of milk by the breasts

Legislation – laws that have been made

Local management of schools (LMS) – enables a headteacher and the governors of a school to decide how to spend the money and staff the school

Matriarchal family – a family in which women are important and dominant

Medical model – view of disability requiring medical intervention

Melanocytes – pigmented cells

Motor impaired – having an impairment of a function of movement

Multiple disadvantage – the concentration of social problems in one area

National Childcare Strategy – strategy introduced by the government in the UK in May 1998 to ensure good quality, accessible and affordable child care for children up to the age of 14

Neonate – an infant under 1 month old

Norms – behaviours and beliefs accepted by a group

Nuclear family – a family grouping where parents live with their children and form a small group with no other family members living near them

Nutrient – a substance that provides essential nourishment

Oesophagus – the top of the digestive tract, leading from the mouth to the stomach

Omission – not doing those things that should be done, such as protecting children from harm

Oppression – using power to dominate and restrict other people

Orthofunction – a teaching method that involves the whole person physically and mentally, and 'instils in children the ability to function as members of society, and to participate in normal social settings appropriate to their age'

Pancreas – a gland that secretes insulin and enzymes that aid digestion

Parasites – small organisms which live on humans and obtain their food from them

Pathogens – germs such as bacteria and viruses which cause illness

Patriarchal family – a family in which men are dominant and make the important decisions

Percentile charts/centile charts – specially prepared charts that are used to record measurements of a child's growth. There are centile charts for weight, height and head circumference

Perception – the process of interpreting sensory information

Peripatetic – travelling (to see those they work with)

Phagocytosis – process by which white cells absorb pathogens and destroy them

Pinpoint haemorrhages – small areas of bleeding under the surface

Play agenda – what a child wants to achieve in their play

Positive image – image that challenges stereotypes and that extends and increases expectations

Potential hazards – possible dangers and threats to the children's safety

Poverty trap – situation experienced by people if they are receiving state benefits and they find that by earning a small amount more, they lose most of their benefits and become worse off

Preconception – the time between a couple deciding they want to have a baby and when the baby is conceived

Pre-term – born before 37 weeks of pregnancy

Primary health care – first line health care and health promotion

Primary health care team – professionals who are concerned with the delivery of the first-line health care and health promotion

Principles – basic truths, which underpin activities

Private sector – provided by individuals, groups or companies to meet demand and make a financial profit

Prone – position of a baby lying on her front

Referral – the process by which suspected abuse is reported by one person to someone who can take action if necessary

Reflective practitioner – workers who think about what they have done/said with a view to improving practice

Regressive – going back to an earlier developmental stage

Residential care – provision of care both during the day and at night outside the child's home with people other than close relatives

Rights of children – the expectations that all children should have regarding how they are treated within their families and in society

Sacrum – base of the spine

Safety legislation – laws that are created to prevent accidents and to promote safety

Safety mark – shows that equipment has complied with certain guidelines during manufacture

Self-esteem – liking and valuing oneself also referred to as self-respect

Self-reliance – the ability to depend on oneself to manage

Social creation – brought about by society

Social model – a view of disability as a problem within society

Socio-economic group – grouping of people according to their status in society, based on their occupation which is closely related to their wealth and income

Special educational needs (SEN) – children with SEN learn differently from most children of the same age and may need extra or different help to learn. Not all disabled children need extra or different help to learn. It depends on their individuals needs. The term SEN is used by national and local education departments

Special Educational Needs Coordinator (SENCO) – appointed person within the setting who has been trained to take overall responsibility for issues relating to special educational needs

Specific learning difficulties – difficulties in learning to read, write or spell or in doing mathematics, not related to generalised learning difficulties

Specific therapeutic goal – identifies objectives to counteract the effects of the condition or impairment

Spiritual beliefs – what a person believes about the non-material world

Statement of special educational needs – a written report setting out a child's needs and the resources required to meet these needs

Statutory duty – duty required by law

Statutory sector – provided by the state

Stereotyping – when people think that all the individual members of the group have the same characteristics as each other: often applied on the basis of race, gender or disability

Stools – The solid products of digestion passed out from the baby's bowel

Summative assessment – summarised findings of assessments

Supine – position of a baby lying on her back

Transition – the movement of a child from one care situation to another

Vaccine – a preparation used to stimulate the production of antibodies and provide immunity against one or several diseases

Values – beliefs that certain things are important and to be valued for example, a person's right to their own belongings

Voluntary sector – provided by voluntary organisations

Weals – streaks left on the flesh

Weaning – the introduction of solid food to an infant's diet

548